A JEW IN THE ROMAN BATHHOUSE

A Jew in the Roman Bathhouse

CULTURAL INTERACTION IN
THE ANCIENT MEDITERRANEAN

Yaron Z. Eliav

PRINCETON UNIVERSITY PRESS
PRINCETON & OXFORD

Copyright © 2023 by Princeton University Press

Princeton University Press is committed to the protection of copyright and the intellectual property our authors entrust to us. Copyright promotes the progress and integrity of knowledge. Thank you for supporting free speech and the global exchange of ideas by purchasing an authorized edition of this book. If you wish to reproduce or distribute any part of it in any form, please obtain permission.

Requests for permission to reproduce material from this work should be sent to permissions@press.princeton.edu

Published by Princeton University Press
41 William Street, Princeton, New Jersey 08540
99 Banbury Road, Oxford OX2 6JX

press.princeton.edu

All Rights Reserved

ISBN 9780691243436
ISBN (e-book) 9780691243443

British Library Cataloging-in-Publication Data is available

Editorial: Fred Appel and James Collier
Production Editorial: Sara Lerner
Jacket Design: Katie Osborne
Production: Lauren Reese
Publicity: Kate Hensley and Charlotte Coyne

Jacket Credit: *Ancient Ruins Used as Public Baths* by Hubert Robert, 1798. Artefact / Alamy Stock Photo

Epigraph Credit: From "Political Correctness" Munk Debate, May 18, 2018, https://munkdebates.com/debates/political-correctness

This book has been composed in Miller

10 9 8 7 6 5 4 3 2 1

למילכה

שגמלתני טוב

. . . I do relish transgression, and I deeply and instinctively distrust conformity and orthodoxy. Progress is not achieved by preachers and guardians of morality but . . . by "madmen, hermits, heretics, dreamers, rebels, and sceptics."

—STEPHEN FRY

CONTENTS

List of Illustrations · xi
Preface · xiii
A Note on References, Names, Abbreviations, and Translations · xv

	Introduction	1
PART I	SETTING THE STAGE	19
CHAPTER 1	The Miracle of (Hot) Water: The Emergence of the Roman Public Bathhouse as a Cultural Institution	21
CHAPTER 2	A Literary Bathhouse: Realities and Perceptions at a Roman (Jewish) Public Bath	44
CHAPTER 3	Earliest Encounters: Archaeology, Scholarly Debate, and the Shifting Grounds of Interpretation	77
PART II	FILTERED ABSORPTION	105
CHAPTER 4	A Sinful Place? Rabbinic Laws (*Halakhah*) and Feelings about the Public Bathhouse	107
CHAPTER 5	*Tsni'ut* (Rabbinic Modes of Modesty) in the Halls of Promiscuity: Mixed Bathing and Nudity in the Public Bathhouse	138
CHAPTER 6	The Naked Rabbi and the Beautiful Goddess: Engaging with Sculpture in the Public Bathhouse	161

PART III	SOCIAL AND CULTURAL TEXTURES	193
CHAPTER 7	A Social Laboratory: Status and Hierarchy in a Provincial Roman Bathhouse	195
CHAPTER 8	A Scary Place: The Perils of the Bath and Jewish Magic Remedies	226
	In Conclusion	252

Abbreviations · 255
Notes · 257
Bibliography of Primary Sources · 313
Bibliography of Scholarly Works · 323
Index of Ancient Citations · 349
General Index · 355

ILLUSTRATIONS

Maps and Diagrams

Map 1. The Roman Mediterranean	xvi
Map 2. Roman Near East, Mesopotamia, and Babylonia	xvii
Map 3. Judaea/Syria-Palaestina	xviii
Diagram 1. A Typical Roman Public Bathhouse	xix

Figures

Fig. 1. Pont du Gard	22
Fig. 2. Roman Aqueduct near Caesarea Maritima	23
Fig. 3. Pressure Pipe from Hippos/Susita	25
Fig. 4. Hypocaust System (diagram)	27
Fig. 5. Furnace Chamber from Scythopolis/Beth Shean	28
Fig. 6. Baths of Caracalla	30
Fig. 7. Greek Hip-Bath	32
Fig. 8. A Strigil	35
Fig. 9. Latrine from Scythopolis/Beth Shean	38
Fig. 10. Yakto Mosaic	47
Fig. 11. Yakto Mosaic (detail)	48
Fig. 12. Hypocaust System from Scythopolis/Beth Shean	66
Fig. 13. *Apodyterium* in the Stabian Bath, Pompeii	74
Fig. 14. Roman Bath at Masada	79
Fig. 15. *Dianna and Actaeon* by Giuseppe Cesare	139
Fig. 16. The "Bikini Girls" from Piazza Armerina, Sicily	157
Fig. 17. *The Baths of Caracalla* by Virgilio Mattoni de la Fuente	162
Fig. 18. Aphrodite of Knidos	163
Fig. 19. Agora Baths in Side, Turkey	167
Fig. 20. Bathhouse in Scythopolis/Beth Shean	169
Fig. 21. Water Spout from Tiberias, Israel	173
Fig. 22. A Wall Painting from a Latrine in Pompeii	180

Fig. 23. The Projecta Casket 206
Fig. 24. The Matron Mosaic from Piazza Armerina, Sicily 207
Fig. 25. Slaves Attending a Patron in Mosaic from Piazza Armerina, Sicily 208
Fig. 26. The Matron Mosaic from Sidi Ghrib, Tunisia 217

PREFACE

MY FASCINATION WITH communal bathing and its bodily pleasures, not to say transgressions, goes back to my childhood years as an orthodox Jewish kid. Growing up in the ultra-religious town of Bnei Brak, Israel, our teachers instilled fear of sin in us, but they could not eliminate the basic human impulses of lust and desire. The inner conflicts that ensued provoked sorrow and confusion, in particular when encountering physical exposure at the beaches on hot, summer days, or when brushing against another naked body in the dim, narrow confines of the Jewish ritual immersion installation, the *miqveh*. The pounding of the heart, the sexual arousal, and the shame of contravention all converged with water in my personal world. Years later, having thrown off the strictures of Jewish law, I turned those memories into a scholarly pursuit to understand the mechanisms at work when one sheds clothes and submerges in water.

This book has been long time in the making. I first chose the Roman bathhouse as a topic for my master's final project, which I submitted to the Institute of Archaeology and the Department of Jewish History at the Hebrew University in Jerusalem. My background was in Rabbinics, the texts of my childhood that became my passion and vocation. But early on in my academic education, as my teachers made it clear that a single crown would not suffice, I embarked on a lifelong path of preparation in classical languages, studies of the Graeco-Roman world, its texts and cultures, as well as thorough training in archaeology. All these disciplines and fields of study come into play in the current book. After the master's final project on the public bathhouses of Roman Jerusalem, I left the topic to pursue others, only to return to it many years later in the research endeavor that resulted in the current book. Over time many things happened in my life: I rose and fell, achieved and failed, prospered and floundered, but my fascination and love for the topic of Roman baths remained constant and fresh. Engaging it always brought a sense of the calm and accomplishment that I missed so much as a young man.

An academic project is never carried out solo. Numerous institutions and people assisted me over the years. Chief among those is the University of Michigan, which has been my academic home for the past twenty years. Its various units, grants, and endowments offered generous financial support that made this project possible. My students in Ann Arbor provided regular intellectual stimulation and challenge that fueled my work, and some of them also joined me as research assistants, graduate and postgraduate students, and later young colleagues, who read about, commented on, and argued about the various subjects discussed in this book. They are too many to enumerate here but I owe them and the university a huge debt that can never be repaid in full. My gratitude also goes to the many other institutions and individuals who invited me to speak about the Jews and the baths over the years, in conferences, lectures, seminars, and private correspondence. I learned from many of these encounters, as they gave me ideas and insights that I have incorporated in my work. I hope I have remembered to give full credit in the appropriate places to specific ideas that I borrowed from others. I was also blessed with two superb editors, David Lobenstine and Dr. Jeffrey Green, whose wisdom and skill are evident on every page of this book.

Last but not least, none of this would have been possible or worthwhile without the cozy comforts and support of my family: my parents, my late father Yaacov and my mother Esther; my father-in-law, Dov Kahanah; my sister and brother and their families; and my own two children, Avishag and Evyatar. They all enjoyed life with me, listened with admirable patience to my overly long disquisitions on matters ancient, and brought that sweetness to life that makes it all so joyful. But most of my debt of gratitude goes to my wife, Milka, who has stood by me like a lioness for the past thirty years, even when I didn't deserve it. She has picked me up when I've fallen, set me straight when I've gone astray, and been my best friend and most precious advisor. Not knowing how to repay her, I dedicate this book to her with love and admiration.

A NOTE ON REFERENCES, NAMES,
ABBREVIATIONS, AND TRANSLATIONS

THIS BOOK INCLUDES references and quotations from hundreds of ancient sources in most of the spoken languages of the Roman Mediterranean. All passages are brought in English. The translations are mine unless indicated otherwise. When translating full passages I've tried to stay as close as possible to the original literary wording; I use brackets [] to signal the addition of words to make the flow of the translation smoother, and I use parentheses () to mark additional explanations that are not part of the text. The bibliography provides a full list of primary texts with the editions I used and available translations to English where these exist, so readers can consult, compare, and decide about the best rendition of the original. The list of primary texts also provides the abbreviated title used in the notes. In general, for abbreviations I follow the conventions of the *Oxford Classical Dictionary* (4th edition) for the Greek and Latin texts, and the *SBL Handbook of Style* (1999 edition) for the Jewish texts. I also follow the latter in transliteration of the Greek, Hebrew, and Aramaic into English, and regarding the abbreviations of periodicals and series. For personal names I use the common spelling in English; for names of places in Judaea/Palestine I follow the list of the *Tabula imperii romani: Iudaea Palaestina*, ed. Yoram Tsafrir, Leah Di Segni, and Judith Green (Jerusalem: Israel Academy of Sciences and Humanities, 1994), and for all others, the *Barrington Atlas of the Greek and Roman World*, ed. Richard J. A. Talbert (Princeton: Princeton University Press, 2000).

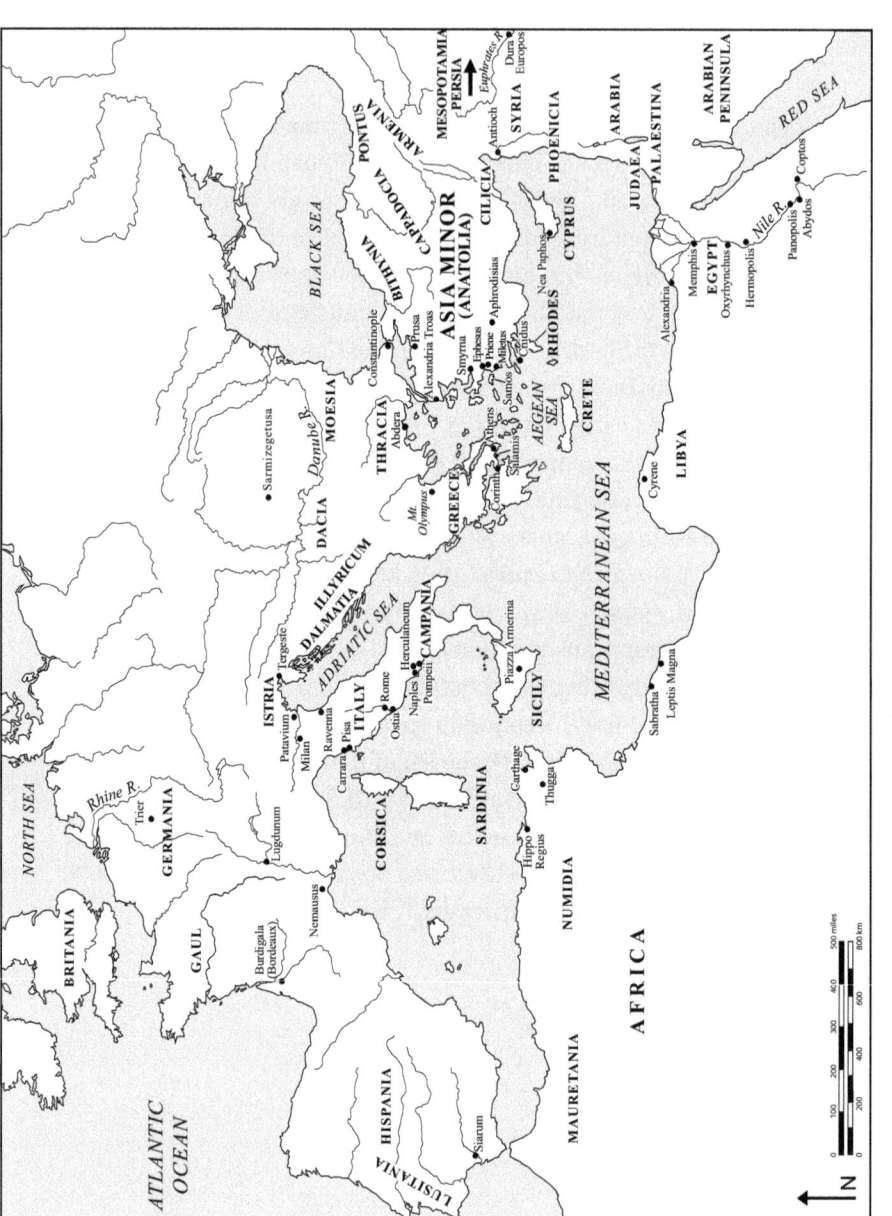

MAP 1. The Roman Mediterranean. *Credit:* Drawn by Lorene Sterner for the author.

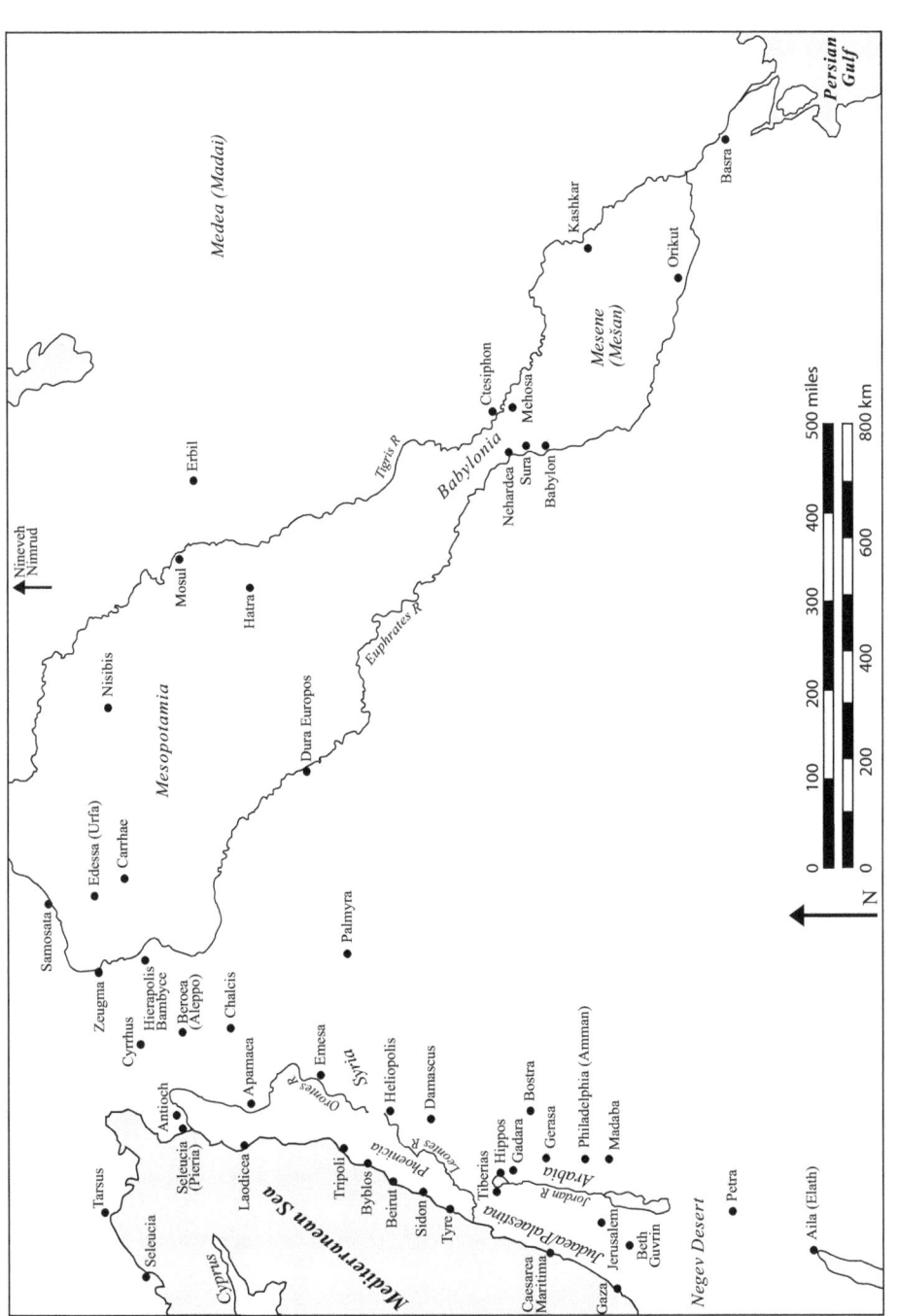

MAP 2. Roman Near East, Mesopotamia, and Babylonia. *Credit*: Drawn by Lorene Sterner for the author.

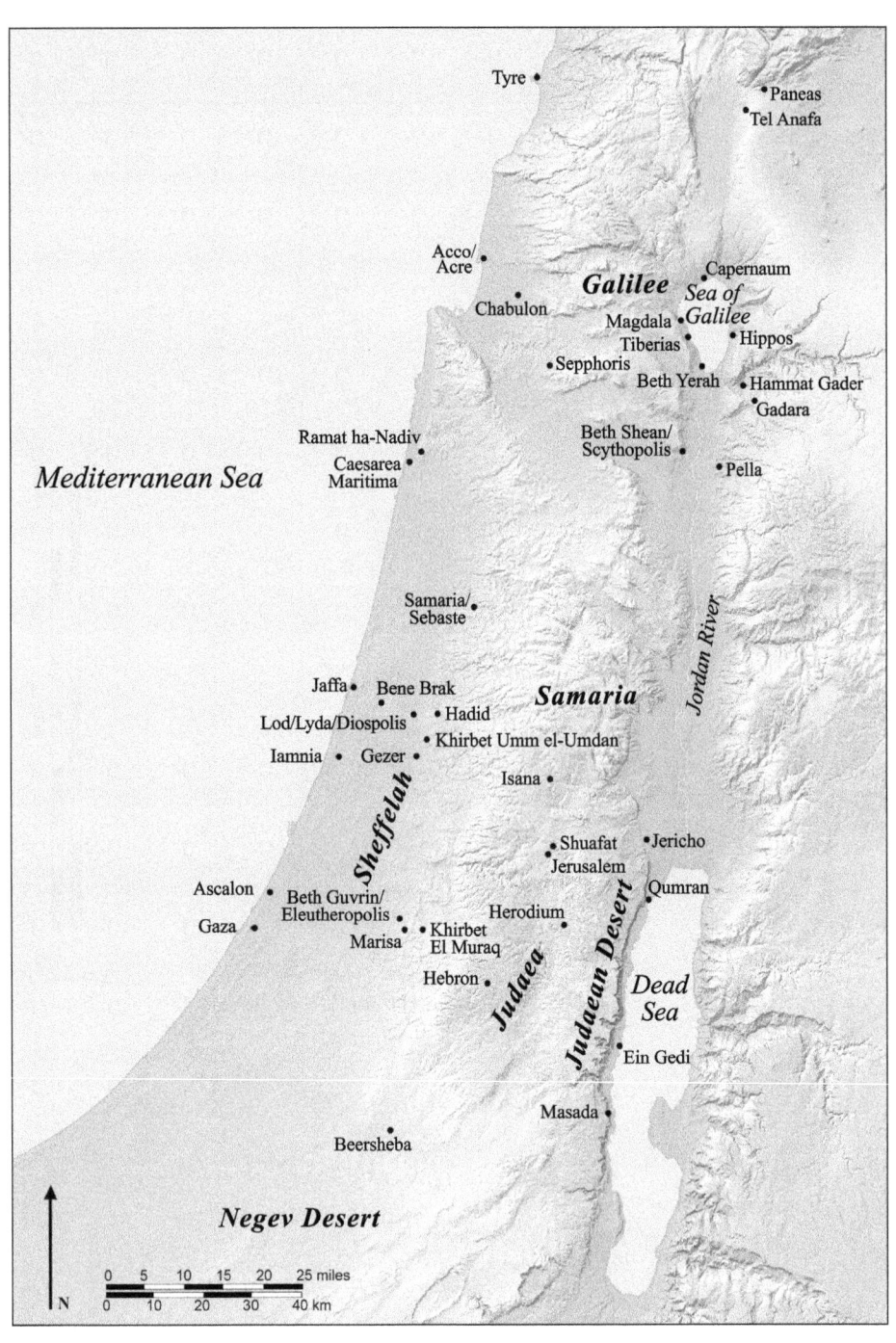

MAP 3. Judaea/Syria-Palaestina. *Credit:* Drawn by Lorene Sterner for the author.

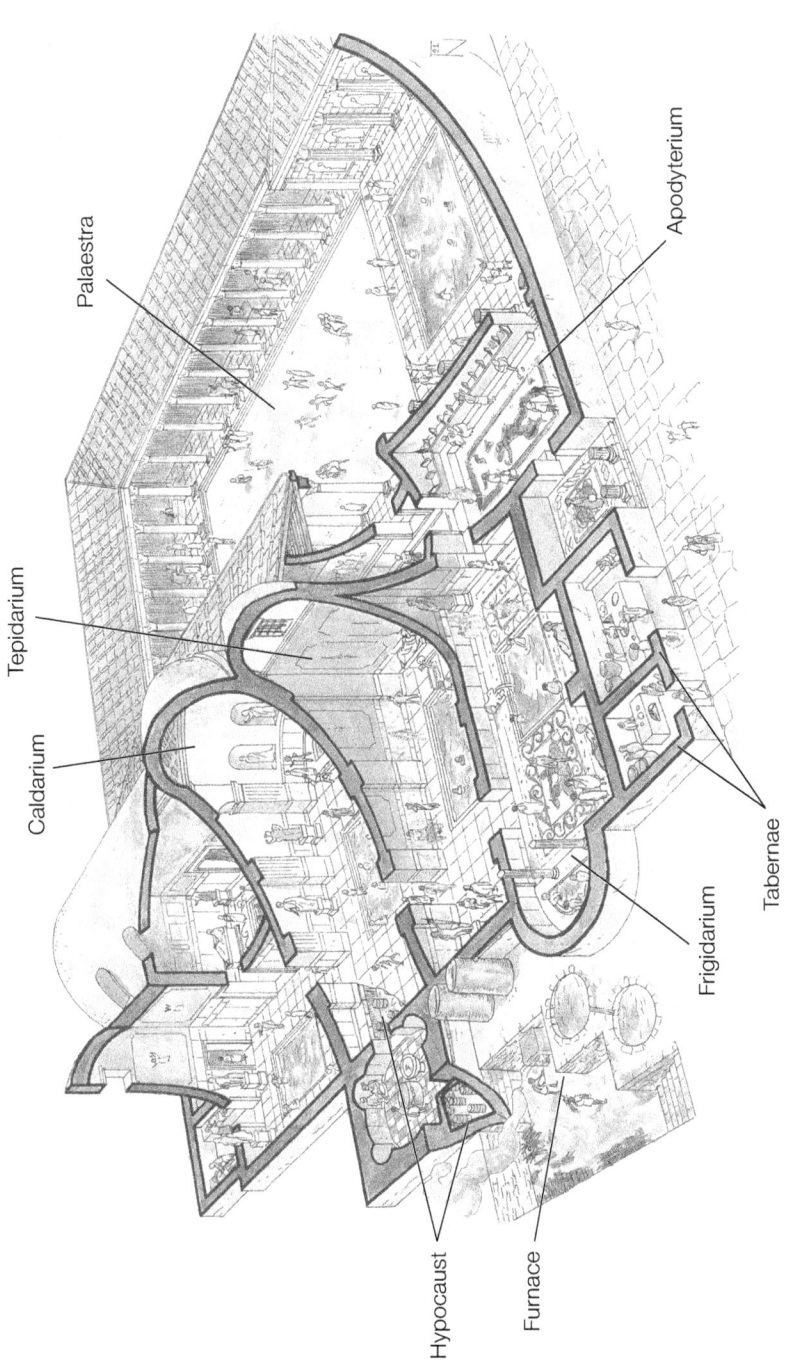

DIAGRAM 1. A typical Roman public bathhouse. Available in full color at https://press.princeton.edu/books/hardcover/9780691243436/a-jew-in-the-roman-bathhouse. *Credit:* Drawn by Yannis Nakas for the author.

A JEW IN THE ROMAN BATHHOUSE

Introduction

EVERY DAY, WE all interact with the world around us in endless ways. We make choices about where we go, what we do, and whom we talk to and how, as well as the places we avoid and the actions we refrain from doing. Sometimes these choices affect us dramatically and alter our lives irrevocably. Most of these judgments, however, are so mundane we don't even think about them. A wide range of principles and perceptions conditions these infinite decisions. We are aware of some of these, while others loom silently in the background, propelling or impeding: ideology, psychology, history, politics, religion, and superstition, all play a role in determining our path. The interminable interactions they lead to are what life consists of. Little by little, person by person, day by day, they mold the experiences and propel the ideas that shape one's existence. Defined broadly, this system—together with its representations in literature, art, and other media—is human culture.

This book dwells on one tiny slice of those cultural interactions—somewhat surprising, seemingly contradictory, and long forgotten. In it, I tell the story of ancient Jews and how they engaged with the Roman public bathhouses that were ubiquitous in their world. It offers a study about cultural interaction in the Roman Mediterranean. On one side stand the Jews, a loosely organized, culturally variegated minority group, living in widely dispersed communities throughout the Mediterranean basin and beyond and defined by their long-established heritage and way of life, anchored in the texts we now call the Hebrew Bible.[1] On the other side rest the mores of the ruling power, the Romans, referred to already in antiquity by the elusive category *romanitas*. While no clear definition ever existed about what it meant to be Roman, a cluster of concepts, behaviors, images, and institutions—shifting in emphasis and extent over time and place and owing much to the Graeco-Hellenistic legacy that preceded them—came to represent Roman identity, lifestyle, and self-image.² How did these two cultural systems, Judaism and *romanitas*, and the people who lived by them engage? Were they utterly distinct entities eyeing each other from across the town square, ancient versions of the Sharks and the Jets, deciding whether to fight or keep the peace? Or were their daily lives enmeshed in ways big and small, a model of intercultural cooperation, albeit uneasy at times? Or is there another, totally different model that better describes their relationship? Modern scholars have long probed and debated this question, whose implications are vast, at the very heart of the evolution of Western civilization.

Frequently, the adoption of Roman habits and norms by minorities subsumed under the effective yet methodologically problematic rubric of "Romanization."³ The current book revisits and reexamines the cultural encounter between Jews and *romanitas* as it took shape in one particular space, the Roman public bathhouse, with special attention to the texts known collectively as rabbinic literature. Most of the figures discussed in this book lived in the Roman province of Judaea, known since the early second century CE as Syria Palaestina (or, in short, throughout this book, Palestine). So, essentially, this book asks: Were the Jewish residents of Judaea/Palestine Romanized, and if so, to what extent, and what model can explain this process and their experiences?

I use the Roman bathhouse as a laboratory to tease out, reconsider, and test the attitudes of the Jews of antiquity toward the Graeco-Roman world. To carry out this task, I utilize the full gamut of available sources—literary, documentary, archaeological, and artistic, both Jewish and not—with special attention and focus on rabbinic literature. I follow some ancient Jews as they patronized the bathhouse, walking in their footsteps and seeing through their eyes. What did they see? What did they do? How did they feel about it? I document their pleasures, examine their anxieties and concerns (occasionally what modern historians imagined to be their concerns), and reconstruct their thoughts, emotions, and convictions about the bathhouse and the activities that took place there. Because the bathhouse was integral to Roman culture, my exploration intersects with a vast swath of topics, from the technology of heating the bath water to the social hierarchies of Roman life, and from nudity and sex to sculpture and magic.⁴ All this allows me to reassess the nature of the cultural encounter between Jews and the Roman way of life and to offer a new model to understand it, which I label "filtered absorption."

Why Bathhouses?

The Roman public bathhouse was a unique institution. It housed and boldly displayed what were arguably the most popular leisure activities in the Roman world. In sprawling cities and small villages, in an empire that extended from modern England and Spain to Egypt and Iraq, people from all walks of life attended the bathhouse on a daily basis. Other structures and spaces were much less inclusive. Only members of a certain religion and followers of a particular god or goddess visited and worshipped at the temples associated with their divinity; similarly, other than occasional visitors and sympathizers, only Jews attended the synagogue, and only those newfangled people called Christians went to church. Places of entertainment such as theaters and hippodromes, although very popular, did not operate daily, and the cost to erect and maintain them precluded many localities, certainly villages but also small cities, from building them altogether. Similarly, only buyers and sellers visited the markets, and other municipal structures, such as the courts, housed in the civic basilicas, served specific needs. The public bathhouse, on the other hand, attracted everyone, and even the smallest of villages spared no effort to build them. Wealthy and poor, prominent citizens and ordinary, men, women, and children, and their household slaves, all came in droves, usually every day. The Jews were no different.

Furthermore, no other space embodied so many different features of the Roman way of life (the *romanitas*): everything from engineering and architecture to food and fashion, from sculpture to sports, from nudity and sex to medicine and magic, to name just a few. Ideas about the human body, about science and metaphysics, about life and its carnal and spiritual pleasures, as well as constructs about fate, aesthetics, social hierarchy, and imperialism, all manifested themselves in the physical environment and the daily experience of the baths. If you want to examine the ways people interacted with each other, and, in particular, how a segment of society engaged with the norms and ways of the Romans, the public bathhouse offers an ideal place, a laboratory of sorts, to carry out this investigation.

Roman bathhouses are also very well documented. Graeco-Roman authors writing in different literary genres and in different locales mention bathhouses time and again. In addition, archaeologists have excavated and studied hundreds of bathing facilities all over the Mediterranean, providing a wealth of information. Researchers have also deciphered hundreds of inscriptions and papyri that refer to bathhouses, highlighting many aspects of their operation and the conduct of people there. During the past decades, great efforts have been made to investigate this rich tapestry of data: archaeologists have organized and dissected the findings from excavations, illuminating the distribution, architecture, and layout of the buildings, as well as the engineering and technological mechanisms that enabled bathhouses to function; literary scholars, social historians, and anthropologists have studied the wide range of behavior that took place at the baths, as well as the imagery of the place and its symbolism in literature and art.[5] The present book owes a great debt to this work, as it laid the foundation for the current study about the Jews and their engagement with the baths, and by extension their attitudes toward Roman culture.

However, most modern studies have neglected one particularly large group of ancient sources that speaks volumes about the Roman baths, in great detail, namely rabbinic literature. This huge corpus of ancient Jewish texts, indeed, the largest that survived from Roman times, frequently alludes to public bathhouses: over five hundred references to the baths and associated activities, which makes the bathhouse the best represented Roman institution in rabbinic material! Modern investigators of bathhouses have mostly ignored this treasure trove of information, partially because of linguistic obstacles—rabbinic texts generally speak Aramaic and Hebrew, languages outside the sphere of most classical experts—and also because of the entrenched misconception that the Jews in general and the rabbis (the authors of this literature) in particular were an isolated and detached element in the Roman world. Furthermore, as I show in great detail in chapters 3 and 4, when modern scholars have attempted to use rabbinic material, even if only sporadically, they have gotten the picture mostly wrong.

A major goal of this book is to break down the long-standing barriers that divide Rabbinics from Classics and Archaeology to both demonstrate how knowledge of classics and archaeology is necessary for the study and understanding of rabbinic material and clearly show the added value that rabbinic material brings to the study of Roman antiquity and its institutions.[6] Studying the Jews in the Roman bathhouse requires placing excerpts from rabbinic literature in direct dialogue with Graeco-Roman texts and with the archaeological and documentary record. This opens a plethora of exciting possibilities. After all, ancient people living their lives, side by side, throughout the Roman Mediterranean—Greek, Roman, Jewish—produced these ancient sources and they naturally relate to each other on many levels. Each group of sources sheds new light on the other, and age-old questions—namely, the relationship between Jews and their Graeco-Roman neighbors—beg for reexamination when seen through the perspective of the bathhouse.

At the same time, this reshuffling of our source material offers other benefits. Rabbinic literature, if properly studied, uniquely enables modern classicists and archaeologists to communicate with a segment of the Roman world that is rarely heard in its own voice and on its own terms. One of the central obstacles to understanding Roman civilization is the absence of sources from the empire's periphery. What do we know about the Celts, about the Palmyrians or other Syrians, and the Arabs, or about the Gallic and German tribes that settled in and out of the empire, other than what Roman authors, such as Julius Caesar or Tacitus, or an occasional local writer who embraced Graeco-Roman ways such as Lucian in Syria and Cyprian in North Africa, as well as Josephus in Judaea, tell us about them? Searching for authentic indigenous voices, we are normally left with archaeology, an occasional inscription (papyri where they are available), and some artistic depictions. In contrast, rabbinic literature offers thousands of pages written by local provincial residents of the Roman world in their own language and in their own words. It can add an abundance of information to elaborate and nuance our understanding of life in this era.

These possibilities have long been recognized by scholars studying rabbinic material in its Graeco-Roman context. The line of inquiry that pays attention to archaeology and brings rabbinic material into conversation with its Graeco-Roman surroundings began with Samuel Krauss in late nineteenth- and early twentieth-century Hungary and Austria. His monumental work, *Talmudische Archäologie* (published 1910–12), remains the entry point for anyone approaching this subject. The great talmudist Saul Lieberman carried on after Krauss, and this direction of research came to full fruition in the work of my teacher Lee Levine at the Hebrew University in Jerusalem and in some of the projects spearheaded by Peter Schäfer in Germany and the United States.[7] The current book continues on the path that these scholars and their students have paved. When it comes to the institution of the Roman bathhouse and its appearance in rabbinic texts, here too my book does not operate in a vacuum. Over the past century and a half, several scholars have addressed this topic, chief among them Krauss himself, who devoted long and at times insightful discussions to this place.[8] Earlier scholars, however, could not benefit from the extensive archaeological data that has only become available in the last few decades, and even today, although offering valuable insights at times, scholars seem to be limited by insufficient training in classics and archaeology or misguided by anachronistic misconceptions about the rabbis and Jews. Throughout the current book—the first full-length monograph devoted to Jews and Roman bathhouses—I refer to these earlier studies, use them where appropriate, take issue with them, and reject their conclusions when necessary. I too have studied and written extensively about bathhouses and expect future scholars to disagree with me. Indeed, while writing the current book I found that some of my early arguments and conclusions required adjustment and at times rejection altogether.[9] Such is the nature of scholarship.

Jews and Graeco-Roman Culture

Western civilization shapes much of our way of life today. At its core, even two millennia later, stands the relationship between ancient Judaism (and its later manifestation in Christianity) and Graeco (sometimes also called Hellenistic) Roman norms. Generally speaking, the democracies of North America and Europe have embraced, although in a modified form, the legacies of the Greeks and the Romans—their philosophy and copious literature, their statecraft, government, and conventions about art, architecture, and aesthetics. They have then infused this rich tapestry with ideas, morality, and religious principles adopted from the biblical traditions of the Jews and the Christians. Naturally, endless studies, debates, and discussions explore both components of this heritage—the Graeco-Roman and the Judaeo-Christian—and the confluence between them.

What are the historical roots and what is the nature of this Judaeo-Graeco-Roman hybrid? Judaism came into the orbit of the Greeks with the conquests of Alexander the Great in the early fourth century BCE. In the next thousand years or so—until Islam's emergence in the eastern Mediterranean and North Africa during the seventh century CE—Jews became the largest, and the most widespread, minority in the Graeco-Roman realm, with the Jewish communities of Persia remaining outside this dominion. According to some estimates Jews comprised 10 percent of the Roman Empire's population.[10] For convenience and structure, throughout this book I divide those thousand years into the following four periods: (1) Hellenistic—from the Greek conquest of Alexander to the arrival of the Romans in Judaea under Pompey in 63 BCE; (2) Early Roman—from 63 BCE to the destruction of the Jewish Temple in Jerusalem in 70 CE; (3) the High Empire—from 70 CE to rise of Diocletian in 284; and (4) the Late Empire—from 284 to the Arab conquests in the seventh century. The High and Late Empires, the periods during which public bathhouses proliferated and rabbinic literature produced, stand at the core of the current book.

The encounter between the Jews (if one can even speak of them as one group) and the Roman ruling powers fluctuated between volatility, even violent confrontations at times, and long durations of peaceful and accommodating relations. When Christianity took the helm of the empire in the fourth century CE, communities and individuals throughout the Roman world inherited and then gradually adopted the ideas and mores embedded in ancient Jewish tradition, molding and reshaping them in the process. In the long run a new civilization replaced the old Roman way of life. It has been given many names and taken a variety of forms—medieval, Catholic, Byzantine, to name a few—and, through this long and tortuous process, it came to shape the modern era in which we live.

Because ancient Judaism played a major role in the foundation of our own world, everyone seems eager to explore its origin and development: modern Jews see ancient Jews as their ancestors; Christians seek their roots in ancient Jewish culture; and those cherishing the values of classical antiquity wish to clarify the role of Jews in Roman society. Acknowledging the importance of the issue, however, researchers regularly complain about the scarcity of sources that shed light on it.[11] At the same time they disagree on almost every aspect of it. One group of recent studies champions the argument promoted by Steve Mason and accepted by (too) many that Judaism, as a coherent ethnic and cultural entity, did not exist in the Hellenistic and Early Roman periods. Mason suggests that we should instead use the term "Judaeans," that is, the citizens (even if not the actual residents) of Judaea—a region in the eastern Mediterranean (somewhat but not completely geographically equivalent with modern Israel) where many, but far from all, Jews resided. Other researchers, chief among them the late Jacob Neusner, believe that in antiquity not one form of Judaism existed but rather many, identifying numerous Judaisms and associating each with different ancient texts, which supposedly present a distinct and coherent cluster of ideas and practices that set it apart from other forms of Judaism. These scholars have argued for a Hellenistic Judaism, Enochic Judaism, and later Rabbinic Judaism, to name a few. At the later end of the chronological spectrum, another influential scholar, Seth Schwartz, argued that whereas Judaism flourished in the Early Roman period, during the High and Late Empires it practically evaporated and ceased to exist, only to reemerge from the dead with the rise of Christianity in the fourth century CE. A fourth argument, championed by the vocal and very popular scholar Daniel Boyarin, claims that Judaism never existed in antiquity as a religion or a coherent category of identity and only took shape with the development of Christianity.[12] If these fantastic constructs cause the reader to raise an eyebrow, they should. They are mostly remnants of the overly skeptical and speculative scholarly agenda that took shape in the second half of the twentieth century (itself a reaction to the overly positivistic first half of the century). They raise interesting questions but rely too much on postmodern, theoretical modes of thinking and fail, at least in the eyes of this writer, to make a convincing case.[13]

Surprisingly, while these modern scholars disagree about the nature of the Jews in antiquity, many (although not all) agree that, whoever they were, the Jews opposed the Roman (and earlier Hellenistic) outlook on life and rejected its standards and customs. Many modern scholars typically emphasize that despite mutual influence and cross-fertilization, Judaism and Hellenism, and later, Roman culture, harbored inherent tension, suspicion, and antagonism toward one another, leading to resentment and apprehension, and often degenerating into violence and bloodshed. According to this understanding, ancient Jewish communities lived in what many modern investigators portray as their own bubble (sometimes described as their own turf) and held themselves apart from the larger cultural landscape, rejecting the ties that bound most of the other residents in the Hellenistic and then the Roman world. From that Archimedean point, the imagined ontological exterior of classical Roman civilization, Jews despised Hellenism and resisted the process of Romanization, *romanitas*, at times vigorously. They strove to distance themselves from what they viewed as foreign manners and firmly maintained their unique and exclusive forms of existence. In this reconstruction, scholars acknowledge that some ancient Jews, those living in the Diaspora, for example (referring to the millions of Jews living outside Judaea/Palestine), were seduced by the rival lifestyle and became Hellenized, speaking Greek and embracing many of the customs of their neighbors; they were "influenced" by the trappings of an adversarial foe. But those were deviations from the norm, the exception that proved the rule. The ancient Jews are seen as a nation dwelling alone, walled in by their own set of beliefs and guided by an exclusionary practical apparatus.

For centuries this was the prevailing view, championed as recently as 2008 in the best-selling monograph by the British historian Martin Goodman, *Rome and Jerusalem: The Clash of Ancient Civilizations*. In 1990, on the other side of the British Channel, the leading French scholar on the topic, Mireille Hadas-Lebel, published her now classic tome called *Jérusalem contre Rome*, reissued in 2012. The titles say it all. Both authors present a panoramic tour of the Roman world and the Jews in it, aiming to show that in almost every detail of life Judaism conflicted with Roman mores. When it comes to the rabbis, most scholars hold the same view, summarized succinctly by Seth Schwartz: "The rabbis rejected Roman values."[14] Consequently, the paradigm of the great divide between Jews and Roman culture prevails in countless studies and textbooks alike.[15]

To be sure, over the years more than a few scholars voiced their dissent, to some extent or another, from this mainstream model, myself included. The current book joins these recent attempts (and some, like Lee Levine's work, not so recent) to contest the standard currencies of understanding by placing the Jews and their way of life as an integral part of the Roman world.[16] But unlike other works that focus on intellectual, literary, religious, or (less often) social matters, my study locates the entire discussion within the confines of a physical space—the bathhouse—and thus brings into the discussion analytical tools that emerge from the discipline of archaeology. It uses the colorful and multifaceted environment of the public baths to illuminate the place of Jews in the Roman world. In the following chapters I reconstruct the cultural experience of (at least some) Jews in the bathhouse of the Roman Mediterranean in order to take a fresh look at the numerous ways in which they engaged Graeco-Roman culture.

It is anachronistic, in my view, and misleading to position Jews outside the cultural sphere of their time and to explore either their influence on it or its influence on them, as if they were two distinct, antagonistic entities. Such a model essentially projects the situation in modern societies, with well-demarcated lines of separation enforced by nationalism and statehood and possibly informed by medieval competition between Christianity and Islam, on the ancient world. But it is far removed from the lived reality of the Roman Mediterranean, where the blending of cultures was both convoluted and seamless. On the contrary, we must acknowledge that Jews lived in the larger environment of the ancient Mediterranean world,[17] deeply embedded in the texture of its life and sharing its ontological outlooks. Focusing our inquiries on their practices and beliefs within this shared cultural landscape, I reach the conclusion that conflict and amity coexisted and intermingled in the spheres of culture and identity. Counter to the view that insists Jews restricted themselves to their own turf, I show that Jews and non-Jews were densely entangled in the baths, and their ongoing encounters went far beyond the oversimplified binary notions of conflict or influence. I call the subtle complexities and dynamics that the book uncovers "the poetics of culture"; and I call the model used to explain it "filtered absorption." The institution of the public bathhouse serves here as the spatial setting, the stage on which this cultural drama played out.

Filtered absorption places Jews not on the exterior of the Roman realm but rather deep in its interior, embedded in the shared experience of those days and embracing many of its fundamental values and conventions; on many levels, they were part and parcel of the Roman milieu just like everyone else.[18] During the High and Late Empires, numerous Jews, at least those of whom we know much about, lived and functioned in the cities and towns of the Mediterranean. Even those who resided in rural settings—and many did, whether in Roman Judaea (later renamed Palestine) or elsewhere—were closely connected with municipalities. Living for hundreds of years in such a mixed environment, rubbing shoulders daily with their non-Jewish neighbors, meant not just close proximity to but also intimate engagement with the Roman way of life— in commerce, in everyday undertakings on the street and in the markets, in local politics, and in leisure activities. Documentary evidence in the papyri found in the Judaean Desert shows Jews casually interacting with non-Jewish peers in the local courts on matters of business but also on a range of family issues. Similarly, countless references in rabbinic literature testify to such contacts, although not always with approval.[19] Many scholars, especially in the late nineteenth and early twentieth centuries (but some to this day), influenced by the segregated status of Jews in medieval, Christian Europe and by the attitudes of some ghettoized ultra-Orthodox Jews today, project this image of Judaism onto ancient times, failing to appreciate how deeply embedded the Jews were within the Roman world.

In order to live as part of the Roman world while also maintaining their heritage and unique practices, Jews continually identified and assessed features of their surroundings that were inconsistent with their convictions and way of life. To be clear, they never achieved unanimous agreement on which features of Roman life were a problem. However, a few elements of *romanitas*—surprisingly few, considering our widespread assumptions about Judaism—bothered at least some Jews in various parts of the Roman world, and these elements were then either rejected altogether or reframed to adapt to Jewish norms. This process of cultural negotiation, subversion, and appropriation was messy and diverse, neither regulated nor uniform. Rather, different individuals and dispersed communities took assorted paths, sometimes converging under similar principles, overlapping, and crisscrossing, and on other occasions diverging and departing far from each other. This is the disorderly nature of cultural dynamics. Dissent and reluctance are as much a part of the shared discourse in Roman society as praise and acceptance. Indeed, as will be shown in detail, all (or almost all) of the reservations raised by rabbis regarding the baths find equivalent articulation in other segments of Roman society.

At the end of the day, filtered absorption allowed (at least some) Jews to live in peace with the surrounding culture, which from this perspective was also their culture. Minority groups apply similar mechanisms throughout human history, allowing them full, or nearly full, integration in the shared cultural landscape of their time while also maintaining and preserving their own identity and customs. Rabbinic literature, which contains an assortment of views and positions, allows us to follow and chart these dynamics at least partially and to explore the strategies and mechanisms at work as they took shape within some strands of the Jewish world. Far from being texts promoting exclusiveness, I present it here as a literary corpus engaging in cultural negotiation and appropriation.

What Is Rabbinic Literature and Who Were the Rabbis?

The group of texts we call rabbinic literature includes some forty documents of various sizes, about half of them of a legal nature (named *halakhah*, from the Hebrew verb "to go"—in the sense of "the way in which we live"). The other half features non-legal material, known as *haggadah* ("telling"). The latter consists of stories, homilies, parables, proverbs, and other genres. Some of these works, both from *halakhah* and *haggadah*, offer commentaries on the scriptures known today as the Hebrew Bible, which ancient Jews considered sacred and divine in nature. Rabbis labeled these latter exegetical works as *midrash* (from the ancient Hebrew verb that means "to investigate" and find meaning). No strict lines divide the different genres and they often intermix and overlap.

During a long and convoluted process spanning the eras of the High and Late Empires (roughly second to seventh centuries CE), the figures often referred to collectively as "the rabbis" produced and then gathered, collected, and edited the *halakhah*, the *haggadah*, and the *midrash*.[20] Written in Hebrew and Aramaic, although with thousands of words borrowed from Greek and Latin (and less from Persian), the texts reflect nearly every aspect of life in the Roman province of Palestine. As they developed their literature, the authors used their surroundings and their daily lives as the building blocks for the content of their discussions. On the one hand, they only sparsely mention specific historical events; clearly, the authors never aspired to offer a historical narrative. On the other hand, rabbinic texts richly represent the stuff of daily life. Both the non-legal and the legal writings abound with discussions and descriptions of physical structures and artifacts from both urban and agrarian settings; the workings of institutions and organizations (private and public, local, provincial, and imperial, social and communal) and the colorful settings of everyday occurrences (birth, childrearing, marriage and family, education, the entire gamut of work and vocation, the calendar, entertainment and leisure, all the way to death and burial).[21] One of the texts, the Babylonian Talmud, was produced in Sasanian Persia and offers a wealth of information about that realm as well.

The creators of rabbinic literature, whom we now call rabbis, did not use that name to define themselves. Rather, in their own eyes they were learned Jews—scholars. The most common term they applied to introduce who they were was *ḥakhamim*, the plural form of the Hebrew word *ḥakham* (wise), meaning, in this context, scholars, sometimes translated in English as sages. They were erudite individuals who devoted their lives to study. They were active in Roman Palestine in the generations after the destruction of the Second Temple of Jerusalem during the Jewish revolt against the Romans in 70 CE and later, from the third century, also in the Sasanian Persian territories of what are now Iraq and Iran, which they called Babylonia (see map 2). The title "rabbi," which means "my teacher," expressed status and prestige (similar to today's "professor"), and individual scholars and students used the word out of respect for other teachers who were particularly important to them, but none of them utilized it to refer to all of them as a group.[22]

Like other intellectuals throughout history, the *ḥakhamim* were animated by their personalities, in particular their natural proclivity toward learning. The focus of their studies, the foundation texts of their curriculum, consisted of the Jewish scriptures, which later became the Hebrew Bible. Their preferred field of study centered on legal discourse and exegesis (unlike other ancient Jewish scholars, who pursued philosophy, mysticism, and even history). Accordingly, rabbinic scholars endeavored to channel what they believed to be the eternal truth of God, as articulated in the Torah (the Pentateuch, namely the first five, most important, books in what came to be the Bible), into meticulous and well-structured legal formulas—strictures, proscriptions, and directives that came to be known collectively as *halakhah*. But in the course of their learning they also crafted stories and anecdotes, transmitted traditions about innumerable topics, and related plentiful information related to their areas of interest.

For all we know, this small group of intellectuals exerted minimal, if any, influence—let alone official authority—over the Jewish public in Roman Palestine, and even less so on the Jewish communities elsewhere in the Mediterranean regions. They never consisted of more than a few dozen at any given time, and sometimes even fewer.[23] The evidence neither shows the ḥakhamim as judges sitting in courts issuing rulings and offering guidance according to Jewish law nor establishes them as leaders of the Jewish population of their time; those roles emerged only hundreds of years later, mostly in the Islamic and medieval European realms, and also in Persia. Furthermore, when it comes to ancient Jewish society in the Roman world at large, despite the traditional view that sees them as a "nation" living by the laws and norms of the rabbis, the evidence speaks clearly to the contrary. As far as I can tell, rabbinic norms as a whole never prevailed in antiquity, even as specific details did. The term "Rabbinic Judaism," which many modern scholars use to characterize either Jewish society or the mores of the rabbis, is a misnomer and anachronistic; Jews were quite diverse in their ways of life.[24]

Moreover, it is quite clear that for at least 150 years after the Temple's destruction, the ḥakhamim never even constituted an organized group, let alone a movement (as is all too commonly, and mistakenly, presumed today); they had no sense of collective self-awareness, no well-defined political goals, and no coherent, uniform conceptual outlook on Jewish life.[25] For generations, these rabbis functioned as individual scholars, teachers with no sense of a larger community beyond the small number of students they had attracted. Whatever links existed among these teachers and their devotees were loose and limited and generally restricted to intellectual interests and scholarly debate.

The situation gradually began to change only at the beginning of the third century, with the project of redacting and publishing the Mishnah, the first comprehensive compilation of rabbinic legal material, organized thematically and intended to cover all aspects of Jewish life. The so-called "rabbinic movement" did not produce the Mishnah; rather, the creation of the Mishnah began to create the rabbinic movement. Once this text became popular among these scattered circles of learning, their shared admiration for and constant engagement with this text laid the foundation for what became, generations later, something that would be familiar to us today: a wide community of scholars devoted to the study of the Mishnah and the legal traditions associated with it as its core curriculum.

In the few decades after the publication of the Mishnah, some scholars produced an addendum, called exactly that in Aramaic—the Tosefta. Other texts, published over the next few centuries, continued to gather the learning of the ḥakhamim. They called many of them *midrashim* (*midrash* in the singular, after the interpretive activity called by that name), organizing them in sequence with the biblical text. They structured other compendia thematically. Chief among the latter was the Palestinian Talmud (also called *Yerushalmi* in Hebrew). Produced in the fourth century as a large addendum to the Mishnah and following its thematic structure, its editors intended to bring together a century and a half of rabbinic scholarship on the Mishnah. A century later its twin text, the Babylonian Talmud, came out, featuring the learning of rabbinic scholars in Sasanian Persia.[26]

These texts—the Mishnah, the Tosefta, the various *midrashim*, the Palestinian Talmud, and the Babylonian Talmud—stand at the heart of the current book. They contain hundreds of references to public Roman bathhouses. The rabbis never show real interest in providing a full description of bathhouses or all the activities that took place there (in contrast, for example, to their discussion of the Temple in Jerusalem—long gone by their day—to which they devote an entire tractate in the Mishnah). Their attention to the bathhouse emerges only as it pertains to whatever specific legal topic they are dealing with, or if it comes up in a story they are telling or a tradition they are conveying.

Neglect of the bathhouse as a focus of discussion is itself a fascinating part of this story. The modern reader, conditioned by the projection of today's orthodox Jewish views back on antiquity and particularly on the rabbis, expects sustained outrage at a place where nudity and licentiousness prevailed, as well as detailed and strict decrees about what Jews should and should not do in the baths. However, one never finds such judgments. Rather, rabbinic authors offer only passing references to the bathhouse and express its acceptance as a regular part of life. In what follows throughout this book, I discuss these surprising conceptual gaps and what they may tell us about the attitudes toward the bathhouse and the activities that took place there, as well as the plentiful—if scattered—references to this establishment, packed with rich detail and insight, gathered together and analyzed alongside other ancient sources: archaeological and epigraphical remains as well in numerous excerpts in Graeco-Roman literature. The result of this unprecedented triangulation of sources provides a fascinating portrayal of the institution of the Roman bathhouse, its manifold functions in the everyday life, and the perceptions of it held by at least some Jews living on the provincial periphery of the Roman Empire. Between the lines emerges a remarkable story of cultural interaction.

Some Methodological and Theoretical Considerations

In closing this introduction, the central methodological and theoretical principles that guide this book should be presented and clarified.

First, for several decades starting in the mid-twentieth century, a series of methodological disputes rattled the field of Rabbinics, focused mainly on the question of whether rabbinic literature may be used as historical evidence. Many of these methodological debates have long been resolved, at least for most researchers. The romantic, positivistic view that took nearly every reference in rabbinic texts at face value and viewed it as reporting actual events has long been rejected. The opposite view, the extreme skepticism of those who mounted the early criticism against the positivists, chief among them Jacob Neusner, has also been discarded.[27] Most investigators today are comfortable using the rabbinic corpus in historical studies involving society and culture, as well as in inquiries about law, literature, and religion. Using the legal formulations and debates of the rabbis creates challenges for the historian, as the line between reality and legal fiction is seldom clear-cut; one must watch out for what Seth Schwartz calls "moving too easily from prescription to description."[28] Similarly, the numerous anecdotes and stories told by rabbis cannot be taken to recount real-life events. But in truth, the historiographical challenges here are no more difficult than with other genres of the ancient world, such as the satire, the novella, and other types of fiction and legends. Scholars have found productive strategies to deal with these problems and extract whatever information possible. Fergus Millar put it best: "The invented world of fiction may yet represent, perhaps cannot help representing, important features of the real world."[29]

Second, in the same vein, most scholars today agree with the harsh (but mostly justified) criticism directed at many of the early studies of Rabbinics that seamlessly mixed Persian material from the Babylonian Talmud with the literature that emerged from Roman Palestine. Although here too, the categorical rejection of all traditions about Roman Palestine mentioned in the Babylonian Talmud, as if an iron, impenetrable wall separated these two realms of rabbinic activity, is mostly misguided. Many scholars, myself included, have shown that nuggets of information traveled in both directions between Palestine and Persia; used with proper caution, at least some passages preserved in the Babylonian Talmud are undoubtedly informative about the Roman world in general and Jewish society in Palestine in particular.[30]

Third, I do not subscribe to the extreme restrictions that some scholars of Talmud place on the study of rabbinic texts before they are established with philological certainty. Simply put, the philological status of many ancient texts, not only rabbinic, remains quite murky, and it does not (and should not) prevent us from studying them and using them to glean information about the ancient world, always keeping in mind that the echoes we hear may not always be accurate and that future generations may hear and thus conclude differently.

Furthermore, with respect to methodology, it is worth noting that the current book deals solely with Roman public bathhouses (as defined in chapter 1), not with water in general or with other ancient hydraulic installations. Nor does it deal with bathing establishments in other periods, beyond the Roman world. Many scholars bind together different institutions associated with water, such as the thermal baths or the Jewish ritual immersion installation used for purification (called *miqveh*). As I explain later in the book, the sources use distinctive names for each of these installations, though they are all called baths in English. True, they all involve water, but their functions were dissimilar, and they served separate and to a large extent discrete purposes. The people of antiquity regarded them as different from one another, and mixing them together usually leads to erroneous, at times quite far-fetched, conclusions.[31]

Finally, on the theoretical side, various strands of scholarship have influenced my thinking and research. From the French Annales school I took my distaste for the historiography of states and nations, politics, wars, and powerful institutions. In particular my debt goes to Michel de Certeau's seminal work, *L'invention du quotidien I: Arts de faire* (in English *The Practice of Everyday Life*), where he lays out the framework for the study of habitual, daily practices of people as categories of cultural appropriation in a specific time and place. The current book applies de Certeau's version of small history (in contrast to the Big History so fashionable these days) to the study of ancient Judaism; simple people, mundane, everyday moments, and ordinary, seemingly unimportant institutions lie at the heart of this research, which attempts to show the richness they can bring to our understanding of the past.

A second layer of influence comes from current developments in the field of Materiality, or as it is sometimes called, The History of Things, or by others, myself included, Material Culture.[32] This subcategory of cultural studies deals with the agency of physical objects and artifacts and sees them as both carriers and instigators of human experiences. On the practical level, it champions the integration of texts and archaeology (and art where applicable). The central claim here is that by studying people's encounter and engagement with artifacts, in the case of this book with the public bathhouse building, with its various installations, apparatuses, and paraphernalia, we are able to re-create the mindsets and perceptions of ancient people on topics and issues that form their lives.

All in all, this book targets multiple audiences: scholars and students of diverse fields such as Archaeology, Rabbinics, and Classics, as well as Ancient Judaism and the history of the Roman Mediterranean. It also aspires to interest the general public: Jews who wish to understand the roots of their tradition and anyone interested in the ancient world as a whole who wishes to see it from the perspective of one of the largest minorities of the time. As it presents the story of cultural interaction between Jews and Graeco-Romans, it also aims to unpack the vast corpora of rabbinic texts and make them accessible to those not too familiar with their nuances and intricacies. For experts in those texts it strives to show how much more can be gleaned by placing them in close dialogue with classical, Graeco-Roman, and archaeological materials. To achieve this, I have tried to eliminate the technical taxonomy and professional jargon that usually overshadow studies of the rabbis and make the text seem undecipherable and impenetrable to the uninitiated. In May 2006 I participated in a conference at what is arguably the most prestigious academic venue in North America, the Institute for Advanced Study in Princeton. Around the table sat some of the biggest names in the study of the ancient world, and when it came to ancient Judaism, they concluded that "Jews, particularly rabbis, lived on their own planet." I vehemently disagreed then, and I hope to prove them wrong in the following pages.

PART I

Setting the Stage

CHAPTER ONE

The Miracle of (Hot) Water

THE EMERGENCE OF THE ROMAN PUBLIC BATHHOUSE AS A CULTURAL INSTITUTION

In the Beginning There Was Water

Chances are that sometime soon after you woke up today, somewhere early in your morning routine, you found yourself in front of the bathroom sink. There you used your hands to manipulate a faucet, which in turn allowed a stream of water to issue from pipes hidden in the walls, through the output opening and into the basin beneath your hands. Perhaps you fancy your water warm, even scorching; or perhaps you like the jolt of a freezing splash to wake you up. You may take a shower or bath, or you may be content to wash your face and brush your teeth. Such are the many choices we have.

We all use water, usually without recognizing or appreciating its availability. Its presence is so embedded into the texture of our lives that water usually remains an afterthought. If at all, it makes just a faint impression on us, just a sound in the background, the swirl down a toilet or the splash from the faucet. The plentiful and ubiquitous supply of water, like electricity, the internet, clothing, and food, has become an essential component of our lives. The availability of hot running water is a fundamental component of modern society and an integral part of daily experience for most—though far from all—people around the globe. Indeed, we call places that lag behind the standards of the civilized world *backwaters*, pun intended.

Conditions in ancient times differed remarkably. Throughout the early phases of human existence, water remained scarce and thus precious, used

FIGURE 1. The Pont du Gard, a first-century CE Roman bridge, resting on arches and carrying an aqueduct over the Gardon river in southern France; the aqueduct brought water to the Roman colony of Nemausus (today Nîmes). *Credit:* Photograph courtesy of Benh Lieu Song, licensed by Creative Commons (CC BY-SA 3.0), courtesy of Wikimedia Commons.

sparingly and almost entirely for essential purposes like drinking and irrigation. In antiquity, most people accumulated rain in cisterns, dug wells, and drew on natural springs and rivers. Nearly everywhere the accessibility and availability of water presented a constant challenge, determining the location of settlements and limiting their size. Indeed, it is no exaggeration to say that the quantity of water determined the number of people who could live together and the size to which a settlement could grow. Without the abundant, ready-to-use water supply of the modern world, the habits and experiences of people in earlier times were quite different as well; think for instance of the smell, not to stay stench, in sweaty summers or chilly winters when there is not enough water to wash oneself, or of hygiene and its medical ramifications. The hard work needed to obtain water—and the limited supply even when it was accessible—made personal cleanliness a secondary concern. It also necessitated communal action to regulate access to the inevitably scarce supply. Those living in antiquity had to negotiate daily their access to water.[1]

Then came the Romans. To overcome this life-defining dearth, the Romans initiated nothing less than a water revolution, transforming living conditions where water was neither copious nor constant and creating a human environment, mainly urban, overflowing with this ubiquitous but precious liquid.[2] At the core of this new stage in human experience stood the aqueduct (figs. 1 and 2).[3] From the Latin noun *aqua*, water, and the verb *ducere*, to lead or guide, these man-made channels transport water from faraway sources, usually high-volume springs, to large

FIGURE 2. A second-century CE Roman aqueduct bringing water to Caesarea Maritima in Judaea/Palestine. *Credit:* Photograph by Mark87, licensed by Creative Commons, courtesy of Wikimedia Commons.

population centers. The Romans did not invent these water systems, nor were they the first to use them. Hundreds of years prior to Roman adoption, Near Eastern cities in Mesopotamia such as Nimrud and Babylon in the ninth century BCE and Nineveh a few generations later featured large-scale water networks stretching at times over tens of miles and including canals, tunnels, and bridges.[4] Delivery structures of this kind could also be found a bit later in the heavily populated cities in the Greek and Hellenistic world, such as Athens, Samos, and Priene.[5] But all of these early examples were much smaller in scale than the Roman project and less widespread. The need to construct aqueducts rose most immediately from the challenges posed by the growing population in the city of Rome during the last centuries before the Common Era, the period of the Republic. By the first century CE, after the Republic gave way to the Empire, the newly established imperial house in Rome, imitated by local rulers and city councils around the Mediterranean, and enabled by the engineering prowess of military units stationed throughout the empire, was building aqueducts everywhere in the Roman realm. In the relatively peripheral province of Judaea alone, home to about a million people during this time, archaeologists have identified some seventy such water systems (fig. 2).[6] These networks of water supply produced a dramatic shift in lifestyle.

Preparatory to these transformative developments in the ability to deliver water, Roman engineers and architects refined and distributed a range of earlier technological advances, including the increasing use of concrete and the growing employment of the arch.[7] Mixing and then calcining water, clay, and lime—a white, powdery substance produced from the burning of limestone—yields cement. When mixed with aggregates of sand, gravel, or crushed stone, cement forms concrete, a cohesive substance with tantalizing capabilities for building structures that are as flexible in shape as they are large and sturdy. A by-product of this process, cement, can also function as a water-resistant plaster. The second building device, the arch, made possible many of the Romans' greatest architectural achievements as it provided stability and height. Builders could use a series of arches to create arcades, whose still-standing ruins are some of the most famous remnants of Roman civilization (see fig. 1). These semicircular towering structures enabled Roman engineers to control elevation and thus maintain the necessary gradient of the conduit; water could thus gradually flow from its source toward the final destination using gravity alone. Arches also allowed engineers to construct aqueducts across vast landscapes, using fewer materials, without splitting up the countryside. They also supported bridges, necessary to traverse valleys, gorges, or any other acute drop in height that interfered with the clear, straight path needed. Another Roman advance that proved extremely important was the inverted siphon, a device that uses air pressure to push water upward in pipes, which allowed an aqueduct to pass under an obstacle if bringing it over proved too costly or impractical.[8]

If fed by a rich source of water, an aqueduct properly built and efficiently maintained can supply huge amounts of water.[9] In the first century of the Common Era, when eight or nine aqueducts operated in Rome, they provided the capital of the empire—a city of about one million people—with more water on a daily basis than the quantity consumed in New York City in 1985.[10] Furthermore, except during periods of maintenance, aqueducts flowed continuously, producing quantities of water never seen before in urban centers. These cities gathered this incoming volume of water in tanks and basins, or directed it to a distribution hub known in Latin as *castella divisoria*, a term preserved in rabbinic literature as "*Kastalin* that dispenses the water in the cities."[11] The water was then dispensed around the city through lead, stone, or ceramic pipes (fig. 3). These pipes delivered water to a range of destinations, from public fountains to private residences. Some of the public fountains were small and unassuming, called *lacus*; others, known as *nymphaea*, were splendid and highly ornamented, providing the people with drinking water. Sextus Julius Frontinus, the Roman senator appointed as commissioner of the aqueducts (*curator aquarum*) toward the end of the first century CE, reports the existence of 39 ornamental fountains and 591 water basins in Rome alone. About two hundred years later, the number of *nymphaea* drops to fifteen, but the number of small water fountains rises to over a thousand.[12]

FIGURE 3. A first-century CE Roman pressure pipe used for the distribution of water in the Graeco-Roman city of Hippos/Susita, just northeast of Judaea/Palestine. *Credit:* Photograph courtesy of Michael Eisenberg.

Once functioning, aqueducts tend to create a water surplus. After all, unlike modern water supply systems, aqueducts featured no real mechanism to stop the flow of the water. The second-century Greek traveler and writer Pausanias reports the huge water excess in Corinth; other sources speak of the use of spare water to cultivate gardens or operate mills, and archaeological evidence shows that various mini-industries, like cloth dyeing and cleaning, depended on the availability of extra water.[13] Contemporaries expressed their awareness of this abundance of water in many forms.[14] Inscriptions regularly praise the water and the amenities it provides, as do numerous ancient authors. In a similar vein but from a different perspective, toward the end of the fourth century Augustine complained that the noise from the gushing water behind the bathhouse regularly prevented him from falling asleep. Around the same time on the other side of the Mediterranean, a Jewish scholar in Roman Palestine, R. Ḥanina of Caesarea Maritima—a city rich with aqueduct water and bathhouses—expressed gratitude for the abundance of water characteristic of many Roman cities, using water as a metaphor for Torah (the Jewish sacred text believed to contain God's words to his people) and saying that flowing water is brought to the city for its gardens, orchards, latrines, and bathhouses.[15]

The connection between the abundance of water brought by the spread of aqueducts and the rise and proliferation of Roman public bathhouses is not entirely clear. First, as scholars have pointed out, many bathhouses, at least in their initial stages, were not supplied by aqueducts. Rather, they relied on cisterns and wells.[16] Indeed, contrary to the generally accepted cause-and-effect model that sees bathhouses as by-products of aqueducts, perhaps the demand for baths stimulated the need for more water and thus induced the construction of aqueducts.[17] Nevertheless, even if the establishment of bathhouses may not depend directly on aqueducts, it is quite clear that widely diffused bathing habits, requiring a lot of water, whether for hygiene or leisure (that is, for purposes beyond the necessities of life), which were shared across social and geographical divides, would not have been possible without them.[18] In the centuries before Roman expansion, it was unimaginable that practically everyone in a city could attend a public bath with warm water on a nearly daily basis. True, some ancient bathhouses were supplied with water from wells and rivers, but without aqueducts, water would always have been scarce, preventing the development of large-scale and widely distributed bathhouses and the lifestyle associated with them.

Then Came Heat

A typical Roman bathhouse offered a variety of amenities and facilities, but its core consisted of water and heat.[19] Combined with a dependable and abundant supply of water, the capacity to heat large quantities of it altered the way people experienced bathing. No longer a scarce, high-end luxury for the upper echelons of society, bathing establishments became a popular, widespread diversion for the masses. Prior to the Roman period, small amounts of water could be heated on a fire; men and women of means could have their slaves do this for them and then have the warmed water poured on their bodies as they sat in a tub, or even have the bathtub laboriously filled and then plunge in before the water cooled off (which, as anyone who has taken a bath knows, happens quite fast). Slaves heated water for privileged individuals in the courts of kings and the residences of the wealthy from time immemorial, and this was somewhat prevalent in the Greek gymnasium and other Greek public bathing structures that preceded the Roman bath (more on these institutions below).

Prior to the Romans, simple heating devices, such as charcoal braziers, provided some hot water.[20] But Roman times witnessed the development of a mechanism that allowed mass production of warm water as well as

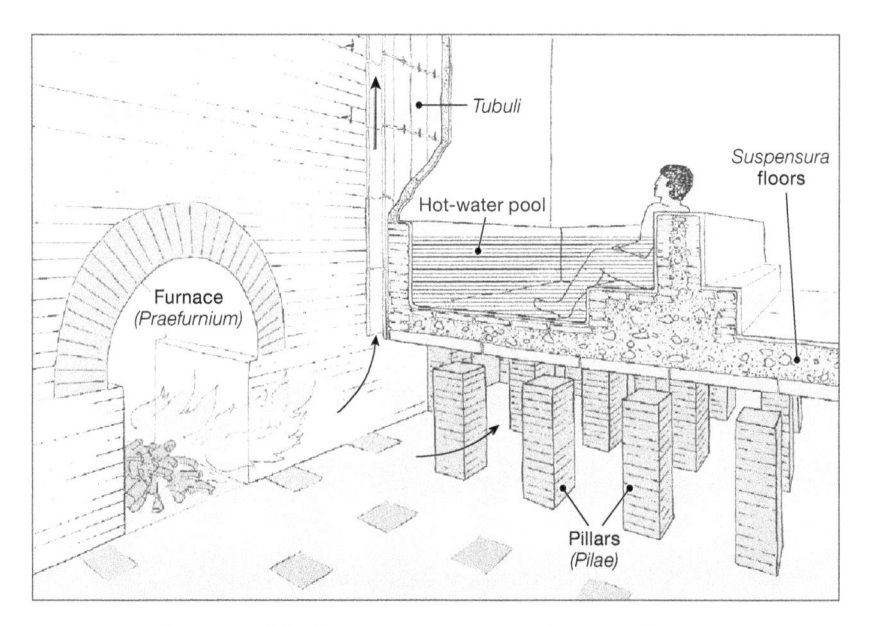

FIGURE 4. A diagram of the hypocaust system. *Credit:* Created by Lorene Sterner for the author, based on drawing by Jean-Pierre Adam, licensed by Creative Commons (CC BY-SA 4.0), courtesy of Wikimedia Commons.

the heating up of large spaces. One ingenious technological innovation made these advancements in heating capabilities easy and widespread: the hypocaust system (from the Greek *hypokauston*, "heating from underneath"; fig. 4).[21] It consisted of a dual-stage heating technique that worked as follows: builders suspended the bathhouse floor (thus named *suspensura*) on a dense mass of small pillars (*pilae*) usually made of layered tiles, either round or square, or at times of monolithic short columns, creating a hollow space underneath the floors (figs. 5 and 12). On top of this "forest" of columns came layers of mortar and plaster and topped by a floor made of stone slabs, mosaic, or marble (giving the bath one of its popular names: *balneae pensiles*, "hanging baths").

In a side furnace chamber (known as *praefurnium*), bronze boilers stood above wood-fed fires; normally, a pipe from the aqueduct or another source filled these boilers with water, which was then heated and, when released, would flow into the basins and pools of the baths. The same furnace also channeled hot air into the cavity under the raised floors, heating them and the entire room above them, with its tubs, basins, and pools, and at the same time maintaining the warmth of the water that flowed from the boilers. Vertical and narrow semi-chimneys at the sides of the bathhouse rooms allowed the hot steam to circulate outside. A system of valves

FIGURE 5. The furnace chamber (at the top of the picture) and the conduit that channeled the hot air to the empty space underneath the hot room (itself not shown), from the western bathhouse in Scythopolis/Beth Shean (fourth to fifth century). *Credit:* Photograph courtesy of Gabi Laron.

and plungers enabled the operators to manipulate and sustain the desired level of heat. At some point toward the end of the first century BCE or a bit later, bathhouse architects added another innovation. By layering the walls with hollow bricks or tiles (known as *tubuli*), with holes at each end, they created a second radiant heating system, where hot air would circulate (see figs. 4 and 14).

Modern scholars disagree about the origin of the hypocaust. Although the famous first-century encyclopedist Pliny the Elder claimed that he knew by name the person who conceived it, one Caius Sergius Orata, a first-century BCE entrepreneur from Campania in southern Italy, the origin of this powerful yet simple invention remains shrouded in mystery.[22] Archaeologists trace the early precursors of the hypocaust throughout the Mediterranean world and far beyond, in places such as Japan and Southeast Asia.[23] Whatever its origins may have been, once adopted and disseminated in the Roman world, the results were astounding. Modern experiments show that the air temperature in the heated rooms of baths with *suspensura* and *tubuli* (as well as solar heat generated from glass windows) could reach 50° C (122° F) and the water temperature could be as high as 40° C (104° F). In rooms without water installations for bathing, the dry heat and low humidity (what we would today call a sauna) could easily climb to 80° C (176° F).[24] Consider the fact that for hundreds, if not thousands, of years, literally from the earliest days of humankind, people for the most part engaged water in its natural, chilly state. Try taking cold showers for only a month; as you shiver, you will appreciate the Roman hot water revolution. The benefits of water were always significant and evident, but conditions confined the enjoyment of water to hot summer days. Imperial Rome transformed all of that, as hot water became available to everyone throughout the year. No wonder people from all walks of life and all strata of society were so fond of public bathhouses; in a world of limited material goods, one often shaped by the burden of manual labor, the bathhouse offered everyone some of the most basic pleasures of life.

Structure and Formation of Public Bathhouses

A bathhouse building and its adjoining courts could take many forms, but certain architectural elements soon became typical and appeared in one way or another in all such structures throughout the Roman Empire (see diagram 1).[25] At the core stood the hot room (known as the *caldarium*), the main benefactor of the hypocaust, which usually included a communal pool (*alveus*), a basin (*labrum*) for cold water, and at times benches around the walls. In addition to the heated nucleus, two other rooms offered engagement with varying temperatures—the *frigidarium*, typically a vaulted room with cold water pools (known as *piscinae*), and the *tepidarium*, an intermediate room between the cold and the hot. Other standard bathhouse features included the changing room (*apodyterium*), which provided niches and shelves for storing clothing (see

FIGURE 6. Remains of the baths of Caracalla in Rome (facing the *caldarium*). *Credit:* Photograph courtesy of Ethan Doyle White, licensed by Creative Commons (CC BY-SA 4.0), courtesy of Wikimedia Commons.

fig. 13), a sauna for both dry and wet sweat (*laconicum* and *sudatorium*, respectively), and a latrine (see fig. 9). Outside the main building, an open court (*palaestra*)—often surrounded by peristyles and porticoes—accommodated sports and exercise and frequently included an open-air swimming pool (*natatio*). Basilicas and spacious halls regularly adjoined the bath complex, serving as reception and dining areas as well as venues for feasts, social gatherings, and celebrations; they were also used for brothels and, even if rarely, libraries. Not all bathhouses included all of these facilities. Builders designed structures in many shapes and sizes as they arranged the basic components of a bathhouse to fit the needs and tastes of their patrons.

Bathhouses were often built in a circular plan, where the bather walked from room to room in a specific direction, moving between the various temperatures and partaking in what became the common bathing cycle (more on this below). In some places, bathhouses were laid out in a more linear fashion, whereas still others were given a more unique layout. The huge, imperial baths of Rome (known as *thermae*) could house thousands of people. The best preserved of these *thermae*, built by and named after the third-century emperor Caracalla, sprawled over 25 hectares (over 2.5 million square feet) and could accommodate some 1,600 visitors at any given time (fig. 6).[26] The facilities in urban centers throughout the empire (normally called *balnea*) were generally more modest, some hosting hundreds of bathers, but the majority of baths found at these centers were smaller, accommodating dozens at a time.

The Romans used their expertise in architecture and technology to add splendor and beauty to many of these bathing facilities; in the words of Cyril Mango, "Some of them could be described as museums of art."[27] Mentioned already were the aqueducts, borne by arches, that brought water from long distances. Inside the building, lofty ceilings, often barrel vaults, and on occasion even round domes, supported by massive piers and columns, rose over immense halls. Towering windows flooded the buildings with light. Mosaic floors, frescoes, stucco, marble, and *opus sectile* ornamentations (a technique using colored materials to create shapes and patterns) decorated the floors and the walls. A great many statues also adorned the bathing facilities.

Before Roman times, people bathed in both private and public settings. A major forerunner to the Roman institution can be seen in the washing enterprises of the Greeks. Starting in the sixth and fifth centuries BCE, public bathing establishments existed throughout the Greek and Hellenistic worlds, either as a stand-alone structure called *balaneion*, a privately owned business serving the public for profit, or those known as *loutra*, facilities incorporated into the gymnasium, the sport and education institution of the Greek city.[28] Nevertheless, the bathing habits of the Greeks and the structures in which this activity took place varied significantly from those of the Romans. On the functional level, Roman baths, for the most part, completely abandoned the Greek practice of washing in hipbaths, known as *pueloi*, where people squatted or sat in an individual tub and had water poured over them (fig. 7). Romans preferred open spaces that allowed people to bathe together in pools and large basins. In addition, with very few exceptions, the Greek bathing establishments also lacked the sophisticated hypocaust heating system of Roman baths and thus the ability to control both the warmth of the water and the environment surrounding it; most Greek facilities simply provided cold water.[29] Furthermore, in the gymnasium, washing the body was secondary and less valued than athletic and intellectual activities[30] and limited to the privileged few who attended this institution. None of this could compare to the Roman experience, where at least in the large cities hundreds of people from all strata of society could enjoy the baths simultaneously and on a regular, daily basis. Essentially, the Greek bathing facility functioned as a practical utility, geared toward cleaning the body after exercise; among the Romans, bathing became a stand-alone feature in the daily experience of people, often a centerpiece in a larger social scene that transpired

FIGURE 7. Greek hip-bath, made of terracotta dated to the second century BCE; on display at the Nafplio Archaeological Museum, Greece. *Credit:* Photograph by Zdenek Kratochvil, licensed by Creative Commons (CC BY-SA 4.0), courtesy of Wikimedia Commons.

within the walls of the public bath. Finally, the Greek bath never achieved the cultural stature it enjoyed in the Roman period, where various activities associated with the baths became fixed features in the texture of city and village life. Whereas numerous inscriptions in cities throughout the Roman world applaud benefactors for building baths, or in which individuals express pride in doing so, with only very few exceptions these are lacking in preceding Greek and Hellenistic epigraphy.[31]

Nevertheless, we should not view the transition from Greek to Roman bathing facilities as a definitive split in which the former ceased to exist after the emergence of the latter. Rather, the two coexisted for centuries, crisscrossed, overlapped, and intersected, swapping characteristics and exchanging features.[32] Deep in the Roman period, gymnasia continued to function, especially in the territories of the Greek/Hellenistic East, which by the first century CE had become the eastern Roman Empire. In the second century, for example, Pausanias sees no problem in listing the gymnasium as one of the essential elements defining a Roman city, together with government offices, a theater, and running water, but he fails to make any specific reference to the public bath, as he probably thought of it as part of the gymnasium.[33] Over a thousand miles to the south, in papyri documenting the upper Egyptian city of Oxyrhynchus, one places a local bath in the gymnasium, while another describes a gymnasium built into a bath.[34] Obviously, ancient people did not categorize these institutions separately, as we do in modern textbooks. On the other hand, ancient authors also differentiated between the two; Pausanias himself discusses the gymnasium and the bath as two distinct buildings, and other Graeco-Roman authors also note the difference.[35] In the end, the relationship between Roman and Greek bathing facilities is complex, and the characteristics that distinguished the two varied greatly from one place to another.

Modern scholars, mainly archaeologists, have invested much effort in pinpointing the origin of the public Roman bathhouse.[36] With some qualifications, most agree that the bathhouse emerged almost simultaneously in Asia Minor and southern Italy in the second century BCE, that it had spread throughout the emerging empire by the end of the following century, and that it had reached its peak in the first few centuries of the Common Era. By the second century CE, hundreds if not thousands of bathing establishments dotted the Mediterranean world in cities, military camps, towns, and even small villages, from Britannia in the west to Dura-Europos on the Persian border in the East.[37] Pliny the Elder states that 170 facilities already existed in Rome alone a century before his time. Three hundred years later, the *Notitia regionum urbis* speaks of over 800 such establishments in Rome. But even the small village (a *vicus* in Latin terminology) near the villa of Pliny the Elder's nephew, Pliny the Younger—himself an author and high-ranking imperial official—contained three. The celebrated second-century scholar and orator Aelius Aristides boasted in a speech that Smyrna, a city on the western Anatolian coast, had so many baths one would never know which to choose.[38]

Beyond the actual numbers, these sources convey the way baths registered in the public imagination: as pervasive and abundant. For those living in the Roman Empire, bathhouses were everywhere. That vision of Roman life extended throughout the Mediterranean world and beyond its limits. One legend claims that upon arrival in Alexandria in the seventh century, the Muslim conquerors encountered four thousand baths. A similar fantastic depiction of the "metropolis of Rome," preserved in the Babylonian Talmud, the sixth-century Jewish Persian text, maintains that "three thousand baths were in [Rome] and five hundred windows [chimneys] were raising its smoke, outside [above the city] wall."[39] Though both of these accounts exaggerate, that amplification is telling; with a few relatively simple technological innovations, the Romans harnessed two of our world's greatest forces—water and fire—and, in the process, prompted a new conception of life and created a new institution, inaugurating a set of experiences that soon became an essential ingredient of daily life.

The Bathing Experience

Over time, bathing routines evolved. By the first century CE, a large segment of the population throughout the Roman world typically attended the bathhouse daily or nearly daily. Public bathing establishments welcomed people from all strata of society (excluding, at least in some places, those with various skin diseases). Surely, certain facilities limited their clientele, restricting entrance to members of a particular guild or other associations, and the wealthy who could afford it incorporated private bathing installations into their villas and mansions. But overall, everyone, including the most affluent and powerful in society, also attended the public baths shared by the rest of the population (see the detailed discussion of these social phenomena in chapter 7). Bathhouses varied on the issue of charging for admission; some evidently did, although always a modest fee, but others, relying on either generous donations from wealthy benefactors or endowments created by the imperial and local governments, allowed people to bathe for free.[40]

Bathers normally arrived during the afternoon or before dinner; both customs are widely documented over the centuries in all areas, although with numerous variations and exceptions.[41] Seneca the Younger, the Stoic scholar and politician of the first century CE, asserts that in the days of Scipio Africanus, three hundred years earlier, Romans used to attend the baths only once a week, but in his time, they went every day.[42] Three hundred or so years after Seneca, in the Syrian city of Antioch on the other side of the Mediterranean, the prolific teacher and scholar Libanius seems to attest to the same practice. In his semi-autobiographical work, he complains about his migraines and says that aside from reading books and composing orations, his only other daily activities are taking his dinner and walking to the baths.[43] Naturally, there were exceptions: Suetonius in his imperial biographies tells us that for reasons of health, the emperor Augustus limited his excursions to the baths, but in another biography Suetonius mentions people who bathed several times a day.[44] Medical considerations can go both ways; centuries after Augustus, the Christian Augustine states that nuns should attend the baths just once a month, but he permits more frequent bathing if their health requires it.[45] So, while

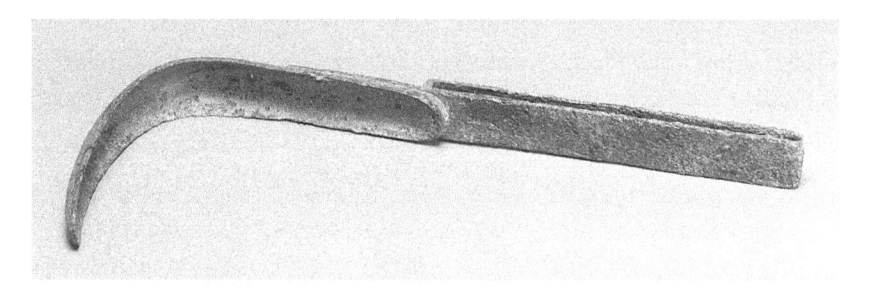

FIGURE 8. A Roman period bronze strigil (*strigilis*), a carved blade used by Greeks and Romans to scrape oil, sweat, and dirt off the skin. *Credit:* On display at the Getty Museum. Los Angeles County Museum of Art, M.80.203.94. Licensed by Wikimedia Commons.

there were exceptions, the norm of daily baths became established and remained in force for centuries.

Once in the bathhouse, the standard routine began with physical exercise in the *palaestra*. Athletic activities ranged from wrestling and lifting weights to all sorts of gymnastic exercises and a wide range of ball games.[46] Physical activity was then followed by alternating immersions in the hot and cold baths in the designated rooms (the *caldarium* and the *frigidarium*) and sitting in the sauna. For people with means, the visit to the baths might end or begin with a massage, followed by a servant or an employee of the bathhouse applying oil and scraping it off with a strigil (*strigilis* in Latin), a sharp tool used to remove the oil after it was applied to the body (figs. 8 and 25).[47] In addition, a wide range of workers plied their trade at the bathhouse. Masseuses, doctors, barbers, hair-pluckers, magicians, and prostitutes, in addition to teachers and lawyers (the latter two less common), all offered their services in the public baths, not to mention the numerous merchants who sold their goods—food, wine, oil, fragrances, and other dealers in trifles—either in stands and stalls inside the baths or in the specialized stores, *tabernae* and *popinae*, that surrounded it.[48] On a wall near the entrance to the well-preserved Suburban bath in Herculaneum, the southern Italian sister city of Pompeii (also engulfed by Mt. Vesuvius's eruption in 79 CE), a merchant scribbled his *carte du jour*, listing prices in the local currency of asses (one-sixteenth of a denarius): nuts, drinks, pork fat, bread, cutlets, and sausages.[49] Garrett Fagan correctly labels the bath a "public recreation center."[50]

The place was crowded, noisy, and smelly, as well as notoriously licentious. Augustine and his friends went to the baths anticipating to spend some time in intellectual discussions, only to come across a "cock fight" that seemed much more appealing than their original plan.[51] Centuries earlier, Seneca the Younger, who once took residence "right over a bathing establishment," complained about the raucous environment just beneath his window:

> So picture to yourself the assortment of sounds, which are strong enough to make me hate my very powers of hearing! When your strenuous gentleman, for example, is exercising himself by flourishing leaden weights; when he is working hard, or else pretends to be working hard, I can hear him grunt; and whenever he releases his imprisoned breath, I can hear him panting in wheezy and high-pitched tones. Or perhaps I notice some lazy fellow, content with a cheap rub-down, and hear the crack of the pummeling hand on his shoulder, varying in sound according as the hand is laid on flat or hollow. Then, perhaps, a professional comes along, shouting out the score; that is the finishing touch. Add to this the arresting of an occasional roisterer or pickpocket, the racket of the man who always likes to hear his own voice in the bathroom, or the enthusiast who plunges into the swimming-tank with unconscionable noise and splashing. Besides all those whose voices, if nothing else, are good, imagine the hair-plucker with his penetrating, shrill voice,—for purposes of advertisement,—continually giving it vent and never holding his tongue except when he is plucking the armpits and making his victim yell instead. Then the cake-seller with his varied cries, the sausageman, the confectioner, and all the vendors of food hawking their wares, each with his own distinctive intonation.[52]

It is hard to say whether Seneca's complaints represent the typical noise that reverberated in bathhouses, but the sheer variety clearly maddened some as it surely delighted others.

Not only loud, bathhouses also reeked. Obviously, ordinary public baths lacked the means available to the immature and short-lived third-century Syrian emperor Elagabalus, who, according to one source, freshened his private bath with roses, spices, and the bitter, aromatic scent of wormwood shrubs.[53] Most baths welcomed their patrons with a rather unpleasant odor: a combination of smoke and gases that leaked from the furnaces, foul smells of human feces, and, most of all, the accumulated stench of people living in Mediterranean climates who lacked modern products such as deodorants and soaps. Whiffs of fragrance and perfumed oils only momentarily masked what amounted to a stinky mess. The Roman satirist Juvenal pokes fun at a man named Boccar, whose body odor prevented everyone in Rome from sharing his bath.[54] But the most colorful, if repulsive, description of human foul odor comes from Juvenal's fellow satirist, Martial:

> (A woman named) Thais smells worse than the veteran crock of a stingy fuller (= the cloth cleaner), recently broken in the middle of the road, or a billy goat fresh from his amours, or a lion's mouth, or a hide from beyond Tiber torn from a dog, or a chicken rotting in an aborted egg, or a jar polluted with putrid garum (= fish oil). In order to exchange this stench for a different odor, whenever she takes off her clothes to get into the bath, the crafty lady is green with depilatory or lurks under a lining of chalk and vinegar, or is coated with three or four layers of thick bean meal. A thousand tricks, and she thinks she's safe. But when all's done, Thais smells of Thais.[55]

The satirist exaggerates in order to poke fun, but he builds his description on what he and other bathers experienced.

The element of the bathhouse that has captured the modern imagination more than any other relates to mixed and nude bathing. As I will show and discuss in great detail in chapter 5, men and women throughout the Roman world normally bathed together, with their bodies fully or partially bare.[56] In general, the Roman landscape was much more revealing, in the carnal sense of the word, than ours, and Roman culture embraced utterly different ideas and perceptions about nudity than those common today.[57] Would the president of the United States pose nude, *Playgirl*-style, for an official portrait? Definitely not. Roman statuary, on the other hand, the equivalent of our mass media, regularly presented emperors in frontal nudity.[58] In Roman cities people exposed themselves in public as they urinated into buckets in the middle of the street (and fullers then collected the urine and used it as detergent). In the public toilets, the latrines, men and women shared rows of open toilets, without any separation or privacy (fig. 9). (Note that while Romans made a distinction between the idea of "public" and "private," the word "privacy" was unknown to them.)[59] Overall, in that pre-underwear age, body parts that we tend to conceal today (indeed, we call them "privates") were much more on display, especially in the hot, Mediterranean summers. Here and there we have found evidence of different hours allocated by gender. But on the whole men and women in the Roman world patronized bathhouses together, and although some people, probably members of the upper strata of society, might have worn certain bathing garments, many, if not most, did not.[60]

Despite the noise, stench, and nudity—or perhaps because of them— people adored the public bath and strove to enjoy its amenities as much as

FIGURE 9. A typical Roman latrine from Scythopolis/Beth Shean, featuring an open space with bathroom seats along the wall and a channel of water underneath to carry away the waste. It is located close to the city center (the original stairs from the main street can still be seen at the top right), open to both men and women who shared the space. *Credit:* Photograph courtesy of Gabi Laron.

they could. They expressed their enthusiasm for baths (as well as criticism) in numerous ways, most of all through their determination to obtain bathing facilities for themselves, even in the most remote and tiny places. A brief inscription from a small village—*vicus* Petra—in the distant and peripheral province of Moesia in the heart of the Balkans captures this commitment and enthusiasm: "What is good, favorable, and lucky. The villagers of Petra who contributed to the building of the bath for the sake of their bodily health."[61]

Similar fondness resonates in numerous other inscriptions, especially on tombs where the dead, or the people writing in their name, sum up the delights of life. The most famous of these epitaphs from Rome declares that "Baths, wine, and sex ruin our bodies but they are the essence of life" (*balnea, vina, venus corrumpunt corpora nostra set vitam faciunt*), a formula that repeats itself throughout the empire in both Latin and Greek, and, as is shown in chapter 4, finds striking parallels in Aramaic-speaking Jewish circles as well.[62] An inscription in the North African province of Numidia calls the baths "the most splendid ornament of the colony," a designation also used hundreds of miles to the east by authors such as Libanius, who writes of the baths as "the beauty" by which one can glorify the city.[63] Many Graeco-Roman authors express similar sentiments: not only lighthearted bath-goers such as Martial, who repeatedly includes going to the baths among his most favorite activities, but also more serious men like Cicero, who made it a top (and indeed sole) priority to ensure that the bathing facilities in his Tuscan villa were awaiting him in good shape before he arrived.[64] By the second century CE, panegyric literary pieces brimming with accolades to the baths were common. The text known as *Hippias* (or *The Bath*) and attributed to the second-century Syrian Greek writer Lucian of Samosata is the prime but far from sole example. Similar poems, known as Bath *Encomia*, were standard rhetorical exercises. They reflect the increasing and widespread approval for this institution among the populace,[65] which prevailed deep into Late Antiquity, even among figures taken over by the mindset of rising Christianity. The fifth-century Gaelic bishop and future saint Sidonius Apollinaris produced poems and prose extolling the baths in a manner and style reminiscent of ancient authors like Lucian (if indeed Lucian wrote the short text known as *Hippias*) and Statius.[66] They all share a fascination for the beauty of the place, from the dim lighting to the gushing water, and infatuation with the joys of bathing. A couple of generations later, and on the eastern shore of the Mediterranean, the Palestinian-born Procopius, the chief historian of Byzantium, maintains the same tone of praise when he labels the public baths of Constantinople as the "ornament of the city."[67] Taken as a whole, these epitaphs and dedications, epigrams and poems, epistles, ekphrasis, and orations represent the shared, abundant love and admiration for the institution of the public bathhouse, cutting across regional and ethnic boundaries throughout the civilization of the ancient Mediterranean known as the Roman Empire. Later in the book I will show that Jews and rabbis shared in this adoration.

Cultural Trajectories

Along with the relatively uniform, though somewhat varied, architectural consolidation of the bathing structure, the similar activities that transpired within its walls, and its growing popularity among the residents of the Roman world, another process—more abstract yet easy to grasp from a distance—gradually took shape: its evolution into a cultural entity. Culture is a perpetually slippery category to define, the unique collective expression—literary, artistic, philosophical, material, linguistic, and so on— of a group of people in a given time. The public bathhouse fulfills the fundamental definition of a cultural institution, in that it embodied aesthetic manifestations and conceptual articulations that represent a shared trait of human experience and habits. Over time it came to encapsulate nothing less than *romanitas*, the essence of the Roman way of life.[68] Among the representations of Roman culture prevalent in the baths (all of which will be dealt with in detail), most conspicuous are the numerous statues that populated and delineated its space (discussed in chapter 6). Sculpture was a central fixture in the visual language of the time, communicating, among other things, multilayered notions about imperialism, mythology, and social hierarchy. Some baths featured other visual, artistic ornamentations as well, such as mosaics and wall paintings. Additionally, conceptions of hedonism, the human body, gender, and sexuality were all embedded in and represented by the activity in the baths, extended and reinforced by other quintessential Roman activities in the realms of sports, medicine, and magic, as well as numerous aspects of the all-embracing experience of religion. Admittedly missing from this collocation, although not entirely absent, are elements of the Roman army (although baths were an essential component of military camps). Nevertheless, when clustered together and coupled with the physical, architectural, and engineering features of the building—the arches, the domes, the aqueducts, and the hypocaust—a public bath offered one of the most condensed expressions of Roman culture in a single space anywhere in the Mediterranean world. Today, the bathhouse is not as evocative of Rome as the more celebrated structures such as the Augustan Pantheon or the Flavian Coliseum. Yet in ancient time, when only a tiny fraction of the population got to visit Rome and engage its monuments, the ubiquity of the public bathhouse, and both its centrality and availability for populations throughout the empire, made it a fundamental representation of the spirit of the people who created it.

Many contemporaries shared this conception and associated the building of the public bath with the mores of the Roman political, imperial system and way of life. The architect and engineer Vitruvius, who lived in the first century BCE and possibly in the early years of the following century, lists the bath as one of the characteristic buildings in a typical Roman city.[69] This view persisted for half a millennium, when Procopius lists baths, along with temples, *stoas* (colonnaded public halls), and markets, as the physical features defining a city.[70] The Roman historian Tacitus, about a century after Vitruvius, in the closing years of the first century CE, describes the Romanization of recently reconquered Britain in relating the deeds of his father-in-law, the general Agricola. It included the introduction of classical, liberal education, the *artes liberales*, the Latin language, and Roman dress to the natives. Equally important was the erection of structures that embodied the human nature (*humanitas*) of the Roman people: temples, markets, Roman-style villas, and public baths.[71] Perhaps not accurate historically, this account provides insight into the mindset of the Roman elite of the time, for whom baths were an indispensable part of Roman identity.

Over the centuries, Roman emperors invested great effort and substantial funds in erecting public bathing facilities all over their realm, propagating this conception of Roman cultural identity. As modern scholars have shown, building projects in all corners of the Mediterranean world functioned as vehicles for Roman imperialism; in the flattering words of the second-century Greek scholar Aelius Aristides, taken from his famous panegyric to Rome and its emperor: "You have filled your whole empire with cities and adornments. . . . Never does the flow of gifts from you to these cities stop . . . [i]ndeed, the cities shine with radiance and grace, and the earth has been adorned like a pleasure garden."[72] Within this context, baths built by the emperors, although only a small fraction of the thousands of baths in operation, feature prominently, and numerous inscriptions have been found, thanking the emperors or local governors for their generosity in erecting these buildings.[73] Authors from different times and places sing the praises of the emperors, especially the good ones, as builders of baths, not only in Rome but throughout the empire. Cicero at the turning point from republic to empire, Pausanias in the second century, the author(s) of the allegedly third-century but more likely fourth-century imperial biographies known as *Scriptores historiae Augustae*, and Procopius, two hundred years later, near the end of antiquity, are representative in expressing the ubiquitous idea that a good Roman ruler builds bathhouses for his people.[74]

But all these examples speak to the Roman point of view. How did those who stood on the other side of the cultural equation—the native provincials, the indigenous residents of the varied locations throughout the Roman Empire—view the cultural identity of the bath? Did they also equate it with *romanitas*? Was it a *Roman* bath in their eyes or just a bath? Sadly, for the most part history has muted their voices and failed to preserve their opinions. Yet, it seems that they shared in love and affection for the baths, as the inscriptions cited testify and their actions confirm. After all, the huge bathing complexes in the provinces surely did not remain empty.

What can be known about the abstract notions and perceptions regarding bathing and the baths that prevailed among residents of Roman provinces? Needless to say, by their nature views and ideas lack homogeneity and vary from one place to another, among different groups and individuals. Some sources do suggest that provincials identified at least some of the bathing establishments that peppered their landscape as specifically Roman. For example, in describing an anti-governmental riot in the Syrian capital of Antioch, the fourth-century, Greek-born Roman historian Ammianus Marcellinus mentions that the violent mob set fire to the baths bearing the name of the emperor Valens.[75] In this instance, particularly because of their close association with the emperor, the baths stood for Rome in the minds of the people of Antioch, like the imperial statues, which tended to be in the first line of fire when dissatisfaction with the government erupted into violence—as they do to this day.[76]

Jewish sources on this subject provide a unique window into the mindsets of ancient people living in the peripheral provinces of the empire. A second- or third-century literary passage in Hebrew, preserved in the much later sixth-century compilation of the Babylonian Talmud, reports the following conversation, which supposedly took place among second-century rabbinic scholars from Roman Palestine:

> R. Judah, R. Jose, and R. Simeon were sitting, and Judah, a son of proselytes, was sitting next to them. R. Judah opened [the discussion] by saying, "How fine are the deeds of this nation [the Romans]; they have established markets, they have built bridges, they have erected baths." R. Jose [remained] silent. R. Simeon b. Yohai replied and said, "All what they made they made for themselves; they established marketplaces, to set prostitutes in them; baths, to rejuvenate themselves; bridges, to levy tolls for them."[77]

Another rabbinic statement maintains that "through four things the [Roman] government devours [their inhabitants]: by their taxes, bathhouses, theatres and annual levies."[78] Clearly, these Jewish scholars saw the baths, whether they liked them or not, as "the deeds of this nation" or "things of this government"—that is, a Roman institution. Similar perceptions resonate in other rabbinic texts. In one case, the author portrays the biblical military hero Joab, the son of Zeruiah, originally a chief commander in the army of King David, as a Roman commander using the spoils of war to treat his people to the luxury of bathhouses. As a consequence, his eventual death left the people as dry "as a desert." Another rabbinical author concocts a parable around the figure of a "king"—that is, a Roman emperor—who, when exalted by the praise bestowed upon him by the residents of a city he visits, promises to reward them by building aqueducts and bathhouses.[79]

These rabbinic texts mirror the imperial propaganda voiced by Aelius Aristides and others and engraved in the numerous adulatory inscriptions thanking emperors for constructing bathhouses. The rabbinic passages testify to the wide reception of the imperial propaganda that associated the Roman Empire with building projects. The Jewish scholars took note of these projects for their own purposes, at times subversively, turning them against the empire with which they were associated. Roman emperors wanted the populations of their far-flung provinces to regard them as great benefactors, builders of bathhouses and providers of the pleasures they offer. For their part, the rabbinic authors of the above passages prove quite receptive and willing to embrace these images of the emperor as builder. However, in a typical anti-colonial maneuver, they often reversed the message behind the images to denounce the authorities and the power that lay behind them.

Interpreted with all due caution, these rabbinic sources confirm that (at least some) Jews in the eastern provinces of the empire identified the bath as a Roman institution.[80] This, in turn, leads to an interesting set of questions: If indeed the bathhouse represented a Roman institution in the minds of Jews, did they attend it? And if so, how did they interact with its various features and how did they feel about it? The rest of the book aims to address these issues.

CHAPTER TWO

A Literary Bathhouse

REALITIES AND PERCEPTIONS
AT A ROMAN (JEWISH) PUBLIC BATH

LET'S IMAGINE FOR a moment that not a single Roman bathhouse had ever surfaced in archaeological excavations or was ever mentioned by surviving ancient sources in Greek or Latin. Surprisingly, we would still know about them from a seemingly unlikely source: rabbinic literature. As seen in the previous chapter and in more detail in chapter 4, rabbinic scholars prized the public bathhouse and frequented it as much as anyone else in the Mediterranean world. Their abundant writings, covering all aspects of Jewish life in the ancient world, include numerous references to the Roman bathhouse: its architecture, the people who built and maintained it, and its technology, furnishings, and paraphernalia. Many of these rabbinic references are terse and isolated, embedded in complex legal discussions, or as the background for stories and statements. But when stitched together, these pieces of evidence comprise one of the fullest descriptions we possess of any Roman institution in the eastern Mediterranean, one replete with nuance and detail. In this chapter, I conjure up an imaginary bathhouse, not the reconstruction of a specific facility but rather the literary construction of a model bathing establishment in Roman times as it existed in the collective rabbinic imagination: a "literary" bathhouse.[1] This discussion will lay the spatial and structural foundation for the rest of the book, as future chapters delve into the cultural and social dynamics that evolved in this facility, and it will also place the authors of this literary creation, the rabbis, at the core of Roman life, deeply embedded in one of its central institutions.

Naming

As early as the second century CE, the Jewish scholars, whom we anachronistically call "rabbis," started to use a new term in Hebrew to refer to public bathing facilities: *merḥats* (*merḥatsa'ot* in the plural). The word does not appear in any text prior to the rabbis, such as the books of the Hebrew Bible or the literature from Qumran, or in any other Semitic text for that matter. Whoever created this name coined a fresh noun, *merḥats*, from an ancient, commonly used Hebrew verb, *lirḥots*, meaning "to bathe/to wash." In the Mishnah, the early third-century CE rabbinic text, which, as far as we know, was the first written document that these ancient scholars ever produced (only the Passover Haggada may have been earlier), this newly created term, *merḥats*, appears two dozen times. It comes up in various formulations of rabbinic law, always referring to a building designed for public bathing.[2] Furthermore, utilizing a grammatical device known as construct-state, rabbinic authors occasionally—only three times in the Mishnah but more in later texts—attach *merḥats* to the noun *bayit* (meaning "house" or "place"), resulting in a second name, a variation of the first one, *beyt merḥats*, literally a house of or a place for washing or bathing: in other words, a bathhouse.[3] In the centuries after the Mishnah, rabbinic scholars in the Persian territories of Mesopotamia (which they called Babylonia) also translate the Hebrew *beyt merḥats* into the Aramaic *bey mas(ḥ) uta'* and use it as another designation for the public bathhouse.[4]

Rabbis were also familiar with a variety of Greek names for bathhouses and used them regularly in their writings. All languages around the Mediterranean adopted the common Greek appellation for the public bathhouse, *balaneion*, chief among them Latin in the west (*balnea*) and Aramaic/Syriac in the east (*balane'*); rabbinic authors, too, often use it, in a variety of forms and spellings (*banyi, balani*, etc.).[5] Rabbinic texts also apply another term to the baths, *dimosin* (*dimosya'ot* or *dimosiyyot* in the plural).[6] This word originally transliterated the Greek *dēmosion*, an adjective meaning "belonging to the people/public/state," into Aramaic and Hebrew. On numerous occasions from the second century CE onward, rabbis use this word, among others, to refer to the physical building that housed the public bath. Subsequent rabbinic texts from the third and fourth centuries—in particular the Palestinian Talmud (the *Yerushalmi*) and the so-called Palestinian haggadic *midrashim*—also utilize this term frequently as a name for the bathhouse, although on other occasions they use it in other ways, simply to denote the category "public" in various contexts unrelated to bathing.[7]

This broad application of the term has confused some modern investigators, especially since several passages use *dimosin* together with the Hebrew name of the public bath, *merḥats*, creating the impression that these are two distinct types of facilities.[8] Greek speakers around the Mediterranean, however, regularly applied *dēmosion* to the bath, as an adjective meaning "public," modifying the words they used for "bathhouse" (mainly *loutron* and *balaneion*). Such combinations as *dēmosion loutron* or *balaneion dēmosion* simply mean "(a/the) public bathhouse" (or sometimes, bathhouses) and were quite common in the Greek vernacular, both before and after the time of the rabbis.[9] In the second century CE, pretty much concurrent with the rabbinic scholars of the Mishnah, Marcus Cornelius Fronto, a famous Roman scholar and orator, born in North Africa, uses the same combination of *loutra* and *dēmosia* when, in a Greek letter to his friend Appian, he speaks of the public baths of his time and distinguishes between public baths, owned by the city and its citizens, and those owned by private individuals.[10] The same phenomenon appears among Aramaic- or Syriac-speaking people of the eastern Mediterranean, where the word *di(e)mosion*, with a range of spelling variations, appears both as an adjective in the general sense of "public" and as a noun referring to the public bathhouse.[11]

Sometime in the next century or two, probably under the influence of the language spoken in the street, people shortened the term and used *dēmosion*, literally "something of the public," as the place-name for a public bathhouse. Modern researchers of rabbinic material have overlooked this transition and development in terminology,[12] but such a sociolinguistic process by which adjectives take the substantive meaning of nouns, known to specialists as "nominalized adjectives," is well attested in both ancient and modern times. The noun "museum," for example, *mouseion* in Greek, is in origin an adjective meaning "of the muses." Similarly, the Latin name for the huge, imperial bathhouse complexes, *thermae*, originally derives from an adjective meaning "warm," itself a loanword from Greek. The English word "pub" is doubly shortened from "public house." All these nouns derive from adjectives that gradually took on a substantive, nominal life of their own.[13]

By the same process, the adjective *dēmosion* mutated into a noun representing the bathhouse. In later centuries, we find this stand-alone adjective-turned-noun in other Greek-speaking places. For example, a mid-fourth-century papyrus from Egypt, in which a city council supervisor instructs one of its members on the delivery of timber to the public bathhouse and warns against fraud, calls the public bathhouse simply a

FIGURE 10. (The white-bordered detail is enlarged in fig. 11.) The late fifth-century CE Yakto mosaic, uncovered in a village by that name, near Daphne, a suburb of the great ancient city of Antioch in what was then northern Syria (today Antakya, in the south corner of Turkey); now at the Hatai Archaeology Museum, Turkey. At the mosaic's center is a medallion of a beautifully dressed woman, crowned with a diadem and holding what is usually interpreted as petals of roses. The Greek inscription defines her as Megalopsychia, an allegoric personification of "greatness of the soul." Around the medallion are various hunting scenes, and on the border of the mosaic is a continuous line of buildings and monuments identified by inscriptions, interspersed with scenes from city life. *Credit:* GM Photo Images, licensed by and permission from Alamy, Inc.

dēmosion.[14] Significantly, the earliest attestation of this linguistic process appears in rabbinical literature, dating to the second century CE, by which time people began calling the bathhouse a *dimosin*.[15] Note also that rabbinic texts dropped the long ending of the word, consisting of two consecutive vowels "i" and "o," and made the word shorter and easier to pronounce with the suffix "in." A few centuries later, the famous Yakto mosaic from Daphne (fig. 10), a suburb of the great city of Antioch (today Antakya, in

FIGURE 11. A detail from the string of buildings depicted on the border of the Yakto mosaic. In the middle is a building titled in Greek *to dēmosin*, a common name for a bathhouse. The building features a red tile roof and a gabled entrance embraced by two white (probably marble) Doric capitals, with another revolving door entrance on the left side. In front stands a dignified figure, wearing a beltless white robe with black stripes, topped with a red mantle accentuating the shoulders, and black shoes. His right hand holds an item, which may be a staff, dagger, or rolled scroll. To his left is a slave wearing a short tunic heading to the bath, hands full with various objects, perhaps bathing paraphernalia. To the right is a merchant wearing a white sleeveless tunic standing behind an outdoor concession stand selling his products. *Credit:* Photograph courtesy of Dick Osseman.

the south corner of Turkey), a magnificent fifth-century hunting scene surrounded by realistic depictions of urban structures, features the splendid facade of a bathhouse with a Greek inscription identifying it as *to dēmosin*, "the public (bathhouse)" (fig. 11). Not only was the adjective nominalized here too, but the spelling matches the Hebrew/Aramaic transliteration of the word in rabbinic literature, without the vowel "o" in the suffix.[16] Another sixth-century inscription from Antioch also refers to a bathhouse as *dēmosin*, without the "o" in the suffix. Other Greek words from this period feature this phonetic phenomenon of shrinking suffixes as well.[17]

The Yakto mosaic and the rabbis share another unique name for the baths. On the same border of the Yakto mosaic, a few structures away from the *dēmosin*, the mosaic depicts another bathhouse: an impressive municipal building with a roof of three small domes. A Greek inscription on top identifies it as "the *pribaton* of Ardabourios."[18] In this case, the name of the establishment derives from the Latin adjectives for "private" (*privus, privatus*), both an adjective modifying nouns and an independent substantive, mainly indicating something removed from the public domain or not belonging to the imperial system. As so often happens, the semantic range of the word extended over time, in our case to denote a privately owned public bath: an institution for public bathing operated by private owners for profit generated from entrance fees and leasing space to food merchants and other providers of goods and services.[19]

The term itself is revealing. As Roman hegemony over Greek-speaking territories endured for centuries, Latin words found their way into the local vernaculars—Greek, Aramaic/Syriac, and other languages—a process that becomes prevalent in the third and fourth centuries CE.[20] Within this period, and within these linguistic and cultural contours, Greek-speaking societies on the eastern reaches of the Mediterranean adopted and nominalized the Latin *privatus* as *pribaton* and made it into one of a variety of Greek names indicating a bathhouse operated as a private business. They used this name to distinguish this type of facility from the *dēmosion*, the public bath owned by the city or the provincial government (and by extension owned by the "public," hence the name *dēmosion*, "of the public"). This differential terminology appears on the Yakto mosaic and in many literary, epigraphic, and papyrological sources in Greek.[21] Rabbinic literature, for the most part a closed book to modern scholars of the Roman world dealing with the *pribaton*, shows that this Latin designation penetrated Semitic languages as well. In a series of rabbinic passages, particularly the fourth-century texts of the *Yerushalmi* and the haggadic *midrashim*, the terms *privata'* in the singular and *privata'ot* in the plural, now written in Hebrew letters in various spellings, appear over half a dozen times, always in association with other names of the public baths (*merḥats* and *dimosin*).[22] By pairing *privata'* and *dimosin*, the rabbinic authors show that they too were aware that the terms refer to different kinds of bathing establishments available to the populace of the cities: the one owned by the city, and by extension belonging to the public, appropriately called *dimosin*; the other privately owned and open to the public for a fee, called *privata'*.²³ In one or two places, rabbinic authors also apply the term *privata'* to a bath attendant (more on that later in this chapter).

Evidently, similar linguistic processes extended over the various regions of the eastern Mediterranean, from Egypt to Roman Palestine all the way to Antioch on the Orontes river in northern Syria, and beyond into Asia Minor and Greece proper. The result is overlapping, although somewhat variable, nomenclature for the bathhouse seen in far-flung locales and disparate societies, thus pointing to shared, although certainly not identical, strands of culture. Some of the names that rabbinic scholars assign to the public bath in their literature, like *merḥats*, were neologisms, possibly coined by the rabbis, while others were adopted into the local Jewish dialect of Roman Palestine from other spoken languages in the region (Greek, Latin, Aramaic/Syriac). Taken together, these terms encapsulate the larger story of this institution as it came to operate among the Jews. Whereas central components of its structure, activity, and cultural perceptions overlap with the common features of this institution throughout the Roman world, others were uniquely tailored for its Jewish users.

The discussion of nomenclature highlights three of the main points of the current chapter. First, names are not created in a vacuum; they represent real entities in people's lives that require a category and a label. Such entities can be either physical structures, large or small, or imagined, spiritual ones, but they must play a significant role and fulfill a function requiring reference. The giving of names runs deep in human experience and reaches back to its most rudimentary stages.²⁴ New names, in our world as in the world of the ancients, often signal innovations, the introduction of something fresh and previously unfamiliar, which requires a label. This applies to words like "phone," "television," and "computer" in our times, as it did to *merḥats* and *dimosin* in the days of the rabbis.

Second, the evolution of names for the Roman public bathhouse in the rabbinic corpus enables us to follow the development of its presence in Jewish life in the eastern provinces of the empire. By collecting and assembling all the fragmentary data in rabbinic literature, we can draw an incomplete but extensive, multidimensional, and colorful picture, providing a penetrating look into one central institution where Jewish life was both lived and shaped during Roman times, and enhance our understanding of ancient Jews and their diverse experiences.

Finally, the foregoing discussion of names and naming highlights another factor that must not be ignored: context. Names and the entities they represent do not function in a vacuum. *Merḥats, balani, dimosin,* and *privata'* gain depth and substance when juxtaposed with *balaneion, dēmosion,* and *pribaton.* Without context, the literary bath as it is depicted in rabbinic literature would remain rather ambiguous. We would know the details but could not grasp their full meaning. Why did the rabbis need to coin a new name for a building that already existed prior to their time? Why did they develop procedures regarding the use of this facility, and what was the purpose and significance of the habits, norms, perceptions, and lore that evolved around the bathhouse? The vast knowledge we possess about the Roman public bathhouse—from thousands of archaeological excavations, and just as many textual references in the ancient Greek and Latin sources that have survived, as well as from minute technical and everyday details in documentary sources, papyri, and inscriptions carved in stone—enhances and deepens our understanding of the rabbinic material. They provide not only thickness to the picture but also the necessary texture to contextualize the literary bath of the rabbis and grasp its connotations.

The rest of this chapter deals with the basic functions of the bathhouse as they are recorded in rabbinic literature, while also providing the context necessary to properly understand these Jewish texts and their significance.

Construction

As shown in detail in chapter 1,[25] when it comes to building public bathhouses (as opposed to owning and running them), a chorus of rabbinic authors credit the Roman authorities and, in particular, the emperor and the imperial coffers as the main resources behind the construction of baths. Such an image functions mainly in the mind of the authors: one hand would suffice to count the opportunities afforded to the Jews of Palestine to see an emperor, let alone one who donated a bathhouse. As I show later in the discussion, local funds rather than the imperial treasury sponsored the construction of most if not all of the bathhouses familiar to rabbis or others, without any real ties to the emperors. However, these texts show that the general public, including at least some of the Jews, viewed the Roman Empire as the prime power responsible for erecting bathhouses.

Building a public bathhouse in Roman times was neither easy nor cheap. The archaeological remains of these structures, scattered throughout the Mediterranean world today, represent the end product, now dilapidated, thus leaving it to our imagination to grasp the magnitude of the operation, the labor involved in erecting such ambitious edifices without modern machines. Only seldom does documentary evidence shed light on specific aspects of construction, like the purchase orders and receipts, from the third and fifth centuries CE, respectively, made out to and by the ironsmiths of Oxyrhynchus in Egypt. These shreds of papyri document the nails manufactured for building the local bath and its appliances.[26] The cost of all other materials—wood, concrete, stone, metal, and eventually marble for the decoration—when combined with shipping costs, manpower, and tools for the design and execution amount to a staggering price tag.

If we take the first and second centuries CE as our benchmark, the sources, references in ancient literature, inscriptions, and papyri, speak of tens of thousands of sesterces (the basic Roman currency, a quarter of a denarius, marked by the modern symbol HS) for the construction of a relatively small and ordinary bathing complex in minor towns, an amount that could easily escalate into six figures and more for elaborate bathhouses in major cities. A typical inscription states that the emperor Hadrian allocated two million sesterces to the port city of Ostia, near Rome, for the erection of a local bath, and his adopted son, the emperor Antoninus Pius, needed to supplement that amount in order to complete the project and its marble decoration.[27] And these were far from the most expensive; in a detailed study, Janet DeLaine estimated the cost of the bath of Caracalla in Rome (see fig. 6), perhaps the greatest public bath ever to be built, at HS 120,000,000, and this covered only the central block of the complex.[28] Such figures put the cheapest price tag on the construction of a single bath, not including future maintenance and repair, at hundreds of times the minimum annual subsistence wage for an average Roman worker, usually calculated at HS 115, and even ten and more times the annual income of a well-to-do, entry-level city councillor, whose property generated an annual income of roughly HS 5,000. At the end of the first century CE, the annual salary of a Roman legionnaire, always seen as a good representation of average income, was 300 denarii, that is, HS 1,200 (a 30 percent rise from a century earlier). It would take about forty such annual salaries to build a modest bathing facility.[29]

Given the high cost, not surprisingly very few institutions could have assumed the task of building public bathhouses. The emperors and provincial magistrates are natural candidates, and certainly records from the first six hundred years of the Common Era affirm that imperial and/or provincial assets occasionally granted funds for this enterprise. The inscription from Ostia mentioned above regarding the patronage of Hadrian and Antoninus Pius offers one example. Likewise, the second-century Greek traveler Pausanias reports that Hadrian also donated a public bath to Corinth. Other records, both literary and documentary, refer to subsidies for baths donated by him and other emperors.[30]

More often than not, however, it was up to local initiatives to enable the residents of a city or town to enjoy the amenities of the baths. City or town councils occasionally voted to allocate funds accumulated in their treasury from local taxes and tariffs for building projects such as public baths.[31] But the costs ran high, the financial resources available to local municipalities were limited, and the empire, when capable and at full strength, exercised a tight grip over local spending, enforced by its provincial governors and their administration. In correspondence from the second century, Pliny the Younger, at the time the governor of Bithynia and Pontus in northern Anatolia, seeks the emperor Trajan's approval on behalf of the townspeople of Prusa (modern Bursa in northwestern Turkey) to build a new public bath to replace an old, dilapidated one. The emperor replies in a businesslike manner that he will grant permission, but only if certain conditions are met, mainly that the funds channeled for this endeavor will not jeopardize the city's other financial obligations.[32]

By far, funding for most bathing facilities came from private hands, part of a process unique to the Graeco-Roman world, called by modern scholars "euergetism" (Greek for benefaction), in which local magnates used their capital for architectural projects that would benefit the public.[33] Wealthy individuals donated large sums to the public for various reasons. The *summa honoraria*, a payment expected from a person appointed to public office, was a factor but surely not the only one. An abundance of epigraphic material from all over the Roman Mediterranean attests to the role of native individuals in establishing bathhouses, either creating them as freely accessible establishments, putting aside hefty endowments to look after their future maintenance, or building them as pay-per-use, private businesses, which the public enjoyed for a nominal entrance fee, while the owners garnered further profit from leasing the place to a manager or renting out space inside to vendors.[34]

Although imperial donations tended to be sporadic and behind only a small fraction of bathing facilities, the public commonly associated bathhouses with the emperor. The builders of many bathing complexes or the cities and communities that enjoyed them often dedicated them to the emperor, even when not funded directly by the imperial treasury, and they often bore the name of that emperor.[35] Furthermore, many writers, in particular those with imperial connections, repeat the cliché about emperors going around the empire establishing bathing complexes. The collection of imperial biographies, known as *Scriptores historiae Augustae*, whose date and reliability modern scholars debate, often associates these hubs of pleasure and recreation with the emperors. The author(s) explicitly articulate what seems to be the standard belief of the era: good emperors, such as Antoninus Pius and Alexander Severus, erect public baths, and bad ones, such as Commodus, do not or, as in the case of the infamous Elagabalus, build them, bathe in them once, and then demolish them.[36]

In the same vein, centuries later, the Christian scholar and imperial historian Procopius often states that the emperor Justinian funded or actually built bathhouses for the public or contributed from the imperial coffers toward their repair, not only in the capital Constantinople but all around the empire.[37] The same seems true in sixth-century Antioch, where, if we are to believe the contemporary, local chronographer and orator John Malalas, different emperors continually endowed the city with public bathhouses, some named after them for centuries.[38]

Rabbinic authors, for their part, generally assumed that the emperors funded the public baths, and one must dig deep to find evidence that they were also aware that other parties contributed to the construction of baths. For example, a fourth- or fifth-century legend, which imagines a discussion between the prominent second-century rabbinic figure Eliezer b. Hyrcanos and a disciple of Jesus, implies that prominent Jews could donate funds to the building of bathhouses. The two men are discussing funds from wealthy Jews, which are sullied in some way and therefore cannot be donated to the Jerusalem Temple. The Christian suggests, with R. Eliezer's approval, that this rich Jew "should make with them bathhouses and latrines."[39] In a somewhat similar vein, another midrashic statement suggests that a rich Jew who amassed his wealth impiously through usury would end up childless. Hence, the imperial government, called *malkhut*, the Hebrew word for kingdom, would confiscate his fortune and channel it back to the public's benefit by building bathhouses and latrines.[40] The assumption at the core of this theoretical debate holds that Jewish money could be put to use, in this case via the Roman authorities, to build bathhouses.

Seeing the full gamut of human and financial resources at play in the erection of bathhouses—individual, municipal, and imperial—clarifies that the association of these buildings (as well as other magnificent municipal structures) with the emperor reflects the public perception surrounding them but not necessarily the facts about their origin. It also bears the imprint of an imperial agenda and propaganda—what we would today call imperialism. From early on, Roman rulers understood that temples and splendid civic edifices, especially those offering leisure and entertainment to the masses, when associated with the empire in the public's mind, fostered admiration, gratitude, loyalty, and alliance. As such, they served as a principal tool to strengthen local alliances with the central government.[41] The first-century Roman senator and historian Tacitus alludes to this strategy when describing the deeds of his father-in-law, Ganeus Julius Agricola, the general-turned-governor of Britain. In his attempt to pacify the "uncivilized" and "belligerent" Britons, says Tacitus, Agricola launched a series of public works, erecting temples, markets, and bathhouses. Romanization and peace in Britain followed, or so Tacitus claims.[42]

For this scheme to work, propaganda must accompany construction, and the public must buy into it. Indeed, the first few centuries of the Common Era witnessed the development of a feedback loop: the emperors encouraged architectural monuments to express their greatness, and the public (wealthy, influential men and local governments) purchased favor and useful connections with the imperial powers by erecting buildings that glorified the emperor. The outcome resembled a multifaceted network of visual expressions, created by a variety of people for a variety of reasons, in which buildings and civic architecture came to represent imperial power.[43]

The rabbinic material should be read within the broad contours of imperial strategy and local obsequiousness. It allows us to observe imperialism as manifested in bathhouse construction from the point of view of the beneficiaries, the residents of a single province, on the eastern edge of the empire. Many native expressions of imperialism and Romanization have survived, but they usually reflect the upper echelons of the cities and the provinces, the people whose interests they served. Numerous inscriptions commissioned by city magistrates and councils or other local potentates praise the empire, as do texts written by local intellectual dignitaries such as the second- and fourth-century orators Aelius Aristides and Libanius, whose speeches and letters hail the empire for the architectural brilliance bestowed on their eastern Mediterranean cities.[44] When the rabbis, themselves neither imperial officials nor provincial elites, discuss the construction of a bathhouse, whether in their legal debates, legends, or proverbs, they reflect the way these ideas about imperialism crystallized in the minds of ordinary provincials. Indeed, Aristides and his second-century contemporary, R. Judah of Palestine, express similar views. The former wrote, "The cities shine with radiance and grace and the whole earth has been adorned like a pleasure garden," and the latter concurs, speaking of the markets, bridges, and bathhouses built by the Romans as examples of "how beautiful are the constructions of this nation."[45] The official agenda of the empire, as pronounced by Aristides, trickled down and found its local expression in the words of R. Judah. Put differently, the strong tie between the erection of bathhouses and the imperial authorities as it appears in rabbinic literature does not reflect the actual realities of construction sites on the ground. However, it does voice the public's perception regarding those projects and the effectiveness of imperial propaganda.

Ownership

Unlike construction, the powers behind it, and the images associated with it, ownership of bathhouses embodies an aspect of property law, a more ordinary issue. As in the modern world, people in antiquity enjoyed the right to acquire and own property: *dominium* in Latin, *qinyan* in rabbinic Hebrew terminology. People bought and sold property everywhere in the Roman world. Some of the most illuminating evidence about real estate transactions comes from Jewish papyri from the Judaean Desert, as well as documents from Transjordan (Petra), Egypt, and elsewhere. As shown there, people spared no effort to carefully document even the smallest parcels of land—witnessed, sealed, and archived. Contestants vigorously pursued disputes in courts and sometimes resolved them less formally, more often than not through violence.[46] Far from being uniform throughout the Roman world, laws of property ranged greatly. Various and occasionally conflicting systems of property law, including Jewish laws, operated simultaneously. The rabbis, a local group of legal scholars in a Roman province, devoted ample intellectual energy to the definitions of, formulations about, and delineations between various aspects of property and ownership.[47] The types of property they discuss include the bathhouse, and in their consideration of its ownership, rabbinic scholars express a specific voice of provincial residents in the Roman Empire, in this case Jews, as they deal with a habitual, widely shared, and economically significant procedure—the transfer of property—while incorporating aspects unique and dear to their own community in the discussion.

Bathhouses appear right in the opening legal prescription of the central chapter devoted to property ownership in the Mishnah—chapter 3, known as *ḥezqat ha-batim* ("possession of houses"), of the third tractate, *Baba Batra* ("the last gate"), in the order Neziqin ("damages," the fourth book of the Mishnah devoted to financial matters). The rabbinic ruling in that passage requires three years of unchallenged possession of real estate in order to validate a claim of ownership that lacks a deed of sale to verify it. It enumerates a variety of assets—olive presses, irrigated fields, and even slaves—to which this rule applies, including bathhouses.[48] The rabbinic scholars who issued this ordinance, and the editors of the Mishnah who included it in their opening statement of *ḥezqat ha-batim*, evidently viewed bathing facilities as the kind of property a Jew may typically own. This ruling refers to a rural setting, the ownership of fields, groves, and olive presses. Hence, it is not clear whether the bathhouse was open to the public, serving the entire community, or a private facility restricted to the owner and his household.

Other rabbinic laws in which the public bathhouse figures offer a much clearer picture. Rabbinic legislators show familiarity with bathhouses owned collectively by the residents of a town or a city: "which is a thing [belonging to the people] of a certain town?" they ask in a *halakhah* dealing with a prohibition connected with vows. They then list these "things": "For example, the [town's central] square, the [public] bathhouse, the synagogue, the ark (holding the scriptures), and the books (purchased by the town for its residents)."[49] The publicly owned bathhouse rubs shoulders here with other communal property, both religious structures and artifacts, such as the synagogue and the ark of the Torah, as well as non-religious spaces, such as the town's central square. Collectively, these represent a standard catalog of possessions of a typical, if legally hypothetical, Jewish commune in the time of the rabbis. The legal formula here is consistent with other places throughout rabbinic literature: it features a public bathhouse as an integral part of what defines a proper village or a city: "It has been taught (in a *baraita*): A town that does not include the following ten things should not be the residence of a scholar: a legal court that [can] impose flagellation and decree penalties; a charity fund collected by two and distributed by three; a synagogue; a public bathhouse; a latrine; a doctor and a surgeon, a scribe; a butcher and a local teacher for children."[50] As shown above, public bathhouses built and maintained by a local municipality, collectively owned by cities or by guilds and other groups within it, are well-documented throughout the Roman world. Everywhere in the Mediterranean, the citizenry, that is, landowning men who constituted the legal core of cities and towns, shared in the communal ownership of municipal property, which regularly included bathhouses. This common arrangement resonates in rabbinic texts and shapes the worldview of their authors regarding the urban landscape of their cities and towns. Hence, their definition of what constitutes a city imitates and replicates the commonly held notions of everyone around them.

But cities and towns did not hold their properties in perpetuity, and at times municipal councils sold off some of their property. Rabbinic literature refers to these transactions too. In establishing provisions for the purchase of a public building that originally housed a synagogue, rabbinic scholars disagree on whether the seller, namely the local citizenry, must set restrictions on the future use of the building. Some rabbis rule that the new owner may not repurpose the property as "a bathhouse, a tannery, a facility for ritual immersion, or a latrine,"[51] because the foul smell of a tannery or lavatory, or the nudity in the bathhouse or the ritual immersion facility, does not sit well with the sanctity of a synagogue building. Countering this position, one rabbinic scholar, R. Judah, disagrees and permits any future use of the former synagogue. At play here are the mechanisms of transferring ownership from the collective body of a municipal community to a private person, and how the concerns of local people—in this case Jews and their feelings about sacred space and the special treatment it requires—should shape such financial transactions.

Setting aside the issue of sacred space, the above *halakhah* also conveys information regarding bathhouses and their ownership: individual Jews indeed owned public bathhouses, and there was nothing exceptional about that. Similarly, in legal directives scattered throughout the Mishnah and later texts, rabbinic scholars aim to regulate the ownership of bathhouses for their Jewish constituencies, mainly by standardizing the financial relationships entailed in selling, buying, renting, or jointly owning such a facility. Bathhouses figure prominently in the chapter of the Mishnah treating movable property on premises being sold. The question there considers whether furniture, tools, and the like are included in the transaction, passing automatically to the new owner or not. After discussing the sale of private houses, courtyards, and olive presses, and before considering fields and towns, the editors of the Mishnah devote a whole *halakhah* to bathhouses:

> He who sells the bathhouse does not [automatically include] the [wooden] planks, the benches, or the [cloth] hangings. But when [the seller stipulates and] says "it (=I am selling the bathhouse) and everything within it"—[this determines that] they (=all the movable items listed above) are all sold. Either way, he has not sold (i.e., automatically

included within the original sale of the bathhouse) the water reservoirs and the wood storage.⁵²

The passage offers a glimpse of the bathhouse's interior, and a subsequent text on the same subject in the Tosefta adds more details (discussed more fully in the next section). Beyond the realistic details about the bath that the text incidentally offers, its authors establish basic rules for transfer of ownership when movable property is associated with the real estate.

Joint ownership of bathhouses also receives ample attention from the rabbis, addressing the question of whether one partner can force division of a shared asset, or, in the case of a gentile and Jew who are partners in a bath, what is the legal status of earnings from operating the bath on the Sabbath, when Jews may not work and, by extension, earn income.⁵³ Similarly, rabbis consider the leasing of bathhouses, recognizing different methods of payment, either for an annual rental fee or for a monthly remittance, as well as the problems that could arise when a non-Jewish lessee operates a Jewish-owned bath and the competition between two bathhouses that offer their services to the public in close proximity.⁵⁴

With regard to renting a bathhouse for an annual fee, problems arose when, in order to synchronize the Hebrew lunar calendar with the solar calendar, a thirteenth, intercalary month was added to a year. The editors of the Mishnah record what seems like an actual case that came before a rabbinic local judge or mediator:

> [A case] so happened in Sepphoris [involving] one who leased a bathhouse from another for twelve golden [denarii] per year, one golden denarius per month. And the case came before Rabban Simeon b. Gamaliel and before R. Jose, and they said: [they should] split [the difference of the additional] intercalated month.⁵⁵

The monthly fee, a golden denarius, also known as *aureus*, appears realistic; at approximately 25 denarii for an *aureus*, the common if fluctuating rate in those years (before it skyrocketed in the years of the later third-century inflation), the total would be about 300 denarii or HS 1,200 a year. While only part of the operating cost of a bathhouse, it falls pretty much in line with the annual salary of the Roman legion soldier, a reasonable fee for a modest bathing facility in a relatively small city such as Sepphoris.⁵⁶ The rulings about ownership discussed above might, however, be theoretical legal abstractions invented for the purpose of discussion, an issue that modern scholars vehemently debate.⁵⁷ Either way, for the present discussion about the literary bath of rabbinic literature, these cases—real or hypothetical—show that rabbinic scholars were familiar with matters of bathhouse ownership by fellow Jews: the fiscal transactions and monetary relationships connected with ownership of public bathhouses, as well as difficulties that may arise from owning a bathhouse and prevent the owners from leading what they regarded as a proper Jewish life. By dealing with these issues, they embrace the bathhouse and bring it into the sphere of their Jewish experience.

The Building and Its Furnishings

Not only does rabbinical literature discuss the people who built, owned, and operated baths, rabbinic authors also present rich portrayals of their physical appearance. Not surprisingly, none of them are as comprehensive and systematic as certain accounts by Latin and Greek authors. The first-century BCE Roman architect and engineer Vitruvius offers the most elaborate presentation, a methodical description of a prototypical public bathhouse, with a thorough understanding of its architectural complexity and meticulous attention to detail. Not far behind, on the Greek, eastern side of the Roman world, texts such as *Hippias*—a second-century CE rhetorical exercise attributed to Lucian of Samosata—praises the bath while carefully delineating its layout and explicating its functions and decoration.[58] These writers pursue the bathhouse as the main topic of this particular literary endeavor, deliberately paying careful attention to its construction and equipment. The rabbinic scholars, by contrast, only refer to the bath in passing, as it intersects with the legal topics they are debating or when they find it relevant to a story they are telling. Still, the sum of the details amounts to a significant exposé of a provincial bath in Roman times, a facility for which, unlike its counterparts in major centers in the Roman world, documented details are scarce and which has received insufficient attention from modern scholars.

The interior of the bathhouse, which consisted of a series of rooms, each designed for a different function in the bathing cycle,[59] stands at the core of a *halakhah* in the Tosefta, a third-century legal compilation, in tractate *Berakhot* (Benedictions), a portion devoted to matters of liturgy and prayer. The passage opens with an explicit reference to the setting: "He, who enters the bathhouse." It goes on to prescribe certain restrictions on Jewish liturgy, such as prayer, that may be carried out in the bath, based on a threefold division of its spatial layout: "a place where people stand dressed," "a place where people stand naked," or "a place where people stand both naked and dressed."[60] The dynamics of naming, discussed at the opening of this chapter, where people label their physical surroundings and, by doing so, reveal the cultural textures that shape their perceptions and consciousness, are at play here as well. The way the rabbinic author classifies the rooms in the bathhouse, showing familiarity with them, reflects his idiosyncrasies. Whereas a Roman engineer or a Greek traveler might sort the rooms of a bathing facility according to the temperature of the water or the activities that take place there, the rabbinic scholar, dealing with rules of Jewish prayer, focuses on the extent of nudity. At play here are the ontological quirks of provincial Jews as they interact with the Roman facility.

The legal segment mentioned before from *ḥezqat ha-batim*, dealing with the selling and buying of a bath, provides further specifics about the architectural makeup of a bathing establishment. In the course of discussing the sale of a bathhouse, it refers to the "inner houses (=rooms)" and "outer houses (=rooms)" of the establishment. This categorization, in both referring to rooms as "houses" and distinguishing between "inner" and "outer," is used in non-Jewish sources as well. The present passage also enumerates other elements of the bathhouse: "the boiler and furnace rooms," "room of the *'olyarin*" (probably the changing room; discussed in detail later in this chapter), and "storage room for the wood," as well as "[water?] towers" and "pools."[61]

In the corresponding, perhaps (but not necessarily) earlier portion of this legal material in the Mishnah, the authors add other, more portable objects under the rubric of "the bath and all its appliances." Among these are: the "benches" of the bath (although some of the textual witnesses and medieval commentators read "cups," a word spelled similarly in Hebrew, *sefel* vs. *safsal*, thus lending to textual variations and confusing readings); "curtains" (represented by the Hebrew *vila'ot*, transliteration of the Latin *velum*, adopted also in Greek as *bēlon*); and wooden planks (*nesarim*).[62] The purpose of these items remains obscure to modern readers, who are far removed from the daily operation of the facility, but they were familiar enough to the rabbinic authors and their audience to obviate the need for further explication. References to these objects elsewhere in the rabbinic corpus shed some light on their role in the bathing apparatus, but not much. A legal segment in the Mishnah, for example, in a tractate dealing with matters of ritual purity, infers that the *nesarim* of the bathhouse were designed so that "water can run underneath them"; the same passage also speaks of the "wooden legs" of the bath's benches.[63] A different extract in Tosefta, tractate *Shabbat*, suggests that the *nesarim* were placed over the hot water pools, either to preserve the heat or to prevent customers from immersing themselves in them on the Sabbath, when Jewish (rabbinic) law forbids it. But no one can guarantee whether one kind of *nesarim* was in use or more.[64] In any event, these passages show that rabbinic authors were quite familiar with Roman bathhouses and described their spatial layout more or less the way everyone did in the Roman world, even adopting some Latin vocabulary.

In engaging with the baths and talking about them, the rabbis always represent a duality, which is at the core of the argument of this book. On the one hand, in physical descriptions of the baths, these Jewish scholars operate within the linguistic contours of their region and culture, labeling a certain structure in the bath by an Aramaic term that shows no connection to neighboring Greek, not to mention Latin. For example, in an anecdote about attending the bath on the Sabbath with R. Judah, R. Isaac recalls asking him about dipping a flask of oil in the warm water of (apparently) the hot pool or basin of the *caldarium*, which he calls the *'agalt'a*, an Aramaic word, stemming from a Semitic root meaning "reservoir."[65] Similarly, a string of unrelated anecdotes in rabbinic literature refers to a room in the public bath by the Aramaic name *'ashuna'*. It portrays the space as hot and steamy, like the Roman *sudatorium*, and *'ashuna'* could be based on the Semitic root for either heat or fire.[66]

On other occasions rabbis rely on the vocabulary of the Graeco-Roman Mediterranean, adopting its taxonomy and redesigning it in Semitic form. One example relates to a bathing installation that they call *'ambeti* or *'abeti*, which stems from the Greek *embatē* and *embasis*, and means bathtub (and sometimes, by extension, the entire bathhouse).[67] Bathtubs have their roots in the Greek bathing culture that preceded the emergence of the Roman bathhouse. Bathers would sit or crouch in what modern scholars call "hip-baths," while slaves or attendants poured water on them (see fig. 7). A passage in the *Yerushalmi* reflects these early, Greek bathing techniques, saying that heating the *'ambeti* required the mixture of hot and cold water, ignoring (or ignorant of) the Roman method of heating great amounts of water with the hypocaust system.[68] The Greek method suffered from lack of control, as we learn from a rabbinic simile that speaks of a "boiling *'ambeti* that no living being can climb into," and those who attempt it are scalded.[69] Although Roman public bathhouses, for the most part, stopped utilizing small tubs, moving to larger pools and basins and to heating large quantities of water at once, tubs surely remained in use, especially in the eastern parts of the empire, where Greek-style baths certainly did not disappear overnight as soon as the Romans arrived. Evidently, these tubs were part of bathhouse furnishings familiar to the rabbis.

Other architectural elements of the bathhouse also surface sporadically throughout rabbinic texts. R. Yoḥanan, a famous third-century scholar, is quoted as comparing the strong arms of the biblical patriarch Jacob with admiration to the two massive columns that stood in the public bathhouse of his hometown of Tiberias.[70] Two hundred years later, on the other side of the Mediterranean, the Gallo-Roman aristocrat and bishop Sidonius Apollinaris expresses a similar sentiment when he extols the size and beauty of the columns in the baths of one of his friends.[71]

Rabbis also refer to the gates of the baths, a prominent architectural feature shown on mosaics and mentioned in papyri correspondence about it (see figs. 11 and 23).[72] A segment in the *Yerushalmi*, relating to people who gather at the entrance of the bath before it opens, mentions the gates as a point of reference.[73] The bathhouse gates play a more important role in another story told in the *Yerushalmi* about a confrontation in the baths between rabbinic scholars and a believer in Jesus (referred to by the pejorative term *min*). In that story (discussed in more detail in chapter 8) the rabbis involved uttered a magic spell, and the gates captured and immobilized the Christian so that everyone who passed him could poke fun at him and beat him.[74]

This same story refers to another architectural element of the bath, calling it *kippah* in Hebrew, normally translated as a dome, although in this case it may be alluding to a carved niche in the walls. The scuffle started when the Christian used a magic spell to capture the rabbinical scholars in the *kippah* of the bath, which they countered with their own magic powers. Indeed, domes, semi-domes, and different kinds of vaults, large and small, often crowned many of the central rooms in the baths, and these unique ceilings captivated the eyes of onlookers, were depicted in art (see fig. 17), and were praised by ancient authors who wrote about bathhouses. Niches too were often built into the walls and housed statues and other decorative elements (see fig. 19).[75]

It remains unclear, however, whether the *kippah* of the bath in rabbinic terminology indeed denoted a dome or a niche. In the story about the duel between the *min* and the rabbis, if *kippah* refers to a dome, the rabbis must have been raised up into it supernaturally, not unthinkable in a story about magic spells but not in keeping with the rest of the story. The term appears in another *halakhah* in the Mishnah, which permits Jews to cooperate with their gentile neighbors in building a bathhouse but requires them to stop when the project reaches construction of the *kippah*, where, according to the author, "[people] set up idolatry (=statues)."[76] Here, the *kippah* seems to be a niche (from the Latin *nidus*, nest), a common ornamental feature in Roman architecture in general and widely in use in bathhouses. It consisted of a shallow, concave recess set in a wall and often crowned by a shell-figured half dome, which housed sculpture and other decorative elements (see fig. 19).[77]

Dome or niche, the numerous references to the structure of the bath, its layout, and the artifacts within it show the familiarity of at least some rabbinic scholars with the institution and its details. They move around it with ease and effortlessly identify its various components. The mixture of terms they use in reference to the baths and their furnishings, some in Hebrew and Aramaic, and others borrowed and transliterated from Greek and Latin, reflects the multilingual, provincial environment in which they lived.

The Heating System

Rabbinic literature often refers to the warm water of the baths, together with the techniques for heating and distributing it.[78] Rabbinic authors use three terms, two of Semitic origin, one borrowed from Greek, to refer to the heating devices associated with the bathhouse: *yorah*, *qamin*, and, rarely, *tannur*.

In the legal passage discussed earlier in the chapter, when the *halakhah* in the Tosefta prescribes the structures and equipment included in sale of a bathhouse, it lists both the *qamin*, a term stemming from a widely used Greek word that means a furnace or an oven, and the more obscure, probably Semitic name *yorah*, together with rooms that house them: "the room of the *qamin* . . . and the room of the *yorot* (pl. of *yorah*)."[79] A legal segment discussing whether it is permissible for Jews to enjoy the public baths on the Sabbath (despite the religious prohibition against lighting fires on this sacred day) states that "at first (Jews) used to plug the *qamin* from the eve of the Sabbath, and (then they were religiously allowed to) enter (the baths) and bathe on the Sabbath." This passage describes the *qamin* as a large heater that people would "stuff with wood," which burned and warmed the water.[80] It was connected to the baths by pipes or channels that, when necessary, could be blocked and sealed ("plugged" in the terminology of the *halakhah*), preventing further heat from entering the main facility.

Another rabbinical legal passage concerning the ritual impurity (*tum'ah*) conferred by a human corpse uses the layout of a public bathhouse and its *qamin* to represent a public building with a separate, yet attached and closely associated, water unit: a single architectural body with two separate limbs. The flow of the water from one to another, when not interrupted, means that the ritual impurity generated by a corpse in one part will impair the purity of the other part.[81]

The kind of spatial organization embedded in these *halakhot* fits well with the known design of Roman bathhouses, where builders usually separated the furnace from the actual structure of the baths, locating it in a chamber of its own (known as *praefurnium*), usually on a lower level than the main building and with separate access through a side entrance (see diagram 1) to protect the bathers from the dangers of smoke and fire. This leads me to believe that the *qamin* and the *yorot*, singular and plural, signify the furnace and the boilers, respectively, the central two devices in the heating system of the Roman bathhouse. One was responsible for creating warm air that would circulate underneath the floor and via ducts in the walls of the warm rooms, and the other refers to large containers in which the water was boiled before flowing to the various pools and basins. Occasionally, rabbis also use a more general term for the source of heat: *tannur*, an ancient Semitic word, which appears already in the Bible, with roots in Akkadian, usually denoting an oven for cooking and baking. In those rare occurrences, it seems to be either a synonym for *qamin* or a different, unknown kind of furnace.[82]

Rabbis also show close familiarity with the second component of the heating arrangements of the Roman bath, the hypocaust (literally, heating from underneath). It consisted of a raised floor, supported by numerous short columns (fig. 12), allowing warm air to flow underneath, warm air and humidity to spread in enclosed bathing spaces, and, most important, the high temperature of the water on the floor in basins, pools, and tubs to be maintained. The hypocaust, under the floor, remained invisible to ordinary bathers and was probably of no interest to them. However, some rabbis, scholars and inspectors of details in their own right, show full awareness of the system, as reflected in a popular anecdote about the fourth-century scholar R. Abbahu on a visit to the public bathhouse in the Galilean city of Tiberias. Three versions of this whimsical tale, combining realistic and fantastical elements, circulated in both Palestinian and Persian/Babylonian rabbinic settings. The hypocaust figures in all three accounts. In one adaptation, the floors of the bathhouse collapse and R. Abbahu miraculously survives by climbing onto one of the hypocaust columns. Other reworkings of the tale exaggerate the incident, but they all confirm that the authors knew about the forest of columns beneath the heated floor of the bath.[83]

Some rabbinic references indicate the authors' awareness that maintaining the heat of the bath required effort and supervision. For example,

FIGURE 12. Pillars (*pilae*) of the hypocaust system from the western bathhouse in Scythopolis/Beth Shean, dated to the fourth or fifth century. Made of ceramic tiles, they supported the floor (now missing) of the hot room. *Credit:* Photograph courtesy of Gabi Laron.

the rabbinic scholars in the Mishnah discussed above about going to the bath at the end of the Sabbath coined a catchy phrase as a unit in the measurement of time: "enough [time] to warm them (= and make them) heated." The phrase refers to the time it took for the workers of the bath to get the heating system up and running and for the cold water to be heated.[84] Another *halakhah* also addresses the heat of water in the baths, ruling that one should be allowed to request the heating or cooling of water, regardless of how those who come afterward would feel about it.[85] Beyond setting guidelines for shared usage of public bathhouses and access to warm water, these *halakhot* voice the pleasure people took from the heated water in the bath. Today we take the availability of hot water for granted. Ancient people could not do so.

The human efforts and the natural resources required to maintain the heat generated by the hypocaust system were never endlessly available. The supply of wood, for example, the fuel used to keep the furnaces burning and maintain the flow of hot water, always presented a major challenge and a financial burden. Numerous papyri attest to the methods, often verging on coercion, that city officials used to compel wealthy individuals to provide timber for the public baths; occasionally the imperial authorities also shared in this task.[86] Rabbinic authors are surprisingly silent about this aspect of city life and civic duties. They are aware of the need of combustible material for the baths, regularly mentioning dried branches, logs, and straw and the basket or container for collecting fuel, known as the *quppah*, associated with the bath attendant, the *ballan* or *ballani* (more on him later).[87] Yet rabbinic literature does not mention the obligation to supply wood or the arrangements made by cities and communities to maintain the supply, an omission similar to the usual rabbinic neglect of the administrative mechanisms that governed the cities where they lived and prospered.

The social dynamics that always surround a rationed commodity, hot water, in this case, also surface in both Graeco-Roman and rabbinic sources. Many ancient texts allude to the privilege of dignitaries—provincial and city officials as well as the wealthy and other luminaries—to have the staff of the bath heat the water especially for them. According to Tacitus, for example, when, during the civil wars of 69 CE, the general Marcus Antonius Primus attended a public bath in northern Italy and "complained of the temperature," a slave from the bath's staff immediately replied that they would heat the water for him right away.[88] On the other side of the Mediterranean, rabbis too were aware of the special treatment that the baths provided for men of power and stature. The legal category of "an important person" as well as that of "a man of shape"—a person who arrives at the bath dressed in attire that proclaims his high status—appears in the Mishnah and other rabbinic sources, which describe the preferential treatment these people received in the public baths.[89] A number of rabbinic stories also evoke the special heating arrangements that certain individuals enjoyed in the baths. In one tale, for example, preserved only in the late (perhaps eighth-century CE) rabbinic compilation *Pirqe de Rabbi Eliezer*, when fate reverses social and political ranks, the wicked biblical figure Haman is forced to carry out the common, yet denigrating, labor of heating the bath for Mordecai, a lowly task normally performed for him. Another rabbinic legend relates that when the emperor Titus arrived in Rome, after the local residents welcomed him with customary praise and glorification, they "immediately warmed the bath for him and he entered and bathed."[90]

Operation and Services

Operating the Roman public bathhouse on a regular basis required meticulous attention to detail and access to financial and human resources. Public baths displayed a complex array of structures and facilities, requiring far more than abundant water and the technology to heat it. Bathhouses around the Roman world opened and closed at certain times, days, and seasons, and someone had to administer this. Managers of this establishment oversaw the collection of an entry fee from the attendees, if required, and they also supervised regular cleaning and maintenance. Other services offered in the baths included guarding the clothes of the bathers, supplying or selling oil, and helping customers apply it and then scrape it from their bodies. The wealthy relied on personal slaves to do this for them (more on slaves in chapter 7), but the less affluent multitudes who regularly frequented the baths needed the help of bathhouse staff or other service providers. Additional services were also available within the bathhouse complex for a fee: massages, a barbershop, food, prostitution, and even medical care. Graeco-Roman sources, the papyri in particular but literary sources as well, portray this exuberant reality with colorful detail and nuanced precision.[91] Lesser known, if at all, rabbinic literature too offers insight and specific information about all of these matters, affording a fresh look at the function of public baths on the eastern reaches of the empire.

A uniform schedule for all the bathhouses in a single city, let alone throughout the Roman world, is unimaginable, though evidence suggests that most, if not all, of them were closed during certain hours, usually at night.[92] Statements and legal formulations preserved in rabbinic sources show awareness of (at least some) people to the operating hours of the bathhouse, which obviously determined when they bathed. One midrashic passage compares bathing with prayer: "Just as the bathhouse is sometimes open and sometimes closed," prayer too must conform to the hours in which the "gates of prayer" are open.[93] Similarly, a *halakhah* dealing with a ritual purity installation, called "the purifier" (*metaheret*), which existed in some public baths that served Jewish communities, explicitly refers to the time when the baths are "locked" and assumes it is during the night.[94]

Some bathing facilities evidently remained open after sundown, at least for several hours. The somewhat exceptional practice of going to the bath in the evening is well-documented in Graeco-Roman sources, in both inscriptions and literary evidence. In some places, slaves and women apparently utilized these extended hours of operation, but the sources are inconsistent in this regard, as they should be.[95] In rabbinic material, I am not familiar with any direct reference to the custom of nocturnal bathing, but a terse legal statement does mention the lighting of lamps in the baths, evidently reflecting an awareness of the use of these facilities after dark. This is reminiscent of a story told about the third-century emperor Alexander Severus, who donated oil for the lamps of the baths so they could remain open after dark.[96] Baths might also have been open before sunrise, as we learn from a story about the third-century rabbinic scholar R. Ḥanina, who happened to walk past the public baths before dawn and encountered early risers who had gone there to perform a ritual immersion for purity.[97]

Rabbinic sources also discuss the availability of baths in the various seasons, confirming trends mentioned in other sources. For example, in a discussion about the performance of Jewish prayer and ritual in the public baths, a question raised by the fourth-century scholar R. Jeremiah assumes that at least some bathing facilities were open only during the summer, a well-known practice elsewhere in the Roman world as well.[98] A *halakhah* in the Mishnah detailing the regulations applying to public Jewish fasts, in response to prolonged droughts, includes "shutting down the (public) baths."[99] A legendary tale, preserved only in a late rabbinic compilation (from perhaps as late as the tenth century CE, though the material is from hundreds of years earlier), speaks of an imaginary king who closed the public baths while he fought against his foes, the barbarians.[100] Even if these texts operate only within the legal and haggadic imagination of some rabbinic scholars, they show clear awareness over a broad span of time that certain circumstances could lead the authorities to close the public baths. Indeed, some Roman inscriptions confirm this. An inscription from Pisa, for example, announces the closure of the public baths, along with local temples and shops, due to the untimely death of Augustus's grandson Gaius Caesar in 4 CE.[101]

Staff

When it came to the maintenance of the baths, rabbinic authors mention different personnel who served the clients of public bathhouses. Sometimes they merely refer to these workers by name. For example, one text mentions a certain Jacob in a scene set in the baths, labeling him with the title *turmesar*. The location of the scene and the similarity of his title to the Greek word meaning "hot" (*thermos*) led some scholars to see him as a bath attendant, one who tends to the bathers and the upkeep of the facility; others believe he was the owner of the bath. A *turmesar* appears in another rabbinic passage together with another member of the bathhouse staff, the *'olyar* (on whom more below), as they negotiate a financial transaction. But other than that, we know nothing about this particular Jacob and his vocation.[102]

Rabbinic authors refer to the major staff member of the bath as *ballan*. This term originates in the Greek *balaneus* and stems from the Greek word that represents the building of the public bath itself, *balaneion*. Many societies and languages around the Roman Mediterranean adopted this term to refer to the public bath's maintenance worker, including Latin (*balneator*) in the west and Aramaic/Syriac (*ba'lonoyo'*) in the east. However, none of these mentions offer a clear-cut definition of the *ballan* and the work he (or, sometimes, though less frequently, she) performs in the bath, leading Inge Nielsen, who collected and discussed the references to this worker, to label him a "Jack of all trades."[103]

Rabbinic literature echoes the same multiplicity of portrayals. Some of the sources in this corpus have the *ballan* collecting admission fees. Rabbis knew, of course, that many, although not all, public baths, whether owned by the city or by private individuals, charged for entrance; they mention the cost as either a *prutah* (the local, probably Aramaic name for the lowest denomination of a bronze coin) or an entry token ("small *prutot* that are given as a token in the baths"), also commonly used in public bathing establishments throughout the Roman world. These sources depict the *ballan* as the doorkeeper of the public bath, the man in charge of admission, and they even record the phrase he used when letting in the people who had paid: "Here's the open bath, enter and bathe."[104]

Rabbinic sources also speak of the "seating place of the *ballan*" by the furnaces of the bath and name him as the person responsible for the heating system. Some rabbis also refer to the *kuppah*, the container for combustible material (mentioned earlier), as "the *kuppah* of the *ballan*."[105] A third group of sources generally associates the *ballan* with responsibilities for general maintenance of the bath, not just the entrance or the furnace. These sources portray him as an employee, or perhaps even the manager, who opened the bath, ensured its water supply, and dealt with the activities and situations that took place during the day. He could be in contact with female clients or chase away thieves.[106]

A similar three-way division, in both terminology and spatial configuration, emerges from rabbinic sources dealing with the station of the *ballan*—what they call the "seating place of the *ballan*"—within the bathhouse building. One passage places him near the furnace; another, dealing with matters of purity, speaks of the "beam (*qorah*) of the *ballan*" and appears to place him and it in the open, public space of the bathhouse, to which fellow Jews have unrestricted access (unlike the confined area of the furnace room, which was kept separate from the public space of the bath); a third rabbinic text speaks of the "box (*teyvah*) of the *ballan*," stating that it was "originally made (in height and shape that would allow the *ballan*) to climb and sit on its top." Although not explicit in this text, a box would be ideal for a doorkeeper, who could sit on it at the entrance and use it to store the collected entrance fees.[107] Needless to say, the entrance to the bath and the furnace rooms span different locations in the bathhouse, and the personnel in charge of them represent two separate vocations, unlike in appearance and skills. Nevertheless, in different passages rabbinic scholars conflate them all as *ballan*, never asserting that one person holds the two jobs.

In smaller institutions that required (and could afford) only a limited staff, the workers, often slaves, did whatever was needed. In this scenario, a *ballan* could attend to the furnace and then move on to other tasks around the facility.[108] However, in larger establishments, where tasks were more specialized, the name *ballan* (literally, the worker at the baths) became a general word that people used to refer to multiple employees of the baths, not feeling the need to discern and distinguish between them, and so it could refer to the doorkeeper or the furnace operator.

Rabbinic authors refer to another employee of the bath by the name '*olyar*. Like *ballan*, this term also stems from the common Graeco-Roman vernacular around the Mediterranean, derived from the name for olive fruit and its tree (*elaia* in Greek and *olea* in Latin) and, more particularly, from olive oil (*elaion* in Greek and *oleum* in Latin). Olive oil was commonly used in the baths, and many Greek words based on the root "olive/olive oil" came to signify the various aspects involved in its distribution and application, both in and outside of the baths, in the Hellenistic *gymnasia*—widespread before the advent of the Roman bathhouse—and elsewhere. The word *elaiothesion*, for example, referred to an oiling room in the *palaestra*, the outdoor training courtyard of the baths; the staff and officials who dispensed olive oil held the title *elaiothetēs* and *elaiochutēs*. Phonetically, the rabbinic term '*olyar* seems closely related to the Latin *olearius*, which refers to the olive oil industry and denotes either a manufacturer or a vendor of oil.[109]

As far as I can tell, other than one exception (in the fourth century CE, in the writings of the Palestine-born Bishop Epiphanius), in the

Greek-speaking world this specific term did not designate a staff member or vendor in the public bathhouse. The rabbinic material, by contrast, consistently places the *'olyar* solely inside the baths. One passage that associates the *'olyar* with the public baths appears in the Palestinian Talmud, in which third-century rabbinic scholars praise the pious behavior of their celebrated predecessor, the first-century Yoḥanan b. Zakkai, who used to wear his phylacteries (two small, black leather boxes containing parchment scrolls with verses from the Torah, which Jews ordinarily wore only while at prayer) all day long. In that passage, one rabbi qualifies the devout practice of Yoḥanan and states that when he arrived at the public bathhouse, he would remove the phylacteries at the station of the *'olyar*.[110] Needless to say, these third-century scholars held no knowledge of bathhouses in the days of Yoḥanan, two centuries before their time, but they did know about their own bathing facilities and staff. Thus these rabbis knew of a member of the bath personnel, or perhaps a peddler, called an *'olyar*, someone commonly found in the public baths of the third century, who could keep watch over items such as Yoḥanan's phylacteries. Along the same lines, the *halakhah* mentioned earlier in this chapter regarding the sale of bathhouses lists among the architectural elements that are transferred in sale of the building, along with the furnace room and the boilers, the "room of the *'olyarin*" (with the Aramaic suffix of the plural).[111] Evidently, some rabbis viewed the *'olyar* as part of the bathhouse staff.

The importance of olive oil in the baths was second only to that of water. According to one rabbinic saying, "[one who] bathes and does not anoint [his body with oil] is like water [poured] over a barrel."[112] Rabbis also describe the various methods of applying oil in the baths: smearing it on yourself, having someone else rub it on your body, or spreading the oil on a special marble table or board (or even the wall) and then brushing your body against it. Some rabbis looked down on this last practice: "anyone who brushes [his body with oil] against marble is the friend of a donkey."[113]

They pay similar attention to the completion of the process, highlighting the instrument used to scrape the oil off the body, *strigilis* in Latin, a scraper, which rabbinic literature calls in Hebrew *magreret* or *magredet*, from the verbs "to drag" or "to scratch." This refers to pulling the curved blade of the *strigilis* along the skin of the body in order to remove the oil with the accumulated sweat and dirt (see fig. 8). Rabbis also mention the "round shape flasks, which are used to carry oil to the baths," they prohibit bringing the oil in glass containers "because of [the] danger (of it breaking)," and they also refer to the "box (stand) on which oil is sold in the baths."¹¹⁴ A number of anecdotes about rabbis who patronized the bathhouse also mention an otherwise unknown custom in which people dipped the oil flask or a saucer containing the oil into the hot water of the bath to warm it and make it more pleasant to the body. It also thins the liquid, making it easier to pour and apply.¹¹⁵ Evidently, just like anywhere else in the Roman world, oil and its application represented an essential and indispensable component of the experience in the public bathhouse and the rabbis clearly recorded its various manifestations.

Despite these frequent references to the use of oil in the bathhouse, only one rabbinic passage (and possibly a second one) connects the *'olyar* to oil. It does so indirectly, when referring to the *strigilis*, calling it in Hebrew: "*migrarot* (in the plural) of *'olyarin*." It also describes the scraper as "suspended," for, as we know from archaeological and artistic depictions, scrapers hung from strings.¹¹⁶ A second, more ambiguous reference appears in one of the anecdotes mentioned above regarding warming the oil: "R. Ḥizkiyah [entered the bath] to bathe. He gave a saucer/flask [of oil?] to Zosimus the *'oryara'* and told him: Bring it up for me to the *'ashuna'*."¹¹⁷

All other appearances of the *'olyar* in rabbinic material, although tied to the baths, lack mention of oil, making the *'olyar* a multitasker that closely resembles the *ballan*. In the discussion of Yoḥanan's phylacteries, the *'olyar* guards the bathers' clothes and other belongings. This seems to place him in the *apodyterium*, the changing room of the public baths. This may also explain an expression that the rabbis use in the laws of purity: "the windows of the *'olyarin*, which open one into the other." This apparently refers to the window-like cubbies where people left their clothes when attending the baths, which have been found in the *apodyteria* in many archaeological excavations (fig. 13). Rabbinic sources also mention a key or a seal that the *'olyar* uses to assure the safekeeping of the clothes, perhaps attesting to a practice not preserved in any other source.¹¹⁸ The fourth-century Epiphanius Bishop of Salamis, himself originally a native of Roman Palestine, records the exact same application in one of his stories when he calls a staff member in the public baths in charge of "taking the bather's clothes" and "watching them" by the Greek title *olearios*.¹¹⁹

Another rabbinic passage designates the *'olyar* as the man responsible for "bringing *balrin* of women to the baths," not revealing the nature of this attire, only its ability "to cover the body and head"; another passage has him responsible for towels and other linens to dry the body.¹²⁰ Rabbis also speak of "coins given to the *'olyar*." Although the reason for the payment is not stated, it could well have been for any of the tasks associated with his job.¹²¹ Finally, another rabbinic tradition puts the *'olyar*

FIGURE 13. *Apodyterium* in the first-century CE Stabian Bath, Pompeii. *Credit:* Photograph courtesy of Bopra77 and Dreamstime, licensed by Dreamstime.

in a completely different area of the baths as the man who handled the charcoal for the furnaces.[122]

Once again we see here the multicultural dynamics of terminology, by which a Roman term, *olearius*, found its way into the domain of the public bathhouse in the eastern reaches of the Mediterranean but lost its original connotation, as the locals endowed it with a range of new meanings. The bathhouse, as we have seen over and over again, was a central arena for this kind of social exchange and linguistic reconfiguration.[123]

Another aspect of the presence of oil in the rabbinic material that sets it apart from other Graeco-Roman sources relates to what the rabbis do not mention: the civic aspect of the oil supply, the funding that city councils and wealthy residents provided for the free distribution of oil. This central feature of the use of oil, mentioned in numerous documentary sources from around the Mediterranean, is not referred to even once in rabbinic literature. On the contrary, the only relevant rabbinic statement, mentioned above, asserts that oil was purchased at a certain counter (box/stand), not freely dispensed, in the baths. I can only speculate about the reason for this silence, even whether it was intentional. In general, rabbinic authors ignored matters of city administration, perhaps because few of them, if any, are documented as serving on city councils. Moreover, the rabbinical legal system, *halakhah*, offers a competing mechanism for running communities.

But something else may be at play here. Some Jews, rabbis included, disapproved of using oil (and wine) produced by non-Jews, due to matters of ritual purity. Jewish laws prohibiting the consumption of "gentile/foreign oil" reach back hundreds of years prior to the rabbis. The first-century Jewish historian Josephus reports that even centuries before his time, a Hellenistic Seleucid king granted permission to any Jews in Asia Minor and Syria who did not wish to anoint themselves with this forbidden product to receive an allowance from the city, through the archon (=magistrate in charge) of the gymnasium, to purchase their own oil. Josephus also states that this custom persisted in his own time, and rabbinic literature too reports an enactment of the court of the third-century rabbinic Patriarch Judah (or his grandson, known as Judah Nessi'ah), attempting to eliminate the ban against the use of gentile olive and wine altogether.[124] Although successful in the long run, it is impossible to determine whether a ban on gentile oil was successfully implemented among Jews in the first few centuries of the Common Era. The rabbis may have avoided mentioning the free distribution of un-kosher oil in the baths because they and perhaps other Jews who attended the bathhouses refused it and bought their own Jewish oil. Admittedly, this is much speculation to hang on the silence of the sources; we will probably never know for sure.

Finally, a couple of rabbinic sources refer to a person who cleans the public bath. In a parable geared to make a specific point in biblical interpretation, the fourth-century rabbinic scholar Abbahu, himself a resident of the Roman port city in Palestine, Caesarea Maritima, mentions a worker in the bathhouse whose job it was to "wash the bath." Similarly, one of the versions of the aforementioned legendary story about Haman being coerced to wash Mordecai also refers to the cleaner of the bath. When Mordecai and Haman arrive in the bath, the manager of the facility was nowhere to be found, and his absence forced the wicked Haman to carry out his chores and "wash the bath" himself.[125]

In sum, the literary bath of the rabbis presents a fully functioning facility with all its amenities, unique structures, furnishings, technological innovations, and staff to cater to the visitors who patronized it. Constructing an ideal bathhouse on the basis of rabbinic texts, as offered in this chapter, centers on the rabbis as everyday life practitioners in a Roman province, east of the Mediterranean, as they engage one of its most celebrated institutions. Collecting and piecing together the details dispersed throughout their literature about bathing facilities enables us to re-create an important aspect of their lives, encompassing the full range of architectural, mechanical, technological, and operational elements. The Roman public bath represents a constant feature of life for everyone in the Roman Empire, and studying how well Jews knew it provides insight into who they were as individuals and about how they functioned as communities. It shows them as part and parcel of the Roman world, at least as it is encapsulated in this one bathing establishment, and integrated in its cultural textures. The discussion here also highlights the innovations, small and great, that provincial residents, in this case Jews, applied to their surroundings, as they coined new words in their vernacular languages to describe the structures and items that functioned in their life and applied their particular conceptual paradigms to interact with and write about them. From Jewish prayer to ideas about purity, communal organization, and magic—all come to life in the literary bath of the rabbis. Although the rabbinic literary bath exists as a whole only on the pages of this book, portions of it were vividly alive among the Jews of antiquity.

CHAPTER THREE

Earliest Encounters

ARCHAEOLOGY, SCHOLARLY DEBATE, AND
THE SHIFTING GROUNDS OF INTERPRETATION

WHO WAS THE FIRST JEW to set foot in a Roman public bathhouse and how did Jews in general feel about this institution?

Was it one of the two envoys sent to Rome by the Hasmonaean leader Judas Maccabaeus in the 160s BCE?[1] If so, a probable occurrence for which we have no record, the baths that these two men would have attended in the capital of the rising empire were by no way significantly different from the Greek-style bathing establishments, known by the Greek name *balaneion* (in the singular), that they doubtless had visited back home in Judaea. Indeed, archaeologists have uncovered remnants, albeit fragmentary, of one such Greek bathing facility—one of a few that were unearthed in the region—at the site of Gezer, just a few miles away from the hometown of the Hasmonaeans.[2] These structures, often labeled "Hellenistic-style" by archaeologists, were the forerunners of the Roman public bathhouse, yet quite different in their layout and function. Here, the washing of the body took place in individual tubs, known as hip-baths, in which an attendant would pour hot water on a crouching bather (see fig. 7). In the years following the envoy to Rome, Hasmonaean rulers made it their habit to include such Hellenistic bathing facilities in all of their palaces.[3] As far as we know, in the first half of the second century BCE the hypocaust— that massive hot water production system and the beating heart of what we think of as the Roman bath—had not even been imagined, let alone invented. Nor was there an ample supply of running water through a vast system of aqueducts. As shown in chapter 1, both of these impressive and signature innovations came into broad use only in the following century;

Roman style bathhouses begin to appear only toward the end of the second century BCE.[4] Therefore, if their Roman hosts took the Hasmonaean ambassadors to the baths in Rome, these structures would not have registered in the minds of the visitors as "Roman" at all.

Four generations later, Herod—an Idumaean Jew, even if a peculiar one—arrived in Rome for the first time, hoping to gain Roman approval for his quest to replace the Hasmonaean dynasty at the helm of Judaea. What he found, in 40 BCE, was a city already brimming with public bathhouses that were distinctly Roman in their style and function, usually referred to by the Latin name *balnea* (stemming, yet different, from the abovementioned Greek name *balaneion*).[5] It is true that the first great imperial bathing facility (called *thermae*), built by Marcus Agrippa, who was to be one of Herod's closest friends, was still a few years away. But, as numerous literary sources testify, many other establishments, smaller in scale but Roman in character, were already open to the public, attracting all strata of society, and designed in what would become the standard Roman model for centuries to come.[6] The public bathhouse was already so entrenched in Roman society by this time that there is no doubt in my mind—though the sources do not mention it—that Herod attended these establishments, whether the public ones or those that his patrons built for their own pleasure in their villas and mansions. Indeed, the remains of his own palaces in Judaea, which he would go on to build over the next thirty years, reveal his enthusiasm for the bathing structures he encountered in Rome. Throughout his reign as king of Judaea (37–4 BCE), Herod made sure to include Roman-style bathing facilities in all his palaces and fortresses (fig. 14). Fourteen of them have been found by archaeologists—the largest archaeological record of bathhouses associated with any one individual from a thousand years of Roman history.[7]

The best known of these Herodian facilities can be seen today at the sites of Masada, Herodium, and Jericho. Even in places—such as Herod's capital, Jerusalem—where his bathhouses have not (yet) been found by archaeologists, literary sources confirm that they indeed existed; the first-century Jewish historian Josephus tells us of two Herodian bathhouses in Jerusalem, one in the Phasael tower, part of the complex of Herod's palace in the west side of the city, and the other in the Antonia fortress on the northern edge of the Temple compound.[8] Herod's bathing structures embody the best of what Roman technology and architecture offered. All were equipped with the most advanced hypocaust systems, with elevated floors (*suspensura*) and channels of hot air (known as *tubuli*) running through the walls (see fig. 14); the walls themselves were constructed using

FIGURE 14. The hot room of the first-century BCE bath in the palace of King Herod at Masada. Note the suspended floor as it rests on the pillars of the hypocaust system and pipes (*tubuli*) that circulate the hot air behind the walls. *Credit:* Photograph courtesy of Guy Shtibel.

the highest standards of the era, combining cement and stone (a variation on the technique known as *opus reticulatum*), and crowned by domes (one of which still stands intact in Herodium) and barrel vaults. Herod's architects designed the different rooms in these baths according to the norm of contemporary Roman bathing structures—hot and sauna, cold and mild, changing rooms and pools—with only slight variations,[9] as articulated in those very years by the influential Roman architect and author Vitruvius. Herod spared no expense to beautify the buildings—lavish frescoes of the so-called first Pompeian style covered the plastered walls as well as stucco decorations; mosaics or large slabs of colorful marble arranged in geometric shapes (a technique known as *opus sectile*) adorned the floors; and niches in the walls accommodated marble washing basins (known as *loutra*) and other ornamentations.

It seems clear that Herod, at least, loved the Roman baths. But what about his subjects? What about the Jewish public, both during his reign and across the generations, and centuries, that followed? Did Herod, and later his sons, grandson, and great-grandson—all rulers over territories with a significant Jewish population—follow in the footsteps of their Roman patrons and erect public bathhouses for the masses? And did the hundreds of thousands of Jews who lived in Judaea, later Roman Palestine, share the king's infatuation with this essential feature of Roman life? How did they feel about and interact with the Roman bath? What about fellow Jews in other places around the Mediterranean? Modern scholars heatedly debate these questions, and no agreement has been reached thus far.

Dispute in Modern Scholarship

There is no scholarship without disagreement. Diverging views on everything and anything—major and minor, large and small—have been a crucial part of the process of human inquiry from the earliest of times. This chapter will explore one of these divergences, a question that has occupied the minds of some modern scholars who study the Jews of the Graeco-Roman world (which, for our purposes, spans roughly from the first century BCE until the first half of the seventh century CE) for over a century. This issue lies at the heart of this entire book: How did Jews engage with the Roman public bath? First, to state the obvious: all the members of any group of people cannot agree about everything. Not all Jews in the Graeco-Roman world viewed bathhouses—or any other establishment for that matter—in the same way. Some Jews surely liked the baths more than others; others may have resented the bathhouse, or aspects within it, to a small or large degree. Varying attitudes are the essence of human diversity. Bearing that in mind, are we able to discern a general, or typical, Jewish attitude toward the baths, whether positive or negative? Did the Jews living in Roman times like public bathhouses? Did they attend them regularly? Did they patronize the services provided there? Or did most Jews dislike this institution? Did they condemn the practices that were carried out within its walls, and were they offended by what the place represented, so that they avoided the baths and the physical and cultural experiences associated with them? Also, just to complicate matters, did the attitudes of Jews change over time?

Answers to these questions can be determined by utilizing a range of sources, textual and archaeological, from the first century BCE and the centuries thereafter, the time in which bathhouses flourished in large numbers throughout the Roman world. It is true that we have relatively little direct evidence about how the baths were used, or not used, by the millions of Jews who lived outside of Judaea/Palestine during this time, inhabiting the cities and towns around the Mediterranean—usually referred to as the Jewish Diaspora. Some aspects of these people's lives have registered in the surviving sources and are thus well known; for example, the institution of the synagogue and its function among Jewish Diaspora communities is documented in hundreds of sources. But other issues, among them Diaspora Jews' engagement with Roman baths, mostly remain unaccounted, and therefore unclear.

On the other hand, when it comes to the regions of Judaea, later known as Syria Palaestina, the combination of written sources and archaeological records provides ample information about Jews and Roman bathhouses. Rabbinic literature, mainly from the third century onward, offers the most valuable data, but it is joined by earlier written sources, like the work of Josephus. Alas, modern scholars disagree on the conclusions that should be drawn from these bodies of ancient writings. Indeed, most who have studied and written on the topic of Jewish interaction with Roman bathhouses have reached a similar, mainly negative conclusion, namely that ancient Jews in Roman times condemned and avoided them. The current chapter—and in various ways, the rest of this book—dissents from this line of scholarship and attempts to dispute their position, arguing against the notion that Jews resented and thus avoided the public baths.

At the core of the scholarly debate regarding Jews and Roman bathhouses stands an archaeological question about the very existence of these facilities among the Jews of the Early Roman period. Did Jews build Roman bathhouses in their settlements, in particular the cities and towns of Judaea and the Galilee during these times? This question is somewhat different from the issue of interaction with the baths, as it pertains to the very action of building the architectural structure that housed this institution. These two topics, however—the existence of the bathhouse building/complex among the Jews on the one hand and the engagement with and attitudes toward it on the other—are closely related; the scholarly position claiming that Jews disapproved of the baths also maintains that due to this negative attitude they refrained from building them in their cities and villages, at least in early Roman times.

A word about chronology is warranted here. The designation "Early Roman" is, of course, a modern construct, one of the several chronological categories that help scholars navigate the long time span of Roman domination. In Judaea, the region at the core of this chapter, it usually refers to the first century and a half of Roman rule, from their conquests in the early 60s BCE up to—depending on whom you ask—either the destruction of the Jewish Temple in Jerusalem in 70 CE or two generations later to the end of the Bar Kokhba revolt in 136 CE. (To simplify matters, we can think of this period as encompassing the first century before and after the Common Era.) Early Roman is followed by the period known as the "High

Empire," covering most of the second and third centuries CE, and then the "Late Empire" from roughly 280 until Rome's demise in the east, in the early seventh century. At a certain point, a fourth designation comes into play, "Late Antiquity," which some scholars see as concurrent with the Late Empire and others define as starting somewhat later and continuing into the era of Arab/Muslim rule in the eastern Mediterranean. Most scholars agree that by the Late Empire, bathhouses were quite prevalent in cities where Jews lived (although disagreement remains as to how Jews regarded them, a topic at the center of the next chapter). In any event, the issue of whether Jewish communities built and/or sponsored Roman bathing facilities for their members in the Early Roman period is highly contested by modern scholars; this will be the focus of the rest of this chapter.

A generation ago, Ronny Reich, a prominent archaeologist studying the spread of Roman bathhouses among the Jews, maintained that "the introduction of the hot bath-house into Eretz-Israel [a modern name used for Roman Judaea] as a public institution caused some reserve and objection within the observant Jewish community."[10] According to Reich's analysis, the institution of the public bath clashed with the Jewish way of life in antiquity. To build his case Reich argues for the absence of public bathhouse buildings from the archaeological record of Early Roman Judaea. He claims that Jews refrained from erecting public bathhouses during those early times because many or most of them rejected communal bathing and other practices associated with these establishments. Reich then presents a list of what he calls, using the rabbinic term, "Halakhic problems" that pertain to the baths and claims that those legal problems led the Jews to avoid and reject the baths. (I discuss Jewish laws pertaining to the baths in detail in the next chapter.)

Other modern scholars, with only slight exceptions, hold similar views.[11] The origin of this understanding, namely that ancient Jews disapproved of the Roman bathhouse, can be traced to the early phases of the academic study of Judaism in the Graeco-Roman world, during the late nineteenth and early twentieth centuries. Samuel Krauss, a Jewish Hungarian scholar writing at the turn of the twentieth century whom many consider the founding father of the field of study now called "Jewish Material Culture in Antiquity," offers the earliest example. He expresses the prevailing contemporary sentiment in his description of the ancient rabbis as "condemning" (*verurteilen*) the bathing culture of the Romans.[12]

Not much changed throughout the twentieth century in the assumption and conclusions held by Krauss. Many scholars embraced Krauss's notion about an essential contradiction between the Roman bathhouse and the Jewish way of life and that widespread animosity toward this institution prevented Jews from embracing and attending the baths. Modern scholars, writing about various aspects of ancient Judaism, about the rabbis, or about Jewish life in the Roman world, have voiced this assertion as a matter of habit, as an undisputed historical truth. One scholar suggested that in the first and second centuries, attending the public bath was "the privilege of the [Jewish] Patriarch [i.e., the supposed official leader of the Jewish community at the time] alone" and that "pious" Jews refrained from the public baths; along the same lines, another scholar claimed that "in the eyes of the pious Jews . . . any public bathhouse, which was not used for ritual purification (*miqveh*) was tainted with idolatry."[13] When archaeologists find bathhouse paraphernalia in Judaean sites that were clearly settled by Jews, they straightaway associate them with non-Jews, perhaps Roman soldiers, since bathhouses were "institutions foreign, apparently, to the ambience of the Jewish village in the late Second Temple period, and the period between the two revolts against the Romans."[14] From here it is but a short leap for archaeologists and scholars of the Roman world in general, who are not necessarily experts about Judaism, to adopt this view about an insurmountable rift between Jews and bathhouses.[15]

Only in the last two decades or so has this mostly uniform stance begun to come under scrutiny. In a series of articles going back to 1995, I began questioning the prevailing scholarly position.[16] Since then, some scholars have accepted my arguments,[17] but others have rejected them and clung to the old assumptions about Jewish repudiation of the Roman baths with reenergized vigor.[18] Twenty years after Reich presented his opinion on the matter, Stefanie Hoss revisited the topic and reached, for the most part, the exact same negative conclusions. Although somewhat more nuanced in her comparative approach, her study follows Reich's reasoning and methodological principle—that the supposed lack of archaeological evidence for public bathhouses means that the local Jewish population refrained from building them. Similarly, she mirrors his position about the allegedly negative attitude of Jews toward the public baths in the Early Roman period, an attitude that caused Jews, says she and Reich, to refrain from building them.[19] Reich's views too, twenty-five years after his first publication, remain unchanged.[20]

These scholars base their conclusion on a two-tier causal structure. The first tier centers on archaeological findings (in this case, the absence thereof); the second tier consists of the attitude of ancient Jews as registered in rabbinic literature. According to this reasoning, the absence of one—archaeological remains of public baths in Early Roman Jewish settlements—both reflects and is caused by the other, that is, by the negative attitudes that Jews harbored against the baths as supposedly registered in rabbinic texts. The current chapter revisits this causal structure with the aim of refuting it. I will focus here on the archaeological side of the argument, namely that Jews did not build bathhouses, reexamining the claim of Reich and Hoss that archaeological evidence shows Jews abstaining from building public bathhouses in the Early Roman period. (The other tier, namely that rabbinic law contains legal "problems" that caused Jews to forsake the bathhouse, is assessed in chapter 4.)

The Missing Baths: A Critique of Archaeological Absence

It should be clear by now that a central component of the discussion about Jews and Roman bathhouses, especially with regard to the early phases of this encounter in the Early Roman period, revolves around archaeological evidence. To make sense of this portion of the debate, some preliminary explanations are necessary. The science of archaeology—excavating the man-made remnants of the ancient world that were buried in the ground, and then documenting, and then interpreting, those finds—has been developing since the days of the Renaissance. The two major methods utilized by archaeologists in their inquiries involve (1) stratigraphy (from the Latin "strata," or layers), the process of identifying and distinguishing between layers in archaeological digs in order to determine relative chronology and change; and (2) typology, namely the study of characteristic physical features of objects and architectural structures and their development over time. By applying these two strategies to large, statistically enabled quantities of archaeological finds and to extended geographical regions, archaeologists are able to classify objects and buildings as characteristic of a certain period or a particular culture. To state the obvious, no Roman temples or Christian basilicas have ever been found in Iron Age sites anywhere in the Near East (roughly the era spanning the last centuries of the second millennium and the first six hundred years of the first millennium BCE). The inverse is true as well: structures built during the Iron Age are absent from the strata of both later and earlier centuries. By identifying different strata of the past, and by documenting what is found in each, archaeologists piece together a portrait of life in different periods. Needless to say, this crude account of the methods of archaeology ignores the intricacies, complexities, and nuances of any archaeologically based historical reconstruction. But at its most basic level, archaeology uncovers the physical evidence of lived experience and thus allows us to follow the dissemination of culture through its material manifestations.

Roman bathhouses are among the most typical buildings of their time and are relatively easy to detect within the array—or perhaps more appropriate, the disarray—of an archaeological dig. Their architectural profile makes them distinctive and with no antecedent in earlier eras. The pools, the special layout of the rooms and open courts, and most prominently the heating system itself, the hypocaust's close-knit rows of small pillars that raised the floors of the hot room (the *caldarium*) to allow hot air to circulate underneath (see fig. 12)—none of these existed before the arrival of the Romans, making the bathhouse building a particularly clear-cut physical marker of this period. Although people occasionally utilized the hypocaust in buildings other than public bathhouses, those were exceptions. As a general rule, a hypocaust, especially when it turns up with these other characteristic features of the baths, identifies the structure as a Roman bathhouse.[21]

Public bathhouse buildings in this particular Roman style began to appear in the Italian peninsula, the heart of the Roman Empire, in the later years of the second century BCE. Pretty much simultaneously, they also emerged in Asia Minor, today's Turkey. One of the earliest examples, the Stabian baths in Pompeii, in southern Italy, dates to the second century BCE. Over the next two centuries public baths gradually spread, following in the footsteps of Roman expansion, throughout the Mediterranean world.[22] The second century BCE, therefore, marks the inception of this institution and the transition, although far from being sharp or immediate, from earlier forms of public bathing, which people carried out mainly in the Greek style, to the Roman bathhouse with its typical layout and habits.

Roman forces conquered, and quickly established Roman rule, in the eastern Mediterranean around the middle of the first century BCE, first in Syria, Phoenicia, and Judaea, and a bit later in Egypt. Pompey the Great's incursions into the region, putting an end to the Seleucid Kingdom and annexing Syria as a province to the Roman Empire in 64 BCE, marks the beginning of this process. As a result, we would expect Roman public bathhouses to start appearing in these territories soon afterward, in the so-called Early Roman period. Yet, when Reich developed his thesis in the 1980s and 1990s, no Early Roman public bathhouses had been found by archaeologists in the regions that today make up the modern state of Israel and the Palestinian autonomous territories (regions which, during the Early Roman times, were heavily, although far from exclusively, populated by Jews). To be sure, Reich took notice of a small number of buildings in these regions that did feature the characteristics of Roman baths and date to the closing decades of the first century BCE and the opening generations of the Common Era. However, at the time most, if not all, of these Early Roman structures had been found within the private domain: those in King Herod's palaces and fortresses were mentioned earlier in the chapter; a few more have been excavated within other wealthy mansions, like at Tel Anafa in northern Galilee, the earliest documented Roman bath in the region, perhaps as early as the late second century BCE, and at two affluent manors—one on the southwestern portions of the Central Hill, west of the city of Hebron, known as Ḥilkiya's Palace (Khirbet el-Muraq), and another on the southern slopes of the Carmel mountain, north of the Roman city of Caesarea Maritima, a place today called Ramat ha-Nadiv (Ḥorvat 'Eleq) (see map 3).[23]

These early baths exhibit the components of typical Roman constructions, in particular the hypocaust heating system and the organization of rooms in keeping with their different functions. But they were all found in the private sphere. The lack of archaeological evidence for public bathing structures from the early centuries of Roman rule led Reich to his conclusion about Jewish rejection of this institution. His logic ran as follows: public bathhouses were not found because Jews did not build them; and they refrained from doing so because they disliked the institution and the activities that took place there (such as nudity and mixed bathing and consequential promiscuity).

As I shall show later in this chapter, the archaeological evidence has changed dramatically in the last twenty years, not in favor of Reich's thesis. But even with just the old evidentiary material that was available to Reich, I find it hard to accept his conclusions. A comparative analysis reveals the problems with his argument. Comparison is essential in any field of study with limited evidence. To understand Judaea in the Early Roman period, one must look at other regions, not inhabited by Jews, at that time to see whether they, in contrast to the Jewish realm, do feature remnants of public bathhouses. Such a comparison will determine whether the absence of Early Roman public bathing facilities is unique to archaeological excavations in areas where Jews lived. If public Roman bathhouses have been found in abundance in excavations outside the areas populated by Jews and are missing only in Jewish territories, one could conclude that this absence is meaningful and may be attributed to something unique to the Jews and their way of life, as Reich claims. My studies have shown that the opposite is true.

All around the eastern Mediterranean, whether in regions close to the Jewish realm of Judaea or farther away, archaeologists have only found a handful of Roman public bathhouses from the Early Roman period.[24] In Judaea this absence is true in mixed cities, where Jews and non-Jews (sometimes called "pagans") regularly rubbed shoulders, such as the port city of Caesarea Maritima on the shores of the Mediterranean or Beth-Shean/Scythopolis on the eastern edge of the region, where the Jezreel and the Jordan valleys meet. The same lack of bathhouses holds true for cities whose populations were largely non-Jewish, such as, from south to north, Marisa, Ascalon, Samaria, Acco/Ptolemais, and Paneas. Needless to say, the presumed Jewish disapproval of the bathhouse could not have played a role in the absence of bathing establishments in the non-Jewish settlements. Bathhouses are also absent from other non-Jewish cities of this period, most notably the urban centers of Transjordan, known at the time as the Decapolis—Bostra, Gadara, Gerasa, and Susita/Hippos. In all of these sites, although public baths from later periods emerge regularly, archaeological excavations have not yielded remnants of Early Roman public baths.[25] This comparative examination produces the same results deep into Syria, as far north as the great city of Antioch, one of the chief metropolises of the Roman world. Here, despite literary evidence for the presence of numerous baths during the Early Roman period, excavations have yielded none; the earliest public bath unearthed by archaeologists in Antioch dates to the second century CE.[26]

These major urban centers of the eastern Mediterranean were all hubs of economic and civic life, embodiments of Roman culture. And they all embraced the physical features of the Graeco-Roman city. Long colonnaded central streets delineated their contours with markets, temples ornamented with Graeco-Roman facades, and statues, theaters, and hippodromes populating their space.[27] Yet public bathhouses built in conformity with the architectural and cultural norms of the Romans, although found in abundance in all of these sites in later periods, have never surfaced in excavations that date to the first century and a half of Roman rule, the Early Roman period. Archaeologists have carried out extensive digs in all of these places, finding plentiful evidence for the presence of Rome, its army, and its culture. But no remnants of public bathhouses have surfaced that date to the closing decades of the first century BCE or the following century. This central institution of Roman life—the public bath—embedded so deeply in the fabric of any typical Roman city, begins to appear in the archaeological record of eastern cities only in the second century CE, and even then, the bath appears only sporadically, absent as often as present. It is not really until the third century CE that this signature building of Rome abounds in the eastern Mediterranean, including Judaea.

The comparative evidence, therefore, undermines the validity of Reich's arguments and refutes his conclusions.[28] The absence of Early Roman public bathhouses in Jewish sites cannot tell us anything specific about Jews and their way of life, since archaeological remnants of early bathhouses were not discovered in any eastern Mediterranean city. Archaeological remains of Early Roman baths, even in places where they surely existed, tend to disappear in the stratification of archaeological excavations. This is not a significant absence, specific to the Jews and shedding light on their way of life and attitudes, but rather a common absence, related to the nature of archaeological preservation in the region at large.

There may be various reasons why archaeologists have not discovered the remains of Early Roman public baths in excavations of big cities in the eastern Mediterranean. Perhaps large municipalities refrained from erecting public bathing institutions immediately upon the arrival of the Romans because builders needed to see to the water supply first; bathhouses, especially the large ones, required large quantities of water. Admittedly, some bathing establishments, as shown in chapter 1, especially the more modest ones, functioned without aqueducts, relying instead on springs or wells, and when available also on nearby rivers; but these could provide only a limited supply of water, inadequate for large cities. Aqueducts were needed, and they had to be financed, planned, and constructed before large public baths could be built—a lengthy process.[29]

A different line of reasoning to explain this absence may be related to the relationship of Early Roman baths with their predecessors, Hellenistic baths. As explained in chapter 1, when the Romans arrived in the eastern Mediterranean they encountered a Greek bathing culture that had functioned for centuries. In Judaea itself some Greek bathing facilities—the so-called hip-baths—have been uncovered by archaeologists.[30] In addition, the institution of the gymnasium, an essential component of any Greek city in the east as elsewhere, which provided a space to pursue Greek education and sports, included bathing facilities. These Greek-style, pre-Roman bathing institutions did not cease to exist with the arrival of the Romans. On the contrary, in numerous places, in particular Greece and Asia Minor but also Egypt, evidence suggests that they persisted deep into Roman times, simultaneously and concurrently with Roman-style baths.[31] The situation in the Roman provinces in northern Europe and Britain and to a similar, if lesser, extent in North Africa was quite different, since there were no earlier public bathing traditions for public bathhouses to replace.³² It may very well be that since the Hellenistic world already featured bathing facilities, it reduced or even eliminated the demand for Roman bathhouses at least at first and locals had less incentive to build them (more on this below).

Finally, from an archaeological standpoint, perhaps Early Roman public bathhouses have not been unearthed because they were incorporated into the more elaborate bathing facilities that replaced them, leaving no clear trace.³³ Even in the city of Rome itself, although abundant literary records testify to the existence of numerous public bathing facilities in the first century BCE, in what is normally called the Republican city, centuries of intense archaeological excavation have not yielded physical evidence for any of these.³⁴ For whatever reasons, the fact remains that Early Roman baths are scarce in all territories of the eastern Mediterranean, and so, contrary to Reich's arguments, their absence in Judaea cannot be attributed to a particular (hypothesized) antagonism of the Jews.

New Light on Old Sources: Josephus

Moving beyond the archaeological argument from silence about inherent Jewish opposition to the Roman bath allows a fresh look at some ancient sources and newly discovered archaeological material, which show that Roman bathhouses existed and perhaps even proliferated among the Jews from the earliest generations of Roman rule.

The Jewish historian Josephus offers one such ancient source. In a series of anecdotes illustrating King Herod's good fortune during his early days, as he fought the last Hasmonaean ruler Antigonus, Josephus includes a dramatic escape scene that takes place in a Roman public bathhouse located in a Jewish settlement. Josephus offers two slightly different versions of this vivid escape tale; one appears in his early book *The Jewish War* (*BJ*), and the second in the later *Jewish Antiquities* (*AJ*).³⁵ In the earlier version of the story, while the soldiers were resting after the battles, Herod headed to the local public bath, which Josephus calls by the common Greek name *balaneion*. According to this account, as Herod was about to enter the bathhouse, a band of enemy combatants, who had escaped the battlefield and taken refuge inside the building, suddenly emerged and assaulted the king. The slightly different account in *AJ* merely has Herod entering an unspecified room or a chamber (*dōmation* in Greek) in order to bathe. Although this second version lacks explicit mention of a bath, the Greek noun that Josephus uses for bathing, *loutron*, belongs to the vocabulary that he ordinarily associates with public bathhouses.³⁶ In this second version, the attack occurs inside the room: the assailants emerge from deeper in the building and catch the king naked and ready for his bath. Such a spatial layout—rooms that the author categorizes as "inner" and, by extension, "outer" chambers—matches the ways that other ancient sources describe bathhouses and their array of rooms. The Tosefta, for example, a Jewish, rabbinic text compiled in the same region as Josephus's homeland about a century after him, when enumerating the various parts of the public bath, speaks of "inner rooms" and "outer rooms," and the same classification of inner and outer occurs in Greek texts as well, which frequently refer to the *caldarium* as the "innermost room" (*endon oikos*).[37]

The two reports of the story in Josephus also disagree as to the exact location of the event. When attacked, Herod was waging a fight against the Hasmonaean king Antigonus and the Jewish supporters who gathered around him. His campaign brought him south from Galilee through the Jordan valley, passing Jericho and heading toward Jerusalem—in other words, within a distinctively Jewish territory. According to *BJ* the incident took place in a village named Cana, unknown in this area; *AJ* seems to preserve the more likely name, Isana, a Jewish town some twelve miles north of Jerusalem.[38] Further ambiguity remains as to whether Herod camped in Isana, while the bathhouse incident happened elsewhere, as seems to be indicated by *BJ*, or whether the "enemy," namely the Jews fighting with Antigonus, and the bathhouse were in Isana itself, as suggested by *AJ*.

It is hard, perhaps impossible, to determine which, if either, of the two versions of this anecdote is true.[39] Did Josephus relate a story that had been preserved in writing or orally, from the days of Herod in the first century BCE, attesting to the existence of a bath in a Jewish settlement? And if so, can we say anything with certainty regarding the nature of this building? Was it a small Roman-style public bathhouse, which, as we have seen, has been found by archaeologists only from slightly later periods and only in private mansions?[40] Or was it an earlier type, a Greek hip-bath? Unfortunately, we cannot know. The Greek word used by Josephus, *balaneion*, applies to both the old, Greek-style baths and the Roman structures, making it impossible to distinguish between the two based on names alone. Nevertheless, the sources offer a clear indication of Josephus's perception and state of mind.

Josephus wrote *BJ* in Rome, in the years just following the Jewish Revolt of 66–70 CE; *AJ* would come some years later. He knew just what Roman public baths were like; he refers to them almost ten times throughout his books, always calling them by their common Greek name (*balaneion*), which he also used in the Herod story.[41] In his narratives Josephus also always takes great pains to present the uniqueness of

Jewish life as he envisioned it and to highlight any deviation from Jewish norms by Herod or anyone else. He does so frequently in his writings: about human representation in art, about statues, about the special nature of the God of Israel, and about the many unique (Romans would say, peculiar) practices of his people, Josephus's fellow Jews.[42] Josephus assumes a clear judgmental tone about Roman institutions and buildings, which came to exist within the Jewish domain and which, in his opinion, deviated from Jewish norms. When discussing Herod's construction of a theater and amphitheater in Jerusalem, for example, he is adamant about their inconsistency with the Jewish way of life. He calls Herod's initiative an "abandonment of the native law" and doesn't shy away from labeling the activities in these buildings as "gentile customs," "incompatible with piety," and "foreign to the Jewish way of life." "To the natives," he says, "it meant an open break with the customs venerated by them."[43] Had he thought that the presence of a bath in a Jewish settlement conflicted with Jewish practice, he would have surely made a point of it. The neutral, uncontested mention of a *balaneion* within a Jewish settlement speaks volumes: Josephus, a representative Early Roman Jew, and one always ready to voice his opinion, saw nothing wrong with the bath. He accepted the presence of this institution among the Jews as normal and expected.

More Recent Discoveries from Galilee and Judaea

New archaeological evidence, stemming from excavations conducted in the last two decades, although at times fragmentary, provides further evidence that public bathhouses operated regularly among the Jews even during Early Roman times. The sites excavated include a variety of municipal settings, a large ancient city as well as smaller towns and villages. And they come from diverse geographical locations, ranging from the Galilee in the north to the heart of Jewish regions on the Central Hill of Judaea and its adjacent territories in the Sheffelah (see map 3). The bathing structures themselves also differ from one another significantly. One is a large urban complex, others are small and modest, but they all share architectural features that define them as Roman establishments, and they all seem to have functioned within a clearly Jewish domain.

MAGDALA

The best documented site is in the Galilean city of Magdala, also known by its Greek name, Taricheae. Writing in the first century CE, Josephus tells us much about this important regional center on the western shores of the

Lake of Galilee, just a few miles north of Tiberias, and about its mostly, although not necessarily solely, Jewish population; other Graeco-Roman authors from roughly the same time, such as Strabo and Pliny the Elder, also knew of the place, as did, about a century later, the Jewish scholars we today call rabbis. One of the followers of Jesus, Mary Magdalene, also came from this city.[44]

Beginning in 2006, the renewed excavations at Magdala uncovered a spacious public bathhouse, well equipped with an elaborate, still standing Roman heating system—a hypocaust—and nicely decorated by mosaic floors and inscriptions (unfortunately only fragmentarily preserved).[45] Reconstructing the stratigraphy of the building, the excavators established its origin in the Hellenistic period, prior to the arrival of the Romans, probably as a Greek-style bathing facility within a local gymnasium. They further showed how it evolved into a typical Roman public bath in the early generations of Roman rule, definitely prior to the war that erupted between the Jews and the Romans in the 60s CE, known as the Great Revolt, in which Magdala participated and was eventually captured by Vespasian and his son Titus.

We have no way of telling who was responsible for its construction or the circumstances in which it opened and then operated. A short line in the correspondence of the famous Roman orator Cicero reveals that in the turbulent year after Julius Caesar's murder, that is in March of 43 BCE, the Roman proconsul Cassius, one of the chief conspirators against Caesar and at the time a central player in the power struggles to gain control of the east, held his court and camp in Taricheae, which was probably, although not definitively, our Magdala.[46] He did not stay there long; two months later, in May of the same year, he wrote another letter to Cicero from elsewhere in Syria.[47] Could it be that the Roman general and his entourage, with the military engineers who surely accompanied them, introduced the Roman bathhouse to this Galilean Jewish city? This is an alluring, perhaps even a reasonable, speculation for which there is no definitive evidence. Regardless of its origin, the institution continued to exist and function within the Jewish city for generations after Cassius and his people were long gone.

The Greek aspect of the city's culture is well reflected in its second name, Taricheae, stemming from a group of Greek words associated with the smoking, pickling, and preservation of fish, a basis of the city's economy (mentioned as early as the first century CE by the Greek-speaking historian and geographer Strabo).[48] As in many other places in the region, the Greek name functioned seamlessly alongside its Aramaic counterpart—*migdal nunya*, "tower of fish," or Magdala for short.[49] The

Greek inscriptions and symbolism of the bathhouse's mosaic floor further demonstrate Greek influence in this community. The inscription offers a common Greek phrase—*kai su* (literally "you too"), usually associated with wishing of good luck and protection to those attending the bath. The mosaic also portrays a host of aquatic, athletic, and other bathing features: a ship, a dolphin, a discus, weights, an *aryballos* (a small flask to carry ointment), and a *strigil*, the sharp scraper used to remove oil after it is rubbed on the body. All of these are part of the standard artistic repertoire and iconography of Roman bathhouse decorations found around the Mediterranean.[50] None of these aspects of Graeco-Roman life embedded deep in the textures of a Jewish city should come as a surprise to anyone, nor are they unique to Magdala in any way.

As discussed in the introduction to this book, by the Early Roman period, Greek culture had been entrenched in the life of the Jews of Judaea, as elsewhere in the eastern Mediterranean, for centuries: the people spoke Greek, some better than others; they used Greek names; and they adopted and adapted Greek mores, norms, and institutions.[51] Modern observers of these phenomena call it Hellenization, and thus may label the Jews living in Magdala as Hellenized Jews. But the residents of Magdala, and the many people living in the villages around it, were not "Hellenized" more or less than anyone else in the Roman world, as these were the norms everywhere and anywhere for many years. Like the Jews of first-century Jerusalem, both BCE and CE, the Jews of Magdala used Greek alongside Aramaic and Hebrew in their inscriptions, buried their dead in tombs constructed and ornamented according to Greek architectural models, and attended a variety of Graeco-Roman institutions that their city hosted and sponsored.[52] They were simply Jews living by the common and widely shared Graeco-Roman customs of their time. The public bathhouse of Magdala sits naturally, and unsurprisingly, within this context of first-century CE Galilee and Judaea. Its uniqueness does not stem from its existence in the ancient world but rather from its resurfacing in our world: a relatively rare finding by modern archaeologists, which further corroborates the assertion that Roman baths were common and habitual among the Jews of the Early Roman period.

SHUAFAT

A second set of Early Roman public bathhouses situated in an unmistakably Jewish settlement comes from the archaeological excavation in Shuafat, the modern Arabic name (the ancient name of the town remains unknown) of a Palestinian neighborhood and refugee camp some two and a half miles north of Jerusalem. Between 2003 and 2007 archaeologists carried out a series of rescue excavations along the route of the main road, both modern and ancient, that traverses the Central Hill north of the city of Jerusalem. In these meticulous archaeological excavations—also known as salvage digs, because they are required by modern Israeli law to precede any building construction in order to assure that no ancient remnants are destroyed before they are properly documented—researchers discovered a string of well-defined buildings, rich with detail and artifacts, that were part of a large town or village. Ancient coins and other chronological markers, found both below and above the floors of these buildings, show that they belonged to a short-lived, although exceptionally well-planned, settlement that was constructed in the years immediately after the Jewish revolt of 66–70 CE and then abandoned two generations later, on the eve of the second Jewish revolt of 132–136 CE. The town would never be settled again.[53] The distinctive Jewish water pools used for ritual immersion (known as *miqveh* in the singular and *miqva'ot* in the plural) appear throughout the site, coupled with typical Jewish stone vessels that the excavators found in abundance in nearly every building. Both of these finds suggest adherence to Jewish laws of ritual purity and are very common in Early Roman Jewish sites, thus marking the clear Jewish character of the residents of this place. Analysis of the bone findings showed the vast majority of animals on the site to be of the kind permitted by Jewish dietary laws, further corroborating the Jewish identity of the people living there.[54]

Yet, at the heart of the Shuafat site stand not one but two exquisitely built Roman public bathhouses. Spacious, one measures over 90 feet long and the other is 60 by 45, and centrally located, these bathing facilities exhibit all the features typical of a Roman public bathhouse. The builders equipped them with the highest standard of hypocaust heating system available at the time, which includes the use of ceramic tiles for the pillars to raise the floors, a relatively rare method in those early days. Both buildings also feature hot and mild bathing rooms (*caldarium* and *tepidarium*), pools, and an outdoor open court (*palaestra*), as well as tubs and even a large, Roman-style toilet (*latrine*) attached to one of the structures. The builders also decorated the floors of the baths with mosaics and colorful stone slabs, the popular Roman technique known as *opus sectile*. Apparently, the Jews living in the Shuafat settlement enjoyed Roman-style bathing at its highest level and with all its common amenities. It is hard to say with certainty who established this settlement or who initiated and then installed the pair of public bathing structures at its heart. Based on the short duration of the place, archaeologists have suggested that the conquering Roman forces built the town, in the wake of the Great Revolt, to resettle refugee Jews from the nearby and just destroyed city of Jerusalem.[55] Despite this uncertainty, all the experts agree that Jews resided in Shuafat, the kind who strictly adhered to purity and dietary laws. It is inconceivable that Roman builders would construct two beautiful, spacious public bathhouses had they thought that the town's population would boycott them. Whoever built these bathhouses obviously knew that at least some Jews did not abhor public bathhouses. The builders did not erect Roman temples at the site, nor did the archaeological excavations unearth even the smallest fragment of a Roman statue, apparently because the local, Jewish residents had no interest in such things, unlike the public bathhouses, which the local Jewish residents of this early Roman town in Judaea welcomed, like their Galilean brethren in Magdala.

THE SHEFFELAH

Traveling twenty miles northwest from Shuafat, one encounters three other sites that feature remains of Roman public bathhouses in what are clearly Jewish villages from the Early Roman period.[56] The three settlements, all excavated in the last twenty years, happen to be very close to one another, within a ten-mile perimeter, and all are located on the western side of Judaea. This is a transitional geographical area known as the Sheffelah, or the Judaean foothills, on the seam between the region's Central Hill and its seashore plains. The excavated sites are in close proximity to the regional center, the large town of Lod/Lydda, which later in the second century CE would officially become a city (*polis*) and be renamed Diospolis. The first site comes from a rescue dig in the modern Israeli city of Modi'in. In a layered series of ruins the size of nearly a football field, called Khirbet Umm el-'Umdan, archaeologists found the remains of a village from the Hellenistic and Early Roman periods. Pottery shards indicate that the settlement in this site began as early as the Persian era (in the fifth to fourth century BCE), but the village reached its peak in Early Roman times, only to be abandoned, like many other towns and settlements, during the Bar Kokhba revolt, the Jewish uprising that engulfed the region in violence and destruction between 132 and 136 CE. Various elements in this settlement identify its residents as Jewish, including a characteristic Jewish ritual immersion pool (*miqveh*) as well as a synagogue, of the type that begins to appear in the years following the destruction of the Jewish Temple in Jerusalem in 70 CE.[57] On the eastern edge of the excavated area stood a Roman bath, only partially excavated and heavily disturbed by later building activity but nevertheless clearly identifiable due to the parts of the hypocaust system that remain intact. The size and orientation of the surviving wall of this building show it to be comparable with the other public building at the site sixty yards to the west, the synagogue. The fragmentary nature of the bath does not allow for many conclusions, other than the simple, yet illuminating, fact of its existence during the Early Roman period in a relatively small Jewish village.

Six miles to the north of Khirbet Umm el-'Umdan, archaeologists have uncovered a second, but this time exquisitely preserved, Roman public bath in the remains of a village now known as Khirbet Krikur.[58] Here too, certain elements point to the Jewish identity of the residents and their life during the Early Roman period, specifically in the generations just before the destruction of the Second Temple and the immediate years thereafter. The excavations unearthed a ritual immersion pool, stone vessels, and ceramic oil lamps of the kind very common among the Jews of the Second Temple period. Just as important, the site features an elaborate series of caves connected by man-made tunnels, hiding places of the kind widely utilized in Jewish settlements that participated in the Bar Kokhba revolt; indeed, a coin found inside this structure bears the inscription "year 2" and is typical of coins struck during the revolt.[59] The Roman bath at this site, with eight-foot walls still standing intact, shows two stages of building. In its infancy it contained a square structure, 31 by 31 feet, subdivided into the typical rooms of a Roman bathhouse: a changing room (*apodyterium*), cold (*frigidarium*) and mild (*tepidarium*) rooms, as well as a hot room (*caldarium*) with two semi-circular, although unsymmetrical, niches that probably accommodated tubs or basins (known as *loutra*). It also had a raised floor supported by arches and pillars accommodating the hypocaust system, which remained intact underneath. The builders arranged the rooms one after the other in a winding line, known by scholars as the angular row type, allowing the bathers to move freely between them, but not in a circular motion. Therefore the attendees had to turn around and come back through the rooms after using the hot room at the end of the row. A separate, smaller room, entered from the outside, hosted the furnace that warmed the water and supplied hot air to the appropriate rooms through ceramic pipes and channels. The builders did not neglect the aesthetics of the place. Archaeologists uncovered remnants of a colorful mosaic floor decorated with geometric shapes in the ruins of two rooms, as well as walls covered by small, nicely carved ceramic tiles. At least one Greek inscription existed as well, perhaps featuring the name

Markus. At some unknown point, the residents of the place initiated a second building, which significantly enlarged the structure, especially by adding a larger space for the entrance with stone benches on its side, perhaps to increase the size of the *apodyterium*, as well as other rooms. They also opened a second entrance, after the *caldarium*, to allow for a circular movement among the rooms. Regarding the date of the bathhouse the archaeologist excavating the site remains somewhat uncommitted. Although the full spectrum of finds on the site—the Bar Kokhba hideout and coin, the stone vessels, the lamps, and the *miqveh*—points to an Early Roman date, the excavator suggests a later date, late second or even third century CE for the bathhouse, although nothing at this site points to anything beyond the Bar Kokhba revolt of 132 CE. Furthermore, in the wake of that rebellion and war with the harsh devastation it brought upon the Jews in Judaea, the population in the region contracted. Many villages were abandoned, and their residents moved either to larger cities or north to Galilee.[60] It is hard, although admittedly not impossible, to imagine a Jewish community affluent enough to invest in a bathhouse during those harsh times. I attribute the archaeologist's reluctance to place the bathhouse within the immediate context of the site (and of numerous other sites in its vicinity of the Sheffelah) to the widespread assumption among modern scholars that Jews avoided bathhouses in the Early Roman period, even though the entire spectrum of evidence presented here, including this very site, suggests otherwise.

A third set of Early Roman bathhouses within a Jewish settlement in this area has been only briefly reported and remains largely unpublished. Archaeologists unearthed it during a large salvage excavation conducted near the new highway interchange of the modern Israeli city of Shoham, just a few miles northwest of Khirbet Krikur. When briefly reporting about this place, the excavator makes a compelling case to identify it with the ancient town of Ḥadid, one of two settlements by that name. As in the other sites, here too the excavator distinguished an Early Roman stratum, including Jewish *miqva'ot*, which was apparently destroyed during the Bar Kokhba revolt. In the middle of the site, two Roman bathhouses are reported to have been found.[61]

The remnants of these seven public bathhouses in five distinctively Jewish settlements of the Early Roman period—two baths each in Shuafat and Ḥadid (Shoham), and one in Magdala, Khirbet Umm el-'Umdan, and Khirbet Krikur, respectively—offer an impressive body of knowledge. What they tell us is clear: Jews accepted the institution of the bath at the earliest phases of its arrival in the region. Obviously, archaeological artifacts per se are limited in the light they can shed on the entirety of groups and people; the ancient voices associated with any building uncovered by modern archaeologists remain mute, but at the same time much can be learned. The different sizes of the bathhouses and the diverse urban profiles of the places that hosted them, from the large sprawling complex at the city of Magdala through the midsize and superbly constructed buildings in the town of Shuafat, all the way to the modest structures in the villages of the Sheffelah, can give us a sense of how dispersed and diffuse Roman public bathhouses were among the Jews of Judaea and Galilee. Moreover, these bathing facilities were broadly dispersed geographically, from the eastern Galilee (Magdala) to the Central Hill region (Shuafat), to the western reaches of the Sheffelah. This shows that Jewish use of Early Roman bathhouses was not limited to a certain community or a particular locale. The architecture, the organization of the rooms, the engineering capabilities embedded in them, and the attention given to their ornamentation and decoration all show that Early Roman Jews in the first century BCE (in Magdala) and unequivocally in the century that followed (as seen in all the other sites), both before and after the destruction of the Second Temple, were familiar with the public baths and, presumably, with the associated practices that took place there, as they also partook in the collective bathing trends of their time.

MORE BATHS IN JUDAEA AND GALILEE

Surely these seven Roman public bathhouses in Jewish settlements are only the tip of the iceberg. These seven were all found by chance. The bathhouse mentioned by Josephus in the village of Isana, discussed above, located at the heart of Jewish territory on the Central Hill only a few miles north of Shuafat, can be seen as the literary equivalent of the recent excavations: a written reflection of the small village facility found almost fully intact in Khirbet Krikur.[62] The early building's angular row arrangement of rooms, each placed deeper in the sequence than the other, fits Josephus's story nicely, as this arrangement would allow the runaway enemy soldiers to hide in an inner room and swiftly emerge to surprise the approaching king Herod. Josephus's bath in Isana, therefore, should be counted as an eighth bathhouse in the Early Roman Jewish realm, even if documented only literarily.

Fragments, admittedly vague and not thoroughly published or studied, of a ninth public bathhouse that seems to go back at least to the first century CE come from the principal Jewish city of Sepphoris in central lower

Galilee.⁶³ From a few generations later, the Mishnah, a third-century compilation that encompasses legal traditions from the second century, records a rabbinic ruling on the distribution of rent from a public bathhouse in the same city of Sepphoris, when one Jew leased it from another.⁶⁴

Indeed, if we include the opening decades of the second century CE in this discussion of Early Roman times, even more information about bathhouses in Jewish settlements emerges. The Tosefta mentions two bathhouses. In one instance it transmits an anecdote about the sons of a famous rabbinic scholar of the late first and early second centuries CE, Rabban Gamaliel, who attended the public bathhouse in the Jewish village of Chabulon, located in western Galilee, some ten miles northwest of Sepphoris.⁶⁵ A second passage speaks of a public bathhouse in Bene Brak, a Jewish village located in close proximity to the other three bathhouses mentioned above in the Sheffelah. According to the legal tradition preserved in this text, two rabbinic scholars known to have lived prior to the Bar Kokhba revolt attended this public facility and enjoyed its amenities.⁶⁶ Even those who might question the historical reliability of these rabbinic sources, myself included, would agree that the authors did not hesitate to locate public bathhouses in Jewish settlements of their time as something quite natural.

Finally, another bathhouse from the early second century comes from the southern reaches of the region, the Jewish village of Ein Gedi, in the Judaean Desert, on the western banks of the Dead Sea.⁶⁷ Archaeologists tend to identify this bathhouse as a military establishment, although no identifying marks of the Roman army have surfaced in the thorough excavations of the site. Once more, this probably reflects the common and erroneous opinion that Jews, in this case at Ein Gedi, would reject this establishment; thus it had to be associated with the Roman army.

The questions regarding who built these ten or so bathing establishments and who provided the architectural expertise and engineering capability, not to mention the funds and manpower required to build them, cannot be answered without further concrete evidence. Did the architects and engineers who originally worked for King Herod, building his palaces (which, as seen earlier in the chapter, were all equipped with high-standard Roman bathhouses), spread knowledge about bathhouses in the region? Or was it army units stationed in Judaea and Galilee, whose engineers were known to construct bathhouses for their units? Maybe both; perhaps neither.

The military explanation, in particular, is one that emerges periodically in the literature and, whether intentionally or not, nearly always seems to divert attention from Jewish involvement. Thus, it deserves a bit of our attention here. One scholar has conjectured that if the bathhouses found near the Shoham interchange belonged to the ancient town of Ḥadid, then their existence could be tied to a military unit, which, according to Josephus, was stationed in that area for a while, during the Great Revolt.[68] The near consensus of identifying the bathhouse in Ein Gedi as a military building stems from information, unrelated to the building itself, about a Roman cohort that resided in the village during those years.[69] Nevertheless, one must keep in mind that, with the exception of Shuafat, there is no evidence whatsoever for the involvement of the Roman army in the construction of the other eight buildings discussed here. Even regarding the three bathhouses for which there is corroboration of some military presence in the area, the two in Shoham/Ḥadid and the one in Ein Gedi, there are no signs in the immediate findings of the baths for the involvement of the army in their construction. Military bathhouses in Judaea—the ones associated with the Roman military camp on the ruins of Second Temple Jerusalem come to mind as an obvious example—or elsewhere in the Near East and around the Mediterranean tend to evince clear signs of their association with the army; tiles stamped with the insignia of the military units usually surface in significant quantities, as do other small artifacts that reflect the presence of soldiers at the site and their participation in the construction of the bath.[70] The *cohors I milliaria Thracum*, the military unit that was stationed in Ein Gedi (whether it was the full unit or only part of it is hard to tell), is known to have stamped ceramic tiles with its name in other places, for example, when it stayed at the city of Hebron.[71] Yet no stamped tiles have emerged in the excavations of the bathhouse in Ein Gedi; nor have any yet surfaced in Shoham. Without such evidence, tying the bathhouses at Ein Gedi and Shoham/Ḥadid to the Roman army remains tenuous and circumstantial at best. It seems to me that lurking behind these hasty conclusions is the general assumption that regards Jewish involvement with Roman bathhouses as inconceivable. Hence, if there is a bathhouse at a Jewish settlement, it "must" be related to the Roman army. Even if the military was responsible for the construction of some of these bathing facilities (unproven, but not unreasonable or impossible), it should not follow that the locals were either excluded from the place or intentionally avoided it. Military bathhouses, in particular when not located within the walls of a large and fully established legion camp, but rather embedded among the local population in a village or town where a small military unit was stationed, were almost never exclusively geared toward soldiers; evidence from all over the empire shows that, when available, the townspeople where the army was stationed or other nearby civilians frequently used and enjoyed those facilities.[72] The Roman cohort that was stationed in Ein Gedi, for example, moved out a few years before the eruption of the Bar Kokhba revolt,[73] yet the bathhouse continued to operate, apparently by and for the local Jewish community.

Finally, we must keep an open mind regarding the large cities of the region, those that hosted either a majority of Jews or at least large Jewish communities alongside other citizens, and for which archaeological excavations have thus far not yielded remnants of public bathhouses from the Early Roman period. Central cities such as Jerusalem, Caesarea Maritima, and Tiberias, flourishing major urban hubs during this era, all contained public bathhouses in the Late Roman period, as is well-documented in both archaeological and literary records, but have thus far not produced evidence for such facilities in earlier times.[74] There is little doubt in my mind that public bathing institutions existed in these urban centers even during the Early Roman period; after all, why would the Jews of Magdala enjoy extensive bathing amenities while their brethren in neighboring Tiberias would not? And the same holds true for Jerusalem, whose residents, as discussed earlier in the chapter, embraced numerous aspects of Graeco-Roman life and whose leaders erected a host of Greek and Roman institutions—a gymnasium going all the way back to pre-Roman times, as well as a variety of entertainment institutions added by Herod.[75]

Caesarea Maritima is a good case in point. In the late first century BCE, King Herod built it almost from the ground up as a full-fledged Roman city, endowing it with all the necessary buildings, facilities, and institutions that constitute such an urban entity: a theater, an amphitheater, a hippodrome, temples, and athletic games were all lavishly bestowed upon Caesarea and operated on a regular basis.[76] Yet, when it comes to bathhouses, Josephus, who is pretty expansive in his description of Herod's buildings, says nothing. Archaeologists who have found bath remnants in excavations of Herod's palaces in the city[77] have not found any evidence of public baths from this period. Does this mean that Herod neglected to build public baths in Caesarea? I find that hard to believe. For one, he surely had to establish a gymnasium, which no proper Greek city can go without, but for which we have no record in either the literature or the archaeology. If it had a gymnasium, it would also have included a public bathing facility. Additionally, in Rome, at the same time, Herod's great friend Marcus Agrippa was in the midst of erecting what would have been the largest public bathhouse ever built at the time (larger ones followed in future centuries). Herod held Marcus Agrippa as the role model to follow and tried hard to emulate his building projects. Why would Herod refrain from erecting a bathhouse in his own primary city? We can only speculate. Perhaps a shortage of water prevented Herod from installing public baths; maybe there were other reasons. Maybe Herod did build a bathhouse in Caesarea just like in other places, large and small, throughout the region, and we simply have not found it yet. Based on everything we have seen in this chapter, we should keep our minds open to the possibility.

The accumulated evidence and analysis presented in this chapter clearly demonstrate that Jews living in Judaea and Galilee during Early Roman times regularly adopted the Roman public bathhouse and readily incorporated it into the textures of their settlements. Reich's argument from absence, that "not a single public bath-house (excluding the palatial ones) dating to the Second Temple Period has been found to date in any contemporary settlement,"[78] was already quite shaky when presented in the late 1980s, since it was not compared to non-Jewish settlements in other regions. Comparative analysis clearly shows that Early Roman bathhouses had not been found anywhere in the eastern Mediterranean. But today, new evidence from the last two decades proves his argument wrong, as Roman public bathhouses from the Second Temple period have surfaced in distinctively Jewish locations such as Magdala (and perhaps Sepphoris), Shuafat, and Ein Gedi, and in the Jewish settlements of the Sheffelah; these bathing facilities also confirm literary evidence from Josephus that corroborates both their existence and the Jewish neutral stance toward them. Hoss's contention that "compared to other provinces, Palestine acquired bathing habits quite late" should be summarily rejected as well, as should her assertion that when public bathhouses were finally erected in the region they emerged in cities with "strong Roman connections" or "a large non-Jewish population."[79] The evidence speaks otherwise. The concentration of Early Roman public bathhouses found in Judaea and Galilee are some of the earliest public structures in the entire Roman east. They also appear in places that are either solely or mostly Jewish and bear no particular connections with the Romans, at least not more than any other place in the Roman realm of the time.

Without the archaeological component of the argument, namely that the absence of archaeological finds proves that the Jews avoided public bathhouses, the scholarly assumption of a general and widespread Jewish negative attitude toward the public Roman bathhouse collapses. The scholars holding this position assumed that the absence of bathhouses from the Jewish realm reflected resentful or dismissive attitudes. But, as is shown here, bathhouses were not absent in Jewish settlements. Rather they were common and widespread. The assumption based on absence has now lost its archaeological foundation.

But the second part of the question remains worth asking: Now that we have established that bathhouses already existed among the Jews in the Early Roman period, and even more in later centuries, how did they feel about them? For the most part, archaeology cannot shed light on feelings and perceptions. We know that the physical structure, the building of a public bathhouse, was erected and operated in quite a few Jewish settlements, but how did the residents of these places view it? What kind of attitudes did they hold about it? What kind of emotions sprung up around it? The existence of a building per se says relatively little about the range of positions that the locals may have held toward the building and about their engagement with the activities that took place there once the establishment was up and running. To answer these questions, we must explore expressions of thoughts and feelings as they were articulated in the ancient written records that present Jewish life and experience in the Roman public bathhouse. That is the goal of the next chapter.

PART II

Filtered Absorption

CHAPTER FOUR

A Sinful Place?

RABBINIC LAWS (*HALAKHAH*) AND
FEELINGS ABOUT THE PUBLIC BATHHOUSE

THIS CHAPTER PICKS UP right where the previous one left off. Chapter 3 showed that, contrary to the long-standing assumption among modern scholars, public bathhouses indeed permeated areas of Judaea/Palestine settled by Jews and regularly operated in the cities and villages where these people lived. Bathing establishments of the Roman kind in these regions date all the way back to the early years of Roman rule in the region (the so-called Early Roman Period). The current chapter treats perceptions and emotions, the feelings and attitudes of the Jewish population in these areas toward these facilities. As mentioned before, even if a public bathing institution stood in the midst of a Jewish town, it does not automatically follow that all or most Jews residing there were happy about its presence. They could have just as well hated, or at least resented, this place, and as a result avoided using it. Archaeological remains can only tell us so much about the mindsets of the people who lived near the baths.

The only written sources that speak at length about the interaction of Jews with Roman public bathhouses are the texts we now categorize as rabbinic literature. In the introduction, I discussed the nature of these texts in some detail and the somewhat misunderstood character of the ancient legal scholars, today referred to as rabbis, who produced them. Many of the complications highlighted there, stemming from the peculiarities of the rabbinic material, which in turn hinder the work of the modern historian who wishes to use them, come into play here. At the outset we must take the chronological gap into account, since the earliest extant rabbinic material comes from the second and third centuries CE (known as the High Empire period) and thus cannot reliably speak to the situation in the Early Roman period—the second half of the first century BCE and the first century CE—when the institution of the Roman public bathhouse first arrived in the region. Furthermore, we cannot know whether the views voiced in the texts of the rabbis represent those of the Jewish masses or just a small segment of Jewish society, and just what that segment was. As emphasized in the introduction, the rabbis in Roman times never achieved the prominence and admiration granted them in future centuries, and their texts held no binding clout over the practice and surely not for the thought and perceptions of Jews at the time. Moreover, since rabbis never coalesced into a homogeneous group in those early days, one cannot speak of a monolithic rabbinic view on a certain matter; rather, rabbinic literature contains an abundance of independent positions that often contradict and negate each other.

Yet, at the same time, the richness of this written material makes it impossible to ignore. These texts open a channel of communication with at least some individual Jews, at the minimum specific rabbinic scholars, during the second and third centuries CE, who lived and operated in Roman Judaea and Galilee, which at the time were part of the Roman province called Palestine. As mentioned and explained in the introduction, the bathhouse appears hundreds of times in rabbinic discussions of Jewish law (known as *halakhah*), as well as in their stories, anecdotes, and maxims. Rabbinic literature therefore offers a treasure trove of information about how certain people (who could be unique or representative) in a specific Roman province lived their lives and viewed their surroundings. When it comes to the institution of the Roman public bathhouse and its function among the Jews, other than the occasional reference in the writings of Josephus, rabbinic material remains the only written documentation on the topic. And this documentation is nothing if not abundant.

As discussed at length in chapter 3, current scholars tend to offer a very simple answer to a complex issue. They portray ancient Jews, en masse, as hostile to both the existence and the experience of the public bathhouse. In their arguments, these modern scholars rely heavily on rabbinic material. They maintain that the rabbis found various halakhic "problems" with use of the baths, which thus fueled the negative view that they and other Jews held toward this institution, and which eventually led them to reject public bathhouses altogether, at least in Early Roman times. In the words of one scholar: "Numerous halakhic problems were a major cause behind the lack of public hot bath-houses in Jewish communities."[1]

Scholars usually mention four areas of the bathing experience that would have troubled Jews who followed rabbinic law:

(1) The heating system of the bath would have undermined observance of the Sabbath, and in particular would have clashed with the halakhic prohibition against heating or enjoying water that was heated on the sacred day, as well as on other Jewish holidays. In addition, maintaining a constant supply of wood and brush for the fire in the bathhouse furnace might have violated the interdictions regarding the Jewish sabbatical year, which forbids the usage of any crops or natural yields during that year.

(2) The common practice in Roman times of bathing in full or partial nudity does not sit well with rabbinic views that regard the exposure of intimate body parts as "undignified." According to this line of argumentation, the *halakhot* that forbid discussion and religious contemplation in the bathhouse reflect the "problems" that Jews may have confronted when attending the facility.

(3) In the bathhouse, people abiding by rabbinic laws of ritual purity were likely to compromise it by coming in contact with men and women who were ritually impure and thus would pass the impurity on to other bathers.

(4) The adornment of the public bathhouse with freestanding statues and other sculptured images would supposedly have offended Jews who followed rabbinic rulings on matters of idolatry. One scholar, Emmanuel Friedheim, takes this argument even further, claiming that Jews and others viewed (some?) bathhouses as consecrated places for worship. According to this view, the bathhouse would be deemed by rabbinic law as a "place/house of idolatry," which Jews would be prohibited from entering.[2]

To modern scholars these halakhic "problems" have a cumulative effect. Taken together, they would lead—seemingly inevitably—to rejection of the bathhouse as a sinful place. Those who wished to live by the rules of *halakhah*, in their mind the correct and sanctified way of life prescribed by the God of Israel, would be compelled to avoid the public bath, due to the incompatibility of its ordinary practices and the more risqué activities that took place there with the laws that defined their lives as Jews. Thus arose the foregone conclusion that has dominated modern scholarship to one degree or another for the past hundred years: Jews resented public bathhouses.

But is this really the case? The current chapter sets out to reject this understanding of ancient rabbinic law and its resulting conclusion about Jewish antagonism toward the Roman public bathhouse. In my view, the situation regarding the baths was exactly the opposite: not only did rabbis, and Jews in general, not despise Roman bathing establishments, they were enchanted by the benefits these places offered and thrilled to participate in its activities. To substantiate these conclusions, I first argue that the entire premise of discerning halakic "problems" and equating them with hostility and rejection is based on a deep misunderstanding of the nature of ancient Jewish law. Second, I demonstrate how the very topics raised by modern scholars—the keeping of the Sabbath, the sabbatical year, and ritual purity, as well as issues of nudity and idolatry—actually show how well Jews integrated the public bathhouse into their communities and way of life. Finally, I conclude by analyzing a variety of sources that illustrate just how fond (at least some) Jews and rabbis alike were of the baths.

These conclusions are the foundation of my proposed alternative model, one that more accurately defines the cultural interaction between Jews and the predominant Roman way of life. I call this model "filtered absorption": a way to understand how minority groups, living among large and appealing civilizations, can embrace the lifestyle of the majority while at the same time preserving and maintaining the mores and habits important to them.

Unproblematic Problems: Halakhah and Rabbinic Laws of the Bath

Jewish law consists of a large body of rules and directives meant to guide the daily lives of Jews as individuals, families, and communities, as well as a nation. It thus operates on a premise different from that of other legal systems, both ancient and modern. With the exception of totalitarian regimes, nearly all other legal systems strive to *minimize* statutory intervention into the lives of individuals; legal prescriptions are limited to areas believed necessary for the proper function of society, the state (or the city), and its institutions, as well as the safety and well-being of its constituents. But all other realms of life are left, at least in theory, to the free and autonomous discretion of the people. In contrast, Jewish law (and later church law functioning on a similar premise) assumes authority and relevance over almost every aspect of human experience, and it aspires to impact the most minute and intimate details of everyday behavior. Ancient Jews embraced a propensity—fluctuating in intensity in different groups, locales, and periods of time—to conduct their lives according to legal directives. As one would expect, matters of private, civil, and criminal law feature prominently in the corpus of Jewish laws governing marriage contracts and writs of divorce, financial transactions, and criminal activity and its sanctions. But Jewish law also extends into spheres we would label today as both religious and private behavior, regulating the minutiae of intimate relations between husbands and wives, and seemingly innumerable aspects of bodily purity, ritual, and worship, as well as the calendar, weekly and annual festivals, dietary restrictions, sexual conduct, clothing, education, and burial, to name some but not all of the topics addressed by *halakhah*.[3]

This vast and convoluted legislative body evolved over centuries, starting long before the rabbis. It lacked precise contours and contained diverse and frequently contradictory tendencies and principles; over time, certain positions and instructions simply nullify others. But this did not prevent Jews, both in ancient and then medieval eras, from assigning divine status to their laws, viewing them as emanating from the will and revelation of their one true god—the God of Israel—as expressed in the ancient books of the Pentateuch (the Torah), which they believed were delivered to them by Moses, "the law giver." Next to their historical heritage and their communal sense of affiliation, many (although by no means all) Jews felt they were defined by allegiance to their judicial corpus. Orthodox Jews today still believe that by following and adhering to these legal strictures, they affirm who they are as a people.[4]

Across the ancient Mediterranean, outsiders, both non-Jewish authors and various ruling powers, often recognized this seemingly intrinsic connection between Jews and their laws. In one of the earliest Greek descriptions of the Jews, by the philosopher and historian Hecataeus of Abdera in the fourth century BCE, the author weaves the laws (*nomoi*) of these people as a leitmotif that runs through his presentation of them. He portrays the laws as stemming from God's commandments (*prostagmata*) and states that, in their importance to the Jews, they are second only to the Temple in Jerusalem.[5] In the same vein, charters and edicts issued by Greek and Roman rulers in various settings throughout the Mediterranean world, both in favor of and against Jewish residents, consistently refer to their ancient, ancestral laws as a central component of their way of life.[6]

By the time of the rabbis, in the second and third centuries CE, the legal tradition of the Jews—now almost a millennium in the making—was comprised of hundreds if not thousands of details. The Pentateuch, the heart of the collection of texts that were canonized in those very centuries as what we now call the Hebrew Bible, contained many legislative principles and directives, which are known in Hebrew as *mitsvot* (and by moderns as "biblical law"). Traditionally there are thought to be 613 of them, and in the days of the rabbis they were already written down and recognized by Jews as sacred, something the Roman authorities were aware of. They were also translated into other languages spoken by Jews around the

Mediterranean, such as Greek and Aramaic.⁷ In addition to these 613 precepts more or less explicitly mentioned in the Torah, hundreds of other legal prescriptions were derived from them, and others were adopted with no explicit biblical basis. In the centuries prior to the rabbis some individuals attempted to gather portions of these latter, what we may call extrabiblical, laws and offer them in a written format (the second-century BCE Book of Jubilees and some of the later texts that emerged from the Qumran community and documented in the Dead Sea Scrolls offer ample examples of this trend). But the overall legal system of the Jews did not coalesce into a single, standard, literary presentation until the great gathering projects of the rabbis.⁸

As explained in the introduction, the rabbis were far from a homogeneous group, and they were certainly not a "movement," as some modern scholars mistakenly characterize them. Yet they defined themselves as scholarly experts (*ḥakhamim* in Hebrew) in Jewish law, for which they coined the term *halakhah*.⁹ These individuals devoted their lives to the study, comprehension, organization, and further elaboration of the legal matrix they received from earlier generations, and which they viewed as the essence of Jewish life and identity. Their devotion to the development of Jewish law embodied a certain urgency, spurred by a huge crisis in the Jewish world caused by the Roman destruction of the Second Temple in Jerusalem in 70 CE. Now without the physical centerpiece of Jewish life, a pressing, indeed existential impetus for legal creativity arose, one that would provide new formulas and prescriptions as well as a spiritual anchor for a suddenly unmoored Jewish community. Rabbinic scholars devoted much attention and energy to filling the chasm created in the ontological and practical infrastructure of Jewish practice in the generations after the Temple's elimination.

Within this context it should come as no surprise that much of rabbinic legal discourse centers around exploring the proper application of old Jewish legal principles, many of which were extracted from the Torah, to the new realities of their time. Their efforts can be divided into two broad categories: the first was innovating replacements for the worship at the Temple and reconfiguring many aspects of Jewish life that centered around it; the second was identifying new aspects of life that emerged in their own time and seeking to bring them under the aegis of Jewish law. As was, and still is, common in many legal circles, much of the discussion in rabbinic discourse verged on the theoretical, abstract, even far-fetched, examining imaginary legal scenarios of all kinds in order to test and tease out an enormous array of legal paradigms and principles. At other times, rabbis addressed real-life situations, which in their mind required legislative application.

In their legal discussions, rabbinic scholars regularly discussed the Roman public bathhouse, different aspects of its function, and the daily events experienced there. In doing so, rabbis took a close look at the technology and equipment that facilitated the operation of these mass bathing installations. They also considered the layout and furnishings of the building, as well as the apparatus and human habits associated with bathing. Compared to other public facilities and institutions, discussions of the bathhouse are extensive, and detailed legislation emerged from them regarding the way Jews should engage with the bathhouse, providing a vivid example of the mechanisms and dynamics that shaped their mentality. The fact that these bathing establishments captured rabbinic attention is natural and necessary. After all, while these scholars toiled in their legal oeuvre, in the second and third centuries CE, Roman public baths gradually grew in number and popularity all over the Mediterranean. As shown in earlier chapters, public bathhouses, small and large, were everywhere to be found—cities, towns, and villages—and their numbers in areas populated by Jews, as in other regions, reached unprecedented levels. Within the all-encompassing parameters of Jewish law, this required reference and legislative guidance, like any other feature of Roman life that impacted the lives of Jews. As explained in chapter 2, rabbis were probably responsible for coining a new name for the public bath in Hebrew, *beit merḥats*. But rabbinic scholars went far beyond assigning the institution a Hebrew name; they considered, over and over again, how various aspects of the bathhouse fit into the principles and instructions of Jewish law or were incompatible with them.

This is the legislative framework for the many rabbinic discussions of the bathhouse. When rabbis bring up an issue related to the baths and question its compatibility with this or that directive of Jewish law, they are not signaling a "problem" in the modern sense of the word. We think of problems as negative: "a matter or situation regarded as unwelcome, harmful, or wrong and needing to be overcome," says the *Oxford English Dictionary*. Such disdainful notions were never, as far as I can tell, on the minds of rabbis hammering out the *halakhah* of the baths. Rather, these legal scholars were identifying areas that had yet to be addressed by Jewish law or had been addressed inadequately in their opinion. Then, with the baths as with any other matter, they would debate, at times disagree, and eventually formulate rulings that spoke to the issue they raised. In doing so, rabbis were discerning the legal threads that could weave the institution of the bath into the fabric of Jewish life.

By equating the numerous legal issues related to the baths that rabbis raise with "problems," modern scholars misconstrue the nature of rabbinic discourse. If discussion of a legal topic necessarily signaled disapproval, one would have to conclude that rabbis disparaged most aspects of life, since they devote most of their literature to exactly that: identifying aspects of life that require legal consideration. As I show in great detail later in this chapter, rabbis and their legal terminology found it easy to condemn what they disliked, usually by prohibiting it altogether and removing it from Jewish experience as they viewed it. For example, rabbinic authors do not go into minute detail about pagan temples—the sale of buildings or grounds of these places, their furniture, or the manner by which one may enter them. They are categorically and summarily forbidden for Jews. By simply barring them from Jewish life, rabbinic scholars voice their disdain. By contrast, rabbinic authors bring the public bath into the folds of Jewish law time after time, weighing, debating, and defining legal formulas that would address its functions, which demonstrate that for these scholars the bath was not a problem. Far from disdain, rabbis show appreciation for this institution and the desire to include it in the landscape of Jewish life. The discussion of the following topics, "problems" according to common modern scholarly jargon, further illustrates and substantiates my contention.

Applying the Laws of the Sabbath to the Roman Public Bathhouse

The editors of the Mishnah—the earliest text arranging the legislative output of rabbinic scholars, composed at the beginning of the third century CE—devoted ample attention to the laws of the Sabbath.[10] They dedicated two full tractates—*Shabbat* and *'Eruvin*—solely to this topic, the former being one of the largest in the entire mishnaic corpus. Further discussion and rulings concerning the Sabbath turn up in other corners of the Mishnah as well as in other rabbinic texts—particularly the Tosefta and the two Talmuds, the *Yerushalmi* and the *Bavli*—that followed. The compilers of these texts gathered hundreds of prescriptions, geared to shape and orchestrate the practice of ancient Jews on this holy day. Within this rich tapestry, among the multitudes of statutes and the numerous decrees and rulings addressing every possible aspect of Sabbath observance, from the imagined to the real, the authors also make a small number of substantial references to the Roman public bathhouse.

In the most general terms, the laws of the Sabbath primarily restrict the normal range of human activity, so that the observant can direct the holy day toward devotion to God. The public bathhouse, of course, is geared toward the opposite: expanding the normal range of people's behavior and luxuriating in the corporeal pleasures of the human body. Hence, one would expect, as many modern scholars have done, that ancient rabbis would have forbidden use of the bathhouse on the Sabbath. The evidence speaks otherwise.

Two features central to the routines of bathhouses would seem to inevitably collide with Jewish laws pertaining to the Sabbath: washing the body with water and heating the water (and the entire establishment) with burning fire.[11] As for the former, today, most observant Jews refrain from bathing on the Sabbath; they will wash their hands and face but avoid taking a shower or a bath or immersing any part of their body in water (in swimming pools, for example). However, it is far from clear whether washing the body per se on the Sabbath in non-heated water was forbidden at all prior to the rabbis. The Hebrew Bible is very clear on certain prohibitions. You cannot make a fire on the Sabbath. You cannot perform any physical labor on the Sabbath. And yet the Bible does not mention a ban on washing the body on the Sabbath, nor is it cited or even alluded to in any of the Jewish writings from the five-hundred-year (or so) span between the production of the books of the Hebrew Bible and the rabbis. Only one so-called post-biblical source refers to washing—the sectarian book known as the *Damascus Document*—and it seems to indicate that, all things being equal, washing the body was actually permitted on the holy day.[12]

When it comes to the rabbis, most of their discussion of washing centered on the use of heated water because of the prohibition against lighting a fire, not with washing itself. One rabbinic tradition, however, does preserve a three-way legal disagreement about washing in cold water: the second-century scholar R. Meir forbids washing in either warm or cold water, but two of his colleagues, R. Simeon and R. Judah, disagree and permit bathing in unheated water. Oddly, a different rabbinic text, the *Yerushalmi* (known also as the Palestinian Talmud), suggests that the same R. Meir did in fact attend the bathhouse on the Sabbath; other texts further confirm that the great rabbinic scholar R. Judah the Patriarch also bathed on the Sabbath in cold water.[13] Although it is impossible to ascertain whether these texts reflect the real-life actions of these figures on the sacred weekly day, the mindset of the authors is pretty clear. Apparently, for some, if not all, Jews over the centuries as well as for many rabbis, bathing in and of itself does not contravene the observance of the Sabbath.

On the other hand, the prohibition against igniting and extinguishing a fire on the Sabbath—and by extension, enjoying its direct benefits, such as cooking, lighting, or heating, whether the house or the bathhouse—is unambiguous. The Torah, the most important and most ancient strata of the Hebrew Bible, articulates this ban in the commandments bestowed on the Israelites by the God of Israel. The Book of Exodus, the second book of the Torah, explicitly asserts: "You shall kindle no fire throughout your settlements on the day of the Sabbath."[14] Surprisingly, in the ensuing centuries prior to the rabbis, only the second-century BCE Book of Jubilees echoes this specific command of the Torah, shedding little if any light on its implementation in real life.[15] Nevertheless, it seems clear that ancient Jews indeed adhered to this directive and refrained from lighting a fire on this day. Compelling testimony comes from a couple of non-Jewish writers. In an epigram by the Greek poet Meleager of Gadara, a younger contemporary of the author of the Book of Jubilees, the poet resentfully mourns a past lover's preference for a "Sabbath keeper" over himself and scorns their joys in the burning heat of love during the (bitter) cold, brought upon them by keeping Sabbath rules.[16] A more clear indication comes from the Christian scholar Bardaisan of Edessa, from the northeast regions of Syria, a contemporary of the rabbis from the late second and early third centuries CE. In his presentation of the laws of the Jews, he pays ample attention to the Sabbath and explicitly lists lighting a fire among its prohibitions.[17]

Rabbinic *halakhah*, without exception, follows the biblical interdiction of lighting a fire on the Sabbath. Indeed, these scholars see no reason to even reiterate the prohibition, as they assume its knowledge, veracity, and wide acceptance by all Jews. Accordingly, when it comes to water, the editors of the Mishnah assert conclusively that "heated on the Sabbath [it] is forbidden for [both] drinking and bathing."[18] This prohibition is so clear, so self-evident, it seems, that little more needs to be said. However, beyond the general and ostensibly all-encompassing ban, its implementation remained complicated and nuanced. When we look more closely, we find that rabbinic scholars invested much legislative energy in defining the extent of this rule and nuancing its implementation.

This is the legal context of the passage Reich provides as proof for "problems involved in heating water on the Shabbat" that "causes some reserve and objection" toward the bathhouse "within the observant Jewish community."[19] Specifically, he refers to a *halakhah* in tractate *Makhshirin* of the Mishnah, which reads as follows:

A town inhabited by both Jews (called here "Israelites") and gentiles and in it a [public] bathhouse operates on the Sabbath—if the majority [of its population] are gentile, [a Jew may] bathe in it (=in the bathhouse) immediately [after the Sabbath ends]; if the majority is Jewish, [then, the Jew must] wait [enough time after the end of the Sabbath] to allow [the water] to heat. [In case the population] was split equally, he (=the Jew) must wait [the additional time after the Sabbath enough] to allow the [water] to heat. In the case of a small bath (called here *'ambeti*), if [the town is run by gentile] magistrates, [a Jew may] bathe [in it] immediately [after the Sabbath ends].[20]

The assumption at the heart of this legal record holds that bathing in the public bathhouse on the Sabbath is not allowed for Jews due to the prohibited use of fire for the ongoing heating of the water. The question the passage discusses relates to the timeline for lifting the ban once the Sabbath is over: whether it will happen "immediately," that is, right when the Sabbath concludes on the nightfall of Saturday (known in rabbinic terminology as *mots'ei shabbat*), or whether one must wait another interval, namely the extra amount of time it may take to reheat the water after the end of the Sabbath.[21]

The above *halakhah* in tractate *Makhshirin* ties the proscribed time frame of bathing with the composition of the population at the place where a specific bathhouse operates. In a town with a gentile majority there is no need to wait any additional time because the rabbinic legislators, applying theoretical principles regarding minorities and majorities, view the water as definitively warmed for the non-Jewish majority inhabitants, and thus do not deny its usage for Jews "immediately" after *mots'ei shabbat*. But where a Jewish majority or an evenly split population exists, the water is seen as warmed for Jews specifically, and they are forbidden to enjoy it until enough time passes for new permissible water to be heated after the Sabbath ends. What seems like an abstract, hair-splitting observation is a rather typical legal construction of rabbinic scholars (as well as other systems of jurisprudence).

What remains completely missing from this segment of legislative discourse is any hint of the kind of "problem" implying negative attitudes of Jews toward the public bathhouse as an institution and compelling them to refrain from using it altogether during the regular days of the week. In the mind of the rabbinic legal scholar who composed the above *halakhah* in tractate *Makhshirin*, the public bathhouse operates as a well-known, habitual, and regularly frequented institution among the Jewish population of Roman Palestine (which is where the Mishnah was composed). Nowhere does the rabbinic scholar articulate or even allude to misgivings about the bath or voice any grave concerns about Jews attending it. On the contrary, had the bath been entirely forbidden to Jews, there would have been no reason to discuss the particulars of the application of the Sabbath laws to it. Furthermore, no one would claim that every aspect of life that comes under Sabbath restrictions due to the use of fire—cooking food, for example, or utilizing olive oil for lighting lanterns—would lead Jews to view it as "problematic" and abstain from it altogether at all times. Hence, applying this logic to the bathhouse does not hold water (pun intended).

Moreover, the modern contention, ostensibly supported by the *halakhah* in tractate *Makhshirin*, that Jews (or at least rabbis) never patronized public bathhouses on the Sabbath is far from self-evident. Numerous rabbinic sources seem to indicate a more complex and variegated situation, one that evolved over time. Consider, for example, the following rabbinic tradition preserved in the *Yerushalmi*:

> At first, they (=Jews) would plug the furnace [of the public bathhouse] from the eve of the Sabbath, [and then they would] enter and bathe on the Sabbath. [But as time went by] they (=Jews) were suspected of filling the furnace with wood on the eve and it would continue burning in the Sabbath, [so the rabbis] prohibited to them (=the Jews) bathing [on the Sabbath] but [still] permitted sweating [in the bath]. [Then] they became suspected of entering and bathing [but] saying we were [only] sweating, [so the rabbis] prohibited them from bathing and sweating [altogether].[22]

This segment presents a much broader, intricate, and fluid legal situation regarding Jews' attendance at the public baths on the Sabbath. Whereas the assumption of the *halakhah* in tractate *Makhshirin* maintained a constant, and seemingly permanent, ban, due to the prohibition against using fire, the *Yerushalmi* passage shows a situation in flux. It alludes to a period of time ("at first") when certain rabbis permitted attending the bath and bathing on the Sabbath, only if one made sure not to enjoy the heat generated by the furnace. Avoiding the heat involved blocking the pipes ("plugging the furnace") that transported the heat, or the heated water, from the boiler to the pools and basins. In other texts, rabbis mention another strategy: covering the heated basins and pools with wooden planks to mark them as off limits on the Sabbath and to allow the rest of the bathing facilities, such as the cold-water pools, to be enjoyed.[23] Only at a later stage, according to this text, owing to the difficulties in enforcing this means of eliminating the heat, did rabbis expand the law even further and bar bathing on the Sabbath altogether. The *halakhah* in tractate *Makhshirin* appears to begin at the end point of the legal process represented in the tradition in the *Yerushalmi*.

Unlike the passage in tractate *Makhshirin*, the segment in the *Yerushalmi* presents a more lenient position, allowing bathing on the Sabbath under certain circumstances.[24] Conclusive support for the permissibility of bathing on this day comes from specific anecdotes in rabbinic literature that mention individual rabbis, some very prominent, such as the second-century R. Meir, the third-century R. Judah the Patriarch, and the fourth-century R. Abbahu, who all attended the baths and enjoyed their amenities on the day of the Sabbath, while making sure to abide by the various halakhic restrictions that define the Jewish observance of this day.[25]

It is safe to say that some Jews, rabbis included, did not patronize public bathhouses on the Sabbath, just as some may have not washed their bodies at all on this day. An ancient church treatise from third-century Syria, the *Didascalia apostolorum*, compiling various rules and orders for the conduct of Christian life and its communities, says as much about Jews, namely that they did not bathe on the Sabbath.[26] However, no one can say how widespread these habits were, or how many Jews obeyed the later rabbinic injunction against using the baths on the holy day. Apparently, not even all rabbis followed this rule, and rabbinic tradition itself confirms that this purported decree changed time and again over the years.

Indeed, nothing in rabbinic *halakhah* regarding bathing on the Sabbath supports the contention that there was an inherent problem for Jews with the institution of the public bathhouse or that there was a broader negative attitude among them that led to total avoidance of this establishment. On the contrary, the very passage in tractate *Makhshirin*—as well as numerous other segments in the rabbinic corpus—proves the opposite: namely, that rabbis (and by logical extension, other Jews as well) accepted the Roman public bathhouse and viewed it as an integral part of their life, therefore one that requires attention and legislation about its compatibility with the laws of the Sabbath. In their mind, these laws filter the absorption of the bath so as to make its activities conform to the norms that define Jewish life. Ancient *halakhah*, according to the filtered absorption model, functions not as a "wall" to exclude the outside world, as some modern scholars would have us believe (and as it operates among ultra-Orthodox Jews today who use that exact image—*halakhah* as a protective wall), but rather as a tool for cultural interaction.

Applying the Laws of the Sabbatical Year and of Ritual Purity to the Bathhouse

The same interpretive model by which I explained the incorporation of the bathhouse into the legal framework of the Sabbath also applies to other spheres of Jewish law, such as the sabbatical year and ritual purity. Once again, these issues represent central components of Jewish life in antiquity; the laws defining their observance extend back hundreds of years before the rabbis, and before the arrival of the public Roman bathhouse. Just as rabbinic scholars pondered the compatibility of the laws of the Sabbath with the bathhouse, they also identified its intersection with these other realms of Jewish life and eventually formulated proper procedures by which to integrate the two.

The commandments regarding the sabbatical year (*shemittah* in Hebrew) require that once every seven years Jews leave their land fallow for a full twelve-month period. These practices, like those about the Sabbath, reach back to the earliest strata of Jewish law as explicated in the Torah. In the most general terms, the laws of the Hebrew Bible forbid cultivation of the ground during the sabbatical year; moreover, crops that do grow during this year are considered sacred, which entails numerous restrictions on their use. By tradition, these directives apply only to land owned by Jews in what they viewed as the promised land of Israel—which, in the era discussed in this book, was called Roman Palestine. Various ancient sources, Jewish and non-Jewish, confirm that many Jews (although far from all) in Graeco-Roman times observed *shemittah* and that the reigning authorities around the Mediterranean recognized their ancestral right to do so.[27]

Not surprisingly, rabbinic scholars discuss sabbatical year laws at length, devoting an entire tractate in the Mishnah to this topic. Within this text, only two short lines refer to the Roman public bathhouse.[28] There, the editors of the Mishnah include a *halakhah* that permits Jews to attend a bathhouse during the sabbatical year, even when that facility utilizes as fuel for its furnaces straw and stubble grown during the sacred year, which are normally forbidden to use. It is hard to understand why Reich lists this passage among the cases that led rabbis to reject the bath due to "problems" it raised with regard to observing Jewish law. After all, this *halakhah* eases sabbatical rules in the bathhouse compared to other furnaces, which some rabbis require to be extinguished if fueled with sabbatically sacred burning material.[29] If anything, the authors of the *halakhah* here accommodate Jews and find ways to enable them to continue enjoying hot baths even during the sabbatical year.

Rabbinic laws regarding ritual purity, I believe, have been similarly misinterpreted. The metaphysical states of purity and impurity appear to be universal categories going back to the earliest days of human experience, with some societies still adhering to these notions in our own times. In the view of ancient Jews, people, animals, plants, and man-made objects could all contract impurity from an array of sources and situations. Impurity, as encoded in a variety of *halakhot*, imposes a range of restrictions on the behaviors of individuals and communities. Once an individual contracts impurity, he or she can transmit it to others and to objects. Numerous and varied activities, including entering temples, participating in public and religious ceremonies, going to war, and cohabiting with one's wife, were all affected by the bodily metaphysical status of purity or impurity. The laws also prescribed a series of actions and procedures, known as rituals of purification, by which impurity can be lifted or revoked, only to be acquired again when the causal situation reoccurs.[30]

Jews shared many of these principles and practices with other people of the ancient world, although they regarded their own system as unique. Certainly, like the rules of the sabbatical year, here too the categories of purity and impurity stretch back to the times of ancient Israel in the Iron Age (the first half millennium BCE), predating the rabbis and the appearance of the Roman public bathhouse by nearly a thousand years. Jewish guidelines on purity and impurity evolved greatly over time, with wide variety, debate, and disagreement. They shaped the lives and norms of communities, sects—such as the group that produced the documents known as the Dead Sea Scrolls, which pay considerable attention to the manifestations of purity—and individuals. (The best known of these individuals, of course, is Jesus, who criticized sharply the Jewish purity norms of his time.)[31]

Jewish laws of ritual purity relied heavily on the Temple in Jerusalem. Therefore, by the time of the rabbis in the second and third centuries CE, in the generations after the destruction of the Temple in 70 CE, many of the practices associated with ritual purity became impractical, and their observance among the Jewish public gradually faded (although it never ceased entirely).[32] This did not prevent rabbinic scholars from devoting a tremendous amount of attention and intellectual energy to the topic and devising a framework of purity laws to guide people who wished to live by them. The editors of the Mishnah allocated an entire order, with twelve tractates, to the laws of ritual purity, and they come up regularly in other corners of the rabbinic literary project at large. Apparently, whether popular and applicable in their time or not, rabbinic scholars found purity and impurity a worthy endeavor to pursue.

Given this perennial interest in ritual purity, as one would expect, rabbis also explored the issue of purity laws in the public bathhouse. Reich lists three passages in rabbinic literature that address situations in which issues of ritual purity can arise in the baths, concluding that these "problems" led Jews to avoid attending public baths altogether.[33] But I think he and others misunderstand how ancient societies, steeped in premodern beliefs, functioned in daily life.

In the modern mind, the realm of impurity may seem arcane and intimidating,[34] but also vast and far-reaching, as if one could contract impurity anywhere. But for ancient people, purity and its impure counterpart were simply one of many aspects of life to navigate, day after day. Anyone who entered the public sphere—be it the market, the synagogue, or the bathhouse—might bump into impurity. Impurity could be contracted by, to name a few common examples, contact with a corpse, a menstruating woman, or wine touched by a gentile. Some people who adhered to the laws of ritual purity—and to be sure, many Jews did not, to the dismay and disapproval of rabbis—surely took precautions to avoid impurities of all kinds. For example, patriarchal societies, Jews included, imposed restrictions on the movement of impure women, mainly due to menstruation, and this may have extended to the bathhouse as well, either by preventing women from entering during their monthly cycle or by creating a secluded area for them to bathe separately from others; indeed, some rabbinic sources allude to such procedures and designate that space within the public bath as "the house of impure women."[35] But in general, people did not limit their movements due to anxiety about coming in contact with impurity. The pervasive ancient attitude seemed to have been: you take the necessary precautions and you go about your life, and if you do become impure, there are always ways to rectify the situation and purify. Rabbis did not stop going to synagogue, or to the study house, or to the market, or to funerals at cemeteries to avoid contact with sources of impurity; why would they stop going to the bathhouse?

When a certain rabbinic author lists places that remain impure forever, he clearly excludes the public bathhouse.[36] Like permitting the use of fuel grown during the sabbatical year discussed earlier, leniency in the application of the laws of purity to bathhouses makes attending them possible. Other rabbinic statutes describe precautions that must be taken at the bathhouse to prevent clothes stored in the dressing-room cubicles from contacting sources of impurity. These texts also clarify the status of bathhouse furniture with regard to contracting impurity—benches made of wood may become impure unless connected to the ground, while stone benches do not. Rabbis also discuss various situations that may arise in the public baths, for example, how to treat a blood stain on a bench used by women or how to deal with women who mistakenly mixed up their clothes in the baths.[37] These discussions about ritual purity in bathhouses and instructions to avoid impurity there, whether purely theoretical or addressing actual situations (sometimes it is hard to know), are not remarkable in the corpus of rabbinic literature. Such discussions referring to bathhouses surface countless times alongside discussions about every ordinary aspect of daily life in the house, the shop, the street, and the market. Wherever human beings came in contact with each other, they could contract impurity. The rabbis did not single out the public bathhouse as a particularly "problematic" source of ritual impurity.

Another aspect of ritual purity that has created great confusion among modern scholars with regard to the bathhouse involves the ritual immersion that Jews used to purify themselves. Biblical and then Jewish rules from the earliest days required the removal of impurity by either washing or immersing the body in water. By doing so they eliminate the metaphysical state of impurity and restore the body to its pure state. In English, we call this process purification. Over the centuries, heated disagreements arose among Jewish groups and sects regarding the process of purification and the specifics of the installation that would make it possible.[38] Rabbinic terminology adopts a more ancient biblical word and calls this installation for purification a *miqveh*; it typically consisted of a shallow pool or basin (which, according to rabbinic configuration, must be fully dug into the ground) that collected fresh water and featured steps to allow easy entry and exit. Many *miqva'ot* have been unearthed in archaeological excavations. However, by the time of the rabbis in the second and third centuries CE, as ritual purity itself gradually lost its relevance, they became less common. Nevertheless, many of them still functioned and the rabbis surely discussed the laws applying to them with great care and attention.[39] Indeed, the editors of the Mishnah devoted an entire tractate to the complicated laws regarding the *miqveh*'s structure and function.

The common English translation of *miqveh* is "ritual bath" or, at times, "immersion bath." This phraseology that bonds the *miqveh* and the public bathhouse with the same noun—bath—coupled with the fact that both facilities use water as their major commodity led some modern scholars to equate the two and suggest internal tensions between them. For example, the British scholar Martin Goodman, in his effort to pit Judaism and the Roman way of life as contradictory and clashing systems, claims: "Although in the course of the Roman imperial period Jews were to develop a taste for baths in the Roman style, more important than such *bathing for pleasure*, and indeed cleanliness, was *bathing for purity*" (my emphasis).[40] Note that Goodman uses the word "bathing" for both the bathhouse and the *miqveh* and implies that the latter was more important than the former. Reich goes even further and speaks of some immanent tension and "competition" between these two water-based facilities, the public bathhouse and the *miqveh*.[41]

Contrary to Goodman, Reich, and other modern scholars, I believe ancient rabbis placed the two facilities in utterly separate categories, serving different purposes and operating in different realms of human experience. For one, vocabulary reflects this ancient mindset. The rabbis coined two entirely distinct names for the two places: *merḥats* for the Roman public bathhouse and *miqveh* for the installation providing ritual purification. They also consistently use different verbs to describe what takes place in these establishments: *lirḥots* for bathing in the baths, *litbol* for ritual immersion in the *miqveh*.[42] Nowhere do rabbis equate the two practices. Immersion is always and only for purification, never for cleaning the body or for pleasure; bathing is never for purification. The ancient laws, presumably going back to the days of the Second Temple, require that water for purification must come from a natural source without being "drawn" first by human hands. This stipulation applies only to water used for ritual immersion and does not indicate, as some suggest, condemnation of bathing for the sake of cleanliness or pleasure.[43] Nowhere do we find rabbis contrasting ritual purification and bathing or elevating one above the other; they represent phenomenologically different entities, as distinct as apples and oranges.[44]

With this clear difference in mind, rabbinic scholars raised an interesting question about the use of the bathhouse for ritual immersion. After all, bathhouses offered a plentiful supply of fresh water, a scarce commodity in antiquity. If the legal rules of ritual purification were satisfied, could a bathhouse be used by those who wished to purify themselves? And alternatively, were stand-alone *miqva'ot* incorporated into public bathhouses where Jews bathed? Was it possible to accomplish both things with a single visit? At least to some degree, some rabbis said yes. Among the Romans it was not unheard of to use the water of the baths for ritual purification.[45] Some rabbinic sources mention an apparatus they call the "purifier (*metaheret*)" in the bath, a rather obscure device that somehow, when installed in a bathhouse, makes the water effective for purification. Other interpretations of this term view it simply as a *miqveh* located in a public bathhouse.[46]

An anecdote recorded in the *Yerushalmi* corroborates the possibility that public baths could be used for ritual purification: the third-century rabbinic scholar Ḥanina encountered some people (perhaps younger students) at dawn heading for the public bathhouse and planning to begin their day with ritual purification. Ḥanina expressed disdain for the excessive pursuit of purity and urged them to channel their energy to scholarship. The implication is clear: ritual purification, either as an actual event or in the mindset of the author, could take place in public bathhouses.[47] Finally, rabbinic Babylonian sources, although reflecting a society where ritual purity and the mechanisms to achieve it had lost much of their importance and prevalence, openly endorse using the bath for ritual immersion.[48]

All in all, both rabbinic laws of the sabbatical year and those regarding ritual purity and purification refer to the bathhouse, and nowhere do they condemn it. On the contrary, inclusion of the bathhouse in discussion of these legal topics proves that it was part and parcel of Jewish life at the time.

Was the Roman Bathhouse Considered a Place of Idolatry?

All modern scholars who have studied the Roman public bathhouse agree about its non-religious nature. Inge Nielsen, for example, states unequivocally that "the bathhouses were always secular."[49] One modern scholar, however, Emmanuel Friedheim, in a series of articles in Hebrew and then in a book in French, argues that "the public bathhouse was perceived at times by some of those who attended it as a sacred space." In his work, Friedheim claims that various ritual practices were carried out in bathhouses and then speaks of the "ritual characteristics" and "religious pagan aspects" of this establishment. He concludes that "people perceived the place as a place of cult." He also asserts that "from a halakhic point of view people related very negatively to the Roman bathhouse due to the idolatrous aspects it contained."[50] (It is unclear from this article whether "people" refers to rabbis in particular or Jews in general.)

I believe Friedheim misunderstands religion in the Roman world and that his argument misses something essential about sacred space and the mechanisms that made it possible.[51] Later in chapter 6 I provide some detailed depictions of the all-encompassing nature of religious experience around the Mediterranean. As I show there, people viewed reality through a variety of lenses, all of which we would today call "religious." In the ancient world, the terms and concepts of religion played a role similar to popular science today, providing the templates, paradigms, and vocabulary that allowed people to interact with the world and make sense of it. Many gods of all kinds, associated with multifarious ethnic groups and originating from diverse geographical and cultural settings, surrounded the people of the Roman Mediterranean wherever they went, rubbing shoulders in the public arena and taking numerous shapes in the shared consciousness of people and communities.

In practical terms this means that folks engaged in what we would call religious behavior in every aspect of their daily life. Indeed, for those people the term "religious" itself would not mean much, because for them it was simply behavior. They worshipped household gods (what the Romans called *lares*) in special niches and cubicles in their homes, and they regularly wore amulets imploring the protection of divine powers. Individuals and societies interacted with their gods throughout the day, offering gifts and sacrifices and making bodily and verbal devotional gestures. All year long, people and communities performed more substantial religious ceremonies. Processions, musical and dramatic performances, prayers and hymns all filled the public space of villages and cities: in small shrines set up at crossroads (known in Latin as *compitum*, house of the *compitales*, the deities of the crossroads), at basilicas occupying city centers, near the numerous neighborhood fountains and basins, at the markets, in granaries, in theaters and hippodromes, and even in latrines.[52]

Public bathhouses were no different. It was not unheard of for various groups to dedicate a room in a bathhouse complex to a particular divinity: for worship of the emperor, of the Persian god Mithras, or even Jesus, to name a few documented examples. Certainly, some of the many religious activities that took place everywhere around cities and towns—such as processions and ritual festivities, and the washing of statues on holidays—also found their way into the public bathhouse. Similarly, people erected statues in the bath and dedicated them to divine beings, like "Health," "Fortune" (the goddess *fortuna*), or the *genius thermarum* (the civic divine entity protecting the baths). Naturally, some rituals evolved around these divine effigies, as happened with their counterparts everywhere else in the city.[53] In the festival of the Veneralia, for example, Roman women entered the baths naked and offered incense to the goddess Fortuna virilis in the hope that she would conceal their bodily defects from male bathers; similarly, all the participants in the festival of the Saturnalia would begin the day at dawn with washing in the baths.[54] In the same vein, ancients also perceived bodies of water—lakes, seas, springs—as full of nymphs and other magical beings, and this naturally extended to the water of the baths as well. Finally, just as people often named ships, bridges, and other structures after gods (as well as after emperors, or simply their owners), they also gave baths divine names. Venus ranked among the most popular designations, but faraway gods, like the Egyptian Serapis and other eastern divinities, also lent their names to baths.[55]

In this context, the religious "aspects" and "characteristics" that Friedheim identifies in the baths were not unique to public bathhouses but rather ordinary features of every public space around the Roman world. Just as markets, public latrines, the city forum, or every private house in a Graeco-Roman city or town cannot be classified as places of idolatry, it would be a mistake to label the public bathhouse as such. Firket Yegül puts it correctly: "In a world almost universally permeated with a sense of religiosity, baths and bathing seem definitely to belong to the secular sphere." And Garrett Fagan similarly concludes, "baths of all kinds carried divine associations with deities . . . [b]ut these associations do not appear to have had a specifically spiritual or cultic character."[56]

The omnipresence of religious behavior did not mean that the ancients viewed everything as sacred. Put differently, a religious outlook on life did not result in everything being imbued with the stature and substance of the sacred. The essence of the concept of sacredness in all cultures around the Roman Mediterranean lies in its restriction, in its application to limited and delimited spaces. In chapter 6 I discuss in detail the processes, both formal and informal, that people carried out to define sacred space (the Romans called this *consecratio* and *dedicatio*, with equivalent designations in Greek and other languages around the Mediterranean). For an entire public bathhouse, as an architectural complex and as an institution, to be considered a sacred place of cult, official action would have been required by imperial magistrates, or by city councils, or at least by a specific group of people or a community (a guild, for example) who owned the place. This would entail delimiting and elevating a place to the sacred realm. A special budget would have to be provided for its upkeep, priests would be appointed to manage it, stewards and servants would be hired to maintain it, and numerous actions and restrictions would ensue. Ample documentary evidence—in inscriptions, in papyrological documentation, and in ancient literature and art—points at the various venues in Graeco-Roman cities and towns that acquired such status.[57]

Only a limited number of baths were accorded this sacred status. Those that did were mainly of two kinds. The first kind functioned within the consecrated grounds of sanctuaries. Large and small temple complexes, both for worshippers and for pilgrims, dotted the landscape of the Roman

Mediterranean. They often included, along with the temple edifice and other shrines, additional structures such as porticoes, residences for the priests and slaves who managed and maintained the place, accommodations for visitors, taverns, shops, libraries, gardens and groves, fountains, and medical facilities, as well as public bathhouses. The entire compound with its numerous buildings was consecrated.[58] Sanctuaries owned the bathhouses on their grounds, which, by extension, shared the consecrated status of the place. Sacred complexes that included bathing facilities are documented not only in Italy and Greece but in places on the distant fringes of the Roman world, such as Palmyra in the Syrian desert, Oxyrhynchus in Egypt, and Cyrene in North Africa.[59]

The second kind of baths with religious status were built next to natural, mineral hot springs. The shared, common opinion in Roman times associated the therapeutic nature of these thermal springs with divine powers. Thus their locations regularly developed as sacred, curative spas, centered on the thermo-mineral spring in its midst and run as a sanctuary to one of the healing gods or goddesses, Asclepius and Hygeia being the most popular.[60] The facilities constructed at these healing sanctuaries, at times resembling the architecture of luxurious bathhouses, provided visitors with access to the naturally hot mineral water. They contained a similar layout of rooms, courtyards, pools, and gardens, as well as a generous display of sculpture. This outward similarity led some scholars to confuse them with ordinary public bathhouses.[61] But thematically and conceptually they were very different.[62] The curative spas always emerged in unique geographical sites, with thermal springs, often far removed from urban centers.[63] Visitors had to make an effort to travel and stay at these healing centers, and the visit registered in their mind as a unique and singular event, unlike the regular, daily attendance at the public bathhouse in their hometowns. The sacred status of these thermal springs indicates nothing about ordinary, widespread public bathhouses.

Finally, it is important to emphasize that, had they wished to do so, nothing would have prevented the owners, individuals or groups, of a public bath from consecrating it to one of the gods. In the Graeco-Roman mind, anything could be extracted from mundane and profane and elevated to the realm of the sacred. If they did so with trees, groves, springs, piles of stones, doors, windows, streets, and sometimes even animals, why should they not be able to do so with baths? Indeed, some documentary evidence, mainly inscriptions, attests that this did happen occasionally: people dedicated a bath to a god, a goddess, or to the *numina* (the divine aspect or nature) of the emperor.[64] The question, therefore, is not whether sacred baths existed. It is clear that they did—within sanctuaries, as part of thermal bathing institutions, and sometimes on their own. But rather the important issue is how common the sacred bath was and whether such phenomena extended to many of the thousands of functioning public bathing establishments all around the Mediterranean or registered in the shared, public consciousness about those facilities. Here the answer should be categorically no. Only a handful of dedicatory inscriptions indicate the consecration of a bath, while hundreds, if not thousands, of inscriptions from bathhouses do not attest to consecration. Moreover, hundreds if not thousands of texts refer to public bathhouses in secular terms, showing the same widespread public mindset that viewed them as entirely secular—as much secular as could be imagined in a world as suffused with religiosity as the Roman world was.

No evidence substantiates the assertion that people perceived public baths as places of worship. Other than baths that operated as part of consecrated sanctuaries, or hot springs facilities that functioned as sanctuaries themselves, people associated public bathhouses with ritual practices no more or less than any other public space, and aside from the abovementioned exceptions, baths did not register in their minds as religious spaces. Friedheim argued for the existence of an unofficial, popular perception that nevertheless saw the baths as ritual institutions and viewed them as sacred space. He claims that this mainly manifested itself in the remote provinces, including those where Jews lived. No evidence substantiates this hypothesis.

At least some rabbis seem quite familiar with the distinctions presented here, between the vast majority of secular public bathhouses and those that stood on the sacred grounds of a sanctuary (or turned into a sanctuary themselves). One *halakhah* specifically examines a special case of "(a sanctuary of) idolatry that has (=owns) a bathhouse or a garden."[65] From the very formulation of this unique case, one must conclude that the rabbinic authors clearly differentiated between the special bathhouse of a sanctuary and all other ordinary bathhouses that do not fall into the idolatrous category. Moreover, even in this idolatry-specific case, the rabbinic author does not prohibit Jews from enjoying this bathhouse, as long as they make no monetary contribution to the idolatrous owner.

As I show in detail later in chapter 6, rabbinic scholars viewed idolatry in very harsh and negative terms. They equated the rejection of idolatry with being Jewish. By doing so one recognizes the God of Israel as the one true divinity and vehemently rejects all other religious entities and their adulation. However, whereas all rabbis, as far as we know, agree that

Jews may not enter "houses built for idolatry" or enjoy them in any way,[66] they never include bathhouses in that category. On the contrary, rabbinic authors regularly list public bathhouses among the buildings that Jews may own, and they even allow Jews to be partners with non-Jews in their construction. This latter *halakhah* only enjoins the Jew from taking part in the construction of niches in the bathhouse "where they (= non-Jews) set up idolatry."[67] "Idolatry" here refers to statues of Graeco-Roman gods and goddesses that bath owners and communities regularly displayed in bathhouses. Some rabbis viewed such sculpture as idolatrous and thus prohibited Jews from erecting or helping non-Jews build niches for them. As I show in detail in chapter 6 this view never reached unanimity and many rabbinic scholars did not see a problem in bathhouse sculpture, even statues of divine figures, nor did any rabbinic scholar suggest prohibiting the bathhouse building as a whole, in and of itself, or consider it a "house of idolatry."[68]

Surely, if rabbis or other Jews encountered some ritual activity in the baths, or in any other public space for that matter, they would step away, just as Jews abiding by the law would not participate in the act of building a niche for a divine statue in the baths. But nothing prevented them from enjoying the baths on other occasions. When Reish Lakish, a rabbinic scholar of the third century, encountered non-Jews offering a libation to a goddess in the public baths, he asked the leading rabbinic authority of the time, R. Yoḥanan, about it, and the latter conclusively replied that the bathhouse itself is not affected by the idolatrous acts of individuals (more on this passage in chapter 6).[69] Similarly, the Christian writer Tertullian, a third-century CE contemporary of the rabbis, testifies that he abstained from bathing during the Roman celebration of the Saturnalia but frequented the baths at all other times. In the same vein, a fourth-century Christian inquired in a letter to Augustine whether he may bathe at a bathhouse where sacrifices to idols took place or where pagans washed on one of their holidays. The questioner was concerned about rituals taking place in the public bathhouse, just like Tertullian and the rabbinic Reish Lakish before him. However, he sees the bathhouse as very different from a pagan temple, which, as he himself recognizes in his previous question, was clearly prohibited. In his answer Augustine ignores the issue of the baths and addresses other matters raised in the inquiry. However, I speculate that he might have followed the lines of Yoḥanan's reply above, namely: stay away from the ritual activities if you happen to come across any, but keep enjoying the baths (as he himself did on numerous occasions).[70]

A SINFUL PLACE? [131]

All in all, rabbis and by extension other Jews engaged with the public Roman bathhouse like they did with many other public places of their time: although many religious activities took place there, it remained a permissible venue for them, to attend and enjoy, never obtaining a status of an idolatrous location. Perhaps the greatest proof of the ease with which Jews attended public bathhouses comes from the affection they felt for it, which will be our next topic.

For the Love of the Baths: Emotional Expressions toward the Baths among the Rabbis

Uncovering the feelings of people who lived hundreds of years ago requires delicacy and nuanced observation, but it is not an impossible task. Like any elusive truths, such sentiments—whether positive or negative, ambivalent or straightforward, sincere or deceitful—surface between the lines of stories and anecdotes, in the assumptions behind statements and assertions, and in the principles that are so much taken for granted they are left unsaid. Emotions also loom large in the perceptions that inspire people to act or desist, and they also figure in other forms of human expression, which are less relevant to the rabbis, such as poetry or the visual arts. The rabbis' vast literary output offers plenty of opportunities to inquire into those feelings that at least some of them harbored toward the Roman public bathhouse.

On the most rudimentary level, it boils down to sheer volume. Large numbers of anecdotes and traditions place rabbinic figures in bathhouses, not merely passages where rabbis discuss a *halakhah* concerning the baths or comment on a certain aspect related to its function but rather depictions (whether real or not) or references to rabbinic figures that place them in a public bathhouse. I would wager that in rabbinic literature more rabbis are documented enjoying the bathhouse than attending the synagogue, though to make that determination would require a laborious count to verify it, which I admittedly did not carry out. Rabbinic figures placed in Roman bathhouses by these traditions come from all walks of life and span the entire chronological gamut of Roman times. They include some of the most esteemed and wealthy rabbinic individuals: members of house of the Patriarch (the official leader of Jews in Late Roman times) such as the third-century R. Judah the Patriarch, the venerated compiler and chief editor of the Mishnah; his grandsons, Judah (known as Judah II *Nesi'ah*) and Hillel, or his grandfather Rabban Gamaliel; and even the semi-legendary establisher of their family line, also considered the founding father of the entire scholarly school of the rabbis, Hillel the Elder, who lived in the days of the Second Temple. All of these men, and many others, are said to have frequented public bathhouses, apparently on a regular basis, and clearly with no reservations.[71]

But not only them. Many passages in rabbinic literature place the most respected rabbinic scholars of different generations—R. Aqiva, R. Eliezer, and R. Joshua in the first half of the second century; R. Meir and R. Simeon b. Yoḥai in the second half of that century; Reish Lakish and R. Abbahu, a century later—in public bathhouses. With them numerous other scholars—Ḥiya, Rav, Joshua b. Levi, Ḥizkiya, Aḥa, Jonah, and Zeira, to mention only a sampling—are all said to have patronized bathhouses as a matter of routine.[72] About Joshua b. Levi, a rabbinic scholar of the third century, it is said that he used to travel some fifteen miles (a half-day walk) from his coastal-plain hometown of Lydda to the more southern city of Beth Guvrin/Eleutheropolis so that he could enjoy the baths during the sabbatical year.[73] Nowhere do we hear of a rabbinic figure who avoided the baths or expressed any reservations about them.

Numbers do not lie. Certainly, not all the traditions about rabbis visiting the baths are historically accurate, nor are they intended to be. Nevertheless, they convey the mindset of the authors who composed and transmitted these anecdotes. Moreover, the many authors of these rabbinic texts took it for granted that all rabbis (and by extension all Jews) went to the public bathhouses and, more important, loved it there. The following tale, told of the semi-legendary figure Hillel the Elder, suffices as an illustration:

> Hillel the Elder, as he was departing from his students and walking away, his students said to him: "Rabbi, to where are you heading?" he said to them: "to perform a (religious) commandment [= a *mitsva*]." They said to him: "And which *mitsva* is Hillel performing?" He said to them: "to bathe in the (public) bathhouse." They said to him: "And this is a *mitsva*?!" He said to them: "Yes." (And supported his answer with the following argument): "If statues of kings that are placed in their (= Roman) theaters and circuses, the person in charge of them rubs them [clean] and washes them, and they (= the Roman authorities) give him a salary for it, and he is even respected with (= among) the nobility of the kingdom, (then) we who were created in the image and likeness (of God), as it is said 'In the image of the Lord he (= God) made the man,' should it not be even more clear (that we are required to wash and keep clean)."[74]

The first midrashic compilation to tell this story dates from four hundred years or more after the alleged days of Hillel the Elder. The editors who wrote this story down probably knew nothing about him and his bathing habits. This is clearly a fable that circulated among rabbinic scholars. However, the point its author makes strikes an interesting note by equating attendance of the baths with the performance of a religious obligation, a *mitsva*. Surprisingly, he also refers matter-of-factly to the sculptures, which, as I show in great detail in chapter 6, proliferated in the space of public bathhouses. This kind of talk does not emerge from people hostile to the institution of the bath. Rather, it shows high regard for the bathing experience.

Comparing the attitudes of rabbis toward other Roman institutions and to the attitudes of other groups, in particular Christians, toward the public bath strengthens my argument. Rabbinic authors did not hesitate to express their hostility toward other Roman institutions. For example, in cities throughout the Roman world, including Judaea and later Roman Palestine, the theater and amphitheater (which Jewish sources term *'itstadion*) operated as typical venues of entertainment.[75] Writing in the first century CE, the Jewish historian Josephus, who was the first to describe King Herod's construction of a Roman theater and amphitheater in Jerusalem, reported the dislike and contempt with which some of his fellow Jews received these structures. Josephus condemned Herod's initiative as "an abandonment of the native law," stating that in these two structures "gentile customs were celebrated," which Josephus denounces as incompatible with "piety," and warned that their adoption would "ravage the old way of life." Josephus declared that the theater and amphitheater opposed Judaism, since they offered an experience "foreign to the Jewish way of life." As he presented a list of the events that took place there—theatrical performances, athletic competitions, horse races, gladiatorial combat—he appears to exalt a dignified royal enterprise, but then Josephus reverses his perspective and explains, unambiguously, the way the Jews viewed these activities:

> To the natives it meant an open break with the customs venerated by them. For it seemed glaring impiety to throw men to wild beasts for the pleasure of other men as spectators, and it seemed a further impiety to change their established ways for foreign practices.[76]

In the following generations, rabbinic scholars followed suit. For example, the Tosefta states: "He who sits in an amphitheater, is guilty of bloodshed." In the same passage it also forbids Jews to visit Roman theaters; the only exception made is for communal leaders, who may need to attend to public business there and look after the interests of their congregation.[77] A passage in the Midrash expresses a similar attitude: "Why then does scripture say 'nor shall you follow their laws' (Lev. 18:3)? . . . [F]or example going to their theaters, circuses and amphitheaters."[78] Elsewhere, R. Simeon b. Pazi is quoted: "'Happy is the man that has not walked' (Ps 1:1) i.e. to theaters and circuses of the gentiles," and R. Abba b. Kahana has the nation of Israel boast: "Lord of the ages, in my entire life, I never went into theaters and circuses."[79]

Not all rabbinic statements share these harsh tones. Some offer a more lenient position; they find circumstances and reasons that allow a Jew to frequent Roman places of entertainment, and other rabbinic texts betray familiarity with the goings-on in those places, suggesting that the authors had firsthand knowledge of them.[80] But the overall disapproval on the part of at least some Jews cannot be mistaken, highlighting the absence of similar condemnation of the bathhouse in rabbinic literature. Whereas at least some rabbis resented the theater and amphitheater, none, as far as our sources tell us, harbored such hostility, or anything close to it, toward the public bathhouse.

A second comparison—to views about the bath that circulated at roughly the same time among Christian scholars and communal leaders of this rising new religion—further enhances the lack of animosity among rabbinic figures. Officially, Christianity never declared a sweeping prohibition of the baths. Accounts of Christians patronizing bathhouses extend back to the very beginning of this religious movement in the second century CE. For example, Tertullian's *Apology*, a work from the second and early third centuries CE, hence contemporary with the rabbinic Mishnah, cites Christians' use of baths to refute the accusation of their supposed retreat from society.[81] After Christianity became the official religion of the Roman Empire in the fourth century, bathhouses were still being built and continued to function for centuries.[82] Distinguished Church leaders frequently attended the baths. Not all of them visited as often as Bishop Sissinius of Constantinople, who, according to the church historian Socrates, bathed twice a day. When asked about his habit, he replied that he settled for a double visit because he did not have time for a third! Even if not all Christians patronized the baths so zealously, pious Christians, such as John Chrysostom in the east and Augustine in the west, did not shun the baths, and indeed used them regularly.[83] Given this attitude, not surprisingly, the Church even owned some public baths, with their revenues flowing into the holy treasury.[84]

On the other hand, some major Church luminaries voiced strong objections to attending bathhouses. At the end of the second century, Clement of Alexandria listed the evils of the bathhouse, which, in his opinion, corrupted Christians' morals. In his words, "if the bath has no real benefit to offer, it should be completely avoided."[85] Two hundred years later, the church scholar Jerome expressed a similar sentiment in reference to monastic life: "He who was bathed once in Christ does not need to bathe again."[86] At approximately the same time, Augustine, despite his personal fondness for the baths (as illustrated above), depicted the famous thermal baths at Baiae, south of Naples, as a symbol of worldly vanities. He asserted that a person who has had the truth revealed to him would surely want to avoid them. Likewise, his older contemporary from the East, the bishop Epiphanius of Salamis, pointed out the decadent behavior at the therapeutic baths of Ḥammat Gader, just southeast of the Lake of Galilee.[87] Keeping in mind that the thermal baths constitute a category of their own, these statements still contain a broad condemnation of public bathhouses.

These examples from throughout the Roman Empire express rigid opposition to the institution of the bathhouse, precisely the tone not heard in rabbinic sources. This disparity between Christian and Jewish voices accentuates the favorable attitude toward the bath among rabbis and reflects the difference between these two related groups during antiquity. Risking overgeneralization, I postulate that Christianity, which had only recently arisen, was consolidating its identity by renouncing elements that had formerly been integral parts of their (Roman) life and culture. Jews, on the other hand, whose identity was long-established within the Roman world, were not as threatened by embracing aspects of the surrounding culture.

Indeed, some rabbis explicitly show their appreciation and affection for the bathhouse. In one instance, rabbinic commentators elaborate on the words attributed to the biblical king Solomon: "I acquired male and female singers and [all] pleasures [known] to people" (Eccl. 2:8). Typically the rabbinic interpreter associates these biblical words with concrete details in his own world: "'[all] pleasures [known] to people'—[these are] publicly and privately held bathhouses."[88] In a similar vein, another midrashic compilation preserved a comment by R. Simon b. Gamaliel, a second-century scholar, on the verse in Lamentations where the biblical author mourns how he has "forgotten the good (that was still around not too long ago)" (Lam. 3:17). In order to illustrate a person who forgets the delights he just recently experienced, R. Simon explains: "Forgotten the good—that is [someone] who washes his hands and feet in warm water in the bathhouse (and forgets it)."[89] To paraphrase, it is as if the rabbinic scholar is saying, if you just relished the pleasures of a warm bath and while still in the bathhouse feel the need to obtain additional warm water to wash your hands and legs, you obviously suffer from short-term amnesia.

In both of these statements the bathhouse registers as an enchanting destination that encapsulates the ultimate pleasures of life. Expressing the same sentiment, rabbis occasionally disparage life in Babylonia because of the lack of public bathhouses (although this might not be accurate, as bathing facilities did apparently operate in one form or another in Persia).[90] Similarly, when rabbis lament the dismal life conditions of the most destitute, those forced to live in huts far from centers of civilization, they cite the inaccessibility of public baths as a central reason for their misery.[91] Thus, it should come as no surprise that when rabbis consider the requisite living conditions for a scholar, they state: "it is not allowed to reside in a town that does not have a doctor, a public bathhouse, and a (rabbinic) court that [is authorized to] lash and jail." They also enjoin a man from preventing his wife from attending the baths for more than a week.[92] Clearly these scholars thought of baths as a necessity of life.

This is not to say that some rabbis were not disturbed by certain aspects of the bathhouse. Not all, to say the least, approved of the nudity that prevailed there along with the promiscuous atmosphere, as discussed in detail in the next chapter. When one rabbinic figure lauded the baths as a great achievement of the Romans, another answered that it was a den of prostitutes.[93] Other rabbinic authors complain that overindulgence in the baths may distract rabbinic scholars from studying the Torah.[94] But none of these rather scarce reservations detract from the numerous positive and affectionate comments about the baths surveyed above.

In their sporadic critique, rabbinic authors strike a similar tone to the occasional disapprovals pronounced by the general population around the Mediterranean. Along with overall endorsement and love for the baths comes a limited chorus of reservation and condemnation of certain aspects of the bathing experience. Some Roman leaders, including an emperor or two, and scholarly figures such as the first-century Seneca the Younger, expressed distaste for one feature or another of the bathing experience: overindulgence will detract from Roman masculinity and weaken its military; promiscuity will undermine the strengths of the family; and so forth and so on. Seneca even spoke of the tension between baths as places of low pleasure and temples (together with the forum and the Roman senate) as places of virtue. But even the harshest of critics, Seneca included, continued to patronize the baths and enjoy their amenities.[95]

In summary, the attitude of the rabbinic scholars surveyed here toward the public bathhouse matches the adoration of and endearment for this institution that prevailed elsewhere in the Roman world. Almost everyone throughout the Mediterranean flocked to bathhouses on a regular, often daily basis, and so did many, if not all, rabbis. Indeed, we know of not a single rabbi who avoided them. The public at large expressed its affection for the baths in inscriptions and other literary formats, while rabbis inscribed their feelings in their own literary project: midrashic exegesis, halakhic rulings, and stories. Contrary to modern expectations, rabbis (and most likely other Jews as well) were fully immersed citizens of the Roman Mediterranean, who eagerly embraced the public baths like everyone in that world.

Within *halakhah*, the bread and butter of the rabbinic enterprise, I have found no sign of what modern scholars believed were "problems" that would have deterred Jews from attending bathhouses. On the contrary, where modern eyes see problems, I see strong appreciation for the baths and a concentrated effort to weave them into the fabric of Jewish life. In other words, this is "filtered absorption" at work: the cultural dynamic by which a minority group adopts norms and ways of life from the dominant culture, while attempting to preserve its own unique identity in the process. By discussing the details of bathhouse experience from a halakhic perspective, the rabbis delineated the path by which Jews could engage this Roman institution while maintaining observance of Jewish law. In these discussions, rabbinic scholars take note of aspects of the bathing experience that are inconsistent with the practice of Judaism (as these individual rabbis understood it), such as bathing on the Sabbath, and uphold maintaining ritual purity and avoiding Roman ritual practices that contradict the Jewish way of life. By doing so, rabbinic scholars mark unacceptable areas and enable the filtered absorption of all the rest.

The various halakhic discussions involving the Roman public bathhouse are bound up with the central factors of life in the ancient world: the dimension of time (the Sabbath), the close bond of ancient people with the products of the earth and the realm of agriculture (the sabbatical year), the metaphysical state of the body in the realm of purity, and the dominion of the divine and the gods as articulated in the laws defining and prohibiting idolatry. By placing it in the context of these very different streams of human experience, rabbis imbued the Roman bathhouse with what they saw as the essence of Jewish life: the precepts and statutes of Jewish law, *halakhah*. It is as if they were saying: we are confident that Jewish life can flourish within the confines of this establishment. By doing so they absorbed one of the central institutions of Roman life into the folds of Judaism.

In the foregoing discussion of filtered absorption I left out a central component of human life, indeed a prominent feature of the bathing experience: the human body. It stands at the heart of the following chapter.

CHAPTER FIVE

Tsni'ut (Rabbinic Modes of Modesty) in the Halls of Promiscuity

MIXED BATHING AND NUDITY
IN THE PUBLIC BATHHOUSE

IN ONE OF THE MOST frequently repeated scenes from classical mythology, the young hunter Actaeon stumbles upon the Roman goddess Diana (Artemis in the Greek versions) while she bathes in a spring (fig. 15). Diana is nude. And she is angry. The deity turns the peeping lad into a stag; eventually, his own band of fierce hounds tears him to pieces.[1] Throughout the innumerable retellings, interpretations, and commentaries on this episode, stretching over two millennia, lies the fundamental tension inherent in nudity and erotica: you can't look away, but somehow, more than in any other realm of aesthetics, there is always a price to pay, be it shame and the wrath of society or sin and the fury of the gods.

The strains that inhere in the nude body are alive and well today, just as they were in ancient times. In the Roman world, no better place captured nudity's turbulent social and cultural dynamics than the public bathhouse. In these bathing facilities—which as we know operated throughout the Roman Empire, certainly from the first century CE onward—men, women, and those who do not fall into these gender-binary categories (labeled in modern taxonomy as "queer") normally bathed together, more often than not with their bodies fully exposed.[2] As shown in chapter 1, bathhouses extended well beyond the specifics of a washing facility—whether tubs, basins, or pools. Nearly all of them integrated an expanded

FIGURE 15. *Dianna and Actaeon* (1602–3), painting by the Italian artist Giuseppe Cesare. Today at the Szépművészeti Museum in Budapest. *Credit:* Public domain, licensed by Creative Commons, courtesy of Wikimedia.

apparatus of rooms that provided water at different temperatures and spaces, both indoors and out, that accommodated numerous activities and services: application of oil, massages, barbers, medicine, and food, to name but a few. In one spot within this complex, known as the *apodyterium* and easily identified in archaeological excavations for its wall full of small cubicles (see fig. 13), people disrobed and stored their clothing for safekeeping. The Romans had neither bathing suits nor undergarments, which would not be invented for some centuries. The location of the *apodyterium* in most Roman bathhouse, situated close to the entrance (diagram 1), suggests that most if not all attendees, after removing and storing their clothing, roamed around public bathhouses fully or partially exposed, as in present-day nudist beaches and clubs. But whereas nudism today exists only on the fringe of modern society, in Roman times it was the norm of public bathing.[3]

Once we grasp the extent of physical exposure in the Roman bathhouse, it is hard not to wonder what happened next. What took place when men and women came together in this setting, without any real laws or institutions to govern their conduct? Well, just what we might expect. Numerous sources convey the promiscuous atmosphere of the public baths, as a place suffused with arousal, voyeurism, and sex, consensual and not, as well as prostitution of all kinds. Sometimes people carried out these activities in secret, in the dark corners of the building; on other occasions they transpired on full display in its halls, gardens, and pools. The crudest statement on record comes from Apelles, a chamber-servant (*cubicularius*) of the emperor, and his brother Dexter; the two scribbled a graffito on the wall of the so-called Suburban baths in Herculaneum, boasting that they "had lunch here most pleasantly and fucked at the same time."[4] Other descriptions, though far more subtle, evoke a similarly licentious ambience, one that transcends ethnic and religious boundaries. In the first century CE, the Latin poet Ovid writes of young women who escape the watchful eyes of their servants for trysts in the baths, a well-known, if notorious, activity in this place.[5] Similarly, the fourth-century bishop Epiphanius tells of the Jewish Patriarch's son obsessing over a beautiful woman whom he peeked in on in the hot room of the thermal baths near Gadara.[6] Even as late as the seventh century, on the eve of the Arab conquest, the sexual activity in the baths seems to have persisted. In one of his tales, John Moschus, a monk who spent long stretches in the Byzantine monasteries of Palestine and later traveled throughout the Mediterranean, tells about a nun from Alexandria, possessed by demons no less, who attended the baths and seduced other church members to have intercourse with her.[7] Take away the overtones of religious apologetics, and the bathhouse scene that emerges matches that of Appeles and Dexter half a millennium earlier. As I plan to show throughout this chapter, Jewish commentators were equally clear about sexual license in the baths. A variety of rabbinic sources from the first few centuries of the Common Era allude, sometimes indirectly, to petting, caressing, masturbating, and ejaculating, and perhaps also to homosexuality, all within the context of the public bathhouse. They also attest to the sex trade that some carried out there.[8] All of these references, in one way or another (and often in several ways), portray an erotically charged environment.

As with any and every human custom, nuance and variation no doubt abounded. That inherent disparity of practice is too often overlooked by modern scholars who fall into the trap of positing binary poles: either a thing always occurred or never (or rarely) did. Questions about the universality of the practice (did everyone bathe in the nude?), its chronological scope (did people always bathe in the nude? and if not, when did this phenomenon begin or end?), and its geographical distribution (was nude bathing practiced everywhere?) are, to say the least, complicated and have not received sufficient attention. But with this crucial caveat in mind, a wide array of sources testify to the pervasiveness of nudity in the public bathhouse during the first few centuries of the Common Era.[9]

As for the mingling of the sexes, some Roman facilities, especially in the early days—that is, in the second and first centuries BCE—allowed for, but as far as we know never enforced, some separation between men and women, mostly by offering double facilities for bathing. The Stabian baths in Pompeii are the best documented example.[10] Additionally, some emperors legislated against the sexual licentiousness of the public bath in the form of directives to keep the genders separated, and some literary sources, especially Christian and Jewish texts from the eastern part of the empire, do allude to some separate bathing facilities for men and women (more on the possibilities and implementations of gender separation below). But overall, only a few of the thousands of structures that have been excavated throughout the Mediterranean basin give any indication of a double bathing arrangement that could accommodate the simultaneous but segregated use by men and women.[11] Similarly, very few sources support different timetables for the attendance of men and women. For all we know, most, if not all, of the public bathhouses in the days of the rabbis—the second to fourth centuries CE—operated as mixed-gender facilities, raising the following question: How did Jews, and especially rabbis, cope with this situation?

At first this seems like a non-issue. After all, much of Jewish religious practice seems anchored in the separation of the sexes. It is common knowledge that ultra-Orthodox Jews today, usually referred to as *Ḥasidim* or *Ḥaredim*, practice strict separation between men and women of every age, in the public sphere and in all walks of life. We assume, not surprisingly, that the same must have been true of Judaism in its formative stages, in ancient (Graeco-Roman) and medieval times. Indeed, it is commonly held today that ancient Judaism and the rabbis strongly and unanimously advocated for full and strict concealment of the body, particularly the female physique, from the gaze of men. That notion of modesty about the body is usually referred to by the rabbinic term *tsniʻut* and considered an inherent constituent of the traditional Jewish way of life.[12] Summarizing this consensus, in a discussion of Judaism and Roman culture, the British scholar Martin Goodman stated: "the Roman attitude to the body was exceptionally relaxed," while "the attitudes of Jews to their bodies could not have been more different."[13] But is this really the case? How much *tsniʻut* did the ancient rabbis practice in the promiscuous halls of the Roman public bathhouse?

Nude Rabbis in the Public Baths

The standard view, voiced by various modern scholars over the years, held that Jewish men, and especially rabbis, would never bathe in a room where women were present, especially if there was any kind of nudity.[14] It is now impossible to accept such a categorical position. Simply put, too many sources paint an entirely different picture. They show that Jews who lived in Roman Palestine, rabbis included (and more broadly, Jews all around the Mediterranean, in what is normally termed the Diaspora), clearly knew that men and women bathed together in the nude in public bathhouses; many of the authors of these texts undoubtedly took part in this practice.

References to naked people in the baths resonate in several rabbinic passages. Perhaps equally revealing, these statements are usually objective and non-judgmental, without any overbearing negative tones. For example, one *halakhah* in the Tosefta, aiming to regulate liturgical activities in the baths, demarcates the layout of a public bathhouse based on the degree of nudity experienced in them. Nudity evidently precludes prayer or religious study. Along with spaces where people are still wearing clothes or beginning to undress, the author also lists the "place where people stand naked." A later text that cites this rabbinic categorization of space termed the Roman bath a "house of the nude."[15] At least one modern scholar, Ronny Reich, rationalized these references with the argument that in recognizing the permissiveness of the public baths, these texts implicitly encouraged Jews to avoid them. Yet nothing in these *halakhot* forbids Jews (or rabbis) from using the baths. They simply state, objectively, that certain activities involving the uttering of God's name, studying Torah, or reciting prayers cannot be carried out in the presence of nudity. Rather than implying that all Jews must avoid all baths altogether, I believe that these texts do the opposite: by delineating which specific religious activities may not be carried out in the baths, the rabbis were acknowledging that Jews regularly used them. The very fact that along with the public bath the rabbinic authors of these texts, which list facilities involving nudity, include places that they surely valued and would never dream of forbidding such as the ritual purity installation known as the *miqveh* clearly shows that exposing intimate parts of the body in the bath did not register in their mind (at least for the author of this text) as a reason to avoid the place and its associated activities altogether.[16]

In a similar vein, other rabbinic texts offer additional compelling details testifying to the habitual presence of Jews among naked bathers. A passage in the Tosefta describes rabbis disrobing in the baths and follows their particular habits as they do so—what piece of clothing they remove first, where exactly they undress within the bathing complex, when they must suspend prayer and Torah study in order to bathe. Never do these sources mention anyone keeping an item of clothing on to conceal certain body parts, nor do they mention anything like a bathing suit to preserve bodily modesty (see below on the other means available to cover one's body).[17] Clearly, these rabbinic authors viewed nakedness as an ordinary feature of the bathing experience.

This casual acceptance of nudity appears not just in rabbinic descriptions and proscriptions but also in rabbinic narrative. Undressed bathers and exposed bodies lurk in the background of the famous tale about Rabban Gamaliel's visit to the bathhouse of Aphrodite (discussed in much detail in chapter 6). A bather named Proklos, whom the anecdote identifies as a philosopher, challenged Gamaliel's presence in the bathhouse, since it featured a statue of the goddess Aphrodite. Thus Gamaliel's attendance seemed to violate the Jewish law regarding idolatry. Gamaliel, like his fellow bathers, was naked when Proklos approached him. His bare flesh prevented him, so the story goes, from responding to Proklos on the spot, since rabbinic law prohibits religious activity—such as prayer or discussing *halakhah*—in the presence of nudity.[18] The tone of this tale is significant: the author never presents Gamaliel's inability to respond on matters of *halakhah* while nude as problematic. Of course he could not argue the finer details of *halakhah*, the story tells us, because of his exposed state; but the corollary is just as important—he was naked, the story implicitly tells us, because that is how you appear in Roman public bathhouses!

Other *halakhot* express the same tone and make the same assumptions about nudity. Different directives throughout the rabbinic corpus simply assume that people expose their bodies, including its most intimate parts, in the public bathhouse. For example, rabbinic law forbids bringing a Torah scroll to the bathhouse or placing a mezuzah (a Jewish amulet containing a parchment inscribed with verses from the Bible that mention God's name, which many Jews place at the entrance to buildings and rooms) there. It also disallows Jews to enter the place while wearing phylacteries or to discuss and study *halakhah* there.[19] The rabbinic authors of these directives do not condemn the bath. They simply recognize the universal custom of bathing unclothed; indeed, they often take nudity for granted, and focus only on how nudity impacts various spheres of Jewish practice. As in bathhouses elsewhere around the Mediterranean,[20] those attending public bathhouses in Roman Palestine wore no clothes, and Jews and rabbis alike patronized those bathhouses regularly.

Gender Mixing

Not only did men and women bathe naked in Roman bathhouses, they did so together. Jewish men and women too, like all other people in the Mediterranean world, often—though perhaps not always—intermingled freely in the bathhouse. Some rabbis did not approve. A passage in the tractate *Ketubbot* of the Tosefta, dealing with a wife who "washes and bathes in the public bath with just any man," forbids what is taken to be the wife's licentious behavior and deems it to be the legal basis for divorce, which would also result in the loss of the woman's financial prenuptial securities (known as the *Ketubah*).[21] This *halakhah* assumes that the presence of naked men and women together in the bath would lead to sexual permissiveness. Therefore, a married woman who went to the baths alone would naturally be suspected of adultery. Indeed, as mentioned before, numerous sources testify to debauchery in the baths and document a wide gamut of carnal pleasures that were available in this sexually permissive space. The Palestinian Talmud, for example, elaborates on the passage about the married woman attending the baths with other men and describes a scene in which someone "caresses (*ṭōfḥôt*) her thigh in the bathhouse," a sexual activity that would surely transpire in such a licentious environment.[22]

In ancient times, as would be the case today, this slew of naked bodies registered in the eyes of some as an invitation to sexual promiscuity. Articulating worry about inappropriate (forbidden by Jewish law) sexual behavior, one rabbinic directive states that a "man should not say to his fellow in a bathhouse, 'rub (the oil into) me well with your hand,' and he who says so will not depart from there unscathed." Voicing similar apprehensions, a passage in the Babylonian Talmud refers to semen found in a bathtub (*'ambati*) used by women. Along the same lines, the medieval compilation *Alphabet of Ben Sira* imagines women impregnated by semen in the baths, and also tells a story about the prophet Jeremiah who encountered evil men from the tribe of Ephraim masturbating in the bathhouse. Admittedly, these last two examples discuss the legal consequences of hypothetical situations (probably just fantastic tales), and they were written by rabbinic scholars far removed from the Roman Empire and its realities. Nevertheless, the overall trajectory of these sources captures the sense of degenerate possibilities (in the eyes of the authors) offered by the public baths—the variety and abundance of sexual proclivities as registered in the minds of ancient people. Since the rabbinic authors saw a need to warn about these erotic activities in the baths, we can assume it was prevalent enough to deserve their attention.[23]

Within the sexually permissive setting of the public baths, the directive in Tosefta *Ketubbot* should be read as a cautionary, preemptive guideline, meant to guard the chastity of married women, a prime concern for all patriarchal societies, both ancient and not. Jews and rabbis were not alone in expressing these trepidations. Sounding a similar alarm, Quintilian, the first-century Roman scholar and rhetorician, born in Spain, wrote: "It is a sign of an adulteress that she goes to the baths with the men"—which probably voices what many thought at the time.[24] A bit later, the famous Roman legal scholar Ulpian (a contemporary of the late second- and third-century rabbis, who like them emerged from the eastern shores of the Mediterranean) strikes the same note as the author in the Tosefta when he specifically lists the public bath as a site inviting adultery.[25] Legal authorities, Jews and Romans, were not alone in addressing anxiety about the possible adultery of married women (mind you, not men!) in the baths. In a scene in the popular novel *Metamorphoses* (also known as *The Golden Ass*), written in the later second century and thus contemporary to the work of the rabbis, Barbarus, a married businessman, is determined to protect the chastity of his wife. Thus he makes his slave, Myrmex, swear to follow his wife everywhere, a task that requires particular vigor when the wife attends the baths while the husband is away at work.[26]

This is also the context for understanding the legislation, attributed perhaps apocryphally to some emperors—in particular Hadrian in the second century and a few other "good" emperors after him—to ban mixed bathing and to institute separation of the sexes in the public baths.[27] Modern scholars remain skeptical about the historical validity of these directives, but everyone agrees that such attempts, if they did occur, remained sporadic, merely pro forma and impossible to enforce. All sources show that the practice of mixed bathing persisted in Hadrian's days and for centuries thereafter.[28]

It is impossible to estimate how many married women resigned themselves to the legal limitations of that particular passage in Tosefta *Ketubbot*, or the one prescribed by Ulpian, and refrained from attending the baths with men; while some may have, others surely did not. If we believe the story mentioned earlier, preserved by the fourth-century Church Father Epiphanius, at least one married woman (perhaps a Christian) did not, and she crossed paths with the son of the Jewish Patriarch in the hot room of the thermal baths near Gadara. Transfixed by the charms of her body, the young man went to great pains to seduce her, though in vain. Writers such as the Spanish-turned-resident-of-Rome poet Martial report similar incidents from other corners of the Mediterranean.[29] Rabbinic sources, too, assume that Jewish women, both married and not, regularly attended public bathhouses; they refer to this practice incidentally, with no negative implications, as matter of fact in many unrelated laws.[30]

At least some rabbis had misgivings about what happened in public bathhouses—whether the mixing of genders, the nudity, the sexual permissiveness, or all three—not only in relation to married women but for their own (religious) sake and for the public at large. If so, again, they were certainly not alone in their uneasiness with the dynamics that bubbled up in the baths around nudity and the mixing of the sexes, or about other aspects of bathing, leisure, and cultivation of the body. As mentioned before, several Roman emperors are thought to have shared these apprehensions about nudity and sex. Certainly Graeco-Roman writers and scholars occasionally showed uneasiness with the situation in the baths. Beyond the castigations of married women, perhaps the most famous of all critics of bathing culture was the first-century Stoic philosopher Seneca the Younger, who spared no words in bashing the baths and what he deemed as the spoiled activities that took place there. He was far from alone. Nevertheless, as Garrett Fagan has nicely shown, moralizing never prevented any of these critics from regularly attending the baths and enjoying the very amenities they criticized.[31]

In other areas of the Mediterranean, within the diverse, multiethnic, and multicultural environment that made the Roman world, we must assume that different groups, societies, and communities upheld dissimilar attitudes toward aspects of life, including the body and its proper level of concealment. For example, modern scholars have noticed that some of the great cities of the Roman east, such as Petra and Palmyra, did not conduct regular Greek-style sports competitions. Throughout the Mediterranean, in the prominent cities of Graeco-Roman civilization, residents regarded these events as central features of civic life. So why not in the leading cities of the Roman eastern frontier? The French scholar Maurice Sartre suggested that the nudity associated with these competitions offended the native populations, who were rooted in the norms of non-Greek cultures of the Arabian peninsula.[32] Thus, any discussion of nudity in the ancient world must account for a variety of attitudes embedded in a spectrum of diverse cultures.

But when it comes to Jews and in particular the rabbis, we must recognize a simple, yet clear and significant fact: nowhere in their vast literature and in the many discussions they devote to bathhouses does a rabbinic author take whatever concerns he may have had a step further and suggest that attendance in bathhouses should be prohibited or restricted in any way due to the widespread nudity that prevailed there or because men and women bathed together. Aside from married women, at least according to the single rabbinic author in tractate *Ketubbot*, who ruled that they could be divorced for bathing with men other than their husbands, all other Jews—men and women, young and old—who wished to follow rabbinic rulings had nothing to prevent them from enjoying the baths.

Even the prohibition against studying Torah in the presence of nudity did not deter some rabbis from continuing their learning in the baths. Unlike Gamaliel in the story discussed above, who refrained from answering a philosopher's question while in the nude, a third-century scholar—R. Ḥiya—carried out his studies of the book of Psalms while in the public bath, apparently nude and among other naked bathers.[33] Some rabbinic scholars went as far as to forbid even thinking about matters related to the study of the Torah in the baths, while others, like the senior student identified as Eleazar b. Jacob, would "rehearse his studies" silently while standing and waiting for his sweat to develop at the bathhouse, clearly with his body exposed. The rabbinic author reporting about this custom takes no issue with the location of the study or the apparent nudity, only with the fact that Eleazar should have conducted his review out loud.[34] A third text ridicules the "unwise" who conduct their studies in bathhouses and latrines, but the very criticism perhaps affirms that some people actually did so. Indeed, in one passage a rabbinic author, contemplating the meaning of true love for the Torah, praises those who take their learning everywhere, including the public bathhouse.[35] Apparently, nudity did not present a serious obstacle to these rabbinic scholars, and by engaging in study and learning in public bathhouses they were conforming to a general intellectual norm, prevalent among the learned in many public bathing facilities all around the Roman Mediterranean. Like R. Ḥiya, a century and half earlier Pliny the Elder also took books into the bath and pursued his studies there (although the testimony regarding this habit, made by his nephew Pliny the Younger, might not refer to public baths), and, like Eleazar b. Jacob, Libanius, the fourth-century scholar from Antioch, while awaiting a friend in the baths, used his time to recite Homer.[36]

As I clearly showed in chapter 4, when they felt it necessary, rabbinic scholars knew very well how to express disapproval of a place or an institution, and to explicitly instruct those who listened to them to shun those establishments. However, they neither expressed disapproval of nudity in bathhouses nor instructed Jews to avoid them due to this issue. Furthermore, their lenient acceptance of the baths contrasts strongly with the disapprobation voiced by some (although certainly not all) Christian authors. Within Christian circles, already in the earliest days of the second century CE, certain leaders and authors condemned the immodest and sexually tainted atmosphere of the public baths. Writing in Alexandria at the end of the second century, the Christian teacher and scholar Clement, for example, spared no words in decrying the Roman bathhouse for its immodesty and concupiscence. Consequently, he instructed his followers to limit their visits to the minimum necessary for hygiene and health.[37] In the same vein, a century and a half later, a council of Christian clerics who gathered for a local synod, probably in the city of Laodicea, in what is today western Turkey, decreed categorically: "None of the priesthood, nor clergymen, nor ascetics, nor any Christian or layman shall wash in a bath with women."[38] Precisely this kind of all-inclusive and damning declaration is nowhere to be found in rabbinic texts.

The tolerance shown by ancient rabbis will likely surprise many modern readers, as it runs counter to our deepest assumptions about Judaism. Indeed, this widely held perception of ancient Judaism begs for thorough reconsideration and reevaluation, which in turn requires a whole book of its own. Though I am unable to tackle this topic in its entirety here, the conclusions of the current study remain clear: the rabbis' attitudes toward nudity and the mingling of men and women in the baths reveal a more complex and nuanced understanding of the body and its exposure than we tend to think. Surely some Jews and some rabbis (such as the author of the *halakhah* in the Tosefta regarding married women mixing with men in the baths) were uncomfortable with the nudity and the mixing of the sexes in the baths. A couple of hundred years earlier, in the second century BCE, the Jewish author of the legal text known as the Book of Jubilees explicitly commands his fellow Jews, with direct reference to divine law, to "cover their shame and not uncover themselves as the nations uncover themselves."[39] Closer to the days of the rabbis, the first-century CE Jewish historian Josephus reports that members of the Jewish sect known as the Essenes washed while covering their body—the women wore a full dress while the men covered their genitalia with a loincloth.[40] Similarly, the eminent fourth-century Christian scholar (anachronistically called Church Father) Augustine asserts that the barbarians—that is, members of tribes outside the Roman Empire—also bathed while covering their body.[41] These exceptions are important to acknowledge. But they are exceptions. Indeed, the peculiarity of eschewing nudity is precisely what caught the attention of authors like Josephus and Augustine—proof that ordinary people did not do so. Significantly, moreover, the rabbis do not emphasize these exceptions to nudity in the baths. Despite firm rhetoric in favor of *tsniʿut*, rabbis found ways, conceptual and practical, to live in peace with the promiscuity of the public bathhouse.

Body Shaming in the Baths

Poking fun at a person's physical appearance and embarrassing them because of some bodily defect or their not-so-appealing physique did not begin in the electronic age with Facebook and Instagram. In many ways the public bathhouse represents the ancient equivalent of our social-media outlets: a space, electronic or real, distinct from the rest of our regular activities, open to people from all walks of life, and attended by nearly everyone on a regular, daily basis. Within Roman bathing establishments, just as on the internet, the dynamics and constraints of social hierarchy and differentiation were simultaneously blurred and reaffirmed (more on this in chapter 7). People attending the baths were both exposed and observed. Shaming in general and body shaming in particular are tools of social discourse and mobility, elevating some and demoting others. Physical exposure in the baths aroused sexual excitement and adventure, but vulnerability, harm, and shame were just as essential, if unwelcome, components of bathing in public.

These intimidating elements of nudity were in no way restricted to Jews, or to any other specific ethnic or social group that attended the baths. As modern observers of the ancient world, we must carefully sensitize our ears to catch the menacing tones that arise, here and there, from the ancient sources. For example, in one of his poems, Ovid, the first-century CE Latin poet, tells us that Roman women would offer incense to the goddess Virile Fortune before attending the bathhouse. He explains: "All women strip when they enter that place (= the public baths), and every blemish on the naked body is plain to see; Virile Fortune undertakes to conceal the blemish and to hide it from men."[42] Ovid's lines convey a fundamental anxiety—in this case, for women—of naked, mixed bathing in Roman times. Satirical authors like Juvenal and Martial offer the other side of the equation, namely the kind of bullying that led the women in Ovid's poem to seek the protection of the goddess. They constantly insult both the men and women they come across in the public baths. Their texts tread regularly on vitriolic diatribes regarding physical appearances. Martial, for example, reviles one of his female acquaintances in the coarsest possible terms (caution to reader: skip the following text if you dislike filthy, degrading language directed toward women): "Either your breasts hang from your bosom like rags, or you're afraid of betraying your belly's furrows in the nude, or your split groin yawns with bottomless cavern, or something protrudes from the mouth of your cunt."[43] His younger contemporary Juvenal fires nasty jabs at heavy people, making fun of their flabby stomachs. He also pokes fun at hairy bodies, testicles, and large and small penises.[44] No wonder that at least some people whose bodies exhibited an imperfection, like the women mentioned in Ovid's poem, were exceedingly self-conscious and nervous when attending the public baths. Such anxieties plagued every level of society all the way to the imperial house; according to one story, even Augustus's mother, the formidable Atia, refrained from appearing in the public bath when her body had contracted a mysterious rash.[45]

This daunting element of the baths, the insecurity that emanated from exposure, resonates in rabbinic literature as well. The rabbis did not indulge in the lewd rants found in the writings of Roman authors. Yet they do show acute awareness of the emotional wounds one might endure while attending the baths. Instances of body shaming register in rabbinic law, specifically in the portion devoted to torts and damages. These are complex and nuanced sections of the rabbinic legal project, to which this book cannot do justice. Suffice it to say that rabbinic scholars devoted an inordinate amount of attention and intellectual energy to civil law involving liability for property damage, personal injury, and emotional harm. They referred to emotional injury with the Hebrew term *boshet*, usually translated as indignity, or shame. Broadly speaking, without presenting their convoluted legal and theoretical arguments, if a person is found liable for *boshet*, rabbinic law states that they are obligated to provide monetary compensation for the disgrace and degradation that their victim suffered.[46] Within this legal framework, the public bathhouse is used as a reference point by the early third-century rabbinic editors of the Tosefta:

> If one shames a naked person, he is liable [for damages, but] shaming a naked person is not similar (i.e., as harmful) to shaming [the body] of a person who is dressed (which shows that he does not wish to expose his body and the aggressor shamed him nevertheless). Shaming [someone's body] in the public bathhouse is liable, but shaming in the bath is not similar (i.e., as harmful) to shaming [someone's body] in the market.[47]

There is more than one way to interpret this halakhic passage. Most medieval and modern commentators follow the line of reasoning offered by rabbinic scholars in fourth- and fifth-century Persia (preserved in the Babylonian Talmud), who saw the essence of the indignation as caused by the very exposure of nudity; in other words, the fundamental injustice is committed when one person strips the other, humiliating them by exposing their body unwillingly.[48] But to me, a more plausible explanation is that the "damage" of shaming is shaped by the specific situation. After all, the person in the bathhouse is already naked—they have already shown they are comfortable exposing their body—so the question, I believe, is whether even after willingly exposing their body they are still susceptible to the emotional harm of *boshet*. The rabbinic authors suggest that although nakedness is usual in the baths, shaming is still possible; but they point out that it is not as severe in terms of the halakhic concept of *boshet* as in the market, where people are secure beneath their clothing.

Even if readers reject my line of interpretation, this ruling clearly reveals rabbinic scholars' awareness of the prevalence of body shaming in the public bathhouse, allowing them to use this slice of daily life in exploring the legal concept of shame. As established earlier in this chapter, *halakhah* accepts nudity as the norm in public bathing establishments, thus the question that drives this discussion is not nudity but whether in circumstances where virtually everyone is naked *boshet* is even possible, to which the legal scholars answer in the affirmative. Admittedly, this discussion remains within the clean, almost sterile, boundaries of legal theory, where scholars explore the limits of damages for *boshet* in a place where nakedness is both accepted and expected. Consequently, the rabbinic text does not speak in the raunchy tones of the Latin satirists (similar, say, to jurists who describe rape, referencing penetration and force but without evoking the emotional horror that comes with it). Nevertheless, this piece of legal discourse regarding *boshet* sheds light on the state of mind of at least some people—the rabbinic scholars who developed it—as they allude to public bathhouses and the atmosphere around the nakedness that prevailed there. That ambience included body shaming.

Furthermore, the discussion of *boshet* also highlights an example of how Roman bathhouses registered in the discourse and thinking of provincial people, in this case Jewish legal scholars. Consideration of *boshet* in the baths represents an innovative and culturally independent move on the part of these Jews to deal with an aspect of the baths that they encountered and viewed as problematic. Romans, if we may rely upon Ovid's testimony above, tackled the problem with a sacrifice to their gods, whereas rabbis used the tools of judicial legislation. Whether or not the rabbinic legal directives were applied in real life is a separate issue, just as the frequency of the offerings mentioned by Ovid remains unclear. These references show that people separate and far away from each other, as Ovid and the Jewish rabbis, were aware of the same state of mind, in this case that of body shaming in the baths.

Though anyone was vulnerable to body shaming in the baths, one manifestation of that experience related directly to Jewish men: ridicule and mockery of circumcised penises. Exposed male organs, like female nudity, attracted much attention in the baths. Seneca the Younger reports on one particularly malicious attendee who spent his time in the baths searching for large penises; writers like Martial and Juvenal often aim their derision toward the male member.[49] As is well known, Jews have long embraced the custom of cutting off the foreskin of the penis as a defining aspect of their religious observance and ethnic identity; ancient biblical traditions testifying to the centrality of this practice among the Israelites, the forerunners of the Jews, go as far back as the Iron Age.[50] In Graeco-Roman times, this ritual placed Jews at odds with the accepted norms of the general population, which not only did not circumcise their boys but also viewed the act as mutilating and abhorrent, not to mention aesthetically unpleasing. Testaments to the unease that some Jews felt about their circumcised organs already surface in the Hellenistic period, prior to the arrival of the Romans. From the second century BCE, for example, the Book of Jubilees mentions (disapprovingly) the efforts made by some Jews to conceal their circumcision and at times even undo it (a painful surgical procedure, known as *epispasm*, was meant to extend the skin on the penis and restore the appearance of a foreskin). Throughout Roman times, both circumcision and attempts to hide or forbid it played a central role in the violent conflicts that erupted between the Jewish population and both Greek and Roman authorities.[51]

Appearing in the public baths without clothes immediately revealed whether you were circumcised. Martial gives us a small yet illuminating taste of the scorn and abuse that such an exposure could prompt when, in one of his epigrams, he pokes fun and mounts insults at a certain actor who attempted to cover his penis in the baths, and when the cover fell off everyone saw he was circumcised.[52] This daunting situation of body shaming and the hostile environment it could precipitate gave rise to various responses among the rabbis. On the most rudimentary level, some rabbis—themselves circumcised—surely felt insecure, perhaps even intimidated. Take for example the early fourth-century CE R. Abbahu, whom numerous anecdotes place in the public bathhouses, both in his home city of Caesarea Maritima and elsewhere in Roman Palestine.[53] In one rabbinic statement, the Persian R. Zeira, who is known to have moved to Roman Palestine at one time, testifies that he saw R. Abbahu in the public bathhouse covering his genitals with his hands.[54] It is hard to make much of this tiny detail, since we cannot know, for example, why and how often R. Abbahu did this, if at all. The testimony appears in the Babylonian Talmud, where Persian rabbinic scholars discuss whether and in what circumstances it is permitted to touch the penis, surely a far cry from the original circumstances it describes. Nevertheless, R. Abbahu's efforts are strikingly similar to the act that Martial maliciously mocked (albeit two hundred years earlier and on the other side of the Mediterranean). Once again, two separate sources seem to be singing the same tune.

Other rabbinic statements are more germane. For example, the second-century scholar R. Meir asserts: "There isn't a man of Israel who is not encircled by the divine commandments (the *mitsvot*).... When entering the [public] bath, [the encirclement of the commandments is achieved through] circumcision [that is engraved] on his skin." The passage goes on to tie this situation in the baths to the biblical promise that God's angel rests around those who trust him, namely the Jews; God's angel, it is explained, rescues them from the perils they confront in the baths.[55] The implication is clear: the rabbinic author reverses the potential for humiliation and perturbation caused by exposure of the circumcised penis and turns it into a source of pride and safety. In the rabbinic author's imagination, circumcision, which marks the covenant between God and his people, becomes a safeguard and protection from harms in the public bathhouse. In the hands of the rabbinic scholar, a potential source of social vulnerability in the baths (and thus a cause of trepidation and anxiety) is turned into a foundation of power and a source of safety and assurance.

A different version of this statement adds another layer to the rabbinic configuration of the circumcised Jew in the bathhouse. In a typical literary exercise (known in rabbinic terminology as *Haggadah*), a rabbinic author composed a fictional anecdote about the biblical figure of King David and then attached a parable to it:

> When King David entered the bathhouse, he saw himself naked [and] said "ouch, I am naked of the commandments," [but then] he looked at [his] circumcision, [and immediately] he started compassing about it with praise, as it is said in Psalms (by tradition—David's own poetry): "for the leader, about the eighth (=by implication circumcision, which is carried out on the eighth day after birth), a psalm to David." A

parable: A king flesh and blood said to his wife "beautify yourself with all your jewelry, so you will be desirable to me." In the same way the Holy one, praised be he, said to Israel: "My children, be marked by the commandments, so you will be desirable to me." And he (= scripture) says about this: "you are beautiful my love, like Tirza"—you are beautiful when you are desirable to me (i.e., when observing the commandments and marked by circumcision).[56]

Here the rabbinic author adds the dimension of aesthetics to that of power, as in the previous passage. The circumcised penis, mocked as ugly and disgusting and thus causing shame and humiliation, is turned into a jewel, an ornament that beautifies the body of the Jew and makes him desirable in the eyes of his true lover and protector, the God of Israel. The rabbis in these two segments establish a coping mechanism for the minority group they belong to. They devised a sequence of subversive ideas and images that, if embraced, would provide a way to overcome the intimidation of the baths. They focus on the very bodily feature that causes the anxiety, the circumcised male organ, recognize the angst associated with it, and at the same time imbue it with pride instead. By doing so they offer an imagined zone of safety and tranquility in the very place that caused the opposite.

Options of Tsni'ut, *Nevertheless*

Along with the pervasiveness of nudity and gender mixing in the Roman public bathhouses, it is important to recognize that some partial means to segregate the genders, and certain ways to conceal one's nudity while bathing or strolling the facilities, did exist as well.[57] A handful of sources allude to men and women bathing at different times, and a few archaeological remains show baths with separate facilities, probably for men and women. Jews and rabbis, like everyone else, could have taken advantage of these options.

A well-known Latin inscription from a bathhouse in a mining establishment in Portugal, dating to the first half of the second century CE (first quoted by Jérôme Carcopino and since cited by many others), clearly delineates different bathing hours based on gender. Women attended from dawn till the seventh hour, and men from the eighth hour until the end of the second hour of the night.[58] On the island of Crete, a second inscription confirms the same custom, although without mentioning specific hours.[59] The paucity of the sources that allude to such a possibility seems to indicate its rarity, as the exception that proves the rule. As far as I can ascertain, the rabbis in their literature do not allude to separate bathing, which suggests that they probably did not come across it (admittedly a weak conjecture, as it rests only on the silence of the sources). Be all that as it may, the option of different hours did exist; it was out there and available.

Another way to separate men and women was to provide an entirely distinct space, either a stand-alone bathing facility for women or a section within the larger bathing complex that accommodated only female bathers. Archaeological evidence mentioned earlier in the chapter, from early bathhouse buildings in Italy from the third and second centuries BCE, points to separate sections for women. That practice seems to have continued, albeit sporadically. In later periods, literary evidence from the Italian peninsula (either references in literary texts or mentions in inscriptions) confirms that at least some locations offered separate bathing arrangements for women.[60] Further references to such establishments also surface in other corners of the Mediterranean world, especially in its eastern reaches, showing that mixed bathing was not the only option available to people in those regions. Although not often, Greek papyri from Egypt do mention a "women's bath" (*gynaikon balaneion*) on a few occasions; some of these texts go back to pre-Roman times, but others reflect the situation in Roman institutions of the second and third centuries CE.[61]

Northeast of Egypt, evidence of similar arrangements comes from the regions of Syria. In establishing the proper behavior of married women, the Christian author of the *Didascalia apostolorum*, for example, prescribed: "Be watchful that you do not bathe in a bath with men. When there is a bath of women in the town or in the village, a believing woman shall not bathe in a bath with a man." This directive matches his earlier instruction to married men: "Bathe in a bath of men and not in one of women."[62] The Aramaic term he uses for the women's baths—*baln'a denash'a*—matches the Greek *gynaikon balaneion* from the papyri in Egypt. Clearly, the author was familiar with bathhouses designed specifically for separate use by men and women, although at the same time he confirms that they are not available everywhere. We can also infer, in that the author felt the need to compel men and women to bathe separately, that they probably would not have done so otherwise.

Rabbinic authors, too, seem to be aware that separate bathing facilities could be available. A *halakhah* dealing with the disclosure of a woman's physical defects before marriage implies that women might have been able to bathe separately in public baths used by some Jews at the time. The Mishnah states: "And if there was a bathhouse in that town he (the future husband) may not make complaints even of secret defects (i.e., physical defects that he finds in his wife after they got married), since he can inquire about her from his women kinsfolk."[63] Clearly a theoretical legal formulation, but one that assumes that only women can observe other naked women in the public baths because men are not present. The means by which the division between men and women happened remains vague in this passage; the simple mention of "a bathhouse in that town" apparently indicates only one bathhouse used by everyone, suggesting either a distinct female room or section, or perhaps a segregated schedule. Another halakhic segment from the laws of *niddah* (the impurity assigned to menstruating women) explicitly mentions "bathhouses of women"—a Hebrew equivalent of the Aramaic terminology of the *Didascalia apostolorum* and the Greek papyri from Egypt.[64]

A third way to conceal nudity, for those who wished to do so, was by covering certain parts of the body. At the outset, it must be said that unlike the previous points about separate hours and spaces, discussion of this topic remains entirely speculative and theoretical. There is no clear-cut proof that any garment existed similar to what today would be known as a "swimsuit," or that any such attire was worn specifically when attending a public bath. On the contrary, as mentioned before, numerous literary and representational sources document nude bathing. However, depictions of the way people dressed—or didn't—when they were not in the water are far from consistent.

Several young women performing exercises and wearing what seem similar to our swimsuits appear on one of the mosaics in the Piazza Armerina villa in Sicily, which dates to the beginning of the fourth century CE. Scholars call them the "Bikini Girls" (fig. 16). Another young woman who appears with them seems to wear a type of sheet wrapped diagonally across her body, partially covering her left side while revealing one of her breasts. It remains anyone's guess whether this mosaic displays apparel actually worn in the baths.[65] Another mosaic from the same location depicts three bathers, a patron and two assisting slaves, in full frontal nudity, while two other slaves wear a loincloth (see fig. 24).

A few centuries earlier, when the poet Martial wished to offend the matron Chione, he remarked that she only covered her private parts in the baths but that if decency were really important to her she should cover her face. Nasty insults aside, this epigram indicates that at least one woman covered her body in the baths, at least partially. In other epigrams Martial praises the physical charms of both men and women he encountered in the baths, with their intimate parts fully bare. Thus, according to Martial, some people went completely nude in the baths, and (at least a few) others

FIGURE 16. The fourth-century CE mosaic known as the "Bikini Girls" at Villa Romana del Casale, in Piazza Armerina, Sicily. *Credit:* Photograph by Ludwig 14, licensed by Creative Commons (CC BY-SA 4.0), courtesy of Wikimedia Commons.

covered their "intimate parts." To his mind, the only ones who cover themselves are those with something to hide, whether because of social status such as slaves or cultural conventions. As mentioned above, according to Martial a circumcised penis, for example, is nothing to be proud of, and so likely to be covered, as are unappealing intimate parts of female bathers.[66] The satirists, in their eagerness to insult and exaggerate, are not necessarily reliable witnesses. Yet in this case, the fact that they mention that people occasionally covered their bodies, in passing, as if their readers would take this for granted makes it clear that it was possible to cover one's body, and some people did so.

One such individual happened to be no less than the third-century emperor Alexander Severus, who is said to have worn something called a *vestis balnearis*—literally a garment for the baths. The function of this item of clothing eludes us today. Its design is unknown, nor do we know when and how it was used. However, its name circulated widely and, as will be shown shortly, even found its way into rabbinic vocabulary.[67] In the same vein, even if for completely different reasons, some Christians clearly concealed their bodies, as can be concluded from the criticism in the *Didascalia apostolorum* against women who did not do so.[68] In later centuries, as Christianity and its norms took a deeper and wider hold over the life of people throughout the Roman world, various sources observed that bathers used a type of sheet called a *lention* in Greek to conceal their nakedness while in the public baths.[69]

Rabbinic authors also refer to various types of coverings for the body, such as towels, that could have been used (even if only partially) to assist people who wished to reduce their physical exposure and maintain their bodily modesty. These references make clear that such means existed; however, there is no way of knowing whether they were used widely or at all. One example of a garment of this sort goes by the name *'apiqarsin* or *'afiqresin*. This term, which also appears in Greek as *epikarsion* and Syriac as *'afkroso*, usually denotes a long undergarment made from relatively delicate cloth, similar to the Greek *chitōn*, that people wrapped around the body and tied above the shoulder. Significantly, the only rabbinic text linking this piece of clothing to the baths presents it as a type of undergarment that one removed after entering the bathhouse and before embarking on the bathing cycle.[70] In one place rabbis ponder the habits of one of their revered teachers, R. Yoḥanan, who apparently, as a token of piety, used to wear his phylacteries (the Jewish amulets worn on head and hand, normally only during the morning prayer) throughout the day. Considering what this would entail for his bathing practices, one of Yoḥanan's students conjectures that he got dressed in a hurry, putting on his *'afiqresin* immediately after exiting the water in the bathhouse, so he could quickly resume wearing his phylacteries when he was no longer naked.[71] This hypothetical discussion among Yoḥanan's students (hypothetical because there is no indication, even in the students' discussion, that indeed Yoḥanan acted in the way they describe) illustrates both sides of the issue; *'afiqresin* could be used to avoid nudity in the baths, but no one, perhaps other than Yoḥanan, in his students' minds, actually used it for this purpose.

Rabbis also mention the *'aluntit*, deriving from the Latin *linteum* and the Greek *lention*, a long, rectangular piece of fabric resembling today's towels. People used it to dry and/or oil the body, among other things. Because it could easily be applied to cover the body and because of its proximity to the water of the bathhouse (unlike a person's regular clothing, which would be left at the *apodyterium*), the *'aluntit* could well have been used by bathers seeking to cover themselves. However, it is important to note that the rabbis themselves never tie it specifically to the baths or to preserving bodily modesty there.[72]

The most noteworthy example in rabbinic literature of attire worn in the baths is a garment whose name appears in a few variants—*balare, balnare, balniteh*—all clearly deriving from the Greek name for the public baths, *balaneion*. Samuel Krauss, the founding father of the field that combines the study of rabbinic literature with archaeology and classical studies, already pointed out that the equivalent word in Latin, *balnearia*, signifies a type of clothing or a sheet used in the baths (what he terms *Badewäsche* or *Badezeug*).[73] This is as close as we get to something resembling a bathing garment. Rabbinic authors mention it only a few times, always specifically in reference to female bathers, naming it the "*balnare* of women" (in one instance they say that the *balnare* was used for "covering their heads and the greater parts of their bodies").[74] It seems, from these descriptions, and from the semantic clarity of the word itself, that we finally have reference to a garment used in the public baths to cover the intimate parts of women's bodies and protect their modesty. Such a hypothesis seems quite appealing.

But the apparent certainty here, however beguiling, is also misleading. In truth, we remain on shaky and speculative ground. The references made by rabbinic authors to the *balnare* are, ultimately, vague, either because everyone knew what it was or because they applied this term in a general way that could refer to many articles of clothing. Furthermore, rabbinic discussions of the *balnare* all center on aspects of Jewish law, such as whether it would be permissible to carry *balnare* on the Sabbath or whether other restrictions that relate to clothing but not to pieces of fabric apply to it. These are highly theoretical matters, debated for centuries by jurists and scholars, but have little to do with the bathhouse or with the issue at stake here, namely the possible utility of this item to avoid nudity in the public bathhouse.[75] None of the sources, as far as I can tell, even hint at this potential usage—even though, from our perspective, such practice seems appealing. Furthermore, even the texts quoted above—about the *balnare* covering the bodies and heads of women—relate to the legal theory of Sabbath law, and nothing more. When all is said and done, the item portrayed by these sources—a large piece of cloth that could cover the entire body and at times could have been used exclusively by women in the baths—sounds like some kind of bathrobe. Perhaps the purpose of this garment—if, indeed, "bathrobe" is an accurate comparison—was to protect women's modesty, at least when they strolled around the baths. But again, I can find no direct proof to support this conjecture.

Thus, at the end of this discussion of bathhouse attire we have come full circle to where we began. Clearly, anyone who had wanted to could have found ways to conceal their nudity and maintain their bodily modesty. The ancient sources point to items of clothing that could have fulfilled this purpose. But the more significant question is whether people in ancient times, Jews and rabbis in particular, felt the need to do so. We may want them to, but mainly in order to accommodate our modern sensibilities. The fact that none of the available sources allude to this need and that the rabbis are not troubled by nude or mixed bathing is very telling.

Exploring the landscape of nudity and gender-integrated bathing at the Roman public bathhouse as it was captured in the eyes and minds of rabbinic scholars offers a rare insight into cultural interaction in those times. Complex and contradictory trends intersect here, simultaneously coexisting with and undermining each other. On the one hand, it seems quite clear that in the Jewish portions of Roman Palestine men and women bathed together in the public baths with their bodies mostly exposed, as was the case in most other places in the Roman Empire. Although this defies modern preconceptions about ancient Judaism, many Jews chose to attend the public baths, regardless of the nudity and the mixing of men and women that prevailed there. Moreover, it is apparent that rabbis, just like their fellow Jews, attended these baths, and rabbinic sources allow us to follow the strategies of these Jewish scholars as they partook in this experience and give us an insight into their attitudes. Can we say with certainty that they were elated by the situation? Absolutely not. But they were not the only ones in the Roman world who expressed reservations. Even the emperors occasionally did so. Some Jews may have patronized only the few establishments that allowed for gender segregation. Others may have used some kind of cloth to cover their nude bodies. Yet these appear to be the exceptions that prove the rule.

As is the case with so many issues regarding the ancient world, statistics, proportions, and frequency will remain unknown forever. But the more important—and more interesting—question regards the habits and perceptions that evolved around bodily exposure and the integration of the sexes in the baths. This chapter shows that the practices and mindsets of the rabbis as they negotiated the promiscuous settings of the public baths embody both nuance and variation, which are the characteristics of the model I call "filtered absorption." According to this paradigm, Jews, like other residents of the Roman world, mostly and normally embraced the ways of life common at the time. But they did so selectively, offering a range of options to reconfigure and avoid features of the experience that did not fit their own norms and practices.

CHAPTER 6

The Naked Rabbi and the Beautiful Goddess

ENGAGING WITH SCULPTURE
IN THE PUBLIC BATHHOUSE

Proklos the son of Plaslos asked Rabban Gamaliel in Acre while he was bathing in the bath of Aphrodite [and] he said to him: it is written in your law "and nothing of the *ḥerem* shall stick to your hand" (Deut. 13:17) why [then] are you bathing in the bath of Aphrodite? He [R. Gamaliel] replied: it is not allowed to answer in the bath. When he came out he said to him: I did not come within her limits; she came within my limits. [People] do not say "let us make a bath for Aphrodite," but [rather, they say] "she, Aphrodite, is made an ornament for the bath." Furthermore, [even] if you were given a large sum of money, [would] you enter into your idolatry naked, [or] polluted from semen, [or would you] urinate in front of her?! And she [Aphrodite] is standing by the drainage and all the people are urinating in front of her. It is said only "their gods" (Deut. 12:3), [i.e.,] that which he treats as a god is prohibited, [but] that which he does not treat as a god is permitted.[1]

The unknown author of this anecdote—preserved in the famous third-century rabbinic text, the Mishnah, in the tractate called *Avodah Zarah*, that is, "Idolatry"—sets up an encounter and ensuing debate between a renowned rabbinic figure of the second century, Gamaliel, and the non-Jew Proklos. The two men meet in the public baths of Acre/Ptolemais, the Phoenician city on the northern seashore of today's Israel, at the time a Greek polis and later a Roman colony. The editors of the Mishnah digress here, as they do on occasion, from the dry systematic presentation of legal

FIGURE 17. *The Baths of Caracalla*, an imaginative painting by the nineteenth-century Spanish painter Virgilio Mattoni de la Fuente. *Credit:* Public domain, licensed by Creative Commons, courtesy of Wikimedia Commons.

formulations, in this case related to idolatry, and offer a short narrative, a snapshot, perhaps fictional, of an encounter in the public bathhouse. A prominent rabbi visits the baths named after the Greek goddess Aphrodite, the Roman Venus, whose statue, so the story implies, stood at its center. Other sources confirm that statues of gods and goddesses were often placed in bathhouses, which were then named after these divinities.[2]

While bathing, Proklos needles the rabbi by asking him how he can bathe in the presence of an idol. Undoubtedly a fictional character, although perhaps based on a real man of that name,[3] Proklos exhibits impressive knowledge of Jewish scripture, not to mention fluency in Hebrew, as he substantiates his challenge by quoting from Deuteronomy, the fifth book of the Pentateuch, considered by Jews at the time as the divine revelation of the God of Israel to his people. Gamaliel remains unperturbed and delivers a series of pithy replies to justify his presence in the baths of Aphrodite.

The realities of public baths shine in the details of this snippet. His own nakedness and that of the bathers around him prevent Gamaliel from justifying himself on the spot, because of the prohibition on discussing Jewish law in the nude. His subsequent reply confirms the pervasiveness of nudity in the baths: "[even] if you were given a large sum of money, [would] you enter into your idolatry naked?" No matter how we may otherwise imagine the venerable Rabban Gamaliel, at the start of this short story he stands buck naked before the beautiful, erotic statue of Aphrodite, her bodily charms most probably on full display as well (fig. 18). A

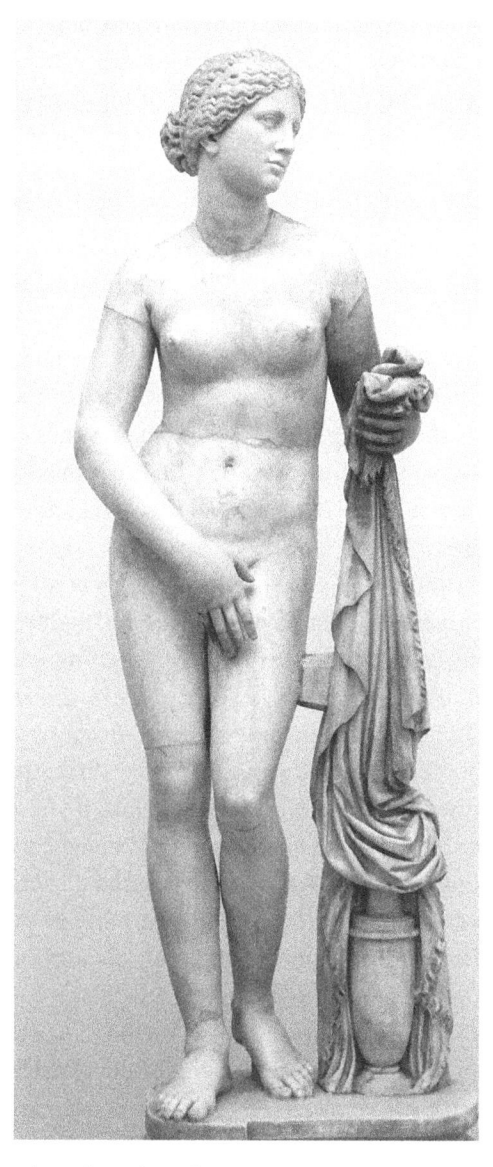

FIGURE 18. Aphrodite of Knidos. This is a Roman copy of one of the most popular statues of the ancient world, made by the Greek sculptor Praxiteles of Athens in the fourth century BCE. The torso and thighs are from the Roman original, whereas the hands, head, legs, drapery, and jar were added by the sixteenth-century Italian restorer Ippolito Buzzi. This is a good visual representation of what Rabban Gamaliel may have seen at the bath. Currently on display in the Ludovisi collection at the Museo Nazionale Romano, in Rome. *Credit:* Photograph by Marie-Lan Nguyen, licensed by Creative Commons (CC BY-SA 4.0), courtesy of Wikimedia Commons.

few centuries later, an Egyptian visitor to Constantinople described a similar statue of the goddess: "And another highborn Aphrodite I saw all of gold, naked, all glittering; and on the breast of the goddess, hanging from her neck, fell in coils the flowing cestus (a kind of a girdle said to be given to the goddess by her husband Hephaestus)." Archaeologists uncovered comparable statues of Venus/Aphrodite all over the Mediterranean, many of them inside or near public baths, where she ranks as one of the most popular sculptured representations.[4] When the naked rabbi and the beautiful goddess meet in the bath, their encounter epitomizes the cultural dynamics that this book explores: conceptions of the body, perceptions of space, tension about identity and its resolution, debates about power and aesthetics. These all converge in a convoluted, at times elusive discourse that emerged from the meeting of cultures in the Roman world in general and in the bathhouse in particular. I call these dynamics "the poetics of cultural interaction."

The story mentions other salacious habits of those attending the public bathhouse. The author alludes to masturbation ("polluted from semen") and also explicitly refers to people's habit of urinating on the statues that stood there, a notorious practice, known to have occurred outside the baths as well.[5] But most of all, the passage reflects two important and interrelated aspects of the bathing experience: first, the abundance of freestanding statues of divinities and mythological figures in public baths; and second, this statue-strewn space prompted many cultural issues. The dialogue in the mishnaic anecdote revolves around questions that arose in Jewish circles regarding engagement with sculpture in the baths. Clearly, such concerns were on the mind of the rabbinic author of the passage and the editors of the Mishnah, who included the short tale in the legal discussion of idolatry. While the author granted Gamaliel and his lenient position the upper hand, allowing bathing in the presence of sculptured divinities, he nevertheless recognized the validity, at least a priori, of the opposing criticism by placing it in the mouth of Proklos. The tension between the challenge of Proklos and the replies of Gamaliel demarcates the spectrum of rationales that circulated among Jews, or at the minimum in rabbinic circles, on this matter.

However, deciphering the precise meaning of these arguments and the positions expressed by this passage proves more difficult than anticipated. Clearly, the position assigned to Gamaliel by the storyteller and the editors of the Mishnah, who included the anecdote in their sequence of idolatry laws, permits Jews to attend the bath despite the presence of a Graeco-Roman statue of a goddess. This apparent leniency is rather remarkable, since we grew accustomed to the idea that the ban on depicting any divinity in any form of art is absolute for Jews. But Gamaliel articulates his reasoning in opaque language. What does he mean when he asserts, "I did not come within her limits; she came within my limits"? What are these limits, who determines them, and how? Furthermore, why does Gamaliel provide a second line of reasoning, referring to the debauched activities of people in the bath, and what is the relation between his two answers? And finally, from the broadest perspective, how does the author of this text understand the term "idolatry," a cultural and legal category frequently employed in discussion of Jewish attitudes toward Roman culture but whose nuances and complexities are rarely investigated? As we seek to understand the multiple facets of the Roman public bathhouse, this last issue is particularly important. Was the bath intrinsically an idolatrous institution, as at least one modern scholar suggests? I discussed that question at length in chapter 4; the current chapter will deal with the cultural perceptions of rabbinic scholars associated with statues in general and in particular those that populated public bathhouses.

In the last century, numerous modern scholars from diverse fields of study engaged Gamaliel's ruling on the bath of Aphrodite. Philologists, philosophers, religious and cultural studies scholars, talmudists, art historians, classicists, and archaeologists have all applied the methodologies of their respective disciplines to the reading and interpretation of this passage.[6] For our purposes, this rabbinic anecdote provides a porthole into the cultural mechanisms and formulas that took shape in the Roman public bathhouse. By unpacking the various contexts in which the Gamliel segment operates, we can come pretty close to the mindset of (some, perhaps only a few) Jews from the ancient world, understand their concerns, and follow the principles that guided their engagement with the baths and its potentially problematic statuary. I label these mechanisms "filtered absorption."

First is the spatial, physical context. The author situates the narrative about Gamaliel and Aphrodite in the space of public baths, a physical environment defined by water, heat, and pleasure, and plentiful statues. What was this space like? What kind of statues stood there, who placed them there, and how aware were Jews of their characteristics and details? As depicted by the storyteller in the Mishnah, Gamaliel seems quite familiar with the sculptured landscape of the baths. Was this typical of Jews?

Second is the legal, halakhic context. We must not forget, and modern scholars who discuss the Gamaliel story often do, that this short narrative functions within the broader context of laws about three-dimensional sculpture in the Mishnah. The editors of the Mishnah tied the Gamaliel portion to the legal statements and formulations that precede it in the third chapter of tractate *Idolatry*. The Gamaliel passage reacts to, negotiates, and modifies those earlier legal formulations, all of which strive to navigate the charged space inhabited by statues. Understanding the broad legislative and literary contexts in relation to the Gamaliel anecdote sheds further light on the experiences of Jews in public bathhouses that contained statuary as well as on the nature of this establishment in their eyes.

Finally, there is the cultural context of the Gamaliel-Aphrodite segment. The ancients, as we shall see, thought a lot about statues. This text in the Mishnah, as well as many others, reveals diverse views regarding statues, but at the same time it shows the common conceptual grounds that Jews shared with other groups and views in diverse corners of the Mediterranean world. Rabbinic writings enable us to trace a cultural discourse—permeated by symbolism, perceptions, and beliefs—that extends beyond the realm of the Jews and the rabbis. Throughout the Roman Empire many ethnic groups encountered statues in the baths, though their voices can no longer be heard. By contrast, the Gamaliel story preserved some peripheral voices from the Roman world, those of Jewish scholars living in Roman Palestine, and as such it may be of use not only to students of the rabbis but to modern scholars of the Roman world in general.

The rest of this chapter attempts to unpack these three different contexts and through them gain a better understanding of how Jews and others interacted with the statues that proliferated in the Roman bathhouse. To do so, the discussion begins and ends with bathhouses, but on the way it extends its sway to the broader manifestations of sculpture in the religious, legal, and everyday realms of Jews and non-Jews alike. The insights gained in those (at times lengthy) detours will then be brought back to the baths and assist in elucidating the cultural dynamics, what this book calls "the poetics of culture," of the place, when Jews encountered and engaged with Roman statues in public bathhouses.

The Sculptural Environment: Statues, Statues, Everywhere!

Throughout the Roman Empire, statues adorned public baths, constituting an essential part of the environment encountered by visitors. Welcoming patrons arriving at ordinary bathhouses, statues were chiseled on the pediment in relief, stood full size on its triangular tip (the *akroterion*), or were placed on the cornice of the building's facade. Inside, sculpture

FIGURE 19. A reconstruction of statues on display around the *frigidarium* pool at the Agora Baths in Side, Turkey. *Credit:* Photograph courtesy of László Szirtesi.

occupied almost every possible spot. Reliefs were engraved on friezes, busts (*protomai*) were carved out of the *abaci* (the square slabs at the top of the column's capital), and life-sized three-dimensional images were placed on beams spanning the columns or in special niches along the walls or were scattered about on pedestals (figs. 17 and 19). As to subjects, these statues and reliefs offered a diverse repertoire: emperors, benefactors, gods, mythological scenes, and important personages, memorialized for various reasons.[7]

Naturally, the number of statues and their quality varied. Few places could compete with the huge imperial baths (the *thermae*), such as the baths of Caracalla in Rome (see fig. 6) or those of Zeuxippos in Constantinople. In a hexametrical *ekphrasis* (a literary description of works of art), the fifth- or sixth-century Egyptian visitor Christodoros of Coptos mentioned about eighty statues just in the baths of Zeuxippos, Constantinople's main bathhouse-gymnasium.[8] In the baths of Caracalla, the existing niches alone held over one hundred standing statues, and of course numerous others stood on their own throughout the open space of the building and in its surrounding courts and gardens.[9] But smaller bathhouses did not lag far behind. The numerous inscriptions that survived from these bathing institutions, most of which carefully document the erection of statues, show that many of these establishments, especially the large urban ones, were crowded with dozens of statues, and we can often, although not always, find quite a few sculptured figures even in small village baths.[10] Public bathhouses in the eastern part of the Roman Empire—including Judaea, later renamed Syria Palaestina—were no different. In the middle Orontes Valley, a second-century inscription from the lavish and well-preserved Syrian city of Apamea enumerates an elaborate program of bronze statues that adorned the baths, including mythological and divine figures such as Theseus and the Minotaur, Apollo, Olympus, one of the sons of Heracles, and the Satyr Marsyas.[11] None have been preserved. But a hundred and sixty miles down on the Syrian-African rift, in the Jordan valley city of Scythopolis, at the heart of Roman Palestine, archaeological excavations in a bathhouse from roughly the same period of time unearthed a series of statues similar in subject and cultural scope. Among them are Dionysius, a nymph, a larger-than-life torso of a ruler, probably one of the emperors, and Aphrodite,[12] the same goddess featured in the contemporaneous mishnaic story about Rabban Gamaliel in Acre discussed at the opening of this chapter. It seems quite clear that most, if not all, bathing establishments throughout the Roman world, especially those located in cities, shared not only a similar architectural layout but also an almost identical, if varied, repertoire of sculptured figures.

Needless to say, statues were hardly limited to bathhouses. Public sculptures were something like the mass media of the Roman world. They populated urban centers throughout the empire. In the words of Paul Zanker, they served as a "visual language" and "pictorial vocabulary"—"visual communication" that articulated and disseminated political, religious, and social messages (more on this below).[13] Sculptural displays conveyed a complex spectrum of emotions and ideas, ranging from fear and loathing to aesthetic admiration, and they offered reflections on everything from the nature of the divine to the implications of social hierarchy, patronage, and power.

Mirroring the situation of the baths (or vice versa), three-dimensional sculptures were the most prominent type: life-sized or even larger representations of mythological figures or real people, carved in marble or other stone, cast in bronze, or carved of wood. They were placed on tall pedestals or atop arches, or installed in *aediculae* (openings framed by columns or pilasters, supporting entablatures and pediments). Of almost equal prominence were relief sculptures that enlivened both the exteriors and interiors of public buildings and temples, animated the capitals of columns, and decorated the entablatures of all sorts of buildings along the

FIGURE 20. A view (looking northeast) of the archaeological remains of the western bathhouse in Scythopolis/Beth Shean, dating to the fourth or fifth century. In the foreground of the picture is the outdoor peristyle court (*palaestra*) with a pool (*natatio*), and under the modern roofs are the various bathing rooms. *Credit:* Photograph courtesy of Gabi Laron.

streets, such as *nymphaea* (water fountains) and *tetrapyla* (colonnaded, arched structures that marked the intersection of streets in many Roman cities). Sculpted images were indeed everywhere in the urban landscape.[14] R.R.R. Smith calls this phenomenon a "strange practice" (in the eyes of the modern viewer) and asserts that "it was a defining practice of Later Greek and Roman city culture" and that "no other societies have invested so heavily in figured public symbols."[15] Elsewhere, I labeled this "the sculptural environment of the Roman world."[16]

The closest (although not identical) parallel in the modern world would be the huge billboards that are ubiquitous along the main streets of many cities, whether they carry a political or cultural message or merely a commercial advertisement. The fascination of a small-town visitor walking through Times Square in New York City for the first time, gaping at its enormous images and neon signs, is likely analogous to the experience of the author of the Book of Acts when he describes Athens as *kateidōlos*. The word literally translates as "full of idols," but Nigel Spivey was on target when he translated it as "a forest of idols."[17] Statues were present outside the city walls as well. They appeared as directional signs at crossroads, as decorations on the *sarcophagi* in the cemeteries, and on triumphal arches that greeted visitors at the city limits. Statues also populated the private sphere. Miniature statues were sold in markets or in sculptors' shops, and sculpted portraits, masks, household utensils, and other objets d'art were common household decor.[18]

Roman Sculpture in the Jewish Realm

Modern scholars have both unconsciously and intentionally downplayed the role of statuary in the lives of ancient Jews. Daniel Sperber, for example, despite organizing his book *The City in Roman Palestine* as an inclusive description of the urban environment of the High and Late Empires (that is, the second to fifth centuries CE), with chapters on the markets, bathhouses, and other public buildings, devotes neither a chapter nor a substantial discussion to statues.[19] In contrast to the impression created by his book and others like it, statues dominated the cityscape of Roman Palestine. It is true that, following the Roman conquest of Judaea by Pompey the Great in 63 BCE, and through the next few generations, many (but not all) local Jews seem to have shunned and resented iconic presentation. The first-century CE Jewish historian Flavius Josephus presents numerous examples of this aniconic tendency, the best known being the crisis in 40 CE. In the winter prior to that year, Jews in the town of Iamnia, on the coastal plains, demolished an altar to the imperial cult. In response the emperor Caligula commanded the erection of a colossal statue of himself in the Jewish temple in Jerusalem. The imperial order stirred tremendous anger and resentment among the Jews throughout the province, who explicitly informed the governor of Syria that they would rather die than allow the desecration of their temple by a statue. The showdown was prevented by the assassination of the emperor in January of 41.[20] Clearly, statues hit a sensitive nerve among the Jews of the time, and they may also have met with disapproval in other neighboring groups, such as the Nabateans.[21]

Similarly, Jewish rulers of the region going back to the Hasmonaeans (also known as the Maccabees), who led the Jews of Judaea during the late Hellenistic period (152–63 BCE), and after them the Jewish client king Herod in the Early Roman period (37–4 BCE), all avoided placing human images on their coins and erecting sculpture in the Jewish cities within their domains (which basically meant Jerusalem, since all other cities contained a mixed Jewish and non-Jewish population). Herod and his sons, however, did not refrain from erecting sculpture in their own palaces.²² Modern historian and archaeologist Lee Levine convincingly suggests that this avoidance of artistic imagery, and its association with the prohibition against worshiping other gods as articulated in the Torah, in the Second Commandment (more on this text and its meaning below), functioned as a political tool in the hands of the Hasmonaeans. For nearly ten decades, these rulers based their reputation on protecting the Jewish way of life from the "threat" of Hellenism (despite their embrace of Greek norms in their palace life and administration).²³ This aniconic tendency persisted into the reign of King Herod, who replaced the Hasmonaeans in the early days of Roman hegemony in the region; outside his immediate Jewish realm Herod felt free to follow the norms of non-Jewish rulers and benefactors, and showered faraway cities throughout the Mediterranean with gifts and patronage, including statues and even temples to Graeco-Roman divinities. But in Jerusalem he adhered strictly to the customs of previous generations, eschewing sculpture or any other form of figurative art. Josephus, writing three generations after Herod, describes this king's practices and articulates one (but by no means the sole) way by which Jews interpreted them at the time:

> Because of his [=Herod's] ambition . . . and the flattering attention which he gave to Caesar and the most influential Romans, he was forced to depart from the customs (of the Jews) and to alter many of their regulations, for in his ambitious spending he founded cities and erected temples—not in Jewish territory, for the Jews would not have put up with this, since we are forbidden such things, including honoring of statues and sculptured forms in the manner of the Greeks—but these he built in foreign and surrounding territory. To the Jews he made the excuse that he was doing these things not on his own account but by command and order, while he sought to please Caesar and the Romans by saying that he was less intent upon observing the customs of his own nation than upon honoring them.²⁴

In the following centuries, as memories of the Hasmonaean regime and its political and cultural strategies faded, Jewish attitudes toward figurative art throughout the Roman world fluctuated dramatically. In the closing decades of the second century CE and during the third century, Jewish life in the region settled into patterns typical of a provincial minority. Jews could be found throughout Roman Palestine, as they lived in mixed cities, large villages and towns, and smaller agricultural hamlets and farms. In particular, urban life, its landscape and institutions, functioned similarly and exhibited a relatively uniform appearance everywhere in the Roman

Mediterranean, which for the current discussion means that bathhouses and public spaces swarmed with statues.

It may very well be that the cities of Palestine, whose size, political status, and economic strength in the second and third centuries were at times rather shaky, featured fewer sculptured pieces than the large and prosperous metropolises of the eastern empire, such as Antioch, Alexandria, or Ephesus, and later Constantinople, or, for that matter, the ancient cities of the Greek world, such as Athens or Rhodes. Even Aphrodisias, in southwest Asia Minor, a smaller and less pivotal urban center, probably displayed more statues than an average Palestinian city, due to its wealth, proximity to the sculpture production hubs of the Roman east, and the relative tranquility of the region during the years of the *pax romana*. Nevertheless, anyone walking in a typical Palestinian city during this period—such as Caesarea Maritima, Scythopolis, Samaria/Sebaste, Paneas (Caesarea Philippi), Aelia Capitolina, or Eleutheropolis (which gained civic status as a colony around 200 CE), to name but a few—would encounter Roman statuary every step of the way. And there is no reason to believe that major cities in regions heavily populated by Jews, such as the mixed cities of the Galilee like Sepphoris and Tiberias, were any different. Archaeological evidence, varied sources in contemporary rabbinical literature dealing with statues, and even bits of information about statues in Palestine mentioned incidentally in non-Jewish sources all confirm the ordinary presence of statues in those Jewish enclaves as well.[25]

Rabbinic authors show full awareness of the "sculptural environment" that surrounded them and frequently allude to it in their writings.[26] They repeatedly mention statues by name—Aphrodite, Mercury, the figures (icons) of kings and emperors—or, on a different note, the "faces which spout water in the towns" (fig. 21).[27] They also refer to the social and political dynamics associated with the erection of statues, and even more broadly, to the ways that statues shaped and were shaped by the larger cultural milieu—the customs, myths, and emotions that inspired the carving of figures and were in turn inspired by the pieces that resulted. For example, the use of statues for imperial propaganda and the practice of *damnatio memoriae*—erasing the visual and epigraphic memory of deposed emperors or contenders—that stemmed from it provided the context for the following rabbinic parable: "A king of flesh and blood entered a province and [the people] set up icons [of him], made statues [of him] and struck coins in his honor. Later on they upset his portraits, broke his statues and defaced his coins, thus diminishing the likenesses of the king."[28]

FIGURE 21. A water spout in the form of a human face from the excavations in Tiberias, Israel. *Credit:* Photograph courtesy of Gabi Laron.

The knowledge of the political significance of sculpture likewise supplied the background for the rabbinic story about an artisan "who [started to] fashion the icon of the king," but the king was "replaced" by another before he had a chance to complete his work.[29] Frequent changes of imperial rule during the political turmoil that plagued the Roman Empire in the third century undoubtedly provided many such occasions, whether following a formal declaration that the former emperor was now a *hostis* (enemy) or simply when, after an emperor was deposed, the statues representing him and his family were demolished spontaneously in the heat of events. Elsewhere, a rabbinic author mentions customs of family statuary; for example, "[A person] goes to a sculptor and says to him, 'Make me a likeness of my father'" or "When the eldest [son] of one of them died they made an icon of him and placed it in their house." Private statues and death masks of family leaders (*imagines maiorum*), or of children who had died prematurely, were extremely popular among affluent families in antiquity.[30]

Rabbinic literature mentions many other details that testify to intimate knowledge of Graeco-Roman sculpture. And even more significantly, those references are not, as we might expect, entirely negative. The engraved inscription that accompanied a statue, for example, an indispensable element of the work and of the way onlookers engaged with it, surfaces in second-century rabbinic terminology as "an inscription that runs under figures and icons." Rabbinic law forbids inspecting such inscribed writings on the Sabbath, apparently as part of the general prohibition against reading texts other than scripture on that sacred day, but the explicit mention of this prohibition suggests that, ordinarily, Jews did read those texts in their day to day.[31] Another example relates to the importance of personal statues in a deceased person's estate, a subject that received attention in Roman law as well. The rabbinic discussion considers the case of a convert who inherited them from his father and remains entirely non-judgmental.[32] Rather unexpectedly, rabbinic scholars also allude to even more spiritual aspects of sculpture and express appreciation of their splendor. Beauty and aesthetics are the underlying theme in Gamaliel's response to Proklos: "she, Aphrodite, is made an ornament for the bath." Another rabbinic story tells of the famous scholar Hillel who referred to his attending the bath as an obligatory requirement from God (*mitsvah*) and compared it to washing and shining statues.[33] Evidently, a legendary tale, not at all historically accurate with reference to Hillel, the story does convey the attitude of its rabbinic author to baths and statues of his own time.

Significantly, many of the rabbinic discussions about Roman three-dimensional figures—indeed, some of the most penetrating insights and innovative formulations about them—surface in relation to those placed in bathhouses. Such is the anecdote about Rabban Gamaliel opening this chapter, which the editors of the Mishnah placed at the culmination of a sophisticated legal discussion about statues and idolatry in general (more on this in the next section). Another passage in the Mishnah, which asks whether Jews may or may be not permitted to take part in the erection of statues in public space, chooses the bathhouse as the location where this issue may arise. The rabbinic scholar deems it permissible to "build with them (i.e., with non-Jews) public bathhouses and [privately owned] baths. [But] when they reach the dome (=probably referring to the niches in the wall that were capped with a semi-dome) in which they set up a [statue of] idolatry, it is prohibited [to continue assisting and collaborating in the] building."[34]

Rabbinic literature also discusses popular rituals related to sculptured figures in association with a visit by a third-century scholar to a bathhouse: "R. Simeon b. Lakish was in (the Arabian provincial capital of) Bostra. He saw [people in the baths] sprinkle (=offer libations) to that Aphrodite. He said to them: 'is this not prohibited?' [When he] came [back to Tiberias he] asked R. Yoḥanan [about this incident]. R. Yoḥanan told him in the name of R. Simeon b. Yehotsadak: 'A thing of (= done by) the public is not prohibited.'"[35] Moreover, the only reference in rabbinic literature to the practice of iconoclasm, namely the deliberate shattering of statues, relates to the bathhouse: "R. Yoḥanan said to bar Drosai: 'Go down and break all those statues inside the public bathhouse.' And he went down and broke all of them but one."[36] Apparently, the statues in the bathhouse captured the attention of the rabbis and occupied their minds more than those in other locations such as Graeco-Roman temple complexes, where, of course, Jews were unlikely to go. This heightened focus on one particular location, although by no means exclusive (rabbinic texts often refer to statues people encounter on the streets of their cities), corroborates the central concept for which I argued in chapter 1: I believe that for Jews, the bathhouse represented the spatial embodiment, the epitome, of Roman culture. Naturally, therefore, discussions about statues centered upon this place.

All in all, rabbis' close acquaintance with these visual, tangible constituents of Roman culture should not be startling. However, it is remarkable and significant for understanding who they were. On the one hand, like everyone in the Mediterranean region, rabbinic scholars inhabited a world shaped by Graeco-Roman mores. Thus, the cultural precepts of this civilization, whether visual or conceptual, naturally seeped into their literary work. On the other hand, the intimate familiarity with statues that some rabbis exhibit is by itself remarkable—after all, they could simply have ignored or refused to discuss the idolatrous stone figures around them. Having demonstrated rabbinic close acquaintance with the sculptural environment of the Roman world, we must now look farther and deeper, and ask: how did they interact with and assess this environment? Cyril Mango, in his influential essay about Byzantine perspectives on statuary, maintains that the Christian position about sculptured figures is indicative of that group's overall approach toward antiquity and Graeco-Roman culture in general.[37] The same approach may apply to Jews as well.

Ancient Rabbinic Laws of Idolatry and Their Reception over the Ages

Any discussion of how Jews in the ancient world viewed, or perceived, or felt about the statues that surrounded them, and of their ideological or conceptual attitudes toward them, must seriously consider the precepts of Jewish law (*halakhah*) derived from the biblical commandment concerning idolatry.[38] Jewish law, as discussed at length in chapter 4, is based primarily, although not solely, on the scriptural books we now call the Bible, and in particular, the Pentateuch, also known as the Torah, the first five books of the corpus, which by the late Roman period had long achieved a foundational and defining status for most if not all Jews. Biblical and then Jewish law are extremely stringent in their opposition to the worship of gods other than the God of Israel, usually called idolatry in English, *'avoda zara* (foreign worship) in Hebrew.

This prohibition against foreign worship receives its earliest expression in the countless warnings in the Torah and in the persistent struggle of the ancient prophets against any manifestation of worshipping other gods. The literary foundation of this negative attitude pivots around the first four verses of the Ten Commandments (Exod. 20:2–5; Deut. 5:6–9), believed at the time to be the direct instruction of the God of Israel to his people. These verses begin with a declarative prelude, known as the First Commandment, "I am the Lord your God," and then specify three prohibitions that follow from that statement: (1) "You shall have no other gods instead of me"; (2) "You shall not make for yourself a statue (*pesel*)"; (3) "You shall not bow to them or worship them."[39]

The relationship between these three interdictions, which came to be known collectively as the Second Commandment, is far from clear, and indeed, over the centuries different groups—from Iron Age Judaeans and Israelites, living roughly in the first four centuries of the first millennium BCE, to the Jews in the Hellenistic and Roman worlds, a period stretching from the fourth century BCE to the seventh century CE—varied greatly on how to interpret these proscriptions, let alone how to implement them.[40] As mentioned earlier in this chapter, in the Early Roman period (63 BCE–70 CE), Jews in faraway places like Alexandria (as reflected in the writings of the local Jewish philosopher Philo) as well as those living in Judaea applied this ban against idols fairly rigorously. Judging from surviving texts and archaeological remains, practically everyone believed that scripture and its underlying divine agenda, as articulated in the Second Commandment, strictly forbade all artistic depictions of the human figure, whether two-dimensional pictures and paintings or three-dimensional statues. Some Jews of that time even extended the sanction to include portrayal of animals. In cities like Jerusalem, which were inhabited primarily by Jews, the archaeological record indeed confirms adherence to this prohibition, shown in the nearly complete artistic void that emerges from the archaeological excavations in such places. Anti-anthropomorphic Jewish positions also inflamed occasional tensions between Jews and their neighbors in the mixed cities of Judaea and elsewhere throughout the Mediterranean as well as with the governing Roman powers.[41]

However, as explained earlier, by the High and Late Empire eras, the second to fifth centuries CE, the period of rabbinic literature, much had changed in Jewish positions regarding Roman sculpture. On the one hand, like their Jewish predecessors, rabbinic scholars still considered the repudiation of idol worship as a foundation of their worldview. They counted idolatry among the three prohibitions for which one should prefer death over transgression; they asserted that "whoever confesses [to belief] in idolatry denies the Ten Commandments"; they deemed any form of idolatry as ritually impure and as the major cause for exile; and they collected statements and regulations forbidding all aspects of idol worship.[42] But on the other hand, when it came to everyday practice, to encounters with statues in the bathhouse and elsewhere, the voices emerging from the rabbinic chorus were rather dissonant—a far cry from the homogeneous anti-sculpture tones that rang in earlier generations of the Early Roman period or from their own high-pitched abhorrence of idolatry.

Chapter 3 of tractate *Avodah Zarah* in the Mishnah, the chapter that includes the anecdote about Gamaliel in the bathhouse, opens with a presentation of three basic, yet quite different legal positions about statues formulated by second-century rabbinic scholars. In the following centuries, deep into the Middle Ages and beyond, these three juristic stances formed the foundation of all rabbinic discussions on the subject. Surprisingly, in this opening, defining statement on idolatry, the Mishnah does not present a wall-to-wall rejection and banishment of all sculptured figures, as one might expect following from the adamant stance of earlier Hellenistic and Early Roman Jews. Rather, the chapter begins with a nuanced yet explicit three-way disagreement on what constitutes an idolatrous statue. It reads as follows:

> "All statues (*tselamim*) are forbidden [as idolatrous] because they are worshipped once a year," such is the statement of R. Meir. [But] the [other] scholars (*ḥakhamim*) say, "[a statue] is not forbidden except one that has a stick or a bird or a ball." R. Simeon b. Gamaliel says, "[a statue] which carries anything in its hand [is forbidden]."[43]

The wording immediately following this passage in the Mishnah mentions "broken pieces," making it clear that *tselem*, the Hebrew used here (in the plural), as in most instances in rabbinic literature, denotes a three-dimensional figure—a statue—that is, one that could be broken into pieces (in contrast to other, two-dimensional images, such as figures woven into cloth, painted on walls, or pieced together into mosaics).[44] Evidently, the two opposing rabbinic positions in this segment—R. Meir's and the anonymous position assigned here to the inclusive designation "the *ḥakhamim*" (=the Scholars)—disagree on the extent of the idolatry prohibition. R. Meir posits that "all statues" are included. But the others take a more restricted view, and thus a more lenient one, and claim that only some statues, defined by very specific visual attributes, are forbidden. The term "attribute" in the terminology of art history refers to a visual element, a symbol added by the artist and well known to the viewers, which will enable the latter to assign meaning or identify what they are seeing. Here, a stick, a bird, or a ball held by the statue is interpreted by the rabbinic scholars as an attribute of idolatry (more on this below). By extension, other statues lacking these attributes are not forbidden.[45] The third position, that of R. Simeon b. Gamaliel, agrees in principle with the *ḥakhamim*'s restricted expanse of the idolatry prohibition but nevertheless extends it: if the statue is holding "anything in its hand," it is idolatrous. The modern reader is left puzzled as to why the item held by the statue makes it idolatrous. The rabbinic scholars do not offer an explanation; later in this chapter, I will attempt to do so.

Another puzzling aspect of this text arises from the causative clause that follows R. Meir's statement and provides the reason for his position: "because they are worshipped once a year." The link it creates between the subject of the sentence—the noun "statues"—and the verb "are worshipped" (in the passive) makes it clear that the issue at the root of R. Meir's view is the specific practice of worshipping statues (what rabbis will call idol worship), which was still common all over the Roman world during the days of the rabbis, carried out in formal and informal ways via sacrifices, incense, and libations.[46] This continued practice of idol worship and the perceived threat it posed to Jews wishing to obey the Second Commandment explain R. Meir's inclusive rejection of statues, because they are all worshipped.

However, the statement that *all* statues were worshipped already seemed inaccurate to rabbinic scholars in the immediate generations following the Mishnah. R. Ḥiyya b. Abba, for example, a rabbinic scholar from the end of the third and early fourth centuries, whose response to and interpretation of the legal formulations of the Mishnah were recorded in the fourth-century text known as the Palestinian Talmud (the *Yerushalmi*), chose to interpret the causative clause of the Mishnah as follows: "because they were worshipped in the big city of Rome twice in seven years." But even this seemingly far-fetched explication (as if in the huge, faraway city of Rome every single statue was worshipped twice every seven years) did not satisfy another talmudic scholar, who asked logically, "and where they are not worshipped are they permitted?" To solve this question he employed a legal principle, formulated by one R. Jose, stating that "since they were forbidden in one place they are forbidden everywhere."[47] This terse back and forth regarding the Mishnah's formulations shows that at least some of these ancient Jewish scholars knew that some statues were *not* worshipped, which made it hard for R. Ḥiyya and the others to accept R. Meir's generalized explanation that *all* statues are "worshipped" and are therefore forbidden. In their attempt to preserve R. Meir's position in its exact formulation (a common aim in rabbinic hermeneutics), they were forced to substantiate it by using a faraway place, a mythological and fantastic location, the great city of Rome, where the people allegedly, at least in the legal imagination of some rabbinic scholars, worshipped all the statues.[48]

It is tempting to dismiss these rabbinical arguments as mere logic-chopping, based at the most on some speculative exegesis of biblical commandments but unconnected to anything beyond their isolated halakhic world.[49] My understanding is exactly the opposite, namely that rabbis in their *halakhah* about statues in general, and in particular about those that populated public bathhouses, engaged in the general—we can almost say global or universal—cultural discourse of their time. These rabbis employed commonly held cultural formulas, notions, and perceptions about sculpture that circulated throughout the Roman Mediterranean, integrated them into their Jewish worldview, and designed sophisticated positions about their surroundings that were then articulated in a particularly Jewish legal vocabulary. As such, rabbis were neither hostile outsiders nor external bystanders in the Roman realm but rather insiders (even if at times critical) embedded in the cultural texture of their time. The following sections will elaborate, flesh out, and illustrate these arguments.

Sacred and Profane: The Graeco-Roman Context of Rabbinic Laws of Idolatry

In ancient times, people perceived reality in categories that today we would call religious. The cosmology of the Graeco-Roman Mediterranean was replete with divine beings: deities, goddesses, spirits, souls, angels, demons, and mythological monsters. Peter Brown characterized this "religious common sense" of the period as "a spiritual landscape rustling with invisible presences—with countless divine beings and their ethereal ministers."[50] Ancient people found these entities everywhere, from the heights of the temples on Mt. Olympus, through the abstractions of philosophical writings, to the lowest of the latrines where people relieved themselves.

FIGURE 22. A wall painting from a latrine in Pompeii, Italy. The goddess Fortuna (Isis) protects a man defecating with the Latin inscription "*cacator cave malum*" (shitter, beware of evil). Today at the National Archaeological Museum of Naples. *Credit:* Photograph by Carole Raddato, licensed by Creative Commons (CC BY-SA 4.0), courtesy of Wikimedia Commons.

One of these public latrines, discovered almost intact in Pompeii, in southern Italy, contains a fresco of the goddess Fortuna in all her glory, with graffito scrawled next to her that reads, "*cacator cave malum*" (shitter, beware of evil).[51] Under Fortuna another drawing showed a man crouching over nothing less than a small altar, likely defecating (fig. 22). For the people of that time this scatological, seemingly salacious artistic expression depicted neither a sacrilege nor a derisive caricature. On the contrary, the elementary human function of excretion, particularly with its inherent odors and the physical exertion, required expression. Just as the modern mind resorts to popular science to regulate the activities of the toilet (for example, we use medicines for constipation), the ancients turned to religion, incarnated (among the Romans) in the guise of Fortuna.[52] Keith Hopkins succinctly captures this all-encompassing presence of religiosity in the title of his book: *A World Full of Gods*.[53]

Consequently, omnipresent manifestations of religion in language and art, in physical structures, and in daily practices both sacred and banal surrounded people wherever they went.[54] They viewed their entire surroundings and everyday routines through the pervasive and invasive lens of religion. Religious vocabulary and imagery penetrated every stratum of language, assisting people in mediating, explaining, and interpreting their interactions with their environment. Myths, legends, and folk beliefs, even the names and characteristics of gods, all fashioned the cognitive templates that explained and validated both natural phenomena and human situations, just as scientific principles and observation underlie the "truth" of today and shape the contours of our world. Religion, or to be more precise, what we today call religion, encompassed all. Indeed, no actual term for "religion" as a set of theological and moral principles that inform a system of practical directives existed in ancient times. For the ancients it was not religion but rather the mentality of daily life, the consciousness that both made the world possible and shaped its continued existence.

Along with and to a certain extent in contrast to this sweeping and unbounded religious landscape stands an equally fundamental and pervasive human tendency, going back to the earliest origins of civilizations and surpassing geographical and political partitions: the impulse to define and delineate boundaries, especially when it comes to physical space and artifacts. Like the familiar distinction between the private and public domain, people all over recognized a fairly clear, though somewhat permeable, boundary between what the Romans termed *locus consecratus* (consecrated space, also known as the *locus sacer*, sacred space) and *locus profanus* (non-consecrated space). The Romans devised various procedures, known as *consecratio* (and a variety of Greek terms using the verb *hieroein*), to transform a place from *profanum* (literally "pre-holy") to a consecrated space, which then received the status of *templum* (*temenos* in Greek). Today we associate the term "temple" with a religious building, but in the ancient world it denoted a place or entity removed from the regular world and offered to the gods. In addition to the buildings we refer to as temples, which the Romans called *aedes sacra*, it referred to a much wider range of venues. For example, the judicial seat of the magistrate known as the *praetor* and the space in which it was placed, and the senate's chamber, were all *templa*. By the same token, a reverse process, *exauguratio*, restored a *templum* to its profane status.[55]

The great Roman/Byzantine legal codices and other texts articulate these categories of holiness and lack thereof, as they preserve laws that set forth formal procedures for conferring sacredness and interacting with it. However, the distinction between sacred and profane goes far beyond the realm of law, and it is not circumscribed geographically. Although Roman law limits its consecration procedures to *ager Italicus*, the territory of Italy,[56] similar measures, though surely more varied, also applied beyond Italy, as attested in inscriptions from all over the Roman world, in the close similarity of the design of sacred structures, in the visual representation of the sacred realm in art, and especially in similar human needs and behaviors.[57]

Taking an example from the Jews: in the days of Augustus some of them applied to the emperor and received his approval to have their own *res sacra*—money consecrated for use in the temple in Jerusalem and their sacred books, which were stored in synagogues, considered sacred under Roman law as well. As a result, this money and these books were protected by Roman laws and its penalties, namely that anyone who stole the money or desecrated the books was guilty of the Roman capital offense of sacrilege, *sacrilegium*.[58] Clearly, this ruling reflects the shared conceptual template about the sacred, although its implementation varied among different peoples and regions of the Roman world. Indeed, the law here reflects the basic human need to identify and distinguish the sacred from the profane. Roman texts document this tendency, enabling us to understand this widely shared strand of ancient culture (more below on how Jews enacted them). The ancient idea of sacredness, therefore, encompassed two complex and at times contradictory aspects: it was both boundless and constricted, it appeared everywhere but in a carefully delineated and rule-bound manner.

When applying these conceptual templates and practical mechanisms to sculpture, we must recognize that some of them obtained sacred status and others did not. A formal process of *consecratio*, ordered by the emperor or decided by a city council, and carried out by the local religious officials (priests), imparted the holy spirit to a statue, the *pneuma* of one of the gods or, alternatively, the *numen* (the divine power and will) of one of the emperors. This made the statue sacred (*res sacra*). Sacred sculpture regularly stood in *templa*, that is within a sacred space, but they could also be erected in the public sphere, both outside and inside municipal structures such as the city forum, courthouse basilica, and the city council (the *boulē*). The public paid homage to these statues of gods and deified emperors in elaborate ceremonies. Priests led processions to and from them; people offered sacrifices and libations at alters erected near them, and they left gifts at their bases. Some of these sacred statues even enrolled their own personal attendants, seeing to their maintenance and safety. Customary care included regular washing, both to keep them clean and for ritual purity. On occasion some statues were removed from their pedestals and taken by hand or by cart to rivers, lakes, or the sea, or to a special pool dug for this purpose (bathhouses were not typically used for this; later I discuss some exceptions).[59] Non-consecrated statues did not receive such treatments.

These ontological categories and the very practical procedures that followed from them provided ancient people with means to distinguish between sacred and non-sacred figures.[60] On the other hand, this does not mean that ordinary people could not themselves set apart statues to gods, a process known in Latin as *dedicatio* and in Greek denoted by various words stemming from the verb *anatithenai*.[61] They could also offer a sacrifice even to a statue lacking a holy spirit or perform some other ritual for it. Such informal practice, even if fundamentally distinct from official consecration, was an inseparable part of religious experience in those times. Varying in intensity and commitment, these private, unofficial, yet common routines of veneration took place daily. For example, an endless series of gestures could be directed toward a statue, any statue, from waving one's hand, touching, or kissing to some more elaborate actions that required preparation. We moderns would regard all of these as "religious acts."[62] Sometimes, after receiving permission from the authorities (under the guidelines of the *lex area*, the set of laws regulating the usage of public space), private citizens erected a small, informal altar in a city street, the forum, or a bathhouse, dedicated to a specific statue. Many differences, however, distinguished unofficially revered figures from consecrated statues. For example, a person who damaged the former was not guilty, under Roman law, of sacrilege.[63]

Surely, the varieties of everyday practices, especially when put into play within the vast array of places, people, and traditions that constituted the far-reaching provinces of the Roman Empire, make it impossible to draw a universal boundary between the sacred and the profane.[64] Nevertheless, the existence of the distinction, the need and the ability to distinguish between different categories of statues, becomes extremely significant as we deepen our understanding of the positions articulated by the rabbis regarding Roman statues and the way they interacted with them, in the bathhouse and elsewhere.

Visual Language of the Sacred

Modern scholars coined the categories "visual language" and "plastic vocabulary" to denote an essential and constant element of human experience, namely a non-spoken and a non-written system of signs that communicates ideas and perceptions not through words but through images. Along with the conceptual and legal distinctions between the sacred and the profane we must consider how people utilized what we call iconography, the visual representations or the system of signs, symbols, and conventions to identify and classify different statues. People constantly engaged with the sculpture around them and combined emotional and spiritual symbolism with this interaction, fostering a plastic language rich in themes and nuances.[65] The ancients did not relate to their sculptures like modern people, who go to museums to appreciate art. In the milieu of the Roman Mediterranean, statues could be many things simultaneously: they were declarations of power and promoters of social status, they marked social hierarchies just as they symbolized the ineffable, they were commemorators as well as "memories," and they functioned as beckoners as well as heralds. In a world suffused with religious vocabulary, every sort of artistic expression, even the seemingly neutral, acquired meaning within a conceptual framework that we now see as religious.[66]

The visual language that evolved around statues applied graphic articulation to distinguish between sacred and profane pieces. It presented symbolic images that triggered notions and emotions, and conveyed concepts, which helped people identify sculptures that were imbued with *pneuma*. In the first century BC, for example, in his essay on the divine (*De natura deorum*), Cicero furnished an explicit expression of these viewing mechanisms: "From our childhood Jupiter, Jove, Minerva, Neptune, Vulcan and Apollo have been known to us by the appearance (*facies*) with which painters and sculptors have chosen to represent them; and not with that appearance only, but having that equipment, age and dress."[67] In the next century, in portions of his encyclopedic work *Naturalis historia* devoted to sculpture, Pliny the Elder takes it for granted that well-defined visual categories separate statues of gods from those of humans.[68] By the early third century, at the same time that rabbinic scholars edited the Mishnah with its views of Roman sculpture, the Greek sophist Philostratus, in his essay on images, seems to know a visual lingua franca: "I do not need to tell you who that is," he says, expecting his reader to be well versed in the symbols artists used to show they were portraying a certain god or mythological figure, "there are countless characteristics of Dionysius for those who wish to represent him in painting or sculpture."[69]

As many modern art historians have noted, these details are not mere *schemata* (patterns to categorize and organize information). Rather they convey meaning and form the "plastic language" mentioned above, shaping the public's perception of statues.[70] The visual strategies to differentiate among statues pervade the Roman Mediterranean. We see them, for example, through the eyes of the second-century Pausanias as he traverses the regions of Greece. By focusing on the sacred and to a large degree ignoring the profane, he reflects the distinction between the two realms as etched in his mind.[71] Lucian of Samosata, perhaps the author of the treatise on the Syrian goddess (*De dea Syria*), shows that similar distinctions applied, at least in his mind, within the northern Syrian cult center of Atargatis, in Hierapolis Bambyce (today Manbij in northern Syria). For example, he writes: "The image of Zeus looks entirely like Zeus in features and clothes and seated posture: you could not identify it otherwise even if you wished."[72] Along the same lines, sporadic yet illuminating statements about the divine quality of certain Egyptian statues in Late Antiquity demonstrate similar awareness of the distinction between sacred statues and ordinary ones.[73] These few, representative examples from different localities in the Mediterranean world show that the use of visual signs to mark the conceptual distinction between the sacred and the profane was widespread and nearly universally embraced, although nuanced and varied in its application.[74] Where were the rabbis within this context?

Back in the Bath: Rabbinic Halakhah *about Statues and the Visual Language of Their Time*

The intricate context of the Graeco-Roman sculptural environment, with its conceptual distinctions between sacred and profane as well as the visual representation (language) of those categories, sheds new light on rabbinic legal positions presented in chapter 3 of tractate *Avodah Zarah* of the Mishnah, discussed earlier in the chapter. Like Cicero, Pliny, and Lucian, the rabbinic scholars whose legal formulations the Mishnah records set out to shape the way those exposed to their words—colleagues, students, perhaps other fellow Jews—would perceive the statues that populated the world around them. (This definition of their efforts disregards the question of how successful they were, as it has no bearing on the present discussion.) Because of their legal background, rabbis used law in this endeavor. The view of the *ḥakhamim* in the Mishnah disagrees with R. Meir's assertion that all statues are worshipped, arguing that "[a statue] is not forbidden except one that has a stick or a bird or a ball." I suggest that this position should be read in light of remarks, such as Cicero's, about people's ability to identify the gods and differentiate them from other statues by using fixed attributes, iconography, that the artists attached to the figures. In other words, this passage shows the awareness of at least some rabbis to "plastic language" principles and their application to differentiate between statues that were worshipped (and thus part of the *res sacra*) and those that were not. In a way, the rabbinic scholars here define their own version of *consecratio*. The items listed by the ḥakhamim in the Mishnah—the stick, the bird, and the ball—functioned, at least in their eyes, as identifying marks of a deity. Thus, the presence of these sculptural elements indicates that non-Jews regarded a certain statue as sacred. In the Tosefta, a text that followed the Mishnah by about a generation, other elements are added to the list, such as a sword, a crown, a ring, and a snake, all conventional symbols in sculptural iconography.[75] The position of the third rabbi in the Mishnah, R. Simon b. Gamaliel, could be explained as expanding the boundaries of the visual formula to include any kind of artistic attribute, which places him midway between the all-inclusiveness of R. Meir and the narrower, iconography-defined position of the ḥakhamim.

The ḥakhamim's position (as well as that of R. Simon b. Gamaliel) results in a more lenient prohibition than does the position of R. Meir because it limits the number of forbidden statues. According to R. Meir, "All statues are forbidden"; according to the ḥakhamim, only a few—with specific attributes—are forbidden. However, according to the explanation presented here, the ḥakhamim did not disagree with R. Meir about the number of forbidden statues but rather with his perception that viewed all statues as worshipped. Understanding the dispute in this way suggests that both sides agreed that *halakhah* prohibits only a worshipped statue. However, R. Meir paired his legal view with the all-inclusive nature of Roman religiosity described above and therefore considered all statues "worshipped idols," whether or not they were actually consecrated. Other rabbinic scholars, referred to as ḥakhamim in this passage, disagreed. Taking a narrower view of the religious experience, they forbid only statues that were originally created to represent deities and thus given a visual "tag" identifying them as *res sacra*. The legal dispute of the rabbinic scholars revolves around two different ways to view the Roman sculptural environment around them. R. Simon b. Gamaliel and the ḥakhamim differentiate between sacred figures and non-sacred figures. R. Meir rejected their distinction, though he did not deny the actual situation. Rather, he perceived and evaluated it differently.[76]

Just a few lines after presenting the disagreement between R. Meir and the ḥakhamim, the editors of the Mishnah offer the anecdote about Rabban Gamaliel and Aphrodite discussed at the beginning of this chapter. Within the well-crafted legal context created by editors of the Mishnah, the anecdotal exchange between this rabbinic scholar and Proklos about the statues of the bathhouse should not be seen as a stand-alone segment. Rather it develops the same issues about which the *hakhamim* disagreed with R. Meir. Rabban Gamaliel's two answers to Proklos take the moderate approach of the *hakhamim* regarding statues a step further. To their view that only those with specifically divine iconography are prohibited, he adds two new criteria: the spatial setting and practical function of a statue. In his first answer, Gamaliel asserts, "I did not come within her limits; she came within my limits." The word "limit" (*gevul* in the Hebrew of the Mishnah) belongs to the semantic field of the Latin term *templum*, both signifying delineation and demarcation of space. It points directly to the prevailing conception of sacred space throughout the Roman world, shared in different languages and among different ethnic groups. In other words: even though Aphrodite was surely a "divine figure," with iconography identifying her as such, and even though similar statues were used in rituals, housed in temples, and so on, Rabban Gamaliel holds that a statue in a given location is forbidden only if that particular place operates as a sacred space, what the Romans called *templum* and what the Mishnah here labels *gevul*, a space confined for ritual worship.[77] Since the bathhouse is not a *templum*, the statue of the goddess inside it is not, in his view, a sacred object. Based on iconography alone, the *hakhamim* of the earlier passage in the Mishnah would declare that the statue of Aphrodite was idolatrous and thus prohibit it, but Rabban Gamaliel's added criteria extend the scope of permitted statues even to gods and goddesses, as long as they are not housed within a space of formal ritual.

When Gamaliel expands on this idea he maintains, "[People] do not say 'let us make a bath for Aphrodite,' but [rather, they say] 'she, Aphrodite, is made an ornament for the bath.'" Here Rabban Gamaliel appeals to what he knows about public opinion to prove that people did not regard the bathhouse as a consecrated space meant to house a sacred object. This statement does not claim that Aphrodite and the other statues crowding the baths were "mere decorations," as some modern scholars have mistakenly maintained (myself included, in some of my earlier studies on this topic);[78] rather it unveils the ritual(less) status of this particular statue based on its spatial surrounding. The Hebrew word "ornament" (*noy*) indicates the statue's lack of ritual status, parallel to the Roman designation, "decorative" (in Latin: *ornamentum*), for a statue that was not formally consecrated.[79]

The second justification that Rabban Gamaliel offers to Proklos presents a somewhat different idea about the treatment of statues in the baths. Gamaliel lists the debased acts that people performed before the statue of Aphrodite in the bathhouse—urinating, masturbating, walking around naked, and the like. He (or the author of this narrative) then associates these behaviors with another rabbinic legal tradition, drawn from verse 12:3 in the book of Deuteronomy (the process of extracting legal instruction from biblical verses was known in rabbinic terminology as *midrash*). From the biblical words "cut down the images of their gods," the midrashic segment concludes: "that which he (that is, the general public) treats as a god is prohibited, [but] that which he does not treat as god is permitted." In other words, even a statue of a deity is not forbidden if people do not treat it with the respect appropriate for consecrated statues. He is not implying that by urinating or exposing themselves people "secularize" the statues, as some modern scholars have suggested,[80] since secularization as such was foreign and unknown in the ancient world. Rather, he means that people's actions before statues indicate their perception of them. For Rabban Gamaliel, or the narrator, the placement of a statue and the activities performed in that place determine its halakhic status. Understood in this way, the Rabban Gamaliel story offers a new set of categories for the interaction with Roman sculpture, different than those of R. Meir and the *ḥakhamim*. The diverse opinions presented by the editors of the Mishnah document varying and opposing responses to the question of what determines the ritual status of a statue, whether it is all-inclusive rituality (R. Meir), the objective identity defined by the statue's iconography (the *ḥakhamim*), or the subjective function and space of a particular statue (Rabban Gamaliel).

The editors of the Mishnah included anecdotes in the legal discussions to add another dimension, often by complicating and diversifying the positions already stated.[81] The short narrative about Rabban Gamaliel in the bathhouse of Acre does exactly that by adding a new set of contextual considerations, which the three opinions presented earlier (R. Meir, the *ḥakhamim*, and R. Simeon) neglected. By setting the story in the public bath, the text reveals the unique cultural dynamics surrounding the encounter with statues in that particular institution. Referring back to the title of this chapter, (at least some) naked rabbis, Rabban Gamaliel in this case, engaged with statues differently from fully clothed rabbis (R. Meir, the *ḥakhamim*, and R. Simeon).

These differing opinions tell us about the ways that some Jews (rabbis in this case) perceived statues, and they also help us understand the much-debated tradition about Reish Lakish in the public bathhouse of Bostra. In that incident, the famous third-century rabbinic scholar R. Simeon b. Lakish encountered a group of people who were sprinkling libations in honor of a statue of Aphrodite in the local bath. He related this incident to his colleague R. Yoḥanan, who responded that the statue remained permissible, because that act did not make that specific Aphrodite sculpture a prohibited idol, or, according to another possible reading, it did not turn the bath into an idolatrous place. To support his position, R. Yoḥanan asserted, "A thing of (=done by) the public is not forbidden."[82] This episode, in which a rabbi witnessed a clear act of pagan worship but did not invoke the prohibition of idolatry, has baffled modern scholars.[83]

It seems to me that this anecdote appears to ratchet the halakhic principle developed in the Rabban Gamaliel story up a notch (or, depending on your perspective, lower it a notch), as that story itself did with the legal prescriptions of R. Meir and the ḥakhamim. The position presented in the Bostra anecdote not only exempts a statue of a deity that stands outside of a ritual context from the prohibition against idolatry (R. Gamaliel's position) but also indicates that even the performance of an informal ritual in its honor, in this case sprinkling a libation, does not make the statue an idol. As I understand the explanation provided for this ruling, "a thing (=an informal act) of (=done by) the public is not forbidden," if a statue of a god stands in a public, non-cultic context and thus is considered non-idolatrous (*profanus*), the unofficial actions of individuals (*dedicatio*) cannot alter its unconsecrated status. This statement must be seen in the context of the pervasive religiosity of the ancient world, as explained earlier, where a wide variety of informal ceremonies in veneration of statues were common. R. Yoḥanan ruled that these informal acts did not change the status of a statue, making it subject to the prohibition of idolatry.

Similar, although not identical, conceptual templates and practical prescriptions regarding bathhouse sculpture are in evidence elsewhere around the Mediterranean. Tertullian, the North African convert, Christian thinker, and lawyer according to some, offers one example. Tertullian, who lived a generation or so before R. Yoḥanan, voiced analogous concerns and comparable solutions. He, unlike the rabbis, listed bathhouses among dubious sites, all potentially blasphemous, because they were decorated with idols; but at the same time he acknowledges that they were but one component of the general environment: "The streets, the market, the baths, the taverns, even our houses, none of these is altogether clear of idols." He also mentions a popular custom of venerating the entrances of bathhouses.[84] Despite his condemnation, and perhaps because he realized that Christians regularly frequented them, Tertullian developed a formula to permit visits, even to pagan temples, on the condition that his Christian readers did not go there to worship.[85] For example, Tertullian mentions ritual activities in the baths during the celebration of the Saturnalia, the ancient Roman festival in the later part of December, when people came to immerse themselves at dawn, simply stating, "I do not bathe at dawn at the Saturnalia—I do not wish to lose both night and day; but I do bathe at the proper and healthful hour."[86] Like the rabbis in Bostra who encountered pagan activities in the public baths, Tertullian eschews the action itself, but he sees no negative implication for the place where it was carried out.

Not all Jews, however, shared the moderate (albeit intolerant) formulations of the ḥakhamim, who dispute R. Meir, of Rabban Gamaliel standing before Aphrodite, or of R. Yoḥanan regarding the libations in the bathhouse of Bostra. As mentioned earlier in this chapter, during the Second Temple period, the centuries immediately preceding these rabbinic opinions, condemnation of sculpture engulfed all or most Jews. Hence, not surprisingly, some Jews destroyed statues and defaced images when they could. According to Josephus's sources, in the first century BCE, when King Herod's illness loosened his iron grip over the people of Judaea, some youths, incited by two highly respected scholars in Jerusalem, tore down the golden eagle erected by the king over the gate to the Temple in the city. Two generations later, on the eve of the Great Revolt, the rebel government ordered Josephus (or so he claims) to demolish the entire palace of Herod's son, Herod Antipas, in Tiberias because of the idolatrous figures of animals that decorated it.[87]

A century and a half later, attitudes had significantly shifted, but not entirely. In opposition to the accommodating voices presented above, some rabbinic scholars vehemently condemned any representation of human figures. One such third-century scholar, R. Naḥum the son of Simai, was nicknamed the Holy of Holies Man, apparently because he refused to look at any depiction of human figures, even on coins. Rabbinic sources present him with praise and high regard and relate the hagiographic tales of others who strove to follow in his footsteps.[88] Regarding sculpture in the public bathhouse, here too some rabbinic positions are unaccommodating, and on one occasion even violent. In the first chapter of tractate *Avodah Zarah* of the Mishnah, in a series of laws dealing with financial and municipal collaboration with non-Jews, the editors include the following directive, mentioned above: "[you may] build with them (= non-Jews) . . . bathhouses. [But] when they reach [in the course of the building project] the dome (= probably referring to the niches in the wall that were capped with a semi-dome) in which they set up a [statue of] idolatry, it is prohibited [to continue assisting and collaborating in the] building."[89] This ruling implies that Jews collaborated with their non-Jewish neighbors in constructing bathhouses. What exactly is labeled in this passage as "idolatry" is not entirely clear. Does the text mean that any statue triggers the prohibition, and by extension that all statues are considered idolatrous? Such a position would coincide with R. Meir's ruling discussed above that "all statues are prohibited" because they were worshipped once a year. However, it might also mean that if and when an idolatrous statue is placed in the bathhouse, then, and just then, and for that portion of the project, Jews may not cooperate. Although nothing is said of bathing in this place later, once the project is complete, the text surely opposes an aspect of bathhouse statuary.

Another rabbinic text, the third-century Palestinian Talmud, presents an anecdote in which the previously mentioned R. Yohanan, who was not put off by the popular rituals around the statue in Bostra, orders a certain Bar Dorsai to "go down and break all those statues of the public bathhouse." Obediently, "he went down and broke them all except one."[90] Several unanswered questions make it difficult to adduce this passage as historical evidence: Who is Bar Dorsai? What is the relationship between him and the prominent rabbinic figure of his time, R. Yohanan? Why would R. Yohanan want these statues shattered? (After all, the editors of the text tied this incident to a legal concept the rabbis call "nullification," the removal of idolatrous status from an artifact, in order to allow the use of the item.) And most curiously, did these actions reported in the *Yerushalmi* actually take place? Breaking statues, especially on such a large scale, never sat well with the imperial and municipal authorities. A similar incident in the public bathhouse of Antioch in the fourth century led to mass arrests, trials, and executions of both the perpetrators and the city councillors, and the city would have suffered much more had not one of its dignitaries been able to appease the emperor.[91] Is that what R. Yohanan had in mind? Probably not. Unfortunately, there is no way of knowing what this terse anecdote means or whether it has any basis in historical reality. Nevertheless, this has not deterred modern scholars from offering fantastic speculations about it.[92] At the very least, it is safe to say that the statues of the bathhouse did not sit well with whoever formulated these lines in the *Yerushalmi*.

To summarize: rabbinic scholars of the High and Late Empire eras convey neither a definitive, unanimous, nor binding view of sculpture. At least from the standpoint of their daily contact with the statues in Roman public baths, these scholars expressed a wide range of opinions, which they based on the common ways of looking at statues in their time. Some rabbis distinguished among types of statues, according to whether or not they were worshipped, a distinction anchored in the conceptual and legal frameworks regarding sacred objects that were prevalent in the Roman world. Their classifications can be seen as halakhic formulations of common ideas about the ways of "viewing" statuary throughout the Mediterranean, in both Jewish and non-Jewish circles. One opinion (R. Meir's view) classified the entire sculptural environment as a homogeneous landscape, solely made up of idols. Other positions, such as the *ḥakhamim*'s stance in the Mishnah, the views voiced by Rabban Gamaliel and later by R. Yoḥanan, placed statues in different categories, distinguishing between those that transgressed the Jewish way of life and those that were tolerable. Their accommodation enabled those who abided by rabbinic law to live a normal life in the presence of Roman sculpture and to attend the bathhouse, easily and comfortably. Here too, we find the model of "filtered absorption" at play; some rabbinic scholars and possibly other Jews absorbed the shared visual language and perceptions about sacred and profane sculpture that prevailed in the Roman Mediterranean. At the same time they filtered these views into Jewish consciousness, enabling them to maintain their unique attitude toward statues.

The model of filtered absorption obviates the necessity to characterize the attitudes of rabbis, and of the Jews in general, toward the Graeco-Roman culture as unrelentingly hostile and overwhelmingly confrontational. The rabbinic rulings on Roman statuary reflect the pragmatic, discerning attitude of a minority group within the Roman world, which forged its own way of life and defined its own uniqueness with profound awareness of the surrounding cultural landscape. I call the dynamics of this process the poetics of cultural interaction.

PART III

Social and Cultural Textures

CHAPTER SEVEN

A Social Laboratory

STATUS AND HIERARCHY
IN A PROVINCIAL ROMAN BATHHOUSE

IN HIS 1881 NOVEL *The Prince and the Pauper*, Mark Twain relies on an age-old trope: the social switcheroo. He extracts the lowly Tom Canty from his poor surroundings and has him change places and roles with Prince Edward VI, his semi-twin lookalike. The narrative device is as simple as it is useful, enabling Twain to fantasize about the stratification of society and the mechanisms that determine one's standing in the pecking order. The book functions as a literary laboratory, a landscape in which to experiment with the factors that shape social dynamics and tease out possibilities for mobility and change that are rarely available in real life. Twain's conclusion clearly resonates with his readers: all other elements being equal—age, looks, even intelligence and talent—a person's social status mirrors the surroundings that form it. Family resources, wealth, political eminence, and the status symbols that reflect them all endow the fortunate with power and prestige. A potent prince, deprived of his trappings, remains as weak and ordinary as the next man on the street.

Needless to say, these explorations of class and social hierarchy stretch back well before Twain's time, or sixteenth-century Tudor England where he sets his novel. Since the earliest phases of human experience, once people realized the advantages of sticking together, some individuals attained more respect and might than others. The difference usually had to do with access to resources, mainly land and its agricultural produce in ancient times, and other forms of capital in later, more modern periods. Whatever the resource, and whenever the era, and whether in a band, or clan, or tribe, or community, or nation, the basic hierarchy has remained the same. With rare exceptions, those on the top block the rungs of the ladder that allow access from below, aiming to prevent mobility and change.[1]

In the Roman Mediterranean, societies maintained clear-cut differentiations—albeit with variations and nuances—among their members, with tight, closely knit gradations that precluded significant change in any individual's social status. Slaves occupied the lowest rungs of the ladder along with children and most women (other than the very affluent). Peasants and the urban poor toiled just a bit above them. Much higher up, just below the imperial family, stood the wealthiest: members of the senatorial ranks in Rome (but also wealthy members of other ranks, such as the equites) and the richest families from around the empire. Usually these included the great estate owners—the landlords who controlled most of the arable land in rural areas—as well as the owners of urban properties such as apartment blocks and shops in cities and large villages. These individuals also wielded political power, occupying seats in the Roman senate, in the provincial administration, or in city councils all over the Roman world, passing privileges and magisterial appointments down to family members over the generations. In between the rich and the poor stood working people, a large segment of society traversing a wide gamut of social affiliations, from welders to scribes to artisans, local merchants, and civil servants. Though neither wealthy nor penurious, they were inherently assiduous and possessed some ability to rise or fall a few rungs on the ladder by joining professional and religious guilds, via marriage, or through other family ties. With rare exceptions, usually surfacing, even erupting, during times of social unrest, society remained rather stagnant—fixed through the convoluted, yet strictly hierarchical, web of patronage ties between powerful, affluent patrons and their clients. Everyone knew their place.[2]

Some opportunities for social mobility came from enlisting in the army; veterans, upon retirement, were regularly granted plots of land and large sums of discharge bonus, and if recruited from the provinces to the auxiliary forces or the fleet, they could even (although not always) be granted Roman citizenship.[3] Another path for social advancement came through the manumission of slaves. Certain freedmen gained immense wealth and status, and the son of one such freedman—Pertinax—even became an emperor in 193 CE, if only for a brief stint.[4] But for the most part, Roman society embodied what Ramsay MacMullen termed "verticality," a hierarchal system that maintained strict distinctions between people of different status and class.[5]

This pecking order exhibited itself in conspicuous ways. The opulent living conditions of the upper echelons, which clients entered regularly when paying tribute to their patrons and beseeching their favor (a performative exercise known as *salutatio*), contrasted with the shabby residences of everyone else. Outdoors, the rich sauntered through the crowded public spaces, clothed in splendid attire, surrounded by slaves and clients, and often carried in litters—all meant to cut them off from the herd and accentuate their elevated status. Even in spaces where people from all classes of society congregated, such as the theater, and even more so in amphitheaters and circuses (hippodromes), which housed popular gladiatorial contests and chariot racing, strict rules determined seating arrangements based on social gradations. Slaves and children stood in the rear, the poor occupied the back seats, and the front rows were reserved for local dignitaries and their families.[6] Symbols, gestures, and tokens of social hierarchy governed almost every aspect of life in Roman cities and towns, enshrined by both law and local custom and accepted by all members of the public.

Within this well-demarcated social environment, the public bathhouse stands out as a fascinating anomaly. Although some small-sized bathing establishments may have restricted access to a particular group,[7] for the most part almost everyone, at times perhaps even emperors, and surely all the people below them in rank, flocked to the baths—both the huge imperial establishments in the city of Rome and the large communal public baths throughout the empire. Unlike other spaces where the masses mingled—the street, the market, or the theaters and hippodromes—where people displayed signs of social status, once inside the bathhouse the powerful left behind nearly all the symbols that marked their distinction and elevated status. Far from their imposing mansions, no longer borne in litters, and stripped of the fine clothing, jewelry, and other insignia that marked their supremacy, dignified members of society, both men and women, were literally left naked, rubbing shoulders with the lowly multitudes. The narrow confines of bathhouses, crowded and rowdy places, effectively erased the otherwise well-maintained barriers that distinguished social classes in the public space.

Modern scholars agree that public bathhouses featured chaotic and disruptive social arenas but differ in assessing their impact on group and class dynamics. Some scholars see the bathhouse as a "social leveler," a subversive space that undermined the mechanisms of order and caste that prevailed everywhere else in the Roman world. Other scholars argue to the contrary: that the blurring of divisions during the bathing experience enabled the dignified and powerful to reassert their status and show off their might. According to this line of thought, by surrounding themselves with slaves who aggressively cleared the crowds and established a "space within a space" for them, they towered over everyone else. In accordance with their elevated status, they also received special treatment such as having someone guard their clothes, fetch them towels, or apply expensive, perfumed olive oil once they left the water, all of which announced their eminence.[8]

As is often the case with such lofty debates, the truth lies somewhere in between, as neither view takes into account differences in regional social circumstances or the way conditions changed over time. Moreover, while some bathhouses may have embodied one of these extreme paradigms, others probably allowed both (and maybe neither). Bathing institutions should be viewed as containing a range of social dynamics, allowing for different behaviors and norms in the communities where they functioned. Indeed, bathhouses should serve as a laboratory allowing us to better understand the social setting in which they were located. The available sources associated with bath-going reveal some of the textures of ancient communities during Roman times and enable us to trace the interactions among groups and the individuals who composed them. As people shed their clothing, and revealed their bodies, they also unveiled their assumptions and prejudices about themselves and about others.

This chapter utilizes the numerous references to Roman public bathhouses in rabbinic literature to glean insights into the social landscape that characterized the places where they lived and to detect the mechanisms for asserting status and establishing hierarchy available to the patrons of public baths. This testimony is unique because of the peripheral nature of the bathhouses frequented by the rabbis, in the province of Palestine on the eastern shore of the Mediterranean. Most of our information about bathing facilities and the people who attended them derives from Roman and Italian writers or from the central cities of the empire, such as Antioch and other major hubs in Greece, Anatolia, and North Africa. The writings of rabbis offer us an opportunity to engage with a provincial establishment, patronized by citizens of a relatively marginal province. Unlike the earlier chapters in the book, which investigate the interaction of Jews with a particular aspect of the bathing culture, such as nudity and sculpture, this chapter and the next broaden the perspective on life in the public bath. The present chapter examines social structure and the experiences associated with it. We ask: What was the social fabric of bathhouses located in predominantly Jewish areas on the eastern edge of the empire, and the dynamics surrounding them, in comparison to other more central areas of the Roman world?

The Social Makeup of the Baths

Rabbinic texts, as shown throughout this book, regularly refer to the people who attended the public baths, including rabbinic figures. They judge their actions and debate and celebrate the experience. They also discuss non-Jewish individuals or groups whom the rabbinic authors encountered in bathhouses or expected to find there. A story set in the bathhouse typically informs us not only about the physical layout of the place, its equipment, and installations but also about its social makeup. Similarly, halakhic rules for attending bathing institutions occasionally mention the folks who frequented them. In other words, rabbinic authors tell us not just about the how and the why and the what of the bathhouse but also about the who and the where. While no single rabbinic text provides a comprehensive picture of the baths or catalogues its patrons systematically, such a picture can be pieced together from the details scattered in numerous passages throughout the rabbinic corpus. Although this composite portrayal is surely incomplete, and we have no guarantee that all the details applied to every bathhouse at all times, nevertheless it can shed light on the social fabric of the bathhouse (or at least bathhouses attended by rabbinic scholars).

Starting at the bottom tier of the social ladder, ample documentation in rabbinic literature indicates that the poor swarmed the baths, begging for whatever charity patrons were willing to part with. Surely beggars could be found everywhere in ancient cities, but the entrance to the public bath, before patrons undressed, was a particularly opportune spot. A rabbinic passage in the fourth-century *Yerushalmi* features this space and comments on the dynamics that transpired there. The text discusses *tsedaqa*, the Jewish ethical and religious obligation for charity. The author recognizes that swindlers sometimes take advantage of the benevolence of others and presents an anecdote about the two famous third-century Galilean scholars, R. Yoḥanan and Reish Lakish, who upon "entering to bathe in the public bathhouse (in the city of) of Tiberias" came across a certain beggar who asked them for charity. The scholars put him off, promising to attend to his needs when they left; but by the time they returned, they found him dead. Wishing at least now to extend him the courtesy they originally denied him, the two scholars start to prepare the poor man's body for burial; in the process they find a hidden pouch full of coins. The vagrant, they conclude, was actually a confidence man.[9]

Putting to the side the moral of the story, or the untenable (and for this discussion, unnecessary) question of whether the incident actually occurred, the setting of this anecdote provides a compelling glimpse into the world of the baths. We see the social mingling that occurred at the entrances of baths, where charitable and indigent members of the community rubbed shoulders. Other non-rabbinic sources reflect the same situation. For one, the Yakto mosaic, which depicts a snippet occurring outside the entrance of the bath, offers a visual representation of this situation that brings together an exquisitely dressed dignitary, a slave, and a merchant (see fig. 11). In the same vein, a sermon by John Chrysostom, a prolific Christian author and archbishop of Constantinople originally born in Syria in the fourth century, refers to the poor who crowd and take shelter at the entrances of public bathhouses, just where the rabbinic scholars encountered their bogus beggar.[10] A later rabbinic text praises the nations of the world who built public bathhouses in which the wealthy and the poor intermingle, and thus provide the opportunity for charity and kindness. Another rabbinic text speaks of other unfortunate members of society, orphans and widows, who take advantage of the presence of rabbinic scholars at the entrance to the baths to ask for communal relief.[11] Again and again we see the essentially same picture: the needy gather in the public baths to beg for alms, a common scene that numerous sources recorded.

Just above this lowest stratum of society, the baths welcomed everyone who lived in the area. As shown in detail earlier, women of all ages and of all ranks, fine ladies and prostitutes, regularly frequented the public bathhouse. Children and slaves accompanied them, as well as a host of men from different walks of life. Some attended to simply enjoy the baths, while others, like doctors and healers, food and oil vendors, and a varied range of service providers (barbers, masseuses, scribes, and even lawyers, to name a few), came to this place to offer their services and make a living off those who wished to use them.[12]

Ancient sources do not pay much attention to children, but their presence in public baths can be inferred. Inscriptions, for example, both exempt them from paying entry fees and mourn their death by drowning and by other hazards.[13] Rabbinic literature confirms the presence of children in bathhouses in a series of passages documenting the way some communities regulated what they regarded as indecent physical exposure among family members in the baths. One passage states that when the two sons of a prominent rabbinic figure arrived in the village of Chabulon, a Jewish settlement in western lower Galilee, and wished to visit the local bath, the residents informed them of a prevailing local custom, which deemed it inappropriate for two brothers to bathe together.[14] A different rabbinic text states that a son should not attend the bath with his father, father-in-law, or teacher, so as to not see them naked.[15] Other groups around the Mediterranean, including the Romans themselves, also deemed it improper for a father and son to bathe in public together. Cicero speaks to that as well as others.[16] Admittedly, none of these literary iterations specifies the age of the brothers or sons involved. Hence, theoretically, they may be speaking of adolescents or adults. However, mention of sons seems to indicate that families with young children attended public bathhouses together.

We are on much more solid footing when it comes to the function of slaves as part of the public bathing experience. Numerous references throughout rabbinic literature attest to their presence in the baths (discussed in detail in the next section of this chapter). Less clear is whether slaves also bathed or whether they were there only to serve their owners. Garrett Fagan's conclusions regarding the Roman world are consistent with the situations reflected in the rabbinic material: for the most part, male slaves and female maids either worked as part of the bath's staff or accompanied their masters—the wealthy patrons who could afford them.[17]

As mentioned earlier, the upper echelons of society often attended the same bathing facilities as everyone else, even though private bathing facilities were available along with the larger public establishments, both those built into villas and mansions of the wealthy and those maintained by specific organizations that limited their access to its members.[18] This may strike modern readers as odd, since members of today's privileged class generally confine themselves to private spaces or exclusive clubs; when was the last time you came across a billionaire, a governor, or any other well-known celebrity at your local community pool or at the public beach? While the existence of private installations shows that the well-off sometimes chose to use them, much evidence affirms that these same wealthy individuals and their family members, perhaps on occasion those as highly placed as emperors, preferred public institutions to their private facilities and attended them regularly.[19] Below I explore the reasons for this unexpected phenomenon.

Rabbinic literature too reaffirms this practice, as it shows its authors were well aware that wealthy and eminent people frequented the public baths together with everyone else. Texts explicitly speak of "rich men" arriving in the bathhouses, or of "important people" and the differential treatment they receive in those communal shared spaces (more on special treatment for the rich below).[20] In one passage a rabbinic scholar mentions a "wealthy woman" who comes to the baths without her husband.[21] Another *halakhah* stipulates the proper way to treat a king in the public baths (it is forbidden to stare at him), and a literary segment concocts a parable around the figure of a slave preparing the public bath for the arrival of a prince. While these passages seem entirely theoretical or fictional, they show that the situations they evoke were feasible in the imaginations of at least some rabbinic authors, which suggests to me they were perhaps feasible in real life as well.[22]

The picture that emerges from these rabbinic texts from the eastern reaches of the empire fits well into the broader social reality prevailing in public bathhouses throughout the Roman world: men, women, and children from all walks of life mingled in the baths in what, at first glance, may seem a seamless mixture. The lowly peasants and artisans swam in the pools and immersed themselves in the basins alongside potent dignitaries; powerful city officials exercised in the courtyards together with the people they governed, while children of all families jumped around and played games together; and female members of highly esteemed families shared the steam rooms or the massage tables with ordinary men and women. But this somewhat idyllic portrayal of social integration and leveling is only partially true.

Devices of Social Differentiation

Everyone went to the baths for more or less the same reason: leisure and socialization—to dip in the water, clean the body, and rest the soul, all while gossiping, bonding, politicking, and advancing financial and communal interests alongside family, friends, and fellow members of the community. But not everyone went to the baths in the same way, nor did they expect to be treated in the same manner. An elaborate system of practices, exceptions, and gestures distinguished esteemed bathers from the rank and file, elevating the former above the latter and announcing their affluence and social acumen.

A closer look at the various activities that took place in public bathhouses, and an analysis of the delicate interactions that transpired there, as well the long-term effects they forged, reveals a fascinating system that established and fostered the social pyramid. This becomes particularly interesting in a space that blurs the customary lines that divided people and announced their relative rank. It is as if the social body, when stricken by a set of afflictions that undermined the pecking order of its limbs, generated alternative devices or adapted existing techniques to overcome the damage. People visiting the baths operated on two different dimensions.

On one level, everyone used the bathhouse and the luxuries it provided in roughly the same way, strolling through the gardens when available, exercising and playing in the outdoor courts (known as the *palaestrae*), swimming in the pools, and passing from one heated room to another as they immersed in basins, washed, and enjoyed massages and saunas. But on another level, as they used the baths, they interacted with other patrons they met there, and those dealings were not the same for everyone. Certain perceptions informed these encounters and required certain conventions and formulations. All of these re-created the temporarily suspended divisions of that community.

Graeco-Roman sources, both literature and art, document these social trajectories in some detail, and the rabbinic corpus offers an opportunity to reexamine them and further decipher their complexities. The rabbis' tidbits, anecdotes, and legal and exegetical discussions serve here as a porthole through which to observe and study social dynamics at the public baths, as they took shape in one particular eastern province of the Roman Empire, and through the lenses of the ancient Jewish scholars, the rabbis.

SLAVES

Slaves provided the most obvious of means available to distinguished members of society who wished to restore their momentarily depleted status in the baths, not those belonging to the private, municipal, or at times even imperial owner of the bathhouse and worked there as part of the facility's staff but the slaves owned by patrons who attended the baths and brought them along.[23] Numerous rabbinic texts recognize the fact, well established in other Graeco-Roman sources as well, that servants accompanied their masters to the public baths. But in these literary segments, even more illuminating than the mere presence of slaves and maids tagging along with their owners are the duties that the rabbinic authors assign to the slaves.

Rabbinic texts typically refer to the task of a servant toward his owner as "carrying his apparel to the public baths."[24] This observation about the role of slaves circulated widely in rabbinic literature from the early third-century texts where it appears first, through numerous variations over a few hundred years of literary attestations, and across the regions of rabbinic activity, from Roman Palestine to the centers of rabbinic learning in Persian Mesopotamia. The image of a servant, male or female, who walks behind or next to his owner, or at times leads the way, while carrying the bathing gear, clothing, and other needed utensils to the public baths surfaces in legal discussions of the rabbis on various topics, often adding other bathhouse duties of the slave. One text includes "putting on his (master's) sandals [and] loosening his sandals," and another extended the activities of the slave even further to encompass the entire bathing process, from start to finish: "undresses him, washes him, anoints him (with oil), scrapes him (=the body from the oil), and dresses him."[25]

This image of a slave servicing his owner in the baths extends beyond rabbinic legal discourse. In a parable that models the bond of the God of Israel and his people on the relationship between a king and his slave, a rabbinic author includes a short segment involving the bathhouse: "once the king enters the city he says to him (=the servant): 'put on my sandals and take my apparel in front of me to the public bath.'"[26] This command echoes almost verbatim orders of owners to their slaves, as recorded in writings from all over the Roman world. For example, the author of the popular Greek story known as the *Life of Aesop*, which most modern scholars date to the second century CE, has the master, Xanthus, instruct his mischievous slave Aesop, "Pick up the oil flask and towels and let's go to the baths."[27] Other literary, non-legal excerpts in the rabbinic corpus follow a similar pattern but add color and variety to the assignments of the slave in the baths. In a midrashic expansion of the biblical story about the matriarch Sarah and her newly acquired maid Hagar, the rabbinic author draws on the widely circulated image of a servant carrying her owner's bathing paraphernalia, saying that Sarah ordered her maid to carry "buckets and bathing apparel" to the public baths.[28] Rabbinic stories also mention still further duties. In one, Gothic slaves escort the aging scholar R. Abbahu to the public baths of Tiberias while providing him support and helping him walk on the slippery floors,[29] and in another a slave pours a cup of wine for the distinguished and wealthy R. Judah the Patriarch as he exits the pool of a public bathhouse (more on the latter text below).[30]

These practices became an everyday spectacle that people routinely and repeatedly witnessed. A slave or a group of them strode ahead or tagged after their owners, carrying the full complement of items needed for bathing, known in Latin as *instrumenta balnei*: clean garments and robes to wear afterward, linen to dry the bodies, caskets holding toiletries, oil flasks, and small bottles made of pottery or glass for perfumes (known as *aryballoi* or *alabastra*), together with the necessary curved blades (known as *strigilēs*) and other tools to scrape the body, combs and cosmetics for women, all topped with buckets to pour water on bathers (known in Latin as *situlae*), a jar of wine and cups, and other foodstuffs. The more slaves a person owned, the more gear they toted.

It was a sight that caught the eye. Indeed, some of the most evocative depictions of bathhouse scenery produced by ancient artists depict a master, male or female, surrounded by servants hauling a collection of objects, both large and small, needed for the bathing experience. A brilliant depiction of this theme has survived in the Esquiline treasure, a trove of silver artifacts from the fourth century CE, unearthed at the foot of the Esquiline Hill in Rome in the late eighteenth century. One of its most fabulous objects is the Projecta Casket, a two-piece silver box and lid, decorated in relief, and used in ancient times to carry toiletries and other items to the baths. On one of the lid panels it shows a train of slaves, led by a distinguished matron, standing at the colonnaded entrance of an impressive bathhouse building, shown in the background crowned by ten domes. Whereas the rich *domina* stands with empty hands, dignified and towering above her servants, the slaves hold small chests (one quite similar to the Projecta Casket itself), clothes, ewers, ladles, and other utensils (fig. 23).[31]

Similarly, although portraying a smaller entourage, a mosaic from a bathhouse in a fourth-century CE Roman Villa del Casale excavated outside of Piazza Armerina in Sicily shows another procession to the baths where a wealthy woman (perhaps the lady of the villa) stands at the center, wearing magnificent clothes and expensive jewelry (more on clothes and jewelry below) and flanked by two boys (her sons, perhaps?) and two maids on the edges (fig. 24). Here too, the artistic composition contrasts the owner and the boys, who walk hands free, and the slaves, one of whom carries a large, shallow casket with folded clothes and the other holds a hanging box for bathing paraphernalia.[32] Other mosaics from the same bathing facility in Piazza Armerina showcase additional stages in the bathing process—undressing and preparing for the bath, oiling and scrubbing the body, and drying it. In all, slaves assist the patron and matron. They stand beside their owners holding sandals, clothes, buckets to pour water, strigils to scrape the oil, and linen for drying the body (fig. 25).[33] Clearly in the public imagination, as captured in these works of art, when wealthy people bathed, slaves attended their needs. The visual language and the literary articulations of both Graeco-Roman and rabbinic texts concur about this feature of the bathing experience.

Observers could not miss the contrast between the slave owner along with his/her family, friends, and clients, strolling to the baths leisurely and freely, or at times even carried on a litter (a practice known to the rabbis as well), and the slaves, with their hands full of gear and equipment, striving to keep up. This was so widely dispersed and engraved in the collective consciousness that people would place bets against each other where the

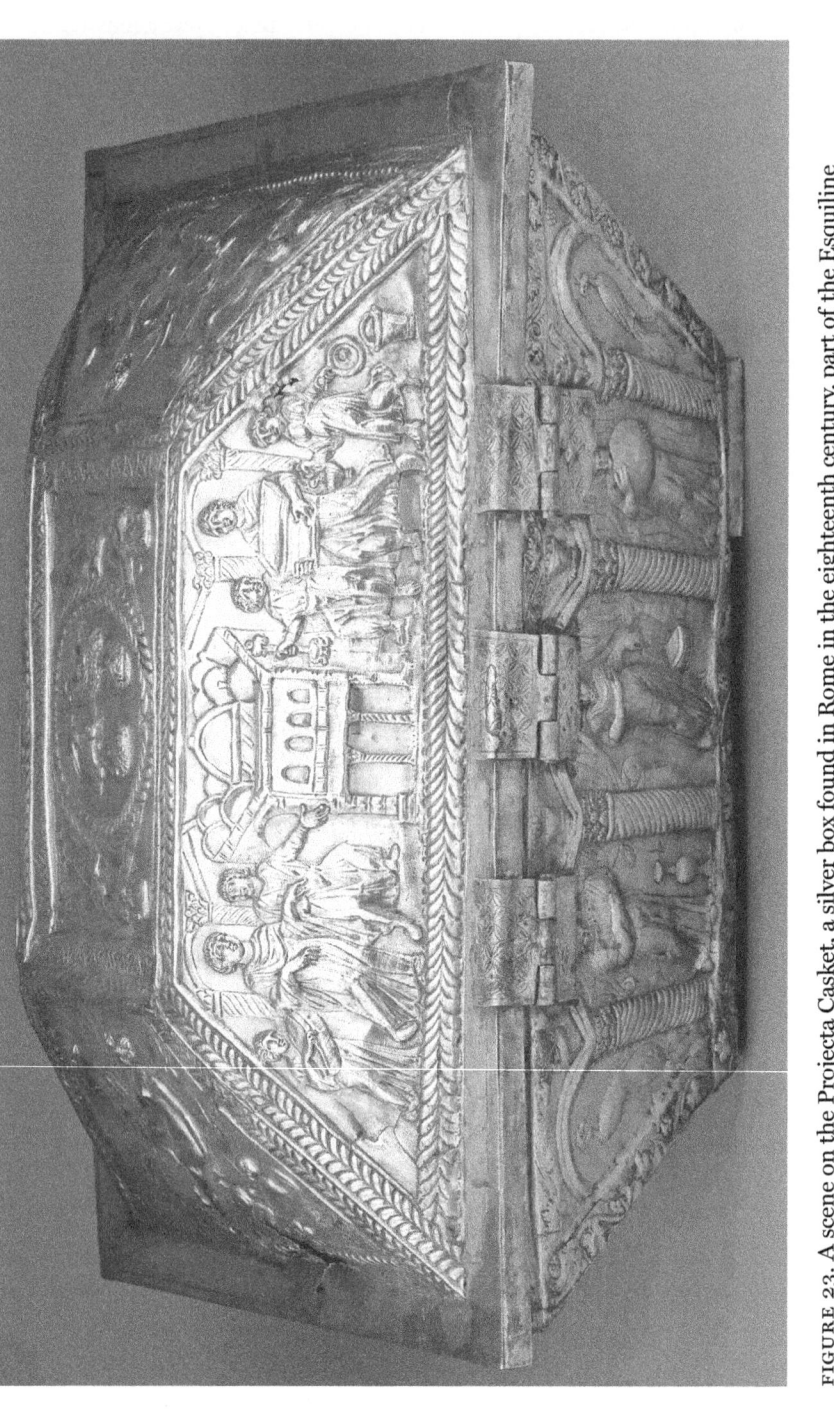

FIGURE 23. A scene on the Projecta Casket, a silver box found in Rome in the eighteenth century, part of the Esquiline Treasure, decorated in the repoussé ("pushed up") technique. It shows a matron (in the middle of the group on left) and her slaves approaching a bathhouse crowned with many domes. *Credit*: The Projecta Casket, Late Roman. Rome, San Francesco di Paola ai Monti. Image courtesy of the British Museum.

FIGURE 24. A fourth-century CE mosaic from Villa Romana del Casale, in Piazza Armerina, Sicily, showing a well-dressed matron, her two sons, and two maids on their way to the baths. The maid on the left carries a casket with folded clean clothes, and the one on the right shoulders a bag (with unknown content) and holds a small stringed box for bathing paraphernalia. *Credit:* Photograph by Ludwig 14, licensed by Creative Commons (CC BY-SA 4.0), courtesy of Wikimedia Commons.

payoff would be for the losing party to carry out these slave-like duties and take the winner's bathing instruments to the public baths. Rabbinic literature preserved the Aramaic articulation of this wager in a popular expression attributed in various forms to third- and fourth-century scholars: "if anyone can explain (a certain complex scholarly matter) to me I will carry his bathing gear to the public bath."[34]

Once in the baths, some owners surely ordered their slaves to wait outside.[35] But servants usually entered the baths with their masters and assumed additional roles inside. Some stood near the open cubicles and shelves of the changing room (the *apodyterium*; see fig. 13) and guarded the clothes of their disrobed owners. Thieves roamed the baths, and although bathing establishments occasionally provided some attendants, also slaves (known as *capsarii*), to keep watch over the clothes and belongings of the customers, personal slaves offered more commitment and enhanced protection.[36] Furthermore, as detailed in the rabbinic references above, slaves attended their masters, assisting and carrying out a range of tasks as needed: undressing and dressing, pouring water from buckets onto their owners, applying oil, scraping their body, fetching food and wine (more on this below), and drying them with towels.

FIGURE 25. Mosaic from Villa Romana del Casale, Piazza Armerina, Sicily, showing slaves attending a patron (probably their owner) in the baths. In the upper register the master stands naked in the middle, with the slave on the left rubbing his shoulder and the slave on the right holding a strigil and a small container of oil. The two slaves in the lower register wear loincloths with their names inscribed (Tite and Cassi), cords knotted around their necks, and anklets on their right leg. The slave on the right also has a cone-shaped hat and holds a stick with a broom-like (or sponge) brush at its end. The one on the left holds a bucket. It is unclear whether these two slaves are cleaning the bathhouse or anointing or washing their owners. *Credit:* Photograph courtesy of Giuseppe Anello and Dreamstime, licensed by Dreamstime.

Owners sometimes assigned other tasks to their slaves. In one famous Graeco-Roman story a master who travels out of town on business instructs his slave to guard the fidelity of his wife, and so when the lady attended the baths, the devoted servant attached himself to her "like glue, holding the hem of her robe in his hand."[37] In other ancient texts, slaves function as bodyguards, shoving people aside and opening a path for their owners to walk through the crowded space of the public baths; on other occasions slaves shielded them from the chaos and violence that could transpire there. In one of his letters, the second-century CE Pliny the Younger reports about one senator, Larcius Macedo, whose slave pushed another bather while clearing the way for his master in the public baths of Rome. The other man, who happened to be an equestrian (a high rank but not as formidable as a senator), aimed a slap at the pugnacious slave but hit the senator, nearly knocking him down (incidentally, this same Macedo would later be murdered by his own slaves while in the private bath of his mansion).[38] Slaves were instrumental to their masters in navigating the mayhem of the baths, at times applying excessive force and engaging in fights and violence of their own making; one such imaginary incident informs the rhetorical exercise in the textbook known as *Rhetorica ad Herennium*, in which a man of lower standing complains to a wealthy patron about the harm he suffered from his violent slave in the baths.[39]

Finally, the sound of the slaves' participation in bathing usually goes unheard. The rowdy environment of the public bathhouse resonates in various sources; at times, the noise rises to deafening decibels. Servants partook in this cacophony. One of the dialogues attributed to the second-century, Syrian-born scholar Lucian of Samosata offers a scathing critique of the pretentious habits of elites in the Roman world, with particular attention to their conduct in the public baths. In one scene he ridicules slaves who walk in front of their masters on the way to the baths, shouting back to warn them about obstacles, bumps, and holes in the road.[40] A few centuries later, the historian Ammianus Marcellinus, another native of the Roman east who became a high imperial official, expresses similar annoyance and distaste for the brash behavior of slaves in the public baths. In a lengthy diatribe against the snobbery of the self-proclaimed elite, Ammianus describes their entourage of servants, at times numbering fifty, the number also mentioned in the previous text by Lucian. Upon arriving at the public baths, they voice loud demands for special treatment for their patrons, bullying the attendants and other women bathers.[41] Similarly, in one of their stories rabbinic authors mention a visit to the baths by a high-ranking Roman official, surrounded by a retinue of slaves.[42]

Taking all this evidence together, the dual function of slaves in the Roman baths becomes very clear. On the practical level, slaves operated in their regular capacity, assisting their owners in the daily tasks involved in going to the baths, a range of chores documented by rabbinic authors and confirmed by other, Graeco-Roman sources. They carried the bathing appliances to and from the baths and lent a hand in undressing their masters, guarding their clothes, applying and scraping oil, and so forth. In this respect, rabbinic sources document the typical duties of slaves in public baths all over the Roman world.

On the social level the function of slaves in public baths, as seen by rabbinic authors and illustrated in the visual presentations of surviving artistic compositions, adds a dimension to the bathing experience that may go unnoticed. Within a social landscape that erased many markers of status and brought people from all strata of society into intimate, unusual proximity, the presence of a coterie of slaves, following certain patrons of the baths and fulfilling their needs, as well as shoving, pushing, and yelling at other bathers, separated those individuals from the crowds and marked them as distinct from the rest of the bathers.

Most people carried out the minutiae of bathing on their own, or paid for services offered by the bathhouse staff, the *capsarii* who guarded cloths, or a masseuse who offered services to those who could afford it. But that kind of paid experience struck a very different cord than that of the affluent, who had personal slaves at their disposal to do all their bidding. An anecdote about the emperor Hadrian in the *Scriptores historiae Augustae* highlights the different experience of the bathers without slaves. According to the story, in the bathhouse, the emperor comes across an army veteran who once served under him. The man was "rubbing his back and the rest of his body against the wall." When asked by the emperor why "the marble (of the wall) [is] rubbing him," the man replied, "because he did not own a slave." The gracious emperor immediately (of course) lent one of his slaves to the veteran to perform this service for him.[43] Rabbis were also aware of the ways ordinary people in the baths had to take care of their own needs. While laying out the laws of the Sabbath, one rabbinic author observes that "a man applies oil on himself" and then rubs it in by scrubbing his body on a piece of leather-cloth. Clearly this individual did not have a slave at his disposal. They also acknowledge the alternative method, mentioning the possibility of paying the *'olyar*, a provider of oil and services associated with it in the baths, to perform certain services.[44]

Fictional or not, the scene about Hadrian and the rabbinic references convey the experience of bathers without slaves. Unless you have servants to pamper you, you must rub your back against the wall like an animal. Slaves walking around their masters, fending off nuisances and standing ready to serve them as needed, carved out an imagined space for their owners within the public layout of the bathhouse. The slaves' bodies elevated their owners above other bathers. In a place that undermined their social status, the presence of slaves offered wealthy and prestigious people a way of displaying and maintaining their prominence. Rabbinic authors corroborate other representations of the importance of a retinue of slaves in art and texts from around the Mediterranean, showing that the social experience of Jews in a peripheral province on the eastern edges of the empire was similar to that of the rest of the Roman world, while at the same time adding substance and nuance to it.

FOOD AND DRINK

Patrons of public bathhouses generally spent the entire afternoon there, and, as one would expect, between dipping in the baths, working out in the courtyards, or enjoying a massage, they also consumed food and beverages. References in ancient texts, documentary evidence from inscriptions, and plenty of archaeological material all confirm that eating and drinking, while not an essential aspect of the bathing experience, regularly took place in public bathing facilities.[45] In Pompeii and Herculaneum, for example, where the eruption of Mt. Vesuvius in 79 CE preserved large portions of these southern Italian cities almost intact, archaeologists unearthed numerous eateries—bars, small restaurants, and shops (known in Latin as *tabernae* and *popinae*), as well as simpler food stands. More than a few of these stood close to the baths and occasionally were even built into the structures' outer walls, facing the adjacent streets. Thus, they could cater to both potential customers outside the baths and the multitudes who flocked to the baths daily (see diagram 1).[46]

Inside the facilities, merchants and vendors offered bathers additional food from permanent and temporary, stationary and movable premises: sturdy stands, improvised kiosks, and carriages of all types and sizes. They displayed fresh food, baked goods, fried fare, and an array of beverages to the hungry crowds. A first-century letter by Seneca the Younger intended to complain about the boisterous environment of the baths but in the process provides a glimpse into the lively food scene that bustled in its courtyards and near its entrances: "The cake-seller with his varied cries, the sausage man, the confectioner, and all the vendors of food hawking their wares, each with his own distinctive intonation."[47] Indeed, graffiti inscriptions from Pompeii confirm this exuberant reality: one message painted on the wall announces a food stand that stood below (now gone); another enumerates a stall's menu items and their prices. It is easy to assume that snacks and fast food are relatively modern inventions, but these findings prove otherwise. Ingredients have surely changed over the centuries but not to the extent you might expect. Sausages, cutlets, hog's fat, bread, nuts, and drinks are all listed, as are hardboiled eggs, a favorite of the ancients.[48] Martial, the first-century satirist and self-proclaimed bathhouse connoisseur in the city of Rome, ridicules the gluttony of one Aemilius, who consumed eggs together with lettuce and some fish while attending the *thermae* in the city.[49] Apparently, if we believe the somewhat unreliable author of the *Scriptores historiae Augustae*, even emperors fancied eggs after bathing, in particular the young Alexander Severus, who took them with milk and bread, rounding off the repast with a sip of mead.[50] When it came to drinking, only the emperor could acquire fresh water straight from one of the city's aqueducts, but ordinary citizens settled for wine, which often resulted in drunken rowdiness, reinforcing the rough image of the baths and exasperating abstemious bathers.[51]

Writers from the East such as Clement of Alexandria refute the notion, mistakenly advanced by some modern scholars, of a clear geographical difference in eating habits between East and West. Some recent scholars imply that patrons of the baths in the eastern parts of the Roman Empire were less insatiable than their western counterparts.[52] In his sharp critique of excess in the baths, Clement, a late second-century Christian scholar, condemns the rich, who "wine and dine" in the baths.[53] Clement's exaggeration of the gluttonous atmosphere in the baths nevertheless confirms that people regularly ate and drank there, and the wealthy stood out by eating more elaborately.

Without the critical tone of their Christian contemporary Clement, rabbinic authors confirm that people ate and drunk at their local bathhouse. Some rabbinic stories take "eating and drinking" in the baths for granted. For example, in a legendary tale about the martyrdom of two second-century scholars, R. Simon and R. Yishmael, the two protagonists reminisce about the time they went into the baths and engaged in "eating and drinking."[54] Clearly, in the author's mind, bathhouse experience included gastronomy.

Some texts are more specific. A third-century rabbinic passage states that olives sprinkled with brine were "sold at the entrances of bathhouses."[55] Another tradition, from the fifth-century Babylonian Talmud (and admittedly murky and perhaps entirely invented or distorted), preserves the recipe of a certain vegetarian snack that people munched on as a refreshment after the heat of the baths. According to those scholars, eating it after bathing would cool their bodies "from the hair of their scalp to the nails of their toes."[56] It may even be that some rabbis were familiar with the baths' favorite snack: hardboiled eggs. In one place the Palestinian Talmud quotes some late third-century rabbinic scholars who praise the taste of hardboiled eggs offered to them as they approached the hot springs of Gadara.[57]

Rabbinic scholars never attempted to provide a full description of the food consumed in public bathhouses. The scanty references above stem from cases in Jewish law (*halakhah*) that they considered and deliberated. Obviously, rabbis saw no point in mentioning food that clearly violated Jewish dietary laws, such as pork sausages or wine produced by gentiles, as there was no doubt that they were prohibited in the baths and everywhere else. Nor did they find any reason to highlight the kosher items prepared and sold by Jews in bathhouses, which they and their fellow Jews gobbled without hesitation. Their few incidental references to food in the bathhouse simply confirm the widespread existence of a food scene in the bathhouses of the Roman east.

Rabbinic literature also mentions drinking wine in the baths, preferably after plunging in the water, which seems to have been a widespread habit in the provinces of the Roman east and beyond. One rabbinic tradition transmits the ingredients of a cocktail called *'aluntit*, which includes old wine, fresh water, and balsam. A comment in the text, which follows the description of the drink, explains: "They prepare it in the bathhouse to chill [the body]." That comment then continues with an anecdote about rabbinic scholars in Persia who went to the baths, imbibed the drink, and experienced that sensation. It cooled their body "from the hair of your scalp to the nails of your toes."[58] While I doubt that this passage can be tied to the bathhouse experience of Roman Palestine, it surely captures the vibe of drinking in the baths, which evidently transcended imperial boundaries.

Other rabbinic traditions, more clearly grounded in the realities of Roman Palestine, locate the drinking of wine as an integral part of the bathhouse routine. I already mentioned the reference to "eating and drinking" in the baths as part of the martyrdom stories of Simon and Yishmael. In a discussion of Jewish custom that prohibits eating in the daytime before Passover (in order to preserve one's appetite for the big celebratory meal of the Seder that evening), the Palestinian Talmud (the *Yerushalmi*) includes a segment about the prominent third-century Rabban Judah II who attended the bathhouse and became thirsty. Rabbinic scholars debated whether drinking falls under the eating ban of the day, but the very question assumes that on ordinary days consumption of wine in the baths was the norm. Similarly, one rabbinic scholar mentions this practice of drinking wine after the bath in another halakhic discussion regarding benedictions over food.[59] Pointing to the same reality, an anecdote about Judah II's grandfather (discussed in more detail below), the illustrious Judah the Patriarch, confirms the habitual drinking of wine in bathhouses. It portrays a scene in a certain public bathhouse, where just as the Patriarch emerges from a basin or a pool his slave promptly pours him a cup of wine, a well-known role of slaves documented elsewhere in the empire as well.[60] Since the tale centers on completely different topics, inclusion of the segment about the wine mainly indicates that the person who told the story did not think it was out of the ordinary.

In the same vein, a rabbinic fable about the emperor Titus places him in a public bath, and as he finishes washing, he promptly receives a drink of wine.[61] The author calls this beverage by the Aramaic term *dipla' potayrin*, which seems to be based on the Greek *diplopotērion*, a double wine goblet, and the reference suggests it is a known custom: "the post-bath double cup of wine."[62] Other passages in rabbinic literature record the practice of taking a double glass of wine after bathing in the exact same way, showing that this had become part of the jargon of bath-goers.[63] Knowledge about this custom reached all the way to the rabbinic centers in Persia; one statement in the Babylonian Talmud speaks of a wine goblet which "in the West (the Bavli's regular term for Roman Palestine) they say is a cup of the bathhouses."[64] Frequent use of the Greek-Aramized name—by multiple rabbinic authors and in varied contexts—shows, in my opinion, that the ancient Jewish scholars in Roman Palestine regularly enjoyed (or at least were familiar with) this popular type of a double drink in the public bathhouses.

As these sources show, Jewish people in the Roman east, like their counterparts elsewhere in the empire, ate food and drank wine in the baths, though the menus were not preserved as in Pompeii, Herculaneum, and Ostia Antica. The distribution techniques of the merchants also go unattested. They were apparently different than the stationary, fully built bars and kiosks of Roman Italy and some other places, which do not appear in the archaeological record of baths in the East. The evidence from rabbinic literature establishes the custom of eating and drinking as regular and widely available in the eastern provinces as it was the western parts of the empire. It also thickens the description of this practice by adding illuminating details about specific foods, their names, and the experiences around them.

In addition to the information they provide about the cuisine in (at least some) public bathhouses in the Roman east, the texts cited here highlight another dimension of bathing, which all too often goes unrecognized: the role of food and drink in the social dynamics of the bathhouse.

Consider the following anecdote, which found its way into a midrashic compilation from Roman Palestine:

> Rabbi (Judah the Patriarch) came out of the bath, wrapped himself in his garments, [and] sat attending to the needs of the people. His slave poured him a cup (of wine), but since he was busy dealing with the needs of the people, he [couldn't] avail himself to take it (=the cup) from him (=the slave). The (ignored) slave became drowsy and (finally) fell asleep. When Rabbi (Judah the Patriarch eventually) turned and looked at him (=the sleeping slave) he exclaimed: "rightly said (the biblical king) Solomon (in Eccl. 5:11): 'sweet is the sleep of the (poor) worker, whether he ate little or much, but the surfeit of the rich does not allow him to fall asleep,' just like us that we attend to the needs of the people, (and so) are not allowed to fall asleep."[65]

The author intended to illustrate the biblical wisdom that contrasts the behavior of the satiated wealthy to the hungry poor. To do so, he enlisted (or perhaps invented—to the current study, it does not make a difference) this anecdote about the famous Judah the Patriarch in the public bathhouse—whereas the illustrious Patriarch diligently attended to his public duties, his less attentive slave dozed off. Whether or not it actually took place, the backdrop of the story captures some of the social dynamics of the baths. With only a few words, as befits the genre of the short anecdote, the author arranges the scene around a prominent local figure, Judah the Patriarch, a wealthy patron of sorts, and his encounter with fellow bathers. In the backdrop, the author creates a theater-like panorama embedded with details and artifacts meant to establish Judah's eminence.

Although the text is silent about this, the Jewish Patriarch presumably started his visit to the bathhouse like everyone else: shedding his clothes, wandering through the pools and rooms, washing his body, and enjoying the comforts of the bathing facilities. The anecdote begins when he emerges from the water. A hierarchy is immediately established: his body is quickly wrapped in robes, a seat is promptly arranged, a slave rushes to offer him a cup of wine, and the people, who had been rubbing shoulders and naked bodies with the eminent personage just a moment earlier, now humbly line up before him to pitch their "needs" and seek his advice and assistance. One can only speculate about the people's appeals: business requests, complaints about disputes that this powerful dignitary can resolve, and perhaps, although not explicitly mentioned in the text, requests for his guidance in matters of Jewish law.

To play out this scene, in which an elite member of society engages with common folks in the public baths, the rabbinic storyteller meticulously re-created the gradations of the social hierarchy within the setting of this establishment. He employed various literary techniques and symbols of power in order to establish the social division and convey the elevated status of the Patriarch. First among these signs of the Patriarch's stature are the clothes with which he is immediately garbed when he exits the water, while the text remains silent about how the other people were dressed. Since the anecdote takes place in the bath and speaks of bathers lining up before the Patriarch and beseeching his help, these common folks may still have been naked or only scantily clad. Furthermore, although not explicitly described in this short anecdote but most likely imagined by the listeners, the garments worn by the Patriarch as he came out of the water would be of a quality that expressed the stature of the man who wore them (more below on clothes as signs of social power). The disparity between the important man garbed in an elegant outfit immediately evident as he emerges from the water and everyone else serves to elevate him above the others.

Another feature that projects social authority in the story involves the chair on which the Patriarch sits, while everyone else evidently stands. Where did that chair come from and what was it like? The author remains sparing with information and detail (as befits his compact literary style). However, a mosaic floor from North Africa, unearthed in the archaeological excavations at a Roman villa in Sidi Ghrib, about twenty-five miles southwest of Carthage in today's Tunisia (fig. 26), suggests what that chair may have looked like, or how the audience of the rabbinic anecdote may have envisioned it. The mosaic depicts a matron in a bathhouse, perhaps on her private estate, surrounded by the typical bathing paraphernalia and flanked by her two maids. In the middle of the artistic composition, she sits on a high-backed chair, elevated on a small podium. Lavishly carved, padded with cushions, and delimited on the sides by two delicate, beaded strings that hold the backrest and the seat base together (perhaps the chair could be folded), it looks more like a miniature throne than a utilitarian chair.[66] It surely accentuates the matron's stature in the mosaic, and it, or something of its kind, could have achieved a similar effect for the seated Judah the Patriarch in the bathhouse scene.

Finally and most illuminating for the discussion here: the wine. Once Judah emerges from the water and is clothed, a slave hurries to pour him a cup of wine. Indeed, as the sources discussed above show, drinking wine after the bath came to be an expected part of the daily routine. But as embedded in this text, the wine becomes part of the symbolic program

FIGURE 26. A mosaic from the late fourth- or early fifth-century Roman villa at Sidi Ghrib, Tunisia. A wealthy matron sits on a throne-like chair (probably at the baths) with two maids, the one on the right holding a mirror and the one on the left with a basket of jewels, and surrounded by bathing paraphernalia—sandals, a casket with folded clean clothes, pitchers, and jars. Today on display at the Bardo National Museum, Tunisia. *Credit:* Photograph by Fabien Dany, licensed by Creative Commons (CC BY-SA 4.0), courtesy of Wikimedia Commons.

intended to convey the Patriarch's unique and lofty social status. Presumably the vessel and the beverage it contained were deluxe, superior to the cheap offerings on sale to the general public. A brasher and more explicit articulation of the symbolism of wine in the public baths and the ways in which it accentuated social distinctions appears in the satirical story about Trimalchio that will be discussed shortly.

All of these elements acting in concert propel a sort of interactive performance, staged against the backdrop of the public baths. The details appearing in the anecdote—the clothes, the chair, and the wine—serve as props to bolster social stratification, making the other bathers aware that a superior member of their community happened to be in their midst and enabling them to offer homage and express deference. Concomitantly, he can resume his social duties and attend to their needs. The entire scene resembles, albeit in less formal settings, the traditional morning audience, the *salutatio*, mentioned earlier in the chapter, that clients all over the

Roman world attended in the homes of their patrons. Rabbinic sources attest that Judah the Patriarch and his descendants carried out similar, if not identical, *salutatio*-like ceremonies, probably in their mansions. Members of the social elite as well as some students are said to have visited their homes for a daily greeting ceremony, where the order of entry was determined by importance and stature.[67] The uniqueness of the anecdote here is that it transfers the social theater into the baths, creating a setting that promotes reverence and enforces social hierarchy in the very place that undermines them.

In his scathing critique of the public baths Clement of Alexandria offers a similar view regarding the social statement associated with food and wine brought to the baths by the wealthy and the flashy utensils in which they were served. Unlike the rabbinic author in the above anecdote, Clement criticized the unseemly behavior of rich women at public bathhouses. His words are indicative of the social mechanisms at work there:

> With utter lack of taste they put their silver plates on display there (= at the public baths), just to make an impression. Perhaps they are displaying their wealth with extravagant ostentation, but they are really displaying their culpable lack of self-discipline . . . and show[ing] that they cannot even sweat without being surrounded with their dishes. Women who are poor share the same baths without indulging in such pomp.[68]

If you ignore Clement's disapproving tone and the biblical interpretations that informed the rabbinic story about Judah the Patriarch, you see they reflect similar social dynamics, crystallized around the consumption of food and the drinking of wine in the baths. In the story about Judah the Patriarch, having the slave serve him wine in a special cup after the bath, while bathers of lower status crowded around to beseech the favor of the Patriarch, serves the same function as the lavish food served in ostentatious silver dishes to the wealthy women in the baths of Alexandria, according to Clement. In both instances, members of the social elite use food, wine, and the vessels they were served in to showcase their wealth and, by extension, reestablish their social standing among fellow bathers.

Another literary segment that strikes a close resemblance to both the anecdote about Judah the Patriarch and the passages from Clement of Alexandria comes from the other side of the Mediterranean: the famous first-century CE Roman novel the *Satyricon*. An episode in that long story takes place in a public bath, where the fictional narrator and his companions meet their dinner host, a wealthy freedman by the name of Trimalchio. This incident, probably a satirical critique of the lower-class freedman's flaunting his wealth, can be read as a catalogue of techniques available to bathers who wish to reestablish their shaky social status in the baths. The scene that unfolds in the *Satyricon* features many of the elements discussed thus far (and some that are discussed below). When Trimalchio plays ball in the courtyard of the bathhouse, his young, long-haired slaves and some eunuchs surround him, and he purposely humiliates them in front of his guests to accentuate his prominence. Later, while getting a massage inside the bathhouse, his slaves show off the most expensive Roman wine, the Falernian, and when he emerges from the water, his slaves dry him off "not with linen but with the softest woolen towels," dress him in a "scarlet gown," and carry him home in a litter. One slave even stands by his ear and plays him soft melodies on the flute.[69]

Setting aside the satirical exaggerations, this incident concurs with the rabbinic anecdote and the passage from Clement. Slaves and preferential treatment, wine, and clothing—all display prestige and stature and characterize the nobility everywhere in the empire. Here too, rabbinic texts provide an important source of evidence for modern scholars wishing to comprehend the social structures that prevailed along the provincial edges of the Roman Empire and the mechanisms associated with them as they were deployed in public bathhouses.

JEWELRY AND ATTIRE

The lady walking to the bath at the center of the mosaic picture in Piazza Armerina (see fig. 23) wears a heavy, magnificent necklace with many strands. Her hair shows an extravagant arrangement, resembling a city wall.[70] Another mosaic composition of the same matron-in-the-bath theme, the one from Roman villa in Sidi Ghrib, North Africa (see fig. 25), provides an even more elaborate representation of an affluent *domina* showcasing her adornments: a double-row necklace, drop earrings, an armlet, and gold bangles.[71] These are luxurious, extremely expensive ornaments well beyond the reach of any but the most wealthy,[72] and they seem entirely out of place in the baths. After all, who would wear a diamond necklace or a ring with a precious stone to the beach today? And what kind of woman would load her hair with the clips and pins needed to maintain her impressive hairdo in order to sit in a room and sweat, let alone take a swim? Well-to-do Roman matrons attending the public baths in the Roman world. Men also wore signs of their status to the baths, though not to the extent of a certain Charinus, ridiculed in a satirical epigram by Martial, who wore six lavish rings as he plunged in the basins of a certain bath.[73] Numerous Graeco-Roman sources attest to the habit of both female and male dignitaries of wearing fine, luxurious attire and expensive jewelry to the baths.[74]

A rabbinic parable confirms that Jews in the eastern provinces followed suit, or at least knew of this trend. In this piece a rabbinic scholar spins his example around a rich woman who wears jewelry made of expensive stones (unclear whether a necklace or bracelet) to the baths, loses one of the gems, and is ashamed to disclose the mishap to her husband.[75] The author could have placed the loss of the jewels anywhere, so his choice of the baths speaks to what he and his audience knew of the place, namely that women wore valuable ornaments to them, despite the high risk of loss and theft. Indeed, archaeologists have found many gemstones, rings, glass beads, and earrings that were swept into the conduits underneath the floors and in the drains and channels of public bathhouses all over the empire.[76] Given the challenge of maintaining stature and prominence in the socially ambiguous environment of the public baths, what better way to demonstrate your reputation and prominence than by wearing signs of it on your neck, arms, or fingers, and in your hair?

Of course, not only jewelry was recruited to flaunt wealth and prominence; clothing was used as well. Even though people disrobed upon entering the facility and left their clothes for safekeeping at the *apodyterium*, they nevertheless spared no effort to show off their fine garments on the way in, before undressing, and after putting them back on again on the way out. The two bathing matrons from Piazza Armerina and Sidi Ghrib—one on the way to the bath and the other sitting in one of its rooms—wear some of the finest items of their wardrobes. The Sidi Ghrib *domina* dresses in a lavish multicolored tunic, generously draped down her body and revealing her shoulders, perhaps with a nod to popular sculptures of the goddess Venus. The assortment of beautiful jewelry adorning her supplements her refined appearance. Her fellow matron from the northern side of the Mediterranean, from the mosaic program at Sicily's Piazza Armerina, maintains a similar extravagant look as she parades to the baths in the midst of her entourage, sporting a floor-length, multistriped dalmatian tunic, rich in both color and texture. Here too, jewelry accentuates the mistress's splendor and distinguishes her from those who accompany her.[77] To dye these wool garments with a blend of so many rich shades, and to execute the stripes of color to such perfection, was no cheap matter in Roman times. Most people settled for much less, wearing monochrome, mostly neutral tones. Thus the bright colors were a sign of limitless resources and exalted social standing.[78]

Many sources also attest to the careful attention paid by people of means to the clothes they put on after they finished bathing. The two mosaics just discussed both feature those outfits in the same manner, folded neatly and carried carefully in a casket by the slaves, surely to be worn by the matrons after the bath. In the box are gleamingly clean white garments—a color hard to achieve and even harder to maintain in the squalid streets of their towns, and thus an indication of refined taste and upper-class ranking—with some dark, probably purple stripes (known in Latin as *clavi*, and used by the wealthy to announce their high rank). The Sidi Ghrib mosaic places the basket and the attire in it among the bathing gear that frame the depiction of the seated lady, whereas in the Piazza Armerina depiction a slave carries the casket holding exactly the same garb, thus pointing to a shared visual language among Roman elites: the use of similar symbolic items to define rank and identity as these matrons strolled toward the bath.[79]

Graeco-Roman literary sources confirm that members of the privileged upper echelons took eye-catching outfits to wear after the baths. In the *Satyricon*, for example, when the ostentatious Trimalchio completes his bathing routines, he dresses in a "scarlet gown" before his slaves carry him home in a litter.[80] Centuries later nothing seems to have changed. When the historian Ammianus Marcellinus criticized what appeared to him as the eccentric behavior of the wealthy in bathhouses, he makes sure to include their habit of bringing loads of tightly pressed clean clothes, carefully folded in boxes, from which they chose what to don after the bath. Ammianus also mentions the numerous rings a wealthy man wears on the way to the bath, before having one of his slaves watch them while bathing, "so that humidity does not harm them," before putting them back on as he is leaving.[81]

Rabbinic authors show acute awareness of these dress codes, and here too, as in the anecdote about Judah the Patriarch or in their treatment of the role of slaves, they highlight the social dynamics associated with them.[82] In a short parable, a rabbinic author evokes an imaginary scene in which a young member of one of the city's elite families (the parable describes him as a resident of the local palace) commits theft in the public bathhouse. One of the bath attendants witnesses the crime but is scared to reveal the identity of the perpetrator, describing him only as "a young man dressed in white."[83] The author clearly took white garments in the baths as a symbol of nobility, as was the case throughout the Roman world. On the other side of the social equation another rabbinic passage, part of a long narrative about the mishaps brought upon the biblical villain Haman, contrasts the lowly garb of the bath attendant, the *ballan*, with the brilliant, imperial attire of Haman, which includes purple garments and a crown.[84] Both of these imaginary passages show awareness of bathhouse attire and its social significance.

GESTURES, SPECIAL TREATMENT, AND DEFERENCE

Numerous other practices, small and large, carried out by individuals who attended public bathhouses, then recognized and embraced by the masses, aimed at reconstituting the social structure so shaken by the messiness and rowdiness of the place. The means of transportation to and from the baths provided one way to display high status. The fictional snobbish Trimalchio in the *Satyricon*, for example, who misses no opportunity to flaunt his wealth, has his slaves carry him home from the baths in a litter, while his guests tagged along on foot.[85] In Roman Palestine too, in a list of elements that distinguish the rich from the poor, a rabbinic author contrasts the latter who walk to the bath by foot to the wealthy "being carried to the baths on a litter."[86] The text, although in Hebrew, uses the Latin *lectica*, and confirms that in the mind of this author this practice indicated social prominence.

Patrons of high social standing received preferential treatment from the owners and staff of the bathhouse. Surely not everyone fared as well as a certain second-century CE consul's wife, who, when traveling with her husband in Campania, in southern Italy, insisted that officials remove everyone from the men's bath at one of the villages so that she could have the entire place to herself. Later, she even had the local magistrate flogged in the forum when he failed to act fast enough. She also wanted the place spotless, and the staff did not meet her standards on that either.[87] Undoubtedly, her eminence registered loud and clear for all residents of that place. Even if not to that extreme, it shows that powerful men and women could voice special requests at the baths and expect them to be fulfilled. Tacitus, in his history of the Roman civil war in 69 CE, recounts an example: when one of the leading generals, Marcus Antonius Primus, walked into a bathhouse and complained that the warmth of the water was not to his liking, it solicited an immediate, and loud, response; a voice immediately reverberated through the chamber of the facility, assuring him that the matter would be attended to promptly.[88]

Rabbinic literature provides ample examples—even if some are entirely fictional or the product of legal theory—of the preferential treatment accorded to people of high social status. The laws in the Mishnah regarding operation of the public bathhouse during the Jewish sabbatical year single out individuals who are identified at the baths as "a person of importance," people whom the bath owner would recognize and handle with special care.[89] During the sabbatical year, rabbinic law forbids a man of stature from attending his regular bathhouse, since his appearance would honor the bath owner. Hence it amounts to an extra benefit not allowed on the sacred year. Indeed, the Palestinian Talmud, perhaps exaggerating, if not inventing, the story whole cloth, reports that the third-century scholar R. Joshua b. Levi traveled on the sabbatical year from his hometown of Lydda (at the time the Roman colony Diospolis) to Beth Guvrin (also a colony, Eleutheropolis), some twenty-three miles to the south, so that he could attend a public bathhouse on the sabbatical without being identified by the crowds.[90] These examples, connected with the singular restrictions of the sabbatical year, reveal the special handling that eminent people expected when visiting public bathhouses in ordinary times. Rabbinic scholars also distinguish between "a man of (real) importance" and one "of (merely) shape" or "form" of eminence, namely an imposter aiming to impress and receive the respect reserved for the upper class by employing some of the techniques discussed in this chapter used by the elite to distinguish themselves in the baths.[91]

Additional details about unique accommodations for people of rank in the baths emerge in other rabbinic stories. One of them mentions a worker in the public bathhouse toiling to clean the place before a prince arrives to visit. As in the anecdote from Tacitus mentioned above, about Marcus Antonius Primus, a couple of rabbinic legends state that when men of authority—like the biblical figure Haman or the emperor Titus—attended the public baths the staff made sure to make the water especially warm.[92]

Finally, rabbinic literature also offers insight into the internal mechanisms at work among these scholars, geared toward maintaining respect and proper decorum between younger and senior rabbis as they cross paths in the baths. As shown in detail in an earlier chapter, most rabbinic scholars refrained from studying Jewish law and lore in the baths as well as carrying out intellectual discussions because they held it prohibited to study Torah in the nude or near naked state. Those who abided by this restriction lost an opportunity to establish their standing in the community by displaying their erudition in a place frequented by nearly everyone on a daily basis. Their Graeco-Roman counterparts, grammarians, teachers and students of rhetoric and law, poets, historians, and sophist philosophers, who had no qualms about exposure to naked bodies, proudly showcased their knowledge and acumen in the public baths. They congregated in large groups in the halls and courtyards of the baths, recited, debated, and argued. Although annoying many, they pronounced themselves as men of *paideia*, bearers of the esteemed Graeco-Roman culture that almost everyone revered.[93] This was a missed opportunity, at least for the rabbis who refrained from Torah study while naked. Perhaps the numerous stories about rabbis going to public bathhouses in groups and with collogues, as well as the tales of rabbis performing miracles in the baths (discussed in the next chapter), which are cited throughout this book, are literary expressions of the frustration that stemmed from their inability to study and debate in the baths or a way to compensate for it.

Aside from the issue of studying in the baths, rabbinic authors pay attention to proper etiquette there. One such guideline speaks of "greetings of peace," a salutation offered to fellow bathers (as well as to acquaintances in general), showing respect and perhaps striving to remind people of dignified, peaceful behavior in an unruly place. The rabbinic directive restricts this token of civility to those in areas of the bath where people were still dressed, probably because the full formula included the utterance of God's name: "peace upon you in the name of God."[94] Rabbis also deal with crowd control in a space frequently filled to overflowing and often confined by narrow hallways: "He who enters the bath," goes the guideline, "gives honor to the one who leaves."[95]

These precepts seem to target the public good rather than establish social hierarchy, but more often than not they involve sensitivity to status and the disparity between the one offering tokens of honor and the ones receiving it. At least one rabbinic author seems familiar with such subtleties. In an oft-repeated tale, like a piece of rabbinic gossip, he tells of R. Ḥiya, a rising star yet still a junior scholar, who met the more senior R. Yishmael in the public bathhouse and "did not submit to him." Needless to say, this greatly offended the senior scholar. He went on to complain before Ḥiya's teacher, Judah the Patriarch, who was inclined to reprimand his negligent protégé; Ḥiya eventually offered an apology and excuse.[96] The account does not divulge what expectations of "submission" Ḥiya failed to meet, though the author and his audience undoubtedly were quite familiar with them: gestures that both defined and reinforced the social ladder among rabbinic scholars even, and perhaps especially, in the public baths.

To summarize: rabbinic texts offer a fascinating portrayal of the social dynamics that transpired in public bathhouses attended by Jews in the eastern parts of the Roman Empire. These Jewish authors shared the concerns and challenges of other communities around the Mediterranean: power, prestige, and hierarchy. Yet at the same time they also strike a unique tone by highlighting issues, norms, perceptions, and habits, as well as terminologies and phrases, unique to the bathing practices of their own communities. They make us privy to the inner workings of their society and show us how the human mechanisms that differentiate among people and ranked them worked in their own times. The stories, legends, and anecdotes that rabbinic authors relate about human interactions at the public bathhouse, along with the laws, regulations, and guidelines that these legal scholars formulated and strove to enforce, all come together to paint a colorful picture of their society, sometimes vivid, with clear contours and sharp distinctions, and sometimes vague and ambiguous.

The bathhouse, as depicted in rabbinic literature, proves to be a laboratory, to use my original metaphor, in which ancient people from all walks of life came together in a single place, on a daily basis, and tested their social distinctions. The slaves who accompanied their owners, the food and wine available only to a select group who could afford them (superior in quality and in the dishes they were served on to the ordinary comestibles offered to the general public), the different garments, jewelry, and means of transportation, the bodily and spoken gestures, all are reactants in this experiment, the product of which is the social ladder that defined hierarchy, status, and power in one confined space on the eastern reaches of the Roman Empire.

CHAPTER EIGHT

A Scary Place

THE PERILS OF THE BATH
AND JEWISH MAGIC REMEDIES

Magic in Context and Culture

Many view magic and religion as fundamentally different categories. Indeed, for much of the nineteenth and early twentieth centuries this was the widely espoused paradigm: that religion and magic represented two distinct, often contradictory realms of human life, manifested in opposing sets of beliefs and experiences about the transcendent powers of the universe. This old view, inherited from medieval theology, contrasted religion, which it saw as a pure form of devotion, with magic, understood as a superstitious perversion, a benighted feature of primitive societies, handicapped by ignorance and cultural backwardness. In the last few decades, however, scholars have proposed a more nuanced view, replacing the binary templates of good and bad ways to engage the divine with a gamut of judgment-free perspectives, in which religion and magic overlap in innumerable ways. Accordingly, both religion and magic operate within a broader platform, nowadays called culture, which, far from being uniform or static, includes countless articulations of human behavior and mentality during a given era and within demarcated geographical boundaries. Everything from language to architecture, science, art, literature, and philosophy, as well as formal (religion) and informal (magic) mechanisms to communicate with deities, all partake in the creation of culture.[1] In what follows, I therefore avoid the counterproductive distinction between magic and religion and the ossified debate distinguishing them. Rather, magic here is simply defined as an informal ritual act, suffused with metaphysical power and meant to set in motion changes in human affairs and their well-being. It informally complements, in other words, the formal ritual acts we know as religion, an expression of culture containing the beliefs and assumptions about life and society at a given time and place.[2]

Applied to Graeco-Roman times, this model offers a fertile field for investigation and insight. In chapter 6 I described the cosmology of the Roman Mediterranean basin as replete with divine beings, animating a world in which magic and organized religious worship operate in tandem and in inseparable ways. Magic, as one modern formula correctly puts it, functioned the way popular science does in our world: offering, if only ostensibly, some degree of control over the forces that dominate life. The powers inspiring and enabling magical acts—angels, demons, and spirits—filled the world of ancient people the way prescription and illegal drugs are embedded in our lives today. These metaphysical beings surrounded humans everywhere, at all times, providing an existential crutch, something to lean on, blame, love, and fear. They were more immediate and accessible than the formal gods, the heavenly forces in the skies (or, for that matter, on Mt. Olympus, or in any temple),[3] whose divine stature separated them from humanity. Magical formulas and techniques enlisted these supernatural, ethereal beings and put them to work in the service of men and women. Whether rooting for the victory of your favorite gladiator in the arena or for your beloved chariot racing team in the hippodrome, capturing the heart of your beloved, soothing pain and healing sickness, inflicting misery on your political enemies and business competition, or soliciting favor and success, magic could help with it all.

Here too, the rift that many scholars claim separated ancient Judaism, especially in the various articulations captured and transmitted in rabbinic literature, from the realm of magic tells only part of the story. Jews resorted to magic like anyone else in the Graeco-Roman world. We know this from multitudes of amulets invoking the name of the Israelite God, not to mention magic spells, curse tablets, incantations in Hebrew and Aramaic, and Jewish magical recipe books, as well as numerous literary traditions, whether preserved independently, as in *Sefer ha-razim* (more on this text below), or captured in the words and actions of rabbis as preserved in the rabbinic corpus. All this evidence shows that ancient Jews embraced magic, like the rest of the population around them.[4] Accordingly, Jews belonged to what may be termed the "magical environment" of the ancient Mediterranean world (a sister term to the "sculptural environment" discussed in chapter 6). Hence, the discussion should focus on their practices and beliefs within this shared cultural landscape.

The current chapter goes in this direction and investigates the procedures of and the perceptions about magic as well as the attitudes toward it as they took shape among Jews, particularly rabbis, but not only them, in the realm of the Roman public bathhouse. It begins by setting the stage and highlighting a rather neglected, dark facet of bathing establishments: they were seen as places suffused with numerous dangers, both physical hazards and human menaces. I discussed some of these threats earlier in the book, but here when brought together with the new material of this chapter they showcase another significant, often overlooked dimension of the bathing experience, which made people feel threatened and vulnerable. To ward off these perils, people felt an urgent need for magical remedies. Most groups in the various corners of the Roman Mediterranean remained silent in the surviving historical record, so their magical practices in the bathhouse are inaccessible to us, but Jewish magical practices, investigated in the second part of this chapter, are attested in rabbinic and other sources and shed light on the useful means available to them and to everyone living in the Roman world to cope with risk, fear, and abuse. The richness of rabbinic literature joins other available sources (like the vast corpus of magical papyri from Egypt) in telling the story of magic and its application within the public bathhouse on the eastern reaches of the Roman Empire. It extends our understanding of magic in the Roman world, and at the same time it adds another dimension to the main theme of this book, namely the interaction of Jews with Graeco-Roman culture.

By now, most readers know that the Roman public bathhouse has drawn the attention of ancient people and modern scholars alike. Being a well-demarcated public space, the latter viewed it as a prime venue through which to grasp and interpret the culture that created it. Understandably, modern scholarship tends to focus on the magnificent baths, in particular fascinated by the great, huge facilities created by the emperors for the populace of Rome (usually known as the imperial *thermae*) or by those, a notch smaller but no less impressive, operating at the center of big cities all around the empire. The luxurious architecture and splendid, spacious surroundings, the ingenious, yet simple heating technology, and the lavish, at times extravagant decorations—statues, wall paintings, and mosaics—all captivated the imagination of modern observers. It stimulated admiration, appreciation, and praise, which in turn translated into the lauding terms usually used to describe this institution. For some, it is the epitome of Roman material culture, the acme of its technological capabilities; others see it as an institution that nurtures the human body, provides bodily pleasure, and even serves as a medical facility; and yet for others it stands for the delights of leisure (as well as inevitable degeneration into hedonistic corruption). The not-so-appealing aspects of the bathhouse (at least in the eyes of modern observers, and to a lesser extent, some ancient people as well), such as the gender mixing and nakedness in the baths, its excessive indulgences, and its filth, were swept aside in favor of the extolling praise. For the most part, the current book, up to this point, has shared this favorable perspective.

Nevertheless, lurking behind the glamorous facade of public bathhouses are some dark and nasty aspects. The soothing comforts of the bath were accompanied by grave physical dangers: serious injury, pain, and even death. These threats, coupled with emotional and social pressures experienced by the bathers, highlight an entirely different facet of the bathing experience. Despite the pleasures and amenities offered by the baths, attending them could involve fear and anxiety. Indeed, in part, the public bathhouse amounts to what anthropologists label a "scary place."[5]

First and foremost, these fears become embedded in the shared consciousness of a society in a given place and time. People's cumulative experiences mark particular structures and spaces as precarious—as locations that pose a threat to the well-being of the population. Visiting places like dense forests or dark and shadowy taverns can invite harm and injury. The perception of the place extends beyond its specific reality. It circulates word to mouth via rumors and tales, amplified by shared notions of fear and intimidation, and disseminated through various networks of communication and expression—literature, poetry, folklore, and art are the most common, but far from the only, channels. Finally, it solidifies in the collective assumptions of the society. Although it is sometimes necessary, obligatory, and even desirable to frequent scary places, doing so incites a rush of fear and a sense of vulnerability, and it must be done with due caution.

Clearly the dangers of the baths were not its sole identifying mark, canceling out all its other, more appealing features. However, danger was an aspect of bathing that comingled with the others, informing, complicating, and curtailing the experience as a whole. While some scholars have noted the unsettling experiences involved in attending the public baths, they did not fully realize, I think, the physical, tangible element that ignited anxiety among bathers or the way these unsettling experiences were connected to the pervasive presence and persistent application of magic.[6] One study of rabbinic material rightly identified the bath as a "dangerous place" but missed the mark by attributing the danger to the demons that supposedly haunted these facilities.⁷ I submit the opposite, that the demons are not the cause of the danger but rather its outcome and embodiment. Risks and fear registered in the ancient mind via demonic language and imagery. In other words, ancient people projected the real hazards of the baths explored below—physical, emotional, sexual, and social—onto demons and then introduced magical practices in the bath as a protective measure.

Physical Dangers in the Baths

On the most rudimentary level, many of the bathing facilities, both in the far reaches of the Roman Empire and even in the city of Rome itself, were a far cry from the huge and glamorous establishments built by the emperors, the imperial *thermae*. Smaller and less impressive bathhouses were far more common.⁸ Whereas the imperial *thermae* featured spacious, well-lit galleries, with high windows that flooded the place with light and delight, the lesser structures contained smaller, often windowless halls that led to poorly lit, dim, and dark interiors, a gloomy and somewhat daunting environment, especially for bathers accustomed to strolling in the open spaces that characterized the Roman urban landscape. In these inferior structures, people often tripped and fell (more on this below), and the atmosphere felt intimidating, if not threatening. The first-century CE Spanish-born poet Martial, a frequent and enthusiastic patron of the baths in Rome, expressed such uneasiness when he complained about the "murky baths" of Lupus and Gryllus.⁹

Even in large and ornate bathhouses, wet and slippery surfaces required constant attention and balance, and uncareful bathers might fall and sustain injury. A rabbinic anecdote from fourth-century CE Roman Palestine offers a glimpse into this somewhat minor, yet emotionally taxing nuisance that confronted bath-goers. It reads as follows:

> R. Abbahu was going down (=came) to bathe in the public bathhouse of Tiberias, and [while there] was leaning on two Goths (=slaves). They stumbled and he steadied them, they stumbled [again] and he stabilized them [for a second time]. They said to him: "How is this so" (that you have so much stamina)? He said to them: "I saved my strength for my old age."¹⁰

The Palestinian Talmud (the *Yerushalmi*) offers this segment not as a piece of gossip but rather as part of an intellectual discussion of geriatrics. It opens with an observation about the challenges faced by seniors: "The stones on which we sat in our youth make war against us in our old age." Characteristic of rabbinic discourse, the editors of the Talmud then move to interrogate this saying through various examples, questioning its validity and refining its message. They include the incident involving R. Abbahu in the bathhouse in one of those discursive segments, showing that the elderly may still possess vigor. R. Abbahu's concluding words, "I saved my strength for my old age," weave his story into the broader tapestry of the Talmud's discussion of old age, showing someone who does not fall prey to the stones that confront him in old age. There is no way, and no need, to determine whether this incident of R. Abbahu really happened. Like any good tale, and in typical rabbinic fashion, the authors reverse the roles, and the supposedly weak old man turns out to be stronger than the powerful Gothic slaves. Unrelated to the topic of old age, the narrator blended numerous everyday details into this scene—bathhouses, their slippery floors, and the accidents they can cause. These loom in the background of the anecdote and provide us with a glimpse of the misfortune that awaits people in the baths. The phrase "leaning on the shoulder of his companion," which surfaces in several other tales about rabbinic figures attending the baths, reflects the same shaky environment and the danger of falls and injury.[11] Similarly, certain regulations recorded in rabbinic texts should be seen as attempts to mitigate the harm that the watery floors can cause, in particular the rule not to bring glass vessels into the public baths "due to the danger."[12] Wet floors caused enough havoc—no need to amplify it with broken glass.

The greatest safety hazard in public baths stemmed from its heating system, the hypocaust, discussed in great detail earlier in the book (see fig. 4). If not properly watched, furnaces and their firewood could easily burst into flames, causing destruction and harm. Indeed, numerous inscriptions from all over the Roman world attest to fires breaking out in bathhouses.[13] The authors of these dense documents, mostly short epitaphs inscribed on stone, focus on the generosity of the individuals who contributed funds to restore the damage, praising and publicizing their euergetism (the philanthropic Roman practice of contributing wealth for public projects that benefit the community). Therefore, they usually neglect to mention the cause of a conflagration or speak of its cost in lives and bodily injuries. In assessing the issue of public safety in the baths, however, we must assume that when fires broke out, as they often did, people got hurt or died.

Setting aside the danger of accidental fires, the hot steam in the ceramic and copper pipes that ran along the walls of the *caldarium* and the other rooms of the public baths could scorch the bare flesh of those packed into its crowded spaces.[14] Indeed, the second-century CE statesman and imperial tutor Fronto says as much when he complains in a letter to Marcus Aurelius, his pupil turned emperor, about his careless slaves who, while carrying him to the public baths, bumped him into the wall and got his knee "scorched" from the heat.[15] If inhaled, the vapor and smoke could even prove lethal, as shown by the suicide of the first-century CE Seneca the Younger, whose slaves assisted his death through "suffocation with the steam of the bath."[16] Fatalities in the baths took many other forms as well. Numerous sources from everywhere in the Roman world report drowning, asphyxiation, slipping, and even murder.[17]

In similar vein, the hot water available to bathers in the pools, basins, and tubs, or the scorching floors of these installations, heated by the searing air pushed underneath the raised floors of the hot rooms (see fig. 4), could become, when not monitored properly, a source of pain, injury, and trepidation. Unlike modern heating systems with thermostats, the furnaces in the Roman public bathhouses, normally serviced by the owner's slaves, featured few means to control the heat. On the one hand, people loved having their water warm, a fondness shared by all, excluding perhaps only some rigorous ascetics or pompous prudes (Livy and Seneca come to mind). Most bathers cheered the hot water and vociferously complained when the temperature did not meet their expectations. This is true of Romans from all walks of life. Marcus Antonius Primus, for example, senator and commander of the Seventh Legion during the civil war of 69 CE, voiced his dismay whenever the water temperature at the bath he happened to be visiting was not to his liking. Ordinary townspeople too spared no words in singing the praises of warm water in their bathing facilities.[18] Jews and rabbis shared this sentiment. In relation to the laws of the Sabbath, the editors of the *Yerushalmi* document a common habit among Jewish bath-goers of splashing each other with warm water. In one anecdote, some of the bathers spattered the prominent scholar R. Abbahu with warm drizzle and he moaned in utter pleasure.[19] While the story may be apocryphal, the text conveys the instinctual feeling of sheer indulgence that comes with warm water.

On the other hand, when temperatures rise out of control, the beloved heated water can become unpleasant and even dangerous. Martial, for example, complains to a certain bath owner that "no one can bear your bath, so hot it is," and in another instance he recommends attending the public baths at only certain hours of the day to avoid contending with water that is "too hot."[20] On the other side of the Mediterranean, rabbis issued similar warnings. For example, a rabbinic parable uses the metaphor of a public bathhouse that is so hot that "no one can step into" it. The parable explains the wickedness of the Amalekites in the biblical story, who were the first to attack the Israelites in the desert after the Exodus. According to the parable, when the crowd in a public bath sees an unruly bather dive into the searing waters in the baths, disregarding the burns his body may sustain, others are encouraged to follow suit.[21] Setting aside the exegetical insights the parable wishes to articulate (namely that attacking a seemingly invincible force—in this parable the water represents the Israelites in the desert—may convince others that victory may yet be achievable, even if you get hurt in the process), the real-life situation it describes matches that of Martial: the danger of overheated water in the baths and the bodily discomfort and even injury it can inflict.

Another precarious situation confronting bath-goers derived from the fragility of the suspended floors of the hot rooms. As explained earlier in the book, the ingenious heating system that Roman engineers perfected for warming the water of the baths hinged on the raised floors of the hot rooms, known as the hypocaust (Greek for "heating from underneath"). The builders used short pillars (*pilae* in Latin), often made of layered bricks, to elevate the stone, occasionally marble, floors of the hot rooms (thus named *suspensura*, suspended) and create a cavity underneath (see figs. 4 and 5). A furnace in a side chamber (known as the *praefurnium*) sent hot air into the void, which heated the raised floors and kept the water warm. The hot air finally flowed outside through vertical pipes that ran inside the side walls of the room. This hot chamber (known as the *caldarium*) usually included a communal pool (*alveus*), a basin (*labrum*) for cold water, and occasionally benches around the walls. The hypocaust was relatively simple and easy to make, a technique that, once introduced, was reproduced thousands of times throughout the Roman world.

The one weakness of this engineering feat lay in its potential for collapse: the heat, water, and humidity of the room, combined with the weight of the bathers, and compounded by poor construction, resulted in the intermittent disintegration of these suspended platforms. In the fifth century CE, the Roman author Macrobius pointed to this design flaw in clear terms: "heat from olive logs promotes the body's health but is destructive for baths and does great harm in loosening the joints of marble."[22] A century earlier, rabbinic traditions document the same situation. In a discussion of actions permissible on Jewish holidays, the Palestinian Talmud mentions a collapse that occurred in the public bathhouses of a certain village in Roman Palestine; the rabbinic scholar Abbahu allowed its repair during the holiday. Another ancient rabbinic dictum recommends, "don't enter a new public bathhouse as [its floor] may collapse."[23]

Indeed, numerous inscriptions and a few literary references record the constant maintenance that public bathhouses required to stave off deterioration.[24] Some of these texts, like the inscription from the Licinian Baths in Thugga (southwest of Carthage in North Africa), complain in general about the faulty work (*inperfecto opera*) of earlier builders, which resulted in ruins and wreckage.[25] Others speak of the dangers of collapse, specifically of the floors, and express the fear people felt; in one example, a fourth-century CE inscription praises Anicius Auchenius Bassus, the governor of Campania in southern Italy, for repairing a public bath:

> The Appearance of the baths was ruinous, [they were] ugly and dirty, and the dangerously unstable overhanging structures threatened to collapse, [all of which] used to keep the bathing populace away out of fear and worry. I repaired the building entirely, shutting out the decay of old, until it was solid, stable, and useable, and made it into a better emblem of the city.[26]

The benefactors who funded the repairs proudly inscribed their deeds for posterity, but imagine the poor individual coming to relax in the baths suddenly falling into the sizzling space underneath the floors. Not a happy prospect, and one that could easily make bath-goers anxious.

It should come as no surprise that such apprehension found its way into literary forms as well. Multiple folktales convey the fear of disintegrating floors in the public bathhouse. They were told independently among different groups throughout the Roman world (and beyond) but express the same apprehension. One example can be seen in later rabbinic accounts of the episode discussed above about R. Abbahu slipping in the bath. In a second version of that incident, preserved only in the Babylonian Talmud (and thus technically beyond the realm of Roman influence), the rabbinic scholar Ravin, known to have traveled back and forth from Persia to Palestine, returned to Babylonia with the following tale: "R. Abbahu was once standing in a bathhouse, two slaves supporting him, when [the floor of] the bathhouse collapsed under him. By chance he was near a column [upon which] he climbed taking up the slaves with him." A third, even more exaggerated version of the events states that "R. Abbahu [once] went into the bathhouse and the floor of the bathhouse gave way beneath him, and a miracle happened to him, and he stood on a pillar and rescued a hundred and one men with one arm."[27] Literary and textual analysis aside, such scenes, in which the structural integrity of the bathhouse fails as floors come crashing down while random pillars from underneath happen to be in the path of the falling R. Abbahu, although fantastic in their very nature, are modeled on this common hazard of the heating system, namely the crumpling floors of the hypocaust.

A similar literary convention informs a tale that circulated among early Christian communities about the Apostle John. In this story, John meets a gnostic heretic named Cerinthus in a public bathhouse in the city of Ephesus on the western coast of today's Turkey, and he proclaims, "Let us flee, lest the bathhouse fall in."[28] This anecdote, from the same time as the rabbinic anecdotes about R. Abbahu, also reflects the common fear of collapsing floors in the bathhouse. Similar anxieties inform the boastful and self-promoting inscription about the fourth-century proconsul governor of Campania mentioned above, who describes the public bath as having "dangerously unstable overhanging structures threatening to collapse, which used to keep the bathing populace away" before he had it repaired.[29]

Despite its many attractions, the public bathhouse clearly embodied structural and technical weaknesses. Taking all these deficiencies together—dim rooms, slippery floors, overheated water, scorching walls, and the real possibility of collapsing floors of the hypocaust—the bathhouse proves to be a dicey physical environment. No wonder people were apprehensive, unsure, and at times simply scared. When the author of the second-century text *Hippias* (or *The Bath*), a text brimming with praise and affection for the public baths, repeatedly emphasizes the "safety" of the ideal bathhouse he is describing, he seems to be contrasting it with the sense of unsafety shared by many in real-life bathing facilities.[30] The first-century CE Seneca the Younger conveys similar insecurity in one of his letters, where he compares the fragile human condition, where unexpected bad fortune can swiftly uproot prosperity, to attending the baths, where without warning something may strike and harm you.[31] In much more perspicuous terms, a chorus of rabbinic texts express this widespread sentiment of insecurity. In one example, they relate the custom of one of their own to leave "instructions" for his household—apparently, a sort of a will—prior to "going to bathe in a heated bathhouse." In a second example, the prominent R. Judah the Patriarch assigns two younger students to accompany the distracted R. Ḥiya in his visits to the public bathhouse due to "danger." Later sources discussing this, both rabbinic and modern commentators, understand that the danger stems from fire or the heat of the *caldarium*.[32]

VIOLENCE

R. Asi, when he moved to Palestine (from Babylon/Persia) he went to the barbershop [and then] wanted to bathe in that public bathhouse of Tiberias. A "clown" (=thug) encountered him (at the entrance to the baths) and gave him a smack. He (=Asi) said (to the person accompanying him to the baths): "The loop around this man's [neck] is loose." And an Archon (=Roman governor) was there, standing and holding a judicial hearing in the case of a certain robber. And [the clown] went and stood (watching the court session and) grinning (=poking fun) at him (at the robber standing trial). The Archon asked (the robber): "who was with you (as an accomplice)?" He (the robber) raised his eyes and saw him who was grinning, he replied to him (=to the Archon): "that [man] that is grinning was with me." And they seized him (=the clown) and tried him (=interrogated him with torture) and he confessed about one [person that he] killed. And as they were taking both of them out, loaded (affixed) to two beams (=heading for execution, perhaps by crucifixion), R. Asi came out of the bath. He said to him (=Asi to the person accompanying him): "the loosened loop [now] tightened." He said to him; "(see the) bad luck of this man, isn't it written [in the Bible]—Therefore refrain from mockery, let your bond be tightened (Isa 28:22)."[33]

The random and quotidian violence depicted in this episode reflects a constant feature of daily experience in the Roman world, one that differentiates it from our way of life, except in gang-controlled neighborhoods or war zones. Ancient societies lacked any meaningful means, such as a standing police force, to protect the weak. They lacked the concept of criminality we associate today with unwarranted violence as well as meaningful laws restricting violence in daily interactions between people on the street. Consequently, arbitrary physical aggression was utterly normal. A slap, a push, a punch, or a kick was often applied by those who had the power to inflict them on those who lacked the power to resist them; although not condoned by the general public or by the authorities, such violence was tolerated as an unavoidable part of life.[34]

Public bathhouses were no different than other venues throughout the Roman Mediterranean. Wherever people congregated, whether for financial and business transactions in markets and fora, for entertainment and leisure in theaters and hippodromes, or in taverns, bars, inns, and even in temples, violence could erupt and escalate in an instant. Whether planned or random, these attacks nearly always caused pain and injury, and—harder to define but perhaps more pervasive—the constant threat of violence perpetrated a sense of insecurity. The lax atmosphere and crowding of public baths, suffused with lascivious ambience and enhanced by the availability of alcohol (see chapters 5 and 7), made them a perfect breeding ground for fights and attacks.

Although, as shown earlier, ancient writers expressed great fondness for the baths and composed many idyllic portrayals of them as havens of comfort and leisure, modern scholars have too often taken these favorable depictions at face value. However, a closer look reveals aggression and physical abuse, casting a shadow on the glowing prestige of this institution. R. Asi was not the only bather who was smacked at the entrance to the baths. Mounting evidence attests to pugnacious crowds, to bullies picking fights, throwing punches, and shoving fellow bathers around. The Roman first-century CE scholar and statesman Seneca the Younger, in his dialogues on anger, takes the baths as an example of a space where violent incidents erupted between strangers, citing an old story about Cato the elder, who was "struck unwittingly" (that is, the attacker did not know who his illustrious victim was) in the public baths.[35] Needless to say, like many similar rabbinic anecdotes about famous people, retold decades (and at times centuries) after the event, the historicity of the account cannot be verified nor does it hold any importance, at least not for our purposes here. Its significance comes from the mindset about and the image of the baths that it conveys as a place where even the most venerable are not shielded from the belligerence of the crowds.

That same perception of the baths, as a place susceptible to violence, emerges from one of the exercises used in a Roman textbook, the *Rhetorica ad Herennium*. The first-century BCE author (at times mistakenly identified as Cicero) evokes a setting where the vulgar speech of the lower classes clashes with the refined manners of the upper echelons. His choice is revealing, though not, by now, surprising: he concocts an incident in the public baths where a common, yet assertive, man rushes up to a wealthy bather and complains that the latter's slaves "just assaulted him," demanding apology and restitution.[36] Placing this incident in a bathhouse speaks to its rowdy reputation.

Rabbinic authors also depict public baths as sites of violence. The tale about R. Asi is just one example. The anecdote mentioned earlier, whether fictional or not, about a rabbinic scholar who used to leave a will with his household before going to the baths is another example. In a story discussed in detail below, a rabbinic author describes a violent confrontation in the baths between a Christian and some prominent rabbinic figures. In one part of that story, the Christian is tied to the doors, and everyone who enters smacks him on the way in. All these snippets reveal a negative aspect of the bathing experience, which is usually drowned out by the chorus of accolades showered upon this institution.

Other references to the public baths strike (pun intended) a similar tone. A few generations after Seneca, in one of Pliny the Younger's letters, he tells about a senator and ex-praetor, Laricius Macedo, who was knocked to the ground in the public baths by an angry bather.[37] A generation or two later, Galen, the Greek physician turned resident of Rome, mentions that a patient of his came across some acquaintances in the public baths (which he calls by the Greek term "gymnasium") who were involved in a skirmish, throwing and receiving punches. Galen goes on to characterize this event as quite common among the youth in the city.[38] On the eastern side of the empire, matters were no different. In a petition from a village in the region of Faiyum, in central Egypt, a local man details a brawl that broke out in the public baths when a small gang of men and women attacked his wife and mother-in-law, "covering their bodies with blows." At least one woman was badly injured, she lost some valuable jewelry, and a bowl was broken.[39] Further north on the Mediterranean eastern coast, the prominent fourth-century scholar Libanius recalls similar violent exchanges from his visits to the public baths. During his early years as a student in the academy of Athens, Libanius recalls that while leaving a bathhouse with a friend, a member of a competing school struck the friend on both cheeks. Like the rabbinic scholar Asi in the tale cited above, Libanius expresses astonishment and fury. Some years later, while leaving the baths on his way to dinner, he, too, sustained a serious injury to his leg when he tried to stop a scuffle, only to find himself wrestled to the ground by one of the quarrelers.[40]

Let there be no misunderstanding: the threat of violence did not deter people from attending the baths. As noted in previous chapters, for the most part people were fond of the baths, enjoyed the activities, and regarded bathing as one of the greatest pleasures of their daily life. I only wish to claim that the bright shiny side of the baths does not account for the entire picture. A dark side of the bathing experience, simmering beneath the surface, but one that the ancients must have considered, nuances and complicates our understanding of this institution. People can love and fear a place simultaneously. Libanius is a striking example. Despite the anxiety, frustration, and anger he harbored toward the baths, he constantly praised them and wrote about them with fondness. In his panegyric speeches, for example, as he sings the praises of his esteemed Antioch, portraying it as an ideal city, or when he lists the pleasures of its prized citizens, he always includes bathing in public bathhouses as a central component.[41] These are two sides of the same coin: public baths offered a wonderful treat for the ancients, but they could also be violent and dangerous.

SEXUAL AND SOCIAL ANXIETIES

As if the physical threats emanating from the structural deficiencies of bathing facilities coupled by the human menaces and fears of violence that confronted people who came to enjoy public bathhouses were not enough, nudity added another layer of discomfort and anxiety. As shown in earlier chapters, men and women throughout the Roman world, Jews included, ordinarily bathed together in public bathhouses, more often than not with their bodies fully exposed. Certain establishments and communities tried to separate the sexes, typically by implementing different bathing hours, less often by creating separate installations for men and women. A few emperors endorsed and reinforced these habits with legislation. But these attempts to segregate remained far from the norm; bathing in the nude, men and women together, endured as the common practice throughout the Roman Empire.

Surely some—perhaps most—bath-goers enjoyed the au naturel, permissive scenery, just as others found the practice offensive. But rather than the response to seeing *others*, here I want to focus on how bathers felt about their own nakedness. Then as now, people run the gamut from pride to shame when it comes to displaying their intimate parts. Stress and apprehension must have been just as common in the Roman bathhouse as they are in gyms and saunas today. Indeed, as discussed earlier, body shaming was an unsurprising by-product of the exposed nature of the baths, causing agitation and agony among certain bathers. It took many forms, from poking fun at someone else's body, his or her weight or smell, to ridicule and mockery of certain body parts or features. One aspect of body shaming specific to Jews manifested in scorn directed at their circumcised penises. Clothes protect people, and once they were off, at least some men and women felt defenseless and helpless.

Quite expectedly, nudity encouraged a wide variety of sexual activities in public bathhouses. As documented in chapter 5, full sexual intercourse and oral sex, as well as touching, caressing, kissing, making out, and masturbating, apparently were common in bathhouses, giving them a lewd image everywhere in the Roman world. These activities may have been expected, accepted, and even desired by some of those attending the baths, but surely not by all. Lacking actual statistics about the frequency of such escapades or subsequent complaints, we can only surmise that not everyone welcomed or reciprocated the inevitable sexual advances. Some were indubitably coerced; the basics of human nature are constant, and thus when given the opportunity men tend to prey sexually on the weaker members of society or flat-out abuse them. The lack of legal protection in Roman times for unwelcome sexual behavior likely increased the vulnerability of many who visited the baths, men and women, boys and girls alike.

Nudity and sex provoked a range of reactions, from agitation to urgency, what some scholars call "the constraints of eros," in ancient people, just as they do in us today.[42] Involuntary bodily reactions—sweat, high pulse rate, and so forth—could give rise to uneasiness and tension. Obviously, for some sexual promiscuity was part of the attraction of going to the baths, but not for someone who was harassed, physically or verbally, who was unable to control his erections, or who was ashamed of their body, and so forth.

Finally, as discussed in chapter 7, in the public baths, for a short while, civic and communal hierarchies melted, as people from all walks of life freely blended with each other, and this added another layer of discomfort and trepidation. Since it catered to people from all stations in life, the public bathhouse became a social arena, a unique environment where the governing class and the elite rubbed shoulders with the lower strata of society, including the poor, women, and slaves. Similar to the dynamics that anthropologists detect in the cafés of nineteenth-century Paris,[43] bathhouses drew people together and eliminated the marks of status that differentiated them in the outside world. The baths separated women from their clothes and jewelry, and stripped away everyone's signs of position and wealth, as well as symbols of social role and status. Many sources document this colorful social mix, as the upper echelons of society freely mingled with the lowest. Such a human jumble obscured the designations of the social pecking order. Unlike Roman theaters and stadiums, where reserved seats and segregated sections delineated social rank and stature, in the public baths (despite some notable exceptions) people shared the space quite equally. Close proximity with others undermined all the usual social boundaries, whether communal, political, or religious, depriving people of the security that such boundaries provide. People exposed not only their ordinarily hidden body parts but also their beliefs and cultural assumptions (think, for example, of the statement implied by circumcision).

The results were myriad, but it is safe to say that the experience in public bathhouses could be quite daunting, at least sometimes and for some people. Especially for members of the upper strata of society, the inevitable erasure of the distinctions that separated them from their inferiors posed a challenge that could lead to emotional intimidation, uneasiness, and dread. For example, the acclaimed scholar and orator Libanius, who undoubtedly stood close to the pinnacle of the social ladder in his hometown of Antioch, articulated this anxiety in its most basic and practical terms. In an autobiographical speech, Libanius reveals that when his body suffered certain illnesses and injuries, so that he was unable to maintain his dignified appearance, he "feared the great baths."[44]

To summarize: although most people greatly enjoyed the wide range of amenities offered by public bathhouses, and frequently attended them, the bathing experience had some negative aspects. The halls might be slippery and dark, and the risk of physical danger or sexual predation, as well as a boundary-less social mix, created constant intimidation and stress. In my view, this conforms to the anthropological model of a "scary place." Not all bathing establishments featured equal threat, but their shared image instigated alarm and propelled people who frequented the place to find mechanisms that would mediate the fear and protect them from dangers, whether imagined or real.

Demonic Manifestations of Fear

Throughout history, people have employed a vast array of strategies to express fear and confront anxiety. One of the most basic techniques, since the earliest days of humankind, involved deflection—what Sigmund Freud called displacement (*Verschiebung*).[45] Ominous threats are easier to manage when diverted from one's own soul and immediate vicinity to somewhere far away and detached from real life. Thrillers and horror movies function this way, as they dramatize a terrifying version of the public's shared phobias, from the medical to the political, from the economic to the criminal, or sexual. It can be exhilarating to watch fictional horrors because we know they will be resolved when the movie is over, the credits roll, and the lights come up.[46]

In ancient times people dealt with menaces in similar ways. Instead of cinematic villains they associated their fears with spirits and demons, supernatural beings that existed everywhere and constantly threatened to cause harm and wreak havoc. Operating within a pre–scientific revolution mindset, people utilized magic to overcome these spirits and demons—that is, they used magic to gain a sense of control over or exempt themselves from looming dangers. Ancient people wore amulets for protection from spirits the way modern people have recourse to popular science to overcome the threatening aspects of their lives. Instead of using over-the-counter medicine for relief from anxiety and pain, or remaining glued to the science channel to watch natural disasters in faraway places, the ancients employed magic spells to gain the same sense of tranquility and imagined safety.

Nowhere in the Roman world were these dynamics more visible than within the precarious environment of the public bath. Freud's *Verschiebung* is at work here. The real physical and emotional hazards of the bath gave rise to the demons that proliferate there, which are the expression and manifestation of the dangers. Indeed, a wide variety of written material—literary, documentary, magical papyri, bowls, and amulets—extending from Graeco-Roman times through the Middle Ages (and even deep into the early modern period), from the Mediterranean world and Europe, refer to the demons that dwelled in bathhouses and to the magical practices people used to protect themselves from them.[47] A wide array of metaphysical beings including mainstream gods and goddesses, along with spirits, ghosts, jinn, nymphs, and mythological monsters, dwelled in the dark corridors of the baths: they plunged into the pools and fountains, pranced in the flames of its furnaces, and hid behind statues in its niches or in the void beneath the suspended floors. They lurked in the dark beneath the benches or hovered in the upper reaches of domes and windows. The real dangers of the bath acquired a demonic dressing.

Inscriptions unearthed in bathhouses throughout the empire evoke an environment permeated by spiritual beings; indeed, the volume of evidence suggests that these supernatural creatures were intrinsic to bathing establishments. The steps of the bathhouse were personified as gods and goddesses; rooms and sometimes entire bath complexes were named after divine, mythological figures; and the pools and basins were widely believed to be the preferred habitat of spirits. One inscription even records a special spiritual being—the *genius thermarum*—residing in baths and (we assume) protecting its clientele.[48]

These beings enabled bathers to express their fears and anxieties. People warned each other with stories about the harm caused by these imps and assigned exotic names to them, often connected to the features associated with a specific creature. Kausatha, for example, a bath demon which the third-century scholar Porphyry is said to have exorcised, received its name from the Greek root *kais* (with the *sigma* falling at times), marking verbs and nouns related to the burning (hence the English caustic).[49] A century before Porphyry, an inscription from Miletus in Asia Minor refers to similar creatures as "fire wedded nymphs," and, a century later, the Christian scholar and bishop Augustine speaks of spirits and demons made of the hot air of the baths.[50]

Other intimidating aspects of the bath, such as the threat of sexual predation, were also assigned to demons. Ancient sources regularly tie the licentious atmosphere and promiscuous activity in the bathhouse to a throng of debauched demons and spirits that caroused there. They also attest to magic spells that helped people join the fun (but at the same time, as shown below, also provided them with the means to protect themselves from unwelcome attention).[51] The exceedingly prevalent idea about haunted public bathhouses mirrors the real dangers that abounded there, allowing people to project their fears onto creatures somewhat removed from their lives.

Rabbinic sources from this period reflect the same vulnerabilities and perceptions. The Jewish authors of these texts depict the bathhouse as populated by threatening spirits and other hostile, metaphysical beings. Like their contemporaries, the pagan scholar Porphyry and the Christian Augustine, the rabbinic author of a commentary preserved in Midrash *Qohelet Rabbah* knows of "male and female demons that were [responsible] for heating the bathhouse."[52] Similarly, a rabbinic story from the same period (translated and discussed in detail below) refers to "the demon of the bath," an entity that neutralizes the hazards of fire and steaming water, naming him Angitaris (and in some versions Antigras/Agentin).[53] Like his counterpart Kausatha in the Porphyry legend, who received his name from the Greek for burning, the rabbis, or whoever coined the name that they used in their story, seem to have drawn it from the Latin *ignis*—fire—which may also be associated with various metaphysical creatures named Agni, all of which are associated with fire.[54] Apparently, when it comes to the demonology of the baths, people of Graeco-Roman times, including both Jews and Christians, share a cosmological worldview and use similar vocabulary to identify the creatures in this cosmos.

One rabbinic story further illustrates how Jews anchored their beliefs about the baths in the widely held assumptions and sensibilities of the time. In this tale, a pious rabbinic scholar from Roman Palestine, Ḥanina b. Papi, is desperate to elude a relentless, rich matron fixated on bedding him; he flees into a bathhouse populated by dangerous spirits (*maziqim* in rabbinic terminology; literally "those who harm"). The story describes the custom of attending the perilous bathhouse in pairs, and only in the daytime, to ward off the menacing spirits. It also ties the safety of R. Ḥanina, who went to the bathhouse alone, to angelic figures bearing the insignia of the Roman emperor (literally in the Hebrew, "two bearers of Caesar guarded me all night").[55] It is probably impossible to pinpoint the precise imagery behind these Roman figures; one option is that they looked like soldiers carrying the standards of one of the legions, which were known to have some divine quality. Be that as it may, the rabbinic storyteller, just like his Graeco-Roman counterparts, presents a dark vision of the bathhouse as a gnarly space besieged by dreadful metaphysical creatures. In doing so, he also draws on the shared visual repertoire of the time, including Roman imagery, probably well known to those who heard the story.

Magical Remedies

The dangers prevailing in public bathhouses, both real and imagined, inspired an abundance of magical activity.[56] As explained earlier, magic enabled ancient people to cope with the threats of everyday life, facing down dangers and gaining some sense of control over them. The practice of magic in the baths varied in intensity, nuance, and detail. On the more extreme side were stories of full-fledged miracles, like the one about the third- and early fourth-century Syrian-born Neoplatonist scholar Iamblichus, who used a magic formula to rescue two boys from the gushing thermal springs in of Hammat Gader, a famous healing resort just northeast of Roman Palestine.[57] Some ancient people surely believed in the feasibility of such wonders. Others may have hoped for miracles to occur, even as they harbored their own doubts, since such fantastic possibilities gave them a sense of safety otherwise lacking.

On the more mundane end of the spectrum, far from outright miracles, magical practices in the baths included a wide variety of gestures, signs, phrases, and catchwords, all meant to provide protection or relief. These included tossing papyri containing a magic spell into the searing chamber of the hypocaust, in order to protect from its hazards, or smearing a papyrus with the blood of an ass and gluing it to the vault of the *caldarium* in order to "attract men to women and women to men, and make virgins rush out of their homes."[58] Another unsettling problem of the baths, theft, also received magical attention. Archaeologists have uncovered many curse tablets (known as *defixiones*) in the ruins of Roman bathing complexes in England, Spain, Greece, and even Jerusalem. People scratched curses on small pieces of lead and sometimes on ceramic lamps or other materials and then deposited them in places requiring protection. The curse tablets address the people's fears, and many target thieves who stole clothes, shoes (mainly sandals), and jewelry, all left behind when bathers undressed at the *apodyterium*.[59]

Bathers also performed magical procedures associated with health and medicine, which, as shown earlier in the book, proliferated in public bathing facilities everywhere in the Roman world.[60] One account, for example, speaks of a young man who moved his fingers back and forth from his chest to a marble plaque on the bathhouse wall while reciting the seven vowels of the alphabet in order to soothe a stomachache, behavior typical of bathers' magical rituals. This unfortunate man happened to live during the days of the zealous fourth-century Christian emperor Valens. Thus, taken for a pagan sorcerer, he paid with his life for his harmless actions, which in every other period would be considered habitual and normal.[61] Needless to say, Christians too, both before they gained imperial power and in the centuries thereafter, resorted to magic in the baths and everywhere else. Christians usually crossed themselves before entering the baths to ward off demons and other evils, and Christian literary traditions record more complex magical procedures as well.[62]

When it comes to magic in public bathhouses, Jews followed the same trajectories as their fellow residents of the Graeco-Roman world. As shown earlier in this chapter, rabbinic literature reveals awareness of the threats awaiting bathers and expresses the anxiety caused by these hazards in vocabulary laden with imagery of demons and spirits. As for dealing with the stressful situations surrounding the bathing experience, here too Jews did not hesitate to tap into the vast reservoir of magical practices to gain protection and peace of mind.

Sefer ha-razim (Book of Secrets), a book of Jewish magic spells from the third and fourth centuries CE, written mostly in Hebrew with some Aramaic, and preserved in multiple copies in the Cairo Genizah, tells how to "extinguish a bath so its blaze does not grow and burn." The text goes on to present a page full of rituals and magical spells that one can recite in order to prevent disaster. These include submerging a salamander—a small amphibian thought to have the ability to withstand fire—in a glass vessel full of oil. Then, the book instructs the reader to invoke the assistance of various "angels of fire" so they "do not allow the fire to come and boil (in) the bath," imploring them to guard the gates, enter the bath, and cool its water.[63] Two of the angels listed on that same page of *Sefer ha-razim* (although their role in the magical ceremony remains vague) are

Agra and Gentes. Phonetically, they resemble the name of the demon Angitaris, who appears in the rabbinic story from more or less the same period of time mentioned above and discussed in full below. That story assigns the demon a similar role in the bathhouse, namely taking control of the fire and protecting bathers from its perils. The similarity of the names of the two angels and that of the demon and their common function in the bath (whether an angel or a demon, bathers relied on them for safety) reflect the people's mentality in dealing with the risks of the bathhouse.

Clearly, fear of fire and heat in the baths led at least some Jews to resort to magical practices practically identical to those of their neighbors. But Jews had other means in their cultural toolbox to protect them from the threats of the baths, chief of which was the God of Israel. Rabbinic literature preserves a prayer, known as the "prayer of the baths," a version of which is found in the fourth-century Palestinian Talmud (the *Yerushalmi*):

> A person who enters a bathhouse recites two prayers, one when he enters and one when he leaves. When he enters he says "May it be your will, Lord my God, that you save me from the burning fire, and from injury by the steam, and from collapse. And may nothing occur to endanger my life. But if something happens, may my death atone for all my sins. And save me from this and similar dangers in times to come." And when he leaves he says "I give thanks to you, Lord my God, for saving me from the fire."[64]

This passage enumerates many of the physical dangers awaiting people in the baths: the fire and the scalding waters, as well as the collapses of the hypocaust's raised floor (and *not* the roof or walls, as medieval commentaries, as well as nineteenth-century scholars, both unfamiliar with the mechanisms of Roman baths, wrongly thought).[65] This rabbinic prayer of the baths should be seen as a magical incantation to ward off the physical threats of the public baths. It marks out a secure (or in contemporary lingo: a stress-free) space by accompanying entry and exit with formulas that invoke divine powers to neutralize the numerous threats. The people reciting this prayer beseech the powerful God of Israel to help them safely navigate the threatening landscape they were about to enter. They then thank him when they emerge from it unscathed. Seeing it this way aligns these prayers with other magical formulas for the same purpose from throughout the Graeco-Roman world.[66] As I argued in the beginning of this chapter, the difference between magic and more formal religious practices was far from clear to ancient people. They took a whatever-works type of approach; if the God of Israel can be recruited to fend off the dangers of the baths, who in their right mind would deny themselves such a resource?

Rabbinic stories provide an even fuller expression of the Jewish mindset regarding the dark sides of the baths and the magical remedies to avoid them. Rich in detail and nuance and colored by the physical and emotional texture of their daily lives, these narratives provide insight into the minds of their authors and their audience. Here is an example of a story from Roman Palestine that recounts an imaginary encounter between two rabbinic scholars—Raban Yudan Nessi'a and Shmuel bar Naḥman—and the emperor Diocletian:

> Diocletian the swineherd—the students of R. Yudan the Patriarch would make fun of him. He became emperor and went to Paneas (Caesarea Philippi, a city in northern Palestine). He sent written orders to the rabbis, [saying]: "Be here in front of me immediately after the end of the [coming] Sabbath." He instructed the messenger (who was to deliver these orders), "Do not give them the document [with the orders] until the eve [of Sabbath], just as the sun is setting." (Diocletian wanted to force the rabbis to miss the appointment, because they could not travel on the Sabbath. Then he could avenge their disrespect for him.) The messenger came to them on the eve [of the Sabbath] as the sun was setting. [After receiving the orders,] R. Yudan the Patriarch and R. Shmuel bar Naḥman went to bathe in the public bathhouse of Tiberias. Angitaris (a bath demon) came before them and R. Yudan the Patriarch wished to rebuke him [and chase him away]. R. Shmuel bar Naḥman said to him (i.e., to Yudan), "Leave him be, as he appears for a trial [and a miracle]." He (the Angitaris) said to them, "What are you rabbis doing (=what is troubling you?)." They told him the story. He said to them, "[Finish] bathing [in honor of the Sabbath]. For your creator is going to perform miracles [for you]." At the end of the Sabbath [the Angitaris miraculously] carried them and brought them in [to Paneas on time]. It was said [to Diocletian], "Those rabbis are outside." He said, "They shall not see my face until they have bathed." There was [there] a bath that was heated for seven days and nights. [The Angitaris] entered before them and overpowered [the heat]. [And afterward] they went in and stood before [Diocletian]. He said to them, "Is it because your creator performs miracles for you that you [allow yourself to] insult the [Roman] Empire?" They said to him, "Diocletian the swineherd we insulted. But Diocletian the king [emperor] we do not insult." [Diocletian said to them], "Even so, you

should not rebuke [anyone], neither a young Roman, nor a young associate of the rabbis (for you never know what greatness that individual will one day attain)."[67]

The plot here revolves around two archetypical bathhouses: a safe one in Tiberias and a hostile one in Paneas. The protagonist, a demon named Angitaris (and in some versions Antigras or Agentin), mediates between the rabbis and the dangers they encounter in the baths. Although he appears in a favorable light here, offering true advice and substantial assistance, the rabbinic narrator's efforts to "convert" the Angitaris by placing the correct views in his mouth ("bathe yourself and your creator will perform miracles") do not detract from his true nature—a demon in charge of the hazards of fire and steaming water and thus able to neutralize them. As argued earlier, I think his name stems from the Latin *ignis* (fire), and he should be associated with other creatures marked by variation on the name Agni, all of which are also associated with fire, as well as other fire-wedded nymphs alluded to in texts and inscriptions. Phonetically, his name also recalls the two angels of *Sefer ha-razim*, Agra and Gente. Magical sources suggest many ways to appease such a spirit, the most popular of which, in the context of the baths, was to toss a magical bowl into the furnaces before entering.[68] The rabbinic narrator based his story on the realistic fear of fire and excess heat in the baths, and shows how at least some Jews, in this case rabbis, embraced magical tools, in literary form and surely also in practice, similar to those of their neighbors.

Another rabbinic story highlights the liminal nature of Roman public bathhouses. Here too magic plays an important role, as the rabbinic scholars encounter people from other segments of society among the mingled public in the bathhouse, in this case a follower of Jesus:

> R. Eliezer, R. Joshua, and R. Aqiva went in to bathe in that [famous] bath of Tiberias. A *min* saw them. He said what he said, and the vault [of one of the bath's halls] seized them, (so they could not move). Said R. Eliezer to R. Joshua, "Joshua b. Ḥaninah, see what you can do." When that *min* was leaving, R. Joshua said what he said, and the doorway [of the bath] seized him [the *min*], and whoever went in gave him a punch, and whoever went out gave him a shove. He said to them, "Undo whatever you have done [to let me go]." They said to him, "Release us, and we will release you." They released one another. Once they got outside, said R. Joshua to that *min*, "Is that all you know?" He said, "Let's go down to the sea [of Galilee]." When they got down to the sea, that *min* said what he said, and the sea split open. He said to

them, "Now is this not what Moses, your teacher, did at the sea?" They said to him, "Do you not admit to us that Moses, our teacher, walked through it?" He said to them, "Yes." They said to him, "[Then] walk through it." He walked through it. R. Joshua instructed the ruler of the sea, who swallowed him up.[69]

This rabbinic story depicts an imaginary confrontation between three leading rabbinic figures, R. Eliezer, R. Joshua, and R. Aqiva, and a *min*, a general term used in rabbinic literature for "heretic," an individual who does not conform to the Jewish way of life (as defined by the rabbis).[70] The way the narrator designed the story leads me to believe that the *min* in this case is a Jewish believer in Jesus.[71] The plot centers on two bodies of water—the public baths and the Sea of Galilee—and the conflict plays out in the spatial layout they create within the urban landscape of the city of Tiberias, a port city of sorts on the narrow shoreline of the large Galilean lake. The power balance between the rabbis and the *min* remains pretty much even while they exchange magic punches in the bathhouse. However, the rabbis gain the upper hand when they meet for a second round on the shore of the big lake, which figures prominently in traditions associated with Jesus, reporting that he performed miracles nearby and even walked on the water.[72] Significantly for the inner logic of the story, when only magic was involved the two sides were at a standoff, but when the heavy powers were brought in—Moses who walked through the Red Sea and Jesus who walked on the water of the Galilee lake—Moses's followers, namely the rabbis, decisively vanquished the believer in Jesus, the *min*.

The author of this short tale arranged the plot as a two-round match between adversaries. Rather than outfitting the two opposing parties with ideologies or scholarly argumentation, he equipped them with magical ammunition. The *min*, upon recognizing the three rabbinic scholars in the bath, "said what he said" (*amar ma demar* in Aramaic)—a regular talmudic formula for pronouncing a magic spell—and captures the rabbis in the bathhouse dome (or, according to another reading, the arched niche for statues), where spirits and demons are known to congregate.[73] He gains the upper hand against the rabbis with his magic, temporarily displaying his superiority in the social arena of the baths. But his victory is short-lived: the rabbis strike back with their own magical powers and add a bit of violent retaliation to the magical tussle. Not only does their magical counterpunch neutralize their opponent, it also exposes him to smacks and ridicule from fellow bathers. Imagine the scene depicted here:

the three distinguished rabbis flail helplessly in the upper reaches of the bath's dome, while the *min*'s body is stuck in the entrance and thrashed by everyone who enters; the space between them, no doubt, is laced with magical aura.

In the next round the adversaries enlist higher powers. Not coincidentally, the *min* attacks the traditional Jewish narrative of God's miraculous splitting of the Red Sea. After all, the *min* suffered violent abuse at the hands of fellow bathers enabled by the rabbis, so what could be more appropriate than to contrast the rabbis' God and his violence against the Egyptians with Jesus's peaceful walk on the water? At the end though, no surprise, the author has his fellow rabbis emerge victorious, as the water of the sea consumes the Christian student.

For the purposes of this book the setting of this confrontation is more important than its outcome. The public bathhouse emerges here as an arena of fierce factional competition. The role of magic in this story is even more illuminating. The author invoked magic to cope with social intimidations and conflict that can erupt in the baths by those who know how to wield it.

To conclude, the study of magic in Roman bathhouses has shed light on some of the dark aspects of this otherwise pleasant and enjoyable facility. Not all was fun in the bathing kingdom; alongside its many amenities and luxuries, a variety of physical hazards, social pressures, and the potential for unwanted sexual attention undermined the good life of the baths. Ancient people associated these risks with the presence of demons and relied on magic to overcome them.

The stories told by and about rabbis show ancient Jews as no strangers to the use of magic in Roman public bathhouses. Traditional scholarship, which portrays them as passive bystanders, at times influenced by Graeco-Roman practices but mostly resisting them, simply does not hold water. The rabbis, when viewed through the prism of the magical practices associated with the Roman bathhouse, emerge as ordinary residents of the Graeco-Roman milieu, part and parcel of its cultural landscape and habitual participants in the mechanisms of its daily life. They attend bathhouses as frequently as any other people in Roman cities and towns, and to cope with its dangers and the anxieties caused by such risks, they resort to the same means as everyone else, namely magical techniques and spells.

Rabbis occasionally put a Jewish spin on these magical practices, in particular by relating the source of their power to the God of Israel. This encapsulates the broader cultural mechanism I call "filtered absorption"; they absorbed the magic around them but filtered it in a way that would align with their own way of life. By doing so, however, they were no different from other ethnic and religious groups in the Roman Mediterranean—followers of Serapis, believers in Mithras (who had a very prominent presence in the baths), or Christians; Syrians, Phoenicians, or Arabs. When the need arose for supernatural assistance, everyone tried to enlist whatever power they had at their disposal to gain some advantage over the mighty, threatening forces. Whereas the evidence for magical practices in bathhouses by many of these groups remains scanty, if it exists at all, the vast material about this topic that survived in rabbinic literature (and in other Jewish texts such as *Sefer ha-razim*) allows for a substantial and rich, if only partial, reconstruction of Jewish magical activities in the bath. It offers rare insight into the mentality of one of the groups, living in an eastern province of the Roman Empire. As any other ordinary denizens of the Roman world, Jews adopted and embraced its widely held practices and cultural norms, while at the same time shaping them and adding their unique voice. This twofold, ambivalent dynamic represents in a nutshell the poetics of cultural interaction in the Roman Mediterranean.

In Conclusion

THIS BOOK PORTRAYS the rabbis of Graeco-Roman times—and by extension other Jews in the Roman Mediterranean—in a decidedly different way. Since Jewish communities all over the world still use the title "Rabbi" today, our conception of ancient rabbis is typically colored by these figures from the immediate past—mainly the couple of centuries before World War II in eastern European ultra-Orthodox circles. (Think *Fiddler on the Roof*, or the numerous other presentations of these bearded men in art and literature.) Clad in black wool suits and white shirts, framed by long beards and hats with wide brims, we imagine these characters as ascetic and pious, and aloof from the pleasures of life. They register in our minds as saintly men who spend their days toiling on the study of the Talmud (which they call the Oral Torah) and instructing their congregations in the divine laws of God (which they still call *halakhah*).

Sharing the same title with the rabbis of the Graeco-Roman world and seeing themselves as the sole legitimate heirs of their tradition, it is only natural that ultra-Orthodox rabbis project themselves on their ancient predecessors. Just as ultra-Orthodox communities struggled (and some still do) to separate themselves from the modern world that surrounded them, with all its carnal temptations and hedonistic evils, so the ancient rabbis, and the Jewish communities they ostensibly led, were supposedly embroiled in the same struggle. For more than a century and a half, since Rabbinics was established as a field of academic study, university-trained scholars have adopted this picture to one degree or another, applying twentieth-century ultra-Orthodox sensitivities and imagery to the ancient rabbis. They tend to view them as "living on their own planet," defined by a worldview suffused with anti-Roman proclivities and detached from the common culture and way of life that engulfed them.

Nothing could be further from the truth. Using the Roman public bathhouse as a laboratory to explore ancient rabbis as well as other Jews, we see a radically different picture. Rabbis enthusiastically patronized the bathhouse and shared its amenities and pleasures, just like all other individuals during their time. Jews built public baths with no hesitation and rabbis frequented them with ease and comfort. They showed deep knowledge of the structure of the facility and voiced great appreciation for its benefits and comforts. They valued the institution and fused it into their way of life by applying numerous *halakhot* to the bathhouse's function and customs. Even more surprising, this investigation shows that certain practices that we would assume to be far removed from rabbinic norms resided quite well with them. It seems clear that female nudity offended ancient rabbis much less than we tend to believe. And rather than condemning all statues as idols, rabbis related to sculpture in nuanced ways that allowed them to engage with these graven images with peace and tranquility. Similarly, rabbis also embraced magic, not as a foreign menace to denounce but rather as one of many tools they applied to cope with the challenges of life.

I hope this book will encourage us to rethink our conception of ancient rabbis and ancient Judaism and to revise our understanding of the ways these people engaged with Graeco-Roman civilization. No longer must we view these cultures as hostile to one another, perpetually negating each other. The model I have offered here, which I call "filtered absorption," explains how different ways of life interact in a relatively peaceful manner. Just as important, it highlights the diversity and disagreement that prevailed among the rabbis themselves about absorption and adaptation. Some of them willingly engaged the surrounding milieu while others resisted it. This entire system of cultural interaction comes to life in the bathhouse as rabbis embraced, absorbed, and accepted it, while at the same time they also rejected, reconfigured, and re-created it. The bathhouse tells an entirely new story about ancient Judaism, offering deeper and richer understanding of its interplay with the common way of life in the Roman Mediterranean. The rabbis who frequented Roman baths remind us that the Judaism of Roman times was not the Orthodox version of Judaism of recent times.

Another aim of this book involves methodology. It demonstrates once more the benefits one can reap from interrogating rabbinic texts alongside archaeology and classical, Graeco-Roman material. Even more significant, it calls for the inclusion of rabbinic literature in the standard corpora of sources used to study the Roman realm. Rabbinic sources are astonishingly rich and give us valuable access to the voices of provincial locals often silenced in our pursuit of the empire; modern scholars owe it to themselves to engage more fully with these texts and integrate them into the exploration of the ancient world. Classicists, historians, archaeologists, and epigraphists can all profit from training in and then incorporating this material just as, decades ago, Sebastian Brock and Peter Brown prompted us to seriously consider materials written in Syriac for the study of Late Antiquity. The voices of the rabbis should be heard, not necessarily for religious reasons but for the historical insights they can offer.

ABBREVIATIONS

AB   Anchor Bible.

ABD   David N. Freedman, ed. *The Anchor Bible Dictionary*. 6 vols. New York: Doubleday, 1992.

ACW   Ancient Christian Writers.

AE   *Archaiologike Ephemeris*.

ANF   Ante-Nicene Fathers.

BJS   Brown Judaic Studies.

BRITANNIA   *Britannia: A Journal of Romano-British & Kindred Studies*.

CFHB   Corpus fontium historiae byzantinae.

CIL   *Corpus inscriptionum latinarum*.

CSCO   Corpus scriptorum christianorum orientalium.

CSEL   Corpus scriptorum ecclesiasticorum latinorum.

EJ   *Encyclopedia Judaica*.

FC   Fathers of the Church.

GCS   Die griechische christliche Schriftsteller der ersten Jahrhunderte.

IJS   Institute for Judaic Studies.

ILS   *Inscriptiones latinae selectae*.

JAOS   *Journal of the American Oriental Society*.

JRA   *Journal of Roman Archaeology*.

LCL   Loeb Classical Library.

LIMC   J. Boardman et al., eds. *Lexicon iconographicum mythologiae classicae*. Zürich: Artemis, 1981–.

LSJ   Henry G. Liddell, Robert Scott, and Henry Stuart Jones. *A Greek-English Lexicon*. 9th ed. with revised supplement. Oxford: Clarendon, 1996.

NEAEHL Ephraim Stern, ed. *The New Encyclopedia of Archaeological Excavations in the Holy Land.* 5 vols. Jerusalem: Israel Exploration Society, 1993–2008.

NPNF Nicene and Post-Nicene Fathers.

OCP *Orientalia christiana periodica.*

PG Jacques-Paul Migne, ed. *Patrologia graeca* [= Patrologiae cursus completus: Series graeca]. 162 vols. Paris: Migne, 1857–86.

SC Sources chrétiennes.

SJ Studia judaica.

TTH Translated Texts for Historians.

NOTES

Introduction

1. Much has been written on Jewish identity and culture in the ancient world. For my own take on this topic with bibliographical references to earlier studies by others, see Eliav, "Jews and Judaism."

2. The literature here is even more vast, especially when exploring the nuances of *romanitas* in various corners of the empire. The three scholars who shaped my view on the subject more than anyone are Erich Gruen on the earlier periods of the Republic, and Maurice Sartre and Peter Brown on later phases. For a glimpse into current discussion, see on the eastern side of the empire, Goldhill, *Being Greek under Rome*; on the west, Revell, *Ways of Being Roman*.

3. For a penetrating glimpse into the voluminous scholarly work on this topic, with a focus on Roman Britain, see Mattingly, "Being Roman." A broader scope, recognizing the problems and offering some interesting solutions, is offered by Revell, *Roman Imperialism and Local Identities*.

4. I do not aim to cover all the topics and sources relevant to the bathhouse—such an endeavor would require more than one volume. The economy of the baths, for example, or the full range of matters associated with medicine, prostitution, or the institution of the thermal baths appears sporadically in this book but could not be fully exhausted.

5. The numerous studies I consulted are all listed in the bibliography. The most important contributions from the last generation and a half include Berger, *Das Bad in der byzantinischen Zeit*; Brödner, *Die römischen Thermen*; Heinz, *Römische Thermen*; Nielsen, *Thermae et balnea*; Yegül, *Baths and Bathing in Classical Antiquity*; Yegül, *Bathing in the Roman World*; and Fagan, *Bathing in Public in the Roman World*. More recently, a new batch of studies has begun to come out, either adding newly discovered material or reassessing older paradigms; see Boussac et al., *25 siècles de bain collectif en Orient*; and Zytka, *A Cultural History of Bathing*. Two recent publications came into my possession too late to be seriously consulted for this book: Sadi Maréchal, *Public Baths and Bathing Habits in Late Antiquity: A Study of the Evidence from Italy, North Africa and Palestine A.D. 285–700*, Late Antique Archaeology supp. 6 (Leiden: Brill, 2020); and Kowalewska, *Bathhouses in Iudaea*.

6. Pace Schwartz, *Were the Jews a Mediterranean Society?*, who claimed that when it comes to the study of rabbinic material, "expertise in the classical literary tradition provides diminishing returns" (113).

7. I have examined these trajectories of modern scholarship, from Krauss in the nineteenth and early twentieth centuries all the way to the present, in a series of articles; see Eliav, "Samuel Krauss"; and Eliav, "From *Realia* to Material Culture."

8. The earliest study about bathing habits in Graeco-Roman Judaea/Palestine is Dechent, "Heilbäder und Badeleben in Palästina." Two decades later, pretty much

simultaneously, two studies about the customs of bathing as reflected in rabbinic material came out; see Preuss, *Biblisch-talmudische Medizin*, 617–42. This chapter on bathing is based on his earlier lecture titled "Waschungen und Bäder nach Bibel und Talmud," which he delivered in 1904. See also Krauss, "Bad und Badewesen"; and Krauss, *Talmudische Archäologie*, 1:209–33. From more recent times, the main studies include Hanoune, "Thermes romains et Talmud"; Sperber, "On the Bathhouse"; Sperber, *The City in Roman Palestine*, 58–72; and Jacobs, "Römische Thermenkultur."

9. My earliest works go back to 1995; see the full list in the bibliography. See, for example, my discussion (p. 136) on Roman bathhouses in territories of the Persian empire ("Babylonia"), where I retract my earlier assertions that no Roman-style bathhouse existed east of the Roman frontier. Another example relates to a broader understanding of the "filtered absorption" model that stands at the heart of this book; over the years, as I tested its validity, in particular responding to criticism voiced by other scholars, I tweaked and changed some of its components.

10. For the historical details, see Eliav, "Jews and Judaism."

11. For one example, see Schwartz, *Were the Jews a Mediterranean Society?* 3–5.

12. See Mason, "Jews, Judaeans, Judaizing, Judaism"; Schwartz, *Imperialism and Jewish Society*, 103–28; and Boyarin, *Judaism*. For a recent articulation of the Judaisms Paradigm, with much-needed nuance and criticism, see Witte, Schröter, and Lepper, *Torah, Temple, Land*.

13. I devoted a detailed piece to argue against Schwartz's claims and in other reviews highlighted some of the shortcomings in the works of Mason and Boyarin (although I did not take the Judaism thesis of the latter two head-on); see Eliav, "The Matrix"; reviews in *Hebrew Studies* 42 (2001): 385–89; and *The Classical Journal—On Line*, October 5, 2017. For a detailed rebuff of Mason's arguments, see Schwartz, *Judeans and Jews*. On Neusner's views and on the erroneous term "Rabbinic Judaism," see my discussion on p. 13. For a detailed critique of the numerous Judaisms model, see Schwartz, "How Many Judaisms Were There?" 221–27.

14. Schwartz, *Were the Jews a Mediterranean Society?* 112. It would be impossible to provide here a full documentation of this scholarly trend. For discussion of the work of some of the leading scholars on this topic in the past century, Saul Lieberman, Martin Hengel, and others, who adhere to the same model, see Eliav, "The Roman Bath as a Jewish Institution," 416–18; and Eliav, "Secularism, Hellenism, and Rabbis in Antiquity," 7–8. For a thorough review of modern scholarly views regarding the encounter of Judaism and Hellenism, see Levine, *Judaism and Hellenism*, 3–32.

15. For two recent and one not-too-recent but central examples, see Millar, *The Roman Near East*, 352; Sartre, *The Middle East under Rome*, 101–2; and Zytka, *A Cultural History of Bathing*, 107, defining the Jews as "somewhat aside from the rest of the population."

16. Lee Levine's work had a serious impact on my own thinking on the topic; see in particular Levine, *Judaism and Hellenism*. Another important study in this direction is Satlow, "Beyond Influence," 37–53. The Hellenistic period remains for the most part outside the confines of the current study, but some scholars challenged the old paradigm in this period as well. For a useful survey of the current state of research on the issue of Jews and Roman culture (and Greek culture before) as well as adjacent

topics, see Dohrmann and Reed, introduction to *Jews, Christians, and the Roman Empire*, 1–22. Cf. also Rosen-Zvi, "Rabbis and Romanization," which quite tellingly does not mention archaeology even once.

17. In these definitions I find myself quite close to the position articulated by Lapin, *Rabbis as Romans*.

18. This positioning of ancient Jews within the cultural landscape of their time, both conceptually and practically, is a central component of my thesis and sets it apart from other formulations offered by scholars trying to explain the same phenomenon. This is why, for example, I avoid the term "neutralization" that many studies (including some of my early work) use to describe Jewish reaction to Graeco-Roman culture. Neutralization is a mechanism of interaction between two separate and opposing entities but not a useful concept when one entity is fully submerged within the other. Cf., for example, Berkowitz, "The Limits of 'Their Laws,'" 121–23, in particular her comment in note 1.

19. For the documentary evidence, see Cotton, "The Impact of the Documentary Papyri."

20. The best modern presentations of these texts in English, including references to editions and translations, are Safrai, *The Literature of the Sages*; and Stemberger and Strack, *Introduction to the Talmud and Midrash*. See also the various chapters on specific rabbinic texts in Katz, *The Cambridge History of Judaism IV*, 299–368, 663–98, 840–76.

21. Krauss, *Talmudische Archäologie* was the first major endeavor to gather and study this information. For a more recent attempt, see Hezser, *The Oxford Handbook of Jewish Daily Life in Roman Palestine*.

22. Much has been written about the evolution of the rabbis as a group; the most solid studies in the eyes of this author, despite some disagreements, are Levine, *The Rabbinic Class*; Hezser, *The Social Structure*; and Lapin, *Rabbis as Romans*.

23. Levine, *The Rabbinic Class*, 66–69. The most balanced study on this topic is Lapin, *Rabbis as Romans*, 98–125.

24. For a detailed presentation of these views, see Eliav, "Jews and Judaism." For the most up-to-date articulation of the opposite view, namely the traditional rabbinic-centered picture of antiquity, see the various articles gathered in Gafni, "Symposium: In the Wake of the Destruction," 163–265.

25. Cf. Hezser, *The Social Structure*, 185–224.

26. For summaries of these texts, reference to editions, translations, and further studies, see the literature listed in note 20 in this chapter.

27. For a multischolarly assessment of Neusner's criticism and contributions to the field as well as its limitations, see the series of studies, "Jacob Neusner and the Scholarship on Ancient Judaism," ed. Eliav.

28. Schwartz, "Ancient Jewish Social Relations," 557.

29. Millar, "The World of the Golden Ass," 75.

30. On the criticism, see Hezser, *The Oxford Handbook of Jewish Daily Life in Roman Palestine*, 11. On the ways to detect information that passed between the two realms, see Eliav, "The Material World of Babylonia."

31. See the examples and discussion late in the book (pp. 123–24).

32. See Eliav, "From *Realia* to Material Culture."

Chapter 1. The Miracle of (Hot) Water: The Emergence of the Roman Public Bathhouse as a Cultural Institution

1. For a general overview of this subject, see Mithen, *Thirst*.

2. Many have discussed this phenomenon: for a study focusing mainly on Britain, see Rogers, *Water and Roman Urbanism*. Cf. Mithen, *Thirst*, 12ff., who locates the "revolution" in an earlier period but, despite the semantics, agrees that the Roman period evinced something totally different in terms of water supply; see ibid., 125. For a recent overview and summary of relevant scholarship, see Rogers, *Water Culture in Roman Society*.

3. The literature on Roman aqueducts is vast: for a detailed summary and updated bibliography, see Wilson, "Hydraulic Engineering."

4. See Bagg, "Wasserhebevorrichtungen im alten Mesopotamien."

5. See, for example, Lewis, "Vitruvius and Greek Aqueducts"; and Tassios, "Water Supply of Ancient Greek Cities."

6. Amit, Patrich, and Hirschfeld, *The Aqueducts of Israel*.

7. See the summaries in Wilson, "Hydraulic Engineering," 285; Hodge, *Roman Aqueducts*, 1–18; and Chanson, "Hydraulics of Roman Aqueducts."

8. On siphons, see Hodge, *Roman Aqueducts*, 147–60.

9. On the need for regular cleaning of channels and conduits in general, see Frontinus, *Aq.* 2.119–122, 124.

10. Scobie, "Slums"; Fagan, *Bathing in Public in the Roman World*, 74.

11. *t. Miqw.* 4:6; cf. Irshai, "Terms and Characteristic Features of Water Installations and Aqueducts in Rabbinical Sources," 75–76, who prefers to translate the Hebrew *kĕrakhim* as villages, a questionable choice given that the etymology of the word refers to a fortified place, which is its meaning in Aramaic; see Sokoloff, *A Dictionary of Jewish Palestinian Aramaic*, 269, s.v. See also *m. B. Bat.* 4:6.

12. Frontinus, *Aq.* 2.78. Numbers for later centuries are provided by appendixes of the regional catalogues known as the *Curiosum* and the *Notitia*; see Jordan and Hülsen, *Topographie*, 2:571–72.

13. Pausanias, *Graeciae descriptio* 2.3.3–5; Palladius, *Op. Agr.* 1.39.4, 1.41; Nielsen, *Thermae et balnea*, 1:24n26. On water and dyeing, see Wilson, "Archaeological Evidence for Textile Production and Dyeing in Roman North Africa."

14. Koloski-Ostrow captured this essential aspect of city life in the Roman world when she said, "Water was everywhere in cities across the Graeco-Roman world. A metaphor for life itself"; see Koloski-Ostrow et al., "Water in the Roman Town," 181. But one must not overlook the exceptions to this rule; for various reasons, many places still suffered from shortages of water. See, for example, Di Segni, "Using Talmudic Sources for City Life in Palestine." Also, one must recall that many aqueducts supplied water for other purposes, in particular agriculture.

15. Fagan, *Bathing in Public in the Roman World*, 312, no. 238; Martial, *Epigrammata* 6.42; Augustine, *De ord.* 1.3.6; *Cant. Rab.* 1:3.

16. For example, Blair et al., "Wells and Bucket-Chains."

17. Fagan, *Bathing in Public in the Roman World*, 57–58, 73; Yegül, *Baths and Bathing in Classical Antiquity*, 391–95; for the second argument, see Wilson, "Hydraulic Engineering," 298.

18. So claim Scobie, "Slums," 424 and Yegül, *Bathing in the Roman World*, 97–100.

19. In seeing the essence of the baths in this way, I follow Yegül, *Baths and Bathing in Classical Antiquity*, 356, who also cites numerous ancient writers that express the same viewpoint.

20. Nielsen, *Thermae et balnea*, 1:14.

21. Vitruvius, *De arch.* 5.10; Yegül, *Baths and Bathing in Classical Antiquity*, 356–62; Nielsen, *Thermae et balnea*, 1:14–18.

22. Pliny, *HN* 9.168.

23. DeLaine, "Some Observations"; Fagan, "Sergius Orata"; Wikander, "Senators and Equites VI." For an early, "primitive hypocaust system" at Tel Anafa in northern Galilee, which predates the arrival of the Romans by a few generations, see Herbert and Ariel, *Tel Anafa I, i*, 67; Herbert suggests that this system has Punic origins (ibid., 17). As Herbert points out correctly, during the Hellenistic period, hypocausts were also common in the palaces of the Hasmonaean kings (ibid., 17n36). See also Brödner, *Die römischen Thermen*, 18–23.

24. The data is collected and summarized in Brödner, *Die römischen Thermen*, 20; Nielsen, *Thermae et balnea*, 1:18.

25. See Brödner, *Die römischen Thermen*, 94–105; Nielsen, *Thermae et balnea*, 1:153–66, for an appendix of common elements of Roman baths. Fagan, *Bathing in Public in the Roman World*, 368ff., provides an inventory of all bathhouse components mentioned in inscriptions.

26. DeLaine, *The Baths of Caracalla*.

27. Mango, "Daily Life in Byzantium," 338. See also Lucian, *Hipp.*; Pliny, *HN* 35.9.26, 34.19.62; Nielsen, *Thermae et balnea*, 1:144–46; Yegül, *The Bath-Gymnasium Complex at Sardis*; and Valeri, "Arredi scultorei dagli edifici termali di Ostia."

28. The classic study of Greek baths remains Ginouvès, *Balaneutikè*, and a good summary in Brödner, *Die römischen Thermen*, 1–12. But research has advanced enormously in the half century since these books came out. For an overview and updated bibliography, see Lucore and Trümper, *Greek Baths and Bathing Culture*; and Wassenhoven, *The Bath in Greece in Classical Antiquity*. The most comprehensive treatment of the Greek gymnasium is still Delorme, *Gymnasion*; on the *loutron*, see ibid., 304ff. For more current research, see Kah and Scholz, *Das hellenistische Gymnasion*.

29. See Trümper, "Urban Context of Greek Public Baths," 35; and DeLaine, "Some Observations." DeLaine argues convincingly that even where fully figured heating systems were found in the Greek world they may have been imported from the Romans (ibid., 123).

30. This is well articulated in Peter Scholz, "Einführung," in *Das hellenistische Gymnasion*, ed. Kah and Scholz, 24.

31. To illustrate this point, compare the inscriptions listed in Günter Schörner, "Stiftungen von Badeanlagen im hellenistischen und kaiserzeitlichen Griechenland," with the collection brought by Fagan, *Bathing in Public in the Roman World*, 233–347.

32. This point has been made by many; see, for example, Fagan, "Bathing in the Backwaters," 523; and Farrington, "The Introduction and Spread of Roman Bathing in Greece," 57.

33. Pausanias, *Graeciae descriptio* 10.4.1.

34. *P.Oxy.* 43, 4441. For one detailed example of such an establishment combining a Hellenistic gymnasium with a Roman public bathhouse, see Yegül, *The Bath-Gymnasium Complex at Sardis*. See also Yegül, "The Roman Baths at Isthmia"; and Yegül, *Baths and Bathing in Classical Antiquity*, 250–313. On the Egyptian phenomena, see Meyer, "'Gymnase' et 'Thermes' dans l'Égypte romaine et byzantine."

35. Pausanias, *Graeciae descriptio* 6:23:8; Martial, *Epigrammata* 3:68; Suetonius, *De vita caesarum: Ner.* 12.3.

36. See, for example, Nielsen, *Thermae et balnea*, 1:6–59; Yegül, *Baths and Bathing in Classical Antiquity*, 48–91; and Yegül, *Bathing in the Roman World*, 40–79.

37. Although far from complete, a broad summary of the distribution of baths throughout the Roman world, accompanied by maps and charts, is offered by Nielsen, *Thermae et balnea*.

38. Pliny, *HN* 36.24.121 (but compare the different reading of this text in Fagan, *Bathing in Public in the Roman World*, 42); 856 is the number cited in the *Curiosum urbis regionum XIV* and the *Notitia regionum urbis XIV*, ed. Jordan and Hülsen, *Topographie*, 2:573; Pliny the Younger, *Ep.* 2.17.26; Aristides, *Or.* 17.11. All sources are gathered and discussed in Fagan, *Bathing in Public in the Roman World*, 40–41, 357. See also Yegül, *Bathing in the Roman World*, 3.

39. Butler, *The Arab Conquest of Egypt*, 402–26; *b. Meg.* 6b.

40. The sources on this topic have been collected and discussed many times; see Nielsen, *Thermae et balnea*, 1:131–35; and Fagan, *Bathing in Public in the Roman World*, 160–61. For the rabbinic sources on this topic, see my discussion on p. 70.

41. For example: Martial, *Epigrammata* 14.60; Apuleius, *Met.* 8.29; Libanius, *Or.* 1.108, 174; Libanius, *Ep.* 29.3. For other times, see, for example, Suetonius, *De vita caesarum: Dom.* 8.2.

42. Seneca the Younger, *Ep.* 86.12.

43. Libanius, *Or.* 1.246.

44. Suetonius, *De vita caesarum: Aug.* 2.82; Suetonius, *Gram. et rhet.* 2.23.

45. Augustine, *Ep.* 211.13.

46. Tacitus, *Ann.* 11.3; *SHA, Alex. Sev.* 30.4.

47. Lucian, *Hipp.*; Nielsen, *Thermae et balnea*, 1:119–52; Yegül, *Bathing in the Roman World*, 12–14.

48. For the various sources mentioning prostitutes in the baths, see Nielsen, *Thermae et balnea*, 1:145n27; and Dauphin, "Brothels, Baths and Babes." On barbers, see Juvenal, *Saturae* 11:150–61; and Fagan, *Bathing in Public in the Roman World*, 199n28. On doctors, see Fagan, *Bathing in Public in the Roman World*, 90, 92n35; and Jackson, "Waters and Spas in the classical World," 9, 9n38. Magicians and scholars will be discussed later in the book; see chap. 8. On dealers in trifles, see Apuleius, *Met.* 4.8.

49. Fagan, *Bathing in Public in the Roman World*, 323–24, no. 277.

50. Ibid., 66.

51. Augustine, *De ord.* 1.8.25.

52. Seneca the Younger, *Ep.* 56.1–2 (trans. Gummere, 1.373–75). See Fagan's comments about this passage and his references to the archaeological evidence, which confirms the occasional close proximity of public baths and city apartment buildings; Fagan, *Bathing in Public in the Roman World*, 12–13.

53. *SHA, Heliogab.* 21.6.
54. Juvenal, *Saturae* 5.85–91.
55. Martial, *Epigrammata* 6.93 (trans. Bailey, 2.73).
56. The most detailed study on this subject remains Ward, "Women in Roman Baths." Cf. Michael Satlow's unpublished paper, "Mixed Bathing in Roman Palestine." Several sources discussed in this chapter are also treated there; however, our general approach, methodology, and conclusions are entirely different. See also Fagan, *Bathing in Public in the Roman World*, 24–29; cf. Yegül, *Bathing in the Roman World*, 27–34, who tries to mediate this custom and put it in line with our own norms. In general, modern suggestions that some bathing garments were worn to cover the body have rightly been rejected; see, for example, Howell, *A Commentary on Book One of the Epigrams of Martial*, 158. If anything, the opposite was the norm. See more about garments on pp. 156–60.
57. The most recent study to make this claim in great detail, illustration, and sophistication is Vout, *Sex on Show*. See also Fagan, *Bathing in Public in the Roman World*, 214–15, esp. n. 80; Brown, *The Body and Society*; and Brown, "Late Antiquity," 245.
58. Hallett, *The Roman Nude*.
59. I discuss these phenomena in detail in "The Material World of Babylonia"; see also Fagan, *Bathing in Public in the Roman World*, 78, 214–15.
60. The best-known source for gender separation is *CIL* 2, suppl. 5181. Other sources, primary and secondary, are collected in Fagan, *Bathing in Public in the Roman World*, 24ff., 214–15, esp. n. 80; also see, in detail, Eliav, "The Roman Bath as a Jewish Institution," 444–48.
61. *AE* 1935.172 = *AE* 1977.758; translated in Fagan, *Bathing in Public in the Roman World*, 272, no. 120.
62. *CIL* 6.15258; translated in Fagan, *Bathing in Public in the Roman World*, 319, no. 261. For a slightly different translation, see Courtney, *Musa lapidaria*, 161. Both cite other parallels to the theme of love of baths in other epitaphs from the eastern parts of the empire.
63. Fagan, *Bathing in Public in the Roman World*, 277, no. 129; see also p. 166; Libanius, *Ep.* 13.7.
64. Martial, *Epigrammata* 2.48, 5.20; Cicero, *Fam.* 14.20 (173 in the Loeb edition). See also Fagan, *Bathing in Public in the Roman World*, 75–81.
65. For a collection and analysis of this literature, see Busch, *Versus balnearum*.
66. Compare Sidonius Apollinaris, *Carm.* 18–19; Sidonius Apollinaris, *Epist.* 2.2.4–9 with Lucian, *Hipp.*; Statius, *Silv.* 1.5.
67. Procopius, *Aed.* 1.11.1.
68. This view is shared by numerous modern scholars. See, for example, Stambaugh, *The Ancient Roman City*, 201; and DeLaine, "Recent Research on Roman Baths," 11.
69. Vitruvius, *De arch.* 1.3.1.
70. Procopius, *Aed.* 1.11.21.
71. Tacitus, *Agr.* 21.
72. Aristides, *Or.* 26.92, 98–99 (trans. Behr, 2.94–95). For a discussion and bibliography, see Longfellow, *Roman Imperialism and Civic Patronage*, in particular pp. 7–8.

73. For example: *CIL* 3.324 = *ILS* 613, Fagan, *Bathing in Public in the Roman World*, 236, no. 13; *CIL* 11.4781 = *ILS* 739, Fagan, *Bathing in Public in the Roman World*, 237, no. 16: "Repairers of the world and restorers of cities, our lords Flavius Julius Constantius, pius, felix, always Augustus, and Julianus, the most noble and victorious Caesar, to make their hallowed name live forever, restored for the Spoletians, with imperial largesse, the baths that had been destroyed by fire some time ago."

74. See Cicero, *Att.* 6.2.5 (116 in the Loeb edition) about the birth of the idea, although without mention of baths; Pausanias, *Graeciae descriptio* 2.3.5 is a good example in writing about Hadrian building baths in Corinth; for the *Scriptores historiae Augustae*, see, for example, the mention of Antoninus Pius raising a bath in Ostia (*SHA, Ant. Pius* 8.3), or the claim that Alexander Severus "built a bath . . . in every region which happened to have none" (*SHA, Alex. Sev.* 39.3; trans. Magie, 2.255). Similarly, "bad" emperors, such as Commodus, do not build baths (*SHA, Comm.* 17.5), or Elagabalus, who built baths, used them once, and then destroyed them (*SHA, Heliogab.* 30.7). On the representation of bathhouses in the *Scriptores historiae Augustae* and the claim that the author(s) use the erection of baths as a test to distinguish between good and bad emperors, see Merten, *Bäder und Badegepflogenheiten*. In Procopius the motif of baths is repeated in almost every city that Justinian establishes; see, for example, Procopius, *Aed.* 2.6.10–11, 2.8.25, 4.1.20–24, 4.10.21.

75. Ammianus Marcellinus, *Res Gesta* 31.1.2.

76. A good, relatively well-documented example of the destruction of statues are the riots of Antioch in 387 CE; see Van Dam, "Imagining an Eastern Roman Empire."

77. *b. Šabb.* 33b. See also *TanḥB*, Shoftim 9; *b. ʿAbod. Zar.* 2b. For more on this passage and the modern scholarly debate around it, see Eliav, "The Roman Bath as a Jewish Institution," 428, 428n21.

78. *ʾAbot R. Nat.* version A, 28 (Schechter, 85).

79. Joab: *y. Mak.* 2 (31d); *Midr. Sam.* 25:3. King exalted by praise: *Lev. Rab.* 26:1 (Margulies, 588); *Num. Rab.* 12:5; *Pesiq. Rab. Kah.* 4:2 (Mandelbaum, 1.55); *Deut. Rab.*, Devarim 13 (Liebermann, 11); *TanḥB*, Ḥukat 5 (in the printed edition 4). In the eastern parts of the Roman Empire, in both Greek texts and rabbinic literature, the term "king" was a common appellation for the emperor; see Mason, *Greek Terms for Roman Institutions*, 120–21. The foundational study for the rabbinic material on this topic remains Ziegler, *Die Königsgleichnisse des Midrasch beleuchtet durch die römische Kaiserzeit*.

80. Pace Lapin, *Rabbis as Romans*, 128.

Chapter 2. A Literary Bathhouse: Realities and Perceptions at a Roman (Jewish) Public Bath

1. I borrow this term from Edmund Thomas's discussion of Lucian's *Hippias* and put my own spin on it; see Thomas, *Monumentality and the Roman Empire*, 221–29.

2. For rabbis as inventors of new terms through the process of nominalization described here, extracting a new noun from a verb, see Fraade, "The Innovation of Nominalized Verbs in Mishnaic Hebrew."

3. For the list of references to *merḥats* in the Mishnah, see Kasovsky, *Thesaurus Mishnae*, 4:1666. The various names of the bath were already gathered and presented

in the pioneering work of Krauss; see "Bad und Badewesen," 180–81, 189–90. But Krauss overlooked the linguistic innovation embedded in those terms and their importance for understanding provincials in the Roman world. In the same vein, more recent scholarly work on bathhouses in Jewish sources either neglected to discuss its names altogether or, when doing so, failed to recognize their cultural significance. For a sample, see Kottek, "Selected Elements," 2915–16; Sperber, *The City in Roman Palestine*, 58–72; and Jacobs, "Römische Thermenkultur," 227–32.

4. For references, see Sokoloff, *A Dictionary of Jewish Babylonian Aramaic*, 215, s.v. In Roman Palestine, the Aramaic verb *saḥi*, to wash or bathe, was known and regularly used by rabbinic scholars, but they, unlike their brethren in Persia, never translated the Hebrew name, *merḥats*, probably their own invention, into Aramaic. Rather, they continued using it even in Aramaic passages; see, for example, *y. Ber.* 4 (8b)—"When R. Mana would go to bathe (*mashey*) in the heated bath (*merḥats*)"; on the usage of this Aramaic verb among rabbis in Roman Palestine, see Sokoloff, *A Dictionary of Jewish Palestinian Aramaic*, 372, s.v. For the question of whether Roman public bathhouses existed in Persian Babylon, see Eliav, "The Material World of Babylonia," 177–78, 177–78n87.

5. On this Greek name and its Latin equivalent, see pp. 30–31. On the various Syriac forms, see Smith, *Thesaurus Syriacus*, 1:536. For the rabbinic material, see Krauss, "Bad und Badewesen," 180; Krauss, *Griechische und lateinische Lehnwörter*, 2:158–60; and Sokoloff, *A Dictionary of Jewish Palestinian Aramaic*, 105–6.

6. With varied spelling attestations but without vowels, the exact pronunciation requires some guesswork. The earliest reference to this term as the name of a public bathhouse is *m. 'Abod. Zar.* 1:5, based on the manuscripts that transmit the more accurate Palestinian textual tradition; see Rosenthal, "Mishna Aboda Zara," 2:17.

7. For a comprehensive, although incomplete, sample of these occurrences, both as related to the baths and not, see Krauss, *Griechische und lateinische Lehnwörter*, 2:205–6.

8. Cf., for example, Zahavy, *The Talmud of the Land of Israel*, 106, section X, which translates *dimosin* as "hot springs," with Neusner's own translation to *m. 'Abod. Zar.* 1:5, which gets it completely right, translating "public bathhouses"; Neusner, *The Mishnah*, 661. Dvorjetski has taken this blunder ad absurdum and relates all references to *dimosin* in the Palestinian Talmud to the thermal springs, mainly of the Galilean city of Tiberias; see Dvorjetski, *Leisure, Pleasure, and Healing*, 34, 136–37. I find no basis for her assertions, in particular because rabbinic terminology consistently refers to these particular springs as *ḥame* (= the hot [waters of]) Tiberias. A closer look at rabbinic discussions of the *dimosin* shows that the authors assumed it was heated by man-made fire with ordinary fuel rather than natural thermal springs; see, for example, *y. Šeb.* 8 (38b–c). In the midst of a discussion about the laws of the Jewish leap year, the rabbinic scholars associate the *dimosin* with the mishnaic law (*m. Šeb.* 8:11) about "a bathhouse (*merḥats*) that was heated with straws and chaff." Other modern scholars were pretty much on the mark regarding this term, starting with the abovementioned Krauss and followed by other lexicons, even if they were not aware of the full linguistic and terminological spectrum presented here.

9. See the references brought in LSJ, 303 (s.v. *balaneion*), 1061 (*loutron* I), to which I would like to add *P.Oxy.* 53, 896, 1889. On the early usage of this terminology

to describe bathhouses already in the Hellenistic period, perhaps even before the emergence of the Roman public bathhouses, see Trümper, "Urban Context of Greek Public Baths," 36, and the references and bibliography she cites in notes 11 and 33. Among later writers from the third century onward, this combination was the norm; see the examples brought in Sophocles, *Greek Lexicon*, 356, s.v. *dēmosios* 2C.

10. Fronto, *Ep.* 5.1 (Haines, 1:268–71).

11. For a range of examples, see the different entries in Smith, *Thesaurus Syriacus*, 1:803, 884–85.

12. See, for example, those listed in note 8 in this chapter.

13. For a broad introduction to this issue and a bibliography, see Kornfilt and Whitman, "Introduction: Nominalizations in Syntactic Theory." For an example of the many studies devoted to this phenomenon in the ancient languages of the Mediterranean, see Myers, "The Use of the Adjective as a Substantive in Horace." See also the short comment in Balme and Lawall, *Athenaze*, 1:113. My assistant Dr. Jelle Verburg contributed to my thinking on this topic and some of the above examples are his.

14. *P.Oxy.* 892, line 11 (Grenfell and Hunt, 6:211). Although admittedly the author of this papyrus wrote *loutron* above the line, apparently thinking the insertion necessary for proper understanding: *to dēmosion loutron* (the public bathhouse). From later centuries, see also the references from sixth-century Antioch on p. 48 and in note 17 of the current chapter.

15. Another early usage of the nominalized adjective *dēmosion*, perhaps referring to a public city structure, although apparently not a bathhouse, comes from the Epistle of the Gallican Churches, a second-century Christian text preserved by the fourth-century Church Historian and native of Roman Palestine Eusebius; see Eusebius, *H.E.* 5.1.37. The text speaks of Christian martyrs taken to their execution in the *dēmosion*, perhaps the local amphitheater, according to Lampe, *A Patristic Greek Lexicon*, 343, s.v. *dēmosios* 2a. If so, this is an interesting, early parallel to the rabbinic nomenclature, although applied to a different urban structure. However, the syntax of the text is somewhat unclear, leading some modern commentators to suspect the Greek is corrupted; see the doubts raised by the various editors of the text, summarized by Lake, *Eusebius*, 425n1.

16. Lassus, "La Mosaïque," 134–36 (no. 14). See also Levi, *Antioch Mosaic Pavements*, 1:323–45 (the *dēmosin* discussed on p. 330), 2:LXXIX, b. But compare the misinterpretation of this specific part of the mosaic in Kondoleon, *Antioch*, 114–15.

17. For the inscription, see Downey, "Greek and Latin Inscriptions," 84–89 (no. 112); for the discussion of our phenomenon with further references and bibliography, see p. 85.

18. Lassus, "La Mosaïque," 131–32 (no. 5); Levi, *Antioch Mosaic Pavements*, 1329, 2:LXXIX, b.

19. For the earlier original meanings of the word, see Lewis and Short, *A Latin Dictionary*, 1147, s.v.; and Ernout and Meillet, *Dictionnare étymologique de la langue latine*, 772–73. For the application of *privatus* to bathhouses in Latin sources, see Merten, *Bäder und Badegepflogenheiten*, 11–15.

20. The topic has been studied extensively, although most of the attention is geared toward demonstrating that Latin was known and used in the eastern parts of the empire. The most comprehensive study, with ample attention and bibliography

regarding the east and the phenomenon discussed here, namely Latinism, the incorporation of Latin in regional languages, is Adams, *Bilingualism and the Latin Language*. See also Horrocks, *Greek*, 124–87.

21. The evidence regarding *pribaton* has been gathered and discussed several times; see a summary and bibliography in Downey, *A History of Antioch in Syria*, 659–60n1. More evidence from early Byzantine times is documented in Berger, *Das Bad in der byzantinischen Zeit*, 28–29, 138–39.

22. For a collection of the references with a proper identification of the term and its Latin roots as well as its Greek parallels, but oblivious to the cultural dynamics presented here, see Krauss, *Griechische und lateinische Lehnwörter*, 2:488. For the Syriac material, where *pribaton* appears but never, as far as I can tell, in relation to the baths, see Smith, *Thesaurus Syriacus*, 2:3259, s.v.

23. Some modern scholars misinterpreted the rabbinic *privata'*, seeing it as a private bathing facility, restricted to the personal use of the wealthy in palaces and the like, a mistake stemming from overly relying on the original, early Latin meaning of the word and not seeing that by extension and in its adoption by Greek and Aramaic vernaculars the meaning of the term was modified. See Kottek, "Selected Elements," 2917; and Jacobs, "Römische Thermenkultur," 227. On the other hand, Berger (unaware of the rabbinic material but writing about *privata* in general) was on the mark when he observed that "Diese kleinen *balneae privatae* waren ... durchaus öffentlich zugänglich, die Bezeichnung *privatae* bezog sich vielmehr auf die Finanzierungsweise: Während die 'Privatbäder' Besitz einer Privatperson waren und nur vom Eintrittsgeld getragen wurden ..., wurde der Betrieb der großen Thermen vom Staat organisiert und subventioniert" (These small *balneae privatae* were ... absolutely publicly accessible, the name of *privatae* refers rather to the way they were financed; while the "private" baths were the property of a private person and were supported only by admission money ... the operation of large therma was organized and subsidized by the state). See Berger, *Das Bad in der byzantinischen Zeit*, 28–29.

24. I wrote about this process in Eliav, *God's Mountain*, xxviii–xxxii and the bibliography listed there.

25. See pp. 24–25.

26. See *P.Oxy.* 2718, 2877.

27. *CIL* 14.98. For a discussion and translation of this inscription, see Fagan, *Bathing in Public in the Roman World*, 173–74, and 234–35, no. 6. The standard discussion of construction costs of baths is still the dissertation by Meusel, "Die Verwaltung und Finanzierung der öffentlichen Bäder zur römischen Kaiserzeit." Good modern discussion can be found in Fagan, *Bathing in Public in the Roman World*, 142–44, 173–35.

28. DeLaine, *The Baths of Caracalla*, 207–24.

29. These calculations are based on Zuiderhoek, "Cities," 175. For the various annual earnings and calculations of subsistence levels, with the variations one must consider for different times and locations throughout the Roman world, see Dominic Rathbone, "Earnings and Costs: Living Standards and the Roman Economy (First to Third Centuries AD)," in *Quantifying the Roman Economy: Methods and Problems*, ed. Alan Bowman and Andrew Wilson (Oxford: Oxford University Press, 2009), 299–326. The standard study on costs and earnings remains, over a generation after it

was first published, Duncan-Jones, *The Economy of the Roman Empire*, with numerous references to bathhouses scattered throughout the book.

30. Pausanias, *Graeciae descriptio* 2.3.5. Fagan, *Bathing in Public in the Roman World*, 137–42 has collected and studied the data from inscriptions about imperial involvement.

31. On the entire topic discussed here, see Zuiderhoek, "Cities," 172–92, with specific reference to bathhouses on p. 180.

32. Pliny the Younger, *Ep.* 10.23–24. See also *P.Oxy.* 3088, a permission letter from the prefect of Egypt to the people of Oxyrhynchus, granting them permission to use local tax money to build a public bath.

33. The foundational study of this phenomenon is by the French archaeologist and historian Paul Veyne, in his 1976 tome, *Le pain et le cirque*; for the most useful rendition of this work, see Veyne, *Bread and Circuses*.

34. The evidence was meticulously gathered and thoroughly studied in Fagan, *Bathing in Public in the Roman World*, 128–75.

35. See ibid., 171 for the wide epigraphic documentation of this phenomenon. It is also confirmed by the papyri; see, for example, *P.Oxy.* 54 and 896, regarding a bath named after Hadrian in Oxyrhynchus in the early third century and well into the fourth century.

36. *SHA, Ant. Pius* 8.3, *Alex. Sev.* 39.3, *Comm.* 17.5, *Heliogab.* 30.7. See Merten, *Bäder und Badegepflogenheiten*, 1–2, 16–34. There is no need for the purposes of this study to consider the veracity of this text, its date, or its nature; see on these matters, for example, Potter, *Literary Texts and the Roman Historian*, 145–47.

37. Procopius, *Aed.* 2.6.10–11, 2.8.24, 4.1.23, 4.10.21.

38. For a full list and discussion of these buildings, see Sartre, *The Middle East under Rome*, 163–64.

39. *Qoh. Rab.* 1:8 (Hirshman, 70–73). An earlier version of this story in *t. Ḥul.* 2:24 (Zuckermandel, 503) does not include the dialogue about the money and the bathhouses, but for the discussion here it is immaterial whether this portion is part of the original story; its relevance stems from the perception of the author, regardless of who he is. For vast bibliography and scholarly discussions regarding this rabbinic tale, including the suggestion that R. Eliezer's interlocutor here is not a Christian (unconvincing to me but also immaterial to my arguments), see the notes in Hirshman's edition. For another late-rabbinic story that incorporates the motif of a Jew erecting baths to benefit the city, see the tale about R. Simeon b. Yoḥai in *b. Šabb.* 33b, but earlier versions of that story do not mention the erection of baths, which seem to have been taken from the earlier *baraita* that the Bavli transmits there, which mentions the baths.

40. Various texts preserve this statement, all in the context of the biblical prohibition against usury, although with varied versions; see *Exod. Rab.* 31:11 (preserved also in the Yemenite compilation *MHG* Deut. 23:20 [Fisch, 528]). Other versions of this passage identify the impious man as the biblical villain Esau; see *Tanḥ Exod., Mishpatim* 14; *TanḥB Exod., Mishpatim* 5 (Buber, 84).

41. From the vast literature on this topic, the following offer a complex and nuanced discussion of the architectural, municipal aspects of imperialism and Romanization: Revell, *Roman Imperialism and Local Identities*; and Longfellow, *Roman Imperialism and Civic Patronage*. On the broad concept of Roman imperialism and its implementation, see Hoyos, *A Companion to Roman Imperialism*.

42. Tacitus, *Agr.* 21.

43. In treating buildings as political statements, I am especially indebted to the ideas developed by Sonne, "Der politische Aspekt von Architektur," 11–16.

44. Aristides, *Or.* 26.93–99; Libanius, *Ep.* 126.9, 149.2. See also Libanius, *Or.* 11. 133–34. For the documentary evidence, see the summary and bibliography in Revell, *Roman Imperialism and Local Identities*, 15–23.

45. Aristides, *Or.* 26.99 (trans. Behr, 2:95); *b. Šabb.* 33b and the literature listed in chapter 1, note 77.

46. For a concise although by no means exhaustive summary and further bibliography on this vast topic, see Du Plessis, "Property."

47. On the phenomenon of local legal traditions in the Roman world, with particular attention to the documentary evidence that comes from Judaea and Nabataea, see Oudshoorn, *The Relation between Roman and Local Law in the Babatha and Salome Komaise Archives*, and the many studies by Hannah Cotton on this topic listed in the bibliography there. For a more recent contribution, see Cotton, "Continuity of Nabataean Law in the Petra Papyri." Several studies of rabbinic law of property have appeared; among them, see Gulak, *Yesode ha-mishpat ha-'ivri*, 1:87–140; and Albeck, *Introduction to Jewish Law in Talmudic Times*, 102–226. For a comparison to Roman law, see Cohen, *Jewish and Roman Law*, 2:457–71.

48. *m. B. Bat.* 3:1.

49. *m. Ned.* 5:5.

50. *b. Sanh.* 17b. Other versions of this *baraita* with similar expressions of the same conceptual outlook on the municipal textures of villages and cities appear in *y. Qidd.* 4 (66b); *S. Eli. Zut.* 16 (Friedmann, 13).

51. *m. Meg.* 3:2.

52. *m. B. Bat.* 4:6. See also *t. B. Bat.* 3:3 (Lieberman, 139).

53. *m. B. Bat.* 1:6; *t. Demai* 6:13 (Lieberman, 96–97).

54. *m. B. Meṣi'a* 8:8; *m. 'Abod Zar.* 1:9; *t. B. Bat.* 2:15 (Lieberman, 136).

55. *m. B. Meṣi'a* 8:8.

56. For more on the price range for such rentals and comparable commodities, see Sperber, *Roman Palestine*, 101–48, with specific reference to our text here on p. 106. On the cost of leasing and maintaining a bathhouse, see Nielsen, *Thermae et balnea*, 122–25.

57. The modern scholarly literature on this topic is vast, largely falling into two camps: those who tend to see the rabbinic, legal material as a reflection of real-life situations and those who are more skeptical. More specifically, see, for example, the introduction and some of the studies collected in Hezser, *Rabbinic Law in Its Roman and Near Eastern Context*, in particular p. 10, and the essay by Moscovitz, "Legal Fictions in Rabbinic Law and Roman Law." The foundational studies of the court cases (*ma'asim*) in the Mishnah and the Tosefta are Cohen, "The Place of the Rabbi in Jewish Society of the Second Century"; Cohen, "The Rabbi in Second-Century Jewish Society"; and Simon-Shoshan, *Stories of the Law*.

58. Vitruvius, *De arch.* 5.10; Lucian, *Hipp.* The Latin and Greek texts mentioned here have been discussed frequently by modern scholars, mostly in the attempt to correlate them with archaeological data and produce a description and history of bathing institutions. See, for example, Nielsen, *Thermae et balnea*, 1:37–59.

59. See pp. 29–30, and diagram 1.

60. *t. Ber.* 2:20 (Lieberman, 10).

61. *t. B. Bat.* 3:3 (Lieberman, 139). Neusner's translation here is ignorant of both philology and the realities of Roman bathhouses; see Jacob Neusner, *The Tosefta*, 6 vols. (New York: Ktav, 1977–86), 4:158. For the numerous textual variants and the interpretation of the terms, see Lieberman, *Tosefta kifshutah*, 10:363. For further suggestions regarding the identification of the various rooms, see Krauss, *Talmudische Archäologie*, 1:218–19; and Jacobs, "Römische Thermenkultur," 237–38. On the classification of inner and outer houses in relation to bathhouses in non-Jewish sources, see my discussion on pp. 89–90.

62. *m. B. Bat.* 4:6. On *vila'ot* and its variants and its identification, see Lieberman, *Tosefta kifshutah*, 10:360–61, 10:360–61n10. On *bēlon*, see Sophocles, *Greek Lexicon*, 307, s.v.

63. *m. Kelim* 22:10.

64. *t. Šabb.* 3:3 (Lieberman, 11–12). Cf. Krauss, "Bad und Badewesen," 188–89. See also my discussion of their utility on p. 118.

65. *y. Šabb.* 3 (6a). On this term and its meaning, see Sokoloff, *A Dictionary of Jewish Palestinian Aramaic*, 395, s.v., 3.

66. *y. Šeb.* 8 (38a); *y. Ned.* 4 (38d); *Gen. Rab.* 33:3 (Theodor and Albeck, 307). On the linguistic side, see Sokoloff, *A Dictionary of Jewish Palestinian Aramaic*, 78, s.v. *'ashun* 2. Modern scholars do not agree about the identification of the room; see Lieberman, *Ha-yerushalmi kifshuto*, introduction, 11; and Brand, *Kele ha-ḥeres besifrut ha-talmud*, 544.

67. For a good collection and discussion of the material, see Krauss, "Bad und Badewesen," 186–87; and Krauss, *Griechische und lateinische Lehnwörter*, 59–60. For the range of meanings associated with the Greek terms, see LSJ, 539, s.v.

68. *y. Šabb.* 3 (6b). On the hypocaust system, see pp. 64–67.

69. *Pesiq. Rab. Kah.* 3:10 (Mandelbaum, 48); *Tanḥ Deut., Ki teste'* 9.

70. *Tanḥ. Gen., Va-yeḥi* 6.

71. Sidonius Apollinaris, *Carm.* 22.136–39.

72. The depictions of the public baths in the Yakto mosaic are one example; see the references for its publication in note 16 in this chapter. For one example from a papyri correspondence, see *P.Oxy.* 896.

73. *y. Ber.* 3 (6c).

74. *y. Sanh.* 7 (25d). The text labels the Christian figure by the term *min*, usually taken to mean a heretic. However, the correct meaning of the word has recently come under reconsideration and scholarly debate; see, for example, Schremer, "Beyond Naming." For our discussion here, this modern dispute does not change much since the passage in question clearly indicates that the *minim* in question are believers in Jesus. For more about this text, see pp. 248–50.

75. See the summaries of the architectural elements in Nielsen, *Thermae et balnea*, 1:153–54 (the *frigidarium*), 1:155–57 (the *tepidarium* and *caldarium*).

76. *m. 'Abod. Zar.* 1:7.

77. For a nice example of these niches and their utility in bathhouse decoration, see Yegül, *Bathing in the Roman World*, 166. See also Krauss, "Bad und Badewesen," 180–81; and Krauss, *Talmudische Archäologie*, 1:217–18. Neusner interprets the passage in the *Yerushalmi* correctly when he translated *kippah* as "vaulting [for use in setting

up an idol]" in Jacob Neusner, ed., *The Talmud of the Land of Israel: A Preliminary Translation and Explanation, Volume 33: Avodah Zarah* (Chicago: University of Chicago Press, 1982), 42. In his translation of the Mishnah, he likewise translated *kippah* as "the vaulting on which they set up an idol" (*The Mishnah*, 661).

78. See fig. 4.

79. *t. B. Bat.* 3:3 (Lieberman, 139). On the Greek roots of *qamin* and its usage in other Semitic languages, see Krauss, *Griechische und lateinische Lehnwörter*, 2:551, s.v.

80. *y. Šabb.* 3 (6a). For a detailed discussion of this important ruling, its literary parallels, and its legal history, see Eliav, "Pyle—Puma—Sfat Medinah." The realistic interpretations of the *halakhah* that I present here and of the following one from *Miqva'ot* are based on insights provided by Saul Lieberman; see Lieberman, *Tosefta kifshutah*, 3:44–45; and in his notes to the new publication of the eighteenth-century commentary of David Pardo. See David Shmu'el ben Ya'aqov Pardo, *Sefer ḥasde David*, ed. Saul Lieberman, 4 vols. (Jerusalem: Bet hamidrash lerabanim shebe'ameriqah; New York: Yad harav Hertsog, 1970–77), 4:3:32, 4:3:32n42.

81. *t. Miqw.* 5:7 (Zuckermandel, 657).

82. See, for example, *m. Kelim* 8:7–8.

83. For the three versions of this story, see *y. Beṣah* 1 (60c); *b. Ketub.* 62a; and *b. Ber.* 60a. And see the detailed analysis in Eliav, "Realia, Daily Life, and the Transmission of Local Stories," 242–52. I come back to these passages later in the book; see pp. 230–31.

84. *m. Makš.* 2:5.

85. *t. B. Meṣi'a* 11:32 (Lieberman, 127).

86. See, for example, *P.Oxy.* 1430, 2015, 2040, together with Nielsen, *Thermae et balnea*, 1.126–27; and Fagan, *Bathing in Public in the Roman World*, 312–13. On the imperial contributions, see, for example, *SHA, Divus Claudius* 14.13–15; and *SHA, Alex. Sev.* 24.5. On the general issue of wood consumption, see the discussion in Hughes, *Environmental Problems of the Greeks and Romans*, 68–87.

87. For example, *m. Šeb.* 8:11; *m. Kelim* 17:1; *Exod. Rab.* 7:4 (Shinan, 195).

88. Tacitus, *Hist.* 3.32.

89. *m. Šeb.* 8:11; *y. Šeb.* 8 (38b–c). More on the social aspects of these dynamics in chapter 7.

90. For the legend on Haman, see *Pirqe R. El.* 50 (Börner-Klein, 699). Other versions of this legend do not mention this detail about heating the bath; see, for example, *b. Meg.* 16a; *Midrash panim aḥerim*, version b, 6 (Buber, 76). On Titus, the earliest version of the legend that includes the bathing component is *Lev. Rab.* 22:3 (Margulies, 501). Margulies provides a list of other versions of this tale in his notes.

91. Modern scholars have collected and discussed the ancient material in multiple studies. See in particular Wissemann, "Das Personal des antiken römischen Bades"; Nielsen, *Thermae et balnea*, 1:125–31 (and the various studies she lists there); and Yegül, *Baths and Bathing in Classical Antiquity*, 46–47.

92. Numerous sources from papyri, inscriptions, and literature all testify to the various customs and practices in this regard; the best comprehensive collection of the relevant Graeco-Roman material and scholarly bibliography on the topic is Nielsen, *Thermae et balnea*, 1:135–38. See also Scobie, "Slums," 409n33; and Yegül, *Bathing in the Roman World*, 11–12.

93. *Lam. Rab.* 3:44 (Buber, 137-38). A different version of this midrashic passage reads *miqveh*, that is, the water immersion facility used for Jewish ritual purity, instead of *merhats*; it was preserved in the printed edition of *Lamentation Rabbah*, as well as in the parallel version in *Pesiq. Rab. Kah.* 24:2 (Mandelbaum, 349). The other body of water used by the rabbinic author of this midrashic simile, the sea, suggests that the original version did not refer to a ritual purity immersion facility but to a public bathhouse, where, unlike the sea, there are time restrictions on use. The next pericope in the midrashic sequence quotes Jeremiah 17:13, where the word *miqveh* appears; this may have caused the manuscript copiers to insert the word in the earlier passage as well.

94. *t. Miqw.* 6:4 (Zuckermandel, 658). See more on ritual purity in the baths in chapter 4.

95. See Fagan, *Bathing in Public in the Roman World*, 203-4, and in particular the inscription he brings in note 45. But the operating charter of the baths in Lusitania, in the southwestern Iberian Peninsula, explicitly assigns the morning hours for women to bathe; see *CIL* 2.5181. Needless to say, if the facility was open in the evening, others may have found their way to it as well; for one example, see Apuleius, *Met.* 1.5.

96. *y. Pesaḥ.* 4 (31a). The version of this *baraita* in *t. Pesaḥ.* 3:17 (Lieberman, 155) does not mention bathhouses. *SHA, Alex. Sev.* 24.6.

97. *y. Ber.* 3 (6c).

98. *y. Ber.* 2 (4c). On seasonal bathhouses around the Roman world, see Nielsen, *Thermae et balnea*, 1:138-40.

99. *m. Ta'an.* 1:6.

100. *'Ag. Ber.* 7:3 (Buber, 19).

101. *CIL* 11.1421, line 23. For further discussion and bibliography on the latter text, see Gordon, *Illustrated Introduction to Latin Epigraphy*, 105-6.

102. *y. Ber.* 2 (4c) with parallel in *Pesiq. Rab.* 22 (Friedmann, 112a); *y. Ma'aś. Š.* 1 (52d). On the various conjectures about his identity, see the entry of the medieval lexicographer Nathan b. Yeḥiel of Rome: Alexander Kohut, ed., *Aruch completum*, 9 vols. (Vienna: Brög, 1878-92; reprint, New York: Pardes, 1955), 8:280, s.v. "bath owner," with the editor, Alexander Kohut, remarking correctly "this word does not appear in Greek sources"; Krauss, *Griechische und lateinische Lehnwörter*, 2:585-86 (bath master); and Sperber, *The City in Roman Palestine*, 60 (bath attendant). But cf. Lieberman, *Tosefta kifshutah*, 2:716n25, who (following Jacob Epstein) sees him as a money changer, not particularly related to the baths, and interprets the word *turmesar* as "small coins" (from the name of the plant *turmus*, i.e., lupine).

103. For the Greek and Latin references, see Nielsen, *Thermae et balnea*, 1:127-28 (quote on 1:127). For a female *ballan*, see Christer Bruun, review of Garrett G. Fagan, *Bathing in Public in the Roman World*, *JRA* 15 (2002): 460n9. On the Syriac, see Smith, *Thesaurus Syriacus*, 435, 536, s.v.; and Sokoloff, *A Syriac Lexicon*, 158, s.v.

104. The first quote is from *t. Ma'ś. Š.* 1:4 (Lieberman, 244). The second quote is from *m. Me'il.* 5:4. See also *m. Šeb.* 8:5. On the *prutah* in general, see Sperber, *Roman Palestine*, 28, 78-79. On the tokens used at certain times, see Lieberman, *Tosefta kifshutah*, 2:715-16, together with Fagan, *Bathing in Public in the Roman World*, 162n68.

105. *m. Kelim* 8:8 (quote), 17:1.

106. Water: *t. Makš.* 3:11 (Zuckermandel, 675). The *halakhah* perceives the *ballan* as closely associated with water, thus his food (an egg in the formulation of the Tosefta) is susceptible to contracting impurity. Thieves: *Num. Rab.* 13:5; *Pesiq. Rab.* 7 (Friedmann, 27b–28a). Women: *baraita* in *b. Qidd.* 82b.

107. Furnace: *m. Kelim* 8:8. Log: *m. Zabim* 4:2; *t. Zabim* 4:7 (Zuckermandel, 679). Box: *t. Kelim b. m.* 10:3 (Zuckermandel, 588); *Sifra, Metsora' perek zavim* 1:2:5 (Weiss, 75b).

108. See Nielsen, *Thermae et balnea*, 1:127. Holding this view among the scholars of rabbinic material are Krauss, "Bad und Badewesen," 191; Krauss, *Talmudische Archäologie*, 1:224–25; and Jacobs, "Römische Thermenkultur," 243–46. Cf. Sperber, *The City in Roman Palestine*, 60, who does not recognize this multiplicity of vocations.

109. For the meanings and variations of all these words, see the specific entries in LSJ, 527–28; Lewis and Short, *A Latin Dictionary*, 1261; and better documentation in Glare, *Oxford Latin Dictionary*, 1370–71. For the *'olyar* in rabbinic literature, see Krauss, *Griechische und lateinische Lehnwörter*, 2:20, s.v.

110. *y. Ber.* 2 (4c). Also appearing in *Pesiq. Rab.* 22 (Friedmann, 112a).

111. *t. B. Bat.* 3:3 (Lieberman, 139).

112. *b. Šabb.* 41a. On the version of this text that reads "does not anoint [his body with oil] first," that is, prior to immersion in water, and the relevance of this addition to the modern debate on the place of anointment in the order of operation in the baths as depicted by the rabbis, see Lieberman, *Ha-yerushalmi kifshuto*, 11. On a second, less picturesque version of this saying—"[He who] bathed and did not anoint, [it is as if he] did not bathe [at all]"—see *Kallah Rab.* 9:16 (Higger, 339). For more on the consumption of oil in the public baths, see Fagan, "Gifts of Gymnasia." The omnipresent production and consumption of olive oil in the ancient world in general, and in the Graeco-Roman Mediterranean in particular, of which its use in the bathhouse is only one facet, have received abundant attention in modern scholarship; for the tip of the iceberg, see Foxhall, *Olive Cultivation in Ancient Greece*, in particular the calculations on 91–92; Mattingly, "First Fruit?"; and the comprehensive bibliography provided in these studies.

113. *t. Ter.* 10:10 (Lieberman, 162). Rubbing oil against marble appears also in *t. Šabb.* 16:14 (Lieberman, 78); *Perek ha-nikhnas la-merḥats* 2 (Higger, 300–301); and *Kallah Rab.* 9:14 (Higger, 338). The latter two contain the sneer about the donkey. See Lieberman's interpretation of this practice with some interesting parallels from classical literature in *Tosefta kifshutah*, 1:473–74. See also his review of Higger's edition to *Kallah Rabbati* in Saul Lieberman, *Studies in Palestinian Talmudic Literature*, ed. David Rosenthal (Jerusalem: Magnes, 1991), 554 (Heb.).

114. *Strigilis*: *m. Šabb.* 22:6; *t. Šabb.* 16:19 (Lieberman, 79). Flasks: *t. Kelim b. q.* 2:9 (Zuckermandel, 571). Prohibition against glass: *Perek ha-nikhnas la-merḥats* 2 (Higger, 302); *Kallah Rab.* 9:16 (Higger, 339).

115. The most explicit expression of this custom appears in *b. Šabb.* 40b. It is also mentioned in as many words in *y. Šabb.* 3 (6a), and even less explicitly, but apparently referring to the same practice, in *y. Šeb.* 8 (38a). Because these traditions mention this practice as part of anecdotes involving named rabbis, they are probably not theoretical constructs.

116. *t. Kelim b. m.* 2:12 (Zuckermandel, 580), and also *m. Kelim* 12:6 (with no mention of the *'olyar*). See also the references to this instrument, without relating it to the *'olyar*, as in the previous note. The connection between the suspension of the scraper and archaeological material was made by Sperber, *The City in Roman Palestine*, 68n13 (with a typographical error, one of many in that book, in the reference to the rabbinic passage). See already Krauss, "Bad und Badewesen," 42–43. Pace Kottek, in "Selected Elements," 2916, who claims that the *'olyar* "brings oil to the bath, he is the one who anoints with oil"; this is a possible, yet not substantiated, conjecture. On a possible second reference to the *'olyar* and oil, based on an ambiguous reading preserved in a partial and rather corrupted manuscript of the *Yerushalmi* (which nevertheless preserved some old, authentic versions), see Lieberman, *Ha-yerushalmi kifshuto*, 11.

117. *y. Šeb.* 8 (38a). As happens many times in the Palestinian Talmud, the passage is terse and ambiguous. Here in particular, signs show that later copyists and editors intervened and changed the words in question. The appellation *'orira'*, based on the Rome manuscript, sometimes appears as a variant of *'olyar*, suggesting that the latter might be the title here as well. For a full apparatus of the versions among the different textual witnesses, as well as discussion and bibliography, see Feliks, *Talmud Yerushalmi Tractate Shevi'it Critically Edited*, 2:172–73.

118. *t. Ṭehar.* 8:7–8 (Zuckermandel, 669). See also *m. Ṭehar.* 7:7. For the interpretation of the "room of the *'olyarin*" as the *apodyterium* and the "the windows of the *'olyarin*" as its cubbies, see Lieberman, *Tosefta kifshutah*, 1:26, 9:363.

119. Epiphanius, *Adv. haeres.* 30.24.2–3, ll. 15–17 (Holl, 365).

120. *Baraitot* in *b. Šabb.* 147b; *b. 'Erub.* 88a. For the documentation of the Graeco-Roman material, see Fagan, *Bathing in Public in the Roman World*, 216n82. Much can be added to the list there; see, for example, *P.Oxy.* 903 (a sort of tote bag for women going to the baths), 921.

121. *y. Ma'aś. Š.* 1 (52d). Lieberman's interpretation of this passage, which sees this payment as an entrance fee to the bath, lacks evidence; see Lieberman, *Tosefta kifshutah*, 2:716n26.

122. *Baraita* in *b. Beṣah* 32a.

123. Many years before me, Lieberman reached the same conclusion (see Lieberman, *Tosefta kifshutah*, 9:363), but he did not apply it to the cultural realm as I strive to do here.

124. Josephus, *AJ* 12.119–20, *BJ* 2.591–92, *Vit.* 74.6; *m. 'Abod. Zar.* 2:6; *y. 'Abod. Zar.* 2 (41d); *b. 'Abod. Zar.* 35b–36a, 37a. On the whole issue, see the studies by Goodman, "Kosher Olive Oil in Antiquity"; and Rosenblum, "Kosher Olive Oil in Antiquity Reconsidered."

125. *Gen. Rab.* 63:8 (Theodor and Albeck, 687, line 7); *Midrash panim aḥerim*, version B 6 (Buber, 76).

Chapter 3. Earliest Encounters: Archaeology, Scholarly Debate, and the Shifting Grounds of Interpretation

1. 1 Macc. 8; Josephus, *AJ* 12.414–19. On this event and the scholarly debates about it, see the summary in Schürer, *The History of the Jewish People*, 1:171–72.

2. Macalister, *The Excavation of Gezer*, 223–28.

3. On these early Greek public baths, see pp. 31–33, and the bibliography there. The archaeological findings from Judaea that pertain to these Hellenistic bathing establishments have been discussed a few times: see Small, "Late Hellenistic Baths in Palestine"; Hoss, *Baths and Bathing*, 38–45; and Birney, "Phoenician Bathing in the Hellenistic East." I owe this last reference to Arleta Kowalewska, who read this chapter and made some important comments and corrections. She also shared with me some chapters of her book, at the time not yet published, for which I am very grateful. See Kowalewska, *Bathhouses in Iudaea*; this book came out too late to fully consult here.

4. See my discussion of these elements and the bibliography about them in chapter 1, pp. 22–29

5. For Herod's first visit to Rome, see Josephus, *BJ* 1.280–85; Josephus, *AJ* 14.377–89. Much has been written about the elusiveness of Herod's Judaism; see, for example, Cohen, "Was Herod Jewish?" 13–24. Much has been written on the various names/titles, Greek and Latin, of bathhouses and their development; for a clear and concise summary, see Nielsen, *Thermae et balnea*, 1:6–9.

6. All the literary references were collected and discussed in Fagan, *Bathing in Public in the Roman World*, 45–55.

7. See Netzer, "Herodian Bath-Houses"; Netzer, *The Architecture of Herod*, 255–58; and Hoss, *Baths and Bathing*, 45–49. The discussion and details in the next paragraph are based on these studies.

8. Josephus, *BJ* 5.168, 241.

9. For example, the possible incorporation of a *miqveh*—an immersion pool meant to serve Jewish purity rituals—into Herod's baths, in particular in the cold room (the *frigidarium*).

10. Reich, "The Hot Bath-House," 103. This is an English version of an earlier lecture in Hebrew that he delivered in 1985 (and eventually published in 1989); see Reich, "Beit ha-merḥaṣ ha-ḥam veha-qehilah ha-yehudit ba-tequfah haromit ha-qedumah." Note the term "observant Jew" in the wording of Reich, used in current Jewish society to distinguish between those who adhere to rabbinic laws (*halakhah*) and those who do not. Applying it to antiquity, in my view, distorts the nature of Jewish experience in those early times, centuries before rabbinic hegemony took over. See Eliav, "Jews and Judaism."

11. For the most articulate exception, see Blidstein, "R. Yohanan, Idolatry, and Public Privilege." Blidstein states that the baths were a "treasured opportunity that the Jews highly esteemed" (155), and he maintains that there were "unobjectionable bath houses" (157) in Tiberias. In that respect, my conclusions in this chapter concur with his, although Blidstein does not deal with the earlier centuries, which this chapter discusses (and see also my reservations regarding his understanding of the sources on p. 303n83).

12. See Krauss, *Monumenta Talmudica V*, ix. Krauss makes this point even though he clearly knows of many rabbinic sources that praise the bath and that numerous (practically all) rabbis attended the bath; see, for example, Krauss, "Bad und Badewesen," 108. On Krauss and his role in the study of Jewish material culture, see Eliav, "Samuel Krauss"; and Eliav, "From *Realia* to Material Culture." For similar assumptions about the bath by a British contemporary of Krauss, see Elmslie, *The Mishnah on Idolatry 'Aboda Zara*, 13–14.

13. Dauphin, "Brothels, Baths and Babes," 64; Oppenheimer, "The Jews in the Roman World," 55. See also Habas-Rubin, "A Poem by the Empress Eudocia,"

115–16n35; and Goodenough, *Jewish Symbols in the Greco-Roman Period*, 4:17. Note that Goodenough and Reich reached opposite conclusions. While Reich asserts that the contradiction between Judaism and the baths caused the Jews to avoid them, at least at the start, Goodenough believes that the Jews went to the baths but overall did not observe the *halakhah*.

14. Zissu and Ganor, "New Finds," 148.

15. For some examples, see Nielsen, *Thermae et balnea*, 1:103n56; Sartre, *The Middle East under Rome*, 102, 174; and Fagan, *Bathing in Public in the Roman World*, 36.

16. Eliav, "Did the Jews"; Eliav, "The Roman Bath as a Jewish Institution," 421–26; Eliav, "Bathhouses as Places of Social and Cultural Interactions."

17. For a sample, see Rosenfeld, *Lod and Its Sages*, 70n254; Jacobs, "Römische Thermenkultur"; and in particular Jacobs's conclusion—"die römische Badekultur im Yerushalmi in hohem Maß reflektiert und weitgehend positive beurteilt wird" (311: "the Roman bath culture is highly reflected in the Yerushalmi, and largely judged positively"). It is not clear if Jacobs borrows this conclusion from my earlier work, which he quotes and which deals precisely with this topic (ibid., 220n6), or whether we both reached the same conclusion independently. Be that as it may, we go in different directions in interpreting this rabbinic positive attitude toward the baths. Jacobs suggests that the rabbis consented to assimilation ("die Rabbinen keineswegs grundsätzlich gegen die 'Assimilation' der palästinischen Juden an die herrschende zeitgenössische Kultur ankämpften"; 311), while the current book argues for the model of cultural interaction. See also Yadin, "Rabban Gamliel, Aphrodite's Bath, and the Question of Pagan Monotheism," 165nn42–43; Fredriksen, *Augustine and the Jews*, 390n11; Levinson, "Enchanting Rabbis," 59; Lapin, *Rabbis as Romans*, 127–32, esp. nos. 4, 9, and 14; Wesler, *An Archaeology of Religion*, 201; Miller, *At the Intersection of Texts*, 43n38, 55n36; Bonnie, *Being Jewish in Galilee*, 132–33; and Kowalewska, *Bathhouses in Iudaea*.

18. In particular Friedheim, "Rabban Gamaliel"; Friedheim, "The Roman Public Bath in Eretz Israel"; and Friedheim, *Rabbinisme et Paganisme*, 69–107. See also Hoss, *Baths and Bathing*. Hoss seems to accept some of my conclusions on pp. 14 and 80 but then on p. 93 embraces Reich's assertions about the lack of early bathhouses in Judaea and about "problems" that Jewish law (*halakhah*) had with this institution. See also her more recent work in the following note. Cf. also Levine, *Jerusalem*, 330, 330n66, who seems to agree with my general argument but sees no sources for baths among the Jews in the pre-70 era. Another middle-of-the-road position is expressed in Safrai and Safrai, *Mishnat Eretz Israel: Tractate Shabbat*, 2:597–99. On the one hand they accept my arguments against Reich (597), but on the other they claim "it seems that the sayings of the Sages show that they refrained from bathhouses due to some of their social characteristics" (598).

19. Hoss, "From Rejection to Incorporation." When she discusses the rabbis (p. 262), all of her central points—unlike Christian literature, rabbis do not condemn the bathhouse; a comparison to how they do condemn the games in the amphitheater; the various adaptations that the rabbis provide for bathing activities—appear in my studies in 1995 ("Did the Jews") and then in 2000 ("The Roman Bath"), but she never references them.

20. See Reich, *Miqva'ot taharah*, 245–47. Although Reich is familiar with my critique and makes reference to it, for the most part he ignores its substance and simply repeats his old views.

21. On the hypocaust, see my discussion and bibliography on pp. 26–29.

22. For an exhaustive, if incomplete, historical survey and analysis, see Nielsen, *Thermae et balnea*.

23. For these sites, see Herbert and Ariel, *Tel Anafa I, i*, 62–74; and Damati, "Muraq, Khirbet El—(Ḥilkiya's Palace)," 1961–63. Hoss's assertion (*Baths and Bathing*, 164, catalogue no. 106) that this bathhouse dates to the first half of the first century BCE contradicts the excavator's conclusion and does not seem founded. For Ramat ha-Nadiv, see Hirschfeld, *Ramat Hanadiv Excavations*, 311–29. An additional bathhouse from this early period was found in the southern region, at Beersheba, but its poor state of preservation and scholarly documentation makes any meaningful conclusions difficult; for literature and discussion, see Eliav, "Did the Jews," 7–8, 7–8n26. The same is the case with the fragments of a bathhouse from Capernaum, on the shores of the Sea of Galilee; see Hoss, *Baths and Bathing*, 46 and 135–36, catalogue no. 31.

24. See the comparative evidence gathered and discussed in Fagan, *Bathing in Public in the Roman World*, 40–44, and in particular n. 11.

25. I collected and examined the data from all these sites in my earlier studies, over twenty years ago; see Eliav, "Did the Jews," 4–8. For later studies and more up-to-date, although not complete, summaries of the material from the region, see the catalogues in Nielsen, *Thermae et balnea*, 2:41–42; Hoss, *Baths and Bathing*; and Kowalewska, *Bathhouses in Iudaea*. For an exception to this chronological model, see the bath in the site of the ancient city of Pella, in Transjordan, although the evidence for dating is rather tenuous and thus speculative; see ibid., 165 (but correct the error there, in the reference to *NEAEHL*; should be vol. 3). For a study on the western baths of Gerasa, the earliest bathing complex out of the ten or so structures uncovered in that city, which reaches the same chronological conclusions, see Lepaon, "The Western Baths of Gerasa of the Decapolis."

26. Antioch's baths were well-documented by the sixth-century chronographer and orator John Malalas. Glanville Downey, Antioch's prime modern scholar, claims, "Construction of baths is a leading motif" for Malalas; see Downey, *A History of Antioch in Syria*, 155. Of the seven Early Roman baths mentioned by Malalas in the city, the earliest of which goes back to the days of Julius Caesar (Malalas, *Chronographia* 9.5 [Thurn, 163 l. 55]), none have been found by archaeologists. The earliest bathing structure, unearthed in the Princeton excavations (Bath C), dates to the second century CE; see Elderkin, *Antioch on-the-Orontes I*, 31. John Malalas and the Antiochian case shed light on the processes of recurrent construction and destruction in the ancient urban environment, and especially the disparity between literary sources and archaeological findings, even in the few instances that both exist. There is no reason to assume that other places would be any different.

27. Much has been written on this topic; for a concise summary and bibliography, see Ball, *Rome in the East*, 246–396.

28. Hoss ("From Rejection to Incorporation," 260) knows of this comparative data from my earlier studies but it leads her to suggest that all "Semitic" populations of the Near East shared some negative attitude toward nakedness and therefore refrained

from building baths. Since she lacks proof for this widespread Near Eastern aversion, the evidence she provides is the lack of archaeological remains of baths. This argument suffers from the logic flaw known as *petitio principii*. It's circular logic; after all, her entire claim is that the lack of baths in Judaea is to be explained by negative attitudes toward aspects of the bath that are found in Jewish texts, but now suddenly she turns the argument around and proves the negative attitudes from the lack of baths. More important, it is hard to fathom where we are to look for this "Semitic" Near East after hundreds of years of Greek rule and the prevalence of Greek culture, in particular in the numerous urban centers of the East—the Decapolis and Syria.

29. This point is clearly made in Owens, "Baths and Water Supply in the Cities of Pisidia: Antioch," and see also his discussion of one documented example, from the city of Alexandria Troas, a Roman colony from the days of Augustus on the northwest coast of Turkey, which received its public baths only a century later, after aqueducts were built during the reign of Hadrian (171). Corinth, the great Greek city on the land bridge (isthmus) between the Greek mainland and the Peloponnesian peninsula, is another example. It was sacked by the Romans in 146 BCE and rebuilt as a colony by Julius Caesar in 44 BCE. Yet the earliest Roman baths in the city date to nearly three generations after its establishment; see Farrington, "The Introduction and Spread of Roman Bathing in Greece," 58–60.

30. See my discussion of these institutions with references to their research and publication on pp. 31–32.

31. The best study of such a gymnasium within the Roman context is Yegül, *The Bath-Gymnasium Complex at Sardis*. And see my detailed discussion and bibliography about this phenomenon on pp. 32–33.

32. On the bathing facilities in northern Europe, see the catalogue in Nielsen, *Thermae et balnea*, 2:211–26, and more recently Bouet, *Les thermes privés et publics en Gaule Narbonnaise*. In North Africa, "because of the relatively late and slow urbanization ... the great majority of the baths ... belong to the prosperous decades of the Antonine and Severan periods," namely, the late second and early third centuries CE; see Yegül, *Baths and Bathing in Classical Antiquity*, 184–249, quote on p. 186. See also Thébert, *Thermes romains d'Afrique du Nord et leur contexte méditerranéen*.

33. Fikret Yegül alludes in this direction when he says, "Rome's position in the early development of public baths has been compromised by its success as a continuously occupied urban center"; see Yegül, "Development of Baths and Public Bathing during the Roman Republic," 30. I owe this reference to Anthony Meyer.

34. For Rome, the literary evidence for Republican public baths, and its contrast with the lack of matching archaeological material, see Nielsen, *Thermae et balnea*, 1:34–35; Yegül, *Bathing in the Roman World*, 66–69; and in more detail Fagan, *Bathing in Public in the Roman World*, 45–51. The evidentiary situation in Rome may be changing as well; see, for example, ibid., 41n5.

35. Josephus, *BJ* 1.340–41; Josephus, *AJ* 14.462–64.

36. The precise meaning of the noun *loutron* in the writings of Josephus remains somewhat ambiguous. Stemming from the verb *louō*, it functions at times as the gerund "bathing" and at others as the toponym "bathhouse," seemingly reflecting a phase in the consolidation of its meaning. The best example in *AJ* comes from the account regarding Agrippa I's imprisonment by the emperor Tiberius (18.203). Antonia, the

emperor's sister-in-law, pleaded on Agrippa's behalf, successfully alleviating some of the incarceration measures, among which is mentioned the permission to bathe (*loutra*) daily. Later, incidentally, Josephus reports on the implementation of this relief, when he says that the news of Tiberius's death reached Agrippa as "he was coming out of the bath (*balaneion*)," making it quite clear that the two terms function interchangeably within the vocabulary he uses for Roman bathhouses. For a fuller discussion of the occurrences of *loutron* and *louō* in Josephus, see Eliav, "Did the Jews," 25nn86, 89.

37. *t. B. Bat.* 3:3 (Lieberman, 138). The same reference to an "outer room" appears in a passage from roughly the same time that was preserved in the later text of the Babylonian Talmud; see *b. Šabb.* 40a (but the term is missing from the parallel text in *t. Šabb.* 3(4):3 [Lieberman, 11–12]). For "room," the sources here use the Hebrew noun *bayit*, which normally means "house" but also attains the connotation of a "room" and a "chamber," similar to other ancient languages, such as the Greek *oikos* and the Syriac *bayto*'; see LSJ, 1205, s.v. 2; Smith, *Thesaurus Syriacus*, 478–79, s.v. 2. For the Greek terminology, see Nielsen, *Thermae et balnea*, 1:156.

38. The transformation of the Greek letters iota and sigma into kappa is a common scribal error in the manuscript tradition, which seems to explain how Cana emerged from Isana. On the latter, its identification and location, see Möller and Schmitt, *Siedlungen Palästinas nach Flavius Josephus*, 111.

39. See, for example, Laqueur, *Der jüdische Historiker Flavius Josephus*, 209–10, who prefers the earlier version of *BJ*.

40. Cf. Bonnie, *Being Jewish in Galilee*, 133, 133n104.

41. See Rengstorf, *A Complete Concordance to Flavius Josephus*, 1:288.

42. Much has been written about Josephus's views regarding the characteristic traits of Jewish life and how he presents them in his writings; for an early bibliography on these topics, see Feldman, *Josephus and Modern Scholarship*, 492–527, 566–72. For the most up-to-date discussion and more recent bibliography, see Schwartz, "Many Sources but a Single Author," 51–55.

43. Josephus, *AJ* 15.267–76. See Eliav, "The Roman Bath as a Jewish Institution," 424–26. A wide array of modern scholars have commented on these passages in Josephus and on whether they represent the prevalent negative view regarding the manifestations of Roman culture among Jews at the time; see the balanced discussion in Levine, *Jerusalem*, 201–6. But compare to the harsh reconstruction of Jewish sensibilities toward anything Roman in Goodman, *Rome and Jerusalem*, 296–98. I find it hard to accept Goodman's portrayal of ancient Jewish society; see my critique on pp. 8–9 and 123–24.

44. For a list of all ancient, Graeco-Roman references (but only a sample of the rabbinic material) and an updated bibliography regarding this place, see Tsafrir, Di Segni, and Green, *Tabula imperii romani*, 173. It is unclear to me why the authors of this volume designate Magdala a town. In particular for the Early Roman period, Josephus (*Vit.* 188) clearly marks it a city (*polis*), counts it together with two other undeniable cities in Galilee, namely Tiberias and Sepphoris, and differentiates it from other places in the region, which he defines as villages (*kōmē*). He also records there the existence of a hippodrome (*BJ* 2.599), a distinctly urban feature. As to a certain confusion in the sources about its precise location, whether north or

south of Tiberias, see the discussion in Schürer, *The History of the Jewish People*, 1:494–95n44. All modern scholars, myself included, seem to agree with the location north of Tiberias.

45. De Luca and Lena, "The Mosaic of the Thermal Bath Complex of Magdala Reconsidered." The term "Thermal" in the title of this article is both misleading and misused, as it normally refers to spas and other healing institutions associated with hot springs, that is, geothermal springs in which the water is believed to have healing qualities, none of which exist in the case of Magdala. Arleta Kowalewska shared with me her reservations about the reconstruction of this bath by the excavators, a critique that is yet to be published. Based on this, the discussion here may need to be modified in the future. See Kowalewska, *Bathhouses in Iudaea*.

46. Cicero, *Fam.* 366. A decade earlier, Cassius had visited Taricheae in the wake of Crassus's famous and devastating defeat by the Parthians in Carrhae, but other than the fact that he took the town by force and enslaved many of its people (apparently in retaliation for their support of the Persians), we know nothing else about his whereabouts and actions there; see Josephus, *BJ* 1.180; Josephus, *AJ* 14.120.

47. Cicero, *Fam.* 387.

48. Strabo, *Geo.* 16.2–46.

49. *b. Pesaḥ* 46a. The full name of the place was also preserved in an ancient list of places, called *The Baraita of Priestly Courses*, now lost but reconstructed by a variety of ancient literary and archaeological sources; see Klein, *Sefer ha-Yishuv*, 162–63.

50. For a detailed presentation and discussion of the items in the mosaic and their interpretation within the context of the bath, see De Luca and Lena, "The Mosaic of the Thermal Bath Complex of Magdala Reconsidered," 12–22.

51. See pp. 6–9.

52. This situation in Jerusalem is well-documented in Levine, "Second Temple Jerusalem."

53. The most comprehensive report of this excavation has appeared thus far only in modern Hebrew; see Bar-Nathan and Sklar-Parnes, "A Jewish Settlement." For an earlier, shorter, and less complete English summary, see Sklar-Parnes, Rapuano, and Bar-Nathan, "Excavations in Northeast Jerusalem." My entire discussion here follows the conclusions of the authors in these publications.

54. For *miqva'ot* in this period, see Reich, *Miqva'ot taharah*. For stone vessels, see Deines, *Jüdische Steingefäße und pharisäische Frömmigkeit*; and Magen, *The Stone Vessel Industry in the Second Temple Period*. On the scholarly debate surrounding the interpretation and chronological scope of artifacts, much of which has no bearing on the questions discussed here, since all sides agree that there is something distinctively Jewish about them, see the thorough discussions and bibliography in Miller, *At the Intersection of Texts*. On the bone findings, see Bouchnick and Bar-Nathan, "Bones as Evidence."

55. See Bar-Nathan and Sklar-Parnes, "A Jewish Settlement," 63; and Cotton, "The Administrative Background to the New Settlement."

56. The first to collect the information about the baths from these three sites and to contemplate their Jewish context was Stiebel, "The Roman Military Bathhouse at En Gedi," 351–52. But other baths that he lists there, from Beth Yerah and Aelia

Capitolina, blur the picture since the first is much later than the Early Roman period and the second clearly has nothing to do with Jews.

57. For the excavation and its findings, see Onn et al., "Khirbet Umm el-'Umdan." On these early second-century synagogues and the scholarly debate about their identification, see Zissu and Ganor, "Horvat 'Ethri," 105–10; Runesson, Binder, and Olsson, *The Ancient Synagogue from Its Origins to 200 C.E.*, 20–79, esp. 57–58; and Hachlili, *Ancient Synagogues*, 23, 34, 43–45.

58. See Hizmi, "A Roman Bath and a Byzantine Farmstead at the Settlement of Menorah (Kh. Krikur)"; all the following details are taken from this publication.

59. For a summary on the phenomenon of Bar Kokhba hiding places, see Mor, *The Second Jewish Revolt*, 221–38. On the coins of the Bar Kokhba revolt, see Meshorer, *Ancient Jewish Coinage*, 2:132–65. For large stone vessel deposits as a characteristic Jewish item in the Early Roman period, see note 54 in this chapter. On characteristic Second Temple oil lamps, see Westenholz, *Let There Be Light*, 25–34; and Sussman, *Roman Period Oil Lamps in the Holy Land*.

60. The data about this particular region was gathered and discussed in Rosenfeld, *Lod and Its Sages*, 218–22. But cf. Schwartz, *Lod (Lydda) Israel*, 101. The population shifts in Judaea after the Bar Kokhba revolt require further investigation and careful reassessment. Some scholars have recently correctly pointed toward the uncertainty, not to say exaggeration, of some of the sources. See, for example, Mor, *The Second Jewish Revolt*, 479–85.

61. Dahari, "Adithaim now Aditha and Betomelgezis in the Madaba Map."

62. Cf. Stiebel, "The Roman Military Bathhouse at En Gedi," 351, who also makes a reference to the passage in Josephus but fails to acknowledge that it was my early studies on Jewish bathhouses that first highlighted the relevance of this forgotten segment in the historical works of Josephus for the study of Roman bathhouses among the Jews; see Eliav, "Did the Jews," 22–27.

63. This is the so-called eastern bathhouse in Sepphoris, not to be confused with other much later bathhouses found at this site. For documentation and bibliography, see Hoss, *Baths and Bathing*, 172, catalogue no. 131. To the literature she lists there one should now add Weiss, "Sepphoris," 2031.

64. *m. B. Meṣi'a* 8:8.

65. *t. Mo'ed Qaṭ.* 2:15 (Lieberman, 372). On Chabulon, see Tsafrir, Di Segni, and Green, *Tabula imperii romani*, 102–3 s.v.

66. *t. Šabb.* 3:3 (Lieberman, 12). Cf. Rosenfeld, *Lod and Its Sages*, 70, who dates this tradition to the early second century based on the names of the scholars mentioned in it; even if this may be methodologically questioned by many scholars, myself included, it is nevertheless a solid, local tradition from the second or third century. On the location of Bene Brak in Ibn Ibreiq, some ten miles west of Khirbet Krikur, see Tsafrir, Di Segni, and Green, *Tabula imperii romani*, 78 s.v.

67. Much has been written about this relatively small bathhouse, which was excavated in the 1960s and then re-excavated in the 1990s; for summaries and discussion, although of varied quality, see the studies gathered in Stern, *En Gedi Excavations*, 301–60. See in particular p. 329, where Orit Peleg raises the possibility that there may have been an earlier bath in Ein Gedi, dating back to Herodian times.

68. Stiebel, "The Roman Military Bathhouse at En Gedi," 351–52.

69. For a survey and discussion of the documentary information regarding the military presence at this site, see Cotton, "Ein Gedi."

70. On the military bathhouse at Ramat Rachel, see Hoss, *Baths and Bathing*, 169–70, catalogue no. 123. On other military bathhouses in the region and in the Near East in general, see Reeves, "The Roman Bath-House."

71. Cotton, "Ein Gedi," 149.

72. On this phenomenon of civilians attending military baths, see Reeves, "The Roman Bath-House," 47; and Nielsen, *Thermae et balnea*, 1:74. For another example from our region, see Davies and Magness, *The 2003-2007 Excavations in the Late Roman Fort at Yotvata*, 61. With regard to Ein Gedi, the possibility of the local Jews attending the military bath was raised by Arbel, "The Roman Bathhouse in En Gedi," 320. Unfortunately, this piece exhibits lack of competence, particularly about Judaism and rabbinic literature, and should be decisively ignored; the author does not know how to quote the texts and never examined them firsthand—e.g., the passage he incorrectly quotes (ibid.) from *y. 'Erub.* 6 (23c) mentions neither the "legionaries" nor the "bath," as Arbel claims. It only speaks of an "inn" (*pundaq*) and of "gentiles" (*goyim*). Similarly, the author's assertion that the Ein Gedi bathhouse was eventually destroyed by the Bar Kokhba rebels is baseless.

73. Cotton, "Ein Gedi," 148–49.

74. On the Late Roman baths in these places, see Hoss, *Baths and Bathing*, 134–35, catalogue no. 29 (Caesarea), 155–57, catalogue nos. 81–88 (Jerusalem), 174, catalogue no. 139 (Tiberias).

75. On the various institutions in Jerusalem, see Levine, *Jerusalem*, 69–75 (gymnasium), 201–6 (Herod's entertainment institutions).

76. On Caesarea Maritima and its buildings, see Levine, *Roman Caesarea*, 18–29; and Holum, Hohlfelder, and Bullet, *King Herod's Dream*, 72–89.

77. Hoss, *Baths and Bathing*, 133–34, catalogue nos. 26–27.

78. Reich, "The Hot Bath-House," 103, repeated again verbatim in Reich, *Miqva'ot taharah*, 246, although the latter study came out years after the baths mentioned here were excavated.

79. Hoss, *Baths and Bathing*, 93; Hoss, "From Rejection to Incorporation," 261.

Chapter 4. A Sinful Place? Rabbinic Laws (Halakhah) and Feelings about the Public Bathhouse

1. Reich, "The Hot Bath-House," 103. And in a somewhat elaborate format in Reich, "Beit ha-merḥaṣ ha-ḥam veha-qehilah ha-yehudit ba-tequfah haromit ha-qedumah." The details and quotations in the following paragraph are all taken from these two publications. On the scholars who followed Reich in this regard and on his later publications on the topic, which are consistent with his earlier views, see pp. 82–83, and notes 13 and 18 in chapter 3.

2. Friedheim, *Rabbinisme et Paganisme*, 69–107, with further references and discussion later in the current chapter.

3. Many modern scholars have tackled the issue of Jewish law and its idiosyncrasy. The most authoritative discussion on the topic from the close of the twentieth century (although in great need of updating and revision) is still Urbach, *The Halakhah*. No

less magisterial is Elon, *Jewish Law*. The most comprehensive bibliography on the topic and its multifaceted dimensions is Rakover, *The Multi-Language Bibliography of Jewish Law* (there are two additional volumes by the same author with bibliographies in Hebrew). For the most recent contributions to the topic, see Saiman, *Halakhah*; and Boyarin, "Is There Jewish Law?" The former is an exposition of the modern Jewish Orthodox take on the subject, the latter an exercise in intellectual juggling with limited merit. More balanced is Albeck, *Introduction to Jewish Law in Talmudic Times*.

4. In addition to the bibliographical material on this subject listed in the previous note, see my own discussion of this issue in Eliav, "Jews and Judaism," 576–78. More recently, and with strong foundation in legal theory, see Vroom, *The Authority of Law in the Hebrew Bible and Early Judaism*.

5. Hecataeus of Abdera *apud* Diodorus Siculus, *Bibliotheca historica* 40.3.1–8. Hecataeus's books were lost. The passage under discussion here was preserved in the fortieth book of the first-century BCE Greek historian Diodorus of Sicily, which in itself was preserved only in fragments, in the compilations, known as the *Bibliotheca*, of the ninth-century Byzantine scholar and Church leader Photius. For commentary on and discussion of this segment, see Stern, *Greek and Latin Authors on Jews and Judaism*, 1:26–35.

6. The Roman material was meticulously collected and studied in Ben Zeev, *Jewish Rights in the Roman World*. About Jewish laws in these documents, see in particular ibid., 409–38, 460–68. For earlier official documents and correspondence from the Hellenistic world, see Stern, *The Documents on the History of the Hasmonaean Revolt*.

7. For comprehensive discussions of these topics, see Mulder and Sysling, *Mikra*. An example of Roman authorities defining Jewish scriptures as sacred is in the law from the days of Augustus, quoted in Josephus, *AJ* 16.164. For the Jewish sentiment about the books of the Torah in the words of the same author, see *Ap*. 1.38–43.

8. Once again, the scholarly research on this topic is too vast to survey here. For a good and insightful summary with references to prior works by others, see Shemesh, *Halakhah in the Making*.

9. On the coining of this new term, see Fraade, "The Innovation of Nominalized Verbs in Mishnaic Hebrew," 140–41.

10. I devoted a separate study to this topic, which involves rather complex discussions of rabbinic *halakhah*; see Eliav, "Pylè—Puma—Sfat Medinah." For a later study that repeats many of my observations, although neglects to acknowledge their source, see Safrai and Safrai, *Mishnat Eretz Israel: Tractate Shabbat*, 1:162–69. The Safrai commentary offers a problematic blend of modern scholarship with traditional, orthodox-style engagement with the mishnaic text, but I cannot discuss its shortcomings in detail here. Another study on the evolution of Sabbath laws related to the bathhouse, with rather different conclusions than mine, is Jacobs, "Römische Thermenkultur," 272–83.

11. Although there may be other infringements as well, such as squeezing water out of wet clothes, these are the main two; for a more complete list and discussion, see Safrai and Safrai, *Mishnat Eretz Israel: Tractate Shabbat*, 1:163–69.

12. *CD* 11:1 (Rabin, 55). On this legal segment, see my discussion in Eliav, "Pylè—Puma—Sfat Medinah," 14n24 and the references I provide there. Supporting my reading is also Wacholder, *The New Damascus Document*, 332.

13. *t. Šabb.* 3:4 (Lieberman, 12). For R. Meir, see *y. Šabb.* 3 (6a); and *b. Šabb.* 40b, and for the anecdote of R. Judah the Patriarch, *t. 'Erub.* 5:24 (Lieberman, 116). Cf. Goldenberg, *The Sabbath Laws of Rabbi Meir*, 38–39, who views even R. Meir's position as a stringency aimed to prevent the use of heated water. I discuss the topic in more detail in Eliav, "Pylè—Puma—Sfat Medinah," 14n25.

14. Exod. 35:3.

15. *Jub.* 50:12 (VanderKam, 326).

16. *Anth. Pal.* 5.160 (Paton, 1:204). My reading follows that of Stern, *Greek and Latin Authors on Jews and Judaism*, 1:139–40. For a slightly different interpretation of this passage, with no real bearing on my point, see Jacobson, "Demo and the Sabbath."

17. Bardaisan, *Liber legum regionum* 604 (Drijvers, 58 line 12).

18. *m. Šabb.* 3:4.

19. Reich, "The Hot Bath-House," 103.

20. *m. Makš.* 2:5. For textual variants and further discussion, see Eliav, "Pylè—Puma—Sfat Medinah," 15–16, 15–16n29. In translating the rabbinic term *'ir* into "town," despite its modern Hebrew meaning as "city," I follow Ze'ev Safrai; see Safrai, *The Economy of Roman Palestine*, 17–19.

21. This legal concept of waiting an additional amount of time before going back to enjoying or using the outcome of a permissible action that was prohibited on the Sabbath is called in rabbinic legal terminology *bikhdei sh-ye'asu*.

22. *y. Šabb.* 3 (6a).

23. See, for example, *t. Šabb.* 3:3 (Lieberman, 12).

24. See, for example, *t. Šabb.* 16:16–17 (Lieberman, 78–79), or the *baraita* in *b. Šabb.* 147a (also *b. 'Erub.* 87b–88a), which states that it is permissible to dry oneself with a piece of cloth or to anoint the body with oil on the Sabbath. From the mention of the bath attendant it seems clear that this *halakhah* assumes that there is no problem with attending the bath on the Sabbath. For a full discussion of these legal developments and a classification of the many rabbinic sources associated with it, see Eliav, "Pylè—Puma—Sfat Medinah," 13–19. But cf. Safrai and Safrai, *Mishnat Eretz Israel: Tractate Shabbat*, 2:526–27, 599; and Jacobs, "Römische Thermenkultur," 279–82.

25. *y. Šabb.* 3 (6a); *b. Šabb.* 40b.

26. *Didascalia apostolorum* 21 (Vööbus, 2:216 lines 14–15). Pace Safrai and Safrai, *Mishnat Eretz Israel: Tractate Shabbat*, 2:599.

27. The best historical overview about the sabbatical year and its observance, despite its over-reliance on and at times naïve acceptance of rabbinic references as historically valid, remains Safrai, "The Practical Implementation of the Sabbatical Year," reprinted in Safrai, *In Times of Temple and Mishnah*, 2:421–66. For concise summaries, see also the entries in *ABD* (5:857–61) and *EJ* (14:574–86).

28. *m. Šeb.* 8:11.

29. *t. Šeb.* 5:19 (Lieberman, 189) with references to Reich's position in note 1 of this chapter. Modern scholars strained to explain the legal difference between a regular furnace and that of the baths; see the literature listed in Eliav, "Did the Jews," 11n43, as well as Safrai and Safrai, *Mishnat Eretz Israel: Tractate Shevi'it*, 276–79.

30. All this has been endlessly studied and rehearsed in numerous fields of modern scholarship—sociology, anthropology, religion, and folklore, to name but a few.

From the seemingly infinite studies devoted to this topic, I remember the relatively short but pathbreaking treatise by Douglas, *Purity and Danger*. For more recent studies with elaborate bibliographies, see Bley, Jaspert, and Köck, *Discourses of Purity in Transcultural Perspective*. More focused on the Roman realm is Lennon, *Pollution and Religion in Ancient Rome*.

31. Here too the literature is vast. For a sample of some more recent studies in English, see Poorthius and Schwartz, *Purity and Holiness*; Harrington, *The Purity Texts*; Klawans, *Impurity and Sin in Ancient Judaism*; and Kazen, *Jesus and Purity Halakha*.

32. Recent scholarship has taken a keen interest in these developments and abundant work has been published about it in the last twenty years, much of which has no bearing on the topics discussed in the present book. For a comprehensive presentation including a good summary and bibliography of earlier studies, see Furstenberg, *Purity and Community in Antiquity*. For a more limited presentation in English, see Balberg, *Purity, Body, and Self*.

33. See the references to his study in note 1 in this chapter. Also Reich, *Miqva'ot taharah*, 245–47.

34. For a peek into the modern mindset, see the memoir of the Jewish writer Bella Rosenfeld Chagall, cited in Brödner, *Die römischen Thermen*, 269–70. Chagall attended the *miqveh* regularly with her mother in the Belarusian city of Vitebsk and provides a vivid description of its horrors.

35. Based on the good textual witnesses to *m. Nid.* 7:4, with discussion of the textual variants in Eliav, "Did the Jews," 21n81; *t. Nid.* 6:15 (Zuckermandel, 648). On the general custom of restricting the movement of menstruating women, see Dinary, "The Impurity Customs of the Menstruate Woman," 308–18, and to the sources he lists there, one should add *Temple Scroll* (*11Q19*) 48:14-16 (Yadin, 147–48).

36. *m. 'Ohal.* 18:10; *t. 'Ohal.* 18:12 (Zuckermandel, 617).

37. *m. Ṭehar.* 7:7; *m. Kelim* 22:10; *m. Nid.* 9:3; a *baraita* in *b. Ḥag.* 20a.

38. For a summary up to the days of the rabbis, see Lawrence, *Washing in Water*.

39. The major study on the archaeological remains of *miqva'ot* is Reich, *Miqva'ot taharah*. The development of ritual purity practices after the destruction of the Second Temple, and its impact on the distribution of *miqva'ot*, has been debated in recent years; some prevalent opinions have been challenged and reevaluated, but the topic is of no direct relevance to the current study. For a summary of old and new trends, see Miller, *At the Intersection of Texts*; and Adler, "The Decline of Jewish Ritual Purity Observance in Roman Palaestina."

40. Goodman, *Rome and Jerusalem*, 278. For others who share this notion, see Oppenheimer, "The Jews in the Roman World," 55. Like Goodman, Oppenheimer stumbles on the translation of the text he provides as proof—*t. Miqw.* 6:3 (Zuckermandel, 658), where he translated the verb as "bathed," whereas the Hebrew verb is the one designated for ritual immersion *taval*. The passage actually deals with ritual immersion for purification in the water of a bathhouse in gentile areas. The *halakhah* expresses reservation about this particular act, due to the association with non-Jews and their presumed ritual impurity, but it says nothing to support Oppenheimer's notion about overall misgivings regarding bathing for cleanliness and pleasure. For similar confusions, see Brödner, *Die römischen Thermen*, 268–70.

41. Reich, *Miqva'ot taharah*, 247. In a similar tone to Reich, although in disagreement with him regarding the factors that caused the development of the early *miqva'ot*, is Adler, "The Hellenistic Origins of Jewish Ritual Immersion." In his attempt to reconstruct the early beginnings of *miqva'ot*, Adler ties them to Greek bathing practices and views the Jewish practices of purification as a response to Greek bathing experiences. I find his argument thought-provoking but speculative and lacking any evidence.

42. For the coining of the name *merḥats*, see my discussion on p. 45. For the terminologies of the *miqveh*, see Miller, *At the Intersection of Texts*, 32–44.

43. m. 'Ed. 1:3, discussed in many other laws in the Order of Purities. Pace Reich, *Miqva'ot taharah*, 247.

44. The only exceptions I know of to this rule are some rabbinic Babylonian sources that mention a ban, possibly on the entrance of Jews to bathhouses, and tie it to ritual immersion. See b. Nid. 66b; b. Yebam. 63b. Much remains unclear about who initiated this injunction and the reasons behind it. If Persian religious authorities forbade Jews from entering local bathhouses, the situation may have been similar to the one mentioned by the fourth-century church historian Eusebius, in which Christians were similarly excluded. See Eusebius, *H.E.* 5.1.5. For more discussion and bibliographical references, see Eliav, "Did the Jews," 33–34.

45. See, e.g., Cicero, *Vat.* 13.31; and Apuleius, *Met.* 11.23.

46. The sources on this point are few and the picture they draw is quite vague. See t. *Miqw.* 5:8 (Zuckermandel, 657), 6:4 (Zuckermandel, 658); t. 'Erub. 8:8 (Lieberman, 133–34); m. *Miqw.* 6:11. The most comprehensive study of the *metaheret* as well as of the presence of *miqva'ot* in bathhouses, which pays close attention to the archaeological evidence and unpacks the complex laws associated with this situation, is Grossberg, "A Mikveh in the Bathhouse"; see also Miller, *At the Intersection of Texts*, 41–42n35.

47. y. Ber. 3 (6c).

48. E.g., b. Ber. 22a in traditions about R. Huna and R. Zeira.

49. Nielsen, *Thermae et balnea*, 1:146. Similarly, see Yegül, *Baths and Bathing in Classical Antiquity*, 124; and Fagan, *Bathing in Public in the Roman World*, 5.

50. Friedheim, *Rabbinisme et Paganisme*, 69–107, and in particular p. 82 and note 263, where the quote about the cult place comes from. See also Friedheim, "Rabban Gamaliel," quote about negative halakhic attitudes on p. 32; and Friedheim, "The Roman Public Bath in Eretz Israel." The citation on the bathhouse as a sacred place comes from p. 180. The only other scholar I am aware of who shares these views is Aupert, "Les thermes comme lieux de culte." For a critique on Aupert's view, see chapter 6, note 3. Other scholars, although not as sharp in their condemnation of the bath as Friedheim, nevertheless seem to share some of his understandings; for a recent example, see Kattan-Gribetz, "'Lead Me Forth in Peace,'" 307, who calls the public bath "a locus of idolatry," and others listed throughout the discussion in chapter 6.

51. I published a detailed critique of Friedheim; see Eliav, "Two Comments on Idolatry," to which he responded in Friedheim, "The Roman Public Bath in Eretz Israel."

52. In addition to the bibliography and references I provide in chapter 6, see, in particular, Bakker, *Living and Working with the Gods*; Bowes, *Private Worship*, 38–44.

53. The examples for these phenomena are too numerous to list. For a sample, see Nielsen, *Thermae et balnea*, 1:146–47; van der Meer, *Ostia Speaks*, 68–69 (Mithraeum and Christian chapel in a bath); and Courtney, *Musa lapidaria*, 68–69 (#40), consecrating a statue to health in the baths (but note the inscription specifies that the consecration is in the place of the bath but not of the entire structure!).

54. Ovid, *Fast.* 4.139–50; Tertullian, *Apol.* 42.4.

55. The information was gathered and discussed in Fagan, *Bathing in Public in the Roman World*, 138, 171–72, and in particular 324, no. 302 (bath named after Serapis), 339, no. 317 (baths named after eastern deities).

56. Yegül, *Baths and Bathing in Classical Antiquity*, 124; Fagan, *Bathing in Public in the Roman World*, 5. See also Nielsen, *Thermae et balnea*, 1:146.

57. For a sample of such indications of sacred places, see, for example, van der Meer, *Ostia Speaks*, 42, 45 (an inscription indicating sacredness associated with Venus, the exact type of expression we don't find in baths), 80, 103.

58. The basic study on Roman sanctuaries remains Stambaugh, "The Functions of Roman Temples."

59. Most of the evidence was collected in Fagan, *Bathing in Public in the Roman World*, 154, together with 234, no. 4. For the bath in Oxyrhynchus, see Strobel, "Baths in Roman and Byzantine Egypt," 3:863. See also Scheid, "Sanctuaires et thermes sous l'empire"; and Bruun, "Lotores: Roman Bath-Attendants," 226–28.

60. For a good summary of these facilities, see Yegül, *Baths and Bathing in Classical Antiquity*, 92–127.

61. See Friedheim, *Rabbinisme et Paganisme*, 77; Friedheim, "Rabban Gamaliel," 9–10; and my critique of this point in Eliav, "Two Comments on Idolatry," 180. Another book that makes this typological mistake is Dvorjetski, *Leisure, Pleasure and Healing*, 273–314, where the author constantly lists rabbinic sources dealing with bathhouses as evidence for healing spas.

62. As clearly understood by Nielsen, *Thermae et balnea*, 1:5; and Yegül, *Baths and Bathing in Classical Antiquity*, 125.

63. On the location of healing centers far from populated areas in order to keep disease at a distance, see Graf, "Heiligtum und Ritual," 168–78, and the discussion in *Le sanctuaire grec*, ed. Olivier Reverdin and Bernard Grange, Entretiens sur l'antiquité classique 37 (Geneva: Foundation Hardt, 1992), 201–2.

64. The relatively few inscriptions and even fewer literary segments that attest to this were collected in Nielsen, *Thermae et balnea*, 1:146, no. 9. And see also Fagan, *Bathing in Public in the Roman World*, 287, no. 161; 288, no. 165; 327, no. 285; 329, no. 289.

65. *m. 'Abod. Zar.* 4:3.

66. *m. 'Abod. Zar.* 3:7.

67. *m. 'Abod. Zar.* 1:7. A similar concept of this process, where the bathhouse is neutral and even positive, and only later an idolatrous figure emerges, is depicted in *Cant. Zuttah* 1:15 (Buber, 19–20).

68. The only trace I can find in rabbinic literature for the position that may consider the entire bathhouse structure a "house of idolatry" comes from the mindset of the figure who questions Rabban Gamaliel's attendance at the bathhouse of Aphrodite in Acre (*m. 'Abod. Zar.* 3:4). I discuss this passage at length in chapter 6. In any

case, without further evidence it is hard to determine whether that position (attributed to the non-Jewish literary figure Proqlos) reflects anyone's real view or is a literary device meant to highlight its dismissal by the directives of Rabban Gamaliel.

69. *y. Šeb.* 8.38b–c.

70. Tertullian, *Apol.* 42.2.4; Augustine, *Ep.* 46.15 (and Augustine's reply in 46). On Augustine's positive view of the baths and his own frequent visits, see *Conf.* 9.12; *C. acad.* 3.1.1, 3.4.9; *De ord.* 1.8.25, 2.11.31; and *De beata vita* 1.6, 4.23. Although the setting in the Cassiciacum dialogues is probably not a large public bath but rather a bathing facility within a private villa, the affinity for this establishment nevertheless shines through.

71. Some sample references (by no means a full catalogue): Judah the Patriarch bathing with R. Isaac, *y. Šabb.* 3 (6a) (= *b. Šabb.* 40b); eating and drinking in the bath and attending to public business, *Qoh. Rab.* 5:11 (Hirshman, 315–16); R. Judah II in a legendary story with demons in the bath, *y. Ter.* 8 (46b–c) (= *Gen. Rab.* 63 [Theodor and Albeck, 688–90]). I discuss this anecdote in detail in Eliav, "A Scary Place," 93–94, and also later in chapter 8. See also *t. Mo'ed Qat.* 2:15 (Lieberman, 372). The anecdote about Rabban Gamaliel in the bathhouse is discussed at length later, in the opening of chapter 6. For the anecdote about Hillel the Elder, see the passage discussed in the next paragraph and the references in note 74 in this chapter.

72. Many of these traditions are collected in *y. Šabb.* 3 (6a) (= *b. Šabb.* 40b). See also *y. Kil.* 9 (32b); *y. Šeb.* 8 (38a, 38b–c); *y. Šeb.* 9 (38d); *y. Sanh.* 7 (25d); *b. Ber.* 22a; *b. Pesaḥ.* 4a.

73. *y. Šeb.* 8 (38a, 38b–c). As mentioned earlier, rabbinic law restricted the usage of the public bath in the sabbatical year; however, attending it in a locality where one was unknown circumvented the restriction, which is what led Joshua b. Levi to travel to Beth Guvrin. On these two cities in Roman times, see the entries in Tsafrir, Di Segni, and Green, *Tabula imperii romani*, 118 (Eleutheropolis), 171 (Lydda).

74. *Lev. Rab.* 34:3 (Margulies, 776–77), with my discussion of parallel versions and content in Eliav, "Did the Jews," 30–31.

75. On these institutions within the landscape of Roman Judaea/Palestine, see Weiss, *Public Spectacles in Roman and Late Antique Palestine*; much of the material I discuss below appears in Weiss's chapter 5 (195–226).

76. Josephus, *AJ* 15.267–76. For the most part I follow the translation of Markus, but occasionally I slightly deviate from it and suggest my own.

77. *t. 'Abod. Zar.* 2:7 (Zuckermandel, 462).

78. *Sifra, 'Aḥare mot* 13 (Weiss, 86a). Cf. Neusner, *Sifra*, 3:78, who translates *'istariyot* as "playing fields" although it is actually a textual variant of *'itstadion*.

79. *b. 'Abod. Zar.* 18b; *Pesiq. Rab Kah.* 15:2 (Mandelbaum, 250).

80. On the attitude of Jews and rabbis toward the theater, on top of Weiss's discussion (reference in note 75 in this chapter), see also Jacobs, "Theatres and Performances as Reflected in the Talmud Yerushalmi."

81. Tertullian, *Apol.* 42.2. Another aspect of Tertullian's position appears in note 70 in this chapter. The sources depicting the Church's position toward the baths were collected and discussed in Zellinger, *Bad und Bäder*; and Berger, *Das Bad in der byzantinischen Zeit*, 34–45. See also Yegül, *Baths and Bathing in Classical Antiquity*, 314–20 and my discussion of Christian positions about the nudity in the baths in chapter 5.

82. For the literary evidence, see Berger, *Das Bad in der byzantinischen Zeit*. For the archaeological material, see Yegül, *Baths and Bathing in Classical Antiquity*, 322–39.

83. Socrates Scholasticus, *H.E.* 6.22. For an account of Chrysostom conducting an Easter service at the public baths when he was restricted from the church and even permitting the baptism of *catechumenoi* there, see ibid., 6.18; Palladius Monachus, *v. Chrys.* 9.162–64. On Augustine's frequent visits to the public bathhouse, see note 70 in this chapter.

84. E.g., *Liber pontificalis* 39 (Duchesne, 213 l. 2), 42 (Duchesne, 222 l. 3). See also Yegül, *Baths and Bathing in Classical Antiquity*, 314.

85. Clement of Alexandria, *Paed.* 3.9.46.4 (Stählin, 262 ll. 16–17); trans. Simon, 237. Even though the translation is not literal, it is an accurate expression of the mood of the text.

86. Jerome, *Ep.* 14.10. Apparently, the monastic disapproval of the baths dates to a much earlier period and could be found, for example, in the account of Hegesippus about James, the brother of Jesus, as early as the second century. In this source, James is portrayed as a Nazarite (i.e., the biblical prototype of a monastic) and one of his customs was to avoid the baths; see Eusebius, *H.E.* 2.23.5. See also Zellinger, *Bad und Bäder*, 47–67. But cf. Berger, *Das Bad in der byzantinischen Zeit*, 35–36; and Hirschfeld, *The Judean Desert Monasteries in the Byzantine Period*, 44.

87. Augustine, *C. acad.* 2.2.6; Epiphanius, *Adv. haeres.* 30.7.5–6. See also Jerome, *Ep.* 45.4.

88. *Qoh. Rab.* 2:8 (Hirshman, 132). This segment was preserved in several midrashic compilations; see the references listed in Eliav, "Did the Jews," 32n122. On the terminology used here by the rabbinic commentator to signify publicly and privately held bathhouses, see my detailed discussion on pp. 45–50.

89. *Lam. Rab.* 3:17 (Buber, 66a). I am quoting this passage following the version preserved in a Genizah fragment (TS C6.62). My thanks to Paul Mandel, who shared with me a photograph of this fragment. On the numerous other versions of this passage that were transmitted in various rabbinic texts, see my summary and discussion in Eliav, "Did the Jews," 33, 33n125.

90. *y. Ber.* 4 (7b) = *Gen. Rab.* 37:4 (Theodor and Albeck, 346), together with other sources, discussion, and bibliography I list in Eliav, "Did the Jews," 33n126. Cf. *b. 'Erub.* 55b, where a Persian rabbinic scholar sneers at the destitute who reside in shacks and huts, that is, in locations remote from organized communities, for not having bathhouses. For bathing facilities in Persian territories outside of the Roman Empire, see Eliav, "The Material World of Babylonia," 178, 178n87.

91. Admittedly this saying was preserved only in the Babylonian Talmud, although in the name of a rabbinic scholar from Roman Palestine ('Ulah), leaving doubt as to whether it reflects the mindset of people in Palestine. See *b. Erub.* 55b (cf. *y. Erub.* 5 [22c]).

92. *y. Qidd.* 4 (66d); *y. Ketub.* 7 (31b). For another version of the former dictum, see the *baraita* in *b. Sanh.* 17b, together with Eliav, "Did the Jews," 29–30, for numerous other rabbinic sources that place the public bathhouse as an integral part of the imagined ideal Jewish community.

93. *Baraita* in *b. Šabb.* 33b, and its discussion on pp. 42–43.

94. E.g., *y. Šabb.* 1 (3a) (=*y. Qidd.* 1 [61a]); *b. Šabb.* 147b.

95. For the general public's love of the public baths, see my discussion on pp. 37–39. And compare to Seneca the Younger, *Ep.* 86.4–13; Seneca, *Dial.: De vita beata* 7.3. For other examples, see Livy, *His.* 23.18.12 and the various legislations of Hadrian against mixed bathing, discussed in the next chapter. Fagan was on the mark in exposing Seneca's hypocrisy, berating the baths as a moralist while enjoying it as a human being; see Fagan, *Bathing in Public in the Roman World*, 52, 100n20.

Chapter 5. Tsni'ut (Rabbinic Modes of Modesty) in the Halls of Promiscuity: Mixed Bathing and Nudity in the Public Bathhouse

1. For one detailed version, see Ovid, *Met.* 3.138–52. For the many versions of this tale, literary and artistic, see *LIMC* 1:1:454–69.

2. The material (both archaeological and literary evidence) has been gathered and is often discussed; see Meusel, "Die Verwaltung und Finanzierung der öffentlichen Bäder zur römischen Kaiserzeit," 158–68; Nielsen, *Thermae et balnea*, 1:146–48; Ward, "Women in Roman Baths," 131–39; Fagan, *Bathing in Public in the Roman World*, 24–29; and Yegül, *Bathing in the Roman World*, 27–34. For queers and Roman bathing culture, see Eger, "Age and Male Sexuality." Since this group does not appear in the sources I discuss in this chapter, I will not regularly refer to it.

3. See my further insights and more comparative material about this throughout this chapter.

4. *CIL* 4.10677; translated in Fagan, *Bathing in Public in the Roman World*, 324, no. 278. There are additional inscriptions written by the same philandering brothers and others. The jury is still out on whether that specific room in the baths functioned as a brothel. See the many sources cited by Fagan, *Bathing in Public in the Roman World*, 34–35; Nielsen, *Thermae et balnea*, 1:146n4.

5. Ovid, *Ars am.* 3.639–40. See also Tacitus, *Hist.* 1.72, where Tigellinus receives the announcement of his imminent death in the midst of lovemaking in the public baths (prompting him to cut his own throat). Further sources are collected in Ward, "Women in Roman Baths," 134–38; and Yegül, *Bathing in the Roman World*, 27–34.

6. Epiphanius, *Adv. haeres.* 30.7.5–6 (Holl, 342).

7. John Moschus, *Pratum spirituale* 11 (Mioni, 92–93; section 242 in Wortley's translation). See also Magoulias, "Bathhouse, Inn, Tavern, Prostitution and the Stage," 236.

8. Prostitution requires an entire discussion of its own, which the confines of this book did not allow; for now, see Jacobs, "Römische Thermenkultur," 256–58; and Dauphin, "Brothels, Baths and Babes." For other references in rabbinic literature, see my discussion later in this chapter.

9. For some excellent articulations of the required nuance in this matter, see Fagan, *Bathing in Public in the Roman World*, 27, and again in his summary on p. 29; Yegül, *Bathing in the Roman World*, 34.

10. See Eschebach, *Die Stabianer Thermen in Pompeji*, 8–26, for the specific separation of bathing rooms for men and women, and again in the summary, pp. 70–72; Ward, "Women in Roman Baths," 128–29; Nielsen, *Thermae et balnea*, 1:26–28; and Yegül, *Bathing in the Roman World*, 61–63.

11. Listed in Nielsen, *Thermae et balnea*, 1:147n24.

12. Many have discussed this topic over the years. For a good collection of the most relevant sources, a nuanced discussion, and bibliography of earlier studies, see Satlow, "Jewish Constructions of Nakedness in Late Antiquity."

13. Goodman, *Rome and Jerusalem*, 274–75. Based on this position he later reaches an unfounded conclusion: "Thus, although in the course of the Roman imperial period Jews were to develop a taste for baths in the Roman style, more important than such bathing for pleasure, and indeed for cleanliness, was bathing for purity" (278). For similar recent conclusions, see Fonrobert, "Regulating the Human Body," 277, where she refers to "the overall rabbinic valuation of female modesty and the care taken to cloak the female body."

14. For some examples of these apologetic views, see Krauss, "Bad und Badewesen," 182, 192–94; Krauss, *Talmudische Archäologie*, 1:225; Preuss, *Biblisch-talmudische Medizin*, 636–38; and Epstein, *Sex Laws and Customs in Judaism*, 29–30. Reich too shares this error. See Reich, "The Hot Bath-House," 103, where the only problem he raises in regard to nudity relates to discussion and religious contemplation; thus, it must be that in his mind mixed nudity per se did not exist in the bathhouses attended by Jews. A similar apologetic trend surfaces among modern classicists who cannot entertain the possibility that ancient norms were so removed from modern standards, thus assigning these behaviors only to low-class individuals; for a list of examples and solid critique, see Ward, "Women in Roman Baths," 135, 135n37.

15. *t. Ber.* 2.20 (Lieberman, 10); *y. Ber.* 2 (4c). For the term "house of the nude," see *Tep.* 17 (Higger, 47*–48*). For a suggestion dating this latter passage to the earliest strata of the rabbinic texts, see Lerner, "The External Tractates," 400–401.

16. For the inclusion of *miqveh*, see, for example, *m. Ber.* 3:5 and compare with *SifreDeut* 258 (Finkelstein, 282). For more on these sources and other examples, see Eliav, "Did the Jews," 16–21.

17. See *y. Šabb.* 1 (3a) = *y. Qidd.* 1 (61a); *Perek ha-nikhnas la-merḥats* 1 (Higger, 296–99); *Kallah Rab.* 9:13 (Higger, 336); *Der. Er. Rab.* 7:11 (Higger, 133–34); *Gen. Rab.* 14:5 (Theodor and Albeck, 129).

18. *m. ʾAbod. Zar.* 3:4.

19. See, for example, *SifreDeut* 258 (Finkelstein, 282); *t. Sanh.* 4:8 (Zuckermandel, 422); and *y. Šabb.* 3 (6a).

20. The material has been collected and discussed more than a few times; see, for example, Fagan, *Bathing in Public in the Roman World*, 34–36, and the inscription he collects and translates on p. 324, nos. 278–79, 281. See also Ward, "Women in Roman Baths," 134–39; and Yegül, *Bathing in the Roman World*, 27–34.

21. *t. Ketub.* 7:6 (Lieberman, 80); *t. Soṭah* 5:9 (Lieberman, 179).

22. *y. Ketub.* 7 (31c). The passage is vague regarding the people participating in this erotic activity, especially since the verb appears in the feminine. Since this passage survived in a sole textual witness, it is unclear whether this is an inflectional correction by a scribe who could not fathom men and women bathing together in the bath (or who read this text in light of the preceding passage in *m. Ketub.* 7:8, where the author suggests that men and women bathed separately). Against this line of reasoning stands the immediate context of the laws enumerated in the Palestinian Talmud, all of which refer to the married woman carrying out impermissible acts

with another man. Heinrich Guggenheimer, one of the modern translators of the *Yerushalmi*, favors the latter, whereas David Fränkel, one of the leading eighteenth-century commentators on this text, seems to have gotten it right, saying that it was a male-female affair, happening as both "stood naked in the baths." See Guggenheimer, *The Jerusalem Talmud: Third Order*, 351; cf. Fränkel, *Qorban ha-'edah*.

23. *Der. Er. Rab.* 10:4; translated in Cohen, 2:561–62; *b. Ḥag.* 15a; *Alphabet of Ben Sira* (Yassif, 198).

24. Quintilian, *Inst.* 5.9.14; translation following Russell, 365.

25. *Dig.* 48.5.10(9). For later manifestations of this legal stipulation, see Berger, *Das Bad in der byzantinischen Zeit*, 44, and again in Zytka, *A Cultural History of Bathing*, 45–46.

26. Apuleius, *Met.* 9.17.

27. The two main sources for Hadrian's act are a short sentence in the abbreviated, eleventh-century version of the third-century historian Cassius Dio's *Hist.* (69.8.2) and another reference in the fourth-century anthology known as *Scriptores historiae Augustae*—SHA, Hadr. 18.10. This latter text also mentions similar actions on behalf of other emperors after Hadrian; see *M. Ant.* 23:8; and *Alex. Sev.* 24:2.

28. The best study on this matter remains Merten, *Bäder und Badegepflogenheiten*, 79–100, in particular 92–93, where she raises serious doubts about its historical credibility. Many other scholars have discussed the topic and the sources; see the references provided in note 25 in this chapter, as well as Ward, "Women in Roman Baths," 139–42.

29. Epiphanius, *Adv. haeres.* 30.7.5–6 (Holl, 342); Martial, *Epigrammata* 1.62. See other texts mentioned on p. 37.

30. See, e.g., *m. Qidd.* 2:3 (and the explanation regarding this law provided in *y. Qidd.* 2 [62c], which sees the bathhouse as a frequent destination for the married woman); *t. Nid.* 6:9 (Zuckermandel, 648); *baraita* in *b. 'Abod. Zar.* 38a–b (equating women going to the bath with men going to the synagogue); and *y. Ketub.* 7 (31b), regarding the amount of time a husband can forbid his wife to go to the bath.

31. On Seneca, see the references and penetrating analysis in Fagan, *Bathing in Public in the Roman World*, 52–53. For others who expressed misgivings, although not necessarily about the nudity, see Livy, *His.* 23.18.12; Tacitus, *Agr.* 21.2; and Suetonius, *De vita caesarum: Aug.* 82.2.

32. See Sartre, "The Nature of Syrian Hellenism in the Late Roman and Early Byzantine Periods," 39–40.

33. *y. Kil.* 9 (32b) = *y. Ketub.* 12 (35a). The sources on studying Torah in the baths were collected and discussed in Jacobs, "Römische Thermenkultur," 283–88. His conclusions support mine, but Jacobs overlooked some of the sources cited here and unconvincingly applied the thesis to some other sources that merely mention a discussion of *halakhah* on the way to bathhouses but not necessarily in them.

34. Compare the prohibition on "reflecting" or thinking on matters associated with Torah study in the bath, brought in the name of R. Yoḥanan in *b. Šabb.* 40b, with the more lenient views, in particular that of R. Ḥizkiyah in *y. Ber.* 3 (6a). For Eleazar's rehearsal, see *TanḥB Gen., Miqets* 2 (Buber, 199). For a discussion of the various rabbinic sources on the topic of intellectual reflection in the baths and the chronological and thematic relationship between them, see Eliav, "Did the Jews," 16–17n68.

35. The ridicule in *Qoh. Rab.* 1:7 (Hirshman, 60). Other versions of this statement are listed in Hirshman's edition. Admittedly, it is not clear from this passage whether the author had in mind other "unwise" rabbis who did study in baths, for he could just as well have been thinking about non-Jewish scholars, or of no one in particular. The praise in *Midr. Pss.* 119:41 (Buber, 498).

36. Pliny the Younger, *Ep.* 3.5.14; Libanius, *Ep.* 11.10. And see Fagan, *Bathing in Public in the Roman World*, 217.

37. Clement of Alexandria, *Paed.* 3.5.32 (Stählin, 254–55), 3.9.46 (Stählin, 263).

38. Fulton, *Index canonum The Greek Text*, 258–59. There is some doubt regarding the location and time of the council that produced these rulings, but this has no bearing on our discussion here.

39. *Jub.* 3:31; trans. VanderKam, 1:21. For more on the background of this statute and its possible association with the encounter with Hellenism in general, and the gymnasium built in Jerusalem in particular (where athletes supposedly practiced in the nude) in this early period, see VanderKam, *Jubilees*, 1:230–31.

40. Josephus, *BJ* 2.161.

41. Augustine, *De civ. Dei* 14.17 (McCracken, 4:360).

42. Ovid, *Fast.* 4.150–55 (trans. Goold, 199).

43. Martial, *Epigrammata* 3.72 (trans. Bailey, 1:255). And see another example in chapter 1, note 55.

44. Juvenal, *Saturae* 1.138–47, 6:413–26, 11:150–61, as well as Martial, *Epigrammata* 12.83.

45. Suetonius, *De vita caesarum: Aug.* 94.4.

46. See Albeck, *Introduction to Jewish Law in Talmudic Times*, 402–3. The central question for us, which Albeck does not consider, concerns verbal shaming that does not involve actual corporal damage and whether it can stand on its own as a category of damages in rabbinic law. The issue is not completely clear; on the one hand, the *halakhah* in the Tosefta indicates that *boshet* can stand on its own—see *t. B. Qam.* 9:1 (Lieberman, 42)—but on the other hand, the *Yerushalmi* preserved a statement by the second-century scholar R. Jose that "he who shames another person with words is not liable." This latter statement was accepted by later generations of rabbinic jurists as grounds for excluding plain verbal shaming. Be that as it may, this ruling is not relevant to our topic of the bathhouse since it is rather clear that shaming in the bathhouse, related to the nudity prevalent there, was indeed a relevant topic for the rabbis. See further discussion in note 48 in this chapter, as well as other methods used by later generations of rabbis to include verbal shaming; see also Berlin and Zevin, *Talmudic Encyclopedia III*, 49–50.

47. *t. B. Qam.* 9:12 (Lieberman, 44–45).

48. The relevant segment in the Babylonian Talmud is *b. B. Qam.* 86b. For a summary of this line of explanation, see Lieberman, *Tosefta kifshutah*, 9:100. My reservation about this explanation stems from the fact that it doesn't sit well with the plain words of the original rabbinic dictum, which says "one who shames another person naked"; according to the common interpretation, this must be read as shaming a naked person by making him or her even more naked. But such a reading adds an entire facet, completely stripping a partially naked person, which does not exist in the original phrasing of the statute. See also the issues brought up in note 46 in this chapter.

49. Seneca the Younger, *QNat.* 1.16.3, together with Martial, *Epigrammata* 1.96, 2.52.

50. For a concise history of the practice of circumcision, its significance, and the debates around it (with ample bibliography to earlier literature), see Cohen, *Why Aren't Jewish Women Circumcised?* 3–54.

51. *Jub.* 15:33–35, with Cohen, *Why Aren't Jewish Women Circumcised?* 25–26 (and the bibliography cited there). On the various ancient conflicts involving circumcision to one degree or another, see Schäfer, "The Bar Kokhba Revolt and Circumcision," and further bibliography he cites there.

52. Martial, *Epigrammata* 7.82, with the debate around its interpretation in Schäfer, "The Bar Kokhba Revolt and Circumcision," 127–28. See also Martial, *Epigrammata* 7.35.

53. On R. Abbahu and his experiences in the baths, see Eliav, "Realia, Daily Life, and the Transmission of Local Stories," 242–52.

54. *b. Šabb.* 41a.

55. *t. Ber.* 6:25 (Lieberman, 40).

56. *SifreDeut* 36 (Finkelstein, 68). Numerous versions of this haggadic segment about David are preserved in rabbinic literature, all without the closing parable, which leads me to question whether the parable was originally part of this literary piece. In any event, the connection was made either by the editors of the Sifre, who included the parable, or by the author who originally composed it, and it reflects his or their state of mind. For other versions, see, *y. Ber.* 9 (14d); *Midr. Pss.* 6:1 (Buber, 58); and *b. Menaḥ* 43b.

57. I explored the possibilities listed below (for maintaining bodily modesty in the public baths) in an early study: see Eliav, "The Roman Bath as a Jewish Institution," 438–49. Years later, Monika Trümper followed the same route in her interrogation of earlier Greek bathing facilities, apparently without knowledge of my study, which could have provided a stimulating parallel to hers; see Trümper, "Gender Differentiation in Greek Public Baths." My current discussion benefits from further insights I gained from Trümper's work.

58. *CIL* 2, suppl. 5181 (p. 789 ll. 19–24). For a reconstructed version of the inscription, including supplements and corrections, see Carcopino, *Daily Life in Ancient Rome*, 258, 258n63. For a survey of the research on this issue, both before and after Carcopino (especially the enormous influence his remarks had upon the ongoing research on this question), see Ward, "Women in Roman Baths," 140–41. Ward's criticism of the disproportionate weight assigned to this single source by Carcopino and his followers is justified. Indeed, a conclusion regarding a widespread custom (of any kind) cannot be drawn from a single source. In this case there is abundant evidence for mixed bathing. However, in my opinion, Ward's desire to prove the prevalence of mixed bathing caused him to miss the main point. The issue is not whether mixed bathing existed, since it is clear that it did, but whether segregated bathing also existed. The significance of the inscription from Portugal, even if it was unique (and below I show that by all means it was not), was to upset the belief that all bathing was always mixed. Apparently, even in the second century CE, when mixed bathing prevailed, there were those who bathed separately.

59. For this inscription, see Ducrey and van Effenterre, "Un règlement d'époque romaine sur les bains d'Arcadès."

60. As far as I know, this admittedly sparse material is yet to be gathered and studied together. For now, see Aulus Gellius, *NA* 10.3.1–3; Martial, *Epigrammata* 7.35; *SHA, Alex. Sev.* 53.2; *CIL* 9.3677 (with translation of this text in Fagan, *Bathing in Public in the Roman World*, 284, no. 151); and *CIL* 14.2121 (ibid., 246, no. 46).

61. The material was gathered and studied by Meyer, "Les femmes et les bains publics."

62. For men: *Didascalia apostolorum* 2 (Vööbus, 1.19 ll. 12–13); for women: ibid., 3 (Vööbus, 1.26 ll. 12–14).

63. *m. Ketub.* 7.8. In my translation I considered some minute textual variants; see Hershler, *The Babylonian Talmud with Variant Readings*, 199. Similar conclusions about this text were reached by Krauss, *Talmudische Archäologie*, 1:225; and Jacobs, "Römische Thermenkultur," 253–55.

64. *t. Nid.* 6.15 (Zuckermandel, 648). On the complex textual history of this passage and some of the difficulties it raises, see Eliav, "The Roman Bath as a Jewish Institution," 44n65.

65. On the mosaic, see Pace, *I mosaici di Piazza Armerina*, 77–81. On the girl with the revealed breast, see ibid., 74. On the term "Bikinimädchen," see, e.g., Heinz, *Römische Thermen*, 129. As to the question of whether this mosaic depicts a bathing suit, see Nielsen, *Thermae et balnea*, 1:141.

66. Martial, *Epigrammata* 3:87, as well as other references in ibid., 1.23, 1.96, 2.14, 2.48, 2.52, 3.3, 3.20, 3.51, 3.68, 3.72, 3.87, 6.93, 7.35, 7.82, 9.33, 11.52, 11.75, 12.83.

67. *SHA, Alex. Sev.* 42.1. The text does not allow us to deduce how this garment was used; see Nielsen, *Thermae et balnea*, 1:141n9.

68. *Didascalia apostolorum* 3 (Vööbus, 26).

69. The material about bathing habits in these later periods, also referred to by modern scholars as Byzantine, are collected in Berger, *Das Bad in der byzantinischen Zeit*. On the *lention*, see ibid., 115.

70. *Perek ha-nikhnas la-merḥats* 1 (Higger, 296–98). For more on this term, the sources that mention it, and its various usages, see Brand, *Kele zekhukhit be-sifrut ha-talmud*, 176–77. For the Greek, see LSJ, 636 (s.v. *epikarsios* III). For the Syriac, see Smith, *Thesaurus Syriacus*, 1:349–50 (s.v. *'afkroso*). See also Krauss, *Griechische und lateinische Lehnwörter*, 2:113 s.v. *'afiqresin*.

71. *y. Ber.* 2 (4c) = *Pesiq. Rab.* 22 (Friedmann, 112a).

72. Presently, there is no inclusive discussion on the sources regarding this item. On its use for drying and rubbing oil (although not exclusively at the baths), see, e.g., *m. Šabb.* 22:5; *t. Šabb.* 6:15–17 (Lieberman, 78–79); and *t. 'Erub.* 5:24 (Lieberman, 116–17). On the Latin derivation, see Lewis and Short, *A Latin Dictionary*, 1069 (s.v. *linteum*). For the Greek, LSJ, 1038 (s.v. *lention*). See also Krauss, *Griechische und lateinische Lehnwörter*, 2:51–52.

73. Krauss, *Griechische und lateinische Lehnwörter*, 2:158–59 s.v. *balnerin*; Krauss, *Talmudische Archäologie*, 1:231. This was adopted by all other lexicographers; see, e.g., Sokoloff, *A Dictionary of Jewish Palestinian Aramaic*, 104 (s.v. *balani*). For the argument that the various forms of spelling actually denote the same object, see Lieberman, *Tosefta kifshutah*, 2:657–58, 2:657–58n47. On Krauss and his contributions to the field of rabbinic material culture, see my discussion on p. 5.

74. A *baraita* in *b. Šabb.* 147b. The other two references are *y. Kil.* 9 (32a) and *y. Mo'ed Qat.* 3 (82a).

75. I gathered the various sources mentioning the *balnare* and discussed the legal theoretical frameworks associated with them in Eliav, "The Roman Bath as a Jewish Institution," 447–48.

Chapter 6. The Naked Rabbi and the Beautiful Goddess: Engaging with Sculpture in the Public Bathhouse

I have dealt with this topic in a series of articles over the last two decades; see "The Roman Bath as a Jewish Institution," 444–48; "Viewing the Sculptural Environment"; "Roman Statues, Rabbis, and Graeco-Roman Culture"; and "Two Comments on Idolatry." My views have changed somewhat, and the current presentation conveys my most recent understanding of this contested subject.

1. *m. 'Abod. Zar.* 3:4–5; based on ms. Kaufmann 50A fol. 167r; see Georg Beer, ed., *Faksimile-Ausgabe des Mischnacodex Kaufman A 50* (Budapest: Hungarian Academy of Sciences; reprint, Jerusalem: Mekorot, 1968).

2. See, for example, the sources collected in Nielsen, *Thermae et balnea*, 1:146–47n9.

3. Pace Friedheim, *Rabbinisme et Paganisme*, 99, who seems to think that Proklos is a real non-Jewish figure and the views he voices in the Mishnah to be an authentic "pagan" position. One can forgive Pierre Aupert, a French archaeologist with minimal knowledge, if any, of rabbinic literature (who at one point quotes a passage from the Mishnah and calls it the Talmud), for misunderstanding the literary nature of figures featured in rabbinic stories and thus attributing historical veracity to these fictional characters; see Aupert, "Les thermes comme lieux de culte," 192. But to have someone with training in rabbinic literature like Friedheim err on such trivial matters is quite surprising. On the other hand, the fictional nature of the anecdote is quite clear to Jacobs, "Römische Thermenkultur," 260–66, esp. 262 (where he speaks of the "fiktiven Charakter" of the encounter described in the text) and again on p. 264 (where he concludes that the text displays "keine realen Dispute" [no real disputes]). On the identity of Proklos or lack thereof, see also Zlotnick, "Proklos ben Plaslos"; Wasserstein, "Rabban Gamliel and Proclus the Philosopher"; and Yadin, "Rabban Gamliel, Aphrodite's Bath, and the Question of Pagan Monotheism."

4. *Anth. Pal.* 2.99–101 (trans. Paton, 1:67), but note other statues of the same goddess that this visitor sees and writes about in the same text. On the many statues of Aphrodite that were unearthed, see Havelock, *Aphrodite of Knidos and Her Successors*. On her representations in public bathhouses, see Manderscheid, *Die Skulpturenausstattung*, 32–33.

5. E.g., Dio Chrysostomus, *Orationes* 37.41; Juvenal, *Saturae* 6.309–10. See also Hobson, *Latrinae et foricae*, 105–6; and Van Dam, *The Roman Revolution of Constantine*, 257–58. For a different interpretation of the semen in this story, see Jacobs, "Römische Thermenkultur," 265–66.

6. For a partial, incomplete list, see the studies listed in note 3 in this chapter, as well as Blidstein, "Nullification of Idolatry in Rabbinic Law," 4–6; Hadas-Lebel, "Le paganisme," 398; Millar, *The Roman Near East*, 268–69; Halbertal, "Coexisting,"

167; Schwartz, "Gamaliel in Aphrodite's Bath," 203–17; Schwartz, *Imperialism and Jewish Society*, 167–74; Eliav, "Viewing the Sculptural Environment," 424–25; Eliav, "Roman Statues, Rabbis, and Graeco-Roman Culture," 112–14; Fine, *Art and Judaism*, 111–12; Levine, "Figural Art in Ancient Judaism," 18–19; Furstenberg, "The Rabbinic View," 355–60; and Stern, "Images," 121–22. See also the numerous references to this passage made by the participants in the conference on the sculptural environment of the Roman east in Eliav, Friedland, and Herbert, *The Sculptural Environment of the Roman Near East*, index s.v. Gamaliel. Finally, see also Neis, *The Sense of Sight in Rabbinic Culture*, 197–98, with a clumsy mistake about the location of Acre; but more seriously, when Neis sees in this text a "curious blend of rabbinic and Roman conceptions of the sacred" (198), she is borrowing, without acknowledgment, my early interpretations of the text; as far as I know, no one ever associated this text with Roman conceptions of the sacred before my 2004 review, Eliav, "The Matrix of Ancient Judaism," 125–26, then further developed in Eliav, "Roman Statues, Rabbis, and Graeco-Roman Culture."

7. The comprehensive study of sculpture in the bathhouse is Manderscheid, *Die Skulpturenausstattung*. See also DeLaine, "Recent Research on Roman Baths," 25–27. On "living" statues, see Hersey, *Falling in Love with Statues*, 1–17.

8. These were collected in book 2 of the so-called *Anthologia Palatina*; see *Anth. Pal.* 2 (Paton, 1:58–91). See also Stupperich, "Das Statuenprogramm in den Zeuxippos-Thermen"; and Bassett, "*Historiae custos*."

9. DeLaine, *The Baths of Caracalla*, 265–67; Marvin, "Freestanding Sculptures from the Baths of Caracalla."

10. Fagan, *Bathing in Public in the Roman World*, 170n88. Fagan gathers a wide array of inscriptions from bathhouses throughout the Roman world (see pp. 225–347).

11. Rey-Coquais, "Inscriptions grecques d'Apameé," 41–46; Balty, *Guide d'Apamée*, 205–6, no. 20.

12. *NEAEHL*, 5:1639–40; Foerster, "A Modest Aphrodite from Bet Shean."

13. Zanker, *The Power of Images in the Age of Augustus*, 3, 101; Fagan, *Bathing in Public in the Roman World*, 88–90.

14. For a detailed study, although focused mostly on the western part of the empire, see Stewart, *Statues*. And more recently with a focus on the later centuries of the Roman Empire, see Bauer and Witschel, *Statuen in der Spätantike*; and Gehn, *Ehrenstatuen in der Spätantike*.

15. Smith, "Statue Life in the Hadrianic Baths at Aphrodisias," 203.

16. Eliav, Friedland, and Herbert, introduction to *The Sculptural Environment of the Roman Near East*, 1–11.

17. Acts 17:16. See Spivey, *Understanding Greek Sculpture*, 13; Von Ehrenkrook, *Sculpting Idolatry*, 114–18. The experience of Paul interacting with sculpture in Athens stands at the heart of my documentary, *Paul in Athens* (2018); see https://paul-in-athens.nes.lsa.umich.edu.

18. These are surveyed time and again with ample examples in the various introductory textbooks on Roman art. See, e.g., Kleiner, *A History of Roman Art*.

19. For other problems related to the ways this book attempts to depict the reality of Roman times, see Di Segni, "Using Talmudic Sources for City Life in Palestine." See also Stern, "Images," 119, who believes that statues were uncommon in Jewish territories (but compare with his assertion on page 116, near note 30).

20. Two ancient writers record the details of this event: the Jewish philosopher Philo, a native of Alexandria, who was in Rome at the time, and the historian Josephus, who most likely used Philo as one of his sources; see Philo, *Legat.* 188, 197–348; Josephus, *BJ* 2.184–87, 192–203; and Josephus, *AJ* 18.261–309. The best modern reconstruction of the event is still Smallwood, *The Jews under Roman Rule*, 174–80. For a detailed study of the way statues operate in the narrative of Josephus, see Von Ehrenkrook, *Sculpting Idolatry*. For some speculation on how the Caligula crisis might have ended had the emperor not died, see Eck, *Judäa—Syria Palästina*, 51–52, and my critique of this in *JAOS* 138 (2018): 198–200.

21. See Patrich, *The Formation of Nabatean Art*.

22. Cf. Josephus's description of Herod's palace in Jerusalem that mentions statues (*BJ* 5.181) and also the account of the palace of his son Herod Antipas in Tiberias (*Vit.* 65–67); but significantly, no statuary fragments were found in any of the extensive excavations in Herod's palaces in Herodium and Masada or in the Hasmonaean palaces in Jericho. See Netzer, *The Architecture of Herod*; and Netzer, *The Palaces of the Hasmoneans and Herod the Great*.

23. For the most recent formulation of this argument, see Levine, *Visual Judaism*, 37–45, with references to his earlier studies on the topic. Cf. Fine, *Art and Judaism*, 60–73. Fine begins his chapter with the (correct) warning not to apply the modern term "art" to ancient Jewish societies that were unfamiliar with it, but then moves to use the category "idolatry" as the centerpiece in his reconstruction of the mindset of Jews in Hasmonaean times; as a result, he falls into the anachronistic trap he himself warned against.

24. Josephus, *AJ* 15.328–330 (trans. Marcus, 8:157–59).

25. Fischer, *Marble Studies*, provides the most comprehensive summary of statuary in Roman Palestine, though this monograph focuses solely on marble. See also the studies on specific sites: Friedland, *The Roman Marble Sculptures*; Gersht, "Caesarean Sculpture in Context"; and Weiss, "Sculptures and Sculptural Images in Urban Galilee." On non-Jewish literary sources discussing statuary in the Roman colony of Aelia Capitolina, see Eliav, "The Desolating Sacrilege."

26. Keeping my focus here on the statues of the baths, the sources that will follow are only a tiny sample; for a typical rabbinic tradition that speaks of third-century rabbis walking the streets of a city, probably Tiberias, and encountering a series of statues along the way, see *y. 'Abod. Zar.* 3 (43b). For scholarly discussions of this reality, see Krauss, *Paras ve-Romi ba-Talmud uva-midrashim*, 47–65; and Lieberman, *Hellenism in Jewish Palestine*, 128–52. References to and discussion of more recent studies will come in the notes below.

27. *t. 'Abod. Zar.* 6:6 (Zuckermandel, 469).

28. *Mek.*, tractate *Baḥodesh* 8 (Horovitz and Rabin, 233); translation with slight changes based on Lauterbach, 2:262. For the association of this text with the *damnatio memoriae*, see Lieberman, *Tosefta kifshutah*, 3:281n3. On the familiarity of the rabbis with the processes of *damnatio memoriae*, see in great detail in Furstenberg, "The Rabbinic View."

29. *Lev. Rab.* 23:12 (Margulies, 2:547).

30. *Mek.*, tractate *Pisḥa* 13 (Horovitz and Rabin, 44); ibid., tractate *Beshallaḥ* 8 (Horovitz and Rabin, 144). See Flower, *Ancestor Masks and Aristocratic Power in Roman Culture*.

31. *t. Šabb.* 17:1 (Lieberman, 80).

32. *m. Demai* 6:10; *t. Demai* 6:13 (Lieberman, 96–97); *Dig.* 34.2.1, 14.

33. *Lev. Rab.* 34:3 (Margulies, 2:776–77), discussed in detail on pp. 132–33.

34. *m. 'Abod. Zar.* 1:7.

35. *y. Šeb.* 8 (38b–c). Although not explicitly stated, it is clear that the story took place in the bathhouse, mainly because of the immediate literary context that deals with a *halakhah* concerning the bath. Cf. Levine, *Judaism and Hellenism*, 109; and Fine, *Art and Judaism*, 112–13. The later parallel in *b. 'Abod. Zar.* 58b–59a blurs the background of the event and does not indicate a bathhouse setting. Cf. Blidstein, "R. Yohanan, Idolatry, and Public Privilege," 155. Blidstein's translation (following Saul Lieberman) that the sprinkling refers to the people who were "washing in the bath of Aphrodite" does not sit well with the demonstrative pronoun *lehada* (=to that) that follows the verb "sprinkling." Other translations of the text have gotten this aspect right; see Alan J. Avery-Peck, trans., *The Talmud of the Land of Israel: A Preliminary Translation and Explanation: Volume 5 Shebiit* (Chicago: University of Chicago Press, 1991), 293; and Guggenheimer, *The Jerusalem Talmud: First Order*, 591. For more on the meaning of this text, the various interpretations of it offered by modern scholars, and the way it fits into the legal framework of idolatry laws, see p. 188–89.

36. *y. 'Abod. Zar.* 4 (43d).

37. Mango, "Antique Statuary and the Byzantine Beholder," 55.

38. This is not to suggest in any way that Jews consistently followed rabbinic *halakhah*, a topic heatedly debated among modern scholars, which I presented on pp. 13–14. I find myself supporting the minimalist view, namely that very few Jews, if at all, followed the rabbis during the periods of the High and Late Empires. Nevertheless, rabbinic or not, to one degree or another Jews adhered to ancient laws, what Josephus calls "our laws" (e.g., *Ap.* 2.277), and so it is highly probable that these laws influenced their perception of statues. The methodological problem is that from the first centuries of the Common Era, the legal corpora of the rabbis are most of what survived of Jewish law. So the historian is left to acknowledge this mishap, hope for more to be recovered, and work with what has survived.

39. In general I follow, with only slight changes, the translation of *The New Oxford Annotated Bible: New Revised Standard Version* (Oxford: Oxford University Press, 1989).

40. Modern scholarship has shown that "Israelite" concepts of idolatry were much more complex than they seem. See, e.g., Schmidt, "The Aniconic Tradition"; also the variety of studies collected in Dietrich and Klopfenstein, *Ein Gott allein?* On the Hellenistic and Early Roman period, see the summary and bibliography in Levine, *Visual Judaism*, 15–65.

41. The literature documenting this phenomenon is vast. See Faur, "The Biblical Idea of Idolatry"; an annotated bibliography on this issue is found in Feldman, *Josephus and Modern Scholarship*, 512–15. On the written sources, see Schürer, *The History of the Jewish People*, 2:58–59, 81–83. See also Hachlili, *Ancient Jewish Art and Archaeology in the Land of Israel*, 65–83; Murphy, "Retelling the Bible"; and Schiffman, "Laws Concerning Idolatry in the *Temple Scroll*," 159–75.

42. Die rather than transgress—*t. Šabb.* 15:17 (Lieberman, 75); *y. Šeb.* 4 (35a) (=*y. Sanh.* 3 [21b]); *b. Sanh.* 74a. Confessing to idolatry—*SifreNum* 111 (Horovitz, 116; trans.

Neusner, 2:160). Impure and cause for exile—*m. Šabb.* 9:1; *m. 'Abod. Zar.* 3:6; *t. 'Abod. Zar.* 6:3 (Zuckermandel, 469); *t. Zabim* 5:6-7 (Zuckermandel, 680); *m. 'Abot* 5:9. Regulations—*m. Ber.* 8:6; *m. Sanh.* 7:6. On the latter, see Schwartz, "Gamaliel in Aphrodite's Bath," 208–10. That this is the common understanding among rabbis, underlying their numerous discussions of idolatry, has been recognized by Weinfeld, "The Uniqueness of the Decalogue and Its Place in Jewish Tradition," 4–6, 6n20. Weinfeld also points to alternative interpretations of these verses circulating among Second Temple Jews (such as Philo and Josephus) and perhaps even among some of the rabbis themselves. See also the sources gathered and discussed in Wallach, "A Palestinian Polemic against Idolatry"; and Furstenberg, "The Rabbinic View."

43. *m. 'Abod. Zar.* 3:1; based on ms. Kaufmann 50A fol. 167r.

44. Most modern scholars have missed this point, as they have tried to generalize from this passage to other forms of figurative art; see, for example, in Jacob Neusner's translation of this passage as "All images"; Jacob Neusner, trans., *The Talmud of the Land of Israel: A Preliminary Translation and Explanation: Abodah Zarah* (Chicago: University of Chicago Press, 1982), 110. See also Levine, *The Ancient Synagogue*, 444, 448, 457. In his later publication, Levine apparently changed his mind and agrees with the reading I offer here; see Levine, *Visual Judaism*, 411–12n33.

45. The question in dispute here—i.e., the extent of the prohibition against idolatry (in which statues are included)—should not be confused with another issue that the rabbis discuss and disagree about, namely the manner of implementing the ban (i.e., how to behave with a statue that is considered an idol), although the same criterion—whether the statue is worshipped—plays an essential role in that discussion. Consider, for example, the rabbinic dispute in *Sifra, Kedoshim* 1 (Weiss, 87a; trans. Neusner, 3:88): "'Do not turn to idols'—do not turn aside to worship them; R. Judah says: certainly do not turn aside even to look at them."

46. Rabbis themselves define the proper and thus prohibited actions of idolatry in that way; see *m. Sanh.* 7:6.

47. *y. 'Abod. Zar.* 3 (42b).

48. The fantastic nature that underlines these rabbinic positions was observed by Goodman, "Palestinian Rabbis and the Conversion of Constantine to Christianity," 6.

49. In a previous study I surveyed and critiqued the central modern interpretations of these laws; see Eliav, "Viewing the Sculptural Environment," 419–21. For alternative explanations to the one presented here, see Urbach, "The Rabbinical Laws of Idolatry," 229–45; Bickerman, "Sur la théologie de l'art figuratif," 137; Blidstein, "R. Yohanan, Idolatry, and Public Privilege"; Hadas-Lebel, "Le paganisme," 398; Goldenberg, *The Nations That Know Thee Not*, 95; Halbertal, "Coexisting," 167; Schwartz, "Gamaliel in Aphrodite's Bath," 213–17; Friedheim, *Rabbinisme et Paganisme*, 70; Furstenberg, "The Rabbinic View"; and Stern, "Images."

50. Brown, "Christianization and Religious Conflict," 632–34; quote on p. 632. For an illuminating articulation of this all-embracing religious spirit that prevailed in the ancient world, with an emphasis on the period under discussion here, see Brown, *The World of Late Antiquity*, 49–112. And more recently, the balanced and authoritative judgment in Cameron, *The Last Pagans of Rome*, 783–801.

51. *CIL* 4.7714–15.

52. See Clement of Alexandria, *Protr.* 4.511 (Stählin, 39). See also Jansen, "Interpreting Images and Epigraphic Testimony," 167–72.

53. The wall painting from Pompeii is reproduced in Hopkins's book in plate 1. See also Belayche, *Iudaea-Palaestina*, 27–31.

54. For a detailed documentation of this phenomenon, although limited to one city in the Roman world, see Bakker, *Living and Working with the Gods*.

55. For a concise but complete summary of these processes, along with a bibliography, see Stambaugh, "The Functions of Roman Temples." On the various meanings of *templum* and its basic etymology as a demarcation of space, both in the heavens and on earth, as a place set aside for sacred purposes, see Catalano, "Aspetti spaziali del sistema giuridico-religioso romano." The most up-to-date, comprehensive treatment of this phenomenon is Lambrinoudakis et al., "Consecration," 3:303–46. See also Bowes, *Private Worship*, 24–27.

56. See, e.g., Bowes, *Private Worship*, 26.

57. On the application of Roman religious norms in the provinces, see Ando, "Exporting Roman Religion." On one of many well-documented places outside of Italy, where similar procedures related to sacred space were applied, see Rogers, *The Sacred Identity of Ephesos*. The central document that sheds light on how sacredness was perceived and enacted in Ephesus, the dedicatory inscription of C. Vibius Salutaris, uses more or less the same categories of sacredness as in Rome. For more on this phenomenon and my refutation of Friedheim's position on the matter, see pp. 125–31.

58. Josephus, *AJ* 16.163–64. For more on *sacrilegium*, see note 63 in this chapter.

59. For a comprehensive summary of the sources, see Linant de Bellefonds et al., "Rites et activités relatifs aux images de culte," 2:419–27.

60. For a more detailed description and analysis of this system, see Stewart, *Statues*, 184–222; and Lambrinoudakis et al., "Consecration," 3:338–39.

61. On the category of dedication, its evolution over time, its overlapping legal and conceptual relationship with consecration, and the non-cultic activities that came to be associated with it, see Mrozek, "Sur la *dedicatio*, la *consecratio* et les dédicants dans les inscriptions du Haut-Empire romain," as well as the articles collected in Bodel and Kajava, *Dediche sacre nel mondo Greco-Romano*.

62. For one example, see Minucius Felix, *Oct.* 2.4.

63. See, e.g., *Dig.* 48.13.11. The language of the law here, which distinguishes between sacred things that belong to the public and those in private possession, strongly resembles the legal position of R. Yoḥanan regarding the statue in the bathhouse mentioned earlier and will be discussed later in the chapter. On the history of this legal concept, see Bauman, "Tertullian and the Crime of *Sacrilegium*," 175–76.

64. Indeed, we find private veneration of statues carried out with the same zeal and devotion as with official *res sacrae*; evidence for this phenomenon was collected and discussed in Bodel, "'Sacred Dedications,'" in particular 22n21, 25–27. Much has been written about the multiple varieties of religious expression and conceptuality in the provinces; see, for example, the studies gathered in Cancik and Rüpke, *Römische Reichsreligion und Provinzialreligion*, in particular Woolf, "Polis-Religion and Its Alternatives in the Roman Provinces."

65. See Spivey, *Understanding Greek Sculpture* (although focusing on a wider and slightly earlier chronological range than discussed here); Elsner, *Art and the Roman Viewer*; and Stewart, *Statues*.

66. For one example from the *ara pacis* in Rome, see Castriota, *The Ara Pacis Augustae*, 5. The vegetal reliefs on the exterior of the *ara pacis* were seen as

representing "images of abundance and fruitfulness intended to evoke the blessings of the *Pax Augusta*" and also as a "visual embodiment of the returning Golden Age, a new era of blessedness in which the limitless flowering of the earth is contingent upon the efficacious presence of a divinely appointed sovereign, Augustus himself."

67. Cicero, *Nat. D.* 1.29.81 (trans. Rackham, 79). I preferred to translate *facies* in this context as "appearance" rather than Rackham's "aspect." See Lewis and Short, *A Latin Dictionary*, 714, s.v. "*facies*" II. It may very well be that the need to place these categories in writing meant that the average viewer of statues had some trouble figuring out whether they were gods or mortals. In fact, the Late Republic of Cicero was beginning to be filled with statues of living people, who stretched the limits of what they are allowed to look like in statuary; Pompey and his crab-claw hair (like the demi-god Alexander) come to mind, as well as Caesar, who claimed to be descended from Venus and is said to have had statues suggesting the lineage. I owe this point to Ryan Hughes.

68. E.g., Pliny the Elder, *HN* 34.17 (38), 19 (89).

69. Philostratus, *Imag.* 1.15 (trans. Fairbanks, 61–63).

70. E.g., Koortbojian, *Myth, Meaning and Memory on Roman Sarcophagi*, 9–22, and the literature he lists on p. 11n27.

71. Eliav, "Viewing the Sculptural Environment," 431–32.

72. Lucian, *Syr. D.* 32 (trans. Lightfoot, 269); the entire work is built on this paradigm.

73. See Frankfurter, "The Vitality of Egyptian Images," 659–78.

74. This should put to rest concerns voiced by some scholars, as if the conceptuality presented here did not encompass the entire Mediterranean world. See, e.g., Stern, "Images," 127–28.

75. *t. ʾAbod. Zar.* 5:1 (Zuckermandel, 468).

76. Sacha Stern has also interpreted rabbinic positions on statues as relating to worship, and to some degree our conclusions, especially regarding the centrality of this "worship" criterion, are quite compatible, but we go in separate ways in understanding the rabbinic sources and in reconstructing their cultural context and significance. See Stern, "Figurative Art and Halakha in the Mishnaic-Talmudic Period," and in its more elaborate formulation, Stern, "Images." For others who use these categories, see Fine, *Art and Judaism*, 111–18 (in particular nn. 244–45, 247); and Neis, *The Sense of Sight*, 170–74. For a different interpretation of the rabbinic laws that also places them in close dialogue with conceptualities prevalent in the Roman world, see Furstenberg, "The Rabbinic View."

77. In response to Stern, "Images," 128n85.

78. For example, Schwartz, *Imperialism and Jewish Society*, 169–74; and my critique of his view in Eliav, "The Matrix of Ancient Judaism."

79. E.g., Suetonius, *De vita caesarum: Tib.* 26 (Rolfe, 1:350–53).

80. Halbertal, "Coexisting," 167.

81. This role of the mishnaic anecdote was clearly defined by the late Yonah Fraenkel; see Fraenkel, *Midrash and Agadah*, 3:694–708. See also Wollfish, "'Iḥud ha-halakhah veha-'agadah," 310, 310n3 (Heb.); and Eliav, "Realia, Daily Life, and the Transmission of Local Stories," 253–54, and see 253–54n38 for references to earlier scholarship on this topic.

82. *y. Šeb.* 8 (8b-c).

83. Cf. Lieberman's commentary on this story (*Hellenism in Jewish Palestine*, 132–33), where he suggests that the bathhouse mentioned here was also a "pagan sanctum" to Aphrodite, but if so I cannot see how a rabbi would permit himself and others to enter it (see chapter 4); Schwartz, "Gamaliel in Aphrodite's Bath," 216–17n33; Jacobs, "Römische Thermenkultur," 267. In my opinion, Blidstein's explanation ("R. Yohanan, Idolatry, and Public Privilege," 155–56) that Rabbi Yohanan's sanction is due to the public nature of the site misses the mark. If it had been built for idolatry, then its "publicans" would not enable it to be sanctioned. Hence, the reason for the dispensation must be that the statue was not made for idol worship in the first place but rather to embellish the baths. That is why the sprinkling of libations would not obligate the rabbis to prohibit the bathhouse as idolatrous. Such an argument also solves the other problem raised by Blidstein—the failure of Reish Lakish and R. Yohanan to rely on the Mishnah regarding R. Gamaliel in Acre. In my opinion, the reason is simple: In R. Gamaliel's case, no idolatrous acts were involved; instead, a statue of Aphrodite was simply placed in the baths (like many other statues). Therefore, R. Gamaliel's act could not be used as precedent in a case where people actually did perform some rituals (in this case libation of water) before one of these statues.

84. Tertullian, *De spect.* 8 (translated with slight changes based on Glover, 253–55); Tertullian, *Idol.* 15.6.

85. Tertullian, *Idol.* 15.6. For more on Tertullian's view of the baths and their relation to views expressed by the rabbis, see Binder, *Tertullian*, 134–35. The connection between Tertullian and the passage regarding R. Gamaliel was pointed out in Dunbabin, "*Baiarum grata voluptas*," 32.

86. Tertullian, *Apol.* 42.4 (trans. Glover, 191).

87. The eagle in Jerusalem: Josephus, *BJ* 1.648; Josephus, *AJ* 17.151–55. Herod Antipas's palace: Josephus, *Vit.* 65.

88. The sources are conveniently collected, presented in English, and thoroughly discussed in Fine, *Art and Judaism*, 113–15.

89. m. 'Abod. Zar. 1:7. In this case, I translate the Hebrew *kippah*, literally a "dome," as the "niche," which in Roman architecture was capped by a semi-dome.

90. y. 'Abod. Zar. 4 (43d; translated with slight changes following Guggenheimer, 413).

91. For a detailed discussion of this event, see Van Dam, "Imagining an Eastern Roman Empire."

92. E.g., Lieberman, "Palestine in the Third and Fourth Centuries," 365–66; Urbach, "The Rabbinical Laws of Idolatry," 234n80; Jacobs, "Römische Thermenkultur," 269–71; and the most fantastic of them all, Friedheim, *Rabbinisme et Paganisme*, 99–102. See also Schwartz, "Gamaliel in Aphrodite's Bath," 216, who rejects the historical reliability of this source altogether.

Chapter 7. A Social Laboratory: Status and Hierarchy in a Provincial Roman Bathhouse

1. The scholarly literature on these social phenomena is too vast to survey here. For the non-specialist in the field of social science and theory, I find most helpful the introductions and collections by the Finnish scholar Peter Kivisto, as well as the concise introduction of Burke, *History and Social Theory*.

2. Here, too, the scholarly work on these topics is immense. For a short introduction to the central facets of social structures and their manifestations with up-to-date bibliographies, see Peachin, *The Oxford Handbook of Social Relations in the Roman World*. My depiction of a well-defined social pyramid echoes the work of Alföldy, *Römische Sozialgeschichte*. On patronage, the central study is still Saller, *Personal Patronage under the Early Empire*, in particular the chapter on the provinces (145–94).

3. See Wesch-Klein, "Recruits and Veterans." For a recent reconsideration of the topic of citizenship that reduces older estimates but still keeps them high, see Lavan, "The Army and the Spread of Roman Citizenship," 1–43.

4. On the social mobility of freed slaves, the best study is still Hopkins, *Conquerors and Slaves*, in particular 133–71.

5. See MacMullen, *Roman Social Relations*, 62.

6. See Rawson, "*Discrimina ordinum*."

7. For a possible bathhouse in Egypt reserved for upper-class women, see Meyer, "Les femmes et les bains publics," 2:55–56. But this was surely far from the norm.

8. Garrett Fagan devotes an entire chapter to the social mechanisms that evolved in the baths and surveys the two views of the debate at length (himself arguing for the latter) with ample bibliography. See Fagan, *Bathing in Public in the Roman World*, 189–219. See also Fagan, "Socializing at the Baths."

9. *y. Pea'ah* 8 (21b), with translation, discussion of textual variants and parallels, and further bibliography in Eliav, *Sites, Institutions and Daily Life in Tiberias*, 24–25. Cf. Jacobs, "Römische Thermenkultur," 306–7, who understands the text but misses the context.

10. John Chrysostom, *De diab. tent.* 3.5.

11. *Cant. Zuttah* 1:15 (Buber, 22); *S. Eli. Rab.* 28 (Friedmann, 153).

12. Food vendors are discussed below. Oil providers and barbers are discussed on pp. 72–73. For all the rest and others, see pp. 34–35.

13. E.g., *CIL* 2.5181, 6.16740, 11.720, and discussion in Fagan, *Bathing in Public in the Roman World*, 197.

14. *T. Mo'ed Qat.* 2:15 (Lieberman, 372), and parallels listed by Lieberman there.

15. *Sem.* 12:12 (Higger, 199); *Lam. Rab.* 3:44 (Buber, 138).

16. Cicero, *Off.* 1.129, and other sources listed in Fagan, *Bathing in Public in the Roman World*, 48n28.

17. Regarding Graeco-Roman sources on slaves in the baths, see the detailed studies of Fagan: "Interpreting the Evidence: Did Slaves Bathe at the Baths?"; and *Bathing in Public in the Roman World*, 199–205. For Fagan's position as cited here, see his conclusions on p. 200. On slaves as part of the bath's staff, see my discussion in various places throughout chapter 2.

18. The documentation of these private facilities, from inscription and papyri as well as archaeological excavations and texts, is vast; see, for example, the summaries in Smith, *Roman Villas*, 24, 197–98, 213–14, 238–39; and Uytterhoeven, "Bathing in a 'Western Style.'"

19. The evidence was collected and meticulously studied in Fagan, *Bathing in Public in the Roman World*, 63n79, 189–96.

20. *SifreDeut* 37 (Finkelstein, 71); *m. Šeb.* 8:11.

21. *'Ag. Ber.* 74:2 (Buber, 144).

22. *m. Sanh.* 2:5; *t. Sanh.* 4:1 (Zuckermandel, 420); *SifreDeut* 157 (Finkelstein, 209); *Gen. Rab.* 63:8 (Theodor and Albeck, 687).

23. On the general function and employment of slaves in the Roman world, the literature is quite vast; see a good summary and further bibliography in Schumacher, "Slaves in Roman Society." Regarding slaves in Jewish society during Roman times, the most comprehensive study is Hezser, *Jewish Slavery in Antiquity*. Many of the rabbinic passages discussed here are also discussed in that book, but not the thesis I develop here regarding the bathhouse.

24. *Mek.*, tractate *Neziqin* 1 (Horovitz and Rabin, 248 ll. 7–8)=*Midr. Tann.* 15:12 (Hoffmann, 85); *Sifra, Behar* 4:7:2 (Weiss, 109c); *SifreNum* 115 (Horovitz, 127 ll. 19–20); *t. Qidd.* 1:5 (Lieberman, 277–78)=*y. Qidd.* 1 (59d); *b. Qidd.* 22b=*b. B. Bat.* 53b; *b. Pesaḥ.* 4a; *'Abot R. Nat.* version A, 14 (Schechter, 59).

25. *t. Qidd.* 1:5 (Lieberman, 277–78)=*y. Qidd.* 1 (59d); *b. Qidd.* 22b=*b. B. Bat.* 53b.

26. *SifreNum* 115 (Horovitz, 127).

27. *VitAes* 38 (trans. Daly, 51). For "towels" the text uses the common Greek word *lention*; on this term and its usage, see my discussion on p. 158.

28. *Gen. Rab.* 45:6 (Theodor and Albeck, 454).

29. On Gothic slaves in baths: *y. Beṣah* 1 (60c), with the discussion and reference to my early work on this passage on pp. 230–31. For other mentions of Gothic slaves in rabbinic literature (in texts unrelated to bathhouses), see Hezser, *Jewish Slavery in Antiquity*, 48–49.

30. *Qoh. Rab.* 5:11 (Hirshman, 315), and more about this in my discussion of food and drink.

31. In reading this panel as a representation of a typical, daily bathhouse scene, I follow Barbier, "La signification du cortège représenté sur le couvercle du coffret de 'Projecta.'" For a discussion of other interpretations of the iconography of this object, mainly seeing it as a sequence of marriage scenery, as well as a presentation of the entire corpus of the treasure, see Shelton, *The Esquiline Treasure*, 26–28 (Shelton, like me, favors the bathhouse interpretation).

32. Carandini, Ricci, and De Vos, *Filosofiana*, 331–34.

33. Ibid., 352–62.

34. *y. B. Qam.* 7 (6a); *b. 'Erub.* 24b; *b. B. Meṣi'a* 41a; *b. Sanh.* 62b. For the term used by the *Yerushalmi* to designate the stuff taken to the baths in this bet—*ba(l)nariye*—see my discussion on p. 159.

35. Plautus, *Pers.* 90–91; *Exod. Rab.* 15:22 = *Tanḥ*, Genesis: *Ḥayei Sara* 3:3. Admittedly, the first source here dates from periods earlier than the ones discussed in this book, and the latter two allude to slaves who might wait outside a bath but did not necessarily walk to the bathhouse with their owner.

36. The evidence for these slaves and their role in guarding clothes was collected and discussed in Fagan, *Bathing in Public in the Roman World*, 38.

37. Apuleius, *Met.* 9.17 (trans. Hanson, 1.157–59).

38. Pliny the Younger, *Ep.* 3.14.6–8. For more on violence in the baths, see pp. 236–39.

39. *Rhet. Her.* 4.14.

40. Lucian, *Nigr.* 34.

41. Ammianus Marcellinus, *Res Gesta* 28.4.9.

42. *Exod. Rab.* 15:17.

43. *SHA, Hadr.* 17 (trans. Magie, 1:53). Also discussed, albeit with an entirely different focus, in Jacobs, "Römische Thermenkultur," 307–9.

44. *t. Šabb.* 3:17 (Lieberman, 15); *y. Ma'aś. Š.* 1 (52d). For more on this staff member and the services he provided, see pp. 71–74.

45. This topic has been studied time and again by modern scholars. See, for example, Nielsen, *Thermae et balnea*, 1:165; Fagan, *Bathing in Public in the Roman World*, 33–34; and Yegül, *Bathing in the Roman World*, 19–20. My discussion in the following paragraphs, when relating to the Graeco-Roman sources, both literary and archaeological, is based on those earlier studies. Needless to say, these scholars were unaware of the rabbinic material I present later on in this section, nor did they develop the argument I present here.

46. See the evidence collected and dissected in Nielsen, *Thermae et balnea*, 1:165; and Fagan, *Bathing in Public in the Roman World*, 32–33n51. But add the important notes and insight in Ellis, "The Distribution of Bars at Pompeii," 382.

47. Seneca the Younger, *Ep.* 56. 2 (trans. Gummere, 1:375). For the full text and further discussion, see p. 36.

48. *CIL* 4.10603, 10674.

49. Martial, *Epigrammata* 12.19.

50. *SHA, Slex. Sev.* 30.5.

51. The many sources on drinking habits were collected in the works listed in note 45 in this chapter. See, in particular, Fagan, *Bathing in Public in the Roman World*, 32n49.

52. For this argument, see Nielsen, *Thermae et balnea*, 1:165.

53. Clement of Alexandria, *Paed.* 3.5.31 (trans. Wood, 225). On Clement's life and the uncertainties about his origins, see Osborn, *Clement of Alexandria*, 1–23. On Clement's negative attitude toward the baths, see my discussion on p. 134.

54. *S. Eli. Rab.* 28 (Friedmann, 153). Other versions of this legend do not include the segment about the bath; see, e.g., *Mek.*, tractate *Mishpatim* 18 (Horovitz and Rabin, 313), and other references listed in the notes there.

55. *t. 'Abod. Zar.* 4:8 (Zuckermandel, 466).

56. *b. 'Abod. Zar.* 38b.

57. *y. Ter.* 2 (41c) = *y. Šabb.* 3 (5d). Admittedly the text does not make the clear connection to the thermal bathing establishment that flourished there, but the connection, based on the parallel with the Graeco-Roman material mentioned above, was convincingly made by Jacobs, "Römische Thermenkultur," 288.

58. *Baraita* in *b. Šabb.* 140a, appearing also in *b. 'Abod. Zar.* 30a and *y. Šabb.* 14 (14c). The latter version does not contain the segment about the *'aluntit*. The portion of the *baraita* in the Babylonian Talmud, in good classical Hebrew, is clearly distinguished from the later Aramaic traditions about use of the drink, which were appended to it by the editors of this portion in the Babylonian Talmud. But the *baraita* itself clearly had more than one version (see the version preserved in the *Yerushalmi*). On the existence of bathhouses outside the boundaries of the Roman world, in particular in Parthian and Sasanian Persia, see Eliav, "The Material World of Babylonia," 177–78, 177–78n87.

59. *y. Pesaḥ.* 10 (37b); *y. Ber.* 6 (10c), together with Benovitz, *Talmud ha-igud*, 508–9, 508–9n16.

60. *Qoh. Rab.* 5:11 (Hirshman, 315–16). For slaves pouring their masters wine as they exit the baths, see, e.g., Juvenal, *Saturae* 11.159.

61. This story has numerous versions in different rabbinic texts; some include the segment about the bath and the wine, some do not. For the most ancient versions that mention the bath and the wine, see *Lev. Rab.* 22:3 (Margulies, 501) and *Qoh. Rab.* 5:8–9 (Hirshman, 300), and see Hirshman in his apparatus criticus for a list of all other versions. Modern scholars devoted plenty of attention to this legendary tradition but for the most part with no discussion of the bathhouse portion and its significance. For the most up-to-date study with detailed references to those that came before him, see Ben Shahar, "Titus in the Holy of Holies." Joshua Levinson's assertion that the bathhouse in the story represents a "space typical of the other [i.e., Roman] culture" stands in stark contrast to the entire premise of the present book, which is to show how embedded the bathhouse was in Jewish culture. Were that not the case, how would the author even know that people drank wine in the baths? Levinson's error is based on the anachronistic views of the Roman bathhouse current among modern scholars of ancient Judaism, which I discuss and reject in chapter 4; see Levinson, "Fatal Charades and the Death of Titus," 39.

62. This was already recognized by Krauss, *Griechische und lateinische Lehnwörter*, 2:210, s.v.

63. *y. Pesaḥ.* 10 (37c); *Gen. Rab.* 51:3 (Theodor and Albeck, 535); *Pesiq. Rab. Kah.* 12:9 (Mandelbaum, 210).

64. *b. Ned.* 38b.

65. *Qoh. Rab.* 5:11 (Hirshman, 315–16).

66. Ennabli, "Les thermes du thiase marin de Sidi Ghrib (Tunisie)," 42–44.

67. E.g., *y. Ta'an.* 4 (68a); *y. Šabb.* 12 (13c). Much has been written on this custom and its identification with the Roman salutation; see Appelbaum, *The Dynasty of the Jewish Patriarchs*, 36–37, and the ample bibliography he lists there. On Roman style patronage among the rabbis in Palestine, in particular in the house of the Patriarch, see Sperber, "Patronage in Amoraic Palestine." For a more recent discussion of this topic, see Schwartz, *Were the Jews a Mediterranean Society?* On the numerous Graeco-Roman sources on these patron-client procedures, see note 2 in this chapter.

68. Clement of Alexandria, *Paed.* 3.5.31 (trans. Wood, 225).

69. Petronius, *Sat.* 27–28 (trans. Schmeling, 111–13). In my understanding of this scene and its cultural setting, I take a note from D'Arms, "Performing Culture," 301–19.

70. Carandini, Ricci, and De Vos, *Filosofiana*, 333–34. In analyzing the visual representations of jewelry and attire in the various mosaics discussed in this section, I follow and heavily borrow from Place, "Clothing Differentiation," 47–61, which also provides further updated and expansive bibliography on these topics.

71. Ennabli, "Les thermes," 43–44; Place, "Clothing Differentiation," 51.

72. See Stout, "Jewelry as a Symbol of Status in the Roman Empire."

73. Martial, *Epigrammata* 11.59.

74. Sources collected in Fagan, *Bathing in Public in the Roman World*, 215–16, 215–16n82. Later Christian authors also confirm this habit; see, e.g., John Chrysostom, *In epistulam ad Colossenses homiliae* 10.4 (*PG* 62:371).

75. *'Ag. Ber.* 74:2 (Buber, 144).

76. Fagan, *Bathing in Public in the Roman World*, 215–16. The most comprehensive study of these findings (although only in the western part of the Mediterranean) is Whitmore, "Small Finds and the Social Environment of the Roman Public Baths"; Whitmore, "Artefact Assemblages from Roman Baths" (my thanks to the author, who forwarded me a copy of this study).

77. Ennabli, "Les thermes," 43–44; Carandini, Ricci, and De Vos, *Filosofiana*, 333–34; Place, "Clothing Differentiation," 51–52.

78. See Croom, *Roman Clothing*, 25–28.

79. On white garments as a fashion choice of the elite, see Croom, *Roman Clothing*, 28. On the shared visual language in mosaic presentations of clothing, see the detailed study of Place, "Clothing Differentiation."

80. Petronius, *Sat.* 28.

81. Ammianus Marcellinus, *Res Gesta* 28.4.9.

82. Much has been written on clothes in Jewish circles in general and about the vast body of information about this topic that was preserved in rabbinic literature, although nothing about clothes in public baths. Krauss devoted an entire section to clothing and jewelry in his magisterial opus; see Krauss, *Talmudische Archäologie*, 1:127–207. See also Roussin, "Costume in Roman Palestine," and the updated summaries in Hezser, *The Oxford Handbook of Jewish Daily Life in Roman Palestine*, 362–402.

83. *Num. Rab.* 13:5 also preserves with some variants in *Pesiq. Rab.* 7 (Friedmann, 27b), and a different version in *TanḥB Num., Koraḥ* 5 (Buber, 86).

84. *Lev. Rab.* 28:6 (Margulies, 664–65); *Esth. Rab.* 10:4 (Tabory and Atzmon, 173–74). See my discussion on this figure and his Graeco-Roman counterparts on pp. 70–71.

85. Petronius, *Sat.* 28.

86. *SifreDeut* 37 (Finkelstein, 71).

87. Aulus Gellius, *NA* 10.3.1–3.

88. Tacitus, *Hist.* 3.32.

89. *m. Šeb.* 8:11. See also my discussion on p. 120.

90. *y. Šeb.* 8 (38b–c).

91. Ibid.

92. *Gen. Rab.* 63:8 (Theodor and Albeck, 687); *Pirqe R. El.* 50 (Börner-Klein, 699). This detail in the story does not appear in the numerous other versions of the Haman legendary cycle. For these versions, see note 86 in chapter 2. For references to the legend about Titus and discussion of its various version, see note 61 in this chapter.

93. The topic of exhibiting *paideia* in the public bathhouse still awaits a more comprehensive study. In addition to the sources that speak to this practice, which were presented in note 36 in chapter 5, see, for example, Martial, *Epigrammata* 3.44, who complains about a poet friend who never stops reciting his material in the baths. Similar complaints about other cultural showoffs appear in Juvenal, *Saturae* 7.232–36. A surprisingly rich source on this topic comes from the writing of the Church scholar and bishop Augustine, who often alludes to intellectual activity that he and his learned colleagues and friends carry out in the baths. See, e.g., Augustine, *De beata vita* 1.6, 4.23; *C. acad.* 3.1, 3.4.9; and *De ord.* 1.8.25, 2.11.31. See, for now, Jacobs, "Römische Thermenkultur," 283–89.

94. *t. Ber.* 2:20 (Lieberman, 10). *Perek ha-nikhnas la-merḥats* 3 (Higger, 303) explains this directive with the clause "due to the danger," the specific meaning of which eludes me.

95. *y. B. Qam.* 3 (3d); *Der. Er. Rab.* 7:12 (Higger, 134). For a different version of the last two rulings, see *Kallah Rab.* 9:15 (Higger, 338–39).

96. *y. Kil.* 9 (32b) = *y. Ketub.* 12 (35a); *Gen. Rab.* 33:3 (Theodor and Albeck, 307); *b. Qidd.* 33a.

Chapter 8. A Scary Place: The Perils of the Bath and Jewish Magic Remedies

This chapter expands on an earlier study of mine by the same title; see Eliav, "A Scary Place." I began exploring the dangers of the baths in much earlier studies; see Eliav, "What Happened to Rabbi Abbahu"; and Eliav, "Realia, Daily Life, and the Transmission of Local Stories," 242–52.

1. For some examples criticizing the old guard and articulating the new notions about magic, see Winkelman, "Magic"; Philips, "The Sociology of Religious Knowledge"; Faraone and Obbink, *Magika Hiera*, vi; and Graf, *Magic in the Ancient World*, 8–19. For an up-to-date discussion of the topic, see Frankfurter, *Guide to the Study of Ancient Magic*.

2. I borrow this formulation from Faraone and Obbink, *Magika Hiera*, vi, who themselves lean on the discussion in Philips, "The Sociology of Religious Knowledge." See also Graf, *Magic in the Ancient World*, 188, and the sources he mentions in note 1.

3. Indeed, etymologically, the word "temple" means exactly that, a space carved out of the world; see Catalano, "Aspetti spaziali del sistema giuridico-religioso romano."

4. For a comprehensive presentation of Jewish magic in Graeco-Roman times, see Bohak, *Ancient Jewish Magic*.

5. See Low and Lawrence-Zúñiga, *The Anthropology of Space and Place*, 225–27.

6. The major study on this topic is Dunbabin, "*Baiarum grata voluptas*." The following discussion owes much to Dunbabin's insights but also takes the topic in new directions. See also Fagan, *Bathing in Public in the Roman World*, 31.

7. See Levinson, "Enchanting Rabbis," 59. In his pioneering studies of rabbinic material culture, Samuel Krauss too noticed this aspect of the public Roman baths but didn't go much beyond pointing it out; see Krauss, "Le traité talmudique 'Déréch Eréç,'" 213; and Krauss, *Talmudische Archäologie*, 1:220, 676n109. See also Hanoune, "Thermes romains et Talmud"; Sperber, "On the Bathhouse," 362–63; Jacobs, "Römische Thermenkultur," 293–94; and Abraham O. Shemesh, "'He Who Enters the Bath-House Utters Two Blessings': On the Evolvement and Decline of an Ancient Jewish Prayer," *Religions* 8, no. 10 (2017), https://doi.org/10.3390/rel8100225. (The latter three articles, as well as the above piece by Levinson, were published after my early studies on the topic.)

8. On these smaller, less assuming structures, see Fagan, *Bathing in Public in the Roman World*, 20–21, 179–80.

9. Martial, *Epigrammata* 1.59, 2.14.11–12.

10. *y. Beṣah* 1 (60c). Other versions of this passage are discussed below. For a full literary and textual analysis, see Eliav, "What Happened to Rabbi Abbahu"; and Eliav, "Realia, Daily Life, and the Transmission of Local Stories," 242–52.

11. E.g., *y. Šabb.* 1 (3a) = *y. Qidd.* 1 (61a).

12. *Perek ha-nikhnas la-merḥats* 2.

13. E.g., *ILPaest* 100; *CIL* 11.4781, 6225. Other examples can be found in the dossier collected in Fagan, *Bathing in Public in the Roman World*, 233–347.

14. On the warm temperatures of the baths, and how they could climb to dangerous levels, see Nielsen, *Thermae et balnea*, 1:18–19. And for a more moderate view, Yegül, *Baths and Bathing in Classical Antiquity*, 380–82.

15. Fronto, *Ep.* 5.44 (Haines, 1:246).

16. For the first set of injuries, see, for example, *CIL* 4.1898 (= Antonio Varone, *Erotica Pompeiana: Love Inscriptions on the Walls of Pompeii*, trans. Ria P. Berg, Studia Archaeologica 116 [Rome: L'Erma di Bretschneider, 2002], 59). On Seneca's suicide, see Tacitus, *Ann.* 15.64.

17. For an inscription mourning the drowning of a young boy, see Fagan, *Bathing in Public in the Roman World*, 197nn19–20, 319, no. 260. See also Juvenal, *Saturae* 1.142–44; *t. Miqw.* 5:7 (Zuckermandel, 657); and Theophanes, *Chronographia*, 498/9 (de-Boor, 142).

18. Tacitus, *Hist.* 3.32. On the habit of going the extra mile in the heating of baths for dignitaries, see pp. 222–23, and on the snobbery of others, see p. 136. For an example of praise of warm water in inscriptions, see Fagan, *Bathing in Public in the Roman World*, 292, no. 175.

19. *y. Šabb.* 3 (6a).

20. Martial, *Epigrammata* 3.25, 10.48.

21. *Pesiq. Rab. Kah.* 3:10 (Mandelbaum, 48, listing later compilations that also preserve this passage).

22. Macrobius, *Sat.* 7.16.24 (trans. Kaster, 3:305).

23. *y. Mo'ed Qat.* 1 (80b); a *baraita* in *b. Pesaḥ.* 112b.

24. The material documenting collapses has been collected and studied several times; see Dunbabin, "*Baiarum grata voluptas*," 35, 35n191; and Fagan, *Bathing in Public in the Roman World*, 164, 180–81. For further testimony about the structural vulnerabilities of bathhouses, increased by natural hazards (rivers) and ongoing neglect, see Procopius, *Aed.* 2.6.10–11, 5.3.7; and Di Segni, "The Greek Inscriptions of Hammat Gader," 186–88.

25. *ILTun* 1500.

26. *CIL* 10.6656; translation following Fagan, *Bathing in Public in the Roman World*, 244, no. 37 with slight changes.

27. *b. Ketub.* 62a; *b. Ber.* 60a. Together with detailed literary and textual analysis in Eliav, "What Happened to Rabbi Abbahu"; Eliav, "Realia, Daily Life, and the Transmission of Local Stories," 242–45. Cf. Krauss, "Bad und Badewesen," 184–85.

28. Eusebius, *H.E.* 3.28.6. See also Irenaeus, *Haer.* 3.3.4; Epiphanius, *Adv. haeres.* 30.24; Berger, *Das Bad in der byzantinischen Zeit*, 47–50; Hanoune, "Thermes romains et Talmud," 257–59; and Jacobs, "Römische Thermenkultur," 300–303.

29. *CIL* 10.6656; translation in Fagan, *Bathing in Public in the Roman World*, 244, no. 37.

30. Lucian, *Hipp.*

31. Seneca the Younger, *Ep.* 107.2.

32. *y. Ber.* 4 (8b) = *Qoh. Zuttah* 3:2 (Buber, 122); *y. Kil.* 9 (32b) = *y. Ketub.* 12 (35a); *Gen. Rab.* 33:3 (Theodor and Albeck, 307), together with the discussion and references in Guggenheimer, *The Jerusalem Talmud: First Order*, 308n90.

33. *y. Ber.* 2 (5c). For my early translation and discussion of this text, see Eliav, *Sites, Institutions and Daily Life in Tiberias*, 23–24. I made some emendations to the text based on Codex Vatican (Vat. Ebr. 135). For an alternative translation, which in my view misses the entire point (and overlooks my aforementioned early treatment of the text), see Jacobs, "Römische Thermenkultur," 304.

34. The literature on this topic, both theory and historiography, is too vast to engage here. For a helpful summary, full of tidbits and insight, as well as useful bibliography, see Fagan, "Violence in Roman Social Relations."

35. Seneca the Younger, *Dial.* 4.32.2.

36. *Rhet. Her.* 4.14.

37. Pliny the Younger, *Ep.* 3.14.6–8. Many of these references, but not all, are listed and discussed in Fagan, "Violence in Roman Social Relations."

38. Galen, *Meth. Med.* 10.3 (Kühn, 672).

39. *P.Rey.* 2.124 (Hunt, 2:119–20).

40. Libanius, *Or.* 1.21, 183.

41. Ibid., 11.212; Libanius, *Decl.* 42.21.

42. Winkler, "The Constraints of Eros."

43. Heise, *Kaffee und Kaffeehaus*, 154–97.

44. Libanius, *Or.* 1.141.

45. Akhtar, *Comprehensive Dictionary of Psychoanalysis*, 82 s.v.

46. There is much to discuss on the theoretical notions behind these human behaviors, going back to the stories of Adam and Eve in the Bible or to Aristotle's concept of katharsis, and then stretching all the way to Freud and other psychoanalysts. Of the rich literature on these topics I found most useful the articles and abundant bibliography collected in Goldstein, *Why We Watch*.

47. The material from Graeco-Roman and Christian sources (but not the Jewish material) regarding the demons of the baths and the magic associated with them has been collected and analyzed numerous times, and my discussion here relies on these studies; see Campbell Bonner, "Demons of the Bath"; Dunbabin, "*Baiarum grata voluptas*," 36–43; Meyer, "Magie et bains publics"; and Fabiano, "I 'demoni dei bagni' tra aqua e fuoco." And more recently, adding new material and updated bibliography, with some of the categories I developed in my earlier studies (with proper reference and credit): Alfayé, "Mind the Bath."

48. *CIL* 8.8926; discussed in Nielsen, *Thermae et balnea*, 1:146, 146n8.

49. Eunapius of Sardis, *VS* 457 (Wright, 358), with LSJ, 761 s.v. *kaiō*.

50. *AE* 1907.177/8; translation in Fagan, *Bathing in Public in the Roman World*, 338–39, no. 315/316; Augustine, *De civ. Dei* 21.10.

51. In addition to the plentiful examples in the studies listed below in note 56, see also Fagan, *Bathing in Public in the Roman World*, 27, 35.

52. *Qoh. Rab.* 2:8 (Hirshman, 132) = *Cant. Rab.* 3:6:5, together with the parallel versions and discussions of this passage in Hirshman, *Midrash Kohelet Rabbah 1–6*, 132–35 (Heb.).

53. *y. Ter.* 8 (64b-c); *Gen. Rab.* 63 (Theodor and Albeck, 688-90).

54. Lurker, *A Dictionary of Gods and Goddesses, Devils and Demons*, 10-11.

55. *b. Qidd.* 39b-40a. This story was preserved only in the Babylonian Talmud, so strictly speaking it derives from the Persian realm, outside the Roman world. However, certain signs convince me that the story originated in Roman Palestine and was transmitted and preserved in the Babylonian text. Not only the name of the scholar, Ḥanina, who is from Palestine, but also the Hebrew used to present the Roman standards point to a Roman-Palestinian origin. On the phenomenon of rabbinic texts moving from Palestine to Persia, see my discussion and further bibliography on p. 15.

56. For the most comprehensive discussions about this magical material, see Dunbabin, *"Baiarum grata voluptas"*; Meyer, "Magie et Bains publics"; and Alfayé, "Mind the Bath."

57. Eunapius of Sardis, *VS* 459 (Wright, 368-70).

58. *PGM2* 2.50, 7.469, 36.69-77; also 127.3-4; *Suppl. Mag.* 42.

59. E.g., Fagan, *Bathing in Public in the Roman World*, 37-38; Alfayé, "Mind the Bath," 28-31.

60. E.g., Meyer and Smith, *Ancient Christian Magic*, 88. For more on medicine in the baths, see p. 35 and note 48 there.

61. Ammianus Marcellinus, *Res Gesta* 29.2.28.

62. References to crossing oneself upon entry are collected in Nielsen, *Thermae et balnea*, 1:147nn10-11. For a more comprehensive discussion of Christian magical activities in general and in bathhouses, and about how demons functioned in their worldview and literature, see Böcher, *Dämonenfurcht und Dämonenabwehr*; Elm and Hartmann, *Demons in Late Antiquity*; and Berger, *Das Bad in der byzantinischen Zeit*, 132ff.

63. *Sefer ha-razim* 3:16-35 (Margalioth, 93-94).

64. *y. Ber.* 9 (14b). Other versions of this prayer appear in *t. Ber.* 6:17 (Lieberman, 38); *Der. Er. Rab.* 10:1; and *b. Ber.* 60a. For a recent study on this prayer, see Shemesh, "'He Who Enters.'"

65. See Eliav, "Realia, Daily Life, and the Transmission of Local Stories," 251n30.

66. Collected in Dunbabin, *"Baiarum grata voluptas,"* 36-42.

67. *y. Ter.* 8 (46b-c); *Gen. Rab.* 63 (Theodor and Albeck, 688-90).

68. Bonner, "Demons of the Bath," 208. On the meaning and origin of the name, cf. Jacobs, "Römische Thermenkultur," 294.

69. *y. Sanh.* 7 (25d). For earlier discussions and analysis of this text, see Eliav, *Sites, Institutions and Daily Life in Tiberias*, 30-31; Jacobs, "Römische Thermenkultur," 298-300; and Levinson, "Enchanting Rabbis," 58-64.

70. For an exhaustive discussion of this term and its evolution, see Schremer, *Brothers Estranged*. On the diverse spectrum of definitions regarding the Jewish way of life in those times, see Eliav, "Jews and Judaism."

71. Pace Levinson, "Enchanting Rabbis," 62-63.

72. Mark 6:45-52 and parallels.

73. For this alternative reading, see Jacobs, "Römische Thermenkultur," 299, somewhat supported by the meaning of the Hebrew word used here, *kippah*, as it appears in earlier rabbinic sources; e.g., *m. ʾAbod. Zar.* 1:7 (as I also translate on pp. 63-64), but detracting from the dramatic effect of the text.

BIBLIOGRAPHY OF PRIMARY SOURCES

'Aggadat Bereshit [*'Ag. Ber.*]. Solomon Buber, *'Aggadat Bereshit*. Cracow: Fischer, 1903; reprint, Jerusalem: n.p., 1973.
Alphabet of Ben Sira. Eli Yassif, *The Tales of Ben Sira in the Middle Ages: A Critical Text and Literary Studies*. Jerusalem: Magnes, 1984.
Ammianus Marcellinus. *Res Gesta*. John C. Rolfe, *Ammianus Marcellinus: History*. 3 vols. LCL. Cambridge, MA: Harvard University Press, 1935-40; rev. ed. 1950-52.
Anthologia Palatina [*Anth. Pal.*]. W. R. Paton, *The Greek Anthology*. 5 vols. LCL. Cambridge, MA: Harvard University Press, 1916; rev. ed. 2014.
Apuleius. *Metamorphoses* [*Met.*]. J. Arthur Hanson, *Apuleius: Metamorphoses (The Golden Ass)*. 2 vols. LCL. Cambridge, MA: Harvard University Press, 1989-96.
Aristides. *Orationes* [*Or.*]. Friedrich Walther Lenz and Charles Allison Behr, eds., *P. Aelii smyrnaei quae supersunt omnia*. 2 vols. Berlin: Weidmann, 1898. Trans. Charles A. Behr, *P. Aelius Aristides: The Complete Works*. 2 vols. Leiden: Brill, 1981-86.
Augustine. *Confessiones* [*Conf.*]. William Watts, *Augustine: Confessions*. 2 vols. LCL. Cambridge, MA: Harvard University Press, 1912; reprint, 1999.
———. *Contra academicos* [*C. acad.*]. Pius Knöll, *Sancti Aureli Augustini opera I:3: Contra academicos*. CSEL 63. Vienna: Hölder Pichler Tempsky, 1922, 1-85. John J. O'Meara, *St. Augustine: Against the Academics*. ACW 12. New York: Newman, 1951.
———. *De beata vita*. Pius Knöll, *Sancti Aureli Augustini opera I:3: De beata vita*. CSEL 63. Vienna: Hölder Pichler Tempsky, 1922, 87-117. Michael P. Foley, *On the Happy Life: St. Augustine's Cassiciacum Dialogues II*. New Haven: Yale University Press, 2019.
———. *De civitate Dei* [*De civ. Dei*]. George E. McCracken, *Augustine: The City of God Against the Pagans*. 7 vols. LCL. Cambridge, MA: Harvard University Press, 1957.
———. *De ordine* [*De ord.*]. Pius Knöll, *Sancti Aureli Augustini opera I:3: De ordine libri duo*. CSEL 63. Vienna: Hölder Pichler Tempsky, 1922, 119-87. Silvano Borruso, *St. Augustine: On Order [De ordine]*. South Bend, IN: St. Augustine's, 2007.
———. *Epistulae* [*Ep.*]. Albert Goldbacher, *S. Aureli Augustini Hipponiensis episcopi epistulae*. CSEL 34, 44, 57-58, 88. Vienna: Verlag der Österreichischen Akademie der Wissenschaften, 1895-1981. Roland J. Teske, John E. Rotelle, and Boniface Ramsey, *The Works of Saint Augustine: A Translation for the 21st Century II: Letters*. 4 vols. Hyde Park, NY: New City Press, 2001-5.
Aulus Gellius. *Noctes Atticae* [*NA*]. John C. Rolfe, *The Attic Nights of Aulus Gellius*. 3 vols. LCL. Cambridge, MA: Harvard University Press, 1927; rev. ed. 1946.
'Avot de Rabbi Nattan [*Abot R. Nat.*]. Solomon Schechter, *Aboth de Rabbi Nathan*. Vienna: Knöpflmacher, 1887; reprint, Hildesheim: Olms, 1979.
Babylonian Talmud (*Bavli*) [*b.* with name of tractate]. Printed edition: *Talmud Bavli*. Wilna: Romm, 1880-86. Isidore Epstein, ed., *The Babylonian Talmud:*

Translated into English with Notes, Glossary and Indices. 36 vols. London: Soncino, 1935-48.
Bardaisan. *Liber legum regionum.* Han J. W. Drijvers, *The Book of the Laws of Countries: Dialogue on Fate of Bardaiṣan of Edessa.* Assen: Van Gorcum, 1965.
Canticles (Song of Songs) Rabbah [*Cant. Rab.*]. Printed edition: *Midrash Rabbah Shir ha-Shirim.* Wilna: Romm, 1887. Harry Freedman and Maurice Simon, eds., *Midrash Rabbah: Song of Songs.* 3rd ed. London: Soncino, 1939.
Canticles (Song of Songs) Zuttah [*Cant. Zuttah*]. Solomon Buber, *Midrasch Zutta 'al Shir ha-Shirim, Ruth, 'Ekhah ve-Qohelet.* Wilna: Romm, 1899; reprint, Tel Aviv, 1925.
Cassius Dio. *Historicus* [*Hist.*]. Earnest Cary, *Dio's Roman History.* 9 vols. LCL. London: W. Heinemann, 1914-27.
Cicero. *De officiis* [*Off.*]. Walter Miller, *Cicero: On Duties.* LCL. Cambridge, MA: Harvard University Press, 1913; rev. ed., 2005.
———. *De natura deorum* [*Nat. D.*]. Harris Rackham, *Cicero: On the Nature of the Gods, Academics.* LCL. Cambridge, MA: Harvard University Press, 1933; rev. ed., 1951.
———. *Epistulae ad Atticum* [*Att.*]. David R. Shackleton Bailey, *Cicero: Letters to Atticus.* 4 vols. LCL. Cambridge, MA: Harvard University Press, 1999.
———. *Epistulae ad familiares* [*Fam.*]. David R. Shackleton Bailey, *Cicero: Letters to Friends.* 3 vols. LCL. Cambridge, MA: Harvard University Press, 2001.
———. *In Vatinium* [*Vat.*]. Robert Gardner, *Cicero Orations: Pro Sestio, in Vatinium.* LCL. Cambridge, MA: Harvard University Press, 1958.
Clement of Alexandria. *Paedagogus* [*Paed.*]. Otto Stählin, ed., *Clemens Alexandrinus I: Protrepticus und Paedagogus.* Rev. ed. Ursula Treu. GCS 12. Berlin: Akademie-Verlag, 1972; reprint, Berlin: De Gruyter, 2013, 87-340; trans. Simon P. Wood, *Clement of Alexandria: Christ the Educator.* FC 23. Washington, DC: Catholic University of America Press, 1954.
———. *Protrepticus* [*Protr.*]. Otto Stählin, ed., *Clemens Alexandrinus I: Protrepticus und Paedagogus.* Rev. ed. Ursula Treu. GCS 12. Berlin: Akademie-Verlag, 1972; reprint, Berlin: De Gruyter, 2013, 1-86. George W. Butterworth, *Clement of Alexandria: Exhortation to the Greeks, The Rich Man's Salvation, To the Newly Baptized.* LCL. Cambridge, MA: Harvard University Press, 1999.
Corpus iuris civilis, digesta (pandectae) [*Dig.*]. Theodor Mommsen and Paul Krüger, eds., *Digesta Iustiniani Augusti.* 2 vols. Berlin: Weidmann, 1870. Alan Watson, ed., *The Digest of Justinian.* 2 vols. Philadelphia: University of Pennsylvania Press, 1985.
Damascus Document [*CD*]. Chaim Rabin, ed., *The Zadokite Documents: I. The Admonition II. The Laws.* Oxford: Clarendon, 1954.
Derekh Ereṣ Rabbah [*Der. Er. Rab.*]. Michael Higger, *The Treatises Derek Erez: Masseket Derek Erez, Pirke Ben Azzai, Tosefta Derek Erez, Edited from Manuscripts with an Introduction, Notes, Variants and Translation.* New York: Moinester, 1935. Abraham Cohen, *The Minor Tractates of the Talmud: Massektoth Ḳeṭannoth.* 2 vols. London: Soncino, 1965.
Deuteronomy Rabbah [*Deut. Rab.*]. Printed edition: *Sefer Midrash Rabbah: Midrash Rabbah 'al hamisah humshe torah ve-hamesh megillot.* Wilna: Romm, 1887. Saul Lieberman, *Midrash Debarim Rabbah.* 2nd ed. Jerusalem: Wahrmann, 1964.

Harry Freedman and Maurice Simon, eds., *Midrash Rabbah: Deuteronomy*. 3rd ed. London: Soncino, 1939.

Didascalia apostolorum. Arthur Vööbus, ed. and trans., *The Didascalia Apostolorum in Syriac*. 2 vols. in 4. CSCO 401-2, 407-8. Scriptores syri 175-76, 178-80. Louvain: Secrétariat du CorpusSCO, 1979.

Digesta. See *Corpus iuris civilis*.

Dio Chrysostomus. *Orationes*. James W. Cohoon and H. Lamar Crosby, *Dio Chrysostom: Discourses*. 5 vols. LCL. Cambridge, MA: Harvard University Press, 1932-51.

Epiphanius. *Panarion (Adversus haereses)* [*Adv. haeres.*]. Karl Holl, ed., *Epiphanius: Panarion haer*. Rev. ed. Jürgen Dummer. 3 vols. GCS 25, 31, 37. Berlin: Akademie-Verlag, 1980-85; reprint, Berlin: De Gruyter, 2013.

Esther Rabbah [*Esth. Rab.*]. Joseph Tabory and Arnon Atzmon, *Modrash Esther Rabbah*. Jerusalem: Schechter Institute, 2014.

Eunapius of Sardis. *Vitae sophistarum* [*VS*]. Wilmer C. Wright, *Philostratus and Eunapius: Life of the Sophists*. LCL. Cambridge, MA: Harvard University Press, 1921, 317-565.

Eusebius. *Historia ecclesiastica* [*H.E.*]. Eduard Schwartz, *Eusebius Werke: Die Kirchengeschichte*. GCS 9:1-2. Leipzig: J. C. Hinrichs, 1903-8. William Wright and Norman McLean, *The Ecclesiastical History of Eusebius in Syriac*. Cambridge: Cambridge University Press, 1898. Kirsopp Lake et al., *Eusebius: The Ecclesiastical History*. 2 vols. LCL. London: W. Heinemann, 1926-32.

Exodus Rabbah [*Exod. Rab.*]. Printed edition: Wilna: Romm, 1887. For the first 14 *parashot*—Avigdor Shinan, *Midrash Shemot Rabbah: Chapters I-XIV*. Jerusalem: Devir, 1984. Harry Freedman and Maurice Simon, eds., *Midrash Rabbah: Exodus*. 3rd ed. London: Soncino, 1939.

Frontinus. *De aquaeductu urbis Romeanae* [*Aq.*]. Charles E. Bennet and Mary B. McElwain, *Frontinus: Strategems, Aqueducts of Rome*. LCL. Cambridge, MA: Harvard University Press, 1925.

Fronto. *Epistulae* [*Ep.*]. Charles R. Haines, *The Correspondence of Marcus Cornelius Fronto*. 2 vols. LCL. Cambridge, MA: Harvard University Press, 1919; rev. ed., 1928.

Galen. *De methodo medendi* [*Meth. Med.*]. Carl G. Kühn, *Claudii Galeni opera omnia*. 22 vols. Leipzig: Cnobloch, 1821-33. Vol. 10 (1825). Ian Johnston and G.H.R. Horsley, *Galen: Method of Medicine*. LCL. Cambridge, MA: Harvard University Press, 2011.

Genesis Rabbah [*Gen. Rab.*]. Printed edition: Wilna: Romm, 1887. Judah Theodor and Chanoch Albeck, *Midrash Bereshit Rabba: Critical Edition with Notes and Commentary*. 2nd ed. Jerusalem: Wahrmann, 1965. Harry Freedman and Maurice Simon, eds., *Midrash Rabbah: Genesis*. 2 vols. 3rd ed. London: Soncino, 1939.

ILPaest. Marrio Mello and Giuseppe Voza, eds., *Le iscrizioni latine de Paestum*. 2 vols. Naples: Università degli studi di Napoli, 1968-69.

ILTun. Alfred Merlin, ed., *Inscriptions latines de la Tunisie*. Paris: Presses universitaires de France, 1944.

Irenaeus. *Adversus haereses* [*Haer.*]. Adelin Rousseau et al., *Irénée de Lyon: Contre les hérésies* (Livre 1; SC 264; Paris: Cerf, 1979); (Livre 2; SC 294; Paris: Cerf, 1982); (Livre 3; SC 211; Paris: Cerf, 1974); (Livre 4; SC 100:2; Paris: Cerf, 1965); (Livre 5; SC 153; Paris: Cerf, 1969); ANF 1:315-567.

Jerome. *Epistulae* [*Ep.*]. Isidorus Hilberg, *Sancti Eusebii Hieronymi epistulae*. 2nd ed. CSEL 54–56. Vienna: Verlag der Österreichischen Akademie der Wissenschaften, 1996; *NPNF*², VI, pp. 1–295.

John Chrysostom. *De diabolo tentatore* [*De diab. tent.*]. *PG* 49:241–76. Bryson Sewell, *John Chrysostom: Three Homilies on the Devil*. Published online by Roger Pearse at https://www.roger-pearse.com/weblog/wp-content/uploads/2014/05/chrysostom-devil-bryson-2014.pdf.

———. *In epistulam ad Colossenses homiliae 1–12*. *PG* 62:299–392; *NPNF*¹13:257–321.

———. *In epistulam i ad Corinthios argumentum et homiliae 1–44*. *PG* 61:9–382; *NPNF*¹ 12:1–269.

John Malalas. *Chronographia*. Ioannes Thurn, *Ioannis Malalae: Chronographia*. CFHB 35. Berlin: Gruyter, 2000. Elizabeth Jeffreys et al., *The Chronicle of John Malalas: A Translation*. Byzantina Australiensia 4. Melbourne: Australian Association for Byzantine Studies, 1986.

John Moschus. *Pratum spirituale*. Elpidio Mioni, "Il *Pratum spirituale* di Giovanni Mosco." *OCP* 17 (1951): 61–94. Trans. John Wortley, *John Moschos: The Spiritual Meadow (Pratum spirituale)*. Cistercian Studies 139. Kalamazoo, MI: Cistercian Publications, 1992.

Josephus. *Antiquitates Judaicae* [*AJ*]. Henry St. J. Thackeray, Ralph Marcus, and Louis H. Feldman, *Josephus: Jewish Antiquities*. 9 vols. LCL. Cambridge, MA: Harvard University Press, 1930–65; rev. ed. 1998.

———. *Bellum Judaicum* [*BJ*]. Henry St. J. Thackeray, *Josephus: The Jewish War*. 3 vols. LCL. Cambridge, MA: Harvard University Press, 1927–89; rev. ed. 1997.

———. *Vita* [*Vit.*]. Henry St. J. Thackeray, *Josephus: The Life, Against Apion*. LCL. Cambridge, MA: Harvard University Press, 1926.

———. *Contra Apionem* [*Ap.*]. Henry J. Thackeray, *Josephus: The Life, Against Apion*. LCL. Cambridge, MA: Harvard University Press, 1926.

Jubilees [*Jub.*]. James C. VanderKam, *The Book of Jubilees*. 2 vols. CSCO 510–11. Leuven: E. Peeters, 1989.

Juvenal. *Saturae*. Susanna Morton Braund, *Juvenal and Persius*. LCL. Cambridge, MA: Harvard University Press, 2004.

Kallah Rabbati [*Kallah Rab.*]. In Michael Higger, *Massekhtot Kalla vehen Massekhet Kallah, Massekhet Kllah Rabbati*. New York: Benei-Rabanan, 1936; reprint, Jerusalem: Makor, 1970), 169–344. Abraham Cohen, *The Minor Tractates of the Talmud: Massektoth Ketannoth*. 2 vols. London: Soncino, 1965, 415–528.

Lamentations Rabbah [*Lam. Rab.*]. Solomon Buber, *Midrasch Echa Rabbati*. Wilna: Romm, 1899; reprint, Hildesheim: G. Olms, 1967. Harry Freedman and Maurice Simon, eds., *Midrash Rabbah: Lamentations*. 3rd ed. London: Soncino, 1939.

Leviticus Rabbah [*Lev. Rab.*]. Mordecai Margulies, *Midrash Wayyikra Rabbah: A Critical Edition Based on Manuscripts and Genizah Fragments with Variants and Notes*. 5 vols. Jerusalem: Ararat, 1953–60; reprint, New York: Jewish Theological Seminary of America, 1993. Harry Freedman and Maurice Simon, eds., *Midrash Rabbah: Leviticus*. 3rd ed. London: Soncino, 1939.

Libanius. *Declemationes* [*Decl.*]. Richard Förster and Eberhard Richtsteig, *Libanii opera*. 12 vols. in 13. Leipzig: Teubner, 1903–27, vols. 5–7. Donald A. Russell, *Libanius Imaginary Speeches: A Selection of Declamations*. London: Duckworth, 1996.

———. *Epistulae* [*Ep.*]. Albert F. Norman, *Libanius: Autobiography and Selected Letters*. 2 vols. LCL. Cambridge, MA: Harvard University Press, 1992.

———. *Orationes* [*Or.*]. Richard Förster and Eberhard Richtsteig, *Libanii opera*. 12 vols. in 13. Leipzig: Teubner, 1903–27, vols. 1–4. Albert F. Norman, *Libanius: Selected Orations*. 2 vols. LCL. Cambridge, MA: Harvard University Press, 1969–77. Albert F. Norman, *Antioch as a Centre of Hellenic Culture as Observed by Libanius*. TTH 34. Liverpool: Liverpool University Press, 2000.

Liber pontificalis. Louis Duchesne and Cyrille Vogel, *Le liber pontificalis: Texte, introduction et commentaire*. 3 vols. Paris: Thorin and Boccard, 1886–1957. Raymond Davis, *The Book of Pontiffs (Liber Pontificalis): The Ancient Biographies of the First Ninety Roman Bishops to AD 715*. TTH 6. Rev. ed. Liverpool: Liverpool University Press, 2000.

Life of Aesop [*VitAes*]. Ben E. Perry, *Aesopica*. Urbana: University of Illinois Press, 2007, 33–208. Lloyd W. Daly, *Aesop without Morals: The Famous Fables and a Life of Aesop*. New York: Yoseloff, 1961.

Livy. *Ab urbe condita libri* [*His.*]. Benjamin O. Foster, *Livy History of Rome*. 13 vols. LCL. Cambridge, MA: Harvard University Press, 1919–59.

Lucian. *De dea Syria* [*Syr. D.*]. Jane L. Lightfoot, *Lucian: On the Syrian Goddess: Edited with Introduction, Translation and Commentary*. Oxford: Oxford University Press, 2003.

———. *Hippias vel balaneion* [*Hipp.*]. Austin M. Harmon, *Lucian: Volume 1*. LCL. Cambridge, MA: Harvard University Press, 1913.

———. *Nigrinus* [*Nigr.*]. Austin M. Harmon, *Lucian: Volume 1*. LCL. Cambridge, MA: Harvard University Press, 1913.

1 Maccabees [1 Macc.]. Werner Kappler, *Maccabaeorum liber I*. Septuaginta: Vetus Testamentum Graecum 9.1. Göttingen: Vandenhoeck & Ruprecht, 1936. Trans. Jonathan A. Goldstein, *1 Maccabees: A New Translation with Introduction and Commentary*. AB. Garden City, NY: Doubleday, 1976.

Macrobius. *Saturnalia* [*Sat.*]. Robert A. Kaster, *Macrobius: Saturnalia*. 3 vols. LCL. Cambridge, MA: Harvard University Press, 2011.

Martial. *Epigrammata*. David R. Shackleton Bailey, *Martial: Epigrams*. 3 vols. LCL. Cambridge, MA: Harvard University Press, 1993.

Mekhilta de-Rabbi Ishmael [*Mek.*]. Haim S. Horovitz and Israel A. Rabin, *Mechilta D'Rabbi Ismael cum variis lectionibus et adnotationibus*. 2nd ed. Jerusalem: Wahrmann, 1970. Jacob Z. Lauterbach, *Mekilta de-Rabbi Ishmael: A Critical Edition on the Basis of Manuscripts and Early Editions with an English Translation, Introduction and Notes*. 3 vols. Philadelphia: Jewish Publication Society of America, 1933.

Midrash ha-Gadol [*MHG*]. For Genesis and Exodus: Mordecai Margulies, *Midrash ha-Gadol on the Pentateuch: Genesis–Exodus*. 2 vols. Jerusalem: Mosad ha-Rav Kook, 1967. For *Leviticus*: Adin Steinsaltz, *Mideash ha-Gadol on the Pentateuch: Leviticus*. Jerusalem: Mosad ha-Rav Kook, 1976. For *Numbers*: Z. Meir Rabinowitz, *Mideash ha-Gadol on the Pentateuch: Numbers*. Jerusalem: Mosad ha-Rav Kook, 1967. For *Deuteronomy*: Solomon Fisch, *Mideash ha-Gadol on the Pentateuch: Deuteronomy*. Jerusalem: Mosad ha-Rav Kook, 1972.

Midrash on Psalms [*Midr. Pss.*]. Solomon Buber, *Midrash Tehillim*. Wilna: Romm, 1892; reprint, Jerusalem, 1966.

Midrash on the Book of Samuel [*Midr. Sam.*]. Solomon Buber, *Midrash Shemu'el*. Krakow: Fisher, 1893; reprint, Jerusalem, 1965.

Midrash panim aḥerim. Solomon Buber, *Sifrey de'agadet'a 'al megilat 'ester*. Wilna: Romm, 1886, 54–82.

Midrash Tannaim [*Midr. Tann.*]. David Z. Hoffmann, *Midrash tana'im'al sefer devarim*. 2 vols. Berlin: Ittskovski, 1908–9.

Minucius Felix. *Octavius* [*Oct.*]. Terrot R. Glover, Gerald H. Rendall, and Walter C. A. Kerr, *Tertullian: Apology, De spectaculis, Minucius Felix: Octavius*. LCL. Cambridge, MA: Harvard University Press, 1931.

Mishnah [*m.* with name of tractate]. Georg Beer, ed., *Faksimile-Ausgabe des Mischnacodex Kaufman A 50*. Budapest: Hungarian Academy of Sciences; reprint, Jerusalem: Mekorot, 1968. Herbert Danby, *The Mishnah: Translated from the Hebrew with Introduction and Brief Explanatory Notes*. Oxford: Oxford University Press, 1933.

Numbers Rabbah [*Num. Rab.*]. Printed edition: *Sefer Midrash Rabbah: Midrash Rabbah 'al hamisah Ḥumshe Torah ve-ḥamesh Megillot*. Wilna: Romm, 1887. Harry Freedman and Maurice Simon, eds., *Midrash Rabbah: Numbers*. 2 vols. 3rd ed. London: Soncino, 1939.

Ovid. *Ars amatoria* [*Ars am.*]. John H. Mozley, *Ovid: The Art of Love and Other Poems*. Revised by George P. Goold. LCL. Cambridge, MA: Harvard University Press, 1979.

———. *Fasti* [*Fast.*]. James George Frazer, *Ovid: Fasti*. Revised by George P. Goold. LCL. Cambridge, MA: Harvard University Press, 1996.

———. *Metamorphoses* [*Met.*]. Frank Justus Miller, *Ovid: Metamorphoses*. Revised by George P. Goold. 2 vols. LCL. Cambridge, MA: Harvard University Press, 1977.

Oxyrhynchus Papyri [*P.Oxy.*]. Bernard P. Grenfell and Arthur S. Hunt, *The Oxyrhynchus Papyri*. 74 vols. London: Egypt Exploration Fund, 1898–.

Palladius. *Opus agriculturae* [*Op. Agr.*]. John G. Fitch, *Palladius: Opus agriculturae (The Work of Farming) and Poem on Grafting*. London: Prospect Books, 2013.

Palladius Monachus. *Dialogus de vita sancti Johannis Chrysostomi* [*v. Chrys.*]. Anne Marie Malingrey and Philippe Leclerq, *Dialogue sur la vie de Jean: Introduction, texte critique, traduction et notes*. 2 vols. SC 341–42. Paris: Cerf, 1988. Robert T. Meyer, *Palladius: Dialogue on the Life of St. John Chrysostom*. ACW 45. New York: Newman, 1985.

Pausanias. *Graeciae description*. William H. S. Jones, Henry A. Ormerod, and Richard E. Wycherley, *Pausanias: Description of Greece*. 5 vols. LCL. Cambridge, MA: Harvard University Press, 1918–35.

Perek ha-nikhnas la-merḥats. In Michael Higger, *The Treatises Derek Erez: Masseket Derek Erez, Pirke Ben Azzai, Tosefta Derek Erez, Edited from Manuscripts with an Introduction, Notes, Variants and Translation*. New York: Moinester, 1935, 295–305. Abraham Cohen, *The Minor Tractates of the Talmud: Massektoth Ḳeṭannoth*. 2 vols. London: Soncino, 1965, 560–62.

Pesiqta de Rav Kahana [*Pesiq. Rab. Kah.*]. Bernard Mandelbaum, *Pesikta de Rav Kahana According to an Oxford Manuscript*. 2 vols. 2nd ed. New York: Jewish Theological Seminary, 1987. William G. Braude and Israel J. Kapstein, *Pěsikta dě-Raḇ Kahăna: R. Kahana's Compilation of Discourses for Sabbaths and Festal Days*. Philadelphia: Jewish Publication Society, 1975.

Pesiqta Rabbati [*Pesiq. Rab.*]. Meir Friedmann ('Ish Shalom), *Pesikta Rabbati*. Vienna: n.p., 1880. Rivka Ulmer, *Pesiqta Rabbati: A Synoptic Edition of Pesiqta Rabbati Based upon All Extant Manuscripts and the Editio Princeps*. 2 vols. South Florida Studies in the History of Judaism 200. Atlanta: Scholars, 1999. William G. Braude, *Pesikta Rabbati: Discourses for Feasts, Fasts, and Special Sabbaths*. Yale Judaica Series 18. New Haven: Yale University Press, 1968.

Petronius. *Satyrica* [*Sat.*]. Gareth Schmeling, *Petronius Satyricon*. LCL. Cambridge, MA: Harvard University Press, 2020.

PGM2. Hans D. Betz, ed., *The Greek Magical Papyri in Translation*. 2nd ed. Chicago: University of Chicago Press, 1992.

Philo. *Legatio ad Gaium* [*Legat.*]. Francis H. Colson, *Philo: The Embassy to Gaius*. LCL. Cambridge, MA: Harvard University Press, 1962.

Philostratus. *Imagines* [*Imag.*]. Arthur Fairbanks, *Elder Philostratus: Imagines, Younger Philostratus: Imagines, Callistratus: Descriptions*. LCL. Cambridge, MA: Harvard University Press, 1931.

Pirqe de-Rabbi Eliezer [*Pirqe R. El.*]. Dagmar Börner-Klein, *Pirke de-Rabbi Elieser: Nach der Edition Venedig 1544 unter Berücksichtigung der Edition Warschau 1852*. SJ 26. Berlin: De Gruyter, 2004.

Plautus. *Persa* [*Pers.*]. Paul Nixon, *Plautus: Vol. III*. LCL. Cambridge, MA: Harvard University Press, 1924.

Pliny the Elder. *Naturalis historia* [*HN*]. Harris Rackham, William H. S. Jones, and D. E. Eicholz, *Pliny: Natural History*. 10 vols. LCL. Cambridge, MA: Harvard University Press, 1938–63.

Pliny the Younger. *Epistulae* [*Ep.*]. Betty Radice, *Pliny: Letters, Panegyrics*. 2 vols. LCL. Cambridge, MA: Harvard University Press, 1969.

Plutarch. *Vitae parallelae* [*Vit.*]. Bernadotte Perrin, *Plutarch: Lives*. 11 vols. LCL. Cambridge, MA: Harvard University Press, 1914–26.

Procopius. *De aedificiis* [*Aed.*]. Henry B. Dewing and Glanville Downey, *Procopius: Buildings*. LCL. Cambridge, MA: Harvard University Press, 1940; rev. ed. 1954.

Qoheleth (Ecclesiastes) Rabbah [*Qoh. Rab.*]. Printed edition: *Sefer Midrash Rabbah: Midrash Rabbah 'al ḥamisah Ḥumshe Torah ve-ḥamesh Megillot*. Wilna: Romm, 1887. Marc Hirshman, *Midrash Kohelet Rabbah 1–6: Critical Edition Based on Manuscripts and Genizah Fragments*. Jerusalem: Schechter Institute, 2016. Harry Freedman and Maurice Simon, eds., *Midrash Rabbah: Ecclesiastes*. 3rd ed. London: Soncino, 1939.

Qoheleth (Ecclesiastes) Zuttah [*Qoh. Zuttah*]. Solomon Buber, *Midrasch Zutta 'al Shir ha-Shirim, Ruth, 'Ekhah ve-Qohelet*. Wilna: Romm, 1899; reprint, Tel Aviv, 1925.

Quintilian. *Institutio oratoria* [*Inst.*]. Donald A. Russell, *Quintillian: The Orator's Education*. 5 vols. LCL. Cambridge, MA: Harvard University Press, 2001.

Rhetorica ad Herennium [*Rhet. Her.*]. Harry Caplan, *[Cicero]: Rhetorica ad Herennium*. LCL. Cambridge, MA: Harvard University Press, 1954.

Rylands Papyri [*P.Rey.*]. Arthur S. Hunt et al., *Catalogue of the Greek (and Latin) Papyri in the John Rylands Library Manchester*. 4 vols. Manchester: University Press, 1911–52.

Scriptores historiae Augustae [*SHA*]. David Magie, *Historia Augusta*. 3 vols. LCL. Cambridge, MA: Harvard University Press, 1921–32.

Seder Eliyahu Rabbah [*S. Eli. Rab.*]. Meir Friedmann ('Ish-Shalom), Seder Eliahu Rabba, und Seder Eliahu Zuta (Tanna d'be Eliahu). *Pseudo-Seder Eliahu Zuta.* Vienna: Achiasaf, 1902. Third printing, Jerusalem: Wahrmann, 1969. Willian G. Braude and Israel J. Kapstein, *Tanna dĕḇe Eliyyahu: The Lore of the School of Elijah.* Philadelphia: Jewish Publication Society, 1981.

Seder Eliyahu Zuttah [*S. Eli. Zut.*]. Meir Friedmann ('Ish-Shalom), Seder Eliahu Rabba, und Seder Eliahu Zuta (Tanna d'be Eliahu). *Pseudo-Seder Eliahu Zuta.* Vienna: Achiasaf, 1902. Third printing, Jerusalem: Wahrmann, 1969. Willian G. Braude and Israel J. Kapstein, *Tanna dĕḇe Eliyyahu: The Lore of the School of Elijah.* Philadelphia: Jewish Publication Society, 1981.

Sefer ha-razim. Mordecai Margalioth, *Sepher ha-razim: A Newly Recovered Book of Magic from the Talmudic Period.* Jerusalem: American Academy for Jewish Research, 1966. Michael A. Morgan, *Sepher ha-razim: The Book of Mysteries.* Texts and Translations 25: Pseudepigrapha Series 11. Chico, CA: Scholars, 1983.

Semaḥot [*Sem.*]. Michael Higger, *Treatise Semaḥot and Treatise Semaḥot of R. Ḥiya and Sefer Ḥibbut ha-Ḳeber and Additions to the Seven Minor Tractates and to Traetise Soferim II.* Newark: Bloch, 1931; reprint, Jerusalem: Makor, 1970.

Seneca the Younger. *Dialogi* [*Dial.*]. John W. Basore, *Seneca: Moral Essays.* 3 vols. LCL. Cambridge, MA: Harvard University Press, 1928–35; reprint, 2001, 2:98–179.

———. *Epistulae* [*Ep.*]. Richard M. Gummere, *Seneca: Epistles.* 3 vols. LCL. Cambridge, MA: Harvard University Press, 1917–25.

———. *Quaestiones naturales* [*QNat.*]. Thomas H. Corcoran, *Seneca: Natural Questions Books I–III.* LCL. Cambridge, MA: Harvard University Press, 1971.

Sidonius Apollinaris. *Carmina* [*Carm.*]. William B. Anderson, *Sidonius: Poems, Letters 1–2.* LCL. Cambridge, MA: Harvard University Press, 1936.

———. *Epistulae* [*Epist.*]. William B. Anderson, *Sidonius: Letters 3–9.* LCL. Cambridge, MA: Harvard University Press, 1965.

Sifra. Isaac H. Weiss, *Sifra de-ve Rav hu Sefer Torat Kohanim.* Vienna: Shlosberg, 1862. Trans. Jacob Neusner, *Sifra: An Analytical Translation.* 3 vols. BJS 138–40. Atlanta: Scholars, 1988.

Sifre to Deuteronomy [*SifreDeut*]. Louis Finkelstein, *Siphre ad Deuteronomium.* Berlin: Jüdischer Kulturbund in Deutschland, 1939; reprint, New York, 1969. Reuven Hammer, *Sifre: A Tannaitic Commentary on the Book of Deuteronomy.* New Haven: Yale University Press, 1986.

Sifre to Numbers [*SifreNum*]. Haim S. Horovitz, *Siphre de-ve Rav: Fasciculus primus: Siphre ad Numeros adjecto Siphre Zutta.* Leipzig: Gustav Fock, 1917; reprint, Jerusalem: Wahrmann, 1966. Jacob Neusner, *Sifré to Numbers: An American Translation and Explanation.* BJS 118–19. 2 vols. Atlanta: Scholars, 1986.

Socrates Scholasticus. *Historia ecclesiastica* [*H.E.*]. Günther C. Hansen, *Sokrates Kirchengeschichte.* GCS n.s. 1. Berlin: Akademie-Verlag, 1995. *NPNF*[2], II, pp. 1–178.

Statius. *Silvae* [*Silv.*]. David R. Shackleton Bailey, *Statius: Silvae.* LCL. Cambridge, MA: Harvard University Press, 2003; rev. ed., Christopher A. Parrott, 2015.

Strabo. *Geographica* [*Geo.*]. Horace Leonard Jones, *Strabo: Geography.* 8 vols. LCL. Cambridge, MA: Harvard University Press, 1917–32.

Suetonius. *De grammaticis et rhetoribus* [*Gram. et rhet.*]. John C. Rolfe, *Suetonius: The Lives of Illustrious Men.* LCL. Cambridge, MA: Harvard University Press, 1914, 396–449.

———. *De vita caesarum*. John C. Rolfe, *Suetonius: Lives of the Caesars*. 2 vols. LCL. Cambridge, MA: Harvard University Press, 1914.
Suppl. Mag. Robert W. Daniel and Franco Maltomini, eds., *Supplementum Magicum*. 2 vols. Papyrologica Coloniensia 16. Opladen: Westdeutscher, 1990.
Tacitus. *Agricola* [*Agr.*]. Maurice Hutton and William Peterson, *Tacitus: Agricola, Germania, Dialogus*. LCL. Cambridge, MA: Harvard University Press, 1914; rev. ed., Robert M. Ogilvie, Eric H. Warmington, and Michael Winterbottom, 1970.
———. *Annales* [*Ann.*]. John Jackson, *Tacitus: Annals*. 3 vols. LCL. Cambridge, MA: Harvard University Press, 1931–37.
———. *Historiae* [*Hist.*]. Clifford H. Moore, *Tacitus: Histories*. 2 vols. LCL. Cambridge, MA: Harvard University Press, 1925–31.
Tanḥuma [*Tanḥ*]. Printed edition: Wilna: Romm, 1831.
Tanḥuma Buber [*TanḥB*]. Solomon Buber, ed., *Midrash Tanhuma*. 2 vols. Wilna: Romm, 1885; reprint, Jerusalem: Wahrmann, 1964. John T. Townsend, *Midrash Tanhuma: Translated into English with Introduction, Indices, and brief Notes (S. Buber Recension)*. 2 vols. Hoboken, NJ: Ktav, 1989.
Tefillin [*Tep.*]. Michael Higger, *Seven Minor Treatises*. New York: Bloch, 1930, 42*–49* (Heb.), 24–30 (English translation). Israel W. Slotki in Abraham Cohen, *The Minor Tractates of the Talmud: Massektoth Ḳeṭannoth*. 2 vols. London: Soncino, 1965, 647–54.
Temple Scroll [*11Q19*]. Yigael Yadin, *The Temple Scroll*. 3 vols. Jerusalem: Israel Exploration Society, 1983.
Tertullian. *Apologeticus* [*Apol.*]. Terrot R. Glover, Gerald H. Rendall, and Walter C. A. Kerr, *Tertullian: Apology, De spectaculis, Minucius Felix: Octavius*. LCL. Cambridge, MA: Harvard University Press, 1931.
———. *De idololatria* [*Idol.*]. Jan H. Waszink and J.C.M. van Winden, *Tertullianus: De idololatria: Critical Text, Translation and Commentary*. Supplements to *Vigilae Christianae* 1. Leiden: Brill, 1987.
———. *De spectaculis* [*De spect.*]. Terrot R. Glover, Gerald H. Rendall, and Walter C. A. Kerr, *Tertullian: Apology, De spectaculis, Minucius Felix: Octavius*. LCL. Cambridge, MA: Harvard University Press, 1931.
Theophanes. *Chronographia*. Carl de-Boor, *Theophanis Chronographia*. 2 vols. Leipzig: Teubner, 1883–85. Cyril Mango and Roger Scott, *The Chronicle of Theophanes Confessor: Byzantine and Near Eastern History AD 284–813*. Oxford: Clarendon, 1997.
Tosefta [*t.* with name of tractate]. For *Zeraim, Moed, Nashim*, and the 3 *Babot* of *Neziqin*: Saul Lieberman, *The Tosefta*. 5 vols. New York: Jewish Theological Seminary, 1955–88. For all the rest: Moses Zuckermandel, *Tosephta: Based on the Erfurt and Vienna Codices with Parallels and Variants*. 2nd ed. Jerusalem: Wahrmann, 1970. Jacob Neusner and Richard S. Sarason, eds., *The Tosefta: Translated from the Hebrew*. 6 vols. New York: Ktav, 1977–86.
Vitruvius. *De architectura* [*De arch.*]. Frank Granger, *Vitruvius: On Architecture*. 2 vols. LCL. Cambridge, MA: Harvard University Press, 1931–34; rev. ed. 1998.
Yerushalmi (*Palestinian Talmud*) [*y.* with name of tractate]. Printed edition: *Talmud Yerushalmi*. Venice: Bomberg, 1523–24. Jacob Neusner, ed., *The Talmud of the Land of Israel: A Preliminary Translation and Explanation*. 35 vols. Chicago: University of Chicago Press, 1982–94. Heinrich W. Guggenheimer, ed., *The Jerusalem Talmud*. SJ. 13 vols. Berlin: De Gruyter, 2000–2014.

BIBLIOGRAPHY OF SCHOLARLY WORKS

Adams, James Noel. *Bilingualism and the Latin Language*. Oxford: Oxford University Press, 2002.

Adler, Yonatan. "The Decline of Jewish Ritual Purity Observance in Roman Palaestina: An Archaeological Perspective on Chronological and Historical Context." In *Expressions of Cult in the Southern Levant in the Greco-Roman Period: Manifestations in Text and Material Culture*, ed. Oren Tal and Zeev Weiss, 269–84. Contextualizing the Sacred 6. Turnhout: Brepols, 2017.

———. "The Hellenistic Origins of Jewish Ritual Immersion." *Journal of Jewish Studies* 69 (2018): 1–21.

Akhtar, Salman. *Comprehensive Dictionary of Psychoanalysis*. London: Karnac, 2009.

Albeck, Shalom. *Introduction to Jewish Law in Talmudic Times*. Ramat Gan: Bar Ilan University, 2014. (Heb.)

Alfayé, Sylvia. "Mind the Bath: Magic at the Roman Bath-Houses." In *From Polites to Magos: Studia György Németh sexagenario dedicate*, ed. Ádám Szabó, 28–37. Hungarian Polis Studies 22. Budapest: Könyvgyártó, 2016.

Alföldy, Géza. *Römische Sozialgeschichte*. 4th ed. Wiesbaden: Steiner, 2011.

Amit, David, Joseph Patrich, and Yizhar Hirschfeld, eds. *The Aqueducts of Israel*. Journal of Roman Archaeology Supplementary Series 46. Portsmouth, RI: Journal of Roman Archaeology, 2002.

Ando, Clifford. "Exporting Roman Religion." In *A Companion to Roman Religion*, ed. Jörg Rüpke, 429–45. Oxford: Blackwell, 2007.

Appelbaum, Alan. *The Dynasty of the Jewish Patriarchs*. Texte und Studien zum antiken Judentum 156. Tübingen: Mohr Siebeck, 2013.

Arbel, Yoav. "The Roman Bathhouse in En Gedi." In *En Gedi Excavations 1: Final Report (1961–1965)*, ed. Ephraim Stern, 306–23. Jerusalem: Israel Exploration Society, 2007.

Aupert, Pierre. "Les thermes comme lieux de culte." In *Les thermes romains: Actes de la table ronde organisée par l'École française de Rome (Rome, 11–12 novembre 1998)*, 185–92. Collection de l'École française de Rome 142. Rome: Palais Farnèse, 1991.

Bagg, Ariel M. "Wasserhebevorrichtungen im alten Mesopotamien." *Wasser und Boden* 53, no. 6 (2001): 40–47.

Bakker, Jan Theo. *Living and Working with the Gods: Studies of Evidence for Private Religion and Its Material Environment in the City of Ostia (100–500 AD)*. Dutch Monographs on Ancient History and Archaeology 12. Amsterdam: Gieben, 1994.

Balberg, Mira. *Purity, Body, and Self in Early Rabbinic Literature*. Berkeley: University of California Press, 2014.

Ball, Warwick. *Rome in the East: The Transformation of an Empire*. London: Routledge, 2000.

Balme, Maurice, and Gilbert Lawall. *Athenaze: An Introduction to Ancient Greek*. Rev. ed. James Morwood. 3rd ed. 2 vols. Oxford: Oxford University Press, 2015.

Balty, Jean Ch. *Guide d'Apamée*. Brussels: Centre belge de recherches archéologiques à Apamée de Syrie, 1981.

Bar-Nathan, Rachel, and Deborah A. Sklar-Parnes. "A Jewish Settlement in Orine between the Two Revolts." *New Studies in the Archaeology of Jerusalem and Its Region* 1 (2007): 57–64. (Heb.)

Barbier, Edmond. "La signification du cortège représenté sur le couvercle du coffret de 'Projecta.'" *Cahiers archéologiques* 12 (1962): 7–33.

Bassett, Sarah. "*Historiae custos*: Sculpture and Tradition in the Baths of Zeuxippos." *American Journal of Archaeology* 100 (1996): 491–506.

Bauer, Franz Alto, and Christian Witschel. *Statuen in der Spätantike*. Spätantike—frühes Christentum—Byzanz 2: Studien und Perspektiven 23. Wiesbaden: Reichert, 2007.

Bauman, Richard A. "Tertullian and the Crime of *Sacrilegium*." *Journal of Religious History* 4 (1967): 175–83.

Belayche, Nicole. *Iudaea-Palaestina: The Pagan Cults in Roman Palestine (Second to Fourth Century)*. Religion der römischen Provinzen 1. Tübingen: Mohr Siebeck, 2001.

Benovitz, Mosh. *Talmud ha-igud: BT Berakhot Chapter VI*. Jerusalem: Society for the Interpretation of the Talmud, 2015. (Heb.)

Ben Shahar, Meir. "Titus in the Holy of Holies." In *Josephus and the Rabbis*, ed. Tal Ilan and Vered Noam, 2:741–68. Jerusalem: Yad Ben Zvi, 2017. (Heb.)

Berger, Albrecht. *Das Bad in der byzantinischen Zeit*. Miscellanea Byzantina Monacensia 27. Munich: Institut für Byzantinistik und neugriechische Philologie der Universität, 1982.

Berkowitz, Beth A. "The Limits of 'Their Laws': Ancient Rabbinic Controversies about Jewishness (and Non-Jewishness)." *Jewish Quarterly Review* 99 (2009): 121–57.

Berlin, Meyer, and Shlomo Zevin. *Talmudic Encyclopedia III*. Jerusalem: Yad Harav Herzog, 1981.

Bickerman, Elias J. "Sur la théologie de l'art figuratif: A propos de l'ouvrage de E. R. Goodenough." *Syria* 44 (1967): 131–61.

Binder, Stéphanie E. *Tertullian,* On Idolatry *and Mishnah* Avodah Zarah: *Questioning the Parting of the Ways between Christians and Jews*. Jewish and Christian Perspectives 22. Leiden: Brill, 2012.

Birney, Kathleen. "Phoenician Bathing in the Hellenistic East: Ashkelon and Beyond." *Bulletin of the American Schools of Oriental Research* 378 (2017): 203–22.

Blair, Ian, Robert Spain, Dan Swift, Tony Taylor, and Damian Goodburn. "Wells and Bucket-Chains: Unforeseen Elements of Water Supply in Early Roman London." *Britannia* 37 (2006): 1–52.

Bley, Matthias, Nikolas Jaspert, and Stefan Köck, eds. *Discourses of Purity in Transcultural Perspective (300–1600)*. Dynamics in the History of Religions 7. Leiden: Brill, 2015.

Blidstein, Gerald J. "Nullification of Idolatry in Rabbinic Law." *Proceedings of the American Academy of Jewish Research* 41/42 (1973–74): 1–44.

———. "R. Yohanan, Idolatry, and Public Privilege." *Journal for the Study of Judaism in the Persian, Hellenistic, and Roman Periods* 5 (1974): 154–61.

Böcher, Otto. *Dämonenfurcht und Dämonenabwehr: Ein Beitrag zur Vorgeschichte der christlichen Taufe*. Beiträge zur Wissenschaft vom alten und neuen Testament 90. Stuttgart: Kohlhammer, 1970.

Bodel, John P. "'Sacred Dedications': A Problem of Definitions." In *Dediche sacre nel mondo Greco-Romano: Diffusione, funzioni, tipologie*, ed. John Bodel and Mika Kajava, 17–30. Acta instituti Romani Finlandiae 35. Rome: Institutum Romanum Finlandiae, 2009.

Bodel, John P., and Mika Kajava, eds. *Dediche sacre nel mondo Greco-Romano: Diffusione, funzioni, tipologie*. Acta instituti Romani Finlandiae 35. Rome: Institutum Romanum Finlandiae, 2009.

Bohak, Gideon. *Ancient Jewish Magic: A History*. Cambridge: Cambridge University Press, 2008.

Bonner, Campbell. "Demons of the Bath." In *Studies Presented to F. Ll. Griffith*, ed. Stephen R. K. Glanville, 203–8. London: Egypt Exploration Society, 1932.

Bonnie, Rick. *Being Jewish in Galilee, 100–200 CE: An Archaeological Study*. Studies in Eastern Mediterranean Archaeology 11. Turnhout: Brepols, 2019.

Bouchnick, Ram, and Rachel Bar-Nathan. "Bones as Evidence of the Ethnicity of the Residents of Shuʿfat after the Destruction of the Second Temple." *New Studies on Jerusalem* 18 (2012): 211–24. (Heb.)

Bouet, Alain. *Les thermes privés et publics en Gaule Narbonnaise*. 2 vols. Collection de l'École française de Rome 320. Rome: École française de Rome, 2003.

Boussac, Marie-Françoise, Sylvie Denoix, Thibaud Fournet, and Bérangère Redon. *25 siècles de bain collectif en Orient: Proche-Orient, Égypte et péninsule Arabique*. 4 vols. Études urbaines 9. Cairo: Institut français d'archéologie orientale, 2014.

Bowes, Kim. *Private Worship, Public Values, and Religious Change in Late Antiquity*. Cambridge: Cambridge University Press, 2008.

Boyarin, Daniel. "Is There Jewish Law? The Case of Josephus." In *Looking for Law in All the Wrong Places: Justice Beyond and Between*, ed. Marianne Constable, Leti Volpp, and Bryan Wagner, 189–200. New York: Fordham University Press, 2019.

———. *Judaism: The Genealogy of a Modern Notion*. New Brunswick, NJ: Rutgers University Press, 2018.

Brand, Yehoshua. *Kele ha-ḥeres besifrut ha-talmud*. Jerusalem: Mosad ha-Rav Kook, 1953.

———. *Kele zekhukhit be-sifrut ha-talmud*. Jerusalem: Mosad ha-Rav Kook, 1978.

Brödner, Erika. *Die römischen Thermen und das antike Badewesen: Eine kulturhistorische Betrachtung*. Darmstadt: Wissenschaftliche Buchgesellschaft, 1983.

Brown, Peter. *The Body and Society: Men, Women and Sexual Renunciation in Early Christianity*. 2nd ed. New York: Columbia University Press, 2008.

———. "Christianization and Religious Conflict." In *The Cambridge Ancient History, Volume 13: The Late Empire, AD 337–425*, ed. Averil Cameron and Peter Garnsey, 632–64. Cambridge: Cambridge University Press, 1998.

———. "Late Antiquity." In *A History of Private Life, Volume 1: From Pagan Rome to Byzantium*, ed. Paul Veyne, trans. Arthur Goldhammer, 235–312. Cambridge, MA: Harvard University Press, 1987.

———. *The World of Late Antiquity, AD 150–750*. London: Thames & Hudson, 1971.

Brunck, Rich. Fr. Phil., and Friedrich Jacobs. *Anthologia Graeca, sive poetarum Graecorum lusus ex recensione Brunckii*. 11 vols. in 9. Leipzig: Dyckio, 1794–1804.

Bruun, Christer. "Lotores: Roman Bath-Attendants." *Zeitschrift für Papyrologie und Epigraphik* 98 (1993): 222–28.

Burke, Peter. *History and Social Theory*. Ithaca: Cornell University Press, 1992.

Busch, Stephan. *Versus balnearum: Die antike Dichtung über Bäder und Baden im römischen Reich*. Berlin: De Gruyter, 1999.

Butler, Alfred J. *The Arab Conquest of Egypt and the Last Thirty Years of the Roman Dominion*. Oxford: Clarendon, 1902.

Cameron, Alan. *The Last Pagans of Rome*. Oxford: Oxford University Press, 2011.

Cancik, Hubert, and Jörg Rüpke, eds. *Römische Reichsreligion und Provinzialreligion*. Tübingen: Mohr Siebeck, 1997.

Carandini, Andrea, Andrenia Ricci, and Mariette De Vos. *Filosofiana: The Villa of Piazza Armerina: The Image of a Roman Aristocrat at the Time of Constantine*. Trans. Marie Christine Keith. Palermo: Flaccovio, 1982.

Carcopino, Jérôme. *Daily Life in Ancient Rome*. Trans. Emily O. Lorimer. London: Penguin Books, 1956.

Castriota, David. *The Ara Pacis Augustae and the Imagery of Abundance in Later Greek and Early Roman Imperial Art*. Princeton: Princeton University Press, 1995.

Catalano, Pierangelo. "Aspetti spaziali del sistema giuridico-religioso romano: Mundus, templum, urbs, ager, Latinum, Italia." *Aufstieg und Niedergang der römischen Welt* II.16.1 (1978): 467–79.

Certeau, Michel de. *L'invention du quotidien I: Arts de faire*. Paris: Gallimard, 1980.

———. *The Practice of Everyday Life*. Trans. Steven Rendall. Berkeley: University of California Press, 1984.

Chanson, Hubert. "Hydraulics of Roman Aqueducts: Steep Chutes, Cascades and Dropshafts." *American Journal of Archaeology* 104 (2000): 47–72.

Cohen, Boaz. *Jewish and Roman Law: A Comparative Study*. 2 vols. New York: Jewish Theological Seminary of Americas, 1966.

Cohen, Shaye J. D. "The Place of the Rabbi in Jewish Society of the Second Century." In *The Galilee in Late Antiquity*, ed. Lee I. Levine, 157–73. New York: Jewish Theological Seminary of America, 1994.

———. "The Rabbi in Second-Century Jewish Society." In *The Cambridge History of Judaism, Vol. 3: The Early Roman Period*, ed. William Horbury et al., 922–90. Cambridge: Cambridge University Press 1999.

———. "Was Herod Jewish?" In *The Beginnings of Jewishness: Boundaries, Varieties, Uncertainties*. Berkeley: University of California Press, 1999.

———. *Why Aren't Jewish Women Circumcised?* Berkeley: University of California Press, 2005.

Cotton, Hannah M. "The Administrative Background to the New Settlement Recently Discovered near Giv'at Shaul-Shu'afat Road." *New Studies in the Archaeology of Jerusalem and Its Region* 1 (2007): 12*–19*.

———. "Continuity of Nabataean Law in the Petra Papyri: A Methodological Exercise." In *From Hellenism to Islam: Cultural and Linguistic Change in the Roman Near East*, ed. Hannah M. Cotton et al., 154–74. Cambridge: Cambridge University Press, 2009.

———. "Ein Gedi between the Two Revolts." *Scripta Classica Israelica* 20 (2001): 139–54.

———. "The Impact of the Documentary Papyri from the Judaean Desert on the Study of Jewish History from 70 to 135 CE." In *Jüdische Geschichte in hellenistisch-römischer Zeit: Wege der Forschung: Vom alten zum neuen Schürer*, ed. Aharon Oppenheimer, 221–36. Schriften des Historischen Kollegs 44. Munich: Oldenbourg, 1999.

Coulton, James J. *The Architectural Development of the Greek Stoa*. Oxford: Clarendon, 1976.

Courtney, Edward. *Musa lapidaria: A Selection of Latin Verse Inscriptions*. American Classical Studies 36. Atlanta: Scholars, 1995.

Croom, Alexandra T. *Roman Clothing and Fashion*. Charleston, SC: Tempus, 2000.

Dahari, Uzi. "Adithaim now Aditha and Betomelgezis in the Madaba Map." In *The Madaba Map Centenary 1897-1997: Travelling through the Byzantine Umayyad Period*, ed. Michele Piccirillo and Eugenio Alliata, 246–48. Studium Biblicum Franciscanum Collectio maior 40. Jerusalem: Studium Biblicum Franciscanum, 1998.

Damati, Emanuel. "Muraq, Khirbet El—(Ḥilkiya's Palace)." In *The New Encyclopedia of Archaeological Excavations in the Holy Land*, ed. Ephraim Stern, 5:1961–63. Jerusalem: Israel Exploration Society, 1993–2008.

D'Arms, John H. "Performing Culture: Roman Spectacle and the Banquets of the Powerful." In *The Art of Ancient Spectacle*, ed. Bettina Bergmann and Christine Kondoleon, 300–319. Studies in the History of Art 56. New Haven: Yale University Press, 1999.

Dauphin, Claudine. "Brothels, Baths and Babes: Prostitution in the Byzantine Holy Land." *Classics Ireland* 3 (1996): 47–72.

Davies, Gwyn, and Jodi Magness. *The 2003-2007 Excavations in the Late Roman Fort at Yotvata*. Winona Lake, IN: Eisenbrauns, 2015.

De Luca, Stefano, and Ann Lena. "The Mosaic of the Thermal Bath Complex of Magdala Reconsidered: Archaeological Context, Epigraphy and Iconography." In *Knowledge and Wisdom: Archaeological and Historical Essays in Honour of Leah Di Segni*, ed. Giovanni C. Bottini, L. Daniel Chrupcala, and Joseph Patrich, 1–33. Studium Biblicum Franciscanum Collectio maior 54. Milan: Terra Santa, 2014.

Dechent, Hermann. "Heilbäder und Badeleben in Palästina." *Zeitschrift des deutschen Palästina-Vereins* 7 (1884): 173–210.

Deines, Roland. *Jüdische Steingefäße und pharisäische Frömmigkeit*. Wissenschaftliche Untersuchungen zum Neuen Testament 2:52. Tübingen: Mohr Siebeck, 1993.

DeLaine, Janet. *The Baths of Caracalla: A Study in the Design, Construction, and Economics of Large-Scale Building Projects in Imperial Rome*. Journal of Roman Archaeology Supplementary Series 25. Portsmouth, RI: Journal of Roman Archaeology, 1997.

———. "Recent Research on Roman Baths." *Journal of Roman Archaeology* 1 (1988): 11–32.

———. "Some Observations on the Transition from Greek to Roman Baths in Hellenistic Italy." *Mediterranean Archaeology* 2 (1989): 111–25.

Delorme, Jean. *Gymnasion: Étude sur les monuments consacrés à l'éducation en Grèce (des origines à l'empire romain)*. Paris: De Boccard, 1960.

Di Segni, Leah. "The Greek Inscriptions of Hammat Gader." In *The Roman Baths of Hammat Gader: Final Report*, ed. Yizhar Hirschfeld, 185–266. Jerusalem: Israel Exploration Society, 1997.

———. "Using Talmudic Sources for City Life in Palestine." Review of Daniel Sperber, *The City in Roman Palestine*. *Journal of Roman Archaeology* 13 (2000): 779–88.

Dietrich, Walter, and Martin A. Klopfenstein, eds. *Ein Gott allein? JHWH-Verehrung und biblischer Monotheismus im Kontext der israelitischen und altorientalischen Religionsgeschichte*. Orbis Biblicus et Orientalis 139. Freiburg: Universitätsverlag; Göttingen: Vandenhoeck & Ruprecht, 1984.

Dinary, Yedidya. "The Impurity Customs of the Menstruate Woman: Sources and Development." *Tarbiz* 49 (1980): 302–24. (Heb.)

Dohrmann, Natalie B., and Annette Yoshiko Reed, eds. *Jews, Christians, and the Roman Empire: The Poetics of Power in Late Antiquity*. Philadelphia: University of Pennsylvania Press, 2013.

Douglas, Mary. *Purity and Danger: An Analysis of Concepts of Pollution and Taboo*. London: Routledge, 1966.

Downey, Glanville. "Greek and Latin Inscriptions." In *Antioch on-the-Orontes III: The Excavations of 1937–1939*, ed. Richard Stillwell, 83–115. Princeton: Princeton University Press, 1941.

———. *A History of Antioch in Syria: From Seleucus to the Arab Conquest*. Princeton: Princeton University Press, 1961.

Ducrey, Pierre, and Henry van Effenterre. "Un règlement d'époque romaine sur les bains d'Arcadès." *Krētika Chronika* 25 (1973): 281–90.

Dunbabin, Katherine M. D. "*Baiarum grata voluptas*: Pleasures and Dangers of the Baths." *Papers of the British School at Rome* 57 (1989): 6–46.

Duncan-Jones, Richard. *The Economy of the Roman Empire: Quantitative Studies*. 2nd ed. Cambridge: Cambridge University Press, 1982.

Du Plessis, Paul. "Property." In *The Cambridge Companion to Roman Law*, ed. David Johnston, 175–98. Cambridge: Cambridge University Press, 2015.

Dvorjetski, Estēe. *Leisure, Pleasure, and Healing: Spa Culture and Medicine in Ancient Eastern Mediterranean*. Supplements to the Journal for the Study of Judaism 116. Leiden: Brill, 2007.

Eck, Werner. *Judäa—Syria Palästina: Die Auseinandersetzung einer Provinz mit römischer Politik und Kultur*. Texte und Studien zum antiken Judentum 157. Tübingen: Mohr Siebeck, 2014.

Edelman, Diana Vikander. *The Triumph of Elohim: From Yahwisms to Judaisms*. Grand Rapids, MI: Eerdmans, 1996.

Eger, Alexander A. "Age and Male Sexuality: 'Queer Space' in the Roman Bath-House?" In *Age and Ageing in the Roman Empire*, ed. Mary Harlow and Ray Laurence, 131–52. Journal of Roman Archaeology Supplementary Series 65. Portsmouth, RI: Journal of Roman Archaeology, 2007.

Ehrenkrook, Jason von. *Sculpting Idolatry in Flavian Rome: (An)Iconic Rhetoric in the Writings of Flavius Josephus*. Society of Biblical Literature Early Judaism and Its Literature 33. Atlanta: Society of Biblical Literature, 2011.

Elderkin, George W. *Antioch on-the-Orontes I: The Excavations of 1932*. Princeton: Publication for the Committee by the Department of Art and Archeology, 1934.

Eliav, Yaron Z. "Bathhouses as Places of Social and Cultural Interactions." In *The Oxford Handbook of Jewish Daily Life in Roman Palestine*, ed. Catherine Hezser, 605–22. Oxford: Oxford University Press, 2010.

———. "The Desolating Sacrilege: A Jewish-Christian Discourse on Statuary, Space, and Sanctity." In *The Sculptural Environment of the Roman Near East: Reflections on Culture, Ideology, and Power*, ed. Yaron Z. Eliav, Elise A. Friedland, and Sharon Herbert, 605–27. Interdisciplinary Studies in Ancient Culture and Religion 9. Leuven: Peeters, 2008.

———. "Did the Jews at First Abstain from Using the Roman Bath-House?" *Cathedra* 75 (1995): 3–35. (Heb.)

———. "From *Realia* to Material Culture: The Reception of Samuel Krauss' *Talmudische Archäologie*." In *Arise, Walk through the Land: Studies in the Archaeology and History of the Land of Israel in Memory of Yizhar Hirschfeld*, ed. Joseph Patrich, Orit Peleg-Barkat, and Erez Ben-Yosef, 17–27. Jerusalem: Israel Exploration Society, 2016.

———. *God's Mountain: The Temple Mount in Time, Place, and Memory*. Baltimore: Johns Hopkins University Press, 2005.

———, ed. "Jacob Neusner and the Scholarship on Ancient Judaism." *Henoch* 31 (2009): 247–83.

———. "Jews and Judaism 70–429 CE." In *A Companion to the Roman Empire*, ed. David S. Potter, 565–86. Malden, MA: Blackwell, 2006.

———. "The Material World of Babylonia as Seen from Roman Palestine: Some Preliminary Observations." In *The Archaeology and Material Culture of the Babylonian Talmud*, ed. Markham J. Geller, 153–85. IJS Studies in Judaica 16. Leiden: Brill, 2015.

———. "The Matrix of Ancient Judaism: A Review Essay of Seth Schwartz's *Imperialism and Jewish Society 200 BCE to 640 CE*." *Prooftexts* 24 (2004): 116–28.

———. "Pylè—Puma—Sfat Medinah and a Halacha Concerning Bath-houses." *Sidra* 11 (1995): 5–19. (Heb.)

———. "Realia, Daily Life, and the Transmission of Local Stories during the Talmudic Period." In *What Athens Has to Do with Jerusalem: Essays on Classical, Jewish and Early Christian Archaeology in Honor of Gideon Foerster*, ed. Leonard V. Rutgers, 235–65. Leuven: Peeters, 2002.

———. "The Roman Bath as a Jewish Institution: Another Look at the Encounter between Judaism and the Greco-Roman Culture." *Journal for the Study of Judaism in the Persian, Hellenistic, and Roman Period* 31 (2000): 416–54.

———. "Roman Statues, Rabbis, and Graeco-Roman Culture." In *Jewish Literatures and Cultures: Context and Intertext*, ed. Anita Norich and Yaron Z. Eliav, 99–115. Brown Judaic Studies 349. Providence, RI: Brown Judaic Studies, 2008.

———. "Samuel Krauss and the Early Study of the Physical World of the Rabbis in Roman Palestine." *Journal of Jewish Studies* 65 (2014): 38–57.

———. "A Scary Place: Jewish Magic in the Roman Bathhouse." In *Man Near a Roman Arch: Studies Presented to Prof. Yoram Tsafrir*, ed. Leah Di Segni et al., 88–97. Jerusalem: Israel Exploration Society, 2009.

———. "Secularism, Hellenism, and Rabbis in Antiquity." In *Religion or Ethnicity: Jewish Identities in Evolution*, ed. Zvi Gitelman, 7–23. New Brunswick, NJ: Rutgers University Press, 2009.

Eliav, Yaron Z. *Sites, Institutions and Daily Life in Tiberias during the Talmudic Period: A Source Book*. Mi'tuv T'veria 10. Jerusalem: Ariel and Bar Ilan University Press, 1995. (Heb.)

———. "Two Comments on Idolatry in the Roman Bath House." *Cathedra* 110 (2003): 173–80. (Heb.)

———. "Viewing the Sculptural Environment: Shaping the Second Commandment." In *The Talmud Yerushalmi and Graeco-Roman Culture* III, ed. Peter Schäfer, 411–33. Texts and Studies in Ancient Judaism 93. Tübingen: Mohr Siebeck, 2002.

———. "What Happened to Rabbi Abbahu at the Tiberian Bath-House? The Place of Realia and Daily Life in the Talmudic Aggada." *Jerusalem Studies in Jewish Folklore* 17 (1995): 7–20. (Heb.)

Eliav, Yaron Z., Elise A. Friedland, and Sharon Herbert, eds. *The Sculptural Environment of the Roman Near East: Reflections on Culture, Ideology, and Power*. Interdisciplinary Studies in Ancient Culture and Religion 9. Leuven: Peeters, 2008.

Ellis, Steven J. R. "The Distribution of Bars at Pompeii: Archaeological, Spatial and Viewshed Analyses." *Journal of Roman Archaeology* 17 (2004): 371–84.

Elm, Eva, and Nicole Hartmann, eds. *Demons in Late Antiquity: Their Perception and Transformation in Different Literary Genres*. Transformationen der Antike 54. Berlin: De Gruyter, 2019.

Elmslie, William A. L. *The Mishnah on Idolatry 'Aboda Zara*. Ed. James A. Robinson. Texts and Studies: Contributions to Biblical and Patristic Literature 8. Cambridge: Cambridge University Press, 1911.

Elon, Menachem. *Jewish Law: History, Sources, Principles*. Trans. Bernard Auerbach and Melvin J. Skyes. 4 vols. Philadelphia: Jewish Publication Society, 1994.

Elsner, Jaś. *Art and the Roman Viewer: The Transformation of Art from the Pagan World to Christianity*. Cambridge: Cambridge University Press, 1995.

Ennabli, Abdelmajid. "Les thermes du thiase marin de Sidi Ghrib (Tunisie)." *Monuments et mémoires* 68 (1986): 1–59.

Epstein, Louis M. *Sex Laws and Customs in Judaism*. New York: Bloch, 1948.

Ernout, Alfred, and Antoine Meillet. *Dictionnare étymologique de la langue latine: Histoire des mots*. Paris: Klincksieck, 1932.

Eschebach, Hans. *Die Stabianer Thermen in Pompeji*. Denkmäler antiker Architektur 13. Berlin: De Gruyter, 1979.

Fabiano, Doralice. "I 'demoni dei bagni' tra aqua e fuoco." In *Dans le laboratoire de l'historien des religions: Mélanges offerts à Philippe Borgeaud*, ed. Francesca Prescendi et al., 275–88. Religions en perspective 24. Geneva: Labor et fides, 2011.

Fagan, Garrett G. *Bathing in Public in the Roman World*. Ann Arbor: University of Michigan Press, 1999.

———. "Bathing in the Backwaters." Review of A. Farrington, *The Roman Baths of Lycia*. *Journal of Roman Archaeology* 10 (1997): 520–23.

———. "Gifts of Gymnasia: A Test Case for Reading Quasi-Technical Jargon in Latin Inscriptions." *Zeitschrift für Papyrologie und Epigraphik* 124 (1999): 263–75.

———. "Interpreting the Evidence: Did Slaves Bathe at the Baths?" In *Roman Baths and Bathing: Proceedings of the First International Conference on Roman Baths Held at Bath, England, 30 March–4 April 1992, Part 1: Bathing and Society*, ed. Janet DeLaine and David E. Johnston, 25–34. Journal of Roman Archaeology Supplementary Series 37. Portsmouth, RI: Journal of Roman Archaeology, 1999.

———. "Sergius Orata: Inventor of the Hypocaust?" *Phoenix* 50 (1996): 56–66.
———. "Socializing at the Baths." In *The Oxford Handbook of Social Relations in the Roman World*, ed. Michael Peachin, 358–73. Oxford: Oxford University Press, 2011.
———. "Violence in Roman Social Relations." In *The Oxford Handbook of Social Relations in the Roman World*, ed. Michael Peachin, 467–95. Oxford: Oxford University Press, 2011.
Faraone, Christopher A., and Dirk Obbink, eds. *Magika Hiera: Ancient Greek Magic and Religion*. Oxford: Oxford University Press, 1991.
Farrington, Andrew. "The Introduction and Spread of Roman Bathing in Greece." In *Roman Baths and Bathing: Proceedings of the First International Conference on Roman Baths held at Bath, England, 30 March–4 April 1992*, part 1: Bathing and Society, ed. Janet DeLaine and David E. Johnston, 57–66. Journal of Roman Archaeology Supplementary Series 37. Portsmouth, RI: Journal of Roman Archaeology, 1999.
Faur, José. "The Biblical Idea of Idolatry." *Jewish Quarterly Review* 69 (1978): 1–15.
Feldman, Louis H. *Josephus and Modern Scholarship (1937–1980)*. Berlin: De Gruyter, 1984.
Feliks, Yehuda. *Talmud Yerushalmi Tractate Shevi'it Critically Edited: A Study of the Halachic Topics and Their Botanical and Agricultural Background*. 2 vols. Jerusalem: Rubin Mass, 1986. (Heb.)
Fine, Steven. *Art and Judaism in the Greco-Roman World: Toward a New Jewish Archaeology*. Cambridge: Cambridge University Press, 2005.
Fischer, Moshe L. *Marble Studies: Roman Palestine and the Marble Trade*. Xenia, Konstanzer Althistorische Vorträge und Forschungen 40. Konstanz: Universitätsverlag Konstanz, 1998.
Flower, Harriet I. *Ancestor Masks and Aristocratic Power in Roman Culture*. Oxford: Clarendon, 1996.
Foerster, Gideon. "A Modest Aphrodite from Bet Shean." *Israel Museum Studies in Archaeology* 4 (2005): 3–15.
Fonrobert, Charlotte Elisheva. "Regulating the Human Body: Rabbinic Legal Discourse and the Making of Jewish Gender." In *The Cambridge Companion to the Talmud and Rabbinic Literature*, ed. Charolette Elisheva Fonrobert and Martin S. Jaffee, 270–94. Cambridge: Cambridge University Press, 2007.
Forbes, Robert J. *Studies in Ancient Technology, Volume 1: Bitumen and Petroleum in Antiquity; the Origin of Alchemy; Water Supply*. 3rd ed. Leiden: Brill, 1993.
Foxhall, Lin. *Olive Cultivation in Ancient Greece: Seeking the Ancient Economy*. Oxford: Oxford University Press, 2007.
Fraade, Steven D. "The Innovation of Nominalized Verbs in Mishnaic Hebrew as Marking an Innovation of Concept." In *Studies in Mishnaic Hebrew and Related Fields: Proceedings of the Yale Symposium on Mishnaic Hebrew, May 2014*, ed. Elitzur A. Bar-Asher Siegal and Aaron J. Koller, 129–48. New Haven and Jerusalem: The Program in Judaic Studies of Yale University and the Center for Jewish Languages and Literatures of the Hebrew University, 2017.
Fraenkel, Yonah. *Midrash and Agadah*. 3 vols. Tel Aviv: Open University of Israel, 1996. (Heb.)
Frankfurter, David. *Guide to the Study of Ancient Magic*. Religions in the Graeco-Roman World 189. Leiden: Brill, 2019.

Frankfurter, David. "The Vitality of Egyptian Images in Late Antiquity, Christian Memory and Response." In *The Sculptural Environment of the Roman Near East*, ed. Yaron Z. Eliav, Elise A. Friedland, and Sharon Herbert, 658–78. Leuven: Peeters, 2008.

Fredriksen, Paula. *Augustine and the Jews: A Christian Defense of Jews and Judaism*. New Haven: Yale University Press, 2008.

Friedheim, Emmanuel. "Rabban Gamaliel and the Bathhouse of Aphrodite in Akko: A Study of Eretz-Israel Realia in the 2nd and 3rd Centuries CE." *Cathedra* 105 (2002): 7–32. (Heb.)

———. *Rabbinisme et Paganisme en Palestine romaine: Étude historique des Realia talmudiques (Ier–IVème siècles)*. Religions in the Graeco-Roman World 157. Leiden: Brill, 2006.

———. "The Roman Public Bath in Eretz Israel: Research Dilemmas Relating to Its Definition as a Sacred Institution." *Cathedra* 119 (2006): 173–80. (Heb.)

Friedland, Elise A. *The Roman Marble Sculptures from the Sanctuary of Pan at Caesarea Philippi/Panias (Israel)*. American Schools of Oriental Research Archeological Reports 17. Boston: American Schools of Oriental Research, 2012.

Fulton, James, ed. *Index canonum The Greek Text: An English Translation and a Complete Digest of the Entire Code of Canon Law*. 3rd ed. New York: Thomas Whittaker, 1852.

Furstenberg, Yair. *Purity and Community in Antiquity: Traditions of the Law from Second Temple Judaism to the Mishnah*. Jerusalem: Magnes, 2016. (Heb.)

———. "The Rabbinic View of Idolatry and the Roman Political Conception of Divinity." *Journal of Religion* 90 (2010): 335–66.

Gafni, Isaiah M. "Symposium: In the Wake of the Destruction: Was Rabbinic Judaism Normative?" In *Jewish Identities in Antiquity: Studies in Memory of Menahem Stern*, ed. Daniel R. Schwartz and Lee I. Levine, 163–265. Texte und Studien zum antiken Judentum 130. Tübingen: Mohr Siebeck, 2009.

Gehn, Ulrich. *Ehrenstatuen in der Spätantike: Chlamydati und Togati*. Spätantike—frühes Christentum—Byzanz 2: Studien und Perspektiven 23. Wiesbaden: Reichert, 2012.

Gersht, Rivka. "Caesarean Sculpture in Context." In *The Sculptural Environment of the Roman Near East*, ed. Yaron Z. Eliav, Elise A. Friedland, and Sharon Herbert, 509–38. Leuven: Peeters, 2008.

Ginouvès, René. *Balaneutikè: Recherches sur le bain dans l'antiquité grecque*. Paris: De Boccard, 1962.

Glare, Peter G. W. *Oxford Latin Dictionary*. 2nd ed. Oxford: Oxford University Press, 2012.

Goldenberg, Robert. *The Nations That Know Thee Not: Ancient Jewish Attitudes toward Other Religions*. New York: New York University Press, 1998.

———. *The Sabbath Laws of Rabbi Meir*. Brown Judaic Studies 6. Missoula, MT: Scholars, 1978.

Goldhill, Simon, ed. *Being Greek under Rome: Cultural Identity, the Second Sophistic and the Development of Empire*. Cambridge: Cambridge University Press, 2001.

Goldstein, Jeffrey, ed. *Why We Watch: The Attractions of Violent Entertainment*. Oxford: Oxford University Press, 1998.

Goodenough, Erwin R. *Jewish Symbols in the Greco-Roman Period*. 13 vols. Bollingen Series 37. New York: Pantheon House, 1953-68.
Goodman, Martin. "Kosher Olive Oil in Antiquity." In *A Tribute to Geza Vermes*, ed. Philip R. Davies and Richard T. White, 227-45. Journal for the Study of the Old Testament 100. Sheffield: Sheffield Academic Press, 1990.
———. "Palestinian Rabbis and the Conversion of Constantine to Christianity." In *The Talmud Yerushalmi and Graeco-Roman Culture II*, ed. Peter Schäfer and Catherine Hezser, 1-9. Texte und Studien zum antiken Judentum 79. Tübingen: Mohr Siebeck, 2000.
———. *Rome and Jerusalem: The Clash of Ancient Civilizations*. New York: Vintage, 2008.
Gordon, Arthur E. *Illustrated Introduction to Latin Epigraphy*. Berkeley: University of California Press, 1983.
Graf, Fritz. "Heiligtum und Ritual: Das Beispiel der griechisch-römischen Asklepieia." In *Le sanctuaire grec*, ed. Olivier Reverdin and Bernard Grange, 159-99. Entretiens sur l'antiquité classique 37. Geneva: Foundation Hardt, 1992.
———. *Magic in the Ancient World*. Trans. Franklin Philip. Revealing Antiquity 10. Cambridge, MA: Harvard University Press, 1997.
Grenfell, Berhard P., and Arthur S. Hunt, eds. *The Oxyrhynchus Papyri, Volume 6*. London: Egypt Exploration Fund, 1908.
Grossberg, Asher. "A Mikveh in the Bathhouse." *Cathedra* 99 (2001): 171-84. (Heb.)
Guggenheimer, Heinrich W., ed. *The Jerusalem Talmud: First Order: Zeraïm. Tractates Kilaim and Ševiït*. Berlin: De Gruyter, 2001.
———. *The Jerusalem Talmud: Third Order: Našim, Tractate Ketubot*. Studia Judaica 34. Berlin: De Gruyter, 2006.
Gulak, Asher. *Yesode ha-mishpat ha-'ivri: Seder dine mamonot beyisra'el*. 2nd ed. 4 vols. in 2. Tel Aviv: Devir, 1967.
Habas-Rubin, Ephrat. "A Poem by the Empress Eudocia: A Note on the Patriarch." *Israel Exploration Journal* 46 (1996): 108-19.
Hachlili, Rachel. *Ancient Jewish Art and Archaeology in the Land of Israel*. Handbuch der Orientalistik 7, Kunst und Archäologie 2B4. Leiden: Brill, 1988.
———. *Ancient Synagogues: Archaeology and Art: New Discoveries and Current Research*. Boston: Brill, 2013.
Hadas-Lebel, Mireille. *Jérusalem contre Rome*. Paris: Cerf, 1990. Republished, Paris: CNRS, 2012.
———. "Le paganisme à travers les sources rabbiniques des IIe et IIIe siècles: Contribution à l'étude du syncrétisme dans l'empire romain." *Aufstieg und Niedergang der römischen Welt* II 19.2 (1979): 397-485.
Halbertal, Moshe. "Coexisting with the Enemy: Jews and Pagans in the Mishnah." In *Tolerance and Intolerance in Early Judaism and Christianity*, ed. Graham N. Stanton and Guy G. Stroumsa, 159-72. Cambridge: Cambridge University Press, 1998.
Hallett, Christopher H. *The Roman Nude: Heroic Portrait Statuary, 200 BC-AD 300*. Oxford: Oxford University Press, 2005.
Hanoune, M. Robert. "Thermes romains et Talmud." In *Colloque histoire et historiographie: Clio*, ed. Raymond Chevallier, 255-62. Collection Caesarodunum 15. Paris: Société d'Édition Les Belles Lettres, 1980.

Harrington, Hannah K. *The Purity Texts*. Companion to the Qumran Scrolls 5. London: Clark, 2004.

Havelock, Christine Mitchell. *The Aphrodite of Knidos and Her Successors: A Historical Review of the Female Nude in Greek Art*. Ann Arbor: University of Michigan Press, 1995.

Heinz, Werner. *Römische Thermen: Badewesen und Badeluxus im römischen Reich*. Munich: Hirmer, 1983.

Heise, Ulla. *Kaffee und Kaffeehaus: Eine Kulturgeschichte*. Hildesheim: Olms, 1987.

Herbert, Sharon C., and D. T. Ariel. *Tel Anafa I, i: Final Report on Ten Years of Excavation at a Hellenistic and Roman Settlement in Northern Israel*. Journal of Roman Archaeology Supplementary Series 10. Ann Arbor, MI: Kelsey Museum, 1994.

Hersey, George L. *Falling in Love with Statues: Artificial Humans from Pygmalion to the Present*. Chicago: University of Chicago Press, 2009.

Hershler, Moshe, ed. *The Babylonian Talmud with Variant Readings: Tractate Kethuboth II*. Jerusalem: Institute for the Complete Israeli Talmud, 1977.

Hezser, Catherine. *Jewish Slavery in Antiquity*. Oxford: Oxford University Press, 2006.

———, ed. *The Oxford Handbook of Jewish Daily Life in Roman Palestine*. Oxford: Oxford University Press, 2010.

———, ed. *Rabbinic Law in Its Roman and Near Eastern Context*. Texte und Studien zum antiken Judentum 97. Tübingen: Mohr, 2003.

———. *The Social Structure of the Rabbinic Movement in Roman Palestine*. Texte und Studien zum antiken Judentum 66. Tübingen: Mohr Siebeck, 1997.

Hirschfeld, Yizhar. *The Judean Desert Monasteries in the Byzantine Period*. New Haven: Yale University Press, 1992.

———. *Ramat Hanadiv Excavations: Final Report of the 1984–1998 Seasons*. Jerusalem: Israel Exploration Society, 2000.

Hirshman, Marc. *Midrash Kohelet Rabbah 1–6: Critical Edition Based on Manuscripts and Genizah Fragments*. Jerusalem: Schechter Institute, 2016. (Heb.)

Hizmi, Ḥananyah. "A Roman Bath and a Byzantine Farmstead at the Settlement of Menorah (Kh. Krikur)." *Qadmoniot* 127 (2004): 44–49. (Heb.)

Hobson, Barry. *Latrinae et foricae: Toilets in the Roman World*. London: Duckworth, 2009.

Hodge, A. Trevor. *Roman Aqueducts and Water Supply*. 2nd ed. London: Duckworth, 2002.

Holum, Kenneth G., Robert L. Hohlfelder, and Robert J. Bullet. *King Herod's Dream: Caesarea on the Sea*. New York: Norton, 1988.

Hopkins, Keith. *Conquerors and Slaves*. Cambridge: Cambridge University Press, 1978.

———. *A World Full of Gods: The Strange Triumph of Christianity*. New York: Free Press, 1999.

Horrocks, Geoffrey. *Greek: A History of the Language and Its Speakers*. 2nd ed. Malden, MA: Wiley-Blackwell, 2010.

Hoss, Stefanie. *Baths and Bathing: The Culture of Bathing and the Baths and Thermae in Palestine from the Hasmoneans to the Moslem Conquest*. British Archaeological Reports International Series 1346. Oxford: Archaeopress, 2005.

———. "From Rejection to Incorporation: The Roman Bathing Culture in Palestine." In *SPA, Sanitas per aquam: Tagungsband des Internationalen Frontinus-Symposiums zur Technik- und Kulturgeschichte der antiken Thermen. Aachen, 18.–22. März 2009*, ed. Ralf Kreiner and Wolfram Letzner, 259–64. Bulletin Antieke Beschaving Supplements 21. Leuven: Peeters, 2012.

Howell, Peter. *A Commentary on Book One of the Epigrams of Martial*. London: Athlone, 1980.

Hoyos, B. Dexter, ed. *A Companion to Roman Imperialism*. History of Warfare 81. Leiden: Brill, 2012.

Hughes, Donald J. *Environmental Problems of the Greeks and Romans: Ecology in the Ancient Mediterranean*. 2nd ed. Baltimore: Johns Hopkins University Press, 2014.

Irshai, Oded. "Terms and Characteristic Features of Water Installations and Aqueducts in Rabbinical Sources." In *The Aqueducts of Israel*, ed. David Amit, Joseph Patrich, and Yizhar Hirschfeld, 68–80. Journal of Roman Archaeology Supplementary Series 46. Portsmouth, RI: Journal of Roman Archaeology, 2002.

Jackson, Ralph. "Waters and Spas in the Classical World." In *The Medical History of Waters and Spas*, ed. Roy Porter, 1–13. Medical History, Supplement 10. London: Wellcome Institute for the History of Medicine, 1990.

Jacobs, Martin. "Römische Thermenkultur im Spiegel des Talmud Yerushalmi." In *The Talmud Yerushalmi and Graeco-Roman Culture I*, ed. Peter Schäfer, 219–311. Texte und Studien zum antiken Judentum 71. Tübingen: Mohr Siebeck, 1998.

———. "Theatres and Performances as Reflected in the Talmud Yerushalmi." In *The Talmud Yerushalmi and Graeco-Roman Culture I*, ed. Peter Schäfer, 327–47. Texte und Studien zum antiken Judentum 71. Tübingen: Mohr Siebeck, 1998.

Jacobson, Howard. "Demo and the Sabbath." *Mnemosyne* 30 (1977): 71–72.

Jansen, Gemma C. M. "Interpreting Images and Epigraphic Testimony." In *Roman Toilets: Their Archaeology and Cultural History*, ed. Gemma C. M. Jansen, Ann Olga Koloski-Ostrow, and Eric M. Moormann, 165–81. Babesch Supplements 19. Leuven: Peeters, 2011.

Jordan, Henri, and Christian Hülsen, eds. *Topographie der Stadt Rom im Alterthum*. 2 vols. Berlin: Weidmannsche, 1907.

Kah, Daniel, and Peter Scholz, eds. *Das hellenistische Gymnasion*. Wissenskultur und gesellschaftlicher Wandel 8. Berlin: Akademie Verlag, 2004.

Kasovsky, Chayim Yehoshua. *Thesaurus Mishnae: Concordantiae verborum quae in sex mishnae ordinibus reperiuntur*. 4 vols. Jerusalem: Massadah, 1960.

Kattan-Gribetz, Sarit. "'Lead Me Forth in Peace': The Origins of the Wayfarer's Prayer and Rabbinic Rituals of Travel in the Roman World." In *Journeys in the Roman East: Imagined and Real*, ed. Maren R. Niehoff, 297–327. Tübingen: Mohr Siebeck, 2017.

Katz, Steven T., ed. *The Cambridge History of Judaism IV: The Late Roman Rabbinic Period*. Cambridge: Cambridge University Press, 2006.

Kazen, Thomas. *Jesus and Purity halakha: Was Jesus Indifferent to Impurity?* Coniectanea Biblica: New Testament Series 38. Winona Lake, IN: Eisenbrauns, 2010.

Klawans, Jonathan. *Impurity and Sin in Ancient Judaism*. Oxford: Oxford University Press, 2011.

Klein, Samuel. *Sefer ha-Yishuv*. Tel Aviv: Dvir, 1939.

Kleiner, Fred S. *A History of Roman Art*. Belmont, CA: Thomas Wadsworth, 2007.

Koloski-Ostrow, Ann Olga, N. de Haan, Gerda de Kleijn, and Susanna A. G. Piras. "Water in the Roman Town: New Research from *Cura Aquarum* and the *Frontinus Society*." *Journal of Roman Archaeology* 10 (1997): 181–91.

Kondoleon, Christine, ed. *Antioch: The Lost Ancient City*. Princeton: Princeton University Press, 2000.

Koortbojian, Michael. *Myth, Meaning, and Memory on Roman Sarcophagi*. Berkeley: University of California Press, 1995.

Kornfilt, Jaklin, and John Whitman. "Introduction: Nominalizations in Syntactic Theory." *Lingua* 121 (2011): 1160–63.

Kottek, Samuel S. "Selected Elements of Talmudic Medical Terminology, with Special Consideration to Graeco-Latin Influences and Sources." *Aufstieg und Niedergang der römischen Welt* II.37.3 (1996): 2912–32.

Kowalewska, Arleta. *Bathhouses in Iudaea/Syria-Palaestina and Provincia Arabia from Herod the Great to the Umayyads*. Oxford: Oxbow, 2021.

Krauss, Samuel. "Bad und Badewesen im Talmud." *Hakedem* 1 (1907): 87–110, 171–94; *Hakedem* 2 (1908): 32–50.

———. *Griechische und lateinische Lehnwörter im Talmud, Midrasch und Targum*. 2 vols. Berlin: S. Calvary, 1898–99.

———. *Monumenta Talmudica V: Geschichte*, part 1—*Griechen und Römer*. Monumenta Hebraica 1. Ed. Karl Albrecht, Salomon Funk, and Nivard Schlögl. Vienna: Orion, 1914.

———. *Paras ve-Romi ba-Talmud uva-midrashim*. Jerusalem: Mossad Harav Kook, 1948.

———. *Talmudische Archäologie*. 3 vols. Leipzig: G. Fock, 1910–12. Reprint, Hildesheim: Georg Olms, 1966.

———. "Le traité talmudique 'Déréch Eréç.'" *Revue des études juives* 36 (1898): 205–21.

Lambrinoudakis, Vassilis, et al. "Consecration, Foundation Rites." In *Thesaurus cultus et rituum antiquorum*, 3:303–46. Los Angeles: J. Paul Getty Museum, 2004–12.

Lampe, Geoffrey W. H. *A Patristic Greek Lexicon*. Oxford: Oxford University Press, 1969.

Lapin, Hayim. *Rabbis as Romans: The Rabbinic Movement in Palestine, 100–400 CE*. Oxford: Oxford University Press, 2012.

Laqueur, Richard. *Der jüdische Historiker Flavius Josephus: Ein biographischer Versuch auf neuer quellenkritischer Grundlage*. Giessen: Munich, 1920.

Lassus, Jean. "La Mosaïque de Yakto." In *Antioch on-the-Orontes I: The Excavations of 1932*, ed. George W. Elderin, 114–56. Princeton: Princeton University Press, 1934.

Lavan, Myles. "The Army and the Spread of Roman Citizenship." *Journal of Roman Studies* 109 (2019): 1–58.

Lawrence, Jonathan David. *Washing in Water: Trajectories of Ritual Bathing in the Hebrew Bible and Second Temple Literature*. Society of Biblical Literature 23. Leiden: Brill, 2006.

Lennon, Jack J. *Pollution and Religion in Ancient Rome*. Cambridge: Cambridge University Press, 2014.

Lepaon, Thomas. "The Western Baths of Gerasa of the Decapolis: Original or Standard Building in the Near Eastern Bathing Context?" In *SPA, Sanitas per aquam: Tagungsband des Internationalen Frontinus-Symposiums zur Technik- und Kulturgeschichte der antiken Thermen. Aachen, 18.-22. März 2009*, ed. Ralf Kreiner and Wolfram Letzner, 117–23. Bulletin Antieke Beschaving Supplements 21. Leuven: Peeters, 2012.

Lerner, Myron B. "The External Tractates." In *The Literature of the Sages I*, ed. Shmuel Safrai, 369-403. Compendia Rerum Iudaicarum ad Novum Testamentum 2.3. Assen: Van Gorcum, 1987.

Levi, Doro. *Antioch Mosaic Pavements*. 2 vols. Oxford: Oxford University Press, 1947.

Levine, Lee I. *The Ancient Synagogue: The First Thousand Years*. 2nd ed. New Haven: Yale University Press, 2005.

———. "Figural Art in Ancient Judaism." *Ars Judaica* 1 (2005): 9–26.

———. *Jerusalem: Portrait of the City in the Second Temple Period (538 B.C.E.-70 C.E.)*. Philadelphia: Jewish Publication Society, 2002.

———. *Judaism and Hellenism in Antiquity: Conflict or Confluence*. Seattle: University of Washington Press, 1998.

———. *The Rabbinic Class of Roman Palestine in Late Antiquity*. Jerusalem: Yad Izhak Ben-Zvi, 1989.

———. *Roman Caesarea: An Archaeological-Topographical Study*. Qedem 2. Jerusalem: Hebrew University of Jerusalem Institute of Archaeology, 1975.

———. "Second Temple Jerusalem: A Jewish City in the Greco-Roman Orbit." In *Jerusalem: Its Sanctity and Centrality to Judaism, Christianity, and Islam*, ed. Lee I. Levine, 53–68. New York: Continuum, 1999.

———. *Visual Judaism in Late Antiquity: Historical Contexts of Jewish Art*. New Haven: Yale University Press, 2012.

Levinson, Joshua. "Enchanting Rabbis: Contest Narratives between Rabbis and Magicians in Late Antiquity." *Jewish Quarterly Review* 100 (2010): 54–94.

———. "Fatal Charades and the Death of Titus." *Jerusalem Studies in Hebrew Literature* 19 (2003): 23–45. (Heb.)

Lewis, Charlton T., and Charles Short. *A Latin Dictionary Founded on Andrews' Edition of Freund's Latin Dictionary*. Oxford: Clarendon, 1879. Reprint, 1956.

Lewis, Michael. "Vitruvius and Greek Aqueducts." *Papers of the British School at Rome* 67 (1999): 145–72.

Liddell, Henry G., Robert Scott, and Henry Stuart Jones. *A Greek-English Lexicon*. 9th ed. with revised supplement. Oxford: Clarendon, 1996.

Lieberman, Saul. *Ha-yerushalmi kifshuto: A Commentary—Part 1: Vol. 1*. 3rd ed. Ed. Menachem Katz. New York: Jewish Theological Seminary, 2008. (Heb.)

———. *Hellenism in Jewish Palestine: Studies in the Literary Transmission, Beliefs and Manners of Palestine in the I Century B.C.E.-IV Century C.E.* Texts and Studies of the Jewish Theological Seminary 18. New York: Jewish Theological Seminary of America, 1962. Reprint, 1994.

———. "Palestine in the Third and Fourth Centuries." *Jewish Quarterly Review* 36 (1946): 329–70.

———. *Tosefta kifshutah: A Comprehensive Commentary on the Tosefta*. 10 vols. Jerusalem: Jewish Theological Seminary, 1955–88. (Heb.)

Linant de Bellefonds, Pascale, et al. "Rites et activités relatifs aux images de culte." In *Thesaurus cultus et rituum antiquorum*, ed. Jean Ch. Balty et al., 2:417–507. Los Angeles: J. Paul Getty Museum, 2004–12.

Longfellow, Brenda. *Roman Imperialism and Civic Patronage: Form, Meaning, and Ideology in Monumental Fountain Complexes*. Cambridge: Cambridge University Press, 2011.

Low, Setha M., and Denise Lawrence-Zúñiga, eds. *The Anthropology of Space and Place: Locating Culture*. Malden, MA: Blackwell, 2003.

Lucore, Sandra K., and Monika Trümper, eds. *Greek Baths and Bathing Culture: New Discoveries and Approaches*. Babesch: Annual Papers on Mediterranean Archaeology Supplement 23. Leuven: Peeters, 2013.

Lurker, Martin. *A Dictionary of Gods and Goddesses, Devils and Demons*. Trans. G. L. Campbell. London: Routledge, 1988.

Macalister, Robert A. *The Excavation of Gezer, 1902–1905 and 1907–1909*. London: Published for the Committee of the Palestine Exploration Fund by J. Murray, 1912.

MacMullen, Ramsay. *Roman Social Relations: 50 B.C. to A.D. 284*. New Haven: Yale University Press, 1974.

Magen, Yitzhak. *The Stone Vessel Industry in the Second Temple Period: Excavations at Ḥizma and the Jerusalem Temple Mount*. Judea and Samaria Publications 1. Jerusalem: Israel Exploration Society, 2002.

Magoulias, Harry J. "Bathhouse, Inn, Tavern, Prostitution and the Stage as Seen in the Lives of the Saints of the Sixth and Seventh Centuries." *Epeteris Hetaireias Byzantinon Spudon* 38 (1971): 233–52.

Manderscheid, Hubertus. *Die Skulpturenausstattung der kaiserzeitlichen Thermenanlagen*. Monumenta artis romanae 15. Berlin: Mann, 1981.

Mango, Cyril. "Antique Statuary and the Byzantine Beholder." *Dumbarton Oaks Papers* 17 (1963): 55–75.

———. "Daily Life in Byzantium." In *Byzantium and Its Image: History and Culture of the Byzantine Empire and Its Heritage*, 45–61. London: Variorum, 1984. Reprint of "Daily Life in Byzantium." In *XVI. Internationaler Byzantinistenkongress, Wien, 4–9. Oktober 1981: Akten*, ed. Jørgen Raasted et al., 337–53. Jahrbuch der österreichischen Byzantinistik 32/1. Vienna: Österreichische Akademie der Wissenschaften, 1981.

Marvin, Miranda. "Freestanding Sculptures from the Baths of Caracalla." *American Journal of Archaeology* 87 (1983): 347–84.

Mason, Hugh J. *Greek Terms for Roman Institutions: A Lexicon and Analysis*. American Studies in Papyrology 13. Toronto: Hakkert, 1974.

Mason, Steve. "Jews, Judaeans, Judaizing, Judaism: Problems of Categorization in Ancient History." *Journal for the Study of Judaism in the Persian, Hellenistic, and Roman Period* 38 (2007): 457–512.

Mattingly, David. "Being Roman: Expressing Identity in a Provincial Setting." *Journal of Roman Archaeology* 17 (2004): 5–25.

———. "First Fruit? The Olive in the Roman World." In *Human Landscapes in Classical Antiquity: Environment and Culture*, ed. Graham Shipley and John Salmon, 213–53. Leicester-Nottingham Studies in Ancient Society 6. London: Routledge, 1996.

Merten, Elke W. *Bäder und Badegepflogenheiten in der Darstellung der Historia Augusta*. Antiquitas 4: Beiträge zur Historia-Augusta-Forschung 16. Bonn: Habelt, 1983.

Meshorer, Ya'akov. *Ancient Jewish Coinage*. 2 vols. Dix Hills, NY: Amphora, 1982.

Meusel, Heinrich. "Die Verwaltung und Finanzierung der öffentlichen Bäder zur römischen Kaiserzeit." PhD diss., University of Köln, 1960.

Meyer, Béatrice. "Les femmes et les bains publics dans l'Égypte grecque, romaine et byzantine." In *Proceedings of the XIXth International Congress of Papyrology, Cairo, 2–9 September 1989*, ed. A.H.S. El-Mosalamy, 1:51–60. Cairo: Ain Shams University, Center of Papyrological Studies, 1992.

———. "'Gymnase' et 'Thermes' dans l'Égypte romaine et byzantine." In *Akten des 21. Internationalen Papyrologenkongresses vol. 2. Berlin 1995*. Ed. Bärbel Kramer et al., 691–95. Archiv für Papyrusforschung 3. Stuttgart: Teubner, 1997.

———. "Magie et Bains publics." In *Atti del XXII Congresso internazionale di papirologia: Firenze, 23–29 agosto 1998*, ed. Isabella Andorlini, 2:937–42. Florence: Istituto papirologico G. Vitelli, 2001.

Meyer, Marvin W., and Richard Smith, eds. *Ancient Christian Magic: Coptic Texts of Ritual Power*. San Francisco: Harper, 1994.

Millar, Fergus. *The Roman Near East, 31 BC–AD 337*. Cambridge, MA: Harvard University Press, 1993.

———. "The World of Golden Ass." *Journal of Roman Studies* 71 (1981): 63–75.

Miller, Stuart S. *At the Intersection of Texts and Material Finds: Stepped Pools, Stone Vessels, and Ritual Purity among the Jews of Roman Galilee*. Journal of Ancient Judaism Supplements 16. Göttingen: Vandenhoeck & Ruprecht, 2015.

Mithen, Steven. *Thirst: Water and Power in the Ancient World*. Cambridge, MA: Harvard University Press, 2012.

Möller, Christa, and Götz Schmitt. *Siedlungen Palästinas nach Flavius Josephus*. Tübinger Atlas des vorderen Orients B:14. Wiesbaden: Reichert, 1976.

Mor, Menahem. *The Second Jewish Revolt: The Bar Kokhba War, 132–136 CE*. Brill Reference Library of Judaism 50. Leiden: Brill, 2016.

Moscovitz, Leib. "Legal Fictions in Rabbinic Law and Roman Law: Some Comparative Observations." In *Rabbinic Law in Its Roman and Near Eastern Context*, ed. Catherine Hezser, 105–32. Texte und Studien zum antiken Judentum 97. Tübingen: Mohr, 2003.

Mrozek, Stanislaw. "Sur la *dedicatio*, la *consecratio* et les dédicants dans les inscriptions du Haut-Empire romain." *Epigraphica* 66 (2004): 119–33.

Mulder, Martin Jan, and Harry Sysling, eds. *Mikra: Translation, Reading, Interpretation of the Hebrew Bible in Ancient Judaism and Early Christianity*. Compendia rerum iudaicarum ad Novum Testamentum 2:1. Assen: Van Gorcum, 1988.

Murphy, Frederick J. "Retelling the Bible: Idolatry in Pseudo-Philo." *Journal of Biblical Literature* 107 (1988): 275–87.

Myers, Abraham L. "The Use of the Adjective as a Substantive in Horace." PhD diss., University of Pennsylvania, 1919.

Neis, Rachel. *The Sense of Sight in Rabbinic Culture: Jewish Ways of Seeing in Late Antiquity*. Cambridge: Cambridge University Press, 2013.

Netzer, Ehud. *The Architecture of Herod, the Great Builder.* Texte und Studien zum antiken Judentum 117. Tübingen: Mohr Siebeck, 2006.

———. "Herodian Bath-Houses." In *Roman Baths and Bathing: Proceedings of the First International Conference on Roman Baths Held at Bath, England, 30 March–4 April 1992*, part 1: Bathing and Society, ed. Janet DeLaine and David E. Johnston, 45–55. Journal of Roman Archaeology Supplementary Series 37. Portsmouth, RI: Journal of Roman Archaeology, 1999.

———. *The Palaces of the Hasmoneans and Herod the Great.* Jerusalem: Yad Ben-Zvi, 2001.

Neusner, Jacob. *The Mishnah: A New Translation.* New Haven: Yale University Press, 1988.

———. *Sifra: An Analytical Translation.* 3 vols. Brown Judaic Studies 138–40. Atlanta: Scholars, 1988.

Nielsen, Inge. *Thermae et balnea: The Architecture and Cultural History of Roman Public Baths.* 2 vols. Aarhus: Aarhus University Press, 1990.

Norich, Anita, and Yaron Z. Eliav, eds. *Jewish Literatures and Cultures: Context and Intertext.* Brown Judaic Studies 349. Providence, RI: Brown Judaic Studies, 2008.

Oleson, John Peter, ed. *Oxford Handbook of Engineering and Technology in the Classical World.* Oxford: Oxford University Press, 2009.

Onn, Alexander, Shlomit Wexler-Bdolah, Yehuda Rapuano, and Tzah Kanias. "Khirbet Umm el-ʿUmdan." *Ḥadashot Arkheologiyot-Excavations and Surveys in Israel* 114 (2002): 64*–68*.

Oppenheimer, Aharon. "The Jews in the Roman World." In *The Sculptural Environment of the Roman Near East: Reflections on Culture, Ideology, and Power*, ed. Yaron Z. Eliav, Elise A. Friedland, and Sharon Herbert, 51–68. Interdisciplinary Studies in Ancient Culture and Religion 9. Leuven: Peeters, 2008.

Osborn, Eric. *Clement of Alexandria.* Cambridge: Cambridge University Press, 2008.

Oudshoorn, Jacobine G. *The Relation between Roman and Local Law in the Babatha and Salome Komaise Archives: General Analysis and Three Case Studies on Law of Succession, Guardianship, and Marriage.* Studies on the Texts of the Desert Judah 69. Leiden: Brill, 2007.

Owens, Edwin J. "Baths and Water Supply in the Cities of Pisidia: Antioch." In *SPA, Sanitas per aquam: Tagungsband des Internationalen Frontinus-Symposiums zur Technik- und Kulturgeschichte der antiken Thermen. Aachen, 18.–22. März 2009*, ed. Ralf Kreiner and Wolfram Letzner, 171–76. Bulletin Antieke Beschaving Supplements 21. Leuven: Peeters, 2012.

Pace, Biagio. *I mosaici di Piazza Armerina.* Roma: Casini, 1955.

Patrich, Joseph. *The Formation of Nabatean Art: Prohibition of a Graven Image among the Nabateans.* Jerusalem: Magnes, 1990.

Peachin, Michael, ed. *The Oxford Handbook of Social Relations in the Roman World.* Oxford: Oxford University Press, 2011.

Philips, Robert C. "The Sociology of Religious Knowledge in the Roman Empire to AD 284." *Aufstieg und Niedergang der römischen Welt* II.16.3 (1986): 2677–2773.

Place, Amy. "Clothing Differentiation in a Shared Visual Culture: Dress Imagery in Mosaic Iconography." In *A Globalised Visual Culture?: Towards a Geography of Late Antique Art*, ed. Fabio Guidetti and Katharina Meinecke, 47–62. Oxford: Oxbow Books, 2020.

Poorthius, Marcel J.H.M., and Joshua Schwartz, eds. *Purity and Holiness: The Heritage of Leviticus*. Jewish and Christian Perspectives 2. Leiden: Brill, 2000.
Potter, David S., ed. *A Companion to the Roman Empire*. Malden, MA: Blackwell, 2006.
———. *Literary Texts and the Roman Historian*. London: Routledge, 1999.
Preuss, Julius. *Biblisch-talmudische Medizin: Beiträge zur Geschichte der Heilkunde und der Kultur überhaupt*. Berlin: Karger, 1911.
Pucci Ben Zeev, Miriam. *Jewish Rights in the Roman World: The Greek and Roman Documents Quoted by Josephus Flavius*. Texte und Studien zum antiken Judentum 74. Tübingen: Mohr Siebeck, 1998.
Rakover, Nahum. *The Multi-Language Bibliography of Jewish Law*. Jerusalem: Library of Jewish Law, 1990.
Rawson, Elizabeth. "*Discrimina ordinum*: The *lex Julia theatralis*." *Papers of the British School at Rome* 55 (1987): 83–114.
Reeves, Mary Barbara. "The Roman Bath-House at Humeima in its Architectural and Social Context." MA diss., University of Victoria, 1996.
Reich, Ronny. "Beit ha-merḥaṣ ha-ḥam veha-qehilah ha-yehudit ba-tequfah haromit ha-qedumah (yemey ha-bayit ha-sheny)." In *Greece and Rome in Eretz Israel: Collected Essays*, ed. Avraham Kasher, Gideon Fuks, and Uriel Rappaport, 207–11. Jerusalem: Yad Izhak Ben-Zvi, 1989.
———. "The Hot Bath-House (*balneum*), the Miqweh and the Jewish Community in the Second Temple Period." *Journal of Jewish Studies* 39 (1988): 102–7.
———. *Miqva'ot taharah bitqufat ha-bayit ha-sheni uvitqufot ha-mishnah ve-talmud*. Jerusalem: Israel Exploration Society, 2013.
Rengstorf, Karl H. *A Complete Concordance to Flavius Josephus*. 4 vols. Leiden: Brill, 1973.
Revell, Louise. *Roman Imperialism and Local Identities*. Cambridge: Cambridge University Press, 2009.
———. *Ways of Being Roman: Discourses of Identity in the Roman West*. Oxford: Oxbow, 2016.
Rey-Coquais, Jean-Paul. "Inscriptions grecques d'Apameé." *Annales archéologiques arabes syriennes* 23 (1973): 39–84.
Rives, James B. *Religion and Authority in Roman Carthage from Augustus to Constantine*. Oxford: Clarendon, 1995.
Rogers, Adam. *Water and Roman Urbanism: Towns, Waterscapes, Land Transformation and Experience in Roman Britain*. Mnemosyne Supplements 355. Leiden: Brill, 2013.
Rogers, Dylan K. *Water Culture in Roman Society*. Ancient History 1:1. Leiden: Brill, 2018.
Rogers, Guy M. *The Sacred Identity of Ephesos: Foundation Myths of a Roman City*. London: Routledge, 1991.
Rosenblum, Jordan. "Kosher Olive Oil in Antiquity Reconsidered." *Journal for the Study of Judaism in the Persian, Hellenistic, and Roman Periods* 40 (2009): 356–65.
Rosenfeld, Ben-Zion. *Lod and Its Sages in the Period of the Mishnah and the Talmud*. Jerusalem: Yad Izhak Ben-Zvi, 1997. (Heb.)
Rosenthal, David. "Mishna Aboda Zara: A Critical Edition with Introduction." 2 vols. PhD diss., Hebrew University of Jerusalem, 1981. (Heb.)

Rosen-Zvi, Ishay. "Rabbis and Romanization: A Review Essay." In *Jewish Cultural Encounters in the Ancient Mediterranean and Near Eastern World*, ed. Mladen Popović, Myles Schoonover, and Marijn Vandenberghe, 218–45. Supplements to the Journal for the Study of Judaism 178. Leiden: Brill, 2017.

Roussin, Lucille A. "Costume in Roman Palestine: Archaeological Remains and the Evidence from the Mishnah." In *The World of Roman Costume*, ed. Judith L. Sebesta and Larissa Bonfante, 182–90. Madison: University of Wisconsin Press, 1994.

Runesson, Anders, Donald Binder, and Birger Olsson. *The Ancient Synagogue from Its Origins to 200 C.E.: A Source Book*. Ancient Judaism Early Christianity 72. Leiden: Brill, 2007.

Rüpke, Jörg. *Antike Religionsgeschichte in räumlicher Perspektive: Abschlussbericht zum Schwerpunktprogramm 1080 der Deutschen Forschungsgemeinschaft "Römische Reichsreligion und Provinzialreligion."* Tübingen: Mohr Siebeck, 2007.

Safrai, Shmuel, ed. *The Literature of the Sages*. 2 vols. Compendia Rerum Iudaicarum ad Novum Testamentum 2:3. Assen: Van Grocum, 1987.

———. "The Practical Implementation of the Sabbatical Year after the Destruction of the Second Temple." *Tarbiz* 35 (1966): 304–28, 36 (1966): 1–21. (Heb.)

———. *In Times of Temple and Mishnah: Studies in Jewish History*. 2 vols. Jerusalem: Magnes, 1994. (Heb.)

Safrai, Shmuel, and Ze'ev Safrai. *Mishnat Eretz Israel: Tractate Shabbat (Moed A-B) with Historical and Sociological Commentary*. 2 vols. Jerusalem: Liphshitz, 2008. (Heb.)

———. *Mishnat Eretz Israel: Tractate Shevi'it (Zeraim V) with Historical and Sociological Commentary*. Jerusalem: Liphshitz, 2008. (Heb.)

Safrai, Ze'ev. *The Economy of Roman Palestine*. London: Routledge, 1994.

Saiman, Chaim N. *Halakhah: The Rabbinic Idea of Law*. Princeton: Princeton University Press, 2018.

Saller, Richard P. *Personal Patronage under the Early Empire*. Cambridge: Cambridge University Press, 1982.

Sartre, Maurice. *The Middle East under Rome*. Trans. Catherine Porter and Elizabeth Rawlings. Cambridge, MA: Harvard University Press, 2005.

———. "The Nature of Syrian Hellenism in the Late Roman and Early Byzantine Periods." In *The Sculptural Environment of the Roman Near East: Reflections on Culture, Ideology, and Power*, ed. Yaron Z. Eliav, Elise A. Friedland, and Sharon Herbert, 25–49. Interdisciplinary Studies in Ancient Culture and Religion 9. Leuven: Peeters, 2008.

Satlow, Michael L. "Beyond Influence: Toward a New Historiographic Paradigm." In *Jewish Literatures and Cultures: Context and Intertext*, ed. Anita Norich and Yaron Z. Eliav, 37–54. Brown Judaic Studies 349. Providence, RI: Brown Judaic Studies, 2008.

———. "Jewish Constructions of Nakedness in Late Antiquity." *Journal of Biblical Literature* 116 (1997): 429–54.

Schäfer, Peter. "The Bar Kokhba Revolt and Circumcision: Historical Evidence and Modern Apologetics." In *Jüdische Geschichte in hellenistisch-römischer Zeit: Wege der Forschung—Vom alten zum neuen Schürer*, ed. Aharon Oppheimer, 119–32. Munich: Oldenbourg, 1999.

Scheid, John. "Sanctuaires et thermes sous l'empire." In *Les thermes romains: Actes de la table ronde organisée par l'École française de Rome (Rome, 11–12 novembre 1998)*, 205–16. Collection de l'École française de Rome 142. Rome: Palais Farnèse, 1991.

Schiffman, Lawrence H. "Laws Concerning Idolatry in the *Temple Scroll*." In *Uncovering Ancient Stones: Essays in Memory of H. Neil Richardson*, ed. Lewis M. Hopfe, 159–75. Winona Lake, IN: Eisenbrauns, 1994.

Schmidt, Brian B. "The Aniconic Tradition: On Reading Images and Viewing Texts." In *The Triumph of Elohim: From Yahwisms to Judaisms*, ed. Diana Vikander-Edelman, 75–105. Grand Rapids, MI: Eerdmans, 1996.

Schörner, Günter. "Stiftungen von Badeanlagen im hellenistischen und kaiserzeitlichen Griechenland." In *Civilisations du bassin Méditerranéen: Hommages à Joachim Śliwa*, ed. Krzysztof M. Ciałowicz and Janusz A. Ostrowski, 307–15. Krakow: Université Jagellonne, Institut d'Archéologie, 2000.

Schremer, Adiel. "Beyond Naming: Laws of *Minim* in Tannaic Literature and the Early Rabbinic Discourse of *Minut*." In *Jews and Christians in the First and Second Centuries: How to Write Their History*, ed. Peter J. Tomson and Joshua Schwartz, 383–97. Compendia rerum iudaicarum ad Novum Testamentum 13. Leiden: Brill, 2014.

———. *Brothers Estranged: Heresy, Christianity, and Jewish Identity in Late Antiquity*. Oxford: Oxford University Press, 2010.

Schumacher, Leonhard. "Slaves in Roman Society." In *The Oxford Handbook of Social Relations in the Roman World*, ed. Michael Peachin, 589–608. Oxford: Oxford University Press, 2011.

Schürer, Emil. *The History of the Jewish People in the Age of Jesus Christ (175 B.C.–A.D. 135)*. Ed. Geza Vermes, Fergus Millar, and Matthew Black. 3 vols. Edinburgh: T&T Clark, 1973–87. Based on *Geschichte des jüdischen Volkes im Zeitalter Jesu Christi*. 3rd ed. Leipzig: Hinrichs, 1901.

Schwartz, Daniel R. *Judeans and Jews: Four Faces of Dichotomy in Ancient Jewish History*. Toronto: University of Toronto Press, 2014.

———. "Many Sources but a Single Author: Josephus's *Jewish Antiquities*." In *A Companion to Josephus*, ed. Honora Howell Chapman and Zuleika Rodgers, 36–58. Oxford: Wiley-Blackwell, 2016.

Schwartz, Joshua J. *Lod (Lydda) Israel: From Its Origin through the Byzantine Period 5600 B.C.E.–640 C.E.* British Archaeological Reports International Series 571. Oxford: Tempus Reparatum, 1991.

Schwartz, Seth. "Ancient Jewish Social Relations." In *The Oxford Handbook of Social Relations in the Roman World*, ed. Michael Peachin, 549–62. Oxford: Oxford University Press, 2011.

———. "Gamaliel in Aphrodite's Bath: Palestinian Judaism and Urban Culture in the Third and Fourth Centuries." In *The Talmud Yerushalmi and Graeco-Roman Culture I*, ed. Peter Schäfer, 201–17. Texte und Studien zum antiken Judentum 71. Tübingen: Mohr Siebeck, 1998.

———. "How Many Judaisms Were There? A Critique of Neusner and Smith on Definition and Mason and Boyarin on Categorization." *Journal of Ancient Judaism* 2 (2011): 208–38.

———. *Imperialism and Jewish Society, 200 B.C.E. to 640 C.E.* Princeton: Princeton University Press, 2001.

Schwartz, Seth. *Were the Jews a Mediterranean Society?: Reciprocity and Solidarity in Ancient Judaism*. Princeton: Princeton University Press, 2010.

Scobie, Alexander. "Slums, Sanitation, and Mortality in the Roman World." *Klio: Beiträge zur alten Geschichte* 68 (1986): 399–433.

Shelton, Kathleen J. *The Esquiline Treasure*. London: British Museum Publications, 1981.

Shemesh, Aharon. *Halakhah in the Making: The Development of Jewish Law from Qumran to the Rabbis*. Berkeley: University of California Press, 2009.

Simon-Shoshan, Moshe. *Stories of the Law: Narrative Discourse and the Construction of Authority in the Mishnah*. Oxford: Oxford University Press, 2012.

Sklar-Parnes, Deborah A., Yehudah Rapuano, and Rachel Bar-Nathan. "Excavations in Northeast Jerusalem: A Jewish Site in between the Revolts." *New Studies on Jerusalem* 10 (2004): 35*–41*.

Small, David B. "Late Hellenistic Baths in Palestine." *Bulletin of the American School of Oriental Research* 266 (1987): 59–74.

Smallwood, E. Mary. *The Jews under Roman Rule: From Pompey to Diocletian: A Study in Political Relations*. Studies in Judaism in Late Antiquity 20. Leiden: Brill, 1976.

Smith, John T. *Roman Villas: A Study in Social Structure*. London: Routledge, 1997.

Smith, R.R.R. "Statue Life in the Hadrianic Baths at Aphrodisias, A.D. 100–600: Local Context and Historical Meaning." In *Statuen in der Spätantike*, ed. Franz A. Bauer and Christian Witschel, 203–35. Wiesbaden: Reichert, 2007.

Smith, Robert Payne. *Thesaurus Syriacus*. 2 vols. Oxford: Clarendon, 1879–98. Reprint and enlarged edition, Kenneth C. Hanson. Eugene, OR: Wipf & Stock, 2007.

Sokoloff, Michael. *A Dictionary of Jewish Babylonian Aramaic of the Talmudic and Geonic Periods*. Ramat-Gan: Bar Ilan University Press, 2003.

———. *A Dictionary of Jewish Palestinian Aramaic of the Byzantine Period*. Ramat-Gan: Bar Ilan University Press, 1990.

———. *A Syriac Lexicon: A Translation from the Latin, Correction, Expansion, and Update of C. Brockelmann's Lexicon Syriacum*. Winona Lake, IN: Eisenbrauns, 2009.

Sonne, Wolfgang. "Der politische Aspekt von Architektur." In *Die Griechische Polis: Architektur und Politik*, ed. Wilfram Höpfner and Gerhard Zimmer. Tübingen: Wasmuth, 1993.

Sophocles, Evangelinus A. *Greek Lexicon of the Roman and Byzantine Periods: From B.C. 146 to A.D. 1100*. Cambridge, MA: Harvard University Press, 1914. Reprint, Hildesheim: Olms, 2005.

Sperber, Daniel. *The City in Roman Palestine*. Oxford: Oxford University Press, 1998.

———. "On the Bathhouse." *Classical Studies in Honor of David Sohlberg*, ed. Ranon Katzoff, Yaakov Petroff, and David Schaps, 353–66. Ramat Gan: Bar-Ilan University Press, 1996.

———. "Patronage in Amoraic Palestine (c. 220–400): Causes and Effects." *Journal of the Economic and Social History of the Orient* 14 (1971): 227–52.

———. *Roman Palestine, 200–400: Money and Prices*. 2nd ed. Ramat Gan: Bar Ilan University Press, 1991.

Spivey, Nigel. *Understanding Greek Sculpture: Ancient Meanings, Modern Readings*. New York: Thames & Hudson, 1996.

Stambaugh, John E. *The Ancient Roman City*. Baltimore: Johns Hopkins University Press, 1988.

———. "The Functions of Roman Temples." *Aufstieg und Niedergang der römischen Welt* II.16.1 (1978): 554–608.
Stanton, Graham, and Guy G. Stroumsa, eds. *Tolerance and Intolerance in Early Judaism and Christianity*. Cambridge: Cambridge University Press, 1998.
Stemberger, Günter, and Hermann L. Strack. *Introduction to the Talmud and Midrash.* Trans. Markus Bockmuehl. 2nd ed. Edinburgh: Clark, 1996.
Stern, Ephraim, ed. *En Gedi Excavations I: Final Report (1961–1965)*. Jerusalem: Israel Exploration Society, 2007.
Stern, Menahem. *The Documents on the History of the Hasmonaean Revolt with a Commentary and Introductions*. 3rd ed. Tel-Aviv: Ha-kibuts ha-meuḥad, 1973. (Heb.)
———. *Greek and Latin Authors on Jews and Judaism*. 3 vols. Jerusalem: Israel Academy of Sciences and Humanities, 1974–84.
Stern, Sacha. "Figurative Art and Halakha in the Mishnaic-Talmudic Period." *Zion* 61 (1996): 397–419. (Heb.)
———. "Images in Late Antique Palestine: Jewish and Graeco-Roman Views." In *The Image and Its Prohibition in Jewish Antiquity*, ed. Sarah Pearce, 110–29. Journal of Jewish Studies Supplement Series 2. Oxford: Journal of Jewish Studies, 2013.
Stewart, Peter. *Statues in Roman Society: Representation and Response*. Oxford: Oxford University Press, 2003.
Stiebel, Guy D. "The Roman Military Bathhouse at En Gedi: The Mazar and Dunayevsky Excavations 1964–1966." In *En Gedi Excavations 1: Final Report (1961–1965)*, ed. Ephraim Stern, 344–53. Jerusalem: Israel Exploration Society, 2007.
Stout, Ann M. "Jewelry as a Symbol of Status in the Roman Empire." In *The World of Roman Costume*, ed. Judith L. Sebesta and Larissa Bonfante, 77–100. Madison: University of Wisconsin Press, 1994.
Strobel, Karl. "Baths in Roman and Byzantine Egypt: Evidence from the Papyri." In *25 siècles de bain collectif en Orient: Proche-Orient, Égypte et péninsule Arabique*, ed. Marie-Françoise Boussac, Sylvie Denoix, Thibaud Fournet, and Bérangère Redon, 3:857–66. Études urbaines 9. Cairo: Institut Français d'Archéologie Orientale, 2014.
Stupperich, Reinhard. "Das Statuenprogramm in den Zeuxippos-Thermen." *Istanbuler Mitteilungen* 32 (1982): 210–35.
Sussman, Varda. *Roman Period Oil Lamps in the Holy Land: Collection of the Israel Antiquities Authority*. British Archaeological Reports International Series 2447. Oxford: Archaeopress, 2012.
Tassios, Theodossios P. "Water Supply of Ancient Greek Cities." *Water Science and Technology* 7 (2007): 165–72.
Thébert, Yvon. *Thermes romains d'Afrique du Nord et leur contexte méditerranéen: Études d'histoire d'archéologie*. Bibliothèque des Écoles françaises d'Athènes et de Rome 315. Rome: École française de Rome, 2003.
Thomas, Edmund. *Monumentality and the Roman Empire: Architecture in the Antonine Age*. Oxford: Oxford University Press, 2007.
Trümper, Monika. "Gender Differentiation in Greek Public Baths." In *SPA sanitas per aquam: Proceedings of the International Frontinus-Symposium on the Technical and Cultural History of Ancient Baths, Aachen March 18-22 2009*, 37–45. Babesch: Annual Papers on Mediterranean Archaeology Supplement 21. Leuven: Peeters, 2012.

Trümper, Monika. "Urban Context of Greek Public Baths." In *Greek Baths and Bathing Culture: New Discoveries and Approaches*, ed. Sandra K. Lucore and Monika Trümper, 33–72. Babesch: Annual Papers on Mediterranean Archaeology Supplement 23. Leuven: Peeters, 2013.

Tsafrir, Yoram, Leah Di Segni, and Judith Green. *Tabula imperii romani: Iudaea Palaestina: Eretz Israel in the Hellenistic, Roman, and Byzantine Periods: Maps and Gazetteer*. Jerusalem: Israel Academy of Sciences and Humanities, 1994.

Urbach, Ephraim E. *The Halakhah: Its Sources and Development*. Trans. R. Posner. Tel Aviv: Modan, 1996.

———. "The Rabbinical Laws of Idolatry in the Second and Third Centuries in the Light of Archaeological and Historical Facts." *Israel Exploration Journal* 9 (1959): 149–65, 229–45.

Uytterhoeven, Inge. "Bathing in a 'Western Style': Private Bath Complexes in Roman and Late Antique Asia Minor." *Istanbuler Mitteilungen* 61 (2011): 287–346.

Valeri, Claudia. "Arredi scultorei dagli edifici termali di Ostia." In *Ostia e portus nelle loro relazioni con Roma*, ed. Christer Bruun and Anna Gallina Zevi, 213–28. Acta Instituti Romani Finlandiae 27. Rome: Institutum Romanum Finlandiae, 2002.

Van Dam, Raymond. "Imagining an Eastern Roman Empire: A Riot at Antioch in 387 C.E." In *The Sculptural Environment of the Roman Near East: Reflections on Culture, Ideology, and Power*, ed. Yaron Z. Eliav, Elize A. Friedland, and Sharon Herbert, 451–81. Interdisciplinary Studies in Ancient Culture and Religion 9. Leuven: Peeters, 2008.

———. *The Roman Revolution of Constantine*. Cambridge: Cambridge University Press, 2007.

Van der Meer, Lammert Bouke. *Ostia Speaks: Inscriptions, Buildings and Space in Rome's Main Port*. Leuven: Peeters, 2012.

VanderKam, James C. *Jubilees: A Commentary in Two Volumes*. 2 vols. Minneapolis: Fortress, 2018.

Veyne, Paul. *Bread and Circuses: Historical Sociology and Political Pluralism— Abridged with an Introduction by Oswyn Murray*. Trans. Brian Pearce. London: Penguin, 1990.

Von Ehrenkrook, Jason Q. *Sculpting Idolatry in Flavian Rome: (An)Iconic Rhetoric in the Writings of Flavius Josephus*. Early Judaism and Its Literature 33. Atlanta: Society of Biblical Literature, 2011.

Vout, Caroline. *Sex on Show: Seeing the Erotic in Greece and Rome*. Berkeley: University of California Press, 2013.

Vroom, Jonathan. *The Authority of Law in the Hebrew Bible and Early Judaism*. Supplements to the Journal for the Study of Judaism 187. Leiden: Brill, 2018.

Wacholder, Ben Zion. *The New Damascus Document: The Midrash on the Eschatological Torah of the Dead Sea Scrolls: Reconstruction, Translation, and Commentary*. Studies on the Texts of the Desert Judah 56. Leiden: Brill, 2007.

Wallach, Luitpold. "A Palestinian Polemic against Idolatry: A Study in Rabbinic Literary Forms." In *Essays in Greco-Roman and Related Talmudic Literature*, ed. Henry A. Fischel, 111–26. New York: Ktav, 1977. Reprint of *Hebrew Union College Annual* 19 (1946): 389–404.

Ward, Roy B. "Women in Roman Baths." *Harvard Theological Review* 85 (1992): 125–47.

Wassenhoven, Maria-Evdokia. *The Bath in Greece in Classical Antiquity: The Peloponnese*. Biblical Archaeology Review International Series 2368. Oxford: Archaeopress, 2012.

Wasserstein, Avraham. "Rabban Gamliel and Proclus the Philosopher (Mishna Aboda Zara 3, 4)." *Zion* 45 (1980): 257–67. (Heb.)

Weinfeld, Moshe. "The Uniqueness of the Decalogue and Its Place in Jewish Tradition." In *The Ten Commandments as Reflected in Tradition and Literature throughout the Ages*, ed. Ben-Zion Segal, 1–34. Jerusalem: Magnes, 1985. (Heb.)

Weiss, Ze'ev. *Public Spectacles in Roman and Late Antique Palestine*. Revealing Antiquity 21. Cambridge, MA: Harvard University Press, 2014.

———. "Sculptures and Sculptural Images in Urban Galilee." In *The Sculptural Environment of the Roman Near East: Reflection on Culture, Ideology, and Power*, ed. Yaron Z. Eliav, Elise A. Friendland, and Sharon Herbert, 559–74. Interdisciplinary Studies in Ancient Culture and Religion 9. Leuven: Peeters, 2008.

———. "Sepphoris." In *The New Encyclopedia of Archaeological Excavations in the Holy Land*, ed. Ephraim Stern, 5:2029–35. Jerusalem: Israel Exploration Society, 1993–2008.

Wesch-Klein, Gabriele. "Recruits and Veterans." In *A Companion to the Roman Army*, ed. Paul Erdkamp, 436–50. Malden, MA: Blackwell, 2007.

Wesler, Kit W. *An Archaeology of Religion*. Lanham, MD: University Press of America, 2012.

Westenholz, Joan Goodnick. *Let There Be Light: Oil Lamps from the Holy Land*. Jerusalem: Bible Lands Museum, 2004.

Whitmore, Alissa. M. "Artefact Assemblages from Roman Baths: Expected, Typical, and Rare Finds." In *Thermae in Context: The Roman Bath in Town and in Life*, ed. Heike Pösche, 57–77. Archaeologia Mosellana 10. Luxembourg: Centre National de Recherche Archéologique, 2018.

———. "Small Finds and the Social Environment of the Roman Public Baths." PhD diss., University of Iowa, 2013.

Wikander, Örjan. "Senators and Equites VI: Caius Sergius Orata and the Invention of the Hypocaust." *Opuscula Romana* 20 (1996): 177–82.

Wilson, Andrew I. "Archaeological Evidence for Textile Production and Dyeing in Roman North Africa." In *Purpureae vestes: Textiles y tintes del Mediterráneo en época romana (Ibiza, 8 al 10 de noviembre, 2002)*, ed. Carmen Alfaro Giner, John P. Wild, and Benjamin Costa, 155–64. Valencia: University of Valencia, 2004.

———. "Hydraulic Engineering and Water Supply." In *The Oxford Handbook of Engineering and Technology in the Classical World*, ed. John P. Oleson, 285–318. Oxford: Oxford University Press, 2008.

Winkelman, Michael. "Magic: A Theoretical Reassessment." *Current Anthropology* 23 (1982): 37–66.

Winkler, John J. "The Constraints of Eros." In *Magika Hiera: Ancient Greek Magic and Religion*, ed. Christopher A. Faraone and Dirk Obbink, 214–43. Oxford: Oxford University Press, 1991.

Wissemann, Michael. "Das Personal des antiken römischen Bades." *Glotta* 62 (1984): 80–89.

Witte, Markus, Jens Schröter, and Verena M. Lepper, eds. *Torah, Temple, Land: Constructions of Judaism in Antiquity*. Texte und Studien zum antiken Judentum 184. Tübingen: Mohr Siebeck, 2021.

Wollfish, Avraham. "'Iḥud ha-halakhah veha-'agadah: 'Iyun be-darkhei 'arikhatah shel ha-tosefta." In *Higayon L'Yona: New Aspects in the Study of Midrash, Aggadah and Piyut in Honor of Professor Yonah Fraenkel*, ed. Joshua Levinson et al., 309–31. Jerusalem: Magnes, 2006.

Woolf, Gregory. "Polis-Religion and Its Alternatives in the Roman Provinces." In *Römische Reichsreligion und Provinzialreligion*, ed. Hubert Cancik and Jörg Rüpke, 71–84. Tübingen: Mohr Siebeck, 1997.

Yadin, Azzan. "Rabban Gamliel, Aphrodite's Bath, and the Question of Pagan Monotheism." *Jewish Quarterly Review* 96 (2006): 149–79.

Yegül, Fikret K. *The Bath-Gymnasium Complex at Sardis*. Archaeological Exploration of Sardis 3. Cambridge, MA: Harvard University Press, 1986.

———. *Bathing in the Roman World*. Cambridge: Cambridge University Press, 2010.

———. *Baths and Bathing in Classical Antiquity*. Cambridge, MA: MIT Press, 1992.

———. "Development of Baths and Public Bathing during the Roman Republic." In *A Companion to the Archaeology of the Roman Republic*, ed. Jane DeRose Evans, 14–32. Malden, MA: Wiley-Blackwell, 2013.

———. "The Roman Baths at Isthmia in Their Mediterranean Context." In *The Corinthia in the Roman Period: Including the Papers Given at a Symposium Held at the Ohio State University on 7–9 March, 1991*, ed. Timothy E. Gregory, 95–113. Journal of Roman Archaeology Supplementary Series 8. Ann Arbor, MI: Journal of Roman Archaeology, 1993.

Zahavy, Tzvee. *The Talmud of the Land of Israel: A Preliminary Translation and Explanation, Volume 1: Berakhot*. Ed. J. Neusner. Chicago Studies in the History of Judaism. Chicago: University of Chicago Press, 1989.

Zanker, Paul. *The Power of Images in the Age of Augustus*. Ann Arbor: University of Michigan Press, 1988.

Zellinger, Johannes. *Bad und Bäder in der altchristlichen Kirche: Eine Studie über Christentum und Antike*. Munich: Max Hueber, 1928.

Ziegler, Ignaz. *Die Königsgleichnisse des Midrasch beleuchtet durch die römische Kaiserzeit*. Breslau: Schottlaender, 1903.

Zissu, Boaz, and Amir Ganor. "Horvat 'Ethri—A Jewish Village from the Second Temple Period and the Bar Kokhba Revolt in the Judean Foothills." *Journal of Jewish Studies* 60 (2009): 90–136.

———. "New Finds from the Period of the Bar Kokhba Revolt in the Southern Shephelah of Judaea." In *Judea and Samaria Research Studies 12*, ed. Ya'acov Eshel, 139–56. Ariel: College of Judea and Samaria, 2003. (Heb.)

Zlotnick, Dov. "Proklos ben Plaslos." In *Saul Lieberman Memorial Volume*, ed. Shamma Friedman, 49–52. New York: Jewish Theological Seminary of America, 1993. (Heb.)

Zuiderhoek, Arjan. "Cities, Buildings and Benefactors in the Roman East." In *Public Space in the Post-Classical City: Proceedings of a One Day Colloquium Held at Fransum 23rd July 2007*, ed. Christopher P. Dickenson and Onno M. van Nijf. Leuven: Peeters, 2013.

Zytka, Michal. *A Cultural History of Bathing in Late Antiquity and Early Byzantium*. London: Routledge, 2019.

INDEX OF ANCIENT CITATIONS

'Aggadat Bereshit, 7:3 — 69; 74:2 — 202, 220
Ammianus Marcellinus, Res Gesta, 28.4.9
 — 209, 221; 29.2.28 — 245; 31.1.2 — 42
Anthologia Palatina, 1.99–101 — 164;
 2 — 167; 5.160 — 116
Apuleius, Metamorphoses, 1.5 — 69;
 8.29 — 34; 9.17 — 145, 208; 11.23 — 124
Aristides, Orationes, 26.92 98–99 — 41, 55–56
Augustine
    Confessiones, 9.12 — 130
    Contra academicos, 2.2.6 — 135;
      3.1.1 — 130, 224; 3.4.9 — 130, 224
    De beata vita, 1.6 — 130, 224;
      4.23 — 130, 224
    De civitate Dei, 14.17 — 148;
      21.10 — 243
    De ordine, 1.3.6 — 25; 1.8.25 — 35–36,
      130, 224; 2.11.31 — 130, 224
    Epistulae, 46.14 — 130; 211.13 — 34
Aulus Gellius, Noctes Atticae, 10.3.1–3 — 155, 222
Avot de-Rabbi Nattan, version A, 12 — 203;
 28 — 42

Bardaisan, Liber legum regionum, 604 — 116
Bavli
    'Avodah Zara, 2b — 42; 18b — 134;
      30a — 213; 35b–36a — 75;
      38a-b — 146, 212; 58b–59a — 175
    Bava Batra, 53b — 203–4
    Bava Metsi'a, 41a — 207
    Bava Qama, 86b — 151
    Berakhot, 22a — 125, 132; 60a — 65, 234, 246
    'Eruvin, 24b — 207; 55b — 289n90; 136, 87b–88a — 73, 119
    Ḥagigah, 15a — 144–45; 20a — 123
    Ketubbot, 62a — 65, 234
    Megilah, 16a — 67
    Menaḥot, 43b — 153–54
    Nedarim, 38b — 214
    Niddah, 66b — 286n44
    Pesaḥim, 4a — 132, 203;
      46a — 92–93; 112b — 234

    Qiddushin, 22b — 203–4; 33a — 224;
      39b — 244; 82b — 70
    Sanhedrin, 17b — 57, 136; 62b — 207;
      74a — 177
    Shabbat, 33b — 42, 136, 268n39;
      40a — 90; 40b — 115, 119, 132,
      147; 41a — 72, 153; 140a — 213;
      147a — 119; 147b — 73, 136
    Yevamot, 63b — 286n44
Bible
    Acts, 17:16 — 169
    Deuteronomy, 5:6–9 — 176;
      12:3 — 161, 188; 13:7 — 161
    Ecclesiastics, 2:8 — 135; 5:11 — 215
    Exodus, 20:2–5 — 176; 35:3 — 115–16
    Isaiah, 28:22 — 236
    Lamentations, 3:17 — 135
    Leviticus, 18:3 — 133
    Mark, 6:45–52 — 249
    Psalms 1:1 — 134

Canticles Rabbah, 1:3 — 25; 3:6:5 — 243
Canticles Zuttah, 1:15 — 130, 200
Cassius Dio, Historicus, 69.8.2 — 145
Cicero
    De officiis, 1.129 — 201
    De natura deorum, 1.29.81 — 184
    Epistulae ad Atticum, 6.2.5 — 41
    Epistulae ad familiars, 14.20 — 39;
      366 — 92; 387 — 92
    In Vatinium, 13.31 — 124
Clement of Alexandria,
    Paedagogus, 3.5.31–32 — 148, 212, 218; 3.9.46.4 — 134
    Protrepticus, 4.5111 — 180
Corpus inscriptionum latinarum,
  2.5181 — 69, 200; 2.supp. 5181 — 154;
  3.324 — 41, 264n73; 4.1898 — 232;
  4.7714–5 — 180; 4.10603 — 212;
  4.10674 — 212; 4.10677 — 140;
  6.15258 — 39; 6.16740 — 200; 8.8926
  — 242; 9.3677 — 155; 10.6656 — 234–35;
  11.720 — 200; 11.1421 — 69; 11.4781 — 41, 264n73; 14.98 — 52; 14.2121 — 155

Corpus iuris civilis, digesta (pandectae), 34.2.1 — 174; 48.5.10(9) — 145; 48.13.11 — 183

Damascus Document, 11:1 — 115
Derekh Ereṣ Rabbah, 7:11 — 143; 7:12 — 224; 10:1 — 246; 10:4 — 144-45
Deuteronomy Rabbah, Devarim 13 — 42
Didascalia apostolorum, 2- 155; 3 — 155; 21 — 119
Dio Chrysostomus, *Orationes,* 37.41 — 164

Epiphanius, *Panarion (Adversus haereses),* 30.7.5-6 — 135, 140, 145-46; 30.24 3 — 73, 235
Esther Rabbah, 10:4 — 222
Eunapius of Sardis, *Vitae sophistarum,* 457 — 243; 459 — 244
Eusebius, *Historia ecclesiastica,* 2.23.5 — 289n86; 3.28.6 — 235; 5.1.5 — 286n44; 5.1.37 — 266n15
Exodus Rabbah, 7:4 — 67; 15:17 — 209; 15:22 — 207; 31:11 — 54

Frontinus, *De aquaeductu urbis Romeanae,* 2.78 — 24
Fronto, *Epistulae,* 5.1 — 46; 5.44 — 232

Galen, *De methodo medendi,* 10.3 — 238
Genesis Rabbah, 14:5 — 143; 33:3 — 62, 224, 235; 37:4 — 136; 45:6 — 204; 51:3 — 214; 63 — 75, 132, 202, 223, 243, 247-48

ILPaest, 100 — 231
ILTun, 1500 — 234
Irenaeus, *Adversus haereses,* 3.3.4 — 235

Jerome, *Epistulae,* 14.10 — 135 ; 45.4 — 135
John Chrysostom
    De diabolo tentatore, 3.5 — 200
    In epistulam ad Colossenses homiliae, 10.4 — 22
John Malalas, *Chronographia,* 9.5 — 87
John Moschus, *Pratum spirituale,* 11 — 140
Josephus
    Antiquitates Judaicae, 12.119-120 — 75; 14.120 — 92; 14.377-89 — 78; 14.462-64 — 89-91; 15.267-76 — 133; 15.328-30 — 171; 16.163-64 — 182, 283n7; 17.151 — 190; 18.203 — 278-79n36;
    Bellum Judaicum, 1.180 — 92; 1.280-85 — 78; 1.340-41 — 89-91; 1.648 — 190; 2.161 — 148; 2.591-92 — 75; 5.168-78; 5.181 — 170-71; 5.241 — 78
    Contra Apionem, 1.38-43 — 283n7; 2.277 — 299n38
    Vita, 65-67 — 170-71, 190; 74.6 — 75
Jubilees, 3:31 — 148; 15:33-35 — 152; 50:12 — 116
Juvenal, *Saturae,* 1.138-47 — 150, 232; 5.85-91 — 36; 6.309-10 — 164; 6.413-26 — 150; 7.232-36 — 224; 11.150-61 — 150 214

Kallah Rabbati, 9:13 — 143; 9:14 — 72; 9:15 — 224; 9:16 — 72

Lamentations Rabbah, 3:17 — 135; 3:44 — 68, 201
Leviticus Rabbah, 22:3 — 67, 214; 23:12 — 173; 26:1 — 42; 28:6 — 222; 34:3 — 132, 174
Libanius
    Declemationes, 42.21 — 239
    Epistulae, 11.10 — 147; 13.7 — 39; 29.3 — 34; 126.9 — 55; 149.2 — 55
    Orationes, 1.21 — 238; 1.108 — 34; 1.141 — 241; 1.174 — 34; 1.183 — 238; 1.246 — 34 11.133-134 — 55; 11.212 — 239
Liber pontifificalis, 39 — 134
Life of Aesop, 28 — 204
Livy, *Historiae,* 23.18.12 — 136, 146
Lucian
    De Syria dea, 32 — 185
    Hippias vel balaneion — 35, 39, 60, 235
    Nigrinus, 34 — 209

Macrobius, *Saturnalia,* 7.16.24 — 233;
Martial, *Epigrammata,* 1.23 — 157; 1.59 — 230; 1.62 — 146; 1.96 — 152, 157; 2.14 — 157, 230; 2.48 — 39, 157; 2.52 — 152, 157; 3.3 — 157; 3.20 — 157; 3.25 — 232; 3.44 — 224; 3.51 — 157; 3.68 — 33, 157; 3.72 — 149-50, 157; 3.87 — 157; 6.42 — 25; 6.93 — 37, 157; 7.35 — 155, 157; 7.82 — 152, 157;

9.33 — 157; 10.48 — 232; 11.52 — 157;
11.75 — 157; 12.19 — 212; 12.83 — 150,
157; 14.60 — 34
Mekhilta de-Rabbi Ishmael
    Baḥodesh, 8 — 172
    Mishpatim, 18 — 212
    Neziqin, 1 — 203
    Pisḥa, 13 — 173
Midrash ha-Gadol
    Deuteronomy, 23:20 — 54
Midrash on Psalms, 6:1 — 153-54;
    119:41 — 147
Midrash panim aḥerim, version b 6 — 67,
    75
Midrash Shemuel, 25:3 — 42
Midrash Tannaim, 15:12 — 203
Minucius Felix, *Octavius*, 2.4 — 183
Mishnah
    'Avodah Zara, 1:7 — 63, 130, 173,
        190-91, 312n73; 1:5 — 45,
        265n8; 1:9 — 59; 2:6 — 75;
        3:1 — 177; 3:4-5 — 143, 161-62,
        287n68; 3:6 — 177; 3:7 — 130;
        4:3 — 129
    'Avot, 5:9 — 177
    Bava Batra, 1:6 — 59; 3:1 — 57;
        4:6 — 48-59, 61
    Bava Metsi'a, 8:8 — 59, 99
    Berakhot, 3:5 — 142; 8:6 — 177
    Betsah, 32a — 74
    'Eduyot, 4:3 — 124
    Kelim, 8:7-8 — 65, 70, 71; 12:6 — 73;
        17:1 — 67, 70; 22:10 — 61,
        123
    Ketubbot, 7:8 — 155-56; 291n22
    Makhshirin, 2:5 — 66, 116-17
    Megilah , — 58
    Me'ilah, 5:4 — 70
    Miqva'ot, 6:11 — 124
    Nedarim, 5:5 — 57
    Niddah, 7:4 — 122
    'Ohalot, 18:10 — 122
    Qiddushin, 2:3 — 146
    Sanhedrin, 4:1 — 202; 7:6 — 177-78
    Shabbat, 3:4 — 116; 9:1 — 177;
        22:5 — 158; 22:6 — 72
    Shevi'it, 8:5 — 70; 8:11 — 67, 120,
        201, 223, 265n8
    Ta'anit, 1:6 — 69
    Tohorot, 7:7 — 73, 123
    Zavim, 4:2 — 71

Notitia regionum urbis XIV — 33
Numbers Rabbah, 12:5 — 42; 13:5 — 70, 221

Ovid
    Ars amatoria, 3.639-40 — 140;
        4.150-55 — 149
    Fasti, 4.139-50 — 126
Oxyrhynchus Papyri, 43 — 33; 53 — 46;
    54 — 53-54; 892 — 46-47; 896 — 46,
    53-54; 903 -n 274n1201430 — 67;
    1889 — 46; 2015 — 67; 2040 — 67;
    2718 — 52; 2877 — 52; 3088 — 268n32;
    4441 — 33

Palestinian Talmud. See *Yerushalmi*
Palladius, *Opus agriculturae*, 1.39.4 — 25;
    1.41 — 25
Palladius Monachus, *Dialogus de vita sancti*
    Johannis Chrysostomi, 9.162-64 — 134
Papyri graecae magicae, 2.50 — 244;
    7.469 — 244; 36.69-77 — 244;
    127.3 — 244; *Supplementum*
    magicae 42 — 244
Pausanias, *Graeciae description*, 2.3.3-5 —
    25, 41, 53; 6.23-28 — 33; 10.4.1 — 32
Perek ha-nikhnas la-merḥats, 1 — 143, 158;
    2 — 72, 231; 3 — 224
Pesiqta Rabbati, 7 — 70, 221; 22 — 70,
    72, 158
Pesiqta de Rav Kahana, 3:10 — 62, 233;
    4:2 — 42; 12:9 — 214; 15:2 — 134;
    24:2 — 272n93
Petronius, *Satyrica*, 27-28 — 219,
    221-22
Philostratus, *Imagines*, 1.15 — 184
Pirqe de-Rabbi Eliezer, 50 — 67, 223
Plautus, *Persa*, 90-91 -207
Pliny the Elder, *Naturalis historia*,
    9.168 — 29; 34.17 — 184; 36.42.121 — 33
Pliny the Younger, *Epistulae*, 3.5.14 — 147;
    3.14.6-8 — 238; 10.23-24 — 53
Procopius, *De aedificiis*, 1.11.1 — 39;
    1.11.21 — 40-41; 2.6.10-11 — 41, 54;
    2.8.24-25 — 41, 54; 3.14.6-8 — 209;
    4.1.20-24 — 41, 54; 4.10.21 — 41, 54;

Qoheleth Rabbah, 1:7 — 147; 1:8 — 54;
    2:8 — 135, 243; 5:8-9 — 214; 5:11 — 132,
    204, 214-17
Qoheleth Zuttah, 3:2 — 235
Quintilian, *Institutio oratoria* 5.9.14 — 145

Rhetorica ad Herennium, 4.14 — 209, 237
Rylands Papyri, 2.124 — 238

Scriptores historiae Augustae
    Antoninus Pius, 8.3 — 41, 54, 264n74
    Alexander Severus, 24.2 — 145; 24.5 — 67; 24.6 — 69; 30.4-5 — 35, 212; 39.3 — 41, 54, 264n74; 42.1 — 15753.2 — 155
    Claudius, 14.13-15 — 67
    Commodus, 17.5 — 41, 54, 264n74
    Elagabalus, 21.6 — 36; 30.7 — 41, 54, 264n74
    Hadrian, 17 — 210; 18.10 — 145
    Marcus Antoninus, 23.8 — 145
Seder Eliyahu Rabbah, 28 — 212
Seder Eliyahu zuttah, 16 — 57; 28- 200
Sefer ha-razim, 3:16-35 — 245-46
Semaḥot, 12:12 — 201
Seneca the Younger
    Dialogi: De vita beata, 7.3 — 136; *De ira*, 32.2 — 237
    Epistulae, 56.1-2 — 36, 211; 86.4-13 — 35, 136; 107.2 — 235
    Quaestiones naturales, 1.16.3 — 152
Sidonius Apollinaris
    Carmina, 18-19 — 39
    Epistulae, 2.2.4-9 — 39
Sifre to Deutoronomy, 36 — 153-54; 37 — 201, 222; 157 — 202; 258 — 142-43
Sifre to Numbers, 111 — 177; 115 — 202, 204
Sifra
    'Aḥare mot, 13 — 133-34
    Behar, 4:7:2 — 203
    Kedoshim, 1 — 178
    Metsora'-Zavim, 1:2:5 — 71
Socrates Scholasticus, *Historia ecclesiastica*, 6.18 — 134; 6.22 — 134
Statius, *Silvae*, 1.5 — 39
Strabo, *Geographica*, 16.2-46 — 92
Suetonius
    De grammaticis et rhetoribus, 2.23 — 34
    De vita caesarum, Augustus, 82 — 34, 146; 94 — 150; Tiberius, 26 — 188; Nero, 12.3 — 33; Domitian, 8.2 — 34

Tacitus
    Agricola, 21 — 41, 55, 146
    Annales, 11.3 — 35; 15.64 — 232
    Historiae, 1.72 — 140; 3.32 — 67, 222, 232
Tanḥuma
    Ḥayei Sara, 3:3 — 207
    Ki teste', 9 — 62
    Mishpatim, 14 — 54
    Va-yeḥi, 6 — 63
Tanḥuma Buber
    Ḥukat, 5 — 42
    Kotaḥ, 5 — 221
    Miqets, 2 — 147
    Mishpatim, 5 — 54
    Shoftim, 9 — 42
Tefillin, 17 — 142
Temple Scroll, 48:14-16 — 285n35
Tertullian
    Apologeticus, 42.2.4 — 130, 134; 42.4 — 126, 189-90
    De idololatria, 15.6 — 189-90
    De spectaculis, 8 — 189
Tosefta
    'Avodah Zara, 2:7 — 133; 4:8 — 212; 5:1 — 186; 6:3 — 177; 6:6 — 172
    Bava Batra, 2:15 — 59; 3:3 — 58-59, 61, 64, 72, 90
    Bava Metsiʻa, 11:32 — 66
    Bava Qama, 9:1 — 293n46; 9:12 — 150-51
    Berakhot, 2:20 — 60-61, 142, 224; 6:17 — 246; 6:25 — 153
    Demai, 6:13 — 59, 174
    ʻEruvin, 5:24 — 115, 158; 8:8 — 124
    Ḥullin, 2:24 — 54, 268n39
    Kelim b.m., 2:12 — 73; 10:3 — 71
    Kelim b.q, 2:9 — 72
    Ketubbot, 7:6 — 144
    Maʻaser sheni, 1:4 — 70
    Makhshirin, 3:11 — 70
    Miqvaʼot, 4:6 — 24; 5:7 — 64-65, 232; 5:8 — 124; 6:3 — 285n40; 6:4 — 68, 124
    Moʻed Qattan, 2:15 — 99, 132, 200
    Niddah, 6:9 — 146; 6:15 — 122, 156
    Pesaḥim, 3:17 -69
    Qiddushin, 1:5 — 203-4
    Sanhedrin, 4:1 — 202; :8 — 143

Shabbat, 3:3 — 62, 90, 99, 118;
  3:4 — 115; 3:17 — 210;
  6:15-17 — 158; 15:17 — 177;
  16:14 — 72; 16:16-17 — 119;
  16:19 — 72; 17:1 — 174
Shevi'it, 5:19 — 120
Sotah, 5:9 — 144
Terumot, 10:10 — 72
Tohorot, 8:7-8 — 73
Zavim, 4:7 — 71; 5:6-7 — 177

Vitruvius, *De architectura*, 1.3.1 — 40;
  5.10 — 27, 60
Yerushalmi
  'Avodah Zara, 2 (41d) — 75;
    3 (42b) — 178-79; 3 (43b) — 172;
    4 (43d) — 175, 191
  Bava Qama, 3 (3d) — 224;
    7 (6a) — 207
  Berakhot, 2 (4c) — 69-70, 73, 142,
    158; 2 (5c) — 236; 3 (6a-c) —
    63, 69, 125, 147; 4 (7b) — 136;
    4 (8b) — 235, 265n4; 6 (10c) —
    213; 9 (14b-d) — 153-54,
    246-47
  Betsah, 1 (60c) — 65, 204, 230
  'Eruvin, 5 (22c) — 289n91;
    6 (23c) — 282n72

Ketubbot, 7 (31b-c) — 136, 144,
  146; 12 (35a) — 147, 224, 235
Kila'yim, 9 (32a-b) — 132, 147, 159,
  224, 235
Ma'aser sheni 1 (52d) — 70, 73, 210
Makkot, 2 (31d) — 42
Mo'ed Qattan, 1 (80b) — 234; 3
  (82a) — 159;
Nedarim, 4 (38d) — 62
Pea'ah, 8 (21b) — 199
Pesahim, 4 (31a) — 69;
  10 (37b-c) — 213-14
Qiddushin, 1 (59d) — 203-4; 1
  (61a) — 136, 143, 231;
  2 (62c) — 146; 4 (66b) — 57, 136
Sanhedrin, 3 (21b) — 177; 7 (25d) —
  63, 132, 249-50
Shabbat, 1 (3a) — 136, 143, 231; 3
  (5d) — 213; 3 (6a-b) — 62, 64,
  115, 118-19, 132, 143, 232; 12
  (13c) — 218; 14 (14c) — 213
Shevi'it, 4 (35a) — 177; 8 (38a) — 62,
  73, 132, (38b-c) — 67, 130, 132,
  174-75, 188-89, 223, 265n8; 9
  (38d) — 132
Ta'aniyot, 4 (68a) — 218
Terumot, 2 (41c) — 213; 8 (46b-c) —
  132, 243, 247-48

GENERAL INDEX

Abba b. Kahana, R., 134
Abbahu, R., 65, 75, 119, 132, 152–53, 204, 230–35
Acco/Acre, map 3, 87, 161, 168, 188, 287n68
Actaeon, fig. 15, 138
Acts, Book of, 169
Adultery (in the baths). *See* Families
Aedes sacra. See Temples and Sanctuaries
Aediculae. See Niches
Aelia Capitolina, 172, 280–281n56. *See also* Jerusalem
'Afkroso. See Clothes: garments used in the bath
'agalt'a, 62. See also *Caldarium*
Agrarian Life. *See* Villages
Agricola, 41, 55
Agrippa, Markus, 78, 101–2
Agrippa I, 278–79n36
Aḥa, R., 132
Akkadian, 65
Alabastra. See *Aryballos*
Albeck, Ḥanokh, 293n46
Alexander Severus, 54, 69, 157, 212
Alexander the Great, 6, 302n67
Alexandria, map 1, 33, 134, 140, 148, 172, 176, 218, 298n20
Alexandria Troas, map 1, 278n29
Alföldy, Géza, 304n2
Alphabet of Ben Sira, 144
Altars, 180, 182–83
'Aluntit. See Clothes: garments used in the bath
'Aluntit, drink, 213
Alveus. See Pools
'Ambeti, 62, 117, 144. *See also* Hip-Baths
Ammianus Marcellinus, 42, 209, 221
Amphitheaters, 91, 101, 133–34, 197, 240, 276n19
Amulets, 227, 242
Anafa, Tel, map 3, 86, 261n23
Anatolia. *See* Asia Minor
Angels, 153, 179, 227, 244–46
Annales School, 16
Anointing. *See* Olive Oil

Anthropology (and anthropologists), 4, 240–41, 284n30
Antigonus, Hasmonaean ruler, 89–90
Antioch, maps 1–2, fig. 10–11, 34, 42, 47–48, 50, 54, 87, 147, 172, 191, 198, 239, 241
Antonia, Fortress, 78
Antoninus Pius, 52–53, 54
Apamea, map 2, 168
Aphrodisias, map 1, 172,
Aphrodite, fig. 18, 127, 143, 161, 164–66, 168, 172, 174, 186–89, 287nn57 and 68
Aphrodite of Knidos, fig. 18
'Apiqarsin. See Clothes: garments used in the bath
Apodyterium, diag. 1, fig. 13, 29, 68, 73, 96–97, 122, 139, 158, 207, 220, 245
Apollo, 168, 184
Aqiva, R., 132, 248–49
Aqueducts, fig. 1–2, 22–23, 24, 25, 26, 31, 40, 43, 77, 88, 212, 260n14, 278n29
Arabia, map 2, 5
Arabs, 6, 33, 140, 146, 251
Aramaic, 4, 11, 13, 39, 45–50, 64, 70, 72, 92, 93, 112, 155–56, 207, 227, 245, 249, 265n4. *See also* Syriac
Arbel, Yoav, 282n72
Archaeology (and archaeologists), 3, 4, 5, 9, 14, 16, 17, 29, 33, 44, 51, 77–103, 107, 123, 138, 155, 164, 168, 172, 176, 211, 214, 216, 220, 244, 253–54
Arches, fig. 1–2, 3, 23, 24, 31, 40, 96; triumphal arches, 170
Architecture, 4, 23, 24, 28, 29, 39, 40, 44, 60, 75, 78, 79, 226
Archon, 75, 236
Aristides, Aelius, 33, 41, 43, 55–56
Army, Legions, Military Units, Soldiers, and Their Bathhouses, 40, 42–43, 52, 59, 69, 83, 87, 89, 92, 95, 99, 100–101, 136, 210, 232, 244, 282n72. *See also* Military Camps
Art and Artists, fig. 15, 1, 4, 31, 79, 91, 93, 127, 131, 165, 171, 180, 182, 184, 185, 203, 205–8, 210–11, 216, 226, 229, 298n23

[355]

Artemis. *See* Diana
Artisans, 202
Aryballos, 93, 204. *See also* Bathhouse: paraphernalia
Ascalon, map 3, 87
Asclepius, 128
'Ashunta, 62, 73. *See also* Sauna
Asi, R., 236–38
Asia Minor, 33, 50, 85, 88, 172, 198, 243
Atargatis, 185
Athens, map 1, fig. 18, 23, 169, 172, 238
Athletic Games. *See* Sports and Exercise
Atia, 150
Augustine, 25, 34, 35, 130, 134–35, 148–49, 243
Augustus, 34, 69, 150, 182, 283n7
Aupert, Pierre, 286n50, 296n3
'Avoda zara. *See* Idolatry

Babylon (city), map 2, 23
Babylonia, map 2. *See* Persia, Parthians, Sasanian; Jews: of Babylonia
Babylonian Talmud, 12, 14, 15, 33, 42, 114, 144, 153, 212, 214, 234
Baiae, Baths of, 135
Balaneion. *See* Greek Bathing
Balkans, 38
Ballan (Greek *balaneus*, Latin *balneator*, Syriac *ba'lonoyo'*), 67, 70–71, 73, 222
Balnea, 30, 39, 45, 51, 52, 78, 90–91, 168, 197, 201, 228
Balnearis/Balnari. *See* Clothes: garments used in the bath
Baraita of Priestly Courses, 92–93, 280n49
Barbarians, 69, 148
Barbers, in Baths, 35, 68, 139, 200, 236
Barbier, Edmond, 305n31
Bardaisan of Edessa, 116
Bar-Kokhba Hideouts, 96–97. *See also* Jewish Society: revolts against Rome.
Basins, 24, 27, 29, 31, 62, 65, 79, 96, 126, 138, 202–3, 214, 232–33, 242
Bathhouse: activities in, 2, 3, 30, 31, 34, 35–36, 39, 50, 60, 80, 113–14, 139, 147, 164, 188, 189, 200–205, 207–10, 224, 232, 237–38, 245–50 (*see also specific activities*); admission fees, 34, 49–50, 53, 68, 70, 71, 200; amenities, 37, 75, 99, 203, 215, 229, 232; anxieties, 2, 36, 149–54, 156, 212, 228–30, 232, 234–35, 238–44, 246 (*see also* Body Shaming); attire (*see* Clothes); ceilings, 31, 63, 79 (*see also* Domes); concerns and reservations about, 2, 36, 80, 90–91, 135–36, 146–48, 160, 165, 189–90, 218, 221, 229, 234, 238; construction and costs, 51–56, 57, 63, 67, 86, 91, 99, 100–101, 233–34, 257n4; as cultural entity, 40–43, 50, 76, 85, 87, 164–65, 175, 228–29, 253; dangers in, 65, 200, 204, 209–10, 221, 226–51; decoration, 31, 40, 52, 64, 79, 92, 93, 94, 96, 98, 109, 166–68, 174, 187, 228 (*see also* Marble; Mosaics; Sculpture); eating and drinking in, 30, 35–36, 49, 72, 123, 200, 211–19 (*see also* Food; Wine); furniture (e.g., benches) and equipment, fig. 26, 44, 58–59, 60–64, 71–72, 75, 97, 113, 122–23, 215–17, 242; facades, entrances, gates, fig. 11 and 23; 48, 63, 71, 166–67, 189, 199–200, 205, 229, 236, 238, 245, 248; filth in, 229, 234; fire hazards, 231–35, 243, 245–46, 247–48 (*see also* Fire); floors of, collapses, 65, 233–35, 246; floors of, slippery, 230–31, 235, 241 (see also *Suspensura*); and health, 34, 38, 200, 229, 245 (*see also* Medicine and Medical Services); heating system and wood supply/storage, 2, 26–29, 34, 59, 61, 62, 64–67, 68, 70, 74, 85, 86, 92, 94, 109, 115–17, 120, 139, 165, 228, 231–35, 242, 244–48 (*see also* Hypocaust; *Praefurnium*); imperial baths (see *Thermae*); interior and structure, diag. 1, 29–31, 50, 59, 60–64, 65, 68, 71–72, 78, 81, 85, 86, 89–90, 96–98, 113, 142, 165–66, 203, 242; lighting (through windows), 29, 31, 39, 69, 230, 242 (*see also* Lamps); leisure (pleasures), 2, 3, 29, 38–39, 43, 66, 73, 115, 136, 146, 165, 203, 211, 229, 232, 237; licentious atmosphere, 35, 37, 86, 109, 136, 138–60, 164, 188, 237, 239–41, 243–44; libraries in, 30, 128; love, adoration, and praise for, 37–39, 60, 110, 113, 131–37, 228–29, 232, 237; maintenance, repair, and staff, 28, 44, 50, 52, 57, 67, 68–76, 201, 203, 207, 210, 222–24, 234 (*see also under specific titles*); merchants and vendors in,

fig. 11; 35–36, 49, 53, 68, 200, 211–212, 214; military baths (*see* Army, Legions, Military Units, Soldiers, and Their Bathhouses); names of, 45–50, 54, 124, 127, 155–56, 162, 238, 242 (*see also under specific names*); noise, 25, 35–37, 197, 209–12, 222; odors, 22, 35, 36–37; operating hours, 34, 68–69, 154–55, 244; origins, 33, 77–78, 85, 113; ownership, types of, 46, 49, 56–60, 70, 86, 99, 127–28, 201, 203, 223; paraphernalia, fig. 8, 11, 24, and 26; 17, 44, 70–72, 83, 198, 203–5, 209–10, 216, 218, 221 (*see also specific items by name*); preferential treatment in, 222–25; private baths (*see* Guilds; Mansions; Villas); used for religious rituals, 124–25, 125–31, 183, 190; scholars studying there and exhibiting erudition, 147, 223–24, 238; separate structures for men and women (*see* Mixed (and Separate) Bathing for Men and Women); services in, 80, 200, 210, 222–25 (*see also under specific service*); slaves in (*see* Society: slaves); splendor and beauty, 31, 39, 79, 174, 228; as social arena, 195–225, 240–41, 248–50; thieves in, 198, 207, 221, 236, 244–45; violence in, 209–10, 236–39, 248–50; water supply (*see* Water). *See also specific rooms and features by name*

Beersheba, map 3, 277n23
Beggars, 199–200. *See also* Society: poor
Bene Brak, map 3, 99
Benefaction. *See* Euergetism
Beth Guvrin. *See* Eleutheropolois
Beth Shean. *See* Scythopolis
Beth Yerah, map 3, 280n56
Bible. *See* Hebrew Bible
Bikhdei sh-ye'asu, 284n21
Bishops, 39, 134
Blidstein, Gerald J., 275n11, 299n35, 303n83
Body, Gestures, 222, 225, 244–45
Body, Human, 40, 126, 145–46, 149–50, 156, 164, 224, 229
Body Shaming, 36–37, 126, 149–54, 156, 212, 239–40
Boilers, diag. 1, 27, 61, 65. 72
Boshet, 150–51

Bostra, map 2, 87, 174, 188–89, 191
Boulē, 182. *See also* Cities: administration/councils, magistrates
Boyarin, Daniel, 7, 258n13, 283n3
Braziers, 26
Bridges, fig. 1, 22–23, 24, 42, 56, 126
Britain, map 1, 3, 33, 41, 55, 88, 244, 257n3, 260n1
Brock, Sebastian, 254
Brown, Peter, 179, 254, 257n2
Buckets, fig. 25, 204–5, 207
Burial, 12, 38, 93, 111, 122, 170
Buzzi, Ippolito, fig. 18
Byzantium, 7, 39

Caesarea Maritima, map 2–3, fig. 2, 25, 75, 86, 87, 101–2, 152, 172
Caesarea Philippi. *See* Paneas
Cairo Genizah, 245
Caldarium, diag. 1, fig. 6 and 14, 29, 35, 62, 79, 85, 94, 96–97, 231, 233, 235, 244. *See also 'agalt'a*
Calendar, 59, 111
Caligula, 170
Campania, map 1, 29, 222, 234–35
Capernaum, map 3, 277n23
Caracalla, Baths of, fig. 6 and 17, 30, 52, 167
Carcopino, Jérôme, 154
Carrhae, map 2, 280n46
Carthage, map 1, 216
Caskets, fig. 23–24 and 26, 205, 221
Casparii, 207, 210. *See also Apodyterium*; Bathhouse: maintenance, repair, and staff
Cassius, 92
Castella divisoria, 24
Cato the Elder, 237
Celts, 5
Cement and Concrete, 23–24
Cemeteries. *See* Burial
Ceramic. *See* Pottery
Certeau, Michel de, 16
Chabulon, map 3, 99, 200
Chagall, Bella Rosenfeld, 285n34
Chariot Racing, 197. *See also* Hippodromes
Charity, 57, 199–200
Chitōn. See under Clothes
Christianity, 6, 7, 9, 10, 39, 84, 110, 119, 134–35, 148

Christians, 3, 34, 39, 54, 116, 119, 130, 133–35, 141, 145, 148, 155, 175, 189–90, 200, 212, 235, 238, 243, 245, 248–51, 268n39, 286n44, 287n53, 307n74. See also *Minim*
Cicero, 39, 41, 92, 184–85, 201, 237
Cinema, Horror and Thriller Movies, 241
Circumcision, 152–54, 157, 239–40
Circuses. *See* Hippodromes
Cisterns, 22, 26
Cities, fig. 10, 10, 12, 23, 26, 32, 33, 37, 39, 40–41, 53, 57, 75, 80–82, 87–89, 93, 95, 101, 107, 113, 146, 161, 168–69, 171–72, 176, 183, 191, 196–98, 228; administration/councils, magistrates, 23, 32, 34, 46, 52, 53, 55, 58, 67, 74, 75, 117, 127, 133, 181–83, 191, 202, 222; citizens, 55, 75, 80, 87, 92, 117; colonnaded streets, 87, 183, 189, 197; institutions, 93, 101, 110, 182; layout, buildings, and monuments, fig. 9, 55, 58, 87, 93, 101, 126–27, 168–70, 182–83, 189, 196, 236; and local politics, 10, 227; large baths (see *Balnea*); local small baths, 31, 49, 90–91, 168, 197, 201, 230; properties owned by, 49, 57; slaves of, 203; stoas, 40, 182. *See also* Colonies
Classics, 4, 5, 17, 138, 253–54, 291n14
Clavi, 221. *See* Clothes
Clement of Alexandria, 134, 148, 212, 218–19
Clients. *See* Patronage
Cloth Dyeing and Cleaning, 25, 58, 220
Clothes, fig. 11, 24, and 26, 3, 29, 37, 41, 67, 68, 73, 111, 139, 142–43, 197–98, 203, 205, 215–17, 219–22, 225, 239–40 (*see also* Sandals); bathing suits, fig. 16, 139, 143, 156–60; *chitōn*, 158; garments used in the bath, 73, 157–60, 203–5, 210, 215–17, 219, 221 (*see also* Towels); tunics, fig. 24 and 26, 220
Coins and Currency 73, 94, 96–97, 172, 190, 199; asses, 35; *aureus*, 59; denarius, 35, 52, 59; *prutah*, 70; sesterces, 52, 59
Colonies, 39, 161, 223
Columns and Capitals, fig. 11 and 23; 30, 31, 63, 87, 128, 167–68, 205
Commodus, 54
Compitales, 126
Compitum. *See* Shrines
Consecratio, 127–28, 181–83, 186–88. *See also* Sacred Space

Constantinople, map 1, 39, 54, 134, 164, 166, 172, 200
Corinth, map 1, 25, 53, 278n29
Cosmetics, 204
Cotton, Hannah, 269n47
Courts, 3, 10, 57, 75
Crassus, 280n46
Crete, map 1, 154
Culture, 1, 40, 44, 61, 76, 84, 87, 110, 135, 138, 164–65, 175, 179, 226–27, 353–54; Byzantine, 7, 39; Greek, 2, 7, 32, 92–93, 146, 169, 171, 278n28 (*see also* Hellenism and Hellenistic World); interaction, 1–2, 3, 4, 7, 10, 14, 49–50, 81, 93, 107, 119, 135, 146, 160, 164–65, 175, 251, 253 (*see also* Filtered Absorption); Jewish (*see* Judaism); poetics of, 9, 164, 166, 192, 251; Roman, 1–2, 4, 8, 32, 37, 40, 169, 175, 179, 223–4 (see also *Romanitas*); Western civilization, 6
Curse Tablets, 227, 244–45
Curtains (cloth separators). See *Vila'ot*
Cyprian, 5
Cyrene, map 1, 128

Daily Life, 12, 75, 151, 180, 211, 238, 247, 250
Damascus Document, 115
Damnatio memoriae, 172–73
Daphne, fig. 10–11, 47–48
D'Arms, John H., 307n69
David, King, 42, 153
Dead Sea, map 3, 99
Dead Sea Scrolls, 45, 112, 121, 148
Death, 12, 200, 229, 231–32, 246. *See also* Burial
Decapolis, 87
Dedicatio, 127, 183, 189. *See also* Sacred Space
DeLaine, Janet, 52
Demons, 140, 179, 227, 229–302, 241–44, 246. *See also* Magic, Miracles, and Magicians
Dēmosios (*Dēmosin*), fig. 11, 45–49, 51
Defixiones. *See* Curse Tablets
Diana, fig. 15, 138
Didascalia apostolorum, 119, 155–56
Dietary Restrictions, 111, 213. *See* Food
Dinner Parties, 218–19, 238
Diocletian, 6, 247
Diodorus of Sicily, 283n5
Dionysius, 168, 184

Diospolis. *See* Lod/Lydda
Diplopotērion, 214. *See also* Wine
Divine Beings. *See by specific type (Roman Gods, Angels, Spirits, etc.)*
Doctors, 136, 200, 238. *See also* Medicine and Medical Services
Domes, fig. 23, 31, 40, 49, 63–64, 79, 174, 190, 205, 243, 248–50
Domina, fig. 23 and 26, 205, 219–20. See also Matrons; Society: rich
Dominium. *See* Law and Lawyers: property law
Downey, Glanville, 277n26
Drowning, 200, 232
Dunbabin, Katherine M. D., 309n6
Dura Europos, maps 1–2, 33
Dvorjetski, Estēe, 265n8, 287n61

Edessa, map 2, 116
Egypt, map 1, 3, 33, 46, 50, 56, 85, 88, 127–28, 155–56, 164, 167, 185, 228, 238, 250, 304n7
Ein Gedi, map 3, 99–102, 282n72
Ekphrasis, 167
Elaiothesion, 71
Eleazar b. Jacob, R., 147
Elegabalus, 36, 54
Eleutheropolois, maps 2–3, 132, 172, 223
Eliezer b. Hyrcanos, R., 54, 132, 248–49
Entertainment, 3, 12, 55, 101, 133–34, 236. *See also* Hippodromes; Leisure; Theaters
Ephesus, map 1, 172, 235, 301n57
Epikarsion. *See* Clothes: garments used in the bath
Epiphanius, 70, 73, 135, 140, 145
Esquiline Treasure, fig. 23, 205
Essenes. *See* Dead Sea Scrolls
Euergetism, 41, 43, 53, 74, 231, 234
Exauguratio, 181. *See also* Sacred Space
Executions, 236, 245

Fagan, Garret, 35, 127, 146, 201, 304n8
Falernian Wine, 219. *See also* Wine
Families, 10, 111, 136, 144–47, 154–156, 173–74, 196–97, 200–202, 205, 208, 220, 222, 238
Faraone, Christopher A., 309n2
Filtered Absorption, 2, 9–10, 110, 119, 137, 160, 165, 192, 250–51, 253, 258n9
Fine, Steven, 298n23

Fire, 26–27, 34, 42, 62, 64–65, 115–16, 118, 231–32, 235, 242–43, 245–46, 248, 264n73, 265n8
Fish, 92
Flasks, 62, 72, 73, 204
Folklore, 181, 229, 234, 284n30
Fonrobert, Charlotte Elisheva, 291n13
Food, 3, 35, 68, 111, 128, 138, 140, 200, 207, 211–19, 225
Fortuna, Goddess, fig. 22, 126, 149, 180
Fountains, 24, 126, 128, 169, 242
Fraenkel, Yonah, 302n81
Fragrances. *See* Bathhouse: odors; Perfumes; Scent
Fränkel, David, 292n22
Frescoes. *See* Bathhouse: decoration
Freud, Sigmund, 241–42
Friedheim, Emmanuel, 109, 125, 127, 129, 296n3, 301n57
Frigidarium, diag. 1, fig. 19, 29, 35, 79, 96
Frontinus, Sextus Julius, 24
Fronto, Marcus Cornelius, 46, 232
Fullers, 37
Funerals. *See* Burial
Furnace. See *Praefurnium*

Gadara, maps 2–3, 87, 116, 140, 145, 213
Galen, 238
Galilee, map 3, 81, 85, 90, 91, 93, 95, 97–99, 102, 108, 135, 172, 199–200
Galilee, Sea of, map 3, 92, 277n23
Gamaliel, Rabban, fig. 18, 99, 131, 143, 147, 161–62, 164–66, 168, 174, 186–90, 192, 287n68
Gardens, 25, 56, 128–129, 140, 167, 203
Garum, 37
Gaul, map 2, 5, 39, 63
Genius thermarum, 126, 242
Gerasa, map 2, 87
Germania, map 1, 5
Gezer, map 3; 77
Gladiatorial Contests, 197, 227
Glass, 72, 204, 220, 231, 245
Gnosticism, 235
God of Israel, 91, 109, 111, 115, 116, 129, 132, 142–43, 153–54, 162, 174, 176, 204, 224, 227, 246–48, 250, 252
Gods. See Religion; Roman Society: gods; *and by specific names*
The Golden Ass. See *Metamorphoses*.
Goodenough, Erwin R., 276n13

Goodman, Martin, 8, 123–24, 141, 279n43
Goths, 204, 230–31
Greece, map 1, 50, 88, 128, 185, 198, 244
Greek Bathing, 26, 31–32, 33, 77–78, 85, 88–92. *See also* Hip-Baths
Greek Language, 8, 11, 27, 39, 45–50, 51, 53, 62, 64, 70, 71, 90, 92, 93, 96, 112, 116, 127, 155–56, 233, 243, 279n38
Greeks, 4, 6, 23, 44, 111, 238. *See also* Culture: Greek; Hellenism and Hellenistic World
Grossberg, Asher, 124
Gruen, Erich, 257n2
Guggenheimer, Heinrich, 292n22
Guilds, 34, 57, 127, 196, 201
Gymnasium, 26, 31, 32, 33, 71, 75, 88, 92, 101, 167, 238, 293n39

Hadas-Lebel, Mireille, 8
Ḥadid, map 3, 97, 100
Hadrian, 52–53, 145, 210, 268n35, 278n29, 290n95
Hagar, Biblical Figure, 204
Hair Pluckers, 35–36
Haman, Biblical Figure, 67, 75, 221–23
Ḥammat Gader, map 3, 135, 140, 213, 244
Ḥanina, R., 25, 69, 125, 243–44
Hasmonaeans, 77–78, 89–90, 170–71
Healing Baths. *See* Thermal Baths
Hebrew, 4, 11, 12, 42, 45–50, 64, 93, 113, 156, 162, 177, 187, 227, 245, 306n58, 312n55
Hebrew Bible, 1, 6, 11, 12, 45, 65, 111, 115, 116, 120, 175, 204, 233. *See also* Torah
Hebron, map 3, 86, 100
Hecataeus of Abdera, 111
Hellenism and Hellenistic World, 2, 6, 7, 8, 23, 32, 71, 75, 88–89, 92–93, 152, 170–71, 176, 258n16, 293n39. See also Culture: Greek
Hephaestus, 164
Heracles, 168
Herbert, Sharon, 261n23
Herculaneum, map 1, 35, 140, 211, 214
Herod, fig. 14, 78–80, 86, 89–91, 99, 101–2, 133, 170–71, 190
Herod Antipas, 190
Herodium, map 3, 78,
Hierapolis Bambyce, map 2, 185
Ḥilkiya's Palace. *See* Khirbet el-Muraq
Hillel II, 131,

Hillel the Elder, 132, 174
Hip-Baths, fig. 7, 31, 62, 77, 88, 90. *See also* 'Ambeti; Greek Bathing; Tubs; *Hippias* (or *The Bath*), 39, 60, 235
Hippodromes, 3, 87, 101, 126, 197, 227, 236
Hippos/Susita, maps 2–3, fig. 3, 87
Ḥiya, R., 132, 147, 178–79, 224, 235
Ḥizkiyah, R., 73, 132, 292n34
Homer, 147
Hopkins, Keith, 180
Hoss, Stephanie, 83–84, 102, 276n18–19, 277n23, 277–78n28
Hunting, fig. 10, 48
Hygeia, Goddess, 126, 128
Hygiene, 22, 26, 148
Hypocaust, diag. 1, fig. 4–5 12 and 14, 27–29, 31, 40, 65–66, 77, 78, 85, 86, 92, 96, 231, 233, 235, 244, 246, 261n23. *See also* under specific parts

Iamblichus, 244
Iamnia, map 3, 170
Iconoclasm. *See* Sculpture: destruction of
Ideology, 1
Idolatry, 63, 83, 109–10, 125–31, 137, 143, 161–62, 164–65, 171, 174, 175–79, 187, 189–91, 253; Second Commandment, 171, 175–76
Imagines maiorum. See Sculpture: of family members and ancestors
Incense, 178
Inns, 236, 282n72
Inscriptions, fig. 22, 3, 5, 14, 25, 32, 38–39, 41–42, 43, 48, 49, 51, 53, 55, 68, 69, 92, 93, 96–97, 127–29, 140, 154–55, 167–68, 172–74, 200, 211, 231, 234, 242–43, 248, 287nn53 and 56
Iraq. *See* Mesopotamia
Iron Age, 84, 121, 152, 176
Isaac, R., 62
Isana, map 3, 90, 98
Isis, fig. 22
Islam, 6, 9, 13
Israelites, 152, 233
Italy, map 1, 29, 33, 35, 67, 85, 128, 155, 211, 222, 234

Jacob, Biblical Figure, 63
Jacobs, Martin, 276n17, 283n10, 292n33, 296n3 and 5, 306n57, 312n73
James, Brother of Jesus, 289n86

Japan, 1
Jeremiah, Biblical Prophet, 144,
Jeremiah, R., 69
Jericho, map 3, 78, 90
Jerome, 134–35
Jerusalem, map 2–3, 78, 90, 91, 93, 94–95, 100–101, 111, 133, 170–71, 176, 182, 190, 244293n39. *See also* Aelia Capitolina
Jesus, 54, 63, 92, 121, 126, 135, 248–50, 289n86. See also *Minim*
Jewelry, fig. 24 and 26, 197, 205, 219–22, 225, 238, 240
Jewish Society: communities, 1, 8, 12, 13, 54, 57–58, 76, 81–82, 98, 99, 101–2, 107, 111–12, 116, 119, 121, 200, 225; diaspora, 8, 75, 80–81, 142, 176, 182, 236; holidays/festivals, 109, 111, 213, 233; law, 15, 56, 58, 75, 94, 95, 109–13, 114–16, 120–21, 124, 137, 148, 159, 162, 171, 176, 215, 299n38; life (*see under specific categories (Sabbath, Synagogue, Purity, etc.)*); liturgy (prayer), 60, 61, 68, 69, 76, 111, 121, 142–43, 246–47; magic (*see* Magic, Miracles, and Magicians); revolts against Rome, 81, 90, 92, 94–97, 99, 100, 101, 152, 176, 190, 282n72; society, 14, 15, 54, 79, 110, 199–202; temple (*see* Second Temple); views of Roman institutions and buildings, 91, 93, 95, 101–2, 107, 110, 119, 130, 133–35, 165, 188, 250, 252–53 (*see also specific topics (Idolatry, Nudity etc.)*); views on Roman statues (*see* Idolatry; Sculpture)
Jews, 1, 4, 8, 39, 43, 51, 56–57, 76, 77, 79, 82, 86, 111–13, 121, 129, 164, 171–72, 176, 182, 211, 227, 245–46, 252–54 (*see also* Judaism); of Babylonia, 12, 45, 125, 136, 151, 213, 236, 286n44, 312n55 (*see also* Persia, Parthians, Sasanian); and magic (*see* Magic, Miracles, and Magicians); owning baths, 56–57, 58–60, 81, 99, 102, 174, 253; relationship with gentile neighbors, 59, 63, 87, 101, 117, 152, 174, 176, 182, 190–91, 243
Joab, son of Zeruiah, 42
John, the Apostle, 235
John Chrysostom, 134, 200
John Malalas, 54, 87
John Moschus, 140
Jordan Valley, map 3, 87, 90
Jose, R., 42, 59, 179, 393n46

Josephus, 5, 75, 78, 81, 89–91, 98, 100, 101, 102, 108, 133, 148–49, 170–71, 190, 299n38, 300n42
Joshua, R., 132, 248–49
Joshua B. Levi, R., 132, 223
Jove, 184
Jubilees, Book of, 112, 116, 148, 152
Judaea, maps 1–3, 2, 5, 7, 8, 10, 23, 77–79, 81–83, 85–89, 91, 93, 95, 97–102, 107–8, 133, 168, 170, 176, 190, 269n47. *See also* Palestine
Judaean Desert, map 3, 56, 99
Judah, R., 42, 56, 62, 115, 300n45
Judah II, Nessi'a (the Patriarch), 75, 131, 213–14
Judah III, Nessi'a (the Patriarch). See Yudan Nessi'a
Judah the Patriarch, 75, 115, 119, 131, 204, 214–18, 221, 224, 235
Judaism, 2, 6, 7, 13, 17, 82–83, 141, 148, 171, 176; and Graeco-Roman culture, 7, 8, 9, 10, 17, 75–76, 8, 91, 101, 119, 164–65, 171, 192, 227–28, 243, 245, 250–51, 259n18; Orthodox, 10, 14, 111, 115, 141, 252–53, 283n3
Judas Maccabaeus, 77
Julius Caesar, 5, 92, 278n29, 302n67
Jupiter, 184. *See also* Zeus
Justinian, 54
Juvenal, 36, 149–50, 152

Kastalin. See *Castella divisoria*
Kattan-Gribetz, Sarit, 286n50
Ketubah, 144
Khirbet el-Muraq, map 3, 86
Khirbet Krikur, 96–97, 98
Khirbet Umm el-'Umdan, map 3, 95–97
Kings, 26, 42–43, 54, 69, 132, 154, 172–73, 202, 204, 247, 264n79. *See also* Roman Emperors and Jewish kings by name
Kippah, 63, 248. *See also* Domes; Niches
Kivisto, Peter, 303n1
Knidos, map 1, fig. 18,
Kohut, Alexander, 272n103
Kosher Food. *See* Dietary Restrictions
Kottek, Samuel, 274n116
Kowalewska, Arleta, 275n3, 280n45
Koloski-Ostrow, Ann Olga, 260n14
Krauss, Samuel, 5, 82, 159, 265n3

Labrum. See Basins
Laconicum. See Sauna
Lacus. See Fountains
Lamps, 69, 96–97, 118, 245. *See also* Bathhouse: lighting
Laodicea, 148
Lares, 126
Latin, fig. 22, 11, 39, 41, 44, 49–50, 51, 56, 62, 64, 70, 71, 72, 151, 154, 187, 233, 243, 248
Latrines, fig. 9 and 22, 25, 30, 37, 54, 57, 58, 94, 126–27, 147, 179–80
Law and Lawyers, in the Roman World, 15, 35, 141, 145, 182, 189, 197, 200, 223, 236 (*see also* Rabbinic *Halakhah*); criminal law, 236; inheritance law, 174; local legal traditions, 256, 69n47; property law, 56–60, 72; religious law, 181–84
Lention. See Clothes: garments used in the bath
Levine, Lee, 5, 9, 171, 258n16, 276n18, 300n44
Levinson, Joshua, 229–30, 307n61
Leisure, 10, 12, 26, 55
Lex area, 183. *See also* Cities
Libanius, 34, 39, 55, 147, 238–39, 241
Libations, 130, 174, 178, 182, 188–90
Lieberman, Saul, 5, 271n80, 272n102, 274n116, 293n48, 303n83
Life of Aesop, 204
Linteum. See Clothes: garments used in the bath
Litters, 197, 219, 221–22, 232
Livy, 232
Lod/Lydda, map 3, 95, 132, 223
Loutra. See Greek Bathing
Lucian of Samosata, 5, 39, 60, 185, 209

MacMullen, Ramsey, 196
Macrobius, 233
Magdala, map 3, 91–93, 95, 97–98, 101, 102
Magic, Miracles, and Magicians, 2, 3, 35, 40, 63, 76, 126, 224, 226–51, 242–43, 244–51, 253. *See also* Demons; Metaphysics
Magic Bowls, 242, 248
Mango, Cyril, 31, 175
Mansions, 78, 86, 90, 196–97, 201, 209, 218
Marble, 27, 31, 52, 72, 79, 168, 210, 233, 245. *See also* Bathhouse: decoration

Marcus Aurelius, 232,
Marisa, map 3, 87
Markets, 3, 40, 41, 42, 55, 56, 87, 122–23, 126–27, 170, 189, 197, 236
Marriage and Married Women in the Baths. *See* Families
Marsyas, the Satyr, 168
Martial, 37, 39, 146, 149–50, 152–53, 156–57, 212, 219–20, 230, 232–33
Mary Magdalene, 92
Masada, map 3, fig. 14, 78
Masks, 170, 173
Mason, Steve, 7, 258n13
Massage, in Baths, 35, 36, 68, 139, 200, 202–3, 210–11, 219
Material Culture, 16, 82
Matrons, fig. 23–24 and 26, 205, 216, 219–20, 243. *See also* Society: rich
Maziqim, 243. *See also* Demons; Spirits
Medicine and Medical Services, in Baths, 3, 22, 34, 35, 40, 57, 68, 128, 139, 148, 229, 245, 257n4. *See also* Thermal Baths
Mediterranean, Eastern, 6, 7, 34, 39, 44, 46, 49, 50, 55, 62, 68, 74, 75, 85, 87–89, 93, 102, 145, 155, 168, 172, 198, 202–3, 211–12, 214, 220, 225, 228, 238, 251, 2257n2
Mediterranean, Roman, 1, 4, 9, 10, 13, 17, 23, 33, 36, 40, 41, 44, 46, 53, 80, 85, 93, 100, 111, 113, 120, 125, 126–28, 136–37, 140–44, 146–47, 155, 164, 166, 171–72, 176, 179, 182, 184–85, 189, 196–97, 201, 211, 218, 225, 228, 236, 242, 246, 251, 252
Meir, R., 115, 119, 132, 153, 177–79, 185–90
Meleager of Gadara, 116
Menstruating Women in the Baths, 122–23, 156
Mercury, 172
Mesopotamia, map 1–2, 3, 12, 23, 45, 203
Metaheret, 68, 124. See also Purity, Impurity, Purification
Metamorphoses, 145,
Metaphysics, 3, 121, 123, 227, 242–44
Mezzuzah, 143
Middle Ages, 7, 9, 10, 13, 111, 141, 144, 177, 226, 242, 246
Migreret. See Strigil
Miletus, map 1, 243
Military Baths. See Army, Legions, Military Units, Soldiers, and Their Bathhouses

Military Camps, 33, 40, 100. *See also* Army, Legions, Military Units, Soldiers, and Their Bathhouses
Millar, Fergus, 15
Mills, 25,
Minerva, 184,
Minim, 63, 248–50, 270n74. *See also* Christians
Minotaur, 168
Miqveh, 16, 58, 83, 94, 95, 96–97, 123–24, 142, 272n93, 275n9, 285n34. *See also* Purity, Impurity, Purification
Mirrors, fig. 26
Mishnah, 13, 14, 45–46, 56–57, 58–59, 61, 63, 67, 69, 99, 114, 116–17, 118–19, 120–21, 123, 131, 134, 155, 161–62, 164–66, 168, 174, 177–79, 184–92, 222–23
Mithras and Mithraea, 126, 251, 287n53
Mitsvot, 111, 132–33, 153, 174
Mixed (and Separate) Bathing for Men and Women, 37, 86, 138–60, 202, 229, 239–40
Moesia, map 1, 38
Monasticism, 135, 140, 289n86
Mordecai, Biblical Figure, 67, 75
Mosaics, 27, 31, 40, 79, 92, 93, 94, 96, 177, 216, 219, 228
Moses, 111, 249
Murder, 209, 232, 236
Musical Instruments, 219
Mysticism, 12
Mythology, 138, 164, 167–68, 172, 179, 181, 184, 242. *See also under specific names*

Nabataea and Nabateans, 170, 269n47
Naḥum b. Somai, R., 190
Naples, map 1, 135
Natatio. See Pools
Nazarites, 289n86
Neis, Rachel, 297n6
Nemausus (Nîmes), map 1, fig. 1
Neoplatonism, 244
Neptune, 184
Nesarim (wooden planks), 61, 118
Neusner, Jacob, 7, 15, 265n8, 300n44
Niches, 63–64, 96, 126, 130, 167–68, 174, 190, 249. See also *Kippah*; Sculpture
Nielsen, Inge, 70, 125
Nimrud, map 2, 23

Nineveh, map 2, 23
Nominalized Adjectives, 46, 48–49
North Africa, map 1, 6, 39, 46, 88, 128, 189, 198, 216
Nudity, fig. 25, 2, 3, 37, 60–61, 86, 90, 109–10, 126, 136, 138–60, 161–64, 188, 197–98, 200, 201, 223–24, 229, 239–40, 253
Nullification, 191. *See also* Idolatry
Numidia, map 1, 39
Numina, 128, 182. *See also* Sculpture: as sacred worshipped object
Nymphaea. See Fountains
Nymphs, 126, 168, 242–43, 248

Obbink, Dirk, 309n2
Old Age, 230–31
Olive Oil: consumption in baths and industry, fig. 25, 35, 36, 57, 58, 62, 68, 69, 71–75, 118, 139, 144, 158, 198, 200, 204–5, 207, 210, 233, 245, 273n112, 284n24 (*see also* Strigil); Jewish ban against, 75
'Olyar, 61, 70–74, 210
Olympus, Mt., map 1, 179, 227
Olympus, Mythological Figure, 168
Oppenheimer, Aharon, 285n40
Opus reticulatum, 79
Opus sectile. See Bathhouse: decoration
Ostia, map 1, 52–53, 214
Ovid, 140, 149–52
Oxyrhynchus, map 1, 33, 52, 128, 268n32 and 35

Paideia, 224. See also Roman Society: Scholars and Scholarship; and Culture: Roman
Palaestra, diag. 1, fig. 20, 30, 35, 71, 94, 202–3, 211, 219
Palestine (Syria Palaestina), 2, 8, 10, 11, 12, 13, 15, 25, 50, 51, 65, 71, 73, 75, 79, 81, 107–8, 118, 120, 133, 140, 142, 152–53, 160, 166, 168, 170–72, 198, 203, 213–14, 222, 230, 233–34, 236, 243–44, 247, 265n5
Palestinian Talmud. See *Yerushalmi*
Palaces, fig. 14, 78, 86, 99, 171, 221
Palmyra, map 2, 5, 128, 146
Paneas, map 3, 87, 172, 247–48
Papyri, 3, 5, 32–33, 46, 49, 56, 63, 67, 68, 127, 155–56, 228, 242, 244
Passover Haggada, 45, 213

Patriarchs, Jewish, 75, 83, 131, 140, 145, 215–18, 247
Patronage, 168, 171, 196–97, 215, 217–18
Pausanias, 25, 32, 33, 41, 53, 185
Peleg, Orit, 281n67
Pella, map 3, 277n25
Perfumes, 204,
Peristyles. *See* Columns and Capitals
Persia, Parthians, Sasanian, map 1–2, 6, 12, 13, 14, 15, 33, 45, 65, 95, 126, 136, 151, 153, 203, 213, 214, 234, 236, 265n5, 280n46, 286n44, 312n55; baths in Persia, 289n90
Persian Language, 11
Petra, map 2, 56, 146
Phasael Tower, 78
Philo, 176, 298n20, 300n43
Philosophy and Philosophers, 12, 143, 146–47, 179, 223, 226, 244
Philostratus, 184
Phoenicia, map 1–2, 85, 161, 250
Photius, 283n5
Phylacteries, 72, 73, 143, 158
Piazza Armerina, map 1; fig. 16 and 24–25, 156, 205, 219–21
Pilae, fig. 4, 12 and 14, 27, 65–66, 85, 94, 96, 233–35
Pilgrims, 127
Pipes, fig. 3 and 21, 64–65, 96, 231, 233
Pirqe de-Rabbi Eliezer, 67
Pisa, map 1, 69
Piscina. *See* Pools
Pliny the Elder, 29, 33, 92, 147, 184–85
Pliny the Younger, 33, 53, 147, 209, 238
Pneuma, 182, 184. *See also* Sculpture: as sacred worshipped object
Polis. *See* Cities
Pompeii (city), map 1, fig. 13 and 22, 35, 85, 141, 180, 211, 214
Pompey, 6, 85, 170, 302n67
Pond du Gard, fig. 1
Pontus, map 1, 53
Pools, diag. 1, fig. 4 and 20, 27, 29, 30, 31, 36, 61, 62, 65, 79, 85, 115, 118, 128, 138, 140, 202–4, 211, 214–15, 232–33, 242. *See also* Swimming
Popinae, 35–36, 211. *See also* Food
Porphyry, 242–43
Porticoes. *See* Columns and Capitals
Portugal, 154
Pottery, 95, 204, 245

Praefurnium (furnace), diag. 1, fig. 4–5, 27–28, 36, 61, 64–67, 70, 72, 96, 109, 118, 120, 231–33, 242, 248
Praxiteles, fig. 18
Prayer. *See* Jewish Society: liturgy
Pribaton, 49–50, 51, 267n23
Priene, map 1, 23
Priests, 127–28, 182
Primus, Marcus Anthony, 67, 222–23, 232
Procopius, 39, 40, 41, 54
Profanus. *See* Sacred Space
Projecta Casket, fig. 23, 205
Prophets, 176
Prostitution, 35, 42, 136, 140, 200, 257n4
Prusa, map 1, 53
Psychology, 1
Psalms, Biblical book, 147
Ptolemais (city). *See* Acco/Acre
Pueloi. *See* Hip-Baths
Purity, Impurity, Purification, 61, 64–65, 68, 69, 71, 73, 75, 76, 93, 95, 109–10, 111, 120–25, 137, 142, 156, 177, 182. *See also Miqveh*; Stone Vessels

Qamin. *See Praefurnium*
Qinyan. *See* Law and Lawyers: property law
Qohelet Rabbah, 243
Quintilian, 145
Qumran. *See* Dead Sea Scrolls

Rabbinic Authority, 13, 108, 299n38
Rabbinic Discourse, 12, 112–14, 231
Rabbinic Etiquette, 224
Rabbinic *Haggadah*, 11, 108, 137, 153–54, 172, 247–50
Rabbinic *Halakhah*, 11, 12, 57–60, 62–66, 68, 69, 72, 74, 82, 84, 107–37, 117–19, 120–21, 125, 129–31, 137, 142–43, 148, 150–51, 155–65, 159, 164–66, 175, 177–79, 185–92, 199, 202, 213, 252–53, 269n57. *See also* Jewish Society: law; *Mitsvot*
Rabbinic Literature, 2, 4, 5, 11–14, 15–16. 17, 44, 45, 81, 83, 107, 198–99, 201–2, 227, 253–54. *See also individual texts by name*
Rabbinic *Midrash*, 11, 14, 45, 49, 133, 137, 188, 204, 233, 243
Rabbinic Views. *See under specific topics (Idolatry, Nudity, etc.)*

Rabbis, 4, 9, 11–14, 39, 42–43, 44, 74, 82–83, 92, 108, 111–12, 130, 136, 179, 227, 247–50, 252–4 (*see also individuals by name*); attending the baths, 44, 72–73, 99, 115, 119, 131–37, 142–43, 147, 160, 161–62, 174–75, 188–89, 198–99, 212–18, 223–24, 230–35, 236–37, 247–50, 253; coining new names and categories, 45–50, 51, 62, 66, 76, 113, 123–24, 252, 265n4; knowledge and perception of Roman sculpture, 63–64, 91, 95, 132–33, 172–75, 179, 185–92, 253 (*see also* Idolatry); as legal scholars, 11–14, 51, 56–57, 107, 112–14, 115–19, 136, 143, 177–79, 185–92, 223–25; multilinguals, 45–50, 64; and other Jews, 13, 108–9, 119, 130–31, 142, 160, 185, 188, 192, 225, 227, 232, 236, 252–53; in Persia (*see* Babylonia; Persia, Parthians, Sasanian); as provincial residents of the Roman world, 56, 61, 76, 108, 137, 151, 166, 179, 198, 211, 225, 246, 250–51, 253–54; studying Torah (*see* Torah); titles (*Ḥakham*, Rabbi), 12, 13, 14, 112, 177–78, 185–88, 192, 252–53; views of cities, 57–58, 67, 74; views of the Romans, 9, 42–43, 44, 76, 136, 165, 252–53
Ramat ha-Nadiv, map 3, 86
Ramat Rachel, 282n70
Ravin, R., 234
Red Sea, 249–50
Reich, Ronny, 82–86, 89, 102, 108, 116, 120, 122, 124, 142, 276n13
Reish Lakish, 130, 132, 174–75, 188–89, 199
Religion, 1, 15, 40, 110–11, 121, 125–31, 171, 179–81, 184, 186, 189, 226–27; imperial cult, 170
Religious Ceremonies (Processions, Festivals, Rituals), 126, 130, 137, 152, 174–75, 178, 182–83, 187–90, 227–28, 246–47
Renaissance, 84
Rhetorica ad Herennium, 237
Rhodes, map 1, 172,
Rivers, 22, 26, 88, 183
Roman Civilization, 5, 8, 10, 15, 24, 34, 39, 87, 146, 232; architecture, 3, 22, 31, 40, 64, 79; citizenship, 196; empire and emperors, 5, 6, 12, 23, 29, 39, 41, 43, 49, 51, 52, 53–55, 111, 126–27, 136, 140, 141, 145–46, 160, 167–68, 171–73, 182–83, 191, 196–97, 202–3, 228, 230, 232, 239, 244, 247–48, 254257n2 (*see also specific emperors by name*); engineering, 3, 4, 23, 24, 40, 92, 98, 99, 228–29, 233; gods, 126–28, 130, 138, 149, 151, 161–68, 171, 179, 181–82, 184–85, 189, 226, 242 (*see also* Religion; *under specific names*); government, 6, 34, 42, 53–55, 67, 127, 173, 191, 222, 234–35, 238; imperialism, 3, 41, 43, 55; institutions, 44, 49, 87, 93, 101 (*see also under specific names*); law (*see* Law and Lawyers); norms, 6, 10, 93, 101, 145, 152 (*see also Romanitas*); population, 6, 87, 197; scholars and scholarship, 223–24 (*see also under specific names and subjects*); Republic, 23, 41, 89, 257n2
Roman Provinces: governors, magistrates, and provincials, 2, 5, 12, 41–42, 43, 52, 54, 56, 61, 67, 75, 85, 101, 108, 127, 170–71, 191, 196, 198, 209, 214, 236. *See also* Courts
Romanitas, 1, 2, 3, 8, 10, 40–41
Romanization, 2, 8, 41, 55
Rome (city), map 1, 23, 24, 33, 40, 41, 52, 67, 77–78, 89, 90, 101–2, 146, 178–79, 212, 228, 230, 238, 298n20, 301n57; *ara pacis*, 301n66; baths of, 33, 67, 77–78, 89, 101–2, 197, 212 (*see also* Caracalla, Baths of; Martial); Coliseum, 40; forum, 136; Pantheon, 40; senate, 136, 181, 196

Sabbath, 59, 61–62, 64, 66, 109–10, 114–19, 120, 137, 159, 174, 210, 232, 247
Sabbatical Year, 109–10, 120–21, 122, 125, 137, 223, 288n73
Sacred Space, 58, 109, 125–31, 181–85, 187, 189, 287ns53 and 56. *See also* Sculpture: as sacred worshipped object; Synagogues; Temples and Sanctuaries
Sacrifices, 178, 182–83
Sacrilege (*sacrilegium*), 180, 182–3. *See also* Sacred Space
Safrai, Shmuel and Ze'ev, 276n18, 283n10, 284n26
Safrai, Ze'ev, 284n20
Salamander, 245
Salamis, map 1, 73, 135

Salutatio, 197, 217–8. *See also* Patronage
Samaria (city), map 3, 87, 172
Samos, map 1, 23
Sandals, fig. 26, 204–5, 245
Sarah, Biblical Figure, 204
Sarcophagi. See Burial
Sartre, Maurice, 146, 257n2
Saturnalia, 126, 130, 190
Satyricon, 218–19, 221–22
Satyrs, 168. *See also under specific names*
Sauna, 29, 30, 35, 62, 79, 118, 202, 218–9. *See also* 'Ashunta
Scent, 58, 180. *See also* Bathhouse: odors
Schäfer, Peter, 5
Schwartz, Seth, 7, 9, 15, 257n6, 258n13
Science, 3, 242
Scipio Africanus, 34
Scribes, 200
Scriptores historiae Augustae, 41, 54, 210, 212
Scriptures. *See* Torah
Sculpture, fig. 17–18 and 22, 2, 3, 37, 40, 42, 63–64, 87, 91, 95, 109, 126, 128, 130, 132–33, 161–92, 228, 242, 249; appreciation of beauty, 174; attributes, 177–78, 184–86 (*see also* iconography *in this entry*); in baths, diag. 1, fig. 17 and 19, 2–3, 40, 63–64, 109, 126, 128, 130, 161–62, 165, 167, 174–75, 177, 187–91, 198, 228, 242, 248, 301n63; of benefactors and dignitaries, 167; in cemeteries and on *sarcophagi*, 170; ceremonies and rituals for, 126, 130, 174–75, 177–79, 182–83, 187, 190; in city centers and civic monuments, 87, 126, 132, 164, 168–70, 172, 174–76, 182–83; destruction of, 42, 172, 175, 190–91; of emperors and part of imperial cult, 37, 132, 167, 170, 173, 182 (see also *Damnatio memoriae*); of family members and ancestors, 126, 173–74; of gods, fig. 17 and 22, 126, 161–64, 168, 172, 174–75, 177, 182, 184–87, 190 (*see also under specific names*); iconography, 184–87; inscriptions of, 167–68, 172–74; Jewish views of (*see* Idolatry; Rabbis: knowledge and perception of Roman sculpture); messages, symbolism, and perceptions of, 91, 130, 165–66, 168–69, 171, 175–76, 184–92; mythological scenes, 164, 167–68, 172, 184; in special niches, fig. 19, 63–64, 126, 167–68, 174, 249; on architectural elements of buildings and monuments (columns, capitals, facades, water spouts), 166–67; along roads, 169, 175; as sacred worshipped object (*res sacra*), 182–92; in temples, 128, 168, 182, 187; washing and cleaning of, 132–33, 174, 182–83
Scythopolis, map 3, fig. 5 and 9 and 12 and 20, 87, 168, 172
Sea, 126, 183, 248–50, 272n93. *See also by specific names*
Sea of Galilee, map 3, 248–50
Sebaste. *See* Samaria
Second Temple, 6, 12, 14, 54, 78, 81, 83, 95, 96, 98, 100, 102, 111–12, 121, 124, 132, 170, 182, 190
Sefer ha-razim, 227, 245–46, 248, 250
Seleucids, 75, 85
Seneca the Younger, 34, 36, 136, 146, 152, 211, 232, 235, 237–38
Sepphoris, map 3, 59, 98–99, 102, 172
Serapis, 127, 251
Sex and Sexual Activities (in the baths), 2, 3, 38, 40, 111, 121, 140, 144–46, 149, 188, 230, 239–41, 250
Sheffelah, map 3, 91, 95–98, 99, 102
Ships, 93, 127
Shmuel b. Naḥman, R., 247
Shrines, 126, 128. *See also* Temples and Sanctuaries
Shuafat, map 3, 93–95, 97–98, 100, 102
Sicily, map 1, 156–57, 205, 220
Side, Turkey, fig. 19
Sidi Ghrib, fig. 26, 216, 220–21
Sidonius Apollinaris, 39, 63
Simeon b. Gamaliel, R., 59, 135, 177–78, 186
Simeon b. Lakish, R. *See* Reish Lakish
Simeon b. Pazi, R., 134
Simeon b. Yehotsadak, R., 175
Simeon b. Yoḥai, R., 42, 115, 132, 212–13, 268n39
Siphon, 24
Situlae, 204. *See also* Bathhouse: paraphernalia
Skin Diseases, 34, 241
Slaves. See Society: slaves
Smith, R.R.R., 169
Smyrna, map 1; 33

Social Hierarchy, 3, 149, 157, 168, 184, 195–225, 240–41
Society, 12, 13, 15, 31–32, 34, 138, 195–225, 230 (*see also* Social Hierarchy); children, 3, 196–97, 200–202; communities, 22, 57, 195, 198, 225; elites, 55, 216, 218–19, 221, 240–41; equites, 196, 209; freedmen, 196, 218–19; land owners, 57, 195–96; middle class:, 196; orphans, 200; peasants, 196, 202; poor, 3, 196–97, 199–200, 215, 218, 240; slaves, fig. 23–25 and 26, 3, 26, 35, 57, 68–69, 71, 127–28, 140, 196–97, 200–202, 203–11, 214–16, 218–19, 221–22, 225, 230–32, 240; widows, 200; women, 3, 68–69, 70, 122–23, 144–47, 149, 154–58, 196, 200, 209, 216, 218–22, 227, 240, 244, 253, 304n7 (*see also* Matrons)
Sorcerers, 245. *See also* Medicine and Medical Services
Southeast Asia, 29
Spain (Hispania), map 1, 3, 145, 146, 244
Spells, 227, 245–46, 250
Sperber, Daniel, 170, 274n116
Spirits, 179, 227, 242–44, 248–49
Sports and Exercise, fig. 16, 3, 35, 36, 40, 88, 93, 101, 146, 156, 202, 219
Spouts. *See* Pipes
Springs, 22, 88, 126, 128
Stabian Baths, fig. 13, 85, 141
Statius, 39
Statues. *See* Sculpture
Stern, Sacha, 302n76
Stiebel, Guy, 280–81n56, 281n62
Stone Vessels, 94, 96–97. *See also* Purity, Impurity, Purification
Strabo, 92
Strigil, fig. 8 and 25, 35, 72, 73, 93, 204–5, 207. *See also* Olive Oil
Suburban Baths. *See* Herculaneum
Sudatorium. *See* Sauna
Suetonius, 34
Suicide, 232
Summa honoraria, 53
Superstition, 1, 226
Suspensura (suspended floors), fig. 4 and 14, 27, 29, 78, 85, 94, 96, 232–35, 242
Sweating. *See* Sauna
Swimming, 36, 115, 210. *See also* Pools

Synagogues, 3, 57, 58, 81, 95, 96, 122, 131, 182, 292n30. *See also* Sacred Space
Syria, maps 1–2, 5, 42, 50, 75, 85, 87, 92, 116, 119, 128, 155, 170, 185, 200, 209, 251
Syriac, 45–50, 158, 254

Tabernae, dig. 1, 35–36, 211. *See* Food
Tacitus, 5, 41, 55, 67, 222–23
Tanneries. *See* Cloth Dyeing and Cleaning
Taricheae. *See* Magdala
Taverns, 189, 229, 236
Taxes, 42, 53
Technology, 2, 4, 31, 34, 44, 75, 78
Temples and Sanctuaries, 3, 40, 41, 55, 84, 87, 95, 101, 114, 121, 127–30, 136, 168, 171, 175, 181–83, 187, 189–90, 227, 236. *See also* Sacred Space; Shrines
Tepidarium, diag. 1, 29, 79, 94, 96
Tertullian, 130, 134, 189–90
Tetrapyla, 169
Theaters, 3, 32, 42, 87, 91, 101, 126, 133–34, 197, 236, 240
Thermae, 10, 46, 78, 167, 197, 228, 230. *See also* Caracalla, Baths of
Thermal Baths, 16, 128–29, 135, 140, 213, 244, 257n4, 265n8, 280n45, 287n61
Theseus, 168
Thieves, 36, 70, 221. *See also* Bathhouse: thieves in
Thomas, Edmund, 264n1
Thugga, map 1, 234
Tiberias, map 3, 63, 65, 92, 172, 174, 190, 199, 204, 230, 236, 247–49
Tiberius, Emperor, 278–79n36
Titus, 67, 92, 214, 223
Toiletries, 204–5
Tombs. *See* Burial
Torah (Pentateuch) and Its Study, 12, 25, 57, 111–12, 116, 120, 136, 142–43, 147, 162, 171, 176, 188, 223–24, 283n7
Tosefta, 13–14, 60–62, 64, 90, 99, 114, 133, 142–45, 147–48, 150–51, 186
Towels, 198, 204–5, 207, 219. See also Clothes: garments used in the bath
Towns, 10, 33, 52, 58, 80, 81, 90, 91, 94, 95, 107, 117, 126–27, 155, 171, 197, 250
Trajan, 53
Transjordan, 87
Travel, 61
Trimalchio. See *Satyricon*

Trümper, Monica, 294n57
Tsedaqa. *See* Charity
Tsni'ut. *See* Nudity
Tubs, 26, 27, 62, 65, 77, 138, 232. *See also* Hip-Baths
Tubuli, fig. 4 and 14, 27, 29, 78
Tunisia, 216
Turkey, 47–48, 85, 235
Turmesar, 69–70. *See also* Bathhouse: maintenance, repair, and staff
Tuscany, 39
Twain, Mark, 195

'Ulah, 289n91
Ulpian, 145
Urban Life. *See* Cities
Urinating, 37
Utensils, 215, 218, 225, 238

Valens, 42, 245
Vaults. *See* Domes
Veneralia, Festival of, 126, 149
Venus, 220, 302n67. *See also* Aphrodite
Vespasian, 92
Vesuvius, Mt., 35, 211
Vicus. *See* Villages
Vila'ot (Latin *velum*; Greek *bēlon*), 61
Villages, 3, 12, 33, 38, 57, 91, 93–100, 107, 126, 171, 196, 222, 233
Villas, 34, 39, 41, 78, 201, 288n70
Visual Language, 40, 168, 183–92, 205, 221, 244

Vitruvius, 40, 60, 79
Vulcan, 184

Ward, Roy B., 294n58
Wall Paintings, 40, 177
Water, fig. 9. 16, 21–26, 29, 32, 34, 39, 59, 61, 62, 64, 66, 67, 70, 73, 77, 88, 102, 115–18, 123, 124, 126–27, 139, 165, 213, 233, 235, 243, 245–46
Weinfeld, Moshe, 300n42
Wells, 22, 26, 88
Wine, 35, 38, 75, 122, 204, 207, 211–19, 225
Wooden Planks. See *Nesarim*; Bathhouse: heating system and wood supply/storage

Yakto Mosaic, fig. 10–11, 47–50, 200
Yegül, Firket, 127, 278ns32–33
Yerushalmi (Palestinian Talmud), 14, 45, 49, 62, 63, 72, 114, 118–19, 125, 144, 178–79, 191, 199, 212–13, 223, 230, 232, 246–50
Yishmael, R., 212–22, 224
Yoḥanan, R., 63, 130, 174–75, 189, 191–92, 199, 292n34, 301n63
Yoḥanan b. Zakkai, R., 72, 73, 158
Yudan Nessi'a (the Patriarch), 247–48

Zanker, Paul, 168
Zeira, R., 153
Zeus, 185. See also Jupiter.
Zytka, Michal, 258n16

A NOTE ON THE TYPE

THIS BOOK has been composed in Miller, a Scotch Roman typeface designed by Matthew Carter and first released by Font Bureau in 1997. It resembles Monticello, the typeface developed for The Papers of Thomas Jefferson in the 1940s by C. H. Griffith and P. J. Conkwright and reinterpreted in digital form by Carter in 2003.

Pleasant Jefferson ("P. J.") Conkwright (1905–1986) was Typographer at Princeton University Press from 1939 to 1970. He was an acclaimed book designer and AIGA Medalist.

The ornament used throughout this book was designed by Pierre Simon Fournier (1712–1768) and was a favorite of Conkwright's, used in his design of the *Princeton University Library Chronicle*.

Ingram Content Group UK Ltd.
Milton Keynes UK
UKHW012324140423
420198UK00007B/13/J